If you are frequently puzzled by the complexities of English spelling and pronunciation, then this handy reference work is what you have been waiting for. It contains more than 23,000 entries with special emphasis on:

MAJOR PRONUNCIATION ERRORS

- ☐ Improper enunciation
- ☐ Wrong accent
- ☐ Accent shifts

MAJOR SPELLING ERRORS

- ☐ When to drop the final "e"
- ☐ When to double final letters
- ☐ When to use a hyphen
- ☐ When to use a compound word
- ☐ Correct abbreviations
- ☐ Proper nouns and foreign phrases

If you can spell the word but cannot pronounce it correctly, or if you can pronounce it but cannot spell it correctly, or if you're puzzled by both points, this new unique reference work will enable you to master both problems at once and for all time.

WORDS
MOST OFTEN
MISSPELLED
AND
MISPRONOUNCED

Ruth Gleeson Gallagher and James Colvin

PUBLISHED BY POCKET BOOKS NEW YORK

WORDS MOST OFTEN MISSPELLED AND MISPRONOUNCED

POCKET BOOK edition published August, 1963

13th printing.........................July, 1976

The system of indicating pronunciation is used by permission. From THE NEW MERRIAM-WEBSTER DICTIONARY, copyright, ©, 1964, by G. & C. Merriam Company, publishers of the Merriam-Webster Dictionaries.

Words Most Often Misspelled and Mispronounced was originally published under the imprint of Washington Square Press, a division of Simon & Schuster, Inc.

This original POCKET BOOK edition is printed from brand-new plates made from newly set, clear, easy-to-read type. POCKET BOOK editions are published by
POCKET BOOKS,
a division of Simon & Schuster, Inc.,
A GULF+WESTERN COMPANY
630 Fifth Avenue,
New York, N.Y. 10020.
Trademarks registered in the United States and other countries.

PREFACE

Words Most Often Misspelled and Mispronounced is a quick reference guide to the trickiest words in the English language. Ours being a problem-laden language, the list is long—over 23,000 words. These are the words likeliest to be looked up by the student, secretary, businessman, and writer—in fact, anyone to whom correct spelling and pronunciation are vital in social and business life.

Keep this book handy. A quick reference guide will do little good on a high shelf. *Words Most Often Misspelled and Mispronounced* is compact enough to keep in your desk drawer. Use it every time you have a word question, until "looking it up" is an engrained habit. Never let yourself get away with a sloppy guess. The most important single aid in improving your word skills is the habit of looking up words *as you use them, as questions arise.*

You might find it helpful to circle words you have to look up. Unless your memory is better than most, you will probably be looking up the same word again. When you write the word, look at it for a second or two. You might even jot it down a couple of times on a scratch pad. Next time you have to refer to this word it will come more easily; soon it will be a confident part of your vocabulary.

For pronunciations the same general idea applies. Say the word a time or two; get the sound of it in your ear. This will lead you into the habit of correct usage, so that in future conversation the right pronunciation comes naturally, without doubts or fumbling.

USING THIS BOOK

This book has been designed to clear up everyday problems in spelling and pronunciation and to make it quick and easy to find words.

Problems in Spelling and Pronunciation

Endings. Misspellings commonly result from changes in the root word with the addition of suffixes. For example, *cause* loses its final *e* when the final *-ing* is added; thus:

> **cause,** causing

A word like *block* does not alter the spelling of its root when *-ing* is added:

> **block,** blocking

Obviously, this isn't a problem. But a few endings cause questions even though the root remains the same:

> **canoe,** canoeing

Words like this are considered problems; consequently, the suffixes have been included in the book. The concern here is to leave no question in the user's mind.

Other examples in this category are words in which the final consonant is doubled with the addition of suffixes:

> **essential,** essentially
> **occur,** occurring

. . . or changes that occur in the plural of nouns:

> **ability,** abilities

As in many traditional dictionaries, the simplest endings (*-ed*, *-ing*, and *-ies*) are picked up at the last unchanged syllable and immediately follow the main entry. Other derivatives follow:

accumulate
  -lating
  accumulable
  accumulation
  accumulative
  accumulator

But even the simplest endings are never broken between double letters. Thus, instead of *accede, -ceding,* the word *acceding* is written out in full. This is done to avoid careless omission of the second *c*.

Pronunciations. The major pronunciation errors of English speakers are the result of improper enunciation or accent. This work uses the standard phonetic symbols of the Merriam-Webster Dictionaries. See page x for the list of these symbols.

Both primary and secondary accents are shown:

primary: **′**
secondary: **′**
Example: **aberration** (ab′er • a′shun)

When the accent shifts as a result of a change in the word's form, the editors have included this face in the sub-entry:

apocalypse (a • pok′a • lips)
apocalyptic (a • pok′a • lip′tik)

When the accent has been omitted from one of the sub-entries (for example, *abnormally*), the user should assume the accent is that of the original entry (ab • nor′mal).

Hyphen problems. "Is it one word, two words, or hyphenated?"

In an attempt to answer this question, extended lists of word compounds and combinations are included. Such lists show the preferred form of compounds in commonest usage. Very often these words are so simple there is no other reason for including them. For example:

good-bye
goodhearted
good-humored
good will

Confusing similarities. Brief definitions and cross references are included for words often mistaken for each other, like *disperse-disburse, serge-surge* and *bouillon-bullion.* For example:

> **bouillon** (soup; see *bullion*)

These definitions are intended as quick reference hints. For your knottier word problems, consult a dictionary.

Places, people, brands, and foreign phrases. State names are listed, along with the preferred abbreviations and correct terms for state residents. For example, a native of Michigan may correctly be called a *Michiganite* or a *Michigander.* Town, city, or river names are included if they are sources of spelling or pronunciation difficulties. Also provided are a selected list of world figures like *Khrushchev, Macmillan,* and *Mao Tse-tung;* brand names that are a part of the language like *Kodachrome;* and common foreign phrases like *coup d'état.*

Choice of words to be included in this book. The editors didn't include words so simple you'd never look them up—words like *man, fan,* and *ran;* nor the blockbusters used to stump the experts, like *cuproiodargyrite.* This left room for words that people do look up and for endings that cause questions.

Some of the words may seem much too simple for a "problem list," but consider the following hardy perennials among the most commonly misspelled words in the language:

> there, their
> receive
> exist, existence, existent
> separate, separation
> occur, occurred, occurring, occurrence
> occasion
> definite, definitely
> definition
> believe, belief

Ease of Finding Words

Have you ever hunted up and down a dictionary page for a word you weren't quite sure of? Sometimes a word and its derivatives are widely separated alphabetically. Many reference works put the derivatives with the main entry; others list them alphabetically. For example, *drier* is a long way from *dry*, and it is a derivative that has considerable importance of its own. In this book, the word *drier* is listed both in straight alphabetical order, and under *dry*. This way, you'll find it whichever place you look first.

Ease of finding main entries is further enhanced by the modern system of syllabifying by centered dots, omitting accent marks. Words are less "broken up" this way and more quickly spotted on the page. If you wish to know the correct accent or a word, it is included in the pronunciation that follows the word.

Fast identification is aided by including the context of certain specialized words. Thus, rather than *sleight*, the entry is *sleight of hand*.

The dominating editorial principle of this book has been the ease with which it could be used, still maintaining a maximum of information. Where the user desires further information on the meanings and uses of words he is referred to the Merriam-Webster series of dictionaries.

The concept of this book originated with James Colvin and the late Frederick Gleeson. They saw the need for a convenient reference work that would clarify two of the greatest irregularities in the English language: *spelling* and *pronunciation*. Both Mr. Colvin and Mr. Gleeson were closely associated with the National Spelling Bee, which is administered by the Scripps-Howard Newspapers. When Mr. Gleeson died, his widow completed the book. She had been his research teammate and has since become a faculty member of St. John College of Cleveland.

—The Publisher

KEY TO THE SYMBOLS
USED IN THE RESPELLING
FOR PRONUNCIATION

The system of indication pronunciation used throughout this book is taken from the 1964 *Merriam-Webster Dictionary*.

ā, *as in* āle, fāte, lā′bor, chā′os.

á, *as in* chá·ot′ic, fá·tal′i·ty, in·an′·i·máte.

â, *as in* câre, pâr′ent, com·pâre′, beár, âir.

ă, *as in* ădd, ăm, făt, ăc·cept′.

ă, *as in* ăc·count′, in′fănt, guid′-ănce.

ä, *as in* ärm, fär, fä′ther, pälm.

á, *as in* ásk, gráss, dánce, stáff, páth.

à, *as in* so′fà, i·de′à, à·bound′, di′à·dem.

b, *as in* ba′by, be, bit, bob, but.

ch, *as in* chair, much; *also for* tch *as in* match; *for* ti *as in* ques′tion; *for* te *as in* right′eous.

đ, *as in* đay, add′ed; *also for* ed *as in* robbed.

đů: *for* du *as in* ver′dure; *for* đeu *as in* gran′deur.

ē, *as in* ēve, mēte, se·rēne′.

ę, *as in* hęre, fęar, węird, đeer (dęr).

ê, *as in* ê·vent′, dê·pend′, crê·ate′.

ĕ, *as in* ĕnd, ĕx·cuse′, ĕf·face′.

ĕ, *as in* si′lĕnt, pru′dĕnce, nov′ĕl.

ẽ, *as in* mak′ẽr, pẽr·vert′, in′fẽr·ence.

f, *as in* fill, feel; *for* ph *as in* tri′umph; *for* gh *as in* laugh.

g, (*always* "*hard*"), *as in* go, be·gin′; *also for* gu *as in* guard; *for* gue *as in* plague; *for* gh *as in* ghost.

gz: *for* x *as in* ex·ist′, ex·am′ple.

h, *as in* hat, hot, hurt, a·head′.

hw: *for* wh *as in* what, why, where.

I, *as in* Ice, sīght, in·spīre′, I·de′a.

ĭ, *as in* Ill, ad·mĭt′, hab′ĭt, pit′y (pĭt′ĭ).

ĭ, *as in* char′ĭ·ty, pos′sĭ·ble, dĭ·rect′, A′prĭl.

j, *as in* joke, jol′ly; *also for* "*soft*" g, *as in* gem, gi′ant; *for* gi *and* ge *as in* re·li′gion, pi′geon; *for* đi *as in* sol′dier; *for* dg(e) *as in* edge, judg′ment.

k, *as in* keep; *also for* "*hard*" ch, *as in* cho′rus; *for* "*hard*" c, *as in* cube; *for* ck, *as in* pack; *for* qu *as in* con′quer; *for* que *as in* pique.

к, (*small capital*): *for* ch *as in* German ich, ach, *etc.*

ks: *for* x *as in* vex, ex′e·cute, per·plex′.

kw: *for* qu *as in* queen, quit, qual′-i·ty.

l, *as in* late, leg, lip, hol′ly.

m, *as in* man, mine, hum, ham′mer.

n, *as in* no, man, man′ner; *also for* gn *as in* sign.

N, (*small capital*): *without sound of its own indicates the nasal tone (as in French or Portuguese) of the preceding vowel, as in* bon (bôN)

ng, *as in* sing, long, sing′er; *also for* ngue, *as in* tongue; *for* n *before the sound of* k *or* "*hard*" g, *as in* bank, junc′tion, lin′ger.

ō, *as in* ōld, nōte, cal′i·cō.

ô, *as in* ô·bey′, a·nat′ô·my, prô·pose′.

ô, *as in* ôrb, lôrd, ôr·dain′; law (lô), bought (bôt), caught (kôt). all (ôl).

ŏ, *as in* ŏdd, nŏt, tŏr′rĭd, fŏr′est.

ô, *as in* sôft, dôg, clôth, lôss, côst.

ŏ, *as in* cŏn·nect′, ŏc·cur′, co′lŏn, cŏm·bine′.

oi, *as in* oil, nois′y, a·void′, goi′ter.

x

ōō, *as in* fōōd, fōōl, nōōn; rude (*rōōd*), ru′mor (*rōō′mẽr*).

ŏŏ, *as in* fŏŏt, wŏŏl; put (*pŏŏt*), pull (*pŏŏl*).

ou, *as in* out, thou, de·vour′.

p, *as in* pa′pa, pen, pin, put.

r, *as in* rap, red, rip, hor′rid; *also for* rh *as in* rho′do·den′dron.

s (*always voiceless, or* "*sharp*"), *as in* so, this, haste; *also for* "*soft*" c, *as in* cell, vice; *for* sc *as in* scene, sci′ence; *for* ss *as in* hiss.

sh, *as in* she, ship, shop; *also for* ch *as in* ma·chine′; *for* ce *as in* o′cean; *for* ci *as in* so′cial; *for* sci *as in* con′scious; *for* s *as in* sure; *for* se *as in* nau′seous; *for* si *as in* pen′sion; *for* ss *as in* is′sue; *for* ssi *as in* pas′sion; *for* ti *as in* na′tion.

t, *as in* time, talk; *also for* ed *as in* baked; *for* th *as in* Thom′as.

th (*voiced*): *for* th *as in* then, though, this, smooth, breathe.

th (*voiceless*), *as in* thin, through, wealth, worth, width.

tū̇: *for* tu *as in* na′ture, cul′ture, pic′ture.

ū, *as in* cūbe, pūre, tūne, lūte, dū′ty.

ů, *as in* ů·nite′, for′mů·late, hů-mane′.

û, *as in* ûrn, fûrl, con·cûr′; her (*hûr*), fern (*fûrn*), fir (*fûr*); *for* German ö, oe, *as in* schön (*shûn*), Goe′the (*gû′tĕ*); *for French* eu, *as in* jeu (*zhû*), seul (*sûl*).

ŭ, *as in* ŭp, tŭb, stŭd′y, ŭn′der.

ů̆, *as in* cir′cŭs, dā′tŭm, cir′cŭm-stance, đe′mon (-*mŭn*), na′tion (-*shŭn*).

ü: *for* German ü, *as in* grün; *for* French u, *as in* me·nu′ (*mĕ-nü′*).

v, *as in* van, vote, re·vise′; *also for* f *as in* of.

w, *as in* want, win; *also for* u *as in* per·suade′ (-*swād′*) *or* o *as in* choir (*kwīr*).

y, *as in* yet, be·yond′; *also for* i *as in* un′ion (-*yŭn*).

z, *as in* zone, haze; *also for voiced* ("*soft*") s, *as in* is, lives, wise, mu′sic, ears; *for* x *as in* xy′lo-phone.

zh: *for* z *as in* az′ure; *for* zi *as in* bra′zier; *for* s *as in* pleas′ure, u′su·al; *for* si *as in* vi′sion; *for* ssi *as in* re·scis′sion; *for* g *as in* rouge, mi·rage′.

′ *as in* par′don (*pär′d′n*), eat′en (*ēt″n*), e′vil (*ē′v′l*), *indicates that the following consonant is syllabic.*

SYMBOLS FOR PHONETIC RESPELLING USED IN *WEBSTER'S THIRD INTERNATIONAL DICTIONARY*

Webster's Third International Dictionary, published in 1967, uses a new system of symbols for indicating pronunciation. That system is reproduced on the following page for your convenience in using any dictionary in conjunction with WORDS MOST COMMONLY MISSPELLED AND MISPRONOUNCED.

MERRIAM-WEBSTER
PRONUNCIATION SYMBOLS

ə ....alone, silent, capital, collect, suppose

'ə, ͵ə..humdrum, abut

ə ....(in ᵊl, ᵊn) battle, cotton; (in lᵊ, mᵊ, rᵊ) French table, prisme, titre

ər ....operation, further

a ....map, patch

ā ....day, fate

ä ....bother, cot, father

à ....a sound between \a\ and \ä\, as in an Eastern New England pronunciation of aunt, ask

aù ...now, out

b ....baby, rib

ch ...chin, catch

d ....did, adder

e .....set, red

ē .....beat, nosebleed, easy

f .....fifty, cuff

g ....go, big

h ....hat, ahead

hw ...whale

i .....tip, banish

ī .....site, buy

j .....job, edge

k ....kin, cook

ḵ ....loch as commonly pronounced in Scotland (it is \k\ without actual contact between tongue and palate)

l .....lily, cool

m ....murmur, dim

n ....nine, own

ⁿ ....indicates that a preceding vowel or diphthong is pronounced through both nose and mouth, as in French bon \bōⁿ\

ŋ ....sing, singer, finger, ink

ō ....bone, hollow

ȯ ....saw, cork

œ ....\e\ with lip rounding, as in French bœuf, German Hölle

œ̄ ....\ā\ with lip rounding, as in French feu, German Höhle

ȯi ....toy, sawing

p ....pepper, lip

r .....rarity

s .....source, less

sh ...shy, mission

t .....tie, attack

th ...thin, ether

t̲h̲ ....then, either

ü ....boot, few \'fyü\

ù ....put, pure \'pyùr\

ᵫ ...\i\ with lip rounding, as in German füllen

ᵫ̄ ....\ē\ with lip rounding, as in French rue, German fühlen

v ....vivid, give

w ....we, away

y ....yard, cue \'kyü\

ʸ ....indicates that a preceding \l\, \n\, or \w\ is modified by the placing of the tongue tip against the lower front teeth, as in French digne \dēnʸ\

z .....zone, raise

zh ...vision, pleasure

\.....slant line used in pairs to mark the beginning and end of a transcription: \'pen\

ˈ .....mark at the beginning of a syllable that has primary (strongest) stress: \'pen-mən-͵ship\

ˌ .....mark at the beginning of a syllable that has secondary (next-strongest) stress: \'pen-mən-͵ship\

- .....mark of syllable division in pronunciations (the mark of syllable division in entries is a centered dot •)

() ....indicate that what is symbolized between sometimes occurs and sometimes does not occur in the pronunciation of the word: factory \'fak-t(ə-)rē\ = \'fak-tə-rē, 'fak-trē\

WORDS MOST OFTEN
MISSPELLED
AND MISPRONOUNCED

ABBREVIATIONS USED IN THIS BOOK

abbr.	abbreviated, abbreviation	n.	noun
adj.	adjective	N.C.	North Carolina
&	and	N. Dak.	North Dakota
Afr.	Africa	N. Mex.	New Mexico
Calif.	California	N.Y.	New York
Can.	Canada	O.	Ohio
Cen. Am.	Central America	Pa.	Pennsylvania
coll.	college	pl.	plural
fem.	feminine	riv.	river
Fla.	Florida	S. Afr.	South Africa
Ga.	Georgia	S. Amer.	South America
Ia.	Iowa	sing.	singular
Ill.	Illinois	St.	Saint
Ind.	Indiana	Tenn.	Tennessee
is.	island, islands	Tex.	Texas
Kans.	Kansas	Turk.	Turkey
masc.	masculine	univ. or U.	university
Md.	Maryland	v.	verb
Me.	Maine	Va.	Virginia
Mex.	Mexico	Wash.	Washington
Minn.	Minnesota	Wyo.	Wyoming
mt(s)	mount(s), mountain(s)		

A

ab·a·cus (ăb′ ȧ·kŭs)
  pl. ab·a·ci (-sī)
a·ban·don (ȧ·băn′ dŭn)
  a·ban·don·ment
a·base (ȧ·bās′)
  -bas·ing   a·base·ment
a·bate (ȧ·bāt′)
  -bat·ing   a·bat·a·ble
  a·bate·ment
ab·bey (ăb′ ĭ)
ab·bre·vi·ate (ȧ·brē′ vĭ·āt)
  -at·ing
  ab·bre·vi·a·tion
        (ȧ·brē′ vĭ·ā′ shŭn)
ab·di·cate (ăb′ dĭ·kāt)
  -cat·ing
  ab·di·ca·tion (ăb′ dĭ·kā′ shŭn)
ab·do·men (ăb·dō′ měn)
  ab·dom·i·nal (ăb·dŏm′ ĭ·nȧl)
  -nal·ly
ab·duct (ăb·dŭkt′)
  ab·duc·tion   ab·duc·tor
ab·er·rant (ăb·ĕr′ ȧnt)
  ab·er·rance
  ab·er·ra·tion (ăb′ ĕr·ā′ shŭn)
a·bet (ȧ·bĕt′)
  -bet·ted   -bet·ting
  a·bet·tor
a·bey·ance (ȧ·bā′ ȧns)
ab·hor (ăb·hôr′)
  -horred   -hor·ring
  ab·hor·rence   ab·hor·rent
a·bide (ȧ·bīd′)
  -bid·ing
a·bil·i·ty (ȧ·bĭl′ ĭ·tĭ)
  -ties
ab·ject (ăb′ jĕkt)
a·ble (ā′ b′l)
  a·ble-bod·ied   a·bly

ab·nor·mal (ăb·nôr′ mȧl)
  ab·nor·mal·i·ty
        (ăb′ nôr·măl′ ĭ·tĭ)
  -ties   ab·nor·mal·ly
a·board (ȧ·bōrd′)
a·bode (ȧ·bōd′)
a·bol·ish (ȧ·bŏl′ ĭsh)
  a·bol·ish·a·ble
  a·bol·ish·ment
ab·o·li·tion (ăb′ ō·lĭsh′ ŭn)
  ab·o·li·tion·ist
A-bomb (ā′ bŏm′)
a·bom·i·na·ble (ȧ·bŏm′ ĭ·nȧ·b′l)
  a·bom·i·na·bly
  a·bom·i·na·tion
        (ȧ·bŏm′ ĭ·nā′ shŭn)
ab·o·rig·i·nes (ăb′ ō·rĭj′ ĭ·nēz)
a·bor·tion (ȧ·bôr′ shŭn)
  a·bor·tive
a·bout-face (ȧ·bout′ fās′)
a·bove (ȧ·bŭv′)
  a·bove·board   a·bove-cit·ed
  a·bove·ground
  a·bove-men·tioned
  a·bove-named   a·bove-said
ab·ra·sion (ăb·rā′ zhŭn)
a·breast (ȧ·brĕst′)
a·bridge (ȧ·brĭj′)
  -bridg·ing   a·bridg·ment
a·broad (ȧ·brôd′)
ab·ro·gate (ăb′ rō·gāt)
  -gat·ing
  ab·ro·ga·tion (ăb′ rō·gā′ shŭn)
  ab·ro·ga·tor
ab·rupt (ăb·rŭpt′)
ab·scess (ăb′ sĕs)
ab·scond (ăb·skŏnd′)
ab·sent (ăb′ sĕnt)
  ab·sence
  ab·sen·tee (ăb′ sĕn·tē′)
  ab·sent-mind·ed

1

ab·so·lute (ăb′ sŏ·lūt)
  ab·so·lute·ly
  ab·so·lut·ism (ăb′ sŏ·lūt·ĭz′m)
ab·solve (ăb·sŏlv′)
  -solv·ing
  ab·so·lu·tion (ăb′ sŏ·lū′ shŭn)
ab·sorb (ăb·sôrb′)
  ab·sorb·a·bil·i·ty
        (ăb·sôrb′ à·bĭl′ ĭ·tĭ)
  ab·sorb·a·ble
  ab·sorb·en·cy -ent
  ab·sorp·tion (ăb·sôrp′ shŭn)
ab·stain (ăb·stān′)
ab·ste·mi·ous (ăb·stē′ mĭ·ŭs)
ab·sten·tion (ăb·stĕn′ shŭn)
ab·sti·nence (ăb′ stĭ·nĕns)
  -nent
ab·stract (ăb′ străkt)
        adj., n.
        (ăb·străkt′) v.
  ab·strac·tion (ăb·străk′ shŭn)
ab·struse (ăb·stroōs′)
ab·surd (ăb·sûrd′)
  ab·surd·i·ty (ăb·sûr′ dĭ·tĭ)
a·bun·dance (à·bŭn′ dăns)
  -dant
a·buse (à·būz′) v.
        (à·būs′) n.
  -bus·ing
  a·bu·sive (à·bū′ sĭv)
a·but (à·bŭt′)
  -but·ted -but·ting
  a·but·ment
a·bys·mal (à·bĭz′ măl)
  a·bys·mal·ly
a·byss (à·bĭs′)
ac·a·dem·ic (ăk′ à·dĕm′ ĭk)
  ac·a·dem·i·cal·ly
  a·cad·e·mi·cian
        (à·kăd′ ĕ·mĭsh′ ăn)
  a·cad·e·my (à·kăd′ ĕ·mĭ)
  -mies
ac·cede (ăk·sēd′)
  (to agree; see exceed)
  ac·ced·ing
ac·cel·er·ate (ăk·sĕl′ ĕr·āt)
  -at·ing
  ac·cel·er·a·tion
        (ăk·sĕl′ ĕr·ā′ shŭn)
  ac·cel·er·a·tor
ac·cent (ăk′ sĕnt)
ac·cen·tu·ate (ăk·sĕn′ tū·āt)
  -at·ing
  ac·cen·tu·a·tion
        (ăk·sĕn′ tū·ā′ shŭn)

ac·cept (ăk·sĕpt′)
  ac·cept·a·bil·i·ty
        (ăk·sĕp′ tà·bĭl′ ĭ·tĭ)
  ac·cept·a·ble ac·cept·ance
ac·cess (ăk′ sĕs)
  ac·ces·si·bil·i·ty
        (ăk·sĕs′ ĭ·bĭl′ ĭ·tĭ)
  ac·ces·si·ble (ăk·sĕs′ ĭ·b′l)
ac·ces·sion (ăk·sĕsh′ ŭn)
ac·ces·so·ry (ăk·sĕs′ ŏ·rĭ)
  -ries
ac·ci·dent (ăk′ sĭ·dĕnt)
  ac·ci·den·tal (ăk′ sĭ·dĕn′ tăl)
  -tal·ly
ac·claim (à·klām′)
  ac·cla·ma·tion
        (ăk′ lá·mā′ shŭn)
  (applause; see acclimation)
ac·cli·mate (à·klī′ mĭt)
  -mat·ing
  ac·cli·ma·tion (ăk′ lĭ·mā′ shŭn)
  (of climate; see acclamation)
  ac·cli·ma·tize -tiz·ing
ac·co·lade (ăk′ ŏ·lād′)
ac·com·mo·date
        (à·kŏm′ ŏ·dāt)
  -dat·ing
  ac·com·mo·da·tion
        (à·kŏm′ ŏ·dā′ shŭn)
ac·com·pa·ny (à·kŭm′ pá·nĭ)
  -nied -ny·ing
  ac·com·pa·ni·ment
  ac·com·pa·nist
ac·com·plice (à·kŏm′ plĭs)
ac·com·plish (à·kŏm′ plĭsh)
  ac·com·plish·a·ble
  ac·com·plish·ment
ac·cord (à·kôrd′)
  ac·cord·ance ac·cord·ing·ly
ac·cor·di·on (à·kôr′ dĭ·ŭn)
ac·cost (à·kŏst′)
ac·count (à·kount′)
  ac·count·a·bil·i·ty
        (à·koun′ tà·bĭl′ ĭ·tĭ)
  ac·count·a·ble ac·count·ing
  ac·count·ant (à·koun′ tănt)
  -an·cy
ac·cred·it (à·krĕd′ ĭt)
  -it·ed -it·ing
ac·crete (à·krēt′)
  ac·cret·ing
  ac·cre·tion (à·krē′ shŭn)
ac·crue (à·kroō′)
  ac·cru·ing ac·cru·al

ac·cu·mu·late (ă·kū′ mû·lāt)
 -lat·ing
 ac·cu·mu·la·ble
 ac·cu·mu·la·tion
                  (ă·kū′ mû·lā′ shŭn)
 ac·cu·mu·la·tive
                  (ă·kū′ mû·lā′ tĭv)
 ac·cu·mu·la·tor
ac·cu·rate (ăk′ û·rĭt)
 ac·cu·ra·cy   ac·cu·rate·ly
ac·cuse (ă·kūz′)
 ac·cus·ing   ac·cus·al
 ac·cu·sa·tion (ăk′ û·zā′ shŭn)
 ac·cu·sa·to·ry (ă·kū′ ză·tō′ rĭ)
ac·cus·tom (ă·kŭs′ tŭm)
 -tomed
ac·e·tate (ăs′ ê·tāt)
a·ce·tic (ă·sē′ tĭk)
ac·e·tone (ăs′ ê·tōn)
a·cet·y·lene (ă·sĕt′ ĭ·lēn)
ache (āk)
 ach·ing
a·chieve (ă·chēv′)
 -chiev·ing   a·chiev·a·ble
 a·chieve·ment a·chiev·er
A·chil·les′ ten·don
                  (ă·kĭl′ ēz)
ac·id (ăs′ ĭd)
 ac·id-form·ing
 a·cid·ic (ă·sĭd′ ĭk)
 a·cid·i·fy (ă·sĭd′ ĭ·fī)
 a·cid·i·ty (ă·sĭd′ ĭ·tĭ)
 ac·i·do·sis (ăs′ ĭ·dō′ sĭs)
 a·cid·u·lous (ă·sĭd′ û·lŭs)
ac·knowl·edge (ăk·nŏl′ ĕj)
 -edg·ing   ac·knowl·edge·a·ble
 ac·knowl·edg·ment
ac·me (ăk′ mē)
ac·ne (ăk′ nē)
ac·o·lyte (ăk′ ŏ·līt)
a·cous·tics (ă·kōōs′ tĭks)
 a·cous·ti·cal   -cal·ly
ac·quaint (ă·kwānt′)
 ac·quaint·ance
ac·qui·esce (ăk′ wĭ·ĕs′)
 -esc·ing   ac·qui·es·cence
ac·quire (ă·kwīr′)
 -quir·ing   ac·quir·a·ble
 ac·quire·ment
ac·qui·si·tion (ăk′ wĭ·zĭsh′ ŭn)
 ac·quis·i·tive (ă·kwĭz′ ĭ·tĭv)
 ac·quis·i·tive·ness
ac·quit (ă·kwĭt′)
 -quit·ted   -quit·ting
 ac·quit·tal   ac·quit·tance

a·cre (ā′ kĕr)
 a·cre·age (ā′ kĕr·ĭj)
ac·rid (ăk′ rĭd)
ac·ri·mo·ni·ous
                  (ăk′ rĭ·mō′ nĭ·ŭs)
 ac·ri·mo·**ny** (ăk′ rĭ·mō′ nĭ)
ac·ro·bat (ăk′ rŏ·băt)
 ac·ro·bat·ic (ăk′ rŏ·băt′ ĭk)
a·cross (ă·krŏs′)
ac·tion (ăk′ shŭn)
 ac·tion·a·ble
ac·ti·vate (ăk′ tĭ·vāt)
 -vat·ing
 ac·ti·va·tion (ăk′ tĭ·vā′ shŭn)
ac·tive (ăk′ tĭv)
 ac·tive·ly
 ac·tiv·i·ty (ăk·tĭv′ ĭ·tĭ)
ac·tor (ăk′ tēr)
 ac·tress
ac·tu·al (ăk′ tû·ăl)
 ac·tu·al·ly
 ac·tu·al·i·ty (ăk′ tû·ăl′ ĭ·tĭ)
 -ties
ac·tu·ar·y (ăk′ tû·ĕr′ ĭ)
 -ar·ies
 ac·tu·ar·i·al (ăk′ tû·âr′ ĭ·ăl)
ac·tu·ate (ăk′ tû·āt)
 -at·ing
a·cu·i·ty (ă·kū′ ĭ·tĭ)
 -ties
a·cu·men (ă·kū′ mĕn)
a·cute (ă·kūt′)
 a·cute·ly
ad·age (ăd′ ĭj)
a·da·gio (ă·dä′ jō)
ad·a·mant (ăd′ ă·mănt)
a·dapt (ă·dăpt′)
 (adjust; see adept, adopt)
 a·dapt·a·bil·i·ty
                  (ă·dăp′ tă·bĭl′ ĭ·tĭ)
 a·dapt·a·ble
 ad·ap·ta·tion (ăd′ ăp·tā′ shŭn)
 a·dapt·er   a·dap·tive
ad·den·dum (ă·dĕn′ dŭm)
 pl. ad·den·da
ad·der (ăd′ ēr)
ad·dict (ăd′ ĭkt) n.
                  (ă·dĭkt′) v.
 ad·dict·ed (ă·dĭk′ tĕd)
 ad·dic·tion (ă·dĭk′ shŭn)
ad·di·tion (ă·dĭsh′ ŭn)
 ad·di·tion·al   -al·ly
ad·di·tive (ăd′ ĭ·tĭv)
ad·dle·brained (ăd′′l·brānd′)

ad·dress (ă·drĕs′)
  ad·dress·ee ad·dress·er
  Ad·dres·so·graph
ad·duce (ă·dūs′)
  ad·duc·ing ad·duc·i·ble
ad·e·noid (ăd′ ĕ·noid)
a·dept (ă·dĕpt′)
  (expert; see *adapt, adopt*)
ad·e·quate (ăd′ ĕ·kwĭt)
  ad·e·qua·cy (-kwȧ·sĭ)
  ad·e·quate·ly
ad·here (ăd·hēr′)
  -her·ing
  ad·her·ence -ent
ad·he·sion (ăd·hē′ zhŭn)
  ad·he·sive (ăd·hē′ sĭv)
ad hoc (ăd hŏk′)
a·dieu (ȧ·dū′)
Ad·i·ron·dack (ăd′ ĭ·rŏn′ dăk)
  (mts.)
ad·ja·cent (ă·jā′ sĕnt)
  -cen·cy
ad·jec·tive (ăj′ ĕk·tĭv)
  ad·jec·ti·val (ăj′ ĕk·tī′ văl)
ad·join·ing (ă·join′ ĭng)
ad·journ (ă·jûrn′)
  ad·journ·ment
ad·judge (ă·jŭj′)
  -judg·ing
ad·ju·di·cate (ă·jōō′ dĭ·kāt)
  -cat·ing
  ad·ju·di·ca·tion
         (ă·jōō′ dĭ·kā′ shŭn)
  ad·ju·di·ca·tor
ad·junct (ăj′ ŭngkt)
ad·jure (ă·jōōr′)
  -jur·ing
ad·just (ă·jŭst′)
  ad·just·a·ble ad·just·er
  ad·just·ment
ad·ju·tant (ăj′ ŏŏ·tănt)
ad-lib (ăd′ lĭb′)
  -libbed -lib·bing
ad·min·is·ter (ăd·mĭn′ ĭs·tĕr)
  ad·min·is·tra·ble
ad·min·is·trate (ăd·mĭn′ ĭs·trāt)
  -trat·ing
  ad·min·is·tra·tion
         (ăd·mĭn′ ĭs·trā′ shŭn)
  ad·min·is·tra·tive (-trā′ tĭv)
  ad·min·is·tra·tor (-trā′ tĕr)
ad·mi·ra·ble (ăd′ mĭ·rȧ·b′l)
ad·mi·ral (ăd′ mĭ·răl)
  ad·mi·ral·ty

ad·mire (ăd·mīr′)
  -mir·ing
  ad·mi·ra·tion (ăd′ mĭ·rā′ shŭn)
  ad·mir·er
ad·mis·si·ble (ăd·mĭs′ ĭ·b′l)
ad·mis·sion (ăd·mĭsh′ ŭn)
ad·mit (ăd·mĭt′)
  -mit·ted -mit·ting
  ad·mit·tance ad·mit·ted·ly
ad·mix·ture (ăd·mĭks′ tŭr)
ad·mon·ish (ăd·mŏn′ ĭsh)
  ad·mo·ni·tion (ăd·mŏ·nĭsh′ŭn)
  ad·mon·i·to·ry
         (ăd·mŏn′ ĭ·tō′ rĭ)
ad nau·se·am (ăd nô′ shē·ăm)
a·do (ȧ·dōō′)
a·do·be (ȧ·dō′ bĭ)
ad·o·les·cent (ăd′ ô·lĕs′ ĕnt)
  -cence
a·dopt (ȧ·dŏpt′)
  (to choose; see *adapt, adept*)
  a·dopt·a·ble a·dop·tion
  a·dop·tive
a·dore (ȧ·dōr′)
  -dor·ing a·dor·a·ble
  ad·o·ra·tion (ăd′ ô·rā′ shŭn)
  a·dorn·ment (ȧ·dôrn′ mĕnt)
ad·re·nal (ăd·rē′ năl)
ad·ren·al·ine (ăd·rĕn′ ăl·ĭn)
A·dri·at·ic (ā′ drĭ·ăt′ ĭk)
a·droit (ȧ·droit′)
ad·u·la·tion (ăd′ û·lā′ shŭn)
a·dult (ȧ·dŭlt′)
a·dul·ter·ant (ȧ·dŭl′ tĕr·ănt)
a·dul·ter·ate (ȧ·dŭl′ tĕr·āt)
  -at·ing
  a·dul·ter·a·tion
         (ȧ·dŭl′ tĕr·ā′ shŭn)
a·dul·ter·y (ȧ·dŭl′ tĕr·ĭ)
  a·dul·ter·ess *n.*
  a·dul·ter·er
  a·dul·ter·ous *adj.*
ad·va·lo·rem (ăd·vȧ·lō′ rĕm)
ad·vance (ăd·văns′)
  -vanc·ing ad·vance·ment
ad·van·tage (ăd·văn′ tĭj)
  ad·van·ta·geous
         (ăd′ văn·tā′ jŭs)
ad·ven·ture (ăd·vĕn′ tŭr)
  ad·ven·ture·some
  ad·ven·tur·ess *n.*
  ad·ven·tur·ous *adj.*
ad·verb (ăd′ vûrb)
  ad·ver·bi·al (ăd·vûr′ bĭ·ăl)

ad·ver·sar·y   (ăd′ vĕr·sĕr′ ĭ)
-sar·ies
ad·verse   (ăd·vûrs′)
ad·verse·ly
ad·ver·si·ty   (ăd·vûr′ sĭ·tĭ)
-ties
ad·ver·tise   (ăd′ vĕr·tīz)
-tis·ing
ad·ver·tise·ment
                   (ăd·vûr′ tĭz·mĕnt)
ad·ver·tis·er
ad·vice   (ăd·vīs′) n.
(recommendation)
ad·vise   (ăd·vīz′) v.
(give advice to)
-vis·ing
ad·vis·a·bil·i·ty
                   (ăd·vīz′ à·bĭl′ ĭ·tĭ)
ad·vis·a·ble   ad·vis·ed·ly
ad·vise·ment   ad·vis·er
ad·vi·so·ry
ad·vo·cate   (ăd′ vô·kāt) n.
                   (-kāt) v.
-cat·ing
ad·vo·ca·cy   (ăd′ vô·kà·sĭ)
Ae·ge·an   (ê·jē′ ắn)
ae·gis   (ē′ jĭs)
a·er·ate   (ā′ ĕr·āt)
-at·ing
a·er·a·tion   (ā′ ĕr·ā′ shŭn)
a·er·a·tor
a·e·ri·al   (â·ẽr′ ĭ·ắl)
a·er·i·fy   (ā′ ĕr·ĭ·fī)
-fied   -fy·ing
a·er·o·dy·nam·ics
                   (ā′ ĕr·ô·dī·năm′ ĭks)
a·er·o·nau·tics   (ā′ ĕr·ô·nô′ tĭks)
a·er·o·sol   (ā′ ĕr·ô·sŏl′)
Aes·chy·lus   (ĕs′ kĭ·lŭs)
Ae·sop   (ē′ sŏp)
aes·thete   (ĕs′ thēt)
aes·thet·ic   (ĕs·thĕt′ ĭk)
(of beauty; see ascetic)
aes·thet·i·cism
                   (ĕs·thĕt′ ĭ·sĭz′m)
af·fa·ble   (ăf′ à·b'l)
af·fa·bil·i·ty   (ăf′ à·bĭl′ ĭ·tĭ)
af·fair   (à·fâr′)
af·fect   (à·fĕkt′) v.
(assume; see effect)
af·fec·ta·tion   (ăf′ ĕk·tā′ shŭn)
af·fect·ed·ly
af·fec·tion   (à·fĕk′ shŭn)
-ate·ly

af·fi·da·vit   (ăf′ ĭ·dā′ vĭt)
af·fil·i·ate   (à·fĭl′ ĭ·āt) v.
-at·ing
af·fil·i·a·tion   (à·fĭl′ ĭ·ā′ shŭn)
af·fin·i·ty   (à·fĭn′ ĭ·tĭ)
-ties
af·firm   (à·fûrm′)
af·firm·a·ble
af·fir·ma·tion   (ăf′ ĕr·mā′ shŭn)
af·firm·a·tive   (à·fûr′ mà·tĭv)
-tive·ly
af·fix   (à·fĭks′)
af·flict   (à·flĭkt′)
af·flic·tion   (à·flĭk′ shŭn)
af·flu·ence   (ăf′ lù·ĕns)
-ent
af·ford   (à·fōrd′)
af·fray   (à·frā′)
af·front   (à·frŭnt′)
Af·ghan·i·stan   (ăf·găn′ ĭ·stăn)
a·field   (à·fēld′)
a·float   (à·flōt′)
a·fore·said   (à·fōr′ sĕd′)
a·fore·thought   (à·fōr′ thôt′)
(malice aforethought)
a·fraid   (à·frād′)
Af·ri·can   (ăf′ rĭ·kắn)
aft·er   (ăf′ tĕr)
aft·er·burn·er
aft·er·din·ner speech
aft·er·ef·fect   aft·er·math
aft·er·noon   aft·er·taste
aft·er·thought   aft·er·ward
a·gain   (à·gĕn′)
a·gainst   (à·gĕnst′)
ag·ate   (ăg′ ĭt)
age   (āj)
ag·ing   age·less
age·long
a·gen·da   (à·jĕn′ dà)
a·gent   (ā′ jĕnt)
a·gen·cy   -cies
ag·glom·er·ate   (à·glŏm′ ĕr·āt)
-at·ing
ag·glom·er·a·tion
                   (à·glŏm′ ĕr·ā′ shŭn)
ag·gran·dize·ment
                   (à·grăn′ dĭz·mĕnt)
ag·gra·vate   (ăg′ rà·vāt)
-vat·ing
ag·gra·va·tion   (ăg′ rà·vā′ shŭn)
ag·gre·gate   (ăg′ rĕ·găt) adj.
                   (-gāt) v.
-gat·ing
ag·gre·ga·tion   (ăg′ rĕ·gā′ shŭn)

ag·gres·sive   (ă·grĕs′ ĭv)
    ag·gres·sion   ag·gres·sor
ag·grieved   (ă·grēvd′)
a·ghast   (à·gàst′)
ag·ile   (ăj′ ĭl)
    ag·ile·ly
    a·gil·i·ty   (à·jĭl′ ĭ·tĭ)
ag·i·tate   (ăj′ ĭ·tāt)
    -tat·ing
    ag·i·ta·tion   (ăj′ ĭ·tā′ shŭn)
    ag·i·ta·tor
ag·nos·tic   (ăg·nŏs′ tĭk)
    ag·nos·ti·cism   (-tĭ·sĭz′m)
ag·o·nize   (ăg′ ŏ·nīz)
    -niz·ing
ag·o·ny   (ăg′ ŏ·nĭ)
    -nies
a·grar·i·an   (à·grâr′ ĭ·ăn)
a·gree   (à·grē′)
    a·gree·a·bil·i·ty
       (à·grē′ à·bĭl′ ĭ·tĭ)
    a·gree·a·ble   a·gree·ment
ag·ri·cul·ture   (ăg′ rĭ·kŭl′ tụr)
    ag·ri·cul·tur·al
       (ăg′ rĭ·kŭl′ tụr·ăl)
    ag·ri·cul·tur·ist
       (ăg′ rĭ·kŭl′ tụr·ĭst)
a·gron·o·my   (à·grŏn′ ŏ·mĭ)
    a·gron·o·mist
a·hoy   (à·hoi′)
aid   (ād) v.
    (to help)
aide   (ād) n.
    (assistant)
    aide-de-camp   (ād′ dĕ·kămp′)
ail·ment   (āl′ mĕnt)
air   (âr)
    air base   air·borne
    air-con·di·tion
    air-con·di·tioned
    air-con·di·tion·er
    air-con·di·tion·ing
    air-cooled   air·craft
    air-dried   air drill
    air-driv·en   air·field
    air-filled   air fil·ter
    air force   air·lift
    air·line   air·mail
    air·man   air-mind·eđ
    air·plane   air·port
    air·proof   air raid
    air·strip   air·tight
Aire·dale   (âr′ dāl′)
aisle   (īl)
    (of a church; see *isle*)

---

a·jar   (à·jär′)
a·kim·bo   (à·kĭm′ bō)
a·kin   (à·kĭn′)
Al·a·bam·a   (ăl′ à·băm′ à)
    abbr. Ala.
    Al·a·bam·i·an   (ăl′ à·băm′ ĭ·ăn)
al·a·bas·ter   (ăl′ à·băs′ tēr)
à la carte   (ä lä kärt′)
a·lac·ri·ty   (à·lăk′ rĭ·tĭ)
A·lad·din   (à·lăd′ ĭn)
a·la·mode   (ä′ là·mōd′)
a·larm·ist   (à·lär′ mĭst)
A·las·ka   (à·lăs′ kà)
    A·las·kan
al·ba·tross   (ăl′ bà·trŏs)
al·be·it   (ôl·bē′ ĭt)
al·bi·no   (ăl·bī′ nō)
    -nos
al·bum   (ăl′ bŭm)
al·bu·men   (ăl·bū′ mĕn)
Al·bu·quer·que,
    N. Mex.   (ăl′ bŭ·kûr′ kĕ)
al·che·my   (ăl′ kĕ·mĭ)
    al·che·mist   (-mĭst)
al·co·hol   (ăl′ kŏ·hŏl)
    al·co·hol·ic   (ăl′ kŏ·hŏl′ ĭk)
    al·co·hol·ism   (ăl′ kŏ·hŏl·ĭz′m)
al·cove   (ăl′ kōv)
al·der·man   (ôl′ dēr·măn)
A·leu·tian   (à·lū′ shăn)
al·fal·fa   (ăl·făl′ fà)
al·ga   (ăl′ gà)
    pl. al·gae   (-jē)
al·ge·bra   (ăl′ jĕ·brà)
    al·ge·bra·ic   (ăl′ jĕ·brā′ ĭk)
a·li·as   (ā′ lĭ·ăs)
al·i·bi   (ăl′ ĭ·bĭ)
    -bis
al·ien   (āl′ yĕn)
    al·ien·a·ble   al·ien·ate
    al·ien·a·tion   (āl′ yĕn·ā′ shŭn)
a·lign   (à·līn′)
    a·lign·ment
al·i·men·ta·ry   (ăl′ ĭ·mĕn′ tà·rĭ)
al·i·mo·ny   (ăl′ ĭ·mō′ nĭ)
al·ka·li   (ăl′ kà·lĭ)
    -lies
    al·ka·line   (ăl′ kà·līn)
    al·ka·lin·i·ty   (ăl′ kà·lĭn′ ĭ·tĭ)
    al·ka·loid   (ăl′ kà·loid)
all   (ôl)
    all-A·mer·i·can
    all-out ef·fort
    all·o·ver pat·tern
    all right (*not* alright)

al·lay   (ă·lā′)
al·le·ga·tion   (ăl′ ĕ·gā′ shŭn)
al·lege   (ă·lĕj′)
  al·leg·ing
  al·leg·ed·ly   (ă·lĕj′ ĕd·lĭ)
Al·le·ghe·ny   (ăl′ ĕ·gā′ nĭ)
  (mts.)   -nies
al·le·giance   (ă·lē′ jăns)
al·le·go·ry   (ăl′ ĕ·gō′ rĭ)
  -ries
  al·le·gor·i·cal   (ăl′ ĕ·gŏr′ ĭ·kăl)
al·ler·gy   (ăl′ ēr·jĭ)
  -gies
  al·ler·gic   (ă·lûr′ jĭk)
al·le·vi·ate   (ă·lē′ vĭ·āt)
  -at·ing
  al·le·vi·a·tion   (ă·lē′ vĭ·ā′ shŭn)
al·ley   (ăl′ ĭ)
  al·leys   al·ley·way
al·li·ance   (ă·lī′ ăns)
al·lied   (ă·līd′)
al·li·ga·tor   (ăl′ ĭ·gā′ tēr)
al·lit·er·a·tion   (ă·lĭt′ ēr·ā′ shŭn)
al·lo·cate   (ăl′ ŏ·kāt)
  -cat·ing
  al·lo·ca·tion   (ăl′ ŏ·kā′ shŭn)
al·lot   (ă·lŏt′)
  al·lot·ted   al·lot·ting
  al·lot·ment
al·low   (ă·lou′)
  al·low·a·ble   al·low·ance
al·loy   (ă·loi′)
all right   (ôl rīt)
all·spice   (ôl′ spīs′)
al·lude   (ă·lūd′)
  (to refer; see *elude*)
  al·lud·ing
al·lure   (ă·lûr′)
  al·lur·ing   al·lure·ment
al·lu·sion   (ă·lū′ zhŭn)
  (indirect reference; see *illusion*)
  al·lu·sive
al·lu·vi·al   (ă·lū′ vĭ·ăl)
al·ly   (ă·lī′)
  al·lied   al·ly·ing
Al·ma Ma·ter   (ăl′ mă mā′ tēr)
al·ma·nac   (ôl′ mă·năk)
al·might·y   (ôl·mīt′ ĭ)
  al·might·i·ly
al·mond   (ä′ mŭnd)
al·most   (ôl′ mōst)
alms·house   (ämz′ hous′)
a·lo·ha   (ä·lō′ hä)
a·long·side   (ă·lŏng′ sīd′)
a·loof   (ă·lōōf′)

a·loud   (ă·loud′)
al·pac·a   (ăl·păk′ ă)
al·pha·bet   (ăl′ fă·bĕt)
  al·pha·bet·ic   (ăl′ fă·bĕt′ ĭk)
  al·pha·bet·ize   -iz·ing
al·read·y   (ôl·rĕd′ ĭ)
  (*Already* means previously: "He
  had *already* arrived"; *all ready*
  means prepared.)
Al·sace-Lor·raine
                      (ăl′ săs lŏ·rān′)
  Al·sa·tian   (ăl·sā′ shăn)
al·tar   (ôl′ tēr)
  (in church)
  al·tar·piece
al·ter   (ôl′ tēr)
  (to modify)
  al·ter·a·tion   (ôl′ tēr·ā′ shŭn)
  al·ter·a·ble
al·ter·ca·tion   (ôl′ tēr·kā′ shŭn)
  (quarrel)
al·ter e·go   (ăl′ tēr ē′ gō)
al·ter·nate   (ôl′ tēr·nĭt) *adj.*
                      (-nāt) *v.*
  -nat·ing
  al·ter·nate·ly   (ôl′ tēr·nĭt·lĭ)
  al·ter·na·tion   (ôl′ tēr·nā′ shŭn)
al·ter·na·tive   (ôl·tûr′ nă·tĭv)
  al·ter·na·tive·ly
al·though   (ôl·thō′)
al·tim·e·ter   (ăl·tĭm′ ĕ·tēr)
al·ti·tude   (ăl′ tĭ·tūd)
al·to·geth·er   (ôl′ tōō·gĕth′ ēr)
al·tru·ism   (ăl′ trōō·ĭz′m)
  al·tru·ist
  al·tru·is·tic   (ăl′ trōō·ĭs′ tĭk)
al·um   (ăl′ ŭm)
a·lu·mi·num   (ă·lū′ mĭ·nŭm)
a·lum·na   (ă·lŭm′ nă); *fem.*
  pl. a·lum·nae   (-nē)
a·lum·nus   (ă·lŭm′ nŭs)
  masc.; pl. a·lum·ni (-nī)
al·ways   (ôl′ wăz)
a·mal·gam·ate   (ă·măl′ gă·māt)
  -at·ing
  a·mal·gam·a·tion
                      (ă·măl′ gă·mā′ shŭn)
a·mass   (ă·măs′)
am·a·teur   (ăm′ ă·tûr′)
  am·a·teur·ish
am·a·to·ry   (ăm′ ă·tō′ rĭ)
a·maze   (ă·māz′)
  -maz·ing   a·maz·ed·ly
  a·maze·ment

Ām·a·zon (ăm′ ȧ·zŏn)
  Am·a·zo·ni·an
    (ăm′ ȧ·zō′ nĭ·ȧn)
am·bas·sa·dor (ăm·băs′ ȧ·dẽr)
  am·bas·sa·do·ri·al
    (ăm·băs′ ȧ·dō′ rĭ·ăl)
am·ber (ăm′ bẽr)
am·bi·dex·trous
    (ăm′ bĭ·děk′ strŭs)
am·bi·gu·i·ty (ăm′ bĭ·gū′ ĭ·tĭ)
  -ties
am·big·u·ous (ăm·bĭg′ û·ŭs)
am·bi·tion (ăm·bĭsh′ ŭn)
  am·bi·tious
am·biv·a·lence (ăm·bĭv′ ȧ·lĕns)
  -lent
am·ble (ăm′ b'l)
  -bling
am·bro·si·a (ăm·brō′ zhĭ·ȧ)
  am·bro·si·al
am·bu·lance (ăm′ bů·lȧns)
am·bu·la·tory (ăm′ bů·lȧ·tō′ rĭ)
am·bush (ăm′ bŏŏsh)
a·mel·io·rate (ȧ·mēl′ yŏ·rāt)
  -rat·ing
  a·mel·io·ra·tion
    (ȧ·mēl′ yŏ·rā′ shŭn)
a·men (ā′ měn′)
a·me·na·ble (ȧ·mē′ nȧ·b'l)
a·mend (ȧ·měnd′)
  a·mend·ment
a·men·i·ty (ȧ·měn′ ĭ·tĭ)
  -ties
A·mer·i·ca·na (ȧ·měr′ ĭ·kā′ nȧ)
A·mer·i·can·ism
    (ȧ·měr′ ĭ·kȧn·ĭz'm)
am·e·thyst (ăm′ ĕ·thĭst)
Ām·herst (coll.) (ăm′ ẽrst)
a·mi·a·ble (ā′ mĭ·ȧ·b'l)
  -bly
  a·mi·a·bil·i·ty
    (ā′ mĭ·ȧ·bĭl′ ĭ·tĭ)
am·i·ca·ble (ăm′ ĭ·kȧ·b'l)
  -bly
a·mid (ȧ·mĭd′)
  a·midst (ȧ·mĭdst′)
a·miss (ȧ·mĭs′)
am·i·ty (ăm′ ĭ·tĭ)
  (friendship; see *enmity*)
  -ties
am·mo·ni·a (ă·mō′ nĭ·ȧ)
am·mu·ni·tion (ăm′ ů·nĭsh′ ŭn)
am·ne·si·a (ăm·nē′ zhĭ·ȧ)
am·nes·ty (ăm′ něs·tĭ)

a·moe·ba (ȧ·mē′ bȧ)
  pl. a·moe·bae (-bē)
  a·moe·bic
a·mong (ȧ·mŭng′)
  a·mongst
a·mor·al (ă·mŏr′ ăl)
  a·mo·ral·i·ty (ā′ mŏ·răl′ ĭ·tĭ)
am·o·rous (ăm′ ŏ·rŭs)
a·mor·phous (ȧ·môr′ fŭs)
am·or·tize (ăm′ ẽr·tīz)
  -tiz·ing
  am·or·ti·za·tion
    (ăm′ ẽr·tĭ·zā′ shŭn)
a·mount (ȧ·mount′)
am·phib·ian (ăm·fĭb′ ĭ·ȧn)
  am·phib·i·ous
am·phi·the·a·ter
    (ăm′ fĭ·thē′ ȧ·tẽr)
am·ple (ăm′ p'l)
  -ply
am·pli·fy (ăm′ plĭ·fī)
  -fied   -fy·ing
  am·pli·fi·ca·tion
    (ăm′ plĭ·fĭ·kā′ shŭn)
  am·pli·fi·er
am·pu·tate (ăm′ pů·tāt)
  -tat·ing
  am·pu·ta·tion (ăm′ pů·tā′ shŭn)
  am·pu·tee (ăm′ pů·tē′)
a·muck (ȧ·mŭk′)
am·u·let (ăm′ ů·lĕt)
a·muse (ȧ·mūz′)
  -mus·ing   a·mus·a·ble
  a·muse·ment
a·nach·ro·nism
    (ȧ·năk′ rŏ·nĭz'm)
  a·nach·ro·nis·tic
    (ȧ·năk′ rŏ·nĭs′ tĭk)
an·a·con·da (ăn′ ȧ·kŏn′ dȧ)
an·al·ge·si·a (ăn′ ăl·jē′ zĭ·ȧ)
  an·al·ge·sic (-jē′ sĭk)
an·a·logue (ăn′ ȧ·lŏg)
  com·put·er
a·nal·o·gy (ȧ·năl′ ŏ·jĭ)
  -gies
  an·a·log·i·cal (ăn′ ȧ·lŏj′ ĭ·kăl)
  a·nal·o·gous (ȧ·năl′ ŏ·gŭs)
a·nal·y·sis (ȧ·năl′ ĭ·sĭs)
  pl. a·nal·y·ses (-sēz)
  an·a·lyst (ăn′ ȧ·lĭst)
  an·a·lyt·ic (ăn′ ȧ·lĭt′ ĭk)
  an·a·lyze (ăn′ ȧ·līz)
  -lyz·ing
  an·a·lyz·a·ble (ăn′ ȧ·līz·ȧ·b'l)

an·arch·y (ăn′ ăr·kĭ)
-arch·ies an·arch·ism
an·arch·ist
a·nath·e·ma (ȧ·năth′ ĕ·mȧ)
a·nat·o·my (ȧ·năt′ ŏ·mĭ)
-mies
an·a·tom·i·cal
(ăn′ ȧ·tŏm′ ĭ·kăl)
an·ces·tor (ăn′ sĕs′ tẽr)
an·ces·tral (ăn·sĕs′ trăl)
an·ces·try (ăn′ sĕs′ trĭ)
an·chor (ăng′ kẽr)
an·chor·age (-ĭj)
an·cho·vy (ăn·chō′ vĭ)
-vies
an·cient (ān′ shĕnt)
an·cil·lar·y (ăn′ sĭ·lĕr′ ĭ)
an·ec·dote (ăn′ ĕk·dōt)
(story; see antidote)
an·ec·do·tal (-dō′ tăl)
a·nem·o·ne (ȧ·nĕm′ ŏ·nĕ)
an·es·the·si·a (ăn′ ĕs·thē′ zhĭ·ȧ)
an·es·thet·ic (-thĕt′ ĭk)
an·es·the·tist (ăn·ĕs′ thĕ·tĭst)
an·es·thet·i·za·tion
(ăn′ ĕs·thĕt′ ĭ·zā′ shŭn)
an·es·the·tize (ăn·ĕs′ thĕ·tīz)
-tiz·ing
an·gel (ān′ jĕl)
an·gel·ic (ăn·jĕl′ ĭk)
an·ger (ăng′ gẽr)
an·gle (ăng′ g′l)
-gling an·gler
an·gle·worm
An·gli·can (ăng′ glĭ·kăn)
An·glo-Sax·on (ăng′ glŏ·săk′ s′n)
An·go·la, Afr. (ăng·gō′ lȧ)
An·go·ra (ăng·gō′ rȧ)
an·gry (ăng′ grĭ)
an·gri·er -gri·est
-gri·ly -gri·ness
an·guish (ăng′ gwĭsh)
an·gu·lar (ăng′ gû·lẽr)
an·gu·lar·i·ty (ăng·gû·lăr′ĭ·tĭ)
an·i·mal (ăn′ ĭ·măl)
an·i·mal·i·ty (ăn′ ĭ·măl′ ĭ·tĭ)
an·i·mate (ăn′ ĭ·māt) v.
(-măt) adj.
-mat·ing
an·i·ma·tion (ăn′ ĭ·mā′ shŭn)
an·i·mos·i·ty (ăn′ ĭ·mŏs′ ĭ·tĭ)
-ties
an·ise (ăn′ ĭs)
an·i·seed
An·ka·ra, Turk. (ăng′ kȧ·rȧ)

an·kle (ăng′ k′l)
an·kle·bone an·klet
an·nals (ăn′ ălz)
An·nap·o·lis, (ȧ·năp′ ŏ·lĭs)
Md.
an·neal (ȧ·nēl′)
an·neal·ing
an·nex (ȧ·nĕks′) v.
(ăn′ ĕks) n.
an·nex·a·tion (ăn′ ĕk·sā′ shŭn)
an·ni·hi·late (ȧ·nī′ ĭ·lāt)
-lat·ing
an·ni·hi·la·tion
(ȧ·nī′ ĭ·lā′ shŭn)
an·ni·hi·la·tor
an·ni·ver·sa·ry (ăn′ ĭ·vûr′ sȧ·rĭ)
-sar·ies
an·no·tate (ăn′ ŏ·tāt)
-tat·ing
an·no·ta·tion (ăn′ ŏ·tā′ shŭn)
an·nounce (ȧ·nouns′)
an·nounc·ing
an·nounce·ment
an·nounc·er
an·noy (ȧ·noi′)
an·noy·ance
an·nu·al (ăn′ û·ăl)
an·nu·al·ly
an·nu·i·ty (ȧ·nū′ ĭ·tĭ)
-ties
an·nul (ȧ·nŭl′)
an·nulled an·nul·ling
an·nul·la·ble an·nul·ment
an·nun·ci·a·tion
(ȧ·nŭn′ sĭ·ā′ shŭn)
an·ode (ăn′ ōd)
a·noint (ȧ·noint′)
a·noint·ment
a·nom·a·ly (ȧ·nŏm′ ȧ·lĭ)
-lies
a·nom·a·lous (-lŭs)
a·non (ȧ·nŏn′)
a·non·y·mous (ȧ·nŏn′ ĭ·mŭs)
an·o·nym·i·ty (ăn′ ŏ·nĭm′ ĭ·tĭ)
an·oth·er (ȧ·nŭth′ ẽr)
an·swer (ăn′ sẽr)
an·swer·a·ble
an·tag·o·nize (ăn·tăg′ ŏ·nīz)
-niz·ing
an·tag·o·nism an·tag·o·nist
an·tag·o·nis·tic
(ăn·tăg′ ŏ·nĭs′ tĭk)
Ant·arc·ti·ca (ănt·ärk′ tĭ·kȧ)
an·te- (ăn′ tĕ)
(prefix meaning before)

an·te·bel·lum   an·te·cham·ber
an·te·date
an·te·di·lu·vi·an (-dĭ·lū′ vĭ·ăn)
an·te me·rid·i·em (*abbr.* a.m.)
                  (-mē·rĭd′ ĭ·ĕm)
an·te·room
an·te·ced·ence (ăn′ tē·sēd′ ĕns)
-ent
an·te·lope   (ăn′ tē·lōp)
an·ten·na   (ăn·tĕn′ ȧ)
an·te·ri·or   (ăn·tēr′ ĭ·ēr)
an·them   (ăn′ thĕm)
an·thol·o·gy   (ăn·thŏl′ ŏ·jĭ)
-gies
an·thra·cite   (ăn′ thrȧ·sīt)
an·thro·poid   (ăn′ thrŏ·poid)
an·thro·pol·o·gy
               (ăn′ thrŏ·pŏl′ ŏ·jĭ)
an·thro·pol·o·gist
an·thro·po·mor·phize
               (ăn′ thrŏ·pŏ·môr′ fīz)
-phiz·ing
an·ti·air·craft   (ăn′ tĭ·âr′ kráft′)
an·ti·bi·ot·ic (ăn′ tĭ·bī·ŏt′ ĭk)
an·ti·bod·y   (ăn′ tĭ·bŏd′ ĭ)
-bod·ies
an·tic   (ăn′ tĭk)
an·tic·i·pate   (ăn·tĭs′ ĭ·pāt)
-pat·ing
an·tic·i·pa·tion
               (ăn·tĭs′ ĭ·pā′ shŭn)
an·tic·i·pa·to·ry
               (ăn·tĭs′ ĭ·pȧ·tō′ rĭ)
an·ti·cli·max   (ăn′ tĭ·klī′ măks)
an·ti·cli·mac·tic
               (-klī·măk′ tĭk)
an·ti·dote   (ăn′ tĭ·dōt)
(remedy; see *anecdote*)
an·ti·freeze   (ăn′ tĭ·frēz′)
an·ti·his·ta·mine
               (ăn′ tĭ·hĭs′ tȧ·mēn)
an·ti·ma·cas·sar
               (ăn′ tĭ·mȧ·kăs′ ēr)
an·ti·pa·sto   (ăn′ tē·päs′ tô)
an·tip·a·thy   (ăn·tĭp′ ȧ·thĭ)
-thies
an·ti·quar·i·an
               (ăn′ tĭ·kwâr′ ĭ·ăn)
an·ti·quat·ed   (ăn′ tĭ·kwāt′ ĕd)
an·tique   (ăn·tēk′)
an·tiq·ui·ty   (ăn·tĭk′ wĭ·tĭ)
-ties
an·ti·Sem·i·tism
               (ăn′ tĭ·sĕm′ ĭ·tĭz′m)

an·ti·Se·mit·ic
               (ăn′ tĭ·sĕ·mĭt′ ĭk)
an·ti·sep·tic   (ăn′ tĭ·sĕp′ tĭk)
an·ti·sep·ti·cize (-tĭ·sīz)
-ciz·ing
an·tith·e·sis   (ăn·tĭth′ ē·sĭs)
an·ti·tox·in   (ăn′ tĭ·tŏk′ sĭn)
an·ti·trust   (ăn′ tĭ·trŭst′)
an·vil   (ăn′ vĭl)
anx·i·e·ty   (ăng·zī′ ĕ·tĭ)
-ties
anx·ious   (ăngk′ shŭs)
anx·ious·ly
an·y   (ĕn′ ĭ)
an·y·bod·y   an·y·how
an·y·more   an·y·one
an·y·thing   an·y·way
an·y·where
a·or·ta   (ȧ·ôr′ tȧ)
a·part·heid   (ȧ·pärt′ hāt)
a·part·ment   (ȧ·pärt′ mĕnt)
ap·a·thy   (ăp′ ȧ·thĭ)
ap·a·thet·ic   (ăp′ ȧ·thĕt′ ĭk)
a·pé·ri·tif   (ȧ′ pā′ rē′ tēf′)
ap·er·ture   (ăp′ ēr·tụ̄r)
a·pex   (ā′ pĕks)
aph·o·rism   (ăf′ ŏ·rĭz′m)
aph·ro·dis·i·ac (ăf′ rŏ·dĭz′ ĭ·ăk)
a·pi·ar·y   (ā′ pĭ·ĕr′ ĭ)
-ar·ies
a·piece   (ȧ·pēs′)
ap·ish   (āp′ ĭsh)
a·plomb   (ȧ·plŏm′)
a·poc·a·lypse   (ȧ·pŏk′ ȧ·lĭps)
a·poc·a·lyp·tic
               (ȧ·pŏk′ ȧ·lĭp′ tĭk)
a·poc·ry·phal   (ȧ·pŏk′ rĭ·fȧl)
a·pol·o·gy   (ȧ·pŏl′ ŏ·jĭ)
-gies
a·pol·o·get·ic (ȧ·pŏl′ ŏ·jĕt′ ĭk)
-i·cal·ly   a·pol·o·gist
a·pol·o·gize   -giz·ing
ap·o·plex·y   (ăp′ ŏ·plĕk′ sĭ)
ap·o·plec·tic   (ăp′ ŏ·plĕk′ tĭk)
a·pos·tle   (ȧ·pŏs′ 'l)
ap·os·tol·ic   (ăp′ ŏs·tŏl′ ĭk)
a·pos·tro·phe   (ȧ·pŏs′ trŏ·fē)
a·poth·e·car·y (ȧ·pŏth′ ē·kĕr′ ĭ)
a·poth·e·car·ies′ meas·ure
ap·o·thegm   (ăp′ ŏ·thĕm)
a·poth·e·o·sis (ȧ·pŏth′ ē·ō′ sĭs)
pl. a·poth·e·o·ses (-sēz)
Ap·pa·la·chian (ăp′ ȧ·lā′ chȧn)
(mts.)
ap·pall   (ȧ·pôl′)

ap·pa·ra·tus (ăp′ à·rā′ tŭs)
 n. sing. & pl.
ap·par·el (à·păr′ ĕl)
 -eled, -el·ing
ap·par·ent (à·păr′ ĕnt)
ap·pa·ri·tion (ăp′ à·rĭsh′ ŭn)
ap·peal (à·pēl′)
 ap·peal·ing
ap·pear (à·pēr′)
 ap·pear·ance
ap·pease (à·pēz′)
 ap·peas·ing ap·pease·ment
 ap·peas·er
ap·pel·late (à·pĕl′ ăt)
ap·pel·la·tion (ăp′ ĕ·lā′ shŭn)
ap·pend (à·pĕnd′)
 ap·pend·age (à·pĕn′ dĭj)
ap·pen·dec·to·my
  (ăp′ ĕn·dĕk′ tô·mĭ)
 ap·pen·di·ci·tis
  (à·pĕn′ dĭ·sī′ tĭs)
ap·pen·dix (à·pĕn′ dĭks)
 -dix·es
ap·per·tain (ăp′ ĕr·tān′)
ap·pe·tite (ăp′ ĕ·tīt)
 ap·pe·tiz·er ap·pe·tiz·ing
Ap·pi·an Way (ăp′ ĭ·ăn)
ap·plaud (à·plôd′)
ap·plause (à·plôz′)
ap·ple (ăp′ ′l)
 ap·ple·sauce
ap·pli·ance (à·plī′ ăns)
ap·pli·ca·ble (ăp′ lĭ·kà·b′l)
 ap·pli·ca·bil·i·ty
  (ăp′ lĭ·kà·bĭl′ ĭ·tĭ)
ap·pli·cant (ăp′ lĭ·kănt)
ap·pli·ca·tion (ăp′ lĭ·kā′ shŭn)
ap·pli·ca·tor (ăp′ lĭ·kā′ tĕr)
ap·pli·ca·to·ry (ăp′ lĭ·kà·tō′ rĭ)
ap·pli·qué (ăp′ lĭ·kā′)
ap·ply (à·plī′)
 ap·plied ap·ply·ing
 ap·pli·er
ap·point (à·point′)
 ap·point·ee (à·poin′ tē′)
 ap·poin·tive ap·point·ment
Ap·po·mat·tox, (ăp′ ô·măt′ ŭks)
Va.
ap·por·tion (à·pōr′ shŭn)
 ap·por·tion·ment
ap·praise (à·prāz′)
 (to judge; see apprise)
 ap·prais·ing ap·prais·al
 ap·praise·ment ap·prais·er

ap·pre·ci·a·ble (à·prē′shĭ·à·b′l)
 -bly
ap·pre·ci·ate (à·prē′ shĭ·āt)
 -at·ing
 ap·pre·ci·a·tion
  (à·prē′ shĭ·ā′ shŭn)
 ap·pre·ci·a·tive
  (à·prē′ shĭ·ā′ tĭv)
 ap·pre·ci·a·to·ry
  (-à·tō′ rĭ)
ap·pre·hend (ăp′ rĕ·hĕnd′)
 ap·pre·hen·si·ble (-hĕn′ sĭ·b′l)
 ap·pre·hen·sion (-hĕn′ shŭn)
 ap·pre·hen·sive (-hĕn′ sĭv)
ap·pren·tice (à·prĕn′ tĭs)
 -tic·ing ap·pren·tice·ship
ap·prise (à·prīz′)
 (to inform; see appraise)
 ap·pris·ing
ap·proach (à·prōch′)
 ap·proach·a·ble
ap·pro·ba·tion (ăp′ rŏ·bā′ shŭn)
ap·pro·pri·ate (à·prō′ prĭ·ĭt)
  adj.
  (-āt) v.
 -at·ing
 ap·pro·pri·a·tion
  (à·prō′ prĭ·ā′ shŭn)
ap·prove (à·prōōv′)
 ap·prov·ing ap·prov·a·ble
 ap·prov·al
ap·prox·i·mate (à·prŏk′ sĭ·mĭt)
  adj.
  (-māt) v.
 -mat·ing
 ap·prox·i·mate·ly
  (à·prŏk′ sĭ·mĭt·lĭ)
 ap·prox·i·ma·tion
  (à·prŏk′ sĭ·mā′ shŭn)
ap·pur·te·nance
  (à·pûr′ tĕ·năns)
a·pri·cot (ā′ prĭ·kŏt)
a·pri·o·ri (ā′ prī·ō′ rĭ)
a·pron (ā′ prŭn)
ap·ro·pos (ăp′ rŏ·pō′)
ap·ti·tude (ăp′ tĭ·tūd)
apt·ly (ăpt′ lĭ)
aq·ua (ăk′ wà)
 aq·ua·cade aq·ua·lung
 aq·ua·ma·rine But: aq·ue·duct
a·quar·i·um (à·kwâr′ ĭ·ŭm)
a·quat·ic (à·kwăt′ ĭk)
aq·ue·duct (ăk′ wĕ·dŭkt)
a·que·ous (ā′ kwĕ·ŭs)
aq·ui·line (ăk′ wĭ·lĭn)

A·qui·nas, (*ȧ·*kwī′ nȧs)
St. Thom·as
ar·a·besque (är′ ȧ·bĕsk′)
A·ra·bi·an (*ȧ·*rā′ bĭ·ȧn)
Ar·a·bic (är′ ȧ·bĭk)
ar·a·ble (är′ ȧ·b'l)
ar·a·bil·i·ty (är′ ȧ·bĭl′ ĭ·tĭ)
ar·bi·ter (är′ bĭ·tēr)
ar·bi·tral
ar·bit·ra·ment (är·bĭt′ rȧ·mĕnt)
ar·bi·trar·y (är′ bĭ·trĕr′ ĭ)
ar·bi·trar·i·ly -i·ness
ar·bi·trate (är′ bĭ·trāt)
-trat·ing
ar·bi·tra·tion (är′ bĭ·trā′ shŭn)
ar·bi·tra·tor
ar·bor (är′ bĕr)
ar·bo·re·al (är· bō· rē·ȧl)
ar·bo·re·tum (är′ bō·rē′ tŭm)
ar·bor·vi·tae (är′ bŏr·vī′ tē)
ar·bu·tus (är·bū′ tŭs)
arc (ärk)
(bowlike curve; see *ark*)
arced
ar·cade (är·kād′)
arch (ärch)
arch·bish·op arch·dea·con
arch·di·o·cese arch·duke
arch·duch·ess arch·en·e·my
But: ar·che·type
ar·chae·ol·o·gy
(är′ kĕ·ŏl′ ō·jĭ)
-gist
ar·cha·ic (är·kā′ ĭk)
arch·an·gel (ärk′ ān′ jĕl)
arch·er·y (är′ chēr·ĭ)
ar·che·type (är′ kĕ·tīp)
Ar·chi·me·des (är′ kĭ·mē′ dēz)
Ar·chi·me·de·an
(är′ kĭ·mē′ dē·ȧn)
ar·chi·pel·a·go (är′ kĭ·pĕl′ ȧ·gō)
-goes
ar·chi·tect (är′ kĭ·tĕkt)
ar·chi·tec·tur·al
(är′ kĭ·tĕk′ tụ̄r·ȧl)
ar·chi·tec·ture (är′ kĭ·tĕk′ tụ̄r)
ar·chives (är′ kīvz)
arc·tic (ärk′ tĭk)
(frigid)
Arc·tic (ärk′ tĭk)
(Ocean, Circle, zone)
ar·dent (är′ dĕnt)
-den·cy
ar·dor (är′ dēr)
ar·du·ous (är′ dụ̄·ŭs)

a·re·a (ā′ rē·ȧ)
(flat surface; see *aria*)
a·re·a·way
a·re·na (*ȧ·*rē′ nȧ)
aren't (ärnt)
ar·go·sy (är′ gō·sĭ)
-sies
ar·gue (är′ gū)
-gu·ing ar·gu·a·ble
ar·gu·er
ar·gu·ment (är′ gụ̄·mĕnt)
ar·gu·men·ta·tion
(är′ gụ̄·mĕn·tā′ shŭn)
ar·gu·men·ta·tive
(är′ gụ̄·mĕn′ tȧ·tĭv)
a·ri·a (ä′ rĭ·ȧ)
(melody; see *area*)
ar·id (är′ ĭd)
a·rid·i·ty (*ȧ·*rĭd′ ĭ·tĭ)
a·ris·to·crat (*ȧ·*rĭs′ tō·krăt)
ar·is·toc·ra·cy (är′ ĭs·tŏk′ rȧ·sĭ)
-cies
a·ris·to·crat·ic
(*ȧ·*rĭs′ tō·krăt′ ĭk)
Ar·is·toph·a·nes
(är′ ĭs·tŏf′ ȧ·nēz)
Ar·is·tot·le (är′ ĭs·tŏt′ 'l)
Ar·is·to·te·li·an
(är′ ĭs·tō·tē′ lĭ·ȧn)
a·rith·me·tic (*ȧ·*rĭth′ mĕ·tĭk)
ar·ith·met·i·cal
(är′ ĭth·mĕt′ ĭ·kȧl)
a·rith·me·ti·cian
(*ȧ·*rĭth′ mĕ·tĭsh′ ȧn)
Ar·i·zo·na (är′ ĭ·zō′ nȧ)
abbr. Ariz.
Ar·i·zo·nan *or* Ar·i·zo·ni·an
(-nĭ·ȧn)
ark (ärk)
(ship; see *arc*)
Ar·kan·sas (är′ kȧn·sô)
abbr. Ark.
Ar·kan·san (är·kăn′ zȧn)
ar·ma·da (är·mä′ dȧ)
ar·ma·dil·lo (är′ mȧ·dĭl′ ō)
ar·ma·ment (är′ mȧ·mĕnt)
ar·ma·ture (är′ mȧ·tụ̄r)
arm·ful (ärm′ fo͞ol)
ar·mi·stice (är′ mĭ·stĭs)
ar·mor (är′ mēr)
ar·mor·y (är′ mēr·ĭ)
-mor·ies
ar·my (är′ mĭ)
-mies
a·ro·ma (*ȧ·*rō′ mȧ)

ar·o·mat·ic   (ăr′ ô·măt′ ĭk)
-i·cal·ly
a·round   (a·round′)
a·rouse   (a·rouz′)
-rous·ing
ar·peg·gio   (är·pĕj′ ō)
ar·raign   (a·rān′)
   ar·raign·ment
ar·range   (a·rānj′)
   ar·rang·ing
   ar·range·ment   ar·rang·er
ar·rant   (ăr′ ant)
   (notorious; see *errant*)
ar·ray   (a·rā′)
ar·rears   (a·rērz′)
ar·rest   (a·rĕst′)
ar·rive   (a·rīv′)
   ar·riv·ing   ar·riv·al
ar·ro·gance   (ăr′ ô·găns)
-gant
ar·ro·gate   (ăr′ ô·gāt)
-gat·ing
ar·ro·ga·tion   (ăr′ ô·gā′ shŭn)
ar·row   (ăr′ ō)
   ar·row·head
ar·se·nal   (är′ sĕ·năl)
ar·se·nic   (är′ sĕ·nĭk)
ar·son   (är′ s'n)
   ar·son·ist
ar·te·ri·al   (är·tēr′ ĭ·al)
ar·te·ri·o·scle·ro·sis
     (är·tē′ rĭ·ô·sklē·rō′ sĭs)
ar·ter·y   (är′ tēr·ĭ)
-ter·ies
ar·te·sian well   (är·tē′ zhan)
art·ful   (ärt′ fool)
-ful·ly   -ful·ness
ar·thri·tis   (är·thrī′ tĭs)
   ar·thrit·ic   (-thrĭt′ ĭk)
ar·ti·choke   (är′ tĭ·chōk)
ar·ti·cle   (är′ tĭ·k'l)
ar·tic·u·late   (är·tĭk′ û·lāt)
     adj.
     (-lāt) *v.*
-lat·ing
ar·tic·u·late·ly   (-lāt·lĭ)
ar·tic·u·la·tion
     (är·tĭk′ û·lā′ shŭn)
ar·tic·u·la·tive   (-lā′ tĭv)
ar·tic·u·la·tor   (-lā′ tēr)
ar·ti·fact   (är′ tĭ·făkt)
ar·ti·fice   (är′ tĭ·fĭs)
ar·ti·fi·cial   (är′ tĭ·fĭsh′ al)
ar·ti·fi·ci·al·i·ty
     (är′ tĭ·fĭsh′ ĭ·ăl′ ĭ·tĭ)

ar·ti·fi·cial·ly
ar·til·ler·y   (är·tĭl′ ēr·ĭ)
   ar·til·ler·y·man
ar·ti·san   (är′ tĭ·zăn)
art·ist   (är′ tĭst)
   ar·tis·tic   (är·tĭs′ tĭk)
   art·ist·ry
art·less   (ärt′ lĕs)
Ār·y·an   (âr′ ĭ·an)
as·bes·tos   (ăs·bĕs′ tôs)
as·cend   (a·sĕnd′)
   as·cend·ance   (a·sĕn′ dans)
-an·cy   -ant
as·cen·sion   (a·sĕn′ shun)
as·cent   (a·sĕnt′)
   (rise; see *assent*)
as·cer·tain   (ăs′ ēr·tān′)
   as·cer·tain·a·ble
   as·cer·tain·ment
as·cet·ic   (a·sĕt′ ĭk)
   (self-denying; see *aesthetic*)
   as·cet·i·cism   (-ĭ·sĭz'm)
as·cot tie   (ăs′ kŏt)
as·cribe   (ăs·krīb′)
-crib·ing   as·crib·a·ble
as·crip·tion   (ăs·krĭp′ shŭn)
a·sep·tic   (a·sĕp′ tĭk)
ash   (ăsh)
   ash·en   ash·es
a·shamed   (a·shāmd′)
   a·sham·ed·ly   (a·shām′ ĕd·lĭ)
Ā·sian   (ā·zhan)
   A·si·at·ic   (ā′ zhĭ·ăt′ ĭk)
a·side   (a·sīd′)
as·i·nine   (ăs′ ĭ·nīn)
   as·i·nin·i·ty   (ăs′ ĭ·nĭn′ ĭ·tĭ)
a·skance   (a·skăns′)
a·skew   (a·skū′)
a·sleep   (a·slēp′)
as·par·a·gus   (ăs·păr′ a·gŭs)
as·pect   (ăs′ pĕkt)
as·pen   (ăs′ pĕn)
as·per·i·ty   (ăs·pĕr′ ĭ·tĭ)
-ties
as·per·sion   (ăs·pûr′ shŭn)
as·phalt   (ăs′ fôlt)
as·phyx·i·ate   (ăs·fĭk′ sĭ·āt)
-at·ing   as·phyx·i·a
as·phyx·i·a·tion
     (ăs·fĭk′ sĭ·ā′ shŭn)
as·pic   (ăs′ pĭk)
as·pir·ant   (ăs·pīr′ ant)
as·pi·rate   (ăs′ pĭ·rĭt) *n.*
-rat·ing   (-rāt) *v.*
as·pi·ra·tion   (ăs′ pĭ·rā′ shŭn)

as·pire (ăs·pīr′)
-pir·ing
as·pi·rin (ăs′ pĭ·rĭn)
as·sail (ă·sāl′)
as·sail·a·ble as·sail·ant
as·sas·sin (ă·săs′ ĭn)
as·sas·si·nate
as·sault (ă·sôlt′)
as·sault·er
as·say (ă·sā′)
as·say·er
as·sem·ble (ă·sĕm′ b'l)
-bling
as·sem·blage (-blĭj)
as·sem·bly (ă·sĕm′ blĭ)
-blies as·sem·bly line
as·sem·bly·man
as·sent (ă·sĕnt′)
(agree; see ascent)
as·sent·or
as·sert (ă·sûrt′)
as·ser·tion as·ser·tive·ness
as·sess (ă·sĕs′)
as·sess·a·ble as·sess·ment
as·ses·sor
as·set (ăs′ ĕt)
as·sid·u·ous (ă·sĭd′ û·ŭs)
as·si·du·i·ty (ăs′ ĭ·dū′ ĭ·tĭ)
as·sign (ă·sīn′)
as·sign·a·ble
as·sign·ee (ăs′ ĭ·nē′)
as·sign·er as·sign·ment
as·sig·na·tion (ăs′ ĭg·nā′ shŭn)
as·sim·i·late (ă·sĭm′ ĭ·lāt)
-lat·ing
as·sim·i·la·ble (-lá·b'l)
as·sim·i·la·tion
(ă·sĭm′ ĭ·lā′ shŭn)
as·sim·i·la·tive (-lā′ tĭv)
as·sim·i·la·to·ry (-lá· tō′ rĭ)
as·sist (ă·sĭst′)
as·sist·ance as·sist·ant
as·so·ci·ate (ă·sō′ shĭ·āt) v.
-at·ing (-ăt) n., adj.
as·so·ci·a·ble (-shĭ·á·b'l)
as·so·ci·a·tion (ă·sō′ sĭ·ā′ shŭn)
-tion·al
as·so·ci·a·tive (-shĭ·ā′ tĭv)
as·so·nance (ăs′ ô·năns)
as·sort (ă·sôrt′)
as·sort·ment
as·suage (ă·swāj′)
as·suag·ing as·suage·ment
as·sua·sive

as·sume (ă·sūm′)
as·sum·ing
as·sump·tion (ă·sŭmp′ shŭn)
as·sure (ă·shoŏr′)
as·sur·ing as·sur·ance
as·sur·ed·ly as·sur·ed·ness
as·ter (ăs′ tēr)
as·ter·isk (ăs′ tēr·ĭsk)
as·ter·oid (ăs′ tēr·oid)
asth·ma (ăz′ mà)
asth·mat·ic (ăz·măt′ ĭk)
a·stig·ma·tism (à·stĭg′ mà·tĭz'm)
as·tig·mat·ic (ăs′ tĭg·măt′ ĭk)
as·ton·ish (ăs·tŏn′ ĭsh)
as·ton·ish·ment
as·tound·ing (ăs·tound′ ĭng)
as·tral (ăs′ trăl)
a·stride (à·strīd′)
as·trin·gent (ăs·trĭn′ jĕnt)
as·trin·gen·cy
as·trol·o·gy (ăs·trŏl′ ô·jĭ)
as·tro·log·i·cal
(ăs′ trŏ·lŏj′ ĭ·kăl)
as·tro·naut (ăs′ trŏ·nôt)
as·tron·o·my (ăs·trŏn′ ô·mĭ)
as·tron·o·mer
as·tro·nom·i·cal
(ăs′ trŏ·nŏm′ ĭ·kăl)
as·tro·phys·ics (ăs′ trŏ·fĭz′ ĭks)
as·tute (ăs·tūt′)
as·tute·ness
a·sun·der (à·sŭn′ dēr)
a·sy·lum (à·sī′ lŭm)
a·sym·me·try (à·sĭm′ ĕ·trĭ)
-tries
at·a·vism (ăt′ à·vĭz'm)
a·the·ist (ā′ thĕ·ĭst)
a·the·is·tic (ā′ thĕ·ĭs′ tĭk)
ath·lete (ăth′ lēt)
ath·let·ic (ăth·lĕt′ ĭk)
At·lan·tic (ăt·lăn′ tĭk)
at·las (ăt′ lăs)
at·mos·phere (ăt′ mŏs·fēr)
at·mos·pher·ic (ăt′ mŏs·fĕr′ ĭk)
at·oll (ăt′ ŏl)
at·om (ăt′ ŭm)
a·tom·ic (ă·tŏm′ ĭk)
at·om·ize (ăt′ ŭm·īz)
-iz·ing
a·tone (à·tōn′)
-ton·ing a·tone·ment
a·tro·cious (à·trō′ shŭs)
a·troc·i·ty (à·trŏs′ ĭ·tĭ)
at·ro·phy (ăt′ rŏ·fĭ)
-phied -phy·ing

at·tach (ă·tăch′)
 at·tach·a·ble at·tach·ment
at·ta·ché (ăt′ a·shā′)
at·tack (ă·tăk′)
at·tain (ă·tān′)
 at·tain·a·ble at·tain·ment
at·tain·der (ă·tān′ dĕr)
 (bill of)
at·tar (ăt′ ẽr)
at·tempt (ă·tĕmpt′)
 at·tempt·a·ble
at·tend (ă·tĕnd′)
 at·tend·ance -ant
at·ten·tion (ă·tĕn′ shŭn)
at·ten·tive (ă·tĕn′ tĭv)
 at·ten·tive·ness
at·ten·u·ate (ă·tĕn′ û·āt)
 -at·ing
 at·ten·u·a·tion
    (ă·tĕn′ û·ā′ shŭn)
at·test (ă·tĕst′)
 at·tes·ta·tion (ăt′ ĕs·tā′ shŭn)
at·tic (ăt′ ĭk)
at·tire (ă·tīr′)
 at·tir·ing at·tire·ment
at·ti·tude (ăt′ ĭ·tûd)
at·tor·ney (ă·tûr′ nĭ)
 -neys
at·tract (ă·trăkt′)
 at·tract·a·ble
 at·trac·tion (ă·trăk′ shŭn)
 at·trac·tive (ă·trăk′ tĭv)
 at·trac·tor
at·trib·ute (ă·trĭb′ ût) v.
 -ut·ing
at·tri·bute (ăt′ rĭ·būt) n.
 at·trib·ut·a·ble
    (ă·trĭb′ ût·a·b′l)
 at·tri·bu·tion (ăt′ rĭ·bū′ shŭn)
 at·trib·u·tive (ă·trĭb′ û·tĭv)
at·tri·tion (ă·trĭsh′ ŭn)
at·tune (ă·tūn′)
 at·tun·ing
au·burn (ô′ bĕrn)
Auck·land, (ôk′ lănd)
 New Zea·land
auc·tion (ôk′ shŭn)
 auc·tion·eer (ôk′ shŭn·ẽr′)
au·da·cious (ô·dā′ shŭs)
 au·dac·i·ty (ô·dăs′ ĭ·tĭ)
au·di·ble (ô′ dĭ·b′l)
 au·di·bil·i·ty (ô′ dĭ·bĭl′ ĭ·tĭ)
au·di·ence (ô′ dĭ·ĕns)
au·di·o-vis·u·al
    (ô′ dĭ·ō·vĭzh′ û·ăl)

au·dit (ô′ dĭt)
 -dit·ed -dit·ing
 au·dit·or
au·di·tion (ô·dĭsh′ ŭn)
au·di·to·ri·um (ô′ dĭ·tō′ rĭ·ŭm)
au·di·to·ry (ô′ dĭ·tō′ rĭ)
au·ger (ô′ gĕr)
 (tool; see augur)
aught (ôt)
 (cipher; see ought)
aug·ment (ôg·mĕnt′)
 aug·ment·a·ble
 aug·men·ta·tion
    (ôg′ mĕn·tā′ shŭn)
au gra·tin (ō′ grä′ tăn′)
au·gur (ô′ gĕr)
 (foretell; see auger)
 au·gu·ry
au·gust (ô·gŭst′)
 (stately; see August)
Au·gust (ô′ gŭst)
 (month; see august)
auld lang syne (ôld lăng sīn)
aunt (änt)
au·ral (ô′ răl)
 (of the ear; see oral)
au·re·o·my·cin (ô′ rē·ō·mī′ sĭn)
au re·voir (ō′ rē·vwär′)
au·ro·ra bo·re·a·lis
 (ô·rō′ ră bō′ rē·ā′ lĭs)
aus·pi·ces (ôs′ pĭ·sĕz)
aus·pi·cious (ôs·pĭsh′ ŭs)
aus·tere (ôs·tẽr′)
 aus·tere·ly
 aus·ter·i·ty (ôs·tĕr′ ĭ·tĭ)
Aus·tra·lia (ôs·trāl′ yä)
au·then·tic (ô·thĕn′ tĭk)
 au·then·ti·cal·ly
 au·then·ti·cate -cat·ing
 au·then·tic·i·ty
    (ô′ thĕn·tĭs′ ĭ·tĭ)
au·thor (ô′ thĕr)
 au·thor·ess
au·thor·i·tar·i·an
 (ô·thôr′ ĭ·târ′ ĭ·ăn)
au·thor·i·ty (ô·thôr′ ĭ·tĭ)
 -ties
 au·thor·i·ta·tive
au·thor·ize (ô′ thĕr·īz)
 -iz·ing
 au·thor·i·za·tion
    (ô′ thĕr·ĭ·zā′ shŭn)
au·to·bi·og·ra·phy
    (ô′ tô·bĭ·ŏg′ ră·fĭ)
 -phies

au·to·bi·o·graph·i·cal
    (ô′ tô·bǐ′ ô·grăf′ ǐ·kǎl)
au·to·crat   (ô′ tô·krăt)
  au·toc·ra·cy   (ô·tŏk′ rá·sǐ)
  au·to·crat·ic   (ô′ tô·krăt′ ǐk)
au·to·graph   (ô′ tô·grăf)
au·to·mat   (ô′ tô·măt)
au·to·mat·ic   (ô′ tô·măt′ ǐk)
  au·to·mat·i·cal·ly
au·to·ma·tion   (ô′ tô·mā′ shŭn)
au·tom·a·ton   (ô·tŏm′ á·tŏn)
au·to·mo·bile   (ô′ tô·mô·bēl′)
  au·to·mo·tive   (ô′ tô·mô′ tǐv)
au·ton·o·my   (ô·tŏn′ ô·mǐ)
  au·ton·o·mous
au·top·sy   (ô′ tŏp·sǐ)
-sies
au·to·sug·ges·tion
    (ô′ tô·sŭg·jĕs′ chŭn)
au·tumn   (ô′ tŭm)
  au·tum·nal   (ô·tŭm′ nǎl)
aux·il·ia·ry   (ôg·zǐl′ yá·rǐ)
-ries
a·vail·a·ble   (á·vāl′ á·b′l)
  a·vail·a·bil·i·ty
    (á·vāl′ á·bǐl′ ǐ·tǐ)
av·a·lanche   (ăv′ á·lánch)
a·vant-garde   (ä·vänt′ gärd′)
av·a·rice   (ăv′ á·rǐs)
  av·a·ri·cious   (ăv′ á·rǐsh′ ŭs)
a·venge   (á·věnj′)
-veng·ing   a·veng·er
av·e·nue   (ăv′ ĕ·nū)
a·ver   (á·vûr′)
-verred   -ver·ring
av·er·age   (ăv′ ĕr·ǐj)
a·verse   (á·vûrs′)
  a·verse·ly
a·ver·sion   (á·vûr′ zhŭn)
a·vert   (á·vûrt′)
  a·vert·i·ble
a·vi·ar·y   (ā′ vǐ·ĕr′ ǐ)
-ar·ies
a·vi·a·tion   (ā′ vǐ·ā′ shŭn)
a·vi·a·tor   (ā′ vǐ·ā′ tēr)
a·vi·a·trix   (ā′ vǐ·ā′ trǐks)
av·id   (ăv′ ǐd)
  a·vid·i·ty   (á·vǐd′ ǐ·tǐ)
av·o·ca·do   (ăv′ ô·kä′ dô)
-dos
av·o·ca·tion   (ăv′ ô·kā′ shŭn)
a·void   (á·void′)
  a·void·a·ble   a·void·ance
av·oir·du·pois   (ăv′ ĕr·dŭ·poiz′)

a·vow   (á·vou′)
  a·vow·al   (á·wăk′ ĕn)
a·wak·en   (á·wăk′ ĕn)
a·ware·ness   (á·wâr′ nĕs)
awe   (ô)
  awe·some   awe-strick·en
  aw·ing
a·weigh   (á·wā′)
aw·ful   (ô′ fôôl)
-ful·ly   -ful·ness
awk·ward   (ôk′ wĕrd)
awl   (ôl)
awn·ing   (ôn′ ǐng)
a·wry   (á·rǐ′)
ax   (ăks)
  ax·es
ax·i·al   (ăk′ sǐ·ǎl)
ax·i·om   (ăk′ sǐ·ŭm)
  ax·i·o·mat·ic   (ăk′ sǐ·ô·măt′ ǐk)
ax·is   (ăk′ sǐs)
  pl. ax·es   (-sēz)
ax·le   (ăk′ s′l)
a·zal·ea   (á·zāl′ yá)
az·ure   (ăzh′ ĕr)

B

bab·ble   (băb′ ′l)
  bab·bling
ba·boon   (bă·bōōn′)
ba·bush·ka   (bá·bŏŏsh′·ká)
ba·by   (bā′ bǐ)
-bies   ba·bies'-breath
ba·by·hood   ba·by·ish
ba·by-sit   ba·by sit·ter
Bab·y·lon   (băb′ ǐ·lŏn)
  Bab·y·lo·ni·an
    (băb′ ǐ·lō′ nǐ·ǎn)
bac·ca·lau·re·ate
    (băk′ á·lô′ rê·åt)
bach·e·lor   (băch′ ĕ·lēr)
ba·cil·lus   (bá·sǐl′ ŭs)
  pl. ba·cil·li   (-ī)
back   (băk)
  back·bite   back·bone
  back·gam·mon   back·ground
  back·hand·ed   back·log
  back·stairs   back·stop
  back·stroke   back talk
  back·ward   back·wa·ter
  back·woods
  back·woods·man
ba·con   (bā′ kŭn)

bac·te·ri·a　　(băk·tẽr′ ĭ·à)
　sing. bac·te·ri·um
　bac·te·ri·al
bac·te·ri·ol·o·gy
　　　　(băk·tẽr′ ĭ·ŏl′ ŏ·jĭ)
　bac·te·ri·ol·o·gist
badg·er　　(băj′ ẽr)
bad·i·nage　　(băd′ ĭ·näzh′)
bad·min·ton　　(băd′ mĭn′ t′n)
baf·fle　　(băf′ ′l)
　baf·fle·ment
bag·a·telle　　(băg′ à·tĕl′)
bag·gage　　(băg′ ĭj)
bag·gy　　(băg′ĭ)
Bagh·dad, I·raq　　(băg′ dăd)
ba·guette　　(bă·gĕt′)
Ba·ha·ma is.　　(bà·hä′ mà)
　Ba·ha·mi·an　　(-mĭ′ ăn)
bail　　(bāl)
　(set free; see *bale*)
bail·iff　　(bāl′ ĭf)
bail·i·wick　　(bāl′ ĭ·wĭk)
bait　　(bāt)
　(a lure; see *bate*)
bak·er·y　　(bāk′ ẽr·ĭ)
　-er·ies
bal·ance　　(băl′ ăns)
　-anc·ing
bal·co·ny　　(băl′ kŏ·nĭ)
　-nies
bald-head·ed　　(bôld′ hĕd′ ĕd)
bale　　(bāl)
　(bundle; see *bail*)
　bal·ing
bale·ful　　(bāl′ fŏŏl)
Bal·e·ar·ic (is.)　　(băl′ ĕ·ăr′ ĭk)
Ba·li　　(bä′ lĕ)
　Ba·li·nese　　(bä′ lĕ·nēz′)
balk·y　　(bôk′ ĭ)
ball　　(bôl)
　ball-and-sock·et joint
　ball bear·ing　　ball-point pen
　ball·room
bal·lad　　(băl′ ăd)
bal·last　　(băl′ àst)
bal·le·ri·na　　(băl′ ĕ·rē′ nà)
bal·let　　(băl′ à)
bal·lis·tic　　(bà·lĭs′ tĭk)
bal·loon　　(bà·lŏŏn′)
bal·lot　　(băl′ ŭt)
bal·ly·hoo　　(băl′ ĭ·hŏŏ)
balm　　(bäm)
　balm·i·ness
bal·sa　　(bôl′ sà)
bal·sam　　(bôl′ săm)

bal·us·trade　　(băl′ ŭs·trād′)
bam·boo　　(băm·bŏŏ′)
bam·boo·zle　　(băm·bŏŏ′ z′l)
　-zling
ba·nal　　(bā′ năl)
　ba·nal·i·ty　　(bà·năl′ ĭ·tĭ)
　ba·nal·ly
ba·nan·a　　(bà·năn′ à)
band·age　　(băn′ dĭj)
　-ag·ing
ban·dan·na　　(băn·dăn′ à)
ban·deau　　(băn·dō′)
ban·dit　　(băn′ dĭt)
　ban·dit·ry
band·stand　　(bănd′ stănd′)
ban·dy　　(băn′ dĭ)
　-died　　-dy·ing
　ban·dy-leg·ged
bane·ful　　(bān′ fŏŏl)
Banff, Can.　　(bămf)
Bang·kok,　　(băng′ kŏk)
　Thai·land
ban·ish　　(băn′ ĭsh)
ban·is·ter　　(băn′ ĭs·tẽr)
ban·jo　　(băn′ jō)
　-jos
bank·rupt　　(băngk′ rŭpt)
　bank·rupt·cy　　(-rŭpt·sĭ)
ban·ner　　(băn′ ẽr)
ban·quet　　(băng′ kwĕt)
　-quet·ed
ban·shee　　(băn′ shē)
ban·tam　　(băn′ tăm)
　ban·tam·weight
ban·ter·ing　　(băn′ tẽr·ĭng)
bap·tism　　(băp′ tĭz′m)
　bap·tis·mal　　(băp·tĭz′ măl)
　Bap·tist　　bap·tize
Bar·ba·dos (is.)　　(bär·bā′ dōz)
　bar·bar·i·an　　(bär·bâr′ ĭ·ăn)
　bar·bar·ic　　(bär·băr′ ĭk)
　bar·ba·rism　　(bär′ bà·rĭz′m)
　bar·bar·i·ty　　(bär·băr′ ĭ·tĭ)
　-ties
　bar·ba·rous　　(bär′ bà·rŭs)
bar·be·cue　　(bär′ bĕ·kū)
　-cu·ing
bar·ber　　(bär′ bẽr)
bar·bi·tu·rate　　(bär′ bĭ·tū′ rāt)
bar·ca·role　　(bär′ kà·rōl)
bare　　(bâr)
　bar·ing　　bare·ly
　bare·back　　bare·head·ed
bar·gain　　(bär′ gĭn)
　bar·gain·er

barge (bärj)
  barg·ing
bar·i·tone (băr′ ĭ·tōn)
bar·keep·er (bär′ kēp′ ẽr)
bar·ley (bär′ lĭ)
bar·na·cle (bär′ nȧ·k′l)
ba·rom·e·ter (bȧ·rŏm′ ĕ·tẽr)
  bar·o·met·ric (băr′ ŏ·mĕt′ rĭk)
bar·on (băr′ ŭn)
  (nobleman; see *barren*)
  bar·on·age (-ĭj)
  bar·on·ess
ba·ro·ni·al (bȧ·rō′ nĭ·ȧl)
ba·roque (bȧ·rōk′)
bar·racks (băr′ ȧks)
bar·ra·cu·da (băr′ ȧ·kōō′ dȧ)
  n. sing. & pl.
bar·rage (bȧ·räzh′)
bar·rel (băr′ ĕl)
  bar·reled   bar·rel chair
  bar·rel house   bar·rel or·gan
bar·ren (băr′ ĕn)
  (sterile; see *baron*)
  bar·ren·ness
bar·ri·cade (băr′ ĭ·kād′)
  -cad·ing
bar·ri·er (băr′ ĭ·ẽr)
bar·ris·ter (băr′ ĭs·tẽr)
bar·room (băr′ rōōm′)
bar·tend·er (bär′ tĕn′ dẽr)
bar·ter (bär′ tẽr)
bas·al me·tab·o·lism
      (bās′ȧl mĕ·tăb′ȯ·lĭz′m)
ba·salt (bȧ·sôlt′)
  ba·sal·tic (bȧ·sôl′ tĭk)
base (bās)
  bas·ing   base·ball
  base·board   base·less
  base·ly   base·ment
  base-mind·ed
bash·ful (băsh′ fŏŏl)
  bash·ful·ly   -ful·ness
bas·ic (bās′ ĭk)
  bas·i·cal·ly
bas·il (băz′ ĭl)
ba·sil·i·ca (bȧ·sĭl′ ĭ·kȧ)
ba·sin (bā′ s′n)
ba·sis (bā′ sĭs)
  pl. ba·ses (-sēz)
bas·ket (băs′ kĕt)
  bas·ket·ball   bas·ket·ful
  bas·ket·ry
bas-re·lief (bä′ rĕ·lēf′)
bass (bās)
  bass clef   bass drum

bass vi·ol
bas·set hound (băs′ ĕt)
bas·si·net (băs′ ĭ·nĕt′)
bas·so (bȧs′ ō)
bas·soon (bȧ·sōōn′)
bas·tard (băs′ tẽrd)
baste (bāst)
  bast·ing
bas·tille (băs·tēl′)
bas·tion (băs′ chŭn)
batch (băch)
bate (bāt)
  (to reduce; see *bait*)
  bat·ing
bathe (bāth) *v.*
  bath·ing
ba·tiste (bȧ·tēst′)
ba·ton (bȧ·tŏn′)
Bat·on Rouge, (băt′ 'n rōōzh′)
  La.
bat·tal·ion (bȧ·tăl′ yŭn)
bat·ten (băt′ 'n)
bat·ter·y (băt′ ẽr·ĭ)
  bat·ter·ies
bat·tle (băt′ 'l)
  bat·tling   bat·tle-ax
  bat·tle cruis·er bat·tle cry
  bat·tle·field   bat·tle·ground
  bat·tle·ship
bau·ble (bô′ b′l)
baux·ite (bôks′ ĭt)
bawd (bôd)
  bawd·i·ness   bawd·y
bawl·ing (bôl′ ĭng)
bay·o·net (bā′ ȯ·nĕt)
bay·ou (bī′ ōō)
ba·zaar (bȧ·zär′)
  (market; see *bizarre*)
ba·zoo·ka (bȧ·zōō′ kȧ)
beach (bēch)
  (seashore; see *beech*)
  beach·comb·er beach·head
  beach wag·on
bea·con (bē′ kŭn)
bead·y (bēd′ ĭ)
bea·gle (bē′ g′l)
bear·a·ble (bâr′ ȧ·b′l)
beard (bẽrd)
beast·ly (bēst′ lĭ)
  bes·tial (bĕst′ yȧl)
be·at·i·fy (bē·ăt′ ĭ·fī)
  (canonize)
  -fied   -fy·ing
be·at·i·fi·ca·tion
      (bē·ăt′ ĭ·fĭ·kā′ shŭn)

beau   (bō)
  pl. beaux   (bōz)
beau·ty   (bū′ tǐ)
  -ties
  beau·te·ous   (bū′ tě·ŭs)
  beau·ti·cian   (bŭ·tǐsh′ ǎn)
  beau·ti·ful   -ful·ly
  beau·ti·fy   -fied, -fy·ing
beaux-arts   (bō′ zär′)
bea·ver   (bē′ vẽr)
be·calm   (bě·käm)
be·cause   (bě·kôz′)
Bech·u·a·na·land
            (běch′ ŏŏ·ä′ nȧ·lǎnd′)
beck·on·ing   (běk′ ŭn·ǐng)
be·come   (bě·kŭm′)
  -com·ing
bed   (běd)
  bed·ded   bed·ding
  bed·bug   bed·clothes
  bed·fel·low   bed lamp
  bed lin·en   bed pad
  bed·post   bed·rid·den
  bed·roll   bed·room
  bed sheet   bed·side
  bed·spread   bed·stead
  bed·time   bed warm·er
be·daub   (bě·dôb′)
bed·lam   (běd′ lǎm)
Bed·ou·in   (běd′ ŏŏ·ǐn)
be·drag·gled   (bě·drǎg′ ′ld)
beech   (bēch)
  (tree; see *beach*)
beef·steak   (bēf′ stāk′)
bee·hive   (bē′ hǐv′)
bee·keep·ing   (bē′ kēp′ ǐng)
Be·el·ze·bub   (bě·ěl′ zě·bŭb)
beet   (bēt)
  (vegetable)
Bee·tho·ven,   (vän bā′ tō′ věn)
  Lud·wig van
bee·tle   (bē′ t′l)
  bee·tle-browed
be·fit   (bě·fǐt′)
  -fit·ted   -fit·ting
be·fore·hand   (bě·fōr′ hǎnd′)
be·fud·dle   (bě·fŭd′ ′l)
  -fud·dling   be·fud·dle·ment
beg·gar   (běg′ ẽr)
be·gin   (bě·gǐn′)
  -gan   -gin·ning
  be·gin·ner
be·go·ni·a   (bě·gō′ nǐ·ȧ)
be·grudge   (bě·grŭj′)
  -grudg·ing

be·guile   (bě·gīl′)
  -guil·ing   be·guile·ment
be·half   (bě·häf′)
be·have   (bě·hāv′)
  -hav·ing
  be·hav·ior   (bě·hāv′ yẽr)
be·hest   (bě·hěst′)
be·hind   (bě·hīnd′)
be·hold·en   (bě·hōl′ d′n)
be·hoove   (bě·hŏŏv′)
  -hoov·ing
beige   (bāzh)
be·ing   (bē′ ǐng)
Bei·rut,   (bā·rŏŏt′)
  Leb·a·non
be·la·bor   (bě·lā′ bẽr)
be·lat·ed·ly   (bě·lāt′ ěd·lǐ)
belch   (bělch)
be·lea·guer   (bě·lē′ gẽr)
bel·fry   (běl′ frǐ)
  -fries
Bel·gium   (běl′ jŭm)
  Bel·gian   (běl′ jȧn)
be·lie   (bě·lī′)
  -lied   -ly·ing
be·lief   (bě·lēf′)
be·lieve   (bě·lēv′)
  -liev·ing   be·liev·a·ble
  be·liev·er
be·lit·tle   (bě·lǐt′′ l)
  -lit·tling   be·lit·tle·ment
bel·la·don·na   (běl′ ȧ·dǒn′ ȧ)
belles-let·tres   (běl′ lět′ r′)
bell·hop   (běl′ hǒp)
bel·li·cose   (běl′ ǐ·kōs)
bel·lig·er·ence   (bě·lǐj′ ẽr·ěns)
  -en·cy   -ent
bel·lows   (běl′ ōz)
bell·weth·er   (běl′ wěth′ ẽr)
be·long·ing   (bě·lông′ ǐng)
be·lov·ed   (bě·lŭv′ ěd)
be·low   (bě·lō′)
be·muse   (bě·mūz′)
  -mus·ing
be·neath   (bě·nēth′)
Ben·e·dic·tine   (běn′ ě·dǐk′ tǐn)
  (pron. -tēn when referring to the
  drink of this name.)
ben·e·dic·tion   (běn′ ě·dǐk′ shŭn)
  ben·e·dic·to·ry
ben·e·fac·tor   (běn′ ě·fǎk′ tẽr)
  ben·e·fac·tress
be·nef·i·cence   (bě·něf′ ǐ·sěns)
  -cent

ben·e·fi·cial (běn' ě·físh' ál)
-cial·ly
ben·e·fi·ci·ar·y
(běn' ě·físh' ǐ·ěr' ǐ)
-ar·ies
ben·e·fit (běn' ě·fǐt)
-fit·ed -fit·ing
be·nev·o·lence (bě·něv' ồ·lěns)
-lent
Ben-Gur·ion, (běn' gōōr·yôn')
Da·vid
be·nign (bě·nīn')
be·nig·nant (bě·nǐg' nǎnt)
-nan·cy
be·nig·ni·ty (bě·nǐg' nǐ·tǐ)
-ties
be·numb (bě·nǔm')
-numbed
Ben·zed·rine (běn·zěd' rēn)
ben·zine (běn' zēn)
(cleaning fluid)
be·queath (bě·kwēth')
be·quest (bě·kwěst')
be·rate (bě·rāt')
-rat·ing
be·reave (bě·rēv')
-reav·ing be·reave·ment
be·ret (bě·rā')
ber·i·ber·i (běr' ǐ·běr' ǐ)
Be·ring (strait) (běr' ǐng)
Berke·ley, Calif. (bûrk' lǐ)
ber·ry (běr' ǐ)
ber·ries
ber·serk (bûr' sûrk)
berth (bûrth)
(a bunk; see *birth*)
be·seech·ing (bě·sēch' ing)
be·set (bě·sět')
-set·ting
be·side (bě·sīd')
be·siege (bě·sēj')
-sieg·ing
be·smear (bě·smēr')
be·smirch (bě·smûrch')
be·speak (bě·spēk')
best (běst)
best-known best-liked
best man best sel·ler
best-sell·ing
bes·tial (běst' yál)
bes·ti·al·i·ty (běs' tǐ·ǎl' ǐ·tǐ)
be·stow (bě·stō')
be·ta ray (bē' tà)
Be·thes·da, Md. (bě·thěz' dá)
Beth·le·hem, Pa. (běth' lě·ěm)

be·tide (bě·tīd')
be·tray (bě·trā')
-trayed -tray·ing
be·tray·al be·tray·er
be·troth (bě·trôth')
be·troth·al
bet·ter·ment (bět' ěr·měnt)
be·tween (bě·twēn')
be·twixt (bě·twǐkst')
bev·el (běv' ěl)
-eled -el·ing
bev·er·age (běv' ěr·ǐj)
Bev·er·ly Hills, (běv' ěr·lǐ)
Calif.
bev·y (běv' ǐ)
bev·ies
be·wail (bě·wāl')
-wailed -wail·ing
be·ware (bě·wâr')
be·wil·der·ing (bě·wǐl' děr·ǐng)
be·witch·ing (bě·wǐch' ǐng)
be·yond (bě·yǒnd')
bi·an·nu·al (bī·ǎn' ū·ál)
(occurring twice a year; see
biennial)
bi·an·nu·al·ly
bi·as (bī' ás)
bi·ased
Bi·ble (bī' b'l)
Bib·li·cal (bǐb' lǐ·kál)
bib·li·og·ra·phy
(bǐb' lǐ·ǒg' rá·fǐ)
-phies
bib·li·o·graph·i·cal
(bǐb' lǐ·ô·grǎf' ǐ·kál)
bib·u·lous (bǐb' ů·lǔs)
(tippling; see *bilious*)
bi·cam·er·al (bī·kǎm' ěr·ál)
bi·car·bon·ate (bī·kär' bǒn·āt)
bi·cen·ten·ni·al (bī' sěn·těn' ǐ·ál)
bi·ceps (bī' sěps)
bick·er·ing (bǐk' ěr·ǐng)
bi·cy·cle (bī' sǐk·'l)
bi·cy·cling bi·cy·clist
bid (bǐd)
bid·ding bid·da·ble
bid·den
bide (bǐd)
bid·ing
bi·en·ni·al (bī·ěn' ǐ·ál)
(once in two years; see *biannual*)
bi·en·ni·al·ly bi·en·ni·um
bier (běr)
(coffin)
bi·fo·cal (bī·fō' kál)

big·a·my   (bĭg′ á·mĭ)
  big·a·mist   big·a·mous
big·ot   (bĭg′ ŭt)
  -ot·ed   big·ot·ry
big·wig   (bĭg′ wĭg′)
bi·ki·ni   (bĭ·kē′ nĭ)
bi·lat·er·al   (bĭ·lăt′ ĕr·ăl)
  -al·ly
bilge wa·ter   (bĭlj)
bi·lin·e·ar   (bĭ·lĭn′ ê·ẽr)
bi·lin·gual   (bĭ·lĭng′ gwăl)
  bi·lin·guist
bil·ious   (bĭl′ yŭs)
  (ill-tempered; see *bibulous*)
bilk   (bĭlk)
bill·board   (bĭl′ bōrd′)
bil·let   (bĭl′ ĕt)
  bil·let·ed
bil·let-doux   (bĭl′ â·dōō′)
bill·fold   (bĭl′ fōld′)
bil·liards   (bĭl′ yẽrdz)
bil·lion   (bĭl′ yŭn)
bill of: (bĭl ŏv)
  bill of fare   bill of lad·ing
  bill of rights   bill of sale
bil·low   (bĭl′ ō)
bi·me·tal·lic   (bī′ mê·tăl′ ĭk)
bi·month·ly   (bī·mŭnth′ lĭ)
  (once in two months)
bi·na·ry   (bī′ ná·rĭ)
bin·au·ral   (bĭn·ô′ răl)
bind·er·y   (bīn′ dĕr·ĭ)
  -er·ies
bin·oc·u·lars   (bĭn·ŏk′ û·lẽrz)
bi·o·chem·is·try
        (bī′ ô·kĕm′ ĭs·trĭ)
  bi·o·chem·ist
bi·og·ra·phy   (bī·ŏg′ rá·fĭ)
  -phies
  bi·o·graph·i·cal
        (bī′ ô·graf′ ĭ·kăl)
bi·ol·o·gy   (bī·ŏl′ ô·jĭ)
  bi·o·log·i·cal (bī′ ô·lŏj′ ĭ·kăl)
  -cal·ly
bi·o·syn·the·sis
        (bī′ ô·sĭn′ thê·sĭs)
bi·par·ti·san·ship
      (bī·pär′ tĭ·zăn·shĭp′)
bi·par·tite   (bī·pär′ tīt)
bi·po·lar   (bī·pō′ lẽr)
  bi·po·lar·i·ty (bī′ pô·lär′ ĭ·tĭ)
birch   (bûrch)
bird   (bûrd)
  bird dog   bird·house

bird of par·a·dise
bird of prey   bird's-eye view
bird watch·er
bird·ie   (bûr′ dĭ)
  (golf term)
birth   (bûrth)
  (origin; see *berth*)
  birth·day   birth·mark
  birth·place   birth rate
  birth·right   birth·stone
Bis·cayne Bay,   (bĭs′kān)
  Fla.
bis·cuit   (bĭs′ kĭt)
bi·sect   (bī′ sĕkt′)
  bi·sec·tion·al (bī·sĕk′ shŭn·ăl)
bi·sex·u·al   (bī·sĕk′ shŏō·ăl)
bish·op   (bĭsh′ ŭp)
  bish·op·ric
Bis·marck,   (bĭz′ märk)
  N. Dak.
bi·son   (bī′ s'n)
bisque   (bĭsk)
bite   (bīt)
  bit·ing
  bit·ten   (bĭt′ 'n)
bit·ter   (bĭt′ ẽr)
  bit·ter·ness   bit·ter·sweet
bi·tu·mi·nous   (bī·tū′ mĭ·nŭs)
  coal
biv·ouac   (bĭv′ wăk)
  -ouacked   -ouack·ing
bi·week·ly   (bī·wēk′ lĭ)
bi·zarre   (bī·zär′)
  (odd; see *bazaar*)
  bi·zarre·ly
black   (blăk)
  black·ball   black·ber·ry
  black·board   Black Death
  black·ened
  black-eyed Su·san
  black·head   black-list *v.*
  black mag·ic   black·mail
  black mar·ket·eer
  black·out   black sheep
  black·smith
blad·der   (blăd′ ẽr)
blame   (blām)
  blam·ing   blam·a·ble
  blame·less
  blame·wor·thi·ness
blan·dish·ment   (blăn′ dĭsh·mĕnt)
blan·ket   (blăng′ kĕt)
  -ket·ed   -ket·ing
blar·ney   (blär′ nĭ)
bla·sé   (blä·zā′)

blas·phe·my (blăs′ fĕ·mĭ)
 -mies
 blas·phem·er (blăs·fĕm′ ĕr)
 blas·phe·mous (blăs′ fĕ·mŭs)
bla·tant (blā′ tănt)
 -tan·cy
blaz·er (blāz′ ĕr)
bla·zon (blā′ z′n)
 bla·zon·ry
bleach (blēch)
bleach·ers (blēch′ ĕrz)
bleak (blēk)
blear·y (blĕr′ ĭ)
bleat (blēt)
bleed (blēd)
blem·ish (blĕm′ ĭsh)
bless (blĕs)
 bless·ed·ness
blight (blīt)
blind (blīnd)
 blind·fold
 blind·man's buff
blink·er (blĭngk′ ĕr)
bliss (blĭs)
blis·ter (blĭs′ tĕr)
blithe (blīth)
 blithe·ly
blitz·krieg (blĭts′ krēg′)
bliz·zard (blĭz′ ĕrd)
bloat (blōt)
bloc (blŏk)
 (political group)
block (blŏk)
 block·bust·er block·head
 block·house
block·ade (blŏk·ād′)
 block·ade-run·ner
blond (blŏnd)
 adj. & n. masc.
blonde (blŏnd) n. fem.
blood (blŭd)
 blood·cur·dling
 blood·hound blood·ied
 blood·i·est blood pres·sure
 blood·shed
 blood·thirst·i·ness
 blood ves·sel
bloom·er (blōōm′ ĕr)
blos·som (blŏs′ ŭm)
blot (blŏt)
 blot·ting blot·ter
blotch (blŏch)
 blotch·es blotch·y
blow (blō)

blow·gun blow·out
blow·pipe blow·up
blown (blōn)
blowz·y (blouz′ ĭ)
blub·ber (blŭb′ ĕr)
bludg·eon (blŭj′ ŭn)
blue (blōō)
 blue·ber·ry blue·bird
 blue blood blue·bon·net
 blue book blue chip
 blue-eyed blue·grass
 blue jay blue laws
 blue-pen·cil v. blue·print
bluff (blŭf)
blu·ing (blōō′ ĭng)
blun·der·buss (blŭn′ dĕr·bŭs)
blur (blûr)
 blurred blur·ry
blurb (blûrb)
blurt (blûrt)
boa con·stric·tor (bō′ ä)
boar (bōr)
 (hog; see bore)
board·er (bōr′ dĕr)
 (one who boards; see border)
 board·ing·house
 board·ing school
boast (bōst)
 boast·ful -ful·ly
boat·swain (bō′ s′n)
bob·bin (bŏb′ ĭn)
bob·by-sox (bŏb′ ĭ·sŏks′)
 bobby-sox·er
bob·o·link (bŏb′ ô·lĭngk)
bob·sled (bŏb′ slĕd′)
bob·tail (bŏb′ tāl′)
Bo·ca Ra·ton, (bō′ kȧ rä·tōn′)
 Fla.
bock beer (bŏk)
bode (bōd)
 bod·ing
bod·ice (bŏd′ ĭs)
bod·y (bŏd′ ĭ)
 bod·ies bod·ied
 bod·i·less
 bod·i·ly (bŏd′ ĭ·lĭ)
 bod·y·guard
Boer (bōōr)
bo·gey (bō′ gĭ)
 (golf term) -geys
bog·gle (bŏg′ 'l)
 bog·gling
bo·gus (bō′ gŭs)
bo·gy (bō′ gĭ)
 (goblin) -gies

Bo·he·mi·an   (bō·hē′ mǐ·ɑ̇n)
boil·er   (boil′ ẽr)
bois·ter·ous   (bois′ tẽr·ŭs)
bold-faced   (bōld′ fāst′)
bo·le·ro   (bō·lâr′ ō)
Bo·liv·i·a   (bō·lǐv′ ǐ·ȧ)
boll wee·vil   (bōl)
bo·lo·ney   (bō·lō′ nǐ)
  (also baloney)
Bol·she·vik   (bŏl′ shě·vǐk)
bol·ster   (bōl′ stẽr)
bomb   (bŏm)
  bomb·proof   bomb·shell
  bomb shel·ter   bomb·sight
bom·bard   (bŏm·bärd′)
bom·bard·ier   (bŏm′bẽr·dẽr′)
bom·bast   (bŏm′ băst)
  bom·bas·tic   (bŏm·băs′ tǐk)
bo·na fi·de   (bō′ nȧ fī′ dě)
bo·nan·za   (bō·năn′ zȧ)
Bo·na·parte, Na·po·le·on
       (bō′ nȧ·pärt, nȧ·pō′ lê·ŭn)
bond   (bŏnd)
  bond·hold·er   bond·man
  bond ser·vant
bond·age   (bŏn′ dǐj)
bon·fire   (bŏn′ fīr′)
bon·net   (bŏn′ ĕt)
  bon·net·eđ
bon·ny   (bŏn′ ǐ)
bo·nus   (bō′ nŭs)
  -nus·es
bon voy·age   (bŏN′ vwȧ′ yàzh′)
bon·y   (bŏn′ ǐ)
  bon·i·ness
boob·y trap   (bōō′ bǐ)
book   (bŏŏk)
  book·bind·er   book·case
  book end   book·keep·er
  book·keep·ing   book·let
  book·lov·er
  book·mak·er   (bookie)
  book·mark   book·mo·bile
  book re·view   book·shelf
  book·store   book val·ue
  book·worm
boom·er·ang   (bōōm′ ẽr·ăng)
boon·dog·gle   (bōōn′ dŏg′′ l)
  -dog·gling
boor·ish   (bŏŏr′ ǐsh)
boost·er   (bōōs′ tẽr)
boot   (bōōt)
  boot·black   boot·leg
  boot·leg·ger   boot·lick·er

boot·ee   (bōō′ tē′)
  (baby's boot)
boo·ty   (bōō′ tǐ)
  (plunder)
booze   (bōōz)
bo·rax   (bō′ răks)
Bor·deaux   (bôr′ dō′)
bor·del·lo   (bôr·děl′ ō)
bor·der   (bôr′ dẽr)
  (edge: see boarder)
  bor·der·line adj.
bore   (bōr)
  (dull person; see boar)
  bor·ing   bore·dom
bo·ric acid   (bō′ rǐk)
born   (bôrn)
  (given birth)
borne   (bōrn)
  (carried)
bo·ron   (bō′ rŏn)
bor·ough   (bûr′ ð)
  (town)
bor·row   (bŏr′ ō)
borsch   (bôrsh)
bos·om   (bŏŏz′ ŭm)
boss·y   (bŏs′ ǐ)
  boss·i·ness
bot·a·ny   (bŏt′ ȧ·nǐ)
  bo·tan·i·cal   (bō·tăn′ ǐ·kȧl)
  bot·a·nist   (bŏt′ ȧ·nǐst)
botch   (bŏch)
  botch·er·y
both·er·some   (bŏth′ ẽr·sŭm)
bot·tle   (bŏt′ 'l)
  bot·tling   bot·tle-fed
  bot·tle·neck   bot·tle wash·er
bot·tom   (bŏt′ ŭm)
bot·u·lism   (bŏt′ û·lǐz′m)
bou·clé   (bōō′ klā′)
bou·doir   (bōō′ dwär)
bough   (bou)
bouɣʜt   (bôt)
bouil·la·baise   (bōō(l)′ yȧ·bās′)
bouil·lon   (bōō′ yŏN′)
  (soup; see bullion)
boul·der   (bōl′ dẽr)
bou·le·vard   (bōō′ lě·värd)
bounce   (bouns)
  bounc·ing   bounc·er
bound·a·ry   (boun′ dȧ·rǐ)
  -ries
bound·less   (bound′ lěs)
boun·te·ous   (boun′ tê·ŭs)
boun·ty   (boun′ tǐ)
  -ties

boun·ti·ful   -ful·ly

bou·quet   (boo·kā′)

bour·bon   (boor′ bŭn)

bour·geois   (boor·zhwä′)

bour·geoi·sie   (boor′ zhwä′ zē′)

bou·ton·niere   (boo′ tŏ·nyâr′)

bo·vine   (bō′ vīn)

bowd·ler·ize   (boud′ lĕr·īz)

-iz·ing

Bow·doin (coll.)   (bō′ d′n)

bow·el   (bou′ ĕl)

bow·er   (bou′ ĕr)

bow·er·y   (bou′ ĕr·ĭ)

-er·ies

bow·ie knife   (bō′ ĭ)

bow·knot   (bō′ nŏt′)

bow·leg·ged   (bō′ lĕg′ ĕd)

bowl·ing al·ley   (bōl′ ĭng)

bow·string   (bō′ strĭng′)

box   (bŏks)

box·car   box eld·er

box·ing glove   box kite

box of·fice   box spring

boy·cott   (boi′ kŏt)

boy·sen·ber·ry   (boi′ s′n bĕr′ ĭ)

-ber·ries

brace·let   (brās′ lĕt)

brac·ing   (brās′ ĭng)

brack·et   (brăk′ ĕt)

-et·ed   -et·ing

brack·ish   (brăk′ ĭsh)

brag   (brăg)

brag·ging

brag·ga·do·ci·o

   (brăg′ à·dō′ shĭ·ō)

brag·gart

Brahms, Jo·han·nes

   (brämz, yŏ·hän′ ĕs)

braid   (brād)

Braille   (brāl)

brain   (brān)

brain·i·ness   brain·less

brain storm   brain·wash·ing

brain·y

brake   (brāk)

(to slow down; see *break*)

brak·ing   brake·man

bram·ble   (brăm′ b′l)

bran·dish   (brăn′ dĭsh)

brand-new   (brănd′ nū′)

bran·dy   (brăn′ dĭ)

-died

Bra·si·lia,   (brà·zēl′ yà)

Bra·zil

bras·sière   (brà·zĕr′)

brass·y   (brás′ ĭ)

brass·i·ness

bra·va·do   (brà·vä′ dō)

brav·er·y   (brāv′ ĕr·ĭ)

bra·vo   (brä′ vō)

-voes

bra·vu·ra   (brà·vū′ rà)

brawl   (brôl)

brawl·er

brawn·y   (brôn′ ĭ)

brawn·i·ness

bra·zen   (brā′ z′n)

bra·zen·ness

Bra·zil·ian   (brà·zĭl′ yăn)

breach   (brēch)

(violation; see *breech*)

bread·bas·ket   (brĕd′ bás′ kĕt)

breadth   (brĕdth)

(width)

break   (brāk)

(burst; see *brake*)

break·a·ble   break·age (-ĭj)

break·down   break·through

break·up   break·wa·ter

break·fast   (brĕk′ fást)

breast·bone   (brĕst′ bōn′)

breath   (brĕth)

breath·less   breath-tak·ing

breathe   (brēth) *v.*

breath·ing

breech   (brēch)

(rear; see *breach*)

breech·es   (brĭch′ ĕz)

breed·ing   (brēd′ ĭng)

breeze   (brēz)

breeze·way   breez·y

breez·i·er   -i·est

-i·ly   -i·ness

breth·ren   (brĕth′ rĕn)

bre·vet   (brĕ·vĕt′)

-vet·ted   -vet·ting

bre·vi·ar·y   (brē′ vĭ·ĕr′ ĭ)

-ar·ies

brev·i·ty   (brĕv′ ĭ·tĭ)

brew·er·y   (broo′ ĕr·ĭ)

-er·ies

bribe   (brīb)

brib·ing   brib·a·ble

brib·er·y   -er·ies

bric-a-brac   (brĭk′ à·brăk′)

brick   (brĭk)

brick·bat   brick·lay·er

brick-red *adj.*   brick·yard

bride   (brĭd)

brid·al (of a wedding; see *bridle*)

bride·groom brides·maid
bridge (brĭj)
 bridg·ing bridge·a·ble
 bridge·work
bri·dle (brī′ d′l)
 (harness; see *bridal*)
 -dling bri·dle path
brief (brēf)
 brief case brief·ly
bri·er (brī′ ẽr)
brig (brĭg)
bri·gade (brĭ·gād′)
brig·a·dier (brĭg′ à·dẽr′)
 gen·er·al
brig·and (brĭg′ ănd)
bright (brīt)
 bright·en bright-eyed
Brigh·ton, (brī′ t′n)
 Eng·land
bril·liance (brĭl′ yăns)
brim (brĭm)
 brimmed brim·ming
 brim·ful brim·stone
brine (brīn)
 brin·ish brin·y
bri·quet (brĭ·kĕt′)
bris·ket (brĭs′ kĕt)
bris·tle (brĭs′ ′l)
 -tling
Bris·tol, (brĭs′ t′l)
 Eng·land
Brit·ain (brĭt′ ′n)
Brit·ish (brĭt′ ĭsh)
Brit·on (brĭt′ ŭn)
 (native of Britain)
Brit·ta·ny (brĭt′ ′n·ĭ)
 (region of France)
brit·tle (brĭt′ ′l)
 brit·tle·ness
broach (brōch)
 (to utter first; see *brooch*)
broad (brôd)
 broad·ax broad·cast
 broad·cloth broad·en·ing
 broad-gauge broad jump
 broad-mind·ed broad·side
 broad·sword broad·tail
bro·cade (brổ·kād′)
broc·co·li (brŏk′ ổ·lĭ)
bro·chure (brổ·shŏŏr′)
brogue (brōg)
broil (broil)
 broil·er
bro·ken (brō′ kĕn)
 bro·ken·heart·ed

bro·ker·age (brỏ′ kẽr·ĭj)
bro·mide (brō′ mīd)
bron·chi·al (brŏng′ kĭ·ăl)
 bron·chi·tis (brŏn·kī′ tĭs)
 bron·chit·ic (brŏn·kĭt′ ĭk)
bron·co·bust·er
   (brŏng′ kō·bŭs′ tẽr)
bron·to·sau·rus
   (brŏn′ tổ·sô′ rŭs)
bronze (brŏnz)
brooch (brōch)
 (jewelry; see *broach*)
brood (brōōd)
brook·let (brŏŏk′ lĕt)
Brook·line, (brŏŏk′ līn)
 Mass.
Brook·lyn, (brŏŏk′ lĭn)
 N.Y.
broom·stick (brōōm′ stĭk′)
broth (brŏth)
broth·el (brŏth′ ĕl)
broth·er (brŭth′ ẽr)
 broth·er·hood broth·er-in-law
 broth·ers-in-law
 broth·er·ly
brought (brôt)
brow·beat (brou′ bēt′)
brown (broun)
 brown Bet·ty brown·ie
 brown·stone brown sug·ar
browse (brouz)
 brows·ing
bruise (brōōz)
 bruis·ing
bru·nette (brōō·nĕt′)
brush-off (brŭsh′ ôf′)
brusque (brŭsk)
 brusque·ly
Brus·sels, (brŭs′ ′lz)
 Bel·gium
 Brus·sels lace
 Brus·sels sprouts
bru·tal (brōō′ tăl)
 bru·tal·i·ty (brōō·tăl′ ĭ tĭ)
 bru·tal·ize -iz·ing
 bru·tal·ly
brute (brōōt)
 brut·ish
Bryn Mawr (brĭn′ mär′)
 (coll.)
bub·ble (bŭb′ ′l)
 bub·bling bub·ble gum
 bub·bly
bu·bon·ic (bû·bŏn′ ĭk)
 plague

buc·ca·neer (bŭk′ ȧ·nēr′)
Bu·cha·rest, (bōō′ kȧ·rĕst)
Ro·ma·nia
buck (bŭk)
  buck·board   buck pri·vate
  buck·saw   buck·shot
  buck·skin   buck·tail
  buck·tooth   buck·wheat
buck·a·roo (bŭk′ȧ·rōō′)
buck·et (bŭk′ ĕt)
  buck·et·ful   buck·et seat
buck·le (bŭk′ 'l)
  -ling
buck·ram (bŭk′ rǎm)
bu·col·ic (bŭ·kŏl′ ĭk)
Bud·dha (bōōd′ ȧ)
  Bud·dhism   Bud·dhist
budge (bŭj)
  budg·ing
budg·et (bŭj′ ĕt)
  -et·ed   -et·ing
  budg·et·ar·y
Bue·nos Ai·res, (bwā′ nŭs âr′ ĕz)
  Ar·gen·ti·na
buf·fa·lo (bŭf′ ȧ·lō)
  -loes   buf·fa·lo fish
buff·er state (bŭf′ ēr)
buf·fet (bŭf′ ĕt)
  (slap)
buf·fet (bŏō·fā′)
  (sideboard)
buf·foon·er·y (bŭ fōōn′ ēr·ĭ)
  -er·ies
bug·a·boo (bŭg′ ȧ·bōō′)
bug·gy (bŭg′ ĭ)
  bug·gies
bu·gle (bū′ g'l)
  -gling   bu·gler
build (bĭld)
  build·ing   build-up
  built
bulb (bŭlb)
  bulb·ar (bŭl′ bēr)
  bulb·ous
bulge (bŭlj)
  bulg·ing
bulk·head (bŭlk′ hĕd′)
bulk·y (bŭl′ kĭ)
  bulk·i·ness
bull (bōōl)
  bull·dog   bull·doz·er
  bull·fight   bull·finch
  bull·frog   bull·head·ed
  bull pen   bull's-eye
  bull ter·ri·er   bull·whip

bul·let (bŏōl′ ĕt)
  bul·let·proof
bul·le·tin (bŏōl′ ĕ·tĭn)
bul·lion (bŏōl′ yŭn)
  (gold or silver; see *bouillon*)
bul·rush (bŏōl′ rŭsh′)
bul·wark (bŏōl′ wērk)
bum·ble·bee (bŭm′ b'l·bē′)
bump·kin (bŭmp′ kĭn)
bump·tious (bŭmp′ shŭs)
bun·dle (bŭn′ d'l)
  -dling
bun·ga·low (bŭng′ gȧ·lō)
bun·gle (bŭng′ g'l)
  -gling   bun·gler
bun·ion (bŭn′ yŭn)
bunk·house (bŭngk′ hous′)
Bun·sen burn·er
  (bŭn′ s'n)
bun·ting (bŭn′ tĭng)
buoy (bōō′ ĭ)
  buoy·ant (bōō′ yȧnt)
  -an·cy
bur (bûr)
  (weed; see *burr*)
bur·den (bûr′ d'n)
  bur·den·some
bu·reau (bū′ rō)
bu·reauc·ra·cy (bŭ·rŏk′ rȧ·sĭ)
  -cies
  bu·reau·crat·ic
    (bū′ rŏ·krăt′ ĭk)
bu·rette (bŭ·rĕt′)
bur·geon·ing (bûr′ jŭn·ĭng)
burgh·er (bûr′ gēr)
bur·glar (bûr′ glēr)
  bur·glar·ize   -iz·ing
  bur·gla·ry   -ries
bur·i·al (bĕr′ ĭ·ȧl)
bur·lap (bûr′ lăp)
bur·lesque (bûr·lĕsk′)
bur·ley (bûr′ lĭ)
  (tobacco)
bur·ly (bûr′ lĭ)
  (brawny)
  bur·li·ness
Bur·mese (bûr′ mēz′)
bur·nish (bûr′ nĭsh)
burnt (bûrnt)
burp (bûrp)
burr (bûr)
  (roughness or accent; see *bur*)
bur·ro (bûr′ ō)
  (donkey)
  bur·ros

bur·row   (bûr′ ō)
  (to dig)
bur·sar   (bûr′ sẽr)
burst   (bûrst)
bur·y   (bĕr′ ĭ)
  bur·ied   bur·y·ing
  bur·i·al
bus   (bŭs)
  bus·es   bus boy
bush·el   (boŏsh′ ĕl)
  -eled   -el·ing
bush·y   (boŏsh′ ĭ)
  bush·i·ness
busi·ness   (bĭz′ nĕs)
  busi·ness·like   busi·ness·man
bus·tle   (bŭs′ 'l)
  -tling
bus·y   (bĭz′ ĭ)
  bus·ied   bus·y·ing
  bus·i·er, -i·est, -i·ly, -i·ness
  bus·y·bod·y
butch·er   (boŏch′ ẽr)
  butch·er·y
but   (bŭt)
  (*prep., conj.*; see *butt*)
butt   (bŭt)
  (end)
butte   (būt)
  (hill)
but·ter   (bŭt′ ẽr)
  but·ter·cup   but·ter·fat
  but·ter·fin·gered
  but·ter·fly   -flies
  but·ter·milk   but·ter·scotch
but·tock   (bŭt′ ŭk)
but·ton   (bŭt′ 'n)
  but·ton·hole
but·tress   (bŭt′ rĕs)
buy·er   (bī′ ẽr)
buz·zard   (bŭz′ ẽrd)
by   (bī)
  by-and-by   by·gone
  by·law   by-line
  by·name   by·pass
  by·path   by-prod·uct
  by·stand·er   by·street
  by·way   by·word
By·zan·tine   (bĭ·zăn′ tĭn)

C

ca·bal   (kȧ·băl′)
  cab·a·lis·tic   (kăb′ ȧ·lĭs′ tĭc)
cab·a·ret   (kăb′ ȧ·rā′)

cab·bage   (kăb′ ĭj)
cab·in   (kăb′ ĭn)
  cab·in class   cab·in cruis·er
cab·i·net   (kăb′ ĭ·nĕt)
  cab·i·net·mak·er
ca·ble   (kā′ b'l)
  -bling   ca·ble car
  ca·ble·gram
ca·boose   (kȧ·boōs′)
cache   (kăsh)
ca·chet   (kă·shā′)
cack·le   (kăk′ 'l)
  -ling
ca·coph·o·ny   (kȧ·kŏf′ ō·nĭ)
cac·tus   (kăk′ tŭs)
  pl. cac·ti   (-tī)
ca·dav·er   (kȧ·dăv′ ẽr)
  ca·dav·er·ous
cad·die   (kăd′ ĭ)
  cad·died   cad·dy·ing
cad·dish   (kăd′ ĭsh)
ca·dence   (kā′ dĕns)
  -dent
ca·det   (kȧ·dĕt′)
Cad·il·lac   (kăd′ 'l·ăk)
Cae·sar·e·an   (sĕ·zâr′ ê·ăn)
  (also spelled *Cesarean*)
ca·fé   (kȧ·fā′)
caf·e·te·ri·a   (kăf′ ê·tẽr′ ĭ·ȧ)
caf·fe·ine   (kăf′ ê·ĭn)
cage·y   (kāj′ ĭ)
  cag·i·ness
Cai·ro, E·gypt   (kī′ rō)
Cai·ro, Ill.   (kâr′ ō)
cais·son   (kā′ sŭn)
ca·jole   (kȧ·jōl′)
  -jol·ing   ca·jole·ment
  ca·jol·er·y
cake   (kāk)
  cake·box   cake pan
  cake·walk
cal·a·boose   (kăl′ ȧ·boōs)
cal·a·mine   (kăl′ ȧ·mīn)
ca·lam·i·ty   (kȧ·lăm′ ĭ·tĭ)
  -ties   ca·lam·i·tous
cal·ci·fy   (kăl′ sĭ·fī)
  -fied   -fy·ing
  cal·ci·fi·ca·tion
             (kăl′ sĭ·fĭ·kā′ shŭn)
cal·ci·mine   (kăl′ sĭ·mīn)
cal·ci·um   (kăl′ sĭ·ŭm)
cal·cu·late   (kăl′ kŭ·lāt)
  -lat·ing   cal·cu·la·ble
  cal·cu·la·tion   (kăl′kŭ·lā′ shŭn)
  cal·cu·la·tor

cal·cu·lus (kăl′ kû·lŭs)
  pl. cal·cu·li (-lī)
Cal·cut·ta, (kăl·kŭt′ à)
  In·di·a
cal·dron (kôl′ drŭn)
cal·en·dar (kăl′ ĕn·dẽr)
calf (kăf)
  calves   calf·skin
Cal·ga·ry, (kăl′ gà·rĭ)
  Can.
cal·i·ber (kăl′ ĭ·bẽr)
cal·i·co (kăl′ ĭ·kō)
  -coes
Cal·i·for·nia (kăl′ ĭ·fôrn′ yà)
  abbr. Calif. *or* Cal.
  Cal·i·for·nian
ca·liph (kā′ lĭf)
cal·is·then·ics (kăl′ ĭs·thĕn′ ĭks)
calk (kôk)
cal·lig·ra·phy (kà·lĭg′ rà·fĭ)
cal·lous (kăl′ ŭs) *adj.*
  (unfeeling)
cal·low (kăl′ ō)
cal·lus (kăl′ ŭs) *n.*
  (thickened skin)
calm (käm)
  calm·ly
cal·o·rie (kăl′ ô·rĭ)
ca·lor·ic (kà·lŏr′ ĭk)
cal·um·ny (kăl′ ŭm·nĭ)
  -nies
Cal·va·ry (kăl′ và·rĭ)
Cal·vin·ist (kăl′ vĭn·ĭst)
ca·lyp·so (kà·lĭp′ sō)
ca·ma·ra·de·rie
      (kä′ mà·rä′ dĕ·rē)
cam·el (kăm′ ĕl)
ca·mel·li·a (kà·mĕl′ ĭ·à)
cam·e·o (kăm′ ĕ·ō)
cam·er·a (kăm′ ẽr·à)
cam·i·sole (kăm′ ĭ·sōl)
cam·o·mile tea (kăm′ ô·mīl)
cam·ou·flage (kăm′ ŏŏ·fläzh)
  -flag·ing
cam·paign (kăm·pān′)
camp·fire (kămp′ fīr′)
cam·phor (kăm′ fẽr)
  cam·phor·at·ed
cam·pus (kăm′ pŭs)
Can·a·da (kăn′ à·dà)
  Ca·na·di·an (kà·nā′ dĭ·ăn)
ca·nal (kà·năl′)
  -nalled   -nal·ling
  ca·nal·boat

can·a·pé (kăn′ à·pā)
ca·nard (kà·närd′)
ca·nar·y (kà·nâr′ ĭ)
  -nar·ies
ca·nas·ta (kà·năs′ tà)
Ca·nav·er·al, (kà·năv′ ẽr·ăl)
  Cape
Can·ber·ra, (kăn′ bẽr·à)
  Aus·tra·lia
can·can (kăn′ kăn)
can·cel (kăn′ sĕl)
  -celed   -cel·ing
  can·cel·er
can·cel·la·tion (kăn′ sĕ·lā′ shŭn)
can·cer (kăn′ sẽr)
  can·cer·ous
can·de·la·brum
      (kăn′ dĕ·lä′ brŭm)
  pl. can·de·la·bra
can·des·cence (kăn·dĕs′ ĕns)
  -cent
can·did (kăn′ dĭd)
can·di·date (kăn′ dĭ·dāt)
  can·di·da·cy (kăn′ dĭ·dà·sĭ)
  can·di·da·ture (kăn′ dĭ·dà·tụr)
can·died (kăn′ dĭd)
can·dle (kăn′ d′l)
  can·dle·light   can·dle pow·er
  can·dle·stick
  can·dle·wick bed·spread
can·dor (kăn′ dẽr)
can·dy (kăn′ dĭ)
  -dies, -died, -dy·ing
ca·nine (kā′ nīn)
can·is·ter (kăn′ ĭs·tẽr)
can·ker (kăng′ kẽr)
  can·ker·ous   can·ker sore
  can·ker·worm
can·ner·y (kăn′ ẽr·ĭ)
  can·ner·ies
Cannes, France (kăn)
can·ni·bal (kăn′ ĭ·băl)
  can·ni·bal·ism
  can·ni·bal·is·tic
      (kăn′ ĭ·băl·ĭs′ tĭk)
can·ning (kăn′ ĭng)
can·non (kăn′ ŭn)
  (gun; see *canon*)
  can·non·ade (kăn′ ŭn·ād′)
  can·non ball
  can·non·eer (kăn′ ŭn·ẽr′)
can·not (kăn′ nŏt)
can·ny (kăn′ ĭ)
  can·ni·ness

ca·noe   (ká·nōō′)
  -noed   -noe·ing
  ca·noe·ist

can·on   (kăn′ ŭn)
  (decree; see *cannon*)
  ca·non·i·cal   (ká·nŏn′ ĭ·kál)
  ca·non·ize   -iz·ing
  can·on law

can·o·py   (kăn′ ŏ·pĭ)
  -pies

can't   (kănt)

can·ta·loupe   (kăn′ tá·lōp)

can·tan·ker·ous
         (kăn·tăng′·kĕr·ŭs)

can·ta·ta   (kán·tä′ tá)

can·teen   (kăn·tēn′)

can·ter   (kăn′ tĕr)
  (light gallop; see *cantor*)

Can·ter·bur·y   (kăn′ tĕr·bĕr·ĭ)

can·ti·cle   (kăn′ tĭ·k'l)

can·ti·le·ver   (kăn′ tĭ·lē′ vĕr)

can·to   (kăn′ tō)
  -tos

can·ton   (kăn′ tŏn)

Can·ton·ese   (kăn′ tŏn·ēz′)

can·tor   (kăn′ tôr)
  (singer; see *canter*)

can·vas   (kăn′ vás)
  (cloth)
  can·vas·back duck

can·vass   (kăn′ vás)
  (to solicit)   can·vass·er

can·yon   (kăn′ yŭn)

ca·pa·ble   (kā′ pá·b'l)
  -bly
  ca·pa·bil·i·ty   (kā′ pá·bĭl′ ĭ·tĭ)

ca·pa·cious   (ká·pā′ shŭs)

ca·pac·i·ty   (ká·păs′ ĭ·tĭ)
  -ties

ca·per   (kā′ pĕr)

cape·skin   (kāp′ skĭn′)

cap·il·lar·y   (kăp′ ĭ·lĕr′ ĭ)
  -il·lar·ies

cap·i·tal   (kăp′ ĭ·tál)
  (property)
  cap·i·tal cit·y
  cap·i·tal goods
  cap·i·tal·ism   -ist
  cap·i·tal·i·za·tion
         (kăp′ ĭ·tál·ĭ·zā′ shŭn)
  cap·i·tal·ize   -iz·ing
  cap·i·tal lev·y
  cap·i·tal stock

cap·i·tol   (kăp′ ĭ·tŏl)
  (statehouse)

ca·pit·u·late   (ká·pĭt′ ū·lāt)
  -lat·ing
  ca·pit·u·la·tion
         (ká·pĭt′ ū·lā′ shŭn)

ca·pon   (kā′ pŏn)

ca·price   (ká·prēs′)
  ca·pri·cious   (ká·prĭsh′ ŭs)

cap·size   (kăp·sīz′)
  -siz·ing

cap·sule   (kăp′ sūl)

cap·tain   (kăp′ tĭn)
  cap·tain·cy

cap·tion   (kăp′ shŭn)

cap·tious   (kăp′ shŭs)

cap·ti·vate   (kăp′ tĭ·vāt)
  -vat·ing
  cap·ti·va·tion
         (kăp′ tĭ·vā′ shŭn)
  cap·ti·va·tor

cap·tive   (kăp′ tĭv)
  cap·tiv·i·ty   (kăp·tĭv′ ĭ·tĭ)

cap·tor   (kăp′ tĕr)

cap·ture   (kăp′ tûr)
  -tur·ing

car·a·mel   (kăr′ á·mĕl)

car·at   (kăr′ át)
  (unit of weight; see *caret*, *carrot*)

car·a·van   (kăr′ á·văn)

car·a·way seeds   (kăr′ á·wā)

car·bide   (kär′ bīd)

car·bine   (kär′ bīn)

car·bo·hy·drate   (kär′ bŏ·hī′ drāt)

car·bol·ic ac·id   (kär·bŏl′ ĭk)

car·bon   (kär′ bŏn)
  car·bo·na·ceous
         (kär′ bŏ·nā′ shŭs)
  car·bo·nat·ed
  car·bon·a·tion
         (kär′ bŏn·ā′ shŭn)
  car·bon bi·sul·fide
  car·bon black
  car·bon cop·y
  car·bon di·ox·ide
  car·bon di·sul·fide
  car·bon·ic   (kär·bŏn′ ĭk)
  car·bon·if·er·ous
         (kär′ bŏn·ĭf′ ĕr·ŭs)
  car·bon mon·ox·ide
  car·bon pa·per
  car·bon proc·ess
  car·bon tet·ra·chlo·ride

car·bun·cle   (kär′ bŭng·k'l)

car·bu·ret·or   (kär′ bŭ·rā′ tĕr)

car·cass   (kär′ kás)
  -cass·es

car·ci·no·ma (kär′ sǐ·nō′ má)
  pl. car·ci·no·ma·ta (-má·tá)
car·da·mom (kär′ dá·mŭm)
card·board (kärd′ bōrd′)
car·di·ac (kär′ dǐ·ăk)
car·di·gan (kär′ dǐ·gán)
car·di·nal (kär′ dǐ·nál)
car·di·o·gram (kär′ dǐ·ō·grăm′)
  car·di·o·graph
  car·di·ol·o·gy (kär′ dǐ·ŏl′ ō·jǐ)
card·sharp (kärd′ shärp′)
care (kâr)
  car·ing   care·free
  care·ful, -ful·ly, -ful·ness
  care·less   -less·ly
  care·tak·er   care·worn
ca·reen (ká·rēn′)
  -reen·ing
ca·reer (ká·rẽr′)
ca·ress (ká·rĕs′)
  ca·ress·ing·ly
car·et (kär′ ĕt)
  (proofreaders' mark; see *carat,*
  carrot)
car·go (kär′ gō)
  -goes
Car·ib·be·an (kär′ ǐ·bē′ án)
  (sea)
car·i·bou (kär′ ǐ·bōō)
  n. sing. & pl.
car·i·ca·ture (kär′ ǐ·ká·tūr)
car·i·es (kâr′ ǐ·ēz)
  (tooth decay)
car·il·lon (kär′ ǐ·lŏn)
car·mine (kär′ mǐn)
car·nage (kär′ nǐj)
car·nal (kär′ nál)
  car·nal·i·ty (kär·năl′ ǐ·tǐ)
  car·nal·ly
car·na·tion (kär·nā′ shŭn)
car·ni·val (kär′ nǐ·vál)
car·ni·vore (kär′ nǐ·vōr)
  car·niv·o·rous (kär·nǐv′ ō·rŭs)
car·ol (kär′ ŭl)
  -oled   -ol·ing
car·om shot (kär′ ŭm)
ca·rous·al (ká·rouz′ ál)
  (drunken revel; see *carrousel*)
  ca·rouse   -rous·ing
car·pen·ter (kär′ pĕn·tẽr)
  car·pen·try
car·pet (kär′ pĕt)
  -pet·ed   -pet·ing
  car·pet·bag·ger
  car·pet bee·tle

carp·ing (kär′ pǐng)
car·port (kär′ pōrt′)
car·riage (kär′ ǐj)
car·ri·er pi·geon
              (kär′ ǐ·ẽr)
car·ri·on (kär′ ǐ·ŭn)
car·rot (kär′ ŭt)
  (vegetable; see *carat, caret*)
car·rou·sel (kär′ ŏŏ·zĕl′)
  (merry-go-round; see *carousal*)
car·ry (kär′ ǐ)
  car·ried   car·ry·ing
  car·ri·er   car·ry·all
  car·ry-o·ver
cart·age (kär′ tǐj)
carte blanche (kärt′ blänsh′)
car·tel (kär′ tĕl′)
Car·te·sian (kär·tē′ zhán)
car·ti·lage (kär′ tǐ·lǐj)
  car·ti·lag·i·nous
        (kär′ tǐ·lăj′ ǐ·nŭs)
car·tog·ra·phy (kär·tŏg′ rá·fǐ)
  car·to·graph·i·cal
        (kär′ tō·grăf′ ǐ·kál)
car·ton (kär′ tŏn)
  (box)
car·toon (kär·tōōn′)
  (drawing)   car·toon·ist
car·tridge (kär′ trǐj)
ca·sa·ba mel·on
         (ká·sä′ bá)
Cas·a·blan·ca, (kăs′ á·blăng′ ká)
  Mo·roc·co
cas·cade (kăs·kād′)
  -cad·ing
cas·car·a (kăs·kâr′ á)
ca·se·in (kā′ sē·ǐn)
case·ment (kās′ mĕnt)
case·work·er (kās′ wûrk′ ẽr)
cash (kăsh)
  n. sing. & pl.
  cash·book
  cash reg·is·ter
ca·shew nut (ká·shōō′)
cash·ier (kăsh·ẽr′)
  cash·ier's check
cash·mere (kăsh′ mẽr)
ca·si·no (ká·sē′ nō)
  (gambling place; see *cassino*)
  -nos
cas·ket (kás′ kĕt)
Cas·san·dra (ká·săn′ drá)
cas·se·role (kăs′ ĕ·rōl)
cas·si·a (kăsh′ ǐ·á)

cas·si·no (kȧ·sē′ nō)
  (card game; see *casino*)
Cas·si·o·pe·ia's Chair
      (kăs′ ĭ·ȯ·pē′ yȧz)
cas·sock (kăs′ ŭk)
cast (kȧst)
. (throw; see *caste*)
cas·ta·net (kăs′ tȧ·nĕt′)
cast·a·way (kȧst′ ȧ·wā′)
caste (kȧst)
  (social class; see *cast*)
cast·er (kȧs′ tẽr)
  (wheel; see *castor*)
cas·ti·gate (kăs′ tĭ·gāt)
  -gat·ing
cas·ti·ga·tion (kăs′ tĭ·gā′ shŭn)
cas·ti·ga·tor
cas·tile soap (kăs′ tēl)
cas·tle (kȧs′ 'l)
cast·off (kȧst′ ŏf′)
cas·tor (kȧs′ tẽr)
  (oil; see *caster*)
cas·trate (kăs′ trāt)
  -trat·ing
cas·tra·tion (kăs·trā′ shŭn)
Cas·tro, Fi·del (kăs′ trō)
cas·u·al (kăzh′ ū·ăl)
cas·u·al·ly   cas·u·al·ness
cas·u·al·ty (kăzh′ ū·ăl·tĭ)
  -ties
cas·u·ist (kăzh′ ū·ĭst)
cas·u·ist·ry (kăzh′ ū·ĭs·trĭ)
cat (kăt)
cat·bird   cat·boat
cat·call   cat·fish
cat·gut   cat nap
cat·nip   cat-o'-nine-tails
cat's-eye   cat's-paw
cat·tail   cat·walk
cat·a·clysm (kăt′ ȧ·klĭz′m)
cat·a·clys·mal (kăt′ ȧ·klĭz′ măl)
cat·a·clys·mic (kăt′ ȧ·klĭz′ mĭk)
cat·a·comb (kăt′ ȧ·kōm)
cat·a·lep·sy (kăt′ ȧ·lĕp′ sĭ)
cat·a·lep·tic (kăt′ ȧ·lĕp′ tĭk)
cat·a·log (kăt′ ȧ·lŏg)
  -loged   -log·ing
cat·a·log·er   cat·a·log·ist
ca·tal·pa (kȧ·tăl′ pȧ)
cat·a·lyst (kăt′ ȧ·lĭst)
cat·a·ma·ran (kăt′ ȧ·mȧ·răn′)
cat·a·pult (kăt′ ȧ·pŭlt)
cat·a·ract (kăt′ ȧ·răkt)
  (waterfall, eye defect)
ca·tarrh (kȧ·tär′)

ca·tas·tro·phe (kȧ·tăs′ trō·fē)
cat·a·stroph·ic (kăt′ ȧ·strŏf′ ĭk)
cat·a·ton·ic (kăt′ ȧ·tŏn′ ĭk)
Ca·taw·ba (kȧ·tô′ bȧ)
catch (kăch)
catch·all   catch·er
catch·ment   catch·word
catch·y
cat·e·chism (kăt′ ē·kĭz′m)
cat·e·chize (kăt′ ē·kīz)
  -chiz·ing
cat·e·chu·men (kăt′ ē·kū′ mĕn)
cat·e·go·ry (kăt′ ē·gō′ rĭ)
  -ries
cat·e·go·ri·cal
cat·e·go·ri·cal (kăt·ē·gŏr′ ĭ·kȧl)
  -cal·ly
ca·ter (kā′ tẽr)
  -tered   -ter·ing
ca·ter·er   ca·ter·ess
cat·er-cor·nered
      (kăt′ ẽr·kôr′ nẽrd)
cat·er·pil·lar (kăt′ ẽr·pĭl′ ẽr)
ca·thar·sis (kȧ·thär′ sĭs)
ca·thar·tic
ca·the·dral (kȧ·thē′ drȧl)
cath·e·ter (kăth′ ē·tẽr)
cath·e·ter·ize -iz·ing
ca·thex·is (kȧ·thĕk′ sĭs)
ca·thec·tic (kȧ·thĕk′ tĭk)
cath·ode (kăth′ ōd)
cath·o·lic (kăth′ ȯ·lĭk)
  (universal)
ca·tho·lic·i·ty (kăth′ ȯ·lĭs′ ĭ·tĭ)
Cath·o·lic (kăth′ ȯ·lĭk)
  (church)
Ca·thol·i·cism
      (kȧ·thŏl′ ĭ·sĭz′m)
cat·sup (kăt′ sŭp)
cat·tle (kăt′ 'l)
cat·tle·man
cat·ty (kăt′ ĭ)
cat·ti·ly   cat·ti·ness
Cau·ca·sian (kô·kā′ zhȧn)
cau·cus (kô′ kŭs)
  -cused   -cus·ing
cau·dal (kô′ dȧl)
caught (kôt)
cau·li·flow·er (kô′ lĭ·flou′ ẽr)
caus·al (kôz′ ȧl)
cau·sal·i·ty (kô·zăl′ ĭ·tĭ)
caus·al·ly
cause (kôz)
caus·ing   caus·a·ble
cau·sa·tion (kô·zā′ shŭn)

caus·a·tive (kôz′ a·tĭv)
cause·less cause·way
caus·tic (kôs′ tĭk)
cau·ter·ize (kô′ tĕr·īz)
-iz·ing
cau·tion (kô′ shŭn)
cau·tion·ar·y (kô′ shŭn·ĕr′ ĭ)
cau·tious (kô′ shŭs)
cav·al·cade (kăv′ ăl·kād′)
cav·a·lier (kăv′ a·lẽr′)
cav·al·ry·man (kăv′ ăl·rĭ·măn)
cave (kāv)
cav·ing cave-in
cave man
cav·ern (kăv′ ẽrn)
cav·ern·ous
cav·i·ar (kăv′ ĭ·är)
cav·il (kăv′ ĭl)
-iled -il·ing
cav·i·ty (kăv′ ĭ·tĭ)
-ties
ca·vort (ka·vôrt′)
cay·enne pep·per
(kī·ĕn′)
cease (sēs)
ceas·ing cease·less
ce·dar (sē′ dẽr)
cede (sēd)
(yield)
ced·ing
ces·sion (sĕsh′ ŭn)
ceil·ing (sēl′ ĭng)
Cel·a·nese (sĕl′ a·nēs)
cel·e·brate (sĕl′ ĕ·brāt)
-brat·ing cel·e·brant
cel·e·bra·tion (sĕl′ ĕ·brā′ shŭn)
cel·e·bra·tor
ce·leb·ri·ty (sĕ·lĕb′ rĭ·tĭ)
-ties
ce·ler·i·ty (sĕ·lĕr′ ĭ·tĭ)
cel·er·y (sĕl′ ẽr·ĭ)
ce·les·tial (sĕ·lĕs′ chăl)
cel·i·bate (sĕl′ ĭ·băt)
cel·i·ba·cy (sĕl′ ĭ·ba·sĭ)
cel·lar (sĕl′ ẽr)
cel·lo (chĕl′ ō)
cel·list
cel·lo·phane (sĕl′ ŏ·fān)
cel·lu·lar (sĕl′ û·lẽr)
cel·lu·loid (sĕl′ û·loid)
cel·lu·lose (sĕl′ û·lōs)
ce·ment (sĕ·mĕnt′)
ce·ment·er
cem·e·ter·y (sĕm′ ĕ·tẽr′ ĭ)
-ter·ies

cen·sor (sĕn′ sẽr)
(examiner)
cen·so·ri·al (sĕn·sō′ rĭ·ăl)
cen·so·ri·ous (sĕn·sō′ rĭ·ŭs)
cen·sor·ship
cen·sure (sĕn′ shẽr)
(criticize)
-sur·ing
cen·sur·a·bil·i·ty
(sĕn′ shẽr·a·bĭl′ ĭ·tĭ)
cen·sur·a·ble
cen·sus (sĕn′ sŭs)
cen·taur (sĕn′ tôr)
cen·te·nar·y (sĕn′ tĕ·nĕr′ ĭ)
cen·te·nar·i·an
(sĕn′ tĕ·nâr′ ĭ·ăn)
cen·ten·ni·al (sĕn·tĕn′ ĭ·ăl)
cen·ter (sĕn′ tẽr)
cen·ter·piece
cen·ti- (sĕn′ tĭ-)
cen·ti·grade cen·ti·gram
cen·ti·me·ter cen·ti·pede
cen·tral (sĕn′ trăl)
cen·tral·i·za·tion
(sĕn′ trăl·ĭ·zā′ shŭn)
cen·tral·ize -iz·ing
cen·tral·ly
cen·trif·u·gal (sĕn·trĭf′ û·găl)
(going away from center)
cen·trip·e·tal (sĕn·trĭp′ ĕ·tăl)
(going toward center)
cen·tu·ri·on (sĕn·tū′ rĭ·ŭn)
cen·tu·ry (sĕn′ tû·rĭ)
-ries
ce·phal·ic (sĕ·făl′ ĭk)
ce·ram·ics (sĕ·răm′ ĭks)
ce·re·al (sẽr′ ĕ·ăl)
(grain; see serial)
cer·e·bel·lum (sĕr′ ĕ·bĕl′ ŭm)
cer·e·bral pal·sy
(sĕr′ ĕ·brăl)
cer·e·brum (sĕr′ ĕ·brŭm)
cer·e·mo·ny (sĕr′ ĕ·mō′ nĭ)
-nies
cer·e·mo·ni·al (sĕr′ ĕ·mō′ nĭ·ăl)
cer·e·mo·ni·ous
(sĕr′ ĕ·mō′ nĭ·ŭs)
ce·rise (sĕ·rēz′)
cer·tain (sûr′ tĭn)
cer·tain·ly cer·tain·ty, -ties
cer·tif·i·cate (sẽr·tĭf′ ĭ·kĭt)
cer·ti·fy (sûr′ tĭ·fī)
-fied -fy·ing
cer·ti·fi·a·ble (sûr′ tĭ·fī′ a·b'l)

cer·ti·fi·ca·tion
    (sûr′ tĭ·fĭ·kā′ shŭn)
cer·ti·fi·er
cer·ti·o·ra·ri (sûr′ shĭ·ô·rā′ rĭ)
cer·ti·tude (sûr′ tĭ·tūd)
ce·ru·le·an (sĕ·rōō′ lĕ·ăn)
cer·vix (sûr′ vĭks)
  pl. cer·vi·ces (sûr·vĭ′ sēz)
  cer·vi·cal
Ce·sar·e·an (sĕ·zâr′ ê·ăn)
ces·sa·tion (sĕ·sā′ shŭn)
  (a stop)
ces·sion (sĕsh′ ŭn)
  (yielding; see *session*)
cess·pool (sĕs′ pōōl)
Cey·lon (sê·lŏn′)
Cé·zanne, Paul (sā′ zàn′)
Cha·blis wine (shä′ blē′)
chafe (chāf)
  chaf·ing
chaff (chăf)
cha·grin (shá·grĭn′)
  -grined   -grin·ing
chain (chān)
  chain gang   chain let·ter
  chain mail
  chain-re·act·ing pile
  chain re·ac·tion
  chain re·ac·tor
  chain stitch   chain store
chair·man (châr′ măn)
  chair·man·ship
  chair·wom·an
chaise longue (shāz′ lôNg′)
chal·ced·o·ny (kăl·sĕd′ ô·nĭ)
cha·let (shă·lā′)
chal·ice (chăl′ ĭs)
chalk (chôk)
  chalk·stone   chalk·y
chal·lenge (chăl′ ĕnj)
  chal·leng·ing   chal·lenge·a·ble
  chal·leng·er
chal·lis (shăl′ ĭ)
cham·ber (chăm′ bĕr)
  cham·ber con·cert
  cham·ber·maid
  cham·ber mu·sic
  cham·ber of com·merce
cham·ber·lain (chăm′ bĕr·lĭn)
cham·bray (shăm′ brá)
cha·me·le·on (ká·mē′ lê·ŭn)
cham·fer (chăm′ fēr)
cham·ois (shăm′ ĭ)
  n. sing. & pl.
cham·pagne (shăm·pān′)

Cham·paign, Ill. (shăm·pān′)
cham·pi·on (chăm′ pĭ·ŭn)
  cham·pi·on·ship
Cham·plain, (shăm·plān′)
  Lake, N.Y.
Champs É·ly·sées
      (shäN′-zā′ lē′ zā′)
chance (cháns)
  chanc·ing   chance·ful
  chanc·y   chanc·i·ness
chan·cel (chăn′ sĕl)
chan·cel·lor (chăn′ sĕ·lĕr)
  chan·cel·ler·y -cel·ler·ies
  chan·cel·lor of the ex·cheq·uer
chan·cer·y (chăn′ sĕr·ĭ)
  -cer·ies
chan·de·lier (shăn′ dĕ·lĕr′)
change (chānj)
  chang·ing
  change·a·bil·i·ty
  change·a·ble   change·ful
  change·less   change·ling
chan·nel (chăn′ ĕl)
  chan·neled   chan·nel·ing
chan·teuse (shäN′ tûz′)
chant·ey (shán′ tĭ)
  -eys
chan·ti·cleer (chăn′ tĭ·klĕr)
cha·os (kā′ ŏs)
  cha·ot·ic (kå·ŏt′ ĭk)
chap·ar·ral (shăp′ ă·răl′)
cha·peau (shá′ pō′)
  pl. cha·peaux (-pōz′)
chap·el (chăp′ ĕl)
chap·er·on (shăp′ ĕr·ōn)
  chap·er·on·age
chap·lain (chăp′ lĭn)
  chap·lain·cy
chap·ter (chăp′ tĕr)
char·ac·ter (kăr′ ăk·tĕr)
  char·ac·ter·is·tic
      (kăr′ ăk·tĕr·ĭs′ tĭk)
  -ti·cal·ly
  char·ac·ter·i·za·tion
      (kăr′ ăk·tĕr·ĭ·zā′ shŭn)
  char·ac·ter·ize -iz·ing
cha·rade (shá·rād′)
char·coal (chär′ kōl′)
charge (chärj)
  charg·ing   charge·a·ble
char·gé d′af·faires
      (shär′ zhā′ dá·fâr′)
char·i·ot (chär′ ĭ·ŭt)
  char·i·ot·eer (chär′ ĭ·ŭt·ĕr′)
cha·ris·ma (ká·rĭz′ má)

char·is·mat·ic (kăr′ ĭz·măt′ ĭk)
char·i·ty (chăr′ ĭ·tĭ)
  -ties   char·i·ta·ble
  char·i·ta·ble·ness
cha·ri·va·ri (shä′ rĕ·vä′ rĕ or
              shĭv′ á·rē)
char·la·tan (shär′ lá·tăn)
  char·la·tan·ry
Char·le·magne (shär′ lĕ·män)
Char·ley horse (chär′ lĭ)
char·lotte russe (shär′ lŏt rōōs′)
charm·ing (chärm′ ĭng)
char·nel (chär′ nĕl)
char·ter (chär′ tĕr)
char·treuse (shär·trōōz′)
char·wom·an (chär′ wŏŏm′ ăn)
char·y (châr′ ĭ)
  char·i·ly
chasm (kăz′m)
chas·sis (shăs′ ĭ)
  pl. chas·sis (shăs′ ĭz)
chaste (chāst)
  chaste·ly
  chas·ten (chās′ 'n)
chas·tise (chăs·tīz′)
  -tis·ing
  chas·tise·ment (chăs′ tĭz·mĕnt)
chas·ti·ty (chăs′ tĭ·tĭ)
châ·teau (shă·tō′)
  pl. châ·teaux (-tōz′)
chat·e·laine (shăt′ ĕ·lān)
Chat·ta·noo·ga, (chăt′ á·nōō′ gá)
  Tenn.
chat·tel mort·gage
              (chăt′ 'l)
chat·ter·box (chăt′ ĕr·bŏks′)
chat·ty (chăt′ĭ)
  chat·ti·ness
chauf·feur (shō·fûr′)
chau·vin·ism (shō′ vĭn·ĭz′m)
  chau·vin·is·tic (shō′ vĭn·ĭs′ tĭk)
cheap (chēp)
  cheap·en   cheap·skate
cheat·er (chēt′ ĕr)
check (chĕk)
  check·book   check·mate
  check·room
check·er (chĕk′ ĕr)
  check·er·board
  check·ered
Ched·dar cheese
              (chĕd′ ĕr)
cheek (chēk)
cheer (chēr)
  cheer·ful, -ful·ly, -ful·ness

cheer·y   cheer·i·er
  -i·est, -i·ly, -i·ness
cheese (chēz)
  cheese·cake   cheese·cloth
  chees·y
chee·tah (chē′ tá)
chef (shĕf)
chef·-d′oeu·vre (shĕ′ dû′ vr′)
Che·khov, An·ton
              (chĕ′ ĸŭf)
chem·i·cal (kĕm′ ĭ·kăl)
  chem·i·cal·ly
che·mise (shĕ·mēz′)
chem·ist (kĕm′ ĭst)
  chem·is·try
che·nille (shĕ·nēl′)
cher chez la femme
        (shĕr′ shā′ lá fám′)
cher·ish (chĕr′ ĭsh)
Cher·o·kee (chĕr′ ŏ·kē′)
che·root (shĕ·rōōt′)
cher·ry (chĕr′ ĭ)
  cher·ries
cher·ub (chĕr′ ŭb)
  che·ru·bic (chĕ·rōō′ bĭk)
  pl. cher·u·bim or cher·ubs
cher·vil (chûr′ vĭl)
Ches·a·peake (bay)
              (chĕs′ á·pēk′)
Chesh·ire cat (chĕsh′ ĕr)
chess·board (chĕs′ bōrd′)
ches·ter·field coat
              (chĕs′ tĕr·fēld)
chest·nut (chĕs′ nŭt)
chev·a·lier (shĕv′ á·lẽr′)
chev·ron (shĕv′ rŭn)
Chey·enne, Wyo.
              (shī·ĕn′)
Chi·an·ti wine (kĭ·ăn′ tĭ)
chic (shēk)
  chic·quer   -quest
chi·can·er·y (shĭ·kān′ ĕr·ĭ)
chick·a·dee (chĭk′ á·dē)
chick·en (chĭk′ ĕn)
  chick·en·heart·ed
  chick·en pox
chick·pea (chĭk′ pē′)
chic·le (chĭk′ 'l)
chic·o·ry (chĭk′ ŏ·rĭ)
chide (chīd)
  chid·ing
chief (chēf)
  chief·ly
  chief·tain (chēf′ tĭn)
  chief·tain·cy

chif·fon   (shĭ·fŏn′)
chif·fo·nier   (shĭf′ ô·nẽr′)
chig·ger   (chĭg′ ẽr)
chi·gnon   (shēn′ yŏn)
Chi·hua·hua   (chĕ·wä′ wä)
chil·blain   (chĭl′ blān′)
child   (chīld)
   child·bear·ing   child·birth
   child·hood   child·like
chil·dren   (chĭl′ drĕn)
Chil·e   (chĭl′ ĕ)
   Chil·e·an   (chĭl′ ĕ·ăn)
chil·i   (chĭl′ ĭ)
   chil·i con car·ne
       (chĭl′ ĭ kŏn kär′ nĕ)
   chil·i sauce
chill·y   (chĭl′ ĭ)
   chill·i·ness
chime   (chīm)
   chim·ing
chi·me·ra   (kĭ·mẽr′ ȧ)
   chi·mer·i·cal   (kĭ·mẽr′ ĭ·kȧl)
chim·ney   (chĭm′ nĭ)
   -neys
chim·pan·zee   (chĭm′ păn·zē′)
chi·na   (chī′ nȧ)
   chi·na·ber·ry   Chi·na·town
   chi·na·ware
chinch bug   (chĭnch)
chin·chil·la   (chĭn·chĭl′ ȧ)
Chi·nese   (chī′ nēz′)
Chi·nook   (shĭ·nŏŏk′)
chintz   (chĭnts)
chip·munk   (chĭp′ mŭngk)
Chip·pen·dale   (chĭp′ ĕn·dāl)
Chip·pe·wa   (chĭp′ ĕ·wä)
chi·rop·o·dy   (kĭ·rŏp′ ô·dĭ)
   chi·rop·o·dist
chi·ro·prac·tor   (kī′ rô·prăk′ tẽr)
   chi·ro·prac·tic   (kī′ rô·prăk′ tĭk)
chis·el   (chĭz′ ′l)
   -eled   -el·ing
   chis·el·er
chi-square   (kī′ skwâr′)
chit·chat   (chĭt′ chăt′)
   chat·ted   chat·ting
chit·ter·lings   (chĭt′ ẽr·lĭngz)
chiv·al·ry   (shĭv′ ȧl·rĭ)
   chiv·al·ric   chiv·al·rous
chlo·rine   (klō′ rēn)
   chlo·rin·ate   (klō′ rĭ·nāt)
   -nat·ing
   chlo·rate   (klō′ rāt)
chlo·ride   (klō′ rīd)
chlo·rite   (klō′ rīt)

chlo·ro·form   (klō′ rô·fôrm)
chlo·ro·phyll   (klō′ rô·fĭl)
chock-full   (chŏk′ fŏŏl′)
choc·o·late   (chŏk′ ô·lĭt)
choice   (chois)
choir   (kwīr)
   choir·boy   choir loft
   choir·mas·ter
choke   (chōk)
   chok·ing   choke·cher·ry
   chok·er
chol·er·a   (kŏl′ ẽr·ȧ)
chol·er·ic   (kŏl′ ẽr·ĭk)
cho·les·ter·ol   (kô·lĕs′ tẽr·ōl)
choose   (chōōz)
   choos·ing   choos·i·ness
   choos·y
chop   (chŏp)
   chopped   chop·ping
   chop·house   chop·py
   chop·stick   chop su·ey
cho·ral   (kō′ rȧl)
   cho·ral·ly
chord   (kôrd)
   (music; see cord)
chore   (chōr)
cho·re·og·ra·phy
       (kō′ rĕ·ŏg′ rȧ·fĭ)
   cho·re·og·ra·pher
chor·tle   (chôr′ t′l)
   -tling
cho·rus   (kō′ rŭs)
chose   (chōz)
   cho·sen
Chou En-lai   (jō′ ĕn′ lī′)
chow·der   (chou′ dẽr)
chow mein   (chou′ mān′)
chris·ten   (krĭs′ ′n)
   -ten·ing
Chris·ten·dom   (krĭs′ ′n·dŭm)
Chris·tian   (krĭs′ chȧn)
   Chris·ti·an·i·ty
       (krĭs′ chĭ·ăn′ ĭ·tĭ)
   Chris·tian·ize   -iz·ing
Christ·like   (krīst′ līk′)
Christ·mas   (krĭs′ mȧs)
chro·mat·ic   (krô·măt′ ĭk)
chrome   (krōm)
chro·mi·um   (krō′ mĭ·ŭm)
chron·ic   (krŏn′ ĭk)
   chron·i·cal·ly
chron·i·cle   (krŏn′ ĭ·k′l)
   -cling

chron·o·log·i·cal
        (krŏn' ŏ·lŏj' ĭ·kǎl)
  -cal·ly
chro·nol·o·gy   (krŏ·nŏl' ŏ·ji)
  -gies
chrys·a·lis   (krĭs' ȧ·lĭs)
chrys·an·the·mum
        (krĭs·ăn' thē·mŭm)
chub·by   (chŭb' ĭ)
  chub·bi·ness
chuck·le   (chŭk' 'l)
  -ling
chum·my   (chŭm' ĭ)
  chum·mi·ness
Chung·king, Chi·na
        (chŏŏng' kĭng')
chunk·y   (chŭngk' ĭ)
church   (chûrch)
  church·go·er   church·ly
  church·yard
Church·ill, Win·ston
        (chûrch' ĭl)
churl·ish   (chûr' lĭsh)
churn   (chûrn)
chute   (shōōt)
chut·ney   (chŭt' nĭ)
ci·ca·da   (sĭ·kā' dȧ)
ci·der   (sī' dēr)
ci·gar   (sĭ·gär')
cig·a·rette   (sĭg' ȧ·rĕt')
cinch   (sĭnch)
Cin·cin·nat·i, O.
        (sĭn' sĭ·năt' ĭ)
cin·der   (sĭn' dēr)
Cin·der·el·la   (sĭn' dēr·ĕl' ȧ)
cin·e·ma   (sĭn' ĕ·mȧ)
  cin·e·mat·ic   (sĭn' ĕ·măt' ĭk)
  cin·e·ma·tog·ra·phy
        (sĭn' ĕ·mȧ·tŏg' rȧ·fĭ)
cin·na·bar   (sĭn' ȧ·bär)
cin·na·mon   (sĭn' ȧ·mŭn)
ci·pher   (sī' fēr)
cir·ca   (sûr' kȧ)
  abbr. c.
cir·cle   (sûr' k'l)
  -cling   cir·clet
cir·cuit   (sûr' kĭt)
  -cuit·ed   -cuit·ing
  cir·cu·i·tous   (sēr·kū' ĭ·tŭs)
cir·cu·lar   (sûr' kŭ·lēr)
  cir·cu·lar·i·ty   (sûr' kŭ·lăr' ĭ·tĭ)
  cir·cu·lar·ly
  cir·cu·lar·ize   -iz·ing
cir·cu·late   (sûr' kŭ·lāt)
  -lat·ing

cir·cu·la·tion   (sûr' kŭ·lā·shŭn)
cir·cu·la·to·ry   (sûr' kŭ·lȧ·tō'rĭ)
cir·cum·cise   (sûr' kŭm·sīz)
  -cis·ing
cir·cum·ci·sion
        (sûr' kŭm·sĭzh' ŭn)
cir·cum·fer·ence
        (sēr·kŭm' fēr·ĕns)
cir·cum·flex   (sûr' kŭm·flĕks)
cir·cum·lo·cu·tion
        (sûr' kŭm·lŏ·kū' shŭn)
cir·cum·scribe   (sûr' kŭm·skrīb')
  -scrib·ing
cir·cum·scrip·tion
        (sûr' kŭm·skrĭp' shŭn)
cir·cum·spect   (sûr' kŭm·spĕkt)
cir·cum·stance   (sûr' kŭm·stăns)
  cir·cum·stan·tial
        (sûr' kŭm·stăn' shǎl)
  cir·cum·stan·ti·ate
        (sûr' kŭm·stăn·shĭ·āt)
  -at·ing
cir·cum·vent   (sûr' kŭm·vĕnt')
  cir·cum·ven·tion
        (-vĕn' shŭn)
cir·cus   (sûr' kŭs)
cir·rho·sis   (sĭ·rō' sĭs)
cir·ro·cu·mu·lus
        (sĭr' ŏ·kū' mŭ·lŭs)
cir·ro·stra·tus   (sĭr' ŏ·strā' tŭs)
cir·rus   (sĭr' ŭs)
cis·tern   (sĭs' tĕrn)
cit·a·del   (sĭt' ȧ·dĕl)
ci·ta·tion   (sī·tā' shŭn)
cite   (sīt)
  (quote; see site, sight)
  cit·ing   cit·a·ble
cit·i·zen   (sĭt' ĭ·zĕn)
  cit·i·zen·ry
cit·ric ac·id   (sĭt' rĭk)
cit·ron   (sĭt' rŭn)
cit·ron·el·la   (sĭt' rŭn·ĕl' ȧ)
cit·rus fruit   (sĭt' rŭs)
cit·y   (sĭt' ĭ)
  cit·ies
  cit·i·fied   (sĭt' ĭ·fīd)
  cit·y-born   cit·y·folk
civ·et   (sĭv' ĕt)
civ·ic   (sĭv' ĭk)
civ·il   (sĭv' ĭl)
  civ·il en·gi·neer
  civ·il law   civ·il·ly
  civ·il rights   civ·il serv·ice
ci·vil·ian   (sĭ·vĭl' yǎn)

ci·vil·i·ty   (sĭ·vĭl′ ĭ·tĭ)
  -ties
civ·i·lize   (sĭv′ ĭ·līz)
  -liz·ing   civ·i·liz·a·ble
  civ·i·li·za·tion
                       (sĭv′ ĭ·lĭ·zā′ shŭn)
claim·ant   (klām′ ănt)
clair·voy·ance   (klâr·voi′ ăns)
  -ant
clam·bake   (klăm′ bāk′)
clam·ber   (klăm′ bẽr)
clam·my   (klăm′ ĭ)
  clam·mi·ness
clam·or   (klăm′ ẽr)
  clam·or·ous
clan   (klăn)
  clan·nish   clans·man
clan·des·tine   (klăn·dĕs′ tĭn)
  -tine·ly
clang·or   (klăng′ ẽr)
  clang·or·ous
clap·board   (klăb′ ẽrd)
clap·per   (klăp′ ẽr)
claque   (klăk)
  (paid applauders)
clar·et   (klăr′ ĕt)
clar·i·fy   (klăr′ ĭ·fī)
  -fied,   -fy·ing
  clar·i·fi·ca·tion
                       (klăr′ ĭ·fĭ·kā′ shŭn)
  clar·i·fi·er   (-fī′ ẽr)
clar·i·net   (klăr′ ĭ·nĕt′)
  clar·i·net·ist
clar·i·on   (klăr′ ĭ·ŭn)
clar·i·ty   (klăr′ ĭ·tĭ)
class   (klås)
  class·a·ble   class-con·scious
  class·mate   class·room
clas·sic   (klăs′ ĭk)
  clas·si·cal   -cal·ly
  clas·si·cism   (klăs′ ĭ·sĭz′m)
clas·si·fy   (klăs′ ĭ·fī)
  -fied,   -fy·ing
  clas·si·fi·a·ble   (-fī′ á·b′l)
  clas·si·fi·ca·tion
                       (klăs′ ĭ·fĭ·kā′ shŭn)
clat·ter   (klăt′ ẽr)
clause   (klôz)
claus·tro·pho·bi·a
                       (klôs′ trŏ·fō′ bĭ·á)
clav·i·chord   (klăv′ ĭ·kôrd)
clav·i·cle   (klăv′ ĭ·k′l)
clay   (klā)
  clay·ey   clay pi·geon

clean   (klēn)
  clean·a·ble   clean-cut
  clean·er
  clean·li·ness   (klĕn′ lĭ·nĕs)
  clean·ly   (klĕn′ lĭ)
  clean·ness
cleanse   (klĕnz)
  cleans·ing   cleans·er
clear   (klẽr)
  clear-cut   clear-eyed
  clear·head·ed   clear·ing·house
  clear-sight·ed
clear·ance   (klẽr′ăns)
cleat   (klēt)
cleave   (klēv)
  cleav·ing
  cleav·age   (-ĭj)
  cleav·ers
clef   (klĕf)
  (musical notation; see cliff)
cleft pal·ate   (klĕft)
clem·en·cy   (klĕm′ ĕn·sĭ)
  -ent
clench   (klĕnch)
Cle·o·pat·ra   (klē′ ŏ·păt′ rá)
cler·gy·man   (klûr′ jĭ·mán)
cler·ic   (klĕr′ ĭk)
  cler·i·cal
clev·er   (klĕv′ ẽr)
cli·ché   (klē·shā′)
cli·ent   (klī′ ĕnt)
  cli·en·tele   (klī′ ĕn·tĕl′)
cliff   (klĭf)
  (rock; see clef)
cli·mate   (klī′ mĭt)
  cli·mat·ic   (klī·măt′ ĭk)
cli·max   (klī′ măks)
  cli·mac·tic   (klī·măk′ tĭk)
climb   (klīm)
cling·stone   (klĭng′ stōn′)
clin·ic   (klĭn′ ĭk)
  clin·i·cal   -cal·ly
  cli·ni·cian   (klĭ·nĭsh′ ăn)
clip·per   (klĭp′ ẽr)
clique   (klēk)
  cli·quish
clob·ber   (klŏb′ ẽr)
cloche   (klōsh)
clock·wise   (klŏk′ wīz′)
clod·dish   (klŏd′ ĭsh)
cloi·son·né   (kloi′ zŏ·nā′)
clois·ter   (klois′ tẽr)
close   (klōs) adj
  close·fist·ed   close·ly
  close-up

close (klōz) *v.*
  clos·ing
clos·et (klŏz' ĕt)
  -et·ed   -et·ing
clo·sure (klō' zhẽr)
cloth (klôth) *n.*
clothe (klōth) *v.*
  cloth·ing
clothes (klōthz)
  clothes·bas·ket
  clothes·brush clothes·line
cloth·ier (klōth' yẽr)
cloud·burst (kloud' bûrst')
cloud·y (kloud' ĭ)
  cloud·i·est -i·ness
clout (klout)
clo·ver·leaf (klō' vẽr·lēf')
  adj.
clown·ish (kloun' ĭsh)
cloy·ing (kloi' ĭng)
club (klŭb)
  clubbed   club·bing
  club car   club chair
  club·foot·ed club·room
  club steak
clue (klōō)
  clu·ing
clum·sy (klŭm' zĭ)
  clum·si·er -si·est
  -si·ly   -si·ness
clus·ter (klŭs' tẽr)
clutch (klŭch)
clut·ter (klŭt' ẽr)
coach·man (kōch' măn)
co·ag·u·late (kō·ăg' û·lāt)
  -lat·ing co·ag·u·lant
  co·ag·u·la·tion
    (kō·ăg' û·lā' shŭn)
  co·ag·u·la·tor
coal (kōl)
  coal·bin   coal gas
  coal mine coal tar
  coal·yard
co·a·lesce (kō' á·lĕs')
  -lesc·ing co·a·les·cence,
  -cent
co·a·li·tion (kō' á·lĭsh' ŭn)
coarse (kōrs)
  (rough; see *course*)
  coars·en coarse·ness
coast (kōst)
  coast·al coast ar·til·ler·y
  coast·er coast guard
  coast·ward
co·au·thor (kō·ô' thẽr)

coax (kōks)
co·ax·i·al ca·ble
    (kō·ăk' sĭ·ăl)
cob·bler (kŏb' lẽr)
cob·ble·stone (kŏb' 'l·stōn')
co·bra (kō' brá)
cob·web (kŏb' wĕb')
  cob·web·by
co·caine (kō·kān')
coc·cyx (kŏk' sĭks)
  pl. coc·cy·ges (kŏk·sī' jēz)
  coc·cyg·e·al (kŏk·sĭj' ē·ăl)
cock·a·too (kŏk' á·tōō')
cock·er span·iel
    (kŏk' ẽr)
cock·eyed (kŏk' īd')
cock·le·shell (kŏk' 'l·shĕl')
cock·ney (kŏk' nĭ)
cock·pit (kŏk' pĭt')
cock·roach (kŏk' rōch')
cock·sure (kŏk' shōōr')
cock·tail (kŏk' tāl')
cock·y (kŏk' ĭ)
  cock·i·er -i·est
  -i·ly   -i·ness
co·co mat·ting (kō' kō)
co·coa (kō' kō)
co·co·nut (kō' kō·nŭt')
co·coon (kō·kōōn')
cod·dle (kŏd' 'l)
  cod·dling
co·de·fend·ant (kō' dē·fĕn' dănt)
co·de·ine (kō' dē·ēn)
cod·fish (kŏd' fĭsh')
codg·er (kŏj' ẽr)
cod·i·cil (kŏd' ĭ·sĭl)
cod·i·fy (kŏd' ĭ·fī)
  -fied   -fy·ing
  cod·i·fi·ca·tion
    (kŏd' ĭ·fĭ·kā' shŭn)
cod-liv·er oil (kŏd' lĭv' ẽr)
co·ed (kō' ĕd')
  co·ed·u·ca·tion·al
    (kō' ĕd' û·kā' shŭn·ăl)
co·ef·fi·cient (kō' ĕ·fĭsh' ĕnt)
co·e·qual (kō·ē' kwăl)
co·erce (kō·ûrs')
  -erc·ing
  co·er·ci·ble (kō·ûr' sĭ·b'l)
  co·er·cion (-shŭn)
  co·er·cive (-sĭv)
co·es·sen·tial (kō' ĕ·sĕn' shăl)
co·ex·ec·u·tor
  n. masc. (kō' ĕg·zĕk' û·tẽr)
  co·ex·ec·u·trix (-trĭks) *n. fem.*

co·ex·ist (kō' ĕg·zĭst')
　co·ex·ist·ence
cof·fee (kôf' ĭ)
　cof·fee·house　cof·fee·pot
　cof·fee shop　cof·fee ta·ble
cof·fers (kôf' ērz)
cof·fin (kôf' ĭn)
co·gent (kō' jĕnt)
　co·gen·cy
cog·i·tate (kŏj' ĭ·tāt)
　-tat·ing
　cog·i·ta·tion (kŏj' ĭ·tā' shŭn)
　cog·i·ta·tive (kŏj' ĭ·tā' tĭv)
　cog·i·ta·tor (kŏj' ĭ·tā' tēr)
co·gnac (kō' nyăk)
cog·nate (kŏg' nāt)
cog·ni·tion (kŏg·nĭsh' ŭn)
cog·ni·zant (kŏg' nĭ·zănt)
　-zance
cog·no·men (kŏg·nō' mĕn)
cog·wheel (kŏg' hwēl)
co·hab·it (kō·hăb' ĭt)
　co·hab·i·ta·tion
　　　　(kō·hăb' ĭ·tā' shŭn)
co·here (kō·hēr')
　-her·ing　co·her·ence,
　-ent
co·he·sion (kō·hē' zhŭn)
　co·he·sive　-sive·ly
co·hort (kō' hôrt)
coif (koif)
　coif·fure (kwä·fūr')
coin (koin)
　coin·age (-ĭj)
co·in·cide (kō' ĭn·sīd')
　-cid·ing
　co·in·ci·dence (kō·ĭn' sĭ·dĕns)
　co·in·ci·dent·al
　　　　(kō·ĭn' sĭ·dĕn' tăl)
co·in·her·it·ance
　　　　(kō' ĭn·hĕr' ĭ·tăns)
co·in·sure (kō' ĭn shōōr')
co·i·tion (kō·ĭsh' ŭn)
　co·i·tus (kō' ĭ·tŭs)
col·an·der (kŭl' ăn·dēr)
cold (kōld)
　cold-blood·ed　cold cream
　cold sore　cold war
cole·slaw (kōl' slô')
col·ic (kŏl' ĭk)
col·i·se·um (kŏl' ĭ·sē' ŭm)
　(any stadium; see Colosseum)
co·li·tis (kō·lī' tĭs)
col·lab·o·rate (kŏ·lăb' ō·rāt)
　-rat·ing

col·lab·o·ra·tion
　　　　(kŏ·lăb' ō·rā' shŭn)
col·lab·o·ra·tive
　　　　(kŏ·lăb' ō·rā' tĭv)
col·lab·o·ra·tor
　　　　(kŏ·lăb' ō·rā' tēr)
col·lapse (kŏ' lăps')
　col·laps·ing　col·laps·i·ble
col·lar (kŏl' ēr)
　col·lar·band　col·lar·bone
　col·lar but·ton
col·late (kŏ·lāt')
　col·lat·ing
　col·la·tion (-lā' shŭn)
col·lat·er·al (kŏ·lăt' ēr·ăl)
　-al·ly
col·league (kŏl' ēg)
col·lect (kŏ·lĕkt')
　col·lect·i·ble　col·lec·tion
　col·lec·tive　-tive·ly
　col·lec·tiv·ism
　col·lec·tiv·i·ty
　　　　(kŏl' ĕk·tĭv' ĭ·tĭ)
　col·lec·tiv·ize　-iz·ing
　col·lec·tor
col·lege (kŏl' ĕj)
　col·le·gi·an (kŏ·lē' jĭ·ăn)
　col·le·gi·ate (kŏ·lē' jĭ·ĭt)
col·lide (kŏ·līd')
　col·lid·ing
　col·li·sion (kŏ·lĭzh' ŭn)
col·lie (kŏl' ĭ)
col·lier·y (kŏl' yēr·ĭ)
　col·lier·ies
col·li·sion (kŏ·lĭzh' ŭn)
col·lo·di·on (kŏ·lō' dĭ·ŭn)
col·loid (kŏl' oid)
　col·loi·dal (kŏ·loi' dăl)
col·lo·qui·al (kŏ·lō' kwĭ·ăl)
　-al·ly
　col·lo·qui·al·ism
col·lo·quy (kŏl' ō·kwĭ)
　-quies
col·lude (kŏ·lūd')
　col·lud·ing　col·lu·sion
co·logne (kō·lōn')
Co·lom·bi·a, (kō·lŭm' bĭ·ȧ)
　S. Amer.
　(see Columbia)
co·lon (kō' lŏn)
colo·nel (kûr' nĕl)
　colo·nel·cy
col·on·nade (kŏl' ō·nād')
col·o·ny (kŏl' ō·nĭ)
　-nies

co·lo·ni·al (kŏ·lō′ nĭ·ảl)
col·o·nist
col·o·ni·za·tion
       (kŏl′ ŏ·nĭ·zā′ shŭn)
col·o·nize -niz·ing
col·o·phon (kŏl′ ŏ·fŏn)
col·or (kŭl′ ēr)
col·or·a·tion (kŭl′ ēr·ā′ shŭn)
col·or-blind col·or·ful,
-ful·ly -ful·ness
col·or·less -less·ness
Col·o·ra·do (kŏl′ ŏ·rä′ dō)
  abbr. Colo.
Col·o·ra·dan (-rä′ d′n)
col·o·ra·tu·ra so·pran·o
       (kŭl′ ēr·ả·tū′ rả)
co·los·sal (kŏ·lŏs′ ẳl)
co·los·sal·ly
Col·os·se·um (kŏl′ ŏ·sē′ ŭm)
  (Roman amphitheater; see
  coliseum)
co·los·sus (kŏ·lŏs′ ŭs)
Co·lum·bi·a (kŏ·lŭm′ bĭ·ả)
  (University, River, District of;
  see *Colombia*)
col·um·bine (kŏl′ ŭm·bīn)
Co·lum·bus (kŏ·lŭm′ bŭs)
col·umn (kŏl′ ŭm)
co·lum·nar (kŏ·lŭm′ nēr)
col·um·nist
co·ma (kō′ mả)
  (trance; see *comma*)
com·bat (kŏm′ bắt) *n.*
com·bat (kŏm·bắt′) *v.*
-bat·ing com·bat·a·ble
com·bat·ant (kŏm′ bả·tẳnt)
com·bat·ive
com·bine (kŏm′ bīn) *n.*
com·bine (kŏm·bīn′) *v.*
-bin·ing com·bin·a·ble
com·bi·na·tion
       (kŏm′ bĭ·nā′ shŭn)
com·bus·tion (kŏm·bŭs′ chŭn)
com·bus·ti·ble
com·bus·tive com·bus·tor
come·back (kŭm′ băk′)
co·me·di·an (kŏ·mē′ dĭ·ẳn)
co·me·di·enne (kŏ·mē′ dĭ·ĕn′)
  n. fem.
come·down (kŭm′ doun′)
com·e·dy (kŏm′ ĕ·dĭ)
-dies
come·ly (kŭm′ lĭ)
come·li·er -li·est
-li·ness

com·et (kŏm′ ĕt)
come·up·pance
       (kŭm·ŭp′ ẳns)
com·fort (kŭm′ fẽrt)
com·fort·a·ble
com·ic (kŏm′ ĭk)
com·i·cal -cal·ly
com·ing (kŭm′ ĭng)
com·ma (kŏm′ ả)
  (punctuation; see *coma*)
com·mand (kŏ·mánd′)
com·mand·er com·mand·ment
com·man·dant (kŏm′ ẳn·dẳnt′)
com·man·deer (kŏm′ ẳn·dẽr′)
com·man·do (kŏ·mán′ dō)
-dos
com·mem·o·rate
       (kŏ·mĕm′ ŏ·rāt)
-rat·ing
com·mem·o·ra·tion
       (kŏ·mĕm′ ŏ·rā′ shŭn)
com·mem·o·ra·tive
       (kŏ·mĕm′ ŏ·rā′ tĭv)
com·mence (kŏ·mĕns′)
com·menc·ing
com·mence·ment
com·mend (kŏ·mĕnd′)
com·mend·a·ble
com·mend·a·tion
       (kŏm′ ĕn·dā′ shŭn)
com·mend·a·tory
com·men·su·rate
       (kŏ·mĕn′ shŏŏ·rĭt)
com·men·su·ra·ble
com·men·su·rate·ly
com·men·su·ra·tion
       (kŏ·mĕn′ shŏŏ·rā′ shŭn)
com·ment (kŏm′ ĕnt)
com·men·tar·y
       (kŏm′ ĕn·tĕr′ ĭ)
-tar·ies
com·men·ta·tor (-tā′ tēr)
com·merce (kŏm′ ûrs)
com·mer·cial (kŏ·mûr′ shẳl)
com·mer·cial·ism
com·mer·cial·i·za·tion
       (kŏ·mûr′ shẳl·ĭ·zā′ shŭn)
com·mer·cial·ize
-iz·ing com·merc·ial·ly
com·min·gle (kŏ·mĭng′ g′l)
-gling
com·mis·er·ate
       (kŏ·mĭz′ ēr·āt)
-at·ing

com·mis·er·a·tion
      (kŏ·mĭz′ ĕr·ā′ shŭn)
com·mis·sar   (kŏm′ ĭ·sär′)
com·mis·sar·i·at
      (kŏm′ ĭ·sär′ ĭ·ăt)
com·mis·sar·y (kŏm′ ĭ·sĕr′ ĭ)
com·mis·sar·ies
com·mis·sion (kŏ·mĭsh′ ŭn)
com·mis·sioned of·fi·cer
com·mit   (kŏ·mĭt′)
com·mit·ted com·mit·ting
com·mit·ment com·mit·tal
com·mit·tee (kŏ·mĭt′ ĭ)
com·mit·tee·man
com·mode   (kŏ·mōd′)
com·mod·i·ous
     (kŏ·mō′ dĭ·ŭs)
com·mod·i·ty (kŏ·mŏd′ ĭ·tĭ)
-ties
com·mo·dore (kŏm′ ô·dōr′)
com·mon   (kŏm′ ŭn)
com·mon de·nom·i·na·tor
com·mon·er
com·mon-law mar·riage
com·mon·ly com·mon·ness
com·mon·place
com·mon sense *n.*
com·mon-sense *adj.*
com·mon stock
com·mon weal
com·mon·wealth
com·mo·tion (kŏ·mō′ shŭn)
com·mu·nal (kŏm′ û·nǎl)
com·mu·nal·ly
com·mune   (kŏ·mūn′) *v.*
com·mun·ing (kŏm′ ūn) *n.*
com·mu·ni·cate
      (kŏ·mū′ nĭ·kāt)
-cat·ing
com·mu·ni·ca·ble
      (-ká·b′l)
com·mu·ni·cant
      (-kǎnt)
com·mu·ni·ca·tion
      (kŏ·mū′ nĭ·kā′ shŭn)
com·mu·ni·ca·tive
      (-kā′ tĭv)
com·mu·ni·ca·tor
      (-kā′ tĕr)
com·mun·ion (kŏ·mūn′ yŭn)
com·mu·ni·qué (kŏ·mū′ nĭ·kā′)
com·mu·nist (kŏm′ û·nĭst)
com·mu·nism
com·mu·nis·tic
      (kŏm′ û·nĭs′ tĭk)

com·mu·nize -niz·ing
Com·mu·nist kŏm′ û·nĭst)
  (specific political party)
com·mu·ni·ty (kŏ·mū′ nĭ·tĭ)
-ties
com·mute   (kŏ·mūt′)
com·mut·ing
com·mu·ta·tion
      (kŏm′ û·tā′ shŭn)
com·mut·er
com·pact   (kŏm·păkt′) *adj.*
      (kŏm′ păkt) *n.*
com·pan·ion (kŏm·păn′ yŭn)
com·pan·ion·a·bil·i·ty
      (kŏm·păn′ yŭn·á·bĭl′ ĭ·tĭ)
com·pan·ion·a·ble
com·pan·ion·ate
      (-ăt)
com·pan·ion·ship
com·pa·ny   (kŭm′ pá·nĭ)
-nies
com·pare   (kŏm·pâr′)
-par·ing
com·pa·ra·bil·i·ty
      (kŏm′ pá·rá·bĭl′ ĭ·tĭ)
com·pa·ra·ble (kŏm′ pá·rá·b′l)
com·par·a·tive
      (kŏm·păr′ á·tĭv)
-tive·ly
com·pa·ri·son (kŏm·păr′ ĭ·sŭn)
com·part·ment (kŏm·pärt′ měnt)
com·pass   (kŭm′ pás)
com·pas·sion (kŏm·păsh′ ŭn)
com·pas·sion·ate (-ĭt)
com·pat·i·ble (kŏm·păt′ ĭ·b′l)
com·pat·i·bil·i·ty
      (kŏm·păt′ ĭ·bĭl′ ĭ·tĭ)
com·pa·tri·ot (kŏm·pā′ trĭ·ŭt)
com·pel   (kŏm·pěl′)
-pelled   -pel·ling
com·pen·di·ous
      (kŏm·pěn′ dĭ·ŭs)
com·pen·di·um
      (kŏm·pěn′ dĭ·ŭm)
com·pen·sate (kŏm′ pěn·sāt)
-sat·ing
com·pen·sa·tion
      (kŏm′ pěn·sā′ shŭn)
com·pen·sa·tive
      (kŏm′ pěn·sā′ tĭv)
com·pen·sa·to·ry
      (kŏm′ pěn′ sá·tō′ rĭ)
com·pete   (kŏm·pēt′)
-pet·ing

com·pe·tence (kŏm′ pĕ·tĕns)
-ten·cy, -tent
com·pe·ti·tion
(kŏm′ pĕ·tĭsh′ ŭn)
com·pet·i·tive
(kŏm·pĕt′ ĭ·tĭv)
-tive·ly
com·pet·i·tor (kŏm·pĕt′ ĭ·tĕr)
com·pile (kŏm·pīl′)
-pil·ing
com·pi·la·tion
(kŏm′ pĭ·lā′ shŭn)
com·pla·cent (kŏm·plā′ sĕnt)
(self-satisfied; see *complaisant*)
com·pla·cence
com·plain (kŏm·plān′)
com·plain·ant com·plaint
com·plai·sant (kŏm·plā′ zănt)
(obliging; see *complacent*)
com·plai·sance
com·plect·ed (kŏm·plĕk′ tĕd)
com·ple·ment (kŏm′ plĕ·mĕnt)
(that which completes; see *compliment*)
com·ple·men·tal
com·ple·men·ta·ry
(kŏm′ plĕ·mĕn′ tà·rĭ)
com·plete (kŏm·plēt′)
-plet·ing com·plete·ly
-plete·ness
com·ple·tion (-plē′ shŭn)
com·plex (kŏm·plĕks′) adj
(kŏm′ plĕks) n.
com·plex·i·ty (kŏm·plĕk′ sĭ·tĭ)
com·plex·ion (kŏm·plĕk′ shŭn)
com·plex·ioned
com·pli·ant (kŏm·plī′ đnt)
-ance
com·pli·cate (kŏm′ plĭ·kāt)
-cat·ing
com·pli·ca·tion
(kŏm′ plĭ·kā′ shŭn)
com·plic·i·ty (kŏm·plĭs′ ĭ·tĭ)
com·pli·ment (kŏm′ plĭ·mĕnt)
(flattery; see *complement*)
com·pli·men·ta·ry
(kŏm′ plĭ·mĕn′ tà·rĭ)
com·ply (kŏm·plī′)
-plied -ply·ing
com·pli·a·ble (kŏm·plī′ à·b′l)
com·po·nent (kŏm·pō′ nĕnt)
com·port (kŏm·pōrt′)
com·pose (kŏm·pōz′)
-pos·ing com·posedly
com·pos·er

com·pos·ite (kŏm·pŏz′ ĭt)
com·po·si·tion
(kŏm′ pŏ·zĭsh′ ŭn)
comp·os·i·tor (kŏm·pŏz′ ĭ·tĕr)
com·pos·ure (kŏm·pō′ zhĕr)
com·pote (kŏm′ pōt)
com·pound (kŏm·pound′) v.
(kŏm′ pound) n.,
adj.
com·pound·a·ble
(kŏm·pound′ à·b′l)
com·pound in·ter·est
(kom′ pound)
com·pre·hend (kŏm′ prĕ·hĕnd′)
com·pre·hen·si·ble
(-hĕn′ sĭ·b′l)
com·pre·hen·sion
(-hĕn′ shŭn)
com·pre·hen·sive
(hĕn′ sĭv)
com·press (kŏm·prĕs′) v.
(kŏm′ prĕs) n.
com·press·i·ble
(kŏm·prĕs′ ĭ·b′l)
com·pres·sion (kŏm·prĕsh′ ŭn)
com·pres·sor (kŏm·prĕs′ ĕr)
com·prise (kŏm·prīz′)
-pris·ing
com·pro·mise (kŏm′ prŏ·mīz)
-mis·ing com·pro·mis·er
Comp·tom·e·ter
(kŏmp·tŏm′ ĕ·tĕr)
comp·trol·ler (kŏn·trōl′ ĕr)
com·pul·sion (kŏm·pŭl′ shŭn)
com·pul·sive (-sĭv)
com·pul·so·ry (-sŏ′ rĭ)
com·pul·so·ri·ly
com·punc·tion
(kŏm·pŭngk′ shŭn)
com·pute (kŏm·pūt′)
-put·ing com·put·a·ble
com·pu·ta·tion
(kŏm′ pŭ·tā′ shŭn)
com·put·er
com·rade (kŏm′ răd)
com·rade·ship
con·cave (kŏn′ kāv)
con·cav·i·ty (kŏn·kăv′ ĭ·tĭ)
con·ceal (kŏn·sēl′)
-cealed -ceal·ing
con·ceal·a·ble con·ceal·ment
con·cede (kŏn·sēd′)
-ced·ing
con·ceit (kŏn·sēt′)
-ceit·ed

con·ceive   (kŏn·sēv′)
  -ceiv·ing   con·ceiv·able,
  -bly
con·cen·trate   (kŏn′ sĕn·trāt)
  -trat·ing
  con·cen·tra·tion
        (kŏn′ sĕn·trā′ shŭn)
  con·cen·tra·tor
con·cen·tric   (kŏn·sĕn′ trĭk)
con·cept   (kŏn′ sĕpt)
  con·cep·tion   (kŏn·sĕp′ shŭn)
  con·cep·tu·al   (kŏn·sĕp′ tŭ·ăl)
con·cern   (kŏn·sûrn′)
  -cern·ing
con·cert   (kŏn·sûrt′) v.
        (kŏn′ sûrt) n.
con·cer·ti·na   (kŏn′ sĕr·tē′ nà)
con·cer·to   (kŏn·chĕr′ tō)
  -tos
con·ces·sion   (kŏn·sĕsh′ ŭn)
  con·ces·sion·aire
        (kŏn·sĕsh′ ŭn·âr′)
  con·ces·sion·ar·y
        (kŏn·sĕsh′ ŭn·ĕr′ ĭ)
conch shell   (kŏngk)
con·cil·i·ate   (kŏn·sĭl′ ĭ·āt)
  -at·ing
  con·cil·i·a·tion
        (kŏn·sĭl′ ĭ·ā′ shŭn)
  con·cil·i·a·tor (kŏn·sĭl′ ĭ·ā′ tĕr)
  con·cil·i·a·to·ry
        (kŏn·sĭl′ ĭ·à·tō′ rĭ)
con·cise   (kŏn·sīs′)
  -cise·ly
con·clave   (kŏn′ klāv)
con·clude   (kŏn·klōōd′)
  -clud·ing
  con·clu·sion   (-klōō′ zhŭn)
  con·clu·sive   -sive·ly
con·coct   (kŏn·kŏkt′)
  con·coc·tion   (kŏn·kŏk′ shŭn)
con·com·i·tant
        (kŏn·kŏm′ ĭ·tănt)
  -tance
con·cord   (kŏn′ kôrd)
  con·cord·ance   (kŏn·kôr′ dăns)
con·course   (kŏn′ kōrs)
con·crete   (kŏn′ krēt)
  -crete·ness
con·cu·bine   (kŏng′ kŭ·bĭn)
  con·cu·bi·nage
        (kŏn·kū′ bĭ·nĭj)
con·cu·pis·cent
        (kŏn·kū′ pĭ·sĕnt)
  -cence

con·cur   (kŏn·kûr′)
  -curred   -cur·ring
  con·cur·rence   -cur·rent
con·cus·sion   (kŏn·kŭsh′ ŭn)
con·demn   (kŏn·dĕm′)
  con·dem·na·ble
  con·dem·na·tion
        (kŏn′ dĕm·nā′ shŭn)
  con·dem·na·to·ry
  con·demn·er   (-dĕm′ ēr)
con·dense   (kŏn·dĕns′)
  -dens·ing   con·den·sa·ble
  con·den·sa·tion
        (kŏn′ dĕn·sā′ shŭn)
  con·dens·er
con·de·scend   (kŏn′ dĕ·sĕnd′)
  con·de·scend·ing·ly
  con·de·scen·sion
        (-sĕn′ shŭn)
con·di·ment   (kŏn′ dĭ·mĕnt)
con·di·tion   (kŏn·dĭsh′ ŭn)
  con·di·tion·al -al·ly
con·dole   (kŏn·dōl′)
  -dol·ing
  con·do·lence   (-dō′ lĕns)
con·done   (kŏn·dōn′)
  -don·ing
con·dor   (kŏn′ dēr)
con·duce   (kŏn·dūs′)
  -duc·ing
  con·du·cive   (-dū′ sĭv)
con·duct   (kŏn′ dŭkt) n.
con·duct   (kŏn·dŭkt′) v.
  con·duct·i·ble con·duc·tion
  con·duc·tive   con·duc·tor
con·duit   (kŏn′ dwĭt)
Co·ney Is.   (kō′ nĭ)
con·fec·tion   (kŏn·fĕk′ shŭn)
  con·fec·tion·er, -er·y
con·fed·er·a·cy
        (kŏn·fĕd′ ĕr·à·sĭ)
  -cies
  con·fed·er·ate (-ĭt)
  con·fed·er·a·tion
        (kŏn·fĕd′ ĕr·ā′ shŭn)
con·fer   (kŏn·fûr′)
  -ferred   -fer·ring
  con·fer·ee   (kŏn′ fĕr·ē′)
  con·fer·ence   (kŏn′ fĕr·ĕns)
  con·fer·ra·ble
con·fess   (kŏn·fĕs′)
  con·fess·ed·ly
  con·fes·sion   (kŏn·fĕsh′ ŭn)
  -fes·sion·al   con·fes·sor

con·fet·ti (kŏn·fĕt′ ĭ)
con·fi·dant (kŏn′ fĭ·dănt′)
  n. masc., (friend)
  con·fi·dante (kŏn′ fĭ·dănt′)
  n. fem.
con·fide (kŏn·fīd′)
  -fid·ing
con·fi·dent (kŏn′ fĭ·dĕnt)
  (sure)
  con·fi·dence con·fi·dent·ly
con·fi·den·tial (kŏn′ fĭ·dĕn′ shăl)
  -tial·ly
con·fig·u·ra·tion
       (kŏn·fĭg′ ū·rā′ shŭn)
con·fine (kŏn·fīn′) v.
  -fin·ing con·fin·a·ble
  con·fine·ment
con·fines (kŏn′ fīnz) n.
con·firm (kŏn·fûrm′)
  con·firm·a·ble
  con·fir·ma·tion
       (kŏn′ fĕr·mā′ shŭn)
  con·firm·a·to·ry
       (kŏn· fûr′ mȧ·tō′ rĭ)
con·fis·cate (kŏn′ fĭs·kāt)
  -cat·ing
  con·fis·ca·tion
       (kŏn′ fĭs·kā′ shŭn)
  con·fis·ca·to·ry
       (kŏn· fĭs′ kȧ·tō′ rĭ)
con·fla·gra·tion
       (kŏn′ flȧ·grā′ shŭn)
con·flict (kŏn·flĭkt′) v.
       (kŏn′ flĭkt) n.
con·flu·ence (kŏn′ floo·ĕns)
con·form (kŏn·fôrm′)
  con·form·able
  con·for·ma·tion
       (kŏn′ fôr·mā′ shŭn)
  con·form·ist con·form·ity
con·found (kŏn·found′)
  con·found·ed·ly
con·frere (kŏn′ frâr)
con·front (kŏn·frŭnt′)
  con·fron·ta·tion
       (kŏn′ frŭn·tā′ shŭn)
Con·fu·cius (kŏn·fū′ shŭs)
  Con·fu·cian·ism
       (kŏn·fū′ shăn·ĭz′m)
con·fuse (kŏn·fūz′)
  -fus·ing con·fus·ed·ly
  con·fu·sion (-fū′ zhŭn)
con·fute (kŏn·fūt′)
  -fut·ing

con·fu·ta·tion
       (kŏn′ fū·tā′ shŭn)
con·ga (kŏng′ gȧ)
con·geal (kŏn·jēl′)
  -gealed -geal·ing
  con·geal·a·ble con·geal·ment
con·gen·ial (kŏn·jēn′ yăl)
  (compatible)
  con·ge·ni·al·i·ty
       (kŏn·jē′ nĭ·ăl′ ĭ·tĭ)
  con·gen·ial·ly
con·gen·i·tal (kŏn·jĕn′ ĭ·tăl)
  (inborn) con·gen·i·tal·ly
  con·gen·i·tal id·i·ot
con·gest (kŏn·jĕst′)
  con·ges·tion (-jĕs′ chŭn)
con·glom·er·ate
       (kŏn·glŏm′ ĕr·ĭt) adj.
  -at·ing (-āt) v.
  con·glom·er·a·tion
       (kŏn· glŏm′ ĕr·ā′ shŭn)
con·grat·u·late
       (kŏn·grăt′ ū·lāt)
  -lat·ing
  con·grat·u·la·tion
       (kŏn·grăt′ ū·lā′ shŭn)
  con·grat·u·la·tor (-lā′ tĕr)
  con·grat·u·la·to·ry (-lȧ·tō′ rĭ)
con·gre·gate (kŏng′ grē·gāt)
  -gat·ing
  con·gre·ga·tion
       (kŏng′ grē·gā′ shŭn)
Con·gre·ga·tion·al·ist
    (kŏng′ grē·gā′ shŭn·ăl·ĭst)
con·gress (kŏng′ grĕs)
  con·gres·sion·al
       (kŏn·grĕsh′ ŭn·ăl)
  con·gress·man
con·gru·ent (kŏng′ groō·ĕnt)
  -ence
  con·gru·ity (kŏn·groō′ ĭ·tĭ)
  con·gru·ous (kŏng′ groō·ŭs)
con·ic (kŏn′ ĭk)
  con·i·cal
co·ni·fer (kō′ nĭ·fĕr)
  co·nif·er·ous (kō·nĭf′ ĕr·ŭs)
con·jec·ture (kŏn·jĕk′ tûr)
  con·jec·tur·al
con·ju·gal (kŏn′ joō·găl)
con·ju·gate (kŏn′ joō·găt)
  -gat·ing
  con·ju·ga·tion
       (kŏn′ joō·gā′ shŭn)
con·junc·tion (kŏn·jŭngk′ shŭn)
  con·junc·tive con·junc·ture

con·jure   (kŭn′ jẽr)
  -jur·ing
con·ju·ra·tion
       (kŏn′ jŏŏ·rā′ shŭn)
  con·jur·er   (kŭn′ jẽr·ẽr)
con·nect   (kŏ·nĕkt′)
  con·nect·ed·ly   con·nec·tion
  con·nec·tive   con·nec·tor
Con·nect·i·cut   (kŏ·nĕt′ ĭ·kŭt)
  abbr. Conn.
con·nip·tion fit   (kŏ·nĭp′ shŭn)
con·nive   (kŏ·nīv′)
  con·niv·ing   con·niv·ance
  con·niv·er
con·nois·seur   (kŏn′ ĭ·sûr′)
con·note   (kŏ·nōt′)
  con·not·ing
  con·no·ta·tion (kŏn′ ŏ·tā′ shŭn)
  con·not·a·tive (kŏ·nōt′ å·tĭv)
con·nu·bi·al   (kŏ·nū′ bĭ·ål)
con·quer   (kŏng′ kẽr)
  con·quer·a·ble con·quer·or
con·quest   (kŏng′ kwĕst)
con·quis·ta·dor
       (kŏn·kwĭs′ tå·dôr)
con·san·guin·i·ty
       (kŏn′ săng·gwĭn′ ĭ·tĭ)
  con·san·guin·e·ous (-ê·ŭs)
con·science   (kŏn′ shĕns)
  con·science·less
con·sci·en·tious
       (kŏn′ shĭ·ĕn′ shŭs)
con·scious   (kŏn′ shŭs)
  con·scious·ness
con·script   (kŏn′ skrĭpt)
       adj., n.
       (kŏn·skrĭpt′) *v.*
  con·scrip·tion (kŏn·skrĭp′ shŭn)
con·se·crate   (kŏn′ sĕ·krāt)
  -crat·ing
  con·se·cra·tion
       (kŏn′ sĕ·krā′ shŭn)
  con·se·cra·tor
con·sec·u·tive   (kŏn·sĕk′ ŭ·tĭv)
  -tive·ly
con·sen·sus   (kŏn·sĕn′ sŭs)
  con·sen·su·al   (-shū·ål)
con·sent   (kŏn·sĕnt′)
con·se·quence   (kŏn′ sĕ·kwĕns)
  con·se·quent, -quent·ly
  con·se·quen·tial
       (kŏn′ sĕ·kwĕn′ shål)
  -tial·ly

con·serv·a·to·ry
       (kŏn·sûr′ vå·tō′ rĭ)
  -ries
con·serve   (kŏn·sûrv′)
  -serv·ing
  con·ser·va·tion
       (kŏn′ sẽr·vā′ shŭn)
  -tion·al
  con·serv·a·tism
       (kŏn·sûr′ vå·tĭz′m)
  con·serv·a·tive   (-tĭv)
  -tive·ly
con·sid·er   (kŏn·sĭd′ ẽr)
  con·sid·er·a·ble, -bly
  con·sid·er·ate   (-ĭt)
  -ate·ly
  con·sid·er·a·tion
       (kŏn·sĭd′ ẽr·ā′ shŭn)
con·sign   (kŏn·sīn′)
  con·sign·ee   (kŏn′ sī·nē′)
  con·sign·ment con·sign·or
con·sist   (kŏn·sĭst′)
con·sist·ent   (kŏn·sĭs′ tĕnt)
  con·sist·en·cy   con·sist·ent·ly
con·sole   (kŏn·sōl′) *v.*
  -sol·ing
  con·so·la·tion
       (kŏn′ sŏ·lā′ shŭn)
  con·so·ler
con·sole ta·ble   (kŏn′ sōl)
con·sol·i·date   (kŏn·sŏl′ ĭ·dāt)
  -dat·ing
  con·sol·i·da·tion
       (kŏn·sŏl′ ĭ·dā′ shŭn)
con·som·mé   (kŏn′ sŏ·mā′)
con·so·nance   (kŏn′ sŏ·nåns)
  -nant
con·sort   (kŏn′ sôrt) *n.*
       (kŏn·sôrt′) *v.*
con·spic·u·ous   (kŏn·spĭk′ ū·ŭs)
con·spir·a·cy   (kŏn·spĭr′ å·sĭ)
  -cies
con·spir·a·tor   (kŏn·spĭr′ å·tẽr)
  con·spir·a·to·ri·al
       (kŏn·spĭr′ å·tō′ rĭ·ål)
con·spire   (kŏn·spīr′)
  -spir·ing
con·sta·ble   (kŭn′ stå·b′l)
con·stab·u·lar·y
       (kŏn·stăb′ ŭ·lẽr′ ĭ)
  -lar·ies
con·stant   (kŏn′ stånt)
  -stan·cy
con·stel·la·tion
       (kŏn′ stĕ·lā′ shŭn)

con·ster·na·tion
      (kŏn′ stĕr·nā′ shŭn)
con·sti·pat·ed   (kŏn′ stĭ·pāt′ ĕd)
  con·sti·pa·tion
      (kŏn′ stĭ·pā′ shŭn)
con·stit·u·en·cy
    – (kŏn·stĭt′ û·ĕn·sĭ)
 -ent
con·sti·tute   (kŏn′ stĭ·tūt)
 -tut·ing
con·sti·tu·tion (kŏn′ stĭ·tū′ shŭn)
  con·sti·tu·tion·al, -al·ism,
  -al·ly
  con·sti·tu·tion·al·i·ty
    (kŏn′ stĭ·tū′ shŭn·ăl′ ĭ·tĭ)
con·strain   (kŏn·strān′)
  con·strain·ed·ly
    (-strān′ ĕd·lĭ)
  con·straint
con·strict   (kŏn·strĭkt′)
  con·stric·tion (-strĭk′ shŭn)
  con·stric·tive con·stric·tor
con·struct   (kŏn·strŭkt′)
  con·struc·ter
  con·struc·tion (-strŭk′ shŭn)
  con·struc·tive -tive·ly
con·strue   (kŏn·strōō′)
 -stru·ing
con·sul   (kŏn′ sŭl)
  (diplomat; see *council, counsel*)
  con·su·lar   (kŏn′ sû·lẽr)
  con·su·late (kŏn′ sû·låt)
con·sult   (kŏn·sŭlt′)
  con·sult·ant (-tånt)
  con·sul·ta·tion
    (kŏn′ sŭl·tā′ shŭn)
  con·sul·tive (-tĭv)
con·sume   (kŏn·sūm′)
 -sum·ing   con·sum·a·ble
 con·sum·ers′ goods
con·sum·mate (kŏn·sŭm′ ĭt)
 adj. (perfect)
con·sum·mate (kŏn′ sŭ·māt) *v.*
 (to complete)
 -sum·mat·ing
 con·sum·ma·tion
    (kŏn′ sŭ·mā′ shŭn)
con·sump·tion (kŏn·sŭmp′ shŭn)
con·sump·tive (kŏn·sŭmp′ tĭv)
con·tact   (kŏn′ tăkt)
  con·tact lens con·tact print
con·ta·gion (kŏn·tā′ jŭn)
 con·ta·gious (-jŭs)
con·tain   (kŏn·tān′)
  con·tain·a·ble con·tain·er

con·tam·i·nate (kŏn·tăm′ ĭ·nāt)
 -nat·ing
 con·tam·i·na·tion
    (kŏn·tăm′ ĭ·nā′ shŭn)
 con·tam·i·na·tor
con·tem·plate (kŏn′ tĕm·plāt)
 -plat·ing
 con·tem·pla·tion
    (kŏn′ tĕm·plā′ shŭn)
 con·tem·pla·tive
    (kŏn·tĕm′ plå·tĭv)
con·tem·po·rar·y
    (kŏn·tĕm′ pŏ·rẽr′ ĭ)
 -rar·ies
 con·tem·po·ra·ne·ous
    (-tĕm′ pŏ·rā′ nē·ŭs)
con·tempt   (kŏn·tĕmpt′)
 con·tempt·i·ble
 con·temp·tu·ous
    (-tĕmp′ tû·ŭs)
con·tend   (kŏn·tĕnd′)
 con·tend·er
con·tent   (kŏn′ tĕnt) *n.*
con·tent   (kŏn·tĕnt′) *adj.*
 con·tent·ed con·tent·ment
con·ten·tion (kŏn·tĕn′ shŭn)
con·ten·tious (kŏn·tĕn′ shŭs)
con·ter·mi·nous
    (kŏn·tûr′ mĭ·nŭs)
con·test   (kŏn′ tĕst) *n.*
con·test   (kŏn·tĕst′) *v.*
 con·test·a·ble con·test·ant
con·text   (kŏn′ tĕkst)
con·tig·u·ous (kŏn·tĭg′ û·ŭs)
 con·ti·gu·i·ty (kŏn′ tĭ·gū′ ĭ·tĭ)
con·ti·nence (kŏn′ tĭ·nĕns)
 -nen·cy
con·ti·nent   (kŏn′ tĭ·nĕnt)
 con·ti·nen·tal (kŏn′ tĭ·nĕn′ tål)
con·tin·gent (kŏn·tĭn′ jĕnt)
 -gen·cy
con·tin·ue   (kŏn·tĭn′ û)
 -u·ing
 con·tin·u·al   -al·ly
 con·tin·u·ance
 con·tin·u·a·tion
    (kŏn·tĭn′ û·ā′ shŭn)
 con·tin·u·ous
con·ti·nu·i·ty (kŏn′ tĭ·nū′ ĭ·tĭ)
 -ties
con·tort   (kŏn·tôrt′)
 con·tor·tion·ist
    (-tôr′ shŭn·ĭst)
con·tour   (kŏn′ tōōr)
con·tra·band (kŏn′ trå·bănd)

con·tra·cep·tion
        (kŏn′ trá·sĕp′ shŭn)
  con·tra·cep·tive
con·tract (kŏn′ trăkt) n.
  con·trac·tor
con·tract (kŏn′ trăkt′) v.
  con·tract·i·ble
  con·trac·tion (-trăk′ shŭn)
  con·trac·tu·al (-trăk′ tụ·ắl)
con·tra·dict (kŏn′ trá·dĭkt′)
  con·tra·dic·tion (-dĭk′ shŭn)
  con·tra·dic·to·ry (-dĭk′ tŏ·rĭ)
con·tra·dis·tinc·tion
        (kŏn′ trá·dĭs·tĭngk′ shŭn)
con·tral·to (kŏn′ trăl′ tō)
  -tos
con·tra·ry (kŏn′ trĕr·Ĭ)
  con·tra·ri·ly (-trĕr·ĭ·lĭ)
  con·tra·ri·ness (-Ĭ·nĕs)
  con·tra·ri·wise (Ĭ·wīs′)
con·trast (kŏn′ trăst′) v.
  con·trast·a·ble
con·trast (kŏn′ trăst) n.
con·tra·vene (kŏn′ trá·vēn′)
  -ven·ing
  con·tra·ven·tion
        (kŏn′ trá·vĕn′ shŭn)
con·trib·ute (kŏn·trĭb′ ût)
  -but·ing
  con·trib·ut·a·ble
  con·tri·bu·tion
        (kŏn′ trĭ·bū′ shŭn)
  con·trib·u·tor
  con·trib·u·to·ry
      (-trĭb′ û·tŏ′ rĭ)
con·trite (kŏn′ trīt)
  -trite·ly
  con·tri·tion (kŏn·trĭsh′ ŭn)
con·trive (kŏn·trīv′)
  -triv·ing
  con·triv·ance (kŏn·trīv′ ắns)
con·trol (kŏn·trōl′)
  -trolled -trol·ling
  con·trol·la·ble con·trol·ler
con·tro·ver·sy (kŏn′ trŏ·vûr′ sĭ)
  -sies
  con·tro·ver·sial
        (kŏn′ trŏ·vûr′ shắl)
  -sial·ly
con·tro·vert (kŏn′ trŏ·vûrt)
con·tu·ma·cious
        (kŏn′ tû·mā′ shŭs)
  con·tu·ma·cy (kŏn′ tû·má·sĭ)
con·tu·sion (kŏn·tū′ zhŭn)
co·nun·drum (kŏ·nŭn′ drŭm)

con·va·lesce (kŏn′ vá·lĕs′)
  -lesc·ing
  con·va·les·cent, -cence
con·vec·tion (kŏn·vĕk′ shŭn)
  con·vec·tive (-vĕk′ tĭv)
con·vene (kŏn·vēn′)
  -ven·ing
con·ven·ience (kŏn·vēn′ yĕns)
  -ient
con·vent (kŏn′ vĕnt)
con·ven·tion (kŏn·vĕn′ shŭn)
  con·ven·tion·al, -al·ly
  con·ven·tion·al·i·ty
      (kŏn·vĕn′ shŭn·ăl′ ĭ·tĭ)
con·verge (kŏn·vûrj′)
  -verg·ing
  con·ver·gence (-vûr′ jĕns)
  -gent
con·verse (kŏn·vûrs′) v.
  -vers·ing
  con·ver·sance (kŏn·vĕr·sắns)
  -sant
  con·ver·sa·tion
        (kŏn·vĕr·sā′ shŭn)
  -tion·al
con·verse (kŏn′ vûrs)
  adj., n.
con·ver·sion (kŏn·vûr′ shŭn)
con·vert (kŏn·vûrt′) v.
  con·vert·i·ble (-vûr′ tĭ·b′l)
con·vert (kŏn′ vûrt) n.
con·vex (kŏn′ vĕks)
  con·vex·i·ty (kŏn·vĕk′ sĭ·tĭ)
con·vey (kŏn·vā′)
  con·vey·ance (kŏn·vā′ ắns)
  con·vey·er
con·vict (kŏn′ vĭkt) n.
con·vict (kŏn·vĭkt′) v.
  con·vic·tion (-vĭk′ shŭn)
con·vince (kŏn·vĭns′)
  -vinc·ing con·vin·ci·ble
  con·vinc·ing·ly
con·viv·i·al (kŏn·vĭv′ Ĭ·ắl)
  con·viv·i·al·i·ty
      (kŏn·vĭv′ Ĭ·ăl′ ĭ·tĭ)
  con·viv·i·al·ly
con·vo·ca·tion
        (kŏn′ vŏ·kā′ shŭn)
con·voke (kŏn·vōk′)
  -vok·ing
con·vo·lu·tion (kŏn′ vŏ·lū′ shŭn)
con·voy (kŏn·voi′) v.
     (kŏn′ voi) n.
con·vulse (kŏn·vŭls′)
  -vuls·ing

con·vul·sion (-vŭl′ shŭn)
con·vul·sive (-vŭl′ sĭv)
cook·book (kŏok′ bŏok′)
cook·er·y (kŏok′ ēr·ĭ)
cook·y (kŏok′ ĭ)
  cook·ies
cool (kōol)
  cool·ant (kōol′ ănt)
  cool·er   cool·ly
  cool·ness
coo·lie (kōo′ lĭ)
  (laborer; see *coulee*)
coop·er·age (kōop′ ēr·ĭj)
co·op·er·ate (kŏ·ŏp′ ēr·āt)
  -at·ing
  co·op·er·a·tion
          (kŏ·ŏp′ ēr·ā′ shŭn)
  co·op·er·a·tive
          (kŏ·ŏp′ ēr·ā′ tĭv)
  -tive·ness
co·opt (kŏ·ŏpt′)
  co·op·ta·tion (cŏ′ ŏp·tā′ shŭn)
co·or·di·nate (kŏ·ŏr′ dĭ·nāt) v.
  -nat·ing (-ăt) n., adj.
  co·or·di·na·tion
          (kŏ·ŏr′ dĭ·nā′ shŭn)
co·part·ner (kŏ·pärt′ nēr)
Co·pen·ha·gen, (kŏ′ pĕn·hā′ gĕn)
  Den·mark
Co·per·ni·cus (kŏ·pûr′ nĭ·kŭs)
  Co·per·ni·can (kŏ·pûr′ nĭ·kăn)
cop·ing saw (kŏp′ ĭng)
co·pi·ous (kŏ′ pĭ·ŭs)
cop·per (kŏp′ ēr)
  cop·per·head cop·per·plate
  cop·per·smith
cop·u·late (kŏp′ û·lāt)
  -lat·ing
  cop·u·la·tion (kŏp′ û·lā′ shŭn)
cop·y (kŏp′ ĭ)
  cop·ies cop·y·book
  cop·y·cat cop·y·hol·der
  cop·y·ist cop·y·right
co·quette (kŏ·kĕt′)
  co·quet·ry (kŏ′ kĕ·trĭ)
  co·quet·tish
cor·al (kŏr′ ăl)
  (as in *coral* reef; see *corral*)
cord (kôrd)
  (string; see *chord*)
  cord·age (kôr′ dĭj)
cor·dial (kôr′ jăl)
  cor·dial·i·ty (kôr·jăl′ ĭ·tĭ)
  cor·dial·ly
cor·don (kôr′ dŏn)

cor·do·van (kôr′ dŏ·văn)
cor·du·roy (kôr′ dŭ·roi)
co·re·spond·ent
          (kŏ′ rĕ·spŏn′ dĕnt)
  (legal term; see *correspondent*)
co·ri·an·der (kŏ′ rĭ·ăn′ dēr)
cork·screw (kôrk′ skrōo′)
cor·mo·rant (kôr′ mŏ·rănt)
corn (kôrn)
  corn bor·er corn bread
  corn·cake corn·cob
  corn·flow·er corn pone
  corn sir·up corn starch
  corn sug·ar
cor·ne·a (kôr′ nĕ·à)
  cor·ne·al
cor·ner (kôr′ nēr)
  cor·ner·stone
cor·net (kôr′ nĕt)
  (horn; see *coronet*)
  cor·net·tist (kôr·nĕt′ ĭst)
cor·nice (kôr′ nĭs)
cor·nu·co·pi·a (kôr′ nù·kŏ′ pĭ·à)
cor·ol·lar·y (kôr′ ŏ·lĕr′ ĭ)
  -ol·lar·ies
co·ro·na (kŏ·rō′ nà)
cor·o·nar·y throm·bo·sis
          (kôr′ ŏ·nĕr′ ĭ)
cor·o·na·tion (kôr′ ŏ·nā′ shŭn)
cor·o·ner (kôr′ ŏ·nēr)
cor·o·net (kôr′ ŏ·nĕt)
  (crown; see *cornet*)
cor·po·ral (kôr′ pŏ·răl)
cor·po·rate (kôr′ pŏ·rĭt)
  cor·po·rate·ly
cor·po·ra·tion (kôr′ pŏ·rā′ shŭn)
  cor·po·ra·tive (kôr′ pŏ·rā′ tĭv)
cor·po·re·al (kôr′ pŏ′ rē·ăl)
corps (kôr)
  corps·man (kôr′ măn)
cor·pu·lent (kôr′ pû·lĕnt)
  -lence
Cor·pus Chris·ti,
  Tex. (kôr′ pŭs krĭs′ tĭ)
cor·pus·cle (kôr′ pŭs·'l)
cor·ral (kŏ·răl′)
  (stockade; see *coral*)
  cor·ralled
cor·rect (kŏ·rĕkt′)
  cor·rec·tion·al (-rĕk′ shŭn·ăl)
  cor·rec·tive cor·rec·tor
cor·re·late (kôr′ ĕ·lāt)
  -lat·ing
  cor·re·la·tion (kôr′ ĕ·lā′ shŭn)
  cor·rel·a·tive (kŏ·rĕl′ à·tĭv)

cor·re·spond (kŏr' ĕ·spŏnd')
cor·re·spond·ent
    (kŏr' ĕ·spŏn' dĕnt)
 (letter writer; see *corespondent*)
 cor·re·spond·ence
cor·ri·dor (kŏr' ĭ·dôr)
cor·rob·o·rate (kŏ·rŏb' ô·rāt)
 -rat·ing
cor·rob·o·ra·tion
    (kŏ·rŏb' ô·rā' shŭn)
 cor·rob·o·ra·tive (-rā' tĭv)
cor·rode (kŏ·rōd')
 cor·rod·ing
cor·ro·sion (kŏ·rō' zhŭn)
 cor·ro·sive (-sĭv)
cor·ru·gat·ed i·ron
   (kŏr' ŭ·gāt' ĕd)
 cor·ru·ga·tion (kŏr' ŭ·gā' shŭn)
cor·rupt (kŏ·rŭpt')
 cor·rupt·er cor·rupt·i·ble
 cor·rup·tion cor·rup·tive
cor·sage (kôr·säzh')
cor·sair (kôr' sâr)
cor·set (kôr' sĕt)
cor·tege (kôr·tĕzh')
cor·tex (kôr' tĕks)
 pl. cor·ti·ces (-tĭ·sēz)
 cor·ti·cal (-tĭ·kăl)
cor·ti·sone (kôr' tĭ·sōn)
Cor·vette (kôr·vĕt')
cos·met·ic (kŏz·mĕt' ĭk)
 cos·met·i·cal·ly
cos·mic (kŏz' mĭk)
 cos·mi·cal·ly cos·mic dust
 cos·mic ray
cos·mol·o·gy (kŏz·mŏl' ô·jĭ)
 -gies
 cos·mo·log·i·cal
    (kŏz' mŏ·lŏj' ĭ·kăl)
cos·mo·pol·i·tan
   (kŏz' mŏ·pŏl' ĭ·tăn)
 cos·mop·o·lite (kŏz·mŏp' ô·līt)
cos·mos (kŏz' mŏs)
Cos·sack (kŏs' ăk)
Cos·ta Ri·ca (kŏs' tá rē' ká)
cost·ly (kŏst' lĭ)
 cost·li·ness
cos·tume (kŏs' tūm)
co·te·rie (kō' tĕ·rĭ)
co·til·lion (kŏ·tĭl' yŭn)
cot·tage (kŏt' ĭj)
cot·ter pin (kŏt' ĕr)
cot·ton (kŏt' 'n)
 cot·ton belt cot·ton flan·nel
 cot·ton gin cot·ton·mouth

 cot·ton·seed cot·ton·tail
 cot·ton·wood
couch (kouch)
cou·gar (kōō' gẽr)
cough (kôf)
could (kŏŏd)
cou·lee (kōō' lĭ)
 (deep valley; see *coolie*)
coun·cil (koun' sĭl)
 (assembly; see *consul, counsel*)
 coun·cil·man
coun·sel (koun' sĕl)
 (advice; see *council, consul*)
 -seled -sel·ing
 coun·se·lor
count (kount)
 count·a·ble count·less
coun·te·nance (koun' tĕ·nŏns)
coun·ter- (koun' tẽr-)
 coun·ter·act
 coun·ter·bal·ance
 coun·ter·charge, -charg·ing
 coun·ter·claim
 coun·ter·clock·wise
 coun·ter·cur·rent
 coun·ter·es·pi·o·nage
 coun·ter·feit, -feit·er
 coun·ter·in·tel·li·gence
 coun·ter·ir·ri·tant
 coun·ter·mand
 coun·ter·of·fen·sive
 coun·ter·part
 coun·ter·prop·a·gan·da
 coun·ter·rev·o·lu·tion
 coun·ter·sign
 coun·ter·vail·ing
count·ess (koun' tĕs)
coun·try (kŭn' trĭ)
 -tries
 coun·tri·fied (kŭn' trĭ·fīd)
 coun·try-bred coun·try·man
 coun·try·side coun·try-style
coun·ty (koun' tĭ)
 -ties
coup d'é·tat (kōō dā' tá')
cou·pé (kōō' pā')
cou·ple (kŭp' 'l)
 -pling
 cou·plet (kŭp' lĕt)
cou·pon (kōō' pŏn)
cour·age (kûr' ĭj)
 cou·ra·geous (kŭ·rā' jŭs)
cour·i·er (kŏŏr' ĭ·ẽr)
course (kōrs)
 (path; see *coarse*)

court	(kōrt)
court·house	court-mar·tial
court·room	court·ship
court·yard	
cour·te·ous	(kûr′ tē·ŭs)
cour·te·san	(kōr′ tē·zən)
cour·te·sy	((kûr′ tē·sĭ)
-sies	
court·ly	(kōrt′ lĭ)
court·li·ness	
cous·in	(kŭz′ 'n)
cou·tu·rier	(kōō′ tū·ryā′)
n. masc.	
cou·tu·rière	(kōō′ tū·ryâr′)
n. fem.	
cov·e·nant	(kŭv′ ě·nǎnt)
cov·er·age	(kŭv′ ēr·ĭj)
cov·er·let	(kŭv′ ēr·lět)
cov·ert	(kŭv′ ērt)
cov·et	(kŭv′ ět)
-et·ed	-et·ing
cov·et·ous	(kŭv′ ě·tŭs)
cov·ey	(kŭv′ ĭ)
(flock)	
cow	(kou)
cow·bell	cow·bird
cow·boy	cow·hide
cow·man	
cow·ard	(kou′ ērd)
cow·ard·ice	(kou′ ēr·dĭs)
cow·ard·li·ness	
cow·lick	(kou′ lĭk′)
co-work·er	(kō·wûr′ kēr)
cox·swain	(kŏk′ s'n)
coy·ness	(koi′ něs)
coy·ote	(kī′ ōt)
co·zy	(kō′ zĭ)
co·zi·er	-zi·est
-zi·ly	-zi·ness
crab	(krăb)
crab ap·ple	crab·by
crab grass	
crack	(krăk)
crack·down	crack·pot
crack-up	
crack·er	(krăk′ ēr)
crack·le	(krăk′ 'l)
-ling	crack·ly
cra·dle	(krā′ d'l)
-dling	
craft	(krăft)
crafts·man·ship	
craft·y	craft·i·er
-i·est, -i·ly, -i·ness	

crag	(krăg)
crag·gi·ness	crag·gy
cram·pon	(krăm′ pŏn)
cran·ber·ry	(krăn′ běr′ ĭ)
-ber·ries	
cra·ni·al	(krā′ nĭ·ǎl)
-al·ly	
cra·ni·um	(krā′ nĭ·ŭm)
crank	(krăngk)
crank·case	crank·pin
crank·shaft	crank·y
cran·ny	(krăn′ ĭ)
cran·nied	
crap·pie	(krăp′ ĭ)
crass	(krăs)
crate	(krāt)
crat·ing	
cra·ter	(krā′ tēr)
cra·vat	(krȧ·văt′)
crave	(krāv)
crav·ing	
cra·ven	(krā′ věn)
cra·ven·ly	cra·ven·ness
crawl	(krôl)
cray·fish	(krā′ fĭsh)
cray·on	(krā′ ŏn)
cra·zy	(krā′ zĭ)
cra·zi·er, -zi·est, -zi·ly, -zi·ness	
cra·zy bone	cra·zy quilt
creak	(krēk)
(sound; see *creek*)	
creak·i·ness	creak·y
cream·er·y	(krēm′ ēr·ĭ)
-er·ies	
crease	(krēs)
creas·ing	
cre·ate	(krē·āt′)
-at·ing	cre·a·tion
cre·a·tive	cre·a·tor
crea·ture	(krē′ tŭr)
crèche	(krāsh)
cre·dence	(krē′ děns)
cre·den·tial	(krē·děn′ shǎl)
cred·i·ble	(krěd′ ĭ·b'l)
cred·i·bil·i·ty	(krěd′ ĭ·bĭl′ ĭ·tĭ)
cred·it	(krěd′ ĭt)
-it·ed	-it·ing
cred·it·a·ble	cred·i·tor
cre·do	(krē′ dō)
-dos	
cre·du·li·ty	(krē·dū′ lĭ·tĭ)
cred·u·lous	(krěd′ û·lŭs)
creek	(krēk)
(stream; see *creek*)	

creep	(krēp)	cro·chet	(krō·shā′)
crept	(krĕpt)	-chet·ing	
cre·mate	(krē′ māt)	crock·er·y	(krŏk′ ēr·ĭ)
-mat·ing		croc·o·dile	(krŏk′ ō·dĭl)
cre·ma·tion	(krė·mā′ shŭn)	cro·cus	(krō′ kŭs)
crem a tȯ rɪ um		-cus·es	
	(krĕm á·tō′ rĭ·ŭm)	Croe·sus	(krē′ sŭs)
cre·ole	(krē′ ōl)	Cro-Ma·gnon	(krō·mǎn′ yŏn)
cre·o·sol	(krē′ ō·sōl)	cro·ny	(krō′ nĭ)
cre·o·sote	(krē′ ō·sōt)	-nies	
crepe	(krāp)	crook·ed	(krŏŏk′ ĕd)
crepe pa·per n		cro·quet	(krō·kā′)
crepe-pa·per adj		(game)	
crepe rub·ber		cro·quette	(krō·kĕt′)
crepe su·zette	(krăp′ sŏŏ·zĕt′)	(food)	
cre·scen·do	(krĕ·shĕn′ dō)	cross	(krŏs)
-dos		cross·bar	cross·bow
cres·cent	(krĕs′ ĕnt)	cross·bred	cross-coun·try
crest·fall·en	(krĕst′ fôl′ ĕn)	cross·cut	cross-ex·am·ine
cre·tin	(krē′ tĭn)	cross-eyed	
cre·tonne	(krė·tŏn′)	cross-fer·ti·li·za·tion	
cre·vasse	(krė·vǎs′)	cross fire	cross-grained
crev·ice	(krĕv′ ĭs)	cross in·dex n.	cross-in·dex v.
crib·bage	(krĭb′ ĭj)	cross·o·ver	
crick·et	(krĭk′ ĕt)	cross-pol·li·na·tion	
cried	(krīd)	cross-ques·tion	
cri·er	(krī′ ēr)	cross ref·er·ence	
crim·i·nal	(krĭm′ ĭ·nǎl)	cross·road	cross·ruff
-nal·ly		cross sec·tion	cross-stitch
crim·i·nal·i·ty		cross·walk	cross·wise
	(krĭm′ ĭ·nǎl′ ĭ·tĭ)	cross·word puz·zle	
crim·i·nol·o·gy		crotch·et·y	(krŏch′ ĕ·tĭ)
	(krĭm′ ĭ·nŏl′ ō·jĭ)	crotch·et·i·ness	
crim·son	(krĭm′ z'n)	crouch	(krouch)
cringe	(krĭnj)	croup	(krōōp)
cring·ing		crou·pi·er	(krōō′ pĭ·ēr)
crin·kle	(krĭng′ k'l)	crou·ton	(krōō·tôN′)
-kling		crow·bar	(krō′ bär′)
crin·o·line	(krĭn′ ō·lĭn)	crowd	(kroud)
crip·ple	(krĭp′ 'l)	cru·cial	(krōō′ shǎl)
crip·pling	crip·pler	-cial·ly	
cri·sis	(crī′ sĭs)	cru·ci·ble	(krōō′ sĭ·b'l)
pl. cri·ses	(-sēz)	cru·ci·fix	(krōō′ sĭ·fĭks)
crisp·y	(krĭs′ pĭ)	cru·ci·fix·ion	
criss·cross	(krĭs′ krŏs′)		(krōō′ sĭ·fĭk′ shŭn)
cri·te·ri·on	(krī·tēr′ ĭ·ŭn)	cru·ci·fy	(krōō′ sĭ·fī)
pl. cri·te·ri·a		-fied	-fy·ing
crit·ic	(krĭt′ ĭk)	crude	(krōōd)
crit·i·cal	-cal·ly	crude·ly	
crit·i·cism	(krĭt′ ĭ·sĭz'm)	cru·di·ty	(krōō′ dĭ·tĭ)
crit·i·cize	(-sīz)	cru·el	(krōō′ ĕl)
-ciz·ing		cru·el·ly	cru·el·ty
cri·tique	(krĭ·tēk′)	cru·et	(krōō′ ĕt)
croak	(krōk)	cruise	(krōōz)
		cruis·ing	cruis·er

crul·ler (krŭl′ ĕr)
crum·ble (krŭm′ b'l)
  -bling
crum·ple (krŭm′ p'l)
  -pling
cru·sade (krōō·sād′)
  -sad·ing   cru·sad·er
crus·ta·cean (krŭs·tā′ shăn)
  crus·ta·ceous (-shŭs)
crust·y (krŭs′ tĭ)
  crust·i·ness
crutch (krŭch)
crux (krŭks)
cry (krī)
  cried   cry·ing
  cri·er   cries
crypt (krĭpt)
  cryp·tic (krĭp′ tĭk)
  cryp·tog·ra·phy
    (krĭp·tŏg′ rȧ·fĭ)
crys·tal (krĭs′ tăl)
  crys·tal·line (krĭs′ tăl·ĭn)
  crys·tal·li·za·tion
    (krĭs′ tăl·ĭ·zā′ shŭn)
  crys·tal·lize (krĭs′ tăl·īz)
  -tal·liz·ing
cu·bic (kū′ bĭk)
cu·bi·cal (kū′ bĭ·kăl)
  (cube-shaped)
cu·bi·cle (kū′ bĭ·k'l)
  (compartment)
cuck·old (kŭk′ ŭld)
cuck·oo (kŏŏk′ ōō)
cu·cum·ber (kū′ kŭm·bĕr)
cud·dle (kŭd′ 'l)
  cud·dling   cud·dle·some
  cud·dly
cudg·el (kŭj′ ĕl)
  -geled   -gel·ing
cue (kū)
  (hint; see *queue*)
cue ball (kū)
cuff (kŭf)
cui·rass (kwĕ·răs′)
cui·sine (kwĕ·zēn′)
cul-de-sac (kŏŏl′ dĕ·săk′)
cu·li·nar·y (kū′ lĭ·nĕr′ ĭ)
cul·mi·nate (kŭl′ mĭ·nāt)
  -nat·ing
  cul·mi·na·tion
    (kŭl′ mĭ·nā′ shŭn)
cu·lottes (kū·lŏts′)
cul·pa·ble (kŭl′ pȧ·b'l)
  cul·pa·bil·i·ty (kŭl′ pȧ·bĭl′ ĭ·tĭ)
cul·prit (kŭl′ prĭt)

cult·ist (kŭl′ tĭst)
cul·ti·vate (kŭl′ tĭ·vāt)
  -vat·ing
  cul·ti·va·ble (kŭl′ tĭ·vȧ·b'l)
  cul·ti·va·tion (kŭl′ tĭ·vā′ shŭn)
  cul·ti·va·tor
cul·ture (kŭl′ tûr)
  cul·tur·al
cum·ber·some (kŭm′ bĕr·sŭm)
cum·brous (kŭm′ brŭs)
cum·in (kŭm′ ĭn)
cum lau·de (kŭm lô′ dē)
cum·mer·bund (kŭm′ ĕr·bŭnd)
cu·mu·la·tive (kū′ mû·lā′ tĭv)
cu·mu·lus (kū′ mû·lŭs)
cu·ne·i·form (kû·nē′ ĭ·fôrm)
cun·ning (kŭn′ ĭng)
cup·board (kŭb′ ĕrd)
cup·ful (kŭp′ fŏŏl)
  -fuls
cu·pid·i·ty (kû·pĭd′ ĭ·tĭ)
cu·po·la (kū′ pŏ·lȧ)
cu·ra·çao (kū′ rȧ·sō′)
cu·rate (kū′ răt)
  cu·ra·cy (kū′ rȧ·sĭ)
cu·ra·tor (kû·rā′ tĕr)
curb·stone (kûrb′ stōn′)
cur·dle (kûr′ d'l)
  -dling
cure (kūr)
  cur·ing   cur·a·ble
  cure-all
cu·rette (kû·rĕt′)
cur·few (kûr′ fū)
cu·ri·ous (kū′ rĭ·ŭs)
  cu·ri·os·i·ty (kū′ rĭ·ŏs′ ĭ·tĭ)
  -ties
curl·i·cue (kûr′ lĭ·kū)
curl·y (kûr′ lĭ)
  curl·i·ness
cur·mudg·eon (kĕr·mŭj′ ŭn)
cur·rant (kûr′ ănt)
  (fruit)
cur·rent (kûr′ ĕnt)
  (timely)   cur·ren·cy
cur·ric·u·lum (kŭ·rĭk′ û·lŭm)
cur·ry (kûr′ ĭ)
  cur·ried   cur·ry·ing
curse (kûrs)
  curs·ing
cur·so·ry (kûr′ sŏ·rĭ)
curt (kûrt)
cur·tail·ment (kûr·tāl′ mĕnt)
cur·tain (kûr′ tĭn)

curt·sy   (kûrt′ sĭ)
-sied   -sy·ing
curve   (kûrv)
  curv·ing
  cur·va·ceous   (kûr·vā′ shŭs)
  cur·va·ture   (kûr′ và·tͅûr)
cush·ion   (kŏŏsh′ ŭn)
cus·pi·dor   (kŭs′ pĭ·dôr)
cuss·ed·ness   (kŭs′ ĕd·nĕs)
cus·tard   (kŭs′ tērd)
cus·to·dy   (kŭs′ tŏ·dĭ)
  -dies
  cus·to·di·al   (kŭs·tō′ dĭ·ål)
  cus·to·di·an   (kŭs·tō′ dĭ·ăn)
cus·tom   (kŭs′ tŭm)
  cus·tom·ar·i·ly   (-ĕr′ ĭ·lĭ)
  cus·tom·ar·y   (-ĕr′ ĭ)
  cus·tom·house
cus·tom·er   (kŭs′ tŭm·ēr)
cut   (kŭt)
  cut·ting   cut·a·way
  cut·back   cut·off
  cut·out   cut·o·ver
  cut-rate   cut·throat
cu·ta·ne·ous   (kù·tā′ nĕ·ŭs)
cute   (kūt)
  cute·ness
cu·ti·cle   (kū′ tĭ·k′l)
cut·lass   (kŭt′ làs)
cut·ler·y   (kŭt′ lĕr·ĭ)
cut·let   (kŭt′ lĕt)
cy·an·am·ide   (sĭ′ ăn·ăm′ ĭd)
cy·a·nide   (sĭ′ à·nīd)
cy·cle   (sĭ′ k′l)
  cy·cli·cal   (sĭ′ klĭ·kàl)
  cy·clist   (sĭ′ klĭst)
cy·cloid   (sĭ′ kloid)
cy·clom·e·ter   (sĭ·klŏm′ ĕ·tēr)
cy·clone   (sĭ′ klōn)
cy·clo·pe·di·a   (sĭ′ klŏ·pē′ dĭ·à)
cy·clo·tron   (sĭ′ klŏ·trŏn)
cyg·net   (sĭg′ nĕt)
cyl·in·der   (sĭl′ ĭn·dēr)
  cy·lin·dri·cal (sĭ·lĭn′ drĭ·kàl)
cym·bal   (sĭm′ bàl)
  (musical instrument; see symbol)
  cym·bal·ist
cyn·ic   (sĭn′ ĭk)
  cyn·i·cal   -cal·ly
  cyn·i·cism   (sĭn′ ĭ·sĭz′m)
cy·press   (sĭ′ prĕs)
Cy·prus (is.)   (sĭ′ prŭs)
cyst   (sĭst)
  cyst·ic
cy·tol·o·gy   (sĭ·tŏl′ ŏ·jĭ)

czar   (zär)
Czech·o·slo·va·ki·a
                  (chĕk′ ŏ·slŏ·vä′ kĭ·à)

                  D

dab·ble   (dăb′ ′l)
  dab·bling
Dachs·hund   (däks′ hŏŏnt′)
Da·cron   (dā′ krŏn)
daf·fo·dil   (dăf′ ŏ·dĭl)
dag·ger   (dăg′ ēr)
da·guerre·o·type
                  (dà·gĕr′ ŏ·tĭp)
dahl·ia   (däl′ yà)
Da·ho·mey,   (dà·hŏ′ mĭ)
  Re·pub·lic of
dai·ly   (dā′ lĭ)
  -lies
dain·ty   (dān′ tĭ)
  dain·ti·ly
dair·y   (dâr′ ĭ)
  dair·ies   dair·y cat·tle
  dair·y·ing   dair·y·man
da·is   (dā′ ĭs)
dai·sy   (dā′ zĭ)
  -sies
Da·lai La·ma   (dä·lī′ lä′ mà)
dal·ly   (dăl′ ĭ)
  dal·lied   dal·ly·ing
  dal·li·ance   (dăl′ ĭ·dͅns)
Dal·ma·tian dog   (dăl·mā′ shͅn)
dam   (dăm)
  (water barrier; see damn)
  dammed
dam·age   (dăm′ ĭj)
  -ag·ing   dam·age·able
dam·ask   (dăm′ àsk)
damn   (dăm)
  (to condemn; see dam)
  dam·na·ble   (dăm′ nà·b′l)
  dam·na·tion   (dăm·nā′ shŭn)
dam·sel   (dăm′ zĕl)
dan·de·li·on   (dăn′ dĕ·lī′ ŭn)
dan·druff   (dăn′ drŭf)
dan·ger·ous   (dān′ jēr·ŭs)
dan·gle   (dăng′ g′l)
  -gling
Dan·ish   (dān′ ĭsh)
dap·per   (dăp′ ēr)
dap·pled   (dăp′ ′ld)
Dar·da·nelles   (där′ d′n·ĕlz′)
dare·dev·il   (dâr′ dĕv′ ′l)
dar·ing   (dâr′ ĭng)

dar·ling (där′ lĭng)
Dar·win·i·an (där′ wĭn′ ĭ·ăn)
dash·board (dăsh′ bôrd′)
das·tard·ly (dăs′ tĕrd·lĭ)
da·ta (dā′ tȧ) n. pl.
  sing. da·tum
da·tive (dā′ tĭv)
daub (dôb)
daugh·ter-in-law (dô′ tĕr·ĭn·lô′)
  pl. daugh·ters-in-law
daunt·less (dônt′ lĕs)
dau·phin (dô′ fĭn)
dav·en·port (dăv′ ĕn·pōrt)
Da·vy Jones's lock·er
    (dā′ vĭ jōn′ zĭz)
daw·dle (dô′ d'l)
  -dling
dawn (dôn)
day (dā)
  day·bed   day·break
  day·dream   day·let·ter
  day·light sav·ing
  day·time
daze (dāz)
  daz·ing   daz·ed·ly
daz·zle (dăz′ 'l)
  daz·zling
DDT (dē′ dē′ tē′)
dea·con (dē′ kŭn)
  dea·con·ess
dead (dĕd)
  dead·en·ing   dead·line
  dead·lock
  dead·ly, -li·er, -li·est, -li·ness
  dead weight   dead·wood
deaf (dĕf)
  deaf-and-dumb al·pha·bet
  deaf·en   deaf-mute
deal·er (dē′ lĕr)
dearth (dûrth)
death (dĕth)
  death·bed   death war·rant
de·ba·cle (dĕ·bä′ k'l)
de·bar (dĕ·bär′)
  -barred   -bar·ring
  de·bar·ment
de·bar·ka·tion (dē′ bär·kā′ shŭn)
de·base·ment (dĕ·bās′ mĕnt)
de·bate (dĕ·bāt′)
  -bat·ing   de·bat·a·ble
  de·bat·er
de·bauch (dĕ·bôch′)
  de·bauch·er·y
de·ben·ture (dĕ·bĕn′ tûr)

de·bil·i·tate (dĕ·bĭl′ ĭ·tāt)
  -tat·ing
  de·bil·i·ta·tion
        (dĕ·bĭl′ ĭ·tā′ shŭn)
de·bil·i·ty (dĕ·bĭl′ ĭ·tĭ) -ties
deb·it (dĕb′ ĭt)
deb·o·nair (dĕb′ ŏ·nâr′)
de·bris (dĕ·brē′)
debt·or (dĕt′ ēr)
de·bunk (dĕ·bŭngk′)
de·but (dā′ bū)
deb·u·tante (dĕb′ ū·tänt′)
dec·ade (dĕk′ ād)
de·ca·dence (dĕ·kā′ dĕns)
  -dent
de·cal (dē′ kăl)
de·cant·er (dĕ·kăn′ tēr)
de·cap·i·tate (dĕ·kăp′ ĭ·tāt)
  -tat·ing
  de·cap·i·ta·tion
    (dĕ·kăp′ ĭ·tā′ shŭn)
de·cath·lon (dĕ·kăth′ lŏn)
de·cay (dĕ·kā′)
  -cayed
de·ceased (dĕ·sēst′)
  de·ce·dent (dĕ·sē′ dĕnt)
de·ceit (dĕ·sēt′)
  de·ceit·ful, -ful·ly, -ful·ness
de·ceive (dĕ·sēv′)
  -ceiv·ing   de·ceiv·a·ble
  de·ceiv·er
de·cel·er·ate (dĕ·sĕl′ ĕr·āt)
  -at·ing
De·cem·ber (dĕ·sĕm′ bĕr)
de·cent (dē′ sĕnt)
  de·cen·cy
de·cen·tral·ize (dĕ·sĕn′ trăl·īz)
  -iz·ing
de·cep·tion (dĕ·sĕp′ shŭn)
  de·cep·tive   -tive·ly
dec·i·bel (dĕs′ ĭ·bĕl)
de·cide (dĕ·sīd′)
  -cid·ing   de·cid·ed·ly
de·cid·u·ous (dĕ·sĭd′ ū·ŭs)
dec·i·mal (dĕs′ ĭ·măl)
dec·i·mate (dĕs′ ĭ·māt)
  -mat·ing
de·ci·pher (dĕ·sī′ fĕr)
  de·ci·pher·a·ble
de·ci·sion (dĕ·sĭzh′ ŭn)
de·ci·sive (dĕ·sī′ sĭv)
  -sive·ness
dec·la·ma·tion
        (dĕk′ lȧ·mā′ shŭn)

de·clare   (dĕ·klâr′)
  -clar·ing
  de·clar·a·tion   (dĕk′ lȧ·rā′ shŭn)
  de·clar·a·tive   (dĕ·klăr′ ȧ·tĭv)
  -to·ry
de·clen·sion   (dĕ·klĕn′ shŭn)
de·cline   (dĕ·klīn′)
  -clin·ing
de·cliv·i·ty   (dĕ·klĭv′ ĭ·tĭ)
  -ties
de·code   (dē·kōd′)
  -cod·ing
dé·col·le·té   (dā′ kŏl′ ĕ·tā′)
  dé·col·le·tage   (dā′ kŏl′ ĕ·täzh′)
de·com·pose   (dē′ kŏm·pōz′)
  -pos·ing
  de·com·po·si·tion
                      (dē′ kŏm·pŏ·zĭsh′ ŭn)
de·com·press   (dē′ kŏm·prĕs′)
  de·com·pres·sion   (-prĕsh′ ŭn)
de·con·tam·i·nate
                  (dē′ kŏn·tăm′ ĭ·nāt)
  -nat·ing
  de·con·tam·i·na·tion
                  (dē′ kŏn·tăm′ ĭ·nā′ shŭn)
dé·cor   (dā′ kôr′)
dec·o·rate   (dĕk′ ô·rāt)
  -rat·ing
  dec·o·ra·tion   (dĕk′ ô·rā′ shŭn)
  dec·o·ra·tive   (-rā′ tĭv)
  dec·o·ra·tor
dec·o·rous   (dĕk′ ô·rŭs)
de·co·rum   (dĕ·kō′ rŭm)
de·coy   (dĕ·koi′)
de·crease   (dĕ·krēs′) v.
  -creas·ing   (dē′ krēs) n.
de·cree   (dĕ·krē′)
de·crep·it   (dĕ·krĕp′ ĭt)
  de·crep·i·tude   (dĕ·krĕp′ ĭ·tūd)
de·cry   (dĕ·krī′)
  -cried   -cry·ing
ded·i·cate   (dĕd′ ĭ·kāt)
  -cat·ing
  ded·i·ca·tion   (dĕd′ ĭ·kā′ shŭn)
  ded·i·ca·to·ry   (dĕd′ ĭ·kȧ·tō′ rĭ)
de·duce   (dĕ·dūs′)
  -duc·ing   de·duc·i·ble
de·duct   (dĕ·dŭkt′)
  de·duct·i·ble   de·duc·tion
  de·duc·tive
deem   (dēm)
deep   (dēp)
  deep·en   Deep·freeze
  deep-root·ed   deep-sea div·er
  deep-seat·ed

deer·skin   (dẽr′ skĭn′)
de·face   (dĕ·fās′)
  -fac·ing   de·face·ment
de·fame   (dĕ·fām′)
  -fam·ing
  def·a·ma·tion   (dĕf′ ȧ·mā′ shŭn)
  de·fam·a·to·ry
                      (dĕ·făm′ ȧ·tō′ rĭ)
de·fault   (dĕ·fôlt′)
de·feat   (dĕ·fēt′)
  de·feat·ism   -ist
def·e·cate   (dĕf′ ĕ·kāt)
  -cat·ing
  def·e·ca·tion   (dĕf′ ĕ·kā′ shŭn)
de·fect   (dĕ·fĕkt′)
  de·fec·tion   de·fec·tive
de·fend   (dĕ·fĕnd′)
  de·fend·ant
de·fense   (dĕ·fĕns′)
  de·fense·less   de·fen·si·ble
  de·fen·sive   -sive·ly
de·fer   (dĕ·fûr′)
  -ferred   -fer·ring
  de·fer·ment   de·fer·ra·ble
def·er·ence   (dĕf′ ẽr·ĕns)
def·er·en·tial   (dĕf′ ẽr·ĕn′ shȧl)
de·fi·ance   (dĕ·fī′ ȧns)
  -ant
de·fi·cien·cy   (dĕ·fĭsh′ ĕn·sĭ)
  -cies   de·fi·cient
def·i·cit   (dĕf′ ĭ·sĭt)
de·file   (dĕ·fīl′)
  -fil·ing   de·file·ment
de·fine   (dĕ·fīn′)
  -fin·ing   de·fin·a·ble
def·i·nite   (dĕf′ ĭ·nĭt)
  def·i·nite·ly   -nite·ness
def·i·ni·tion   (dĕf′ ĭ·nĭsh′ ŭn)
de·fin·i·tive   (dĕ·fĭn′ ĭ·tĭv)
de·flate   (dĕ·flāt′)
  -flat·ing
  de·fla·tion   (dĕ·flā′ shŭn)
  de·fla·tion·ary
de·flect   (dĕ·flĕkt′)
  de·flec·tion
de·flow·er   (dĕ·flou′ ẽr)
de·form   (dĕ·fôrm′)
  de·for·ma·tion
                      (dē′ fôr·mā′ shŭn)
  de·formed
  de·form·i·ty   (dĕ·fôr′ mĭ·tĭ)
  -ties
de·fraud   (dĕ·frôd′)
de·fray   (dĕ·frā′)
  de·fray·ment

de·frost (dē·frŏst′)
deft (dĕft)
de·funct (dĕ·fŭngkt′)
de·fy (dĕ·fī′)
 -fied -fy·ing
de Gaulle, Charles
(dē·gōl′)
de·gen·er·ate (dē·jĕn′ ĕr·ĭt)
 adj., n.
 (-āt) *v.*
 -at·ing
 de·gen·er·a·cy (-à·sĭ)
 de·gen·er·a·tion
 (dē· jĕn·ĕr·ā′ shŭn)
de·grade (dĕ·grād′)
 -grad·ing
 deg·ra·da·tion
 (dĕg′ rà·dā′ shŭn)
de·gree (dĕ·grē′)
de·hu·man·ize (dē·hū′ mǎn·īz)
 -iz·ing
 de·hu·man·i·za·tion
 (dē·hū′ mǎn·ĭ·zā′ shŭn)
de·hu·mid·i·fy (dē′ hú·mĭd′ ĭ·fī)
 -fied -fy·ing
 de·hu·mid·i·fi·er
de·hy·drate (dē·hī′ drāt)
 -drat·ing
de·i·fy (dē′ ĭ·fī)
 -fied -fy·ing
deign (dān)
de·i·ty (dē′ ĭ·tĭ)
 -ties
de·is·tic (dē·ĭs′ tĭk)
de·ject (dĕ·jĕkt′)
 de·jec·tion (-jĕk′ shŭn)
Del·a·ware (dĕl′ à·wâr)
 abbr. Del.
 Del·a·war·e·an
 (dĕl′ à·wâr′ ē·àn)
de·lay (dĕ·lā′)
de·lec·ta·ble (dĕ·lĕk′ tà·b'l)
 de·lec·ta·tion (dē′ lĕk·tā′ shŭn)
del·e·gate (dĕl′ ē·gāt)
 -gat·ing
 del·e·ga·tion (dĕl′ ē·gā′ shŭn)
de·lete (dĕ·lēt′)
 -let·ing
 de·le·tion (dĕ·lē′ shŭn)
del·e·te·ri·ous (dĕl′ ē·tēr′ ĭ·ŭs)
delft·ware (dĕlft′ wâr′)
de·lib·er·ate (dĕ·lĭb′ ĕr·ĭt)
 adj. -ate·ly
 -at·ing (-āt) *v.*

de·lib·er·a·tion
(dĕ·lĭb′ ĕr·ā′ shŭn)
del·i·cate (dĕl′ ĭ·kĭt)
 -cate·ly
 del·i·ca·cy (-kà·sĭ)
de·li·cious (dĕ·lĭsh′ ŭs)
de·light (dĕ·līt′)
 de·light·ed·ly de·light·ful
 -ful·ly -ful·ness
de·lim·it (dĕ·lĭm′ ĭt)
 -it·ed -it·ing
 de·lim·i·ta·tion
 (dĕ·lĭm′ ĭ·tā′ shŭn)
de·lin·e·ate (dĕ·lĭn′ ē·āt)
 -at·ing de·lin·e·a·tor
de·lin·quen·cy (dĕ·lĭng′ kwĕn·sĭ)
 de·lin·quent
de·lir·i·ous (dĕ·lĭr′ ĭ·ŭs)
de·lir·i·um (dĕ·lĭr′ ĭ·ŭm)
 de·lir·i·um tre·mens
 (trē′ mĕnz)
de·liv·er (dĕ·lĭv′ ĕr)
 de·liv·er·a·ble de·liv·er·ance
 de·liv·er·y
del·phin·i·um (dĕl·fĭn′ ĭ·ŭm)
de·lude (dĕ·lūd′)
 -lud·ing
 de·lu·sion (-lū′ zhŭn)
del·uge (dĕl′ ûj)
 -ug·ing
de luxe (dĕ·lŏŏks′)
delve (dĕlv)
 delv·ing
de·mag·net·ize (dē·mǎg′ nĕ·tīz)
 -iz·ing
dem·a·gogue (dĕm′ à·gŏg)
 dem·a·gog·uer·y (-gŏg′ ĕr·ĭ)
 dem·a·gog·ic (dĕm′ à·gŏj′ ĭk)
de·mand (dĕ·mànd′)
 de·mand·a·ble
de·mar·cate (dĕ·mär′ kāt)
 -cat·ing
 de·mar·ca·tion
 (dē′ mär·kā′ shŭn)
de·mean (dĕ·mēn′)
de·mean·or (dĕ·mēn′ ĕr)
de·ment·ed (dĕ·mĕn′ tĕd)
de·men·ti·a prae·cox
 (dĕ·mĕn′ shĭ·à prē′ kŏks)
de·mer·it (dĕ·mĕr′ ĭt)
de·mesne (dĕ·mān′)
de·mil·i·ta·rize (dĕ·mĭl′ ĭ·tà·rīz)
 -riz·ing
 de·mil·i·ta·ri·za·tion
 (dē·mĭl′ ĭ·tà·rĭ·zā′ shŭn)

de·mise (dē·mīz′)
dem·i·tasse (dĕm′ ĭ·tăs)
dem·i·urge (dĕm′ ĭ·ûrj)
de·mo·bi·lize (dē·mō′ bĭ·līz)
 -liz·ing
 de·mo·bi·li·za·tion
  (dē·mō′ bĭ·lĭ·zā′ shŭn)
de·moc·ra·cy (dē·mŏk′ rȧ·sĭ)
 -cies
dem·o·crat (dĕm′ ô·krăt)
dem·o·crat·ic (dĕm′ ô·krăt′ ĭk)
de·moc·ra·tize (dē·mŏk′ rȧ·tīz)
 -tiz·ing
de·mol·ish (dē·mŏl′ ĭsh)
dem·o·li·tion (dĕm′ ô·lĭsh′ ŭn)
de·mon (dē′ mŭn)
 de·mo·ni·a·cal
  (dē′ mô·nī′ ȧ·kȧl)
 de·mon·ic (dē·mŏn′ ĭk)
de·mon·e·tize (dē·mŏn′ ē·tīz)
 -tiz·ing
dem·on·strate (dĕm′ ŭn·strāt)
 -strat·ing
 de·mon·stra·ble
  (dē·mŏn′ strȧ·b'l)
 dem·on·stra·tion
  (dĕm′ ŭn·strā′ shŭn)
 de·mon·stra·tive
  (dē·mŏn′ strȧ·tĭv)
 dem·on·stra·tor
de·mor·al·ize (dē·mŏr′ ȧl·īz)
 -iz·ing
 de·mor·al·i·za·tion
  (dē·mŏr′ ȧl·ĭ·zā′ shŭn)
de·mote (dē·mōt′)
 -mot·ing
 de·mo·tion (dē·mō′ shŭn)
de·mur (dē·mûr′)
 (delay)
 -murred
 -mur·ring de·mur·rer
de·mure (dē·mūr′)
 (modest) de·mure·ly
de·na·tion·al·ize
  (dē·năsh′ ŭn·ȧl·īz)
 -iz·ing
de·nat·u·ral·ize
  (dē·năt′ û·rȧl·īz)
 -iz·ing
de·na·ture (dē·nā′ tûr)
 -tur·ing
den·drite (dĕn′ drīt)
de·ni·al (dē·nī′ ȧl)
den·i·grate (dĕn′ ĭ·grāt)
 -grat·ing

den·im (dĕn′ ĭm)
den·i·zen (dĕn′ ĭ·zĕn)
de·nom·i·na·tion·al
  (dē·nŏm′ ĭ·nā′ shŭn·ȧl)
de·nom·i·na·tor
  (dē·nŏm′ ĭ·nā′ tẽr)
de·note (dē·nōt′)
 -not·ing
de·noue·ment (dā·nōō′ mäɴ)
de·nounce (dē·nouns′)
 -nounc·ing de·nounce·ment
dense (dĕns)
 dense·ly
 den·si·ty (dĕn′ sĭ·tĭ)
den·tal (dĕn′ tȧl)
 den·ti·frice (dĕn′ tĭ·frĭs)
 den·tist (dĕn′ tĭst)
 den·ture (dĕn′ tûr)
de·nude (dē·nūd′)
 -nud·ing
de·nun·ci·ate (dē·nŭn′ shĭ·āt)
 -at·ing
 de·nun·ci·a·tion
  (dē·nŭn′ sĭ·ā′ shŭn)
 de·nun·ci·a·to·ry
  (-nŭn′ shĭ·ȧ·tō′ rĭ)
de·ny (dē·nī′)
 -nied -ny·ing
 de·ni·al de·ni·er
de·o·dor·ant (dē·ō′ dẽr·ȧnt)
 de·o·dor·ize -iz·ing
de·ox·i·dize (dē·ŏk′ sĭ·dīz)
 -diz·ing
de·part (dē·pärt′)
 de·par·ture (dē·pär′ tûr)
de·part·ment (dē·pärt′ mĕnt)
 de·part·men·tal
  (dē′ pärt·mĕn′ tȧl)
De Paul (univ.) (dē pôl′)
De Pauw (univ.) (dē·pô′)
de·pend (dē·pĕnd′)
 de·pend·a·bil·i·ty
  (dē·pĕn′ dȧ·bĭl′ ĭ·tĭ)
 de·pend·a·ble (dē·pĕn′ dȧ·b'l)
 de·pend·ence (dē·pĕn′ dĕns)
 -en·cy -ent
de·pict (dē·pĭkt′)
 de·pic·tion (dē·pĭk′ shŭn)
de·pil·a·to·ry (dē·pĭl′ ȧ·tō′ rĭ)
 -tor·ies
de·plete (dē·plēt′)
 -plet·ing
 de·ple·tion (dē·plē′ shŭn)
de·plore (dē·plōr′)
 -plor·ing de·plor·a·ble

de·ploy·ment (dĕ·ploi′ mĕnt)
de·po·lar·ize (dē·pō′ lēr·ĭz)
  -iz·ing
de·pop·u·late (dē·pŏp′ û·lăt)
  -lat·ing
de·port (dē·pōrt′)
  de·por·ta·tion
      (dē′ pŏr·tā′ shŭn)
  de·por·tee (dē′ pōr·tē′)
  de·port·ment
de·pose (dē·pōz′)
  -pos·ing   de·pos·al
de·pos·it (dē·pŏz′ ĭt)
  -it·ed   -it·ing
  de·pos·i·tor (dē·pŏz′ ĭ·tēr)
  de·pos·i·to·ry (dē·pŏz′ ĭ·tō′ rĭ)
dep·o·si·tion (dĕp′ ō·zĭsh′ ŭn)
de·pot (dē′ pō)
dep·ra·va·tion (dĕp′ rá·vā′ shŭn)
  (corruption: see *deprivation*)
de·praved (dē·prāvd′)
  de·prav·i·ty (dē·prăv′ ĭ·tĭ)
  -ties
dep·re·cate (dĕp′ rē·kāt)
  -cat·ing
  dep·re·ca·tion
      (dĕp′ rē·kā′ shŭn)
de·pre·ci·ate (dē·prē′ shĭ·āt)
  -at·ing
  de·pre·ci·a·ble
      (-á·b'l)
  de·pre·ci·a·tion
      (dē·prē′ shĭ·ā′ shŭn)
dep·re·da·tion (dĕp′ rē·dā′ shŭn)
de·press (dē·prĕs′)
  de·pres·sant   de·pres·sive
  de·pres·sor
de·pres·sion (dē·prĕsh′ ŭn)
dep·ri·va·tion (dĕp′ rĭ·vā′ shŭn)
  (loss; see *depravation*)
depth (dĕpth)
dep·u·ta·tion (dĕp′ û·tā′ shŭn)
dep·u·ty (dĕp′ û·tĭ)
  -ties
  dep·u·tize (dĕp′ û·tīz)
de·ranged (dē·rānjd′)
  de·range·ment
der·e·lict (dĕr′ ĕ·lĭkt)
  der·e·lic·tion (dĕr′ ĕ·lĭk′ shŭn)
de·ride (dē·rīd′)
  -rid·ing
  de·ri·sion (dē·rĭzh′ ŭn)
  de·ri·sive (dē·rī′ sĭv)
de·rive (dē·rīv′)
  -riv·ing

der·i·va·tion (dĕr′ ĭ·vā′ shŭn)
de·riv·a·tive (dē·rĭv′ á·tĭv)
der·ma·ti·tis (dûr′ má·tī′ tĭs)
der·ma·tol·o·gy
      (dûr′ má·tŏl′ ō·jĭ)
der·o·gate (dĕr′ ō·gāt)
  -gat·ing
der·o·ga·tion (dĕr′ ō·gā′ shŭn)
de·rog·a·tive (dē·rŏg′ á·tĭv)
de·rog·a·to·ry
      (dē·rŏg′ á·tō′ rĭ)
der·rick (dĕr′ ĭk)
der·ring-do (dĕr′ ĭng-dōō′)
der·vish (dûr′ vĭsh)
des·cant (dĕs·kănt′)
de·scend (dē·sĕnd′)
  de·scend·ant (dē·sĕn′ dănt)
  de·scent (dē·sĕnt′)
  (ancestry; see *dissent*)
de·scribe (dē·skrīb′)
  -scrib·ing   de·scrib·a·ble
  de·scrip·tion (dē·skrĭp′ shŭn)
  de·scrip·tive (dē·skrĭp′ tĭv)
des·e·crate (dĕs′ ē·krāt)
  ·crat·ing
  des·e·cra·tion (dĕs′ ē·krā′ shŭn)
de·seg·re·gate (dē·sĕg′ rē·gāt)
  ·gat·ing
  de·seg·re·ga·tion
      (dē·sĕg′ rē·gā′ shŭn)
de·sen·si·tize (dē·sĕn′ sĭ·tīz)
  -tiz·ing
des·ert (dĕz′ ērt)
  (arid region)
de·sert (dē·zûrt′)
  (to abandon; see *dessert*)
  de·sert·er
  de·ser·tion (dē·zûr′ shŭn)
de·serve (dē·zûrv′)
  -serv·ing
  de·serv·ed·ly (-zûr′ vĕd·lĭ)
des·ic·cate (dĕs′ ĭ·kāt)
  -ic·cat·ing
de·sid·er·a·tum
      (dē·sĭd′ ēr·ā′ tŭm)
  pl. de·sid·er·a·ta
de·sign (dē·zīn′)
  de·sign·er
des·ig·nate (dĕz′ ĭg·nāt)
  -nat·ing
  des·ig·na·tion (dĕz′ ĭg·nā′ shŭn)
de·sire (dē·zīr′)
  -sir·ing
  de·sir·a·bil·i·ty
      (dē·zīr′ á·bĭl′ ĭ·tĭ)

de·sir·a·ble   de·sir·ous
de·sist   (dĕ·zĭst′)
Des Moines, Ia.   (dĕ moin′)
des·o·late   (dĕs′ ô·lĭt) *adj.*
 -lat·ing   (-lāt) *v.*
 des·o·late·ly   (-lĭt·lĭ)
 des·o·la·tion   (dĕs′ ô·lā′ shŭn)
de·spair   (dĕ·spâr′)
 de·spair·ing·ly
des·per·a·do   (dĕs′ pĕr·ā′ dō)
 -does
des·per·ate   (dĕs′ pĕr·ĭt)
 (without hope; see *disparate*)
 des·per·ate·ly
 des·per·a·tion
                  (dĕs′ pĕr·ā′ shŭn)
des·pi·ca·ble   (dĕs′ pĭ·kà·b'l)
de·spise   (dĕ·spīz′)
 -spis·ing
de·spite   (dĕ·spīt′)
de·spoil   (dĕ·spoil′)
 de·spoil·er
de·spond·ence   (dĕ·spŏn′ dĕns)
 -enc·y   -ent
des·pot   (dĕs′ pŏt)
 des·pot·ic   (dĕs·pŏt′ ĭk)
 -i·cal·ly
 des·pot·ism   (dĕs′ pŏt·ĭz'm)
des·sert   (dĭ·zûrt′)
 (sweets; see *desert*)
des·ti·ny   (dĕs′ tĭ·nĭ)
 -nies
 des·ti·na·tion   (dĕs′ tĭ·nā′ shŭn)
 des·tined
des·ti·tute   (dĕs′ tĭ·tūt)
 des·ti·tu·tion   (dĕs′ tĭ·tū′ shŭn)
de·stroy   (dĕ·stroi′)
 de·stroy·er
de·struc·tion   (dĕ·strŭk′ shŭn)
 de·struct·i·ble
 de·struc·tive   -tive·ness
des·ue·tude   (dĕs′ wê·tūd)
des·ul·to·ry   (dĕs′ ŭl·tō′ rĭ)
 des·ul·to·ri·ness
de·tach   (dĕ·tăch′)
 de·tach·a·ble   de·tach·ment
de·tail   (dĕ·tāl′)
 de·tailed
de·tain   (dĕ·tān′)
 de·tain·ment
de·tect   (dĕ·tĕkt′)
 de·tect·a·ble
 de·tec·tion   (dĕ·tĕk′ shŭn)
 de·tec·tor
 de·tec·tive   (dĕ·tĕk′ tĭv)

de·ten·tion   (dĕ·tĕn′ shŭn)
de·ter   (dĕ·tûr′)
 -terred   -ter·ring
 de·ter·ment   de·ter·rent
de·ter·gent   (dĕ·tûr′ jĕnt)
de·te·ri·o·rate   (dĕ·tēr′ ĭ·ô·rāt)
 -rat·ing
 de·te·ri·o·ra·tion
                  (dĕ·tēr′ ĭ·ô·rā′ shŭn)
de·ter·mine   (dĕ·tûr′ mĭn)
 -min·ing
 de·ter·mi·nant
                  (-mĭ·nǎnt)
 de·ter·mi·na·tion
                  (dĕ·tûr′ mĭ·nā′ shŭn)
 de·ter·mined·ly
 de·ter·min·ism
                  (-mĭn·ĭz'm)
de·ter·rent   (dĕ·tûr′ ĕnt)
 -ter·rence
de·test   (dĕ·tĕst′)
 de·test·a·ble
de·throne   (dĕ·thrōn′)
 -thron·ing   de·throne·ment
det·o·nate   (dĕt′ ô·nāt)
 -nat·ing
 det·o·na·tion   (dĕt·ô·nā′ shŭn)
de·tour   (dē′ tōŏr)
de·tract   (dĕ·trăkt′)
 de·trac·tion   (dĕ·trăk′ shŭn)
 de·trac·tor
det·ri·ment   (dĕt′ rĭ·mĕnt)
 det·ri·men·tal   (dĕt′ rĭ·mĕn′ tǎl)
deuce   (dūs)
de·val·u·ate   (dĕ·vǎl′ û·āt)
 -at·ing
 de·val·u·a·tion
                  (dĕ·vǎl′ û·ā′ shŭn)
dev·as·tate   (dĕv′ ǎs·tāt)
 -tat·ing
 dev·as·ta·tion
                  (dĕv′ ǎs·tā′ shŭn)
 dev·as·ta·tor
de·vel·op   (dĕ·vĕl′ ŭp)
 -oped,   -op·ing
 de·vel·op·er   de·vel·op·ment
 de·vel·op·men·tal
                  (dĕ·vĕl′ ŭp·mĕn′ tǎl)
de·vi·ate   (dē′ vĭ·āt)
 -at·ing
 de·vi·ant   (dē′ vĭ·ǎnt)
 de·vi·a·tion   (dē′ vĭ·ā′ shŭn)
de·vice   (dĕ·vīs′) *n.*
 (a scheme)

dev·il (dĕv′ 'l)
  dev·il·ish   dev·il·ment
  dev·il·try
de·vi·ous (dē′ vĭ·ŭs)
de·vise (dĕ·vīz′) v.
  (to invent) -vis·ing
de·vi·tal·ize (dē·vī′ tŭl·īz)
  -iz·ing
de·void (dĕ·void′)
de·volve (dĕ·vŏlv′)
  -volv·ing
de·vote (dĕ·vōt′)
  -vot·ing   de·vot·ed·ly
  dev·o·tee (dĕv′ ō·tē′)
de·vo·tion (dĕ·vō′ shŭn)
  -tion·al
de·vour (dĕ·vour′)
de·vout (dĕ·vout′)
dew·drop (dū′ drŏp′)
dew·y (dū′ ĭ)
  dew·i·ness
dex·ter·i·ty (dĕks·tĕr′ ĭ·tĭ)
  dex·ter·ous (dĕk′ stĕr·ŭs)
dex·trose (dĕks′ trōs)
di·a·be·tes (dī′ å·bē′ tēz)
  di·a·bet·ic (-bĕt′ ĭk)
di·a·bol·ic (dī′ å·bŏl′ ĭk)
  di·a·bol·i·cal (-ĭ·kŭl)
di·a·crit·i·cal mark
          (dī′ å·krĭt′ ĭ·kŭl)
di·a·dem (dī′ å·dĕm)
di·ag·nose (dī′ ăg·nōs′)
  -nos·ing
di·ag·no·sis (dī′ ăg·nō′ sĭs)
  pl. -no·ses (-sēz)
di·ag·nos·tic (dī′ ăg·nŏs′ tĭk)
  di·ag·nos·ti·cian
          (dī′ ăg·nŏs·tĭsh′ ăn)
di·ag·o·nal (dī·ăg′ ō·nŭl)
  di·ag·o·nal·ly
di·a·gram (dī′ å·grăm)
  -gramed   -gram·ing
  di·a·gram·mat·ic
      (dī′ å·grå·măt′ ĭk)
di·al (dī′ ŭl)
  di·aled   di·al·ing
di·a·lect (dī′ å·lĕkt)
di·a·lec·tic (dī′ å·lĕk′ tĭk)
  di·a·lec·ti·cal ma·te·ri·al·ism
di·a·logue (dī′ å·lŏg)
di·am·e·ter (dī·ăm′ ē·tēr)
di·a·met·ric (dī′ å·mĕt′ rĭk)
  di·a·met·ri·cal·ly
di·a·mond (dī′ å·mŭnd)
di·a·per (dī′ å·pēr)

di·aph·a·nous (dī·ăf′ å·nŭs)
di·a·phragm (dī′ å·frăm)
di·ar·rhe·a (dī′ å·rē′ å)
  di·ar·rhet·ic (-rĕt′ ĭk)
di·a·ry (dī′ å·rĭ)
  -ries
di·a·ther·my (dī′ å·thûr′ mĭ)
di·a·tribe (dī′ å·trīb)
dice (dīs) n. pl.
  sing. die
di·chot·o·my (dī·kŏt′ ō·mĭ)
  -mies
  -miz·ing   di·chot·o·mize
dick·ey (dĭk′ ĭ)
  -eys
Dic·ta·phone (dĭk′ tå·fōn)
dic·tate (dĭk′ tāt)
  -tat·ing
  dic·ta·tion (dĭk·tā′ shŭn)
  dic·ta·tor
  dic·ta·to·ri·al (dĭk′ tå·tō′ rĭ·ŭl)
dic·tion (dĭk′ shŭn)
dic·tion·ar·y (dĭk′ shŭn·ĕr′ ĭ)
  -ar·ies
dic·tum (dĭk′ tŭm)
  pl. dic·ta
di·dac·tic (dī·dăk′ tĭk)
  di·dac·ti·cal
die (dī)
  died   dy·ing
die·sel en·gine (dē′ zĕl)
di·et (dī′ ĕt)
  di·e·tar·y (dī′ ĕ·tĕr′ ĭ)
  di·e·tet·ic (dī′ ĕ·tĕt′ ĭk)
  di·e·ti·tian (dī′ ĕ·tĭsh′ ăn)
dif·fer (dĭf′ ēr)
dif·fer·ence (dĭf′ ēr·ĕns)
  -ent
dif·fer·en·tial (dĭf′ ēr·ĕn′ shŭl)
dif·fer·en·ti·ate
      (dĭf′ ēr·ĕn′ shĭ·āt)
  -at·ing
  dif·fer·en·ti·a·tion
      (dĭf′ ēr·ĕn′ shĭ·ā′ shŭn)
dif·fi·cult (dĭf′ ĭ·kŭlt)
  dif·fi·cul·ty
dif·fi·dence (dĭf′ ĭ·dĕns)
  -dent
dif·fract (dī·frăkt′)
  dif·frac·tion (dī·frăk′ shŭn)
dif·fuse (dī·fūs′) adj.
  (-fūz′) v.
  dif·fus·ing
  dif·fu·sion (dī·fū′ zhŭn)
di·gest (dī·jĕst) n.

di·gest (dǐ·jěst′) *v.*
  di·gest·ant (-jěs′ tănt)
  di·gest·i·bil·i·ty
           (dǐ·jěst′ ǐ·bǐl′ ǐ·tǐ)
  di·gest·i·ble   di·ges·tive
dig·it (dǐj′ ǐt)
  dig·it·al com·pu·ter
           (dǐj′ ǐ·tǎl)
dig·i·tal·is (dǐj′ ǐ·tǎl′ ǐs)
dig·ni·fy (dǐg′ nǐ·fī)
  -fied,   -fy·ing
dig·ni·tar·y (dǐg′ nǐ·těr′ ǐ)
  -tar·ies
dig·ni·ty (dǐg′ nǐ·tǐ)
  -ties
di·gress (dǐ·grěs′)
  di·gres·sion (dǐ·grěsh′ ŭn)
dike (dīk)
di·lap·i·dat·ed
           (dǐ·lǎp′ ǐ·dāt′ ěd)
  di·lap·i·da·tion
           (dǐ·lǎp′ ǐ·dā′ shŭn)
di·late (dǐ·lāt′)
  -lat·ing
  di·la·tion (dǐ·lā′ shŭn)
dil·a·to·ry (dǐl′ à·tō′ rǐ)
  dil·a·to·ri·ness
di·lem·ma (dǐ·lěm′ à)
dil·et·tan·te (dǐl′ ě·tǎn′ tě)
  dil·et·tant·ism
           (-tǎn′ tǐz′m)
dil·i·gence (dǐl′ ǐ·jěns)
  -gent
dil·ly·dal·ly (dǐl′ ǐ·dǎl′ ǐ)
  -dal·lied   -dal·ly·ing
di·lute (dǐ·lūt′)
  -lut·ing
  di·lu·tion (dǐ·lū′ shŭn)
di·men·sion (dǐ·měn′ shŭn)
  di·men·sion·al
di·min·ish (dǐ·mǐn′ ǐsh)
dim·i·nu·tion (dǐm′ ǐ·nū′ shŭn)
di·min·u·tive (dǐ·mǐn′ ū·tǐv)
dim·i·ty (dǐm′ ǐ·tǐ)
dim·ple (dǐm′ p'l)
din·er (dīn′ ěr)
din·ette (dǐ·nět′)
din·ghy (dǐng′ gǐ)
  (rowboat)   -ghies
din·gy (dǐn′ jǐ)
  (grimy)
  din·gi·ness
din·ing room (dīn′ ǐng)
din·ner (dǐn′ ěr)
di·no·saur (dī′ nǒ·sôr)

di·o·cese (dī′ ǒ·sēs)
  di·oc·e·san (dī·ǒs′ ě·sǎn)
Di·og·e·nes (dī·ǒj′ ě·nēz)
di·o·ra·ma (dī′ ǒ·rä′ mà)
di·ox·ide (dī·ǒk′ sīd)
diph·the·ri·a (dǐf·thêr′ ǐ·à)
diph·thong (dǐf′ thǒng)
di·plo·ma (dǐ·plō′ mà)
di·plo·ma·cy (dǐ·plō′ mà·sǐ)
  dip·lo·mat (dǐp′ lǒ·mǎt)
  dip·lo·mat·ic (dǐp′ lǒ·mǎt′ ǐk)
dip·per (dǐp′ ěr)
dip·so·ma·ni·a (dǐp′ sǒ·mā′ nǐ·à)
  dip·so·ma·ni·ac
           (-ǎk)
dire (dīr)
  dire·ness   dir·est
di·rect (dǐ·rěkt′)
  di·rec·tion (dǐ·rěk′ shŭn)
  -tion·al   di·rec·tive
  di·rec·tor
di·rec·to·rate (dǐ·rěk′ tǒ·rǐt)
di·rec·to·ry (dǐ·rěk′ tǒ·rǐ)
  -ries
dirge (dûrj)
dir·i·gi·ble (dǐr′ ǐ·jǐ·b′l)
dirn·dl (dûrn′ d'l)
dirt·y (dûr′ tǐ)
  dirt·ied   dirt·y·ing
dis·a·bil·i·ty (dǐs′ à·bǐl′ ǐ·tǐ)
  -ties
dis·a·ble (dǐs·ā′ b'l)
  -bling   dis·a·ble·ment
dis·ad·van·tage
           (dǐs ǎd·văn′ tǐj)
dis·af·fec·tion (dǐs′ à·fěk′ shŭn)
dis·a·gree (dǐs′ à·grē′)
  dis·a·gree·a·ble
  dis·a·gree·ment
dis·al·low (dǐs′ à·lou′)
dis·ap·pear (dǐs′ à·pēr′)
  dis·ap·pear·ance
dis·ap·point (dǐs′ à·point′)
  dis·ap·point·ed
  dis·ap·point·ment
dis·ap·pro·ba·tion
           (dǐs′ ǎp·rǒ·bā′ shŭn)
dis·ap·prove (dǐs′ à·prōōv′)
  -ap·prov·ing   dis·ap·prov·al
dis·ar·ma·ment
           (dǐs·är′ mà·měnt)
dis·arm·ing (dǐs·ärm′ ǐng)
dis·ar·range (dǐs′ à·rānj′)
  -ar·rang·ing

dis·ar·ray (dĭs′ ă·rā′)
dis·as·sem·ble (dĭs′ ă·sĕm′ b'l)
-bling
dis·as·so·ci·ate (dĭs′ ă·sō′ shĭ·āt)
-at·ing
dis·as·ter (dĭ·zăs′ tẽr)
dis·as·trous (-trŭs)
dis·a·vow (dĭs′ ă·vou′)
dis·a·vowal
dis·band (dĭs·bănd′)
dis·bar (dĭs·bär′)
-barred -bar·ring
dis·bar·ment
dis·be·lief (dĭs′ bĕ·lēf′)
dis·be·lieve -liev·ing
dis·burse (dĭs·bûrs′)
(to pay out; see *disperse*)
-burs·ing dis·burs·a·ble
dis·burse·ment
disc (dĭsk)
disc jock·ey
dis·card (dĭs·kärd′) v.
(dĭs′ kärd) n.
dis·cern (dĭ·zûrn′)
dis·cern·i·ble dis·cern·ment
dis·charge (dĭs·chärj′)
-charg·ing
dis·ci·ple (dĭ·sī′ p'l)
dis·ci·pline (dĭs′ ĭ·plĭn)
dis·ci·pli·nar·i·an
(dĭs′ ĭ·plĭ·nâr′ ĭ·ăn)
dis·ci·pli·nar·y
(dĭs′ ĭ·plĭ·nĕr′ ĭ)
dis·claim·er (dĭs·klām′ ẽr)
dis·close (dĭs·klōz′)
-clos·ing
dis·clo·sure (-klō′ zhẽr)
dis·col·or (dĭs·kŭl′ ẽr)
dis·col·or·a·tion
(dĭs·kŭl′ ẽr·ā′ shŭn)
dis·com·fit (dĭs·kŭm′ fĭt)
(embarrass)
dis·com·fi·ture (-fĭ·tụ̂r)
dis·com·fort (dĭs·kŭm′ fẽrt)
dis·com·po·sure
(dĭs′ kŏm·pō′ zhẽr)
dis·con·cert·ing
(dĭs′ kŏn·sûrt′ ĭng)
dis·con·nect (dĭs′ kŏ·nĕkt′)
dis·con·nect·ed·ly
dis·con·so·late (dĭs·kŏn′ sŏ·lĭt)
-late·ly
dis·con·tent·ed
(dĭs′ kŏn·tĕn′ tĕd)

dis·con·tin·ue (dĭs′ kŏn·tĭn′ ū)
-u·ing
dis·con·tin·u·a·tion
(-tĭn′ ū·ā′ shŭn)
dis·con·ti·nu·i·ty
(-tĭ·nū′ ĭ·tĭ)
dis·con·tin·u·ous
(-tĭn′ ū·ŭs)
dis·cor·dant (dĭs·kôr′ dănt)
-dance
dis·count (dĭs′ kount)
dis·cour·age (dĭs·kûr′ ĭj)
-ag·ing
dis·cour·age·ment
dis·course (dĭs·kōrs′)
dis·cour·te·ous (dĭs·kûr′ tĕ·ŭs)
dis·cour·te·sy (dĭs·kûr′ tĕ·sĭ)
-sies
dis·cov·er·a·ble
(dĭs·kŭv′ ẽr·ȧ·b'l)
dis·cov·er·y (dĭs·kŭv′ ẽr·ĭ)
-er·ies
dis·cred·it (dĭs·krĕd′ ĭt)
-it·ed -it·ing
dis·cred·it·a·ble
dis·creet (dĭs·krēt′)
(prudent)
dis·cre·tion (dĭs·krĕsh′ ŭn)
dis·crep·an·cy (dĭs·krĕp′ ăn·sĭ)
dis·crete (dĭs·krēt′)
(separate)
dis·cre·tion (dĭs·krĕsh′ ŭn)
dis·crim·i·nate (dĭs·krĭm′ ĭ·nāt) v.
-nat·ing
dis·crim·i·na·tion
(dĭs·krĭm′ ĭ·nā′ shŭn)
dis·crim·i·na·to·ry
(dĭs·krĭm′ ĭ·nȧ·tō′ rĭ)
dis·cur·sive (dĭs·kûr′ sĭv)
dis·cus (dĭs′ kŭs)
(athletic device)
dis·cuss (dĭs·kŭs′)
(to debate)
dis·cus·sion (-kŭsh′ ŭn)
dis·dain·ful (dĭs·dān′ fŏŏl)
-ful·ly -ful·ness
dis·ease (dĭ·zēz′)
dis·em·bark (dĭs′ ĕm·bärk′)
dis·em·bar·ka·tion
(dĭs·ĕm′ bär·kā′ shŭn)
dis·em·bod·y (dĭs′ ĕm·bŏd′ ĭ)
-bodied -bodying
dis·em·bow·el (dĭs′ ĕm·bou′ ĕl)
-eled -eling

dis·en·chant·ment
      (dĭs′ ĕn·chănt′ mĕnt)
dis·en·cum·ber
      (dĭs′ ĕn·kŭm′ bēr)
dis·en·fran·chise
      (dĭs′ ĕn·frăn′ chīz)
  -chis·ing
  dis·en·fran·chise·ment
dis·en·gage   (dĭs′ ĕn·gāj′)
  -gag·ing
  dis·en·gage·ment
dis·en·tan·gle·ment
      (dĭs′ ĕn·tăng′ g'l·mĕnt)
dis·es·teem   (dĭs′ ĕs·tēm′)
dis·fa·vor   (dĭs·fā′ vēr)
dis·fig·ure·ment
      (dĭs·fĭg′ ûr·mĕnt)
dis·fran·chise (dĭs·frăn′ chīz)
  chis·ing
dis·gorge   (dĭs·gôrj′)
  -gorg·ing
dis·guise   (dĭs·gīz′)
  -guis·ing
dis·gust·ing (dĭs·gŭs′ tĭng)
dis·ha·bille (dĭs′ á·bēl′)
dis·har·mo·ni·ous
      (dĭs′ här·mō′ nĭ·ŭs)
dis·heart·en (dĭs·här′ t'n)
di·shev·eled (dĭ·shĕv′ ĕld)
  di·shev·el·ment
dis·hon·es·ty (dĭs·ŏn′ ĕs·tĭ)
  -ties
dis·hon·or·a·ble
      (dĭs·ŏn′ ēr·á·b'l)
dis·il·lu·sion (dĭs′ ĭ·lū′ zhŭn)
  (to free from illusion; see *dis-solution*)
dis·in·clined (dĭs′ ĭn·klīnd′)
  dis·in·cli·na·tion
      (dĭs·ĭn′ klĭ·nā′ shŭn)
dis·in·fect   (dĭs′ ĭn·fĕkt′)
  dis·in·fect·ant dis·in·fec·tion
dis·in·gen·u·ous
      (dĭs′ ĭn·jĕn′ û·ŭs)
dis·in·her·it (dĭs·ĭn·hĕr′ ĭt)
  -it·ed   -it·ing
  dis·in·her·it·ance
dis·in·te·grate (dĭs·ĭn′ tĕ·grāt)
  -grat·ing
  dis·in·te·gra·tion
      (dĭs′ ĭn′ tĕ·grā′ shŭn)

dis·in·ter·est·ed
      (dĭs′ ĭn′ tēr·ĕs·tĕd)
dis·joint·ed (dĭs·join′ tĕd)
dis·junc·tion (dĭs·jŭngk′ shŭn)
disk   (dĭsk)
  (platelike object; also *disc*)
dis·like   (dĭs·līk′)
  -lik·ing
dis·lo·ca·tion (dĭs′ lō·kā′ shŭn)
dis·loy·al   (dĭs·loi′ ăl)
  dis·loy·al·ty
dis·mal   (dĭz′ măl)
  dis·mal·ly
dis·man·tle (dĭs·măn′ t'l)
  -tling
dis·may   (dĭs·mā′)
dis·mem·ber·ment
      (dĭs·mĕm′ bēr·mĕnt)
dis·miss   (dĭs·mĭs′)
  dis·mis·sal
dis·mount (dĭs·mount′)
dis·o·be·di·ence
      (dĭs′ ō·bē′ dĭ·ĕns)
dis·o·bey   (dĭs′ ō·bā′)
dis·o·blig·ing (dĭs′ ō·blĭj′ ĭng)
dis·or·dered (dĭs·ôr′ dērd)
  dis·or·der·ly -li·ness
dis·or·gan·ized
      (dĭs·ôr′ găn·ĭzd)
dis·o·ri·ent·ed (dĭs·ō′ rĭ·ĕnt·ĕd)
dis·own   (dĭs·ōn′)
dis·par·age (dĭs·păr′ ĭj)
  -ag·ing
  dis·par·age·ment
dis·pa·rate (dĭs′ pá·răt)
  (dissimilar; see *desperate*)
  dis·par·i·ty (dĭs·păr′ ĭ·tĭ)
dis·pas·sion·ate
      (dĭs·păsh′ ŭn·ĭt)
dis·patch   (dĭs·păch′)
dis·pel   (dĭs·pĕl′)
  -pelled   -pel·ling
dis·pen·sa·ble (dĭs·pĕn′ sá·b'l)
  dis·pen·sa·bil·i·ty
      (dĭs·pĕn′ sá·bĭl′ ĭ·tĭ)
dis·pen·sa·ry (dĭs·pĕn′ sá·rĭ)
  -ries
dis·pen·sa·tion
      (dĭs′ pĕn·sā′ shŭn)
dis·pens·er (dĭs·pĕn′ sēr)
dis·perse   (dĭs·pûrs′)
  (to scatter; see *disburse*)
  -pers·ing
  dis·per·sal (-pûr′ săl)
  dis·per·sion (-pûr′ shŭn)

dis·pir·it·ed   (dĭs·pĭr′ ĭt·ĕd)
dis·place   (dĭs·plās′)
  -plac·ing
  dis·placed per·son
  dis·place·ment
dis·play   (dĭs·plā′)
dis·please   (dĭs·plēz′)
  -pleas·ing –
  dis·pleas·ure   (dĭs·plĕzh′ ẽr)
dis·pose   (dĭs·pōz′)
  -pos·ing   dis·pos·al
  dis·po·si·tion   (dĭs′ pŏ·zĭsh′ ŭn)
dis·pos·sess   (dĭs′ pŏ·zĕs′)
dis·pro·por·tion
               (dĭs′ prŏ·pōr′ shŭn)
  dis·pro·por·tion·ate
                    (-ĭt)
dis·prove   (dĭs·prōōv′)
  -prov·ing
dis·pute   (dĭs·pūt′)
  -put·ing   dis·pu·ta·ble
  dis·pu·tant   (dĭs′ pŭ·tănt′)
  dis·pu·ta·tion   (dĭs′ pŭ·tā′ shŭn)
  dis·pu·ta·tious
               (dĭs′ pŭ·tā′ shŭs)
dis·qual·i·fy   (dĭs·kwŏl′ ĭ·fī)
  -fied   -fy·ing
  dis·qual·i·fi·ca·tion
               (dĭs·kwŏl′ ĭ·fĭ′ kā′ shŭn)
dis·qui·et·ing   (dĭs·kwī′ ĕt·ĭng)
dis·re·gard   (dĭs′ rĕ·gärd′)
dis·re·pair   (dĭs′ rĕ·pâr′)
dis·re·pute   (dĭs′ rĕ·pūt′)
  dis·rep·u·ta·ble
               (dĭs·rĕp′ û·tá·b'l)
dis·re·spect   (dĭs′ rĕ·spĕkt′)
dis·rupt   (dĭs·rŭpt′)
  dis·rup·tion   (dĭs·rŭp′ shŭn)
  dis·rup·tive   (-tĭv)
dis·sat·is·fy   (dĭs·săt′ ĭs·fī)
  -fied,   -fy·ing
  dis·sat·is·fac·tion
               (dĭs′ săt·ĭs·făk′ shŭn)
dis·sect   (dĭ·sĕkt′)
  dis·sec·tion   (dĭ·sĕk′ shŭn)
dis·sem·ble   (dĭ·sĕm′ b'l)
  -bling
dis·sem·i·nate   (dĭ·sĕm′ ĭ·nāt)
  -nat·ing
  dis·sem·i·na·tion
               (dĭ·sĕm′ ĭ·nā′ shŭn)
dis·sen·sion   (dĭ·sĕn′ shŭn)
dis·sent   (dĭ·sĕnt′)
  (disagree; see *descent*)
  dis·sen·ter

dis·sen·tient   (dĭ·sĕn′ shĕnt)
dis·ser·ta·tion   (dĭs′ ẽr·tā′ shŭn)
dis·serv·ice   (dĭs·sûr′ vĭs)
dis·si·dence   (dĭs′ ĭ·dĕns)
  -dent
dis·sim·i·lar   (dĭ·sĭm′ ĭ·lẽr)
  dis·sim·i·lar·i·ty
               (dĭ·sĭm′ ĭ·lăr′ ĭ·tĭ)
dis·sim·u·late   (dĭ·sĭm′ û·lāt)
  -lat·ing
dis·si·pate   (dĭs′ ĭ·pāt)
  -pat·ing
  dis·si·pa·tion   (dĭs′ ĭ·pā′ shŭn)
  dis·si·pa·tor
dis·so·ci·ate   (dĭ·sō′ shĭ·āt)
  -at·ing
  dis·so·ci·a·tion
               (dĭ·sō′ sĭ·ā′ shŭn)
dis·so·lute   (dĭs′ ŏ·lūt)
  dis·so·lute·ness
dis·so·lu·tion   (dĭs′ ŏ·lū′ shŭn)
  (disintegration; see *disillusion*)
dis·solve   (dĭ·zŏlv′)
  dis·solv·ing   dis·sol·vent
dis·so·nance   (dĭs′ ŏ·nắns)
  -nant
dis·suade   (dĭ·swād′)
  dis·suad·ing
  dis·sua·sion   (dĭ·swā′ zhŭn)
  dis·sua·sive   (-sĭv)
dis·sym·me·try
               (dĭs·sĭm′ ĕ·trĭ)
dis·taff   (dĭs′ tăf)
dis·tance   (dĭs′ tắns)
dis·taste   (dĭs·tāst′)
  dis·taste·ful   -ful·ly
  -ful·ness
dis·tem·per   (dĭs·tĕm′ pẽr)
dis·tend   (dĭs·tĕnd′)
dis·till   (dĭs·tĭl′)
  dis·til·la·tion   (dĭs′ tĭ·lā′ shŭn)
  dis·til·ler·y   (dĭs·tĭl′ ẽr·ĭ)
  -til·ler·ies
dis·tinct   (dĭs·tĭngkt′)
  dis·tinc·tion   (dĭs·tĭngk′ shŭn)
  dis·tinc·tive   (-tĭngk′ tĭv)
dis·tin·guished   (dĭs·tĭng′ gwĭsht)
  dis·tin·guish·a·ble
dis·tort   (dĭs·tôrt′)
  dis·tor·tion   (-tôr′ shŭn)
dis·tract   (dĭs·trăkt′)
  dis·tract·ed·ly   dis·tract·i·ble
  dis·trac·tion   (-trăk′ shŭn)
dis·traught   (dĭs·trôt′)

dis·tress　　　(dĭs·trĕs′)
　dis·tress·ful　　dis·tress·ing·ly
dis·trib·ute　　(dĭs·trĭb′ ût)
　-ut·ing　　　dis·trib·ut·a·ble
　dis·tri·bu·tion
　　　　　　　(dĭs′·trĭ·bū′ shŭn)
　dis·trib·u·tor
dis·trict at·tor·ney
　　　　　　　(dĭs′ trĭkt)
dis·trust·ful　　(dĭs·trŭst′ fŏŏl)
dis·turb·ance　　(dĭs·tûr′ băns)
dis·un·ion　　(dĭs·ūn′ yŭn)
dis·use　　　(dĭs·ūs′) n.
ditch　　　(dĭch)
dit·to　　　(dĭt′ ō)
dit·ty　　　(dĭt′ ĭ)
　dit·ties
di·ur·nal　　(dī·ûr′ năl)
　-nal·ly
di·van　　　(dī′ văn)
dive bomb·er　　(dīv)
di·verge　　(dī·vûrj′)
　-verg·ing　　di·ver·gence,
　-gent
di·vers　　　(dī′ vērz)
　(several)
di·verse　　(dī·vûrs′)
　(different)
　di·verse·ly
　di·ver·si·fy　　(dī·vûr′ sĭ·fī)
　-fied,　　　-fy·ing
　di·ver·si·ty　　(dī·vûr′ sĭ·tĭ)
　-ties
di·ver·sion　　(dĭ·vûr′ shŭn)
　di·ver·sion·ar·y
di·vert·ing　　(dī·vûrt′ ĭng)
di·vest　　　(dī·vĕst′)
di·vide　　　(dĭ·vīd′)
　-vid·ing　　di·vid·a·ble
　div·i·dend　　(dĭv′ ĭ·dĕnd)
div·i·na·tion　　(dĭv′ ĭ·nā′ shŭn)
di·vine　　　(dĭ·vīn′)
di·vin·i·ty　　(dĭ·vĭn′ ĭ·tĭ)
　-ties
di·vis·i·ble　　(dĭ·vĭz′ ĭ·b'l)
di·vi·sion　　(dĭ·vĭzh′ ŭn)
　di·vi·sion·al
di·vi·sive　　(dĭ·vī′ sĭv)
di·vi·sor　　(dĭ·vī′ zēr)
di·vorce　　(dĭ·vōrs′)
　-vorc·ing
　di·vor·cee　　(dĭ·vōr′ sē′)
div·ot　　　(dĭv′ ŭt)
di·vulge　　(dĭ·vŭlj′)
　-vulg·ing　　di·vul·gence

Dix·ie　　　(dĭk′ sĭ)
diz·zy　　　(dĭz′ ĭ)
　diz·zi·ness
Do·ber·man pin·scher
　　　　　　(dō′ bēr·măn pĭn′ shēr)
doc·ile　　　(dŏs′ ĭl)
　doc·ile·ly
　do·cil·i·ty　　(dō·sĭl′ ĭ·tĭ)
dock·et　　(dŏk′ ĕt)
　-et·ed,　　　-et·ing
dock·yard　　(dŏk′ yärd′)
doc·tor　　(dŏk′ tēr)
　doc·tor·al　　(dŏk′ tēr·ăl)
　doc·tor·ate　　(dok′ tēr·ĭt)
doc·trine　　(dŏk′ trĭn)
　doc·tri·naire　　(dŏk′ trĭ·nâr′)
　doc·tri·nal　　(dŏk′ trĭ·năl)
doc·u·ment　　(dŏk′ û·měnt)
　doc·u·men·ta·ry
　　　　　　　(dŏk′ û·měn′ tȧ·rĭ)
　-ries
　doc·u·men·ta·tion
　　　　　　　(dŏk′ û·měn·tā′ shŭn)
dod·der·ing　　(dŏd′ ēr·ĭng)
dodge　　　(dŏj)
　dodg·ing
do·er　　　(dōō′ ēr)
doe·skin　　(dō′ skĭn′)
does·n't　　(dŭz′ ĕnt)
dog　　　　(dŏg)
　dog days　　dog-eared
　dog·fight　　dog·ged·ly
　dog·house　　dog-tired
　dog·watch　　dog·wood
dog·ger·el　　(dŏg′ ēr·ĕl)
dog·ma　　(dŏg′ mȧ)
　dog·mat·ic　　(dŏg′ măt′ ĭk)
　dog·ma·tism　　(dŏg′ mȧ·tĭz'm)
do-good·er　　dōō′ gŏŏd′ ēr)
doi·ly　　　(doi′ lĭ)
　-lies
dol·drums　　(dŏl′ drŭmz)
dole·ful　　(dōl′ fŏŏl)
　-ful·ly　　　-ful·ness
dol·lar　　(dŏl′ ēr)
dol·lop　　(dŏl′ ŭp)
dol·man sleeve　　(dŏl′ măn)
dol·or·ous　　(dŏl′ ēr·ŭs)
dol·phin　　(dŏl′ fĭn)
dolt·ish　　(dōlt′ ĭsh)
do·main　　(dō·măn′)
do·mes·tic　　(dō·měs′ tĭk)
　do·mes·ti·cate　　(dō·měs′ tĭ·kāt)
　-cat·ing

do·mes·tic·i·ty
    (dō′ mĕs·tĭs′ ĭ·tĭ)
dom·i·cile   (dŏm′ ĭ·sĭl)
dom·i·nant   (dŏm′ ĭ·nănt)
 -nance
dom·i·nate   (dŏm′ ĭ·nāt)
 -nat·ing
 dom·i·na·tion
    (dŏm′ ĭ·nā′ shŭn)
dom·i·neer·ing
    (dŏm′ ĭ·nēr′ ĭng)
Do·min·i·can   (dȯ·mĭn′ ĭ·kȧn)
Re·pub·lic
do·min·ion   (dȯ·mĭn′ yŭn)
dom·i·no   (dŏm′ ĭ·nō)
 -noes
do·nate   (dō′ nāt)
 -nat·ing
 do·na·tion   (dȯ·nā′ shŭn)
Don Juan   (dŏn hwän′)
don·key   (dŏng′ kĭ)
 -keys
do·nor   (dō′ nẽr)
Don Quix·ote   (dŏn kē·hō′ tȧ)
don't   (dōnt)
doo·dle   (dōō′ d'l)
 -dling
dooms·day   (dōōmz′ dā′)
door   (dōr)
 door·keep·er   door·nail
 door·step   door·way
dope fiend   (dōp)
dope·y   (dōp′ ĭ)
dor·mant   (dôr′ mȧnt)
 -man·cy
dor·mer win·dow
    (dôr′ mẽr)
dor·mi·to·ry   (dôr′ mĭ·tō′ rĭ)
 -ries
dor·sal   (dôr′ sȧl)
do·ry   (dō′ rĭ)
 -ries
dos·age   (dōs′ ĭj)
dos·si·er   (dŏs′ ĭ·ā)
Do·sto·ev·ski, Fyo·dor
    (dŏs′ tŭ·yĕv′ skĭ, fyȯ′ dẽr)
dote   (dōt)
 dot·ing
 dot·age   (dōt′ ĭj)
 do·tard   (dō′ tẽrd)
dot·ted swiss   (dŏt′ ĕd)
dou·ble   (dŭb′ 'l)
 -bly
 dou·ble-breast·ed
 dou·ble-deal·ing

dou·ble-deck·er
dou·ble-en·ten·dre
dou·ble-head·er
dou·ble-take   dou·ble talk
dou·ble time
doubt   (dout)
 doubt·er   doubt·ful
 -ful·ly   -ful·ness
 doubt·less
douche   (dōōsh)
dough·boy   (dō′ boi′)
dough·nut   (dō′ nŭt′)
dour   (dōōr)
douse   (dous)
 dous·ing
dove·tail   (dŭv′ tāl′)
 -tailed   -tail·ing
dow·a·ger   (dou′ ȧ·jẽr)
dow·dy   (dou′ dĭ)
 dow·di·ness
dow·el   (dou′ ĕl)
 dow·el·ing
down   (doun)
 down·beat   down·cast
 down·fall   down·heart·ed
 down·pour   down·stairs
 down·town   down·trod·den
 down·ward   down·y
dow·ry   (dou′ rĭ)
 -ries
dox·ol·o·gy   (dŏks·ŏl′ ȯ·jĭ)
 -gies
doze   (dōz)
 doz·ing
doz·en   (dŭz′ 'n)
drach·ma   (drăk′ mȧ)
draft   (drȧft)
 drafts·man
drag·net   (drăg′ nĕt′)
drag·on·fly   (drăg′ ŭn·flī′)
 -flies
drain   (drān)
 drain·age   (drān′ ĭj)
 drain·pipe
dra·ma   (drä′ mȧ)
 dra·ma·tic   (drȧ·măt′ ĭk)
 -i·cal·ly
 dram·a·tist   (drăm′ ȧ·tĭst)
 dram·a·ti·za·tion
    (drăm′ ȧ·tĭ·zā′ shŭn)
dra·per·y   (drā′ pẽr·ĭ)
 -per·ies
dras·tic   (drăs′ tĭk)
 -ti·cal·ly
draw·back   (drô′ băk′)

draw·bridge   (drô′ brĭj′)
draw·er   (drô′ ẽr)
drawl   (drôl)
drawn   (drôn)
dray·age   (drā′ ĭj)
dread·ful   (drĕd′ fŏol)
  -ful·ly   -ful·ness
dread·nought   (drĕd′ nôt′)
dream·land   (drēm′ lănd′)
dream·y   (drēm′ ĭ)
  dream·i·ness
drear·y   (drẽr′ ĭ)
  drear·i·ly   drear·i·some
dredge   (drĕj)
  dredg·ing
dregs   (drĕgz)
drench   (drĕnch)
dress·mak·er   (drĕs′ māk′ ẽr)
dres·sy   (drĕs′ ĭ)
drib·ble   (drĭb′ l)
  drib·bling
dri·er   (drī′ ẽr)
drift·wood   (drĭft′ wŏod′)
drill·mas·ter   (drĭl′ más′ tẽr)
drink·a·ble   (drĭngk′ á·b′l)
drive   (drĭv)
  driv·ing   drive-in
  drive·way
driv·el   (drĭv′ ′l)
  -eled   -el·ing
driz·zle   (drĭz′ ′l)
  driz·zling
droll   (drōl)
  droll·er·y   (drōl′ ẽr·ĭ)
drom·e·dar·y   (drŏm′ ĕ·dẽr′ ĭ)
drone   (drōn)
  dron·ing
droop·y   (drŏōp′ ĭ)
  droop·i·ness
drop   (drŏp)
  dropped   drop·ping
  drop-forge   drop leaf *n.*
  drop-leaf *adj.* drop·let
drop·sy   (drŏp′ sĭ)
  drop·si·cal
drought   (drout)
  (dryness; also *drouth*)
drown   (droun)
  drowned   (dround)
drow·sy   (drou′ zĭ)
  drow·si·er   -si·est
  -si·ly   -si·ness
drudge   (drŭj)
  drudg·er·y

drug   (drŭg)
  drugged   drug·ging
  drug·gist   drug·less
  drug·store
dru·id   (drŏō′ ĭd)
drum   (drŭm)
  drum·head
  drum ma·jor·ette
  drum·mer   drum·ming
  drum·stick
drunk·ard   (drŭngk′ ẽrd)
drunk·en   (drŭngk′ ĕn)
  drunk·en·ly   drunk·en·ness
dry   (drī)
  dried   dry·ing
  dri·er   dri·est
  dry-clean   dry clean·ing
  dry goods   dry·ly
  dry·ness   dry rot
du·al   (dū′ ál)
  (double; see *duel*)
  du·al·ism
  du·al·i·ty   (dū·ăl′ ĭ·tĭ)
  du·al·ly   du·al-pur·pose
du·bi·ous   (dū′ bĭ·ŭs)
du·cal   (dū′ kál)
duc·at   (dŭk′ ăt)
duch·ess   (dŭch′ ĕs)
duch·y   (dŭch′ ĭ)
  duch·ies
duck·ling   (dŭk′ lĭng)
duc·tile   (dŭk′ tĭl)
  duc·til·i·ty   (dŭk·tĭl′ ĭ·tĭ)
duct·less gland
                  (dŭkt′ lĕs)
dude ranch   (dūd)
dudg·eon   (dŭj′ ŭn)
du·el   (dū′ ĕl)
  (fight; see *dual*)
  du·eled   du·el·ing
  du·el·ist
du·en·na   (dū·ĕn′ á)
du·et   (dū·ĕt′)
duf·fel bag   (dŭf′ ĕl)
duf·fer   (dŭf′ ẽr)
dug·out   (dŭg′ out′)
duke·dom   (dūk′ dŭm)
dul·cet   (dŭl′ sĕt)
dul·ci·mer   (dŭl′ sĭ·mẽr)
dull   (dŭl)
  dull·ard   (dŭl′ ẽrd)
  dull·ness
  dul·ly   (dŭl′ lĭ)
du·ly   (dū′ lĭ)
  (in due manner)

dumb·bell (dŭm′ bĕl′)
dum·found (dŭm′ found′)
dum·my (dŭm′ ĭ)
 dum·mies
dump·ling (dŭmp′ lĭng)
Dun·can Phyfe (dŭng′ kăn fīf′)
dun·ga·rees (dŭng′ gȧ·rēz′)
dun·geon (dŭn′ jŭn)
du·o·de·num (dū′ ỏ·dē′ nŭm)
dupe (dūp)
 dup·ing
du·plex (dū′ plĕks)
du·pli·cate (dū′ plĭ·kȧt)
 adj., n.
 (-kāt) v.
 -cat·ing
 du·pli·ca·tion
  (dū′ plĭ·kā′ shŭn)
 du·pli·ca·tor (-kā′ tẽr)
du·plic·i·ty (du·plĭs′ ȷ·tĭ)
 -ties
du·ra·ble (dū′ rȧ·b'l)
 du·ra·bil·i·ty (dū′ rȧ·bĭl′ ȷ·tĭ)
du·ra·tion (dủ·rā′ shŭn)
du·ress (dū′ rĕs)
dur·ing (dūr′ ĭng)
dusk·y (dŭs′ kĭ)
dust (dŭst)
 dust·bin dust bowl
 dust·pan
Dutch ov·en (dŭch)
du·ty (dū′ tĭ)
 -ties
 du·te·ous (dū′ tẽ·ŭs)
 du·ti·ful, -ful·ly, -ful·ness
dwarf (dwôrf)
dwell·ing (dwĕl′ ĭng)
dwin·dle (dwĭn′ d'l)
 -dling
dye (dī)
 dyed dye·ing
 dye·stuff
dy·ing (dī′ ĭng)
 (expiring)
dy·nam·ic (dī·năm′ ĭk)
 dy·nam·i·cal·ly
 dy·na·mism (dī′ nȧ·mĭz′m)
 dy·na·mite (dī′ nȧ·mīt)
 dy·na·mo (dī′ nȧ·mō)
 -mos
dy·nas·ty (dī′ năs·tĭ)
 -ties
 dy·nas·tic (dī·năs′ tĭk)
dys·en·ter·y (dĭs′ ĕn·tĕr′ ĭ)
dys·func·tion (dĭs·fŭngk′ shŭn)

dys·pep·sia (dĭs·pĕp′ shȧ)
 dys·pep·tic (dĭs·pĕp′ tĭk)
dys·tro·phy (dĭs′ trỏ·fĭ)

E

ea·ger (ē′ gẽr)
ea·gle (ē′ g'l)
 ea·glet (ē′ glĕt)
ear (ẽr)
 ear·ache ear·drum
 ear·phone ear·ring
 ear·shot
earl·dom (ûrl′ dŭm)
ear·ly (ûr′ lĭ)
 ear·li·er, -li·est, -li·ness
ear·nest (ûr′ nĕst)
earn·ing (ûr′ nĭng)
earth (ûrth)
 earth·en·ware earth·ling
 earth·ly -li·ness
 earth·quake earth·y
ease (ēz)
 eas·ing
ea·sel (ē′ z'l)
East·er (ēs′ tẽr)
east·ern·er (ēs′ tẽr·nẽr)
east·ward (ēst′ wẽrd)
eas·y (ēz′ ĭ)
 eas·i·er eas·i·est
 eas·i·ly eas·i·ness
 eas·y·go·ing
Eau de Co·logne
  (ō dě kỏ·lōn′)
eaves·drop·per (ēvz′ drŏp′ ẽr)
ebb tide (ĕb tīd)
eb·on·y (ĕb′ ŭn·ĭ)
e·bul·li·ence (ê·bŭl′ ĭ·ĕns)
 e·bul·li·ent
ec·cen·tric (ĕk·sĕn′ trĭk)
 ec·cen·tric·i·ty
  (ĕk′ sĕn·trĭs′ ȷ·tĭ)
Ec·cle·si·as·tes (ě·klē′ zĭ·ăs′ tēz)
ec·cle·si·as·ti·cal
  (ě·klē′ zĭ·ăs′ tĭ·kȧl)
ech·e·lon (ĕsh′ ê·lŏn)
ech·o (ek′ o)
 -oed -o·ing
 ech·oes
é·clair (ȧ·klâr′)
ec·lec·tic (ĕk·lĕk′ tĭk)
 ec·lec·ti·cism (-tĭ·sĭz'm)
e·clipse (ê·klĭps′)
 -clips·ing

ec·logue (ĕk′ lŏg)
e·col·o·gy (ê·kŏl′ ô·jĭ)
　e·col·o·gist (ê·kŏl′ ô·jĭst)
e·con·o·my (ê·kŏn′ ô·mĭ)
　-mies
　e·co·nom·ic (ē′ kô·nŏm′ ĭk)
　e·co·nom·i·cal
　　　　　　　(ē′ kô·nŏm′ ĭ·kâl)
　e·con·o·mist (ê·kŏn′ ô·mĭst)
　e·con·o·mize (ê·kŏn′ ô·mĭz)
　-miz·ing
ec·ru (ĕk′ rōō)
ec·sta·sy (ĕk′ stà·sĭ)
　-sies
　ec·stat·ic (ĕk·stăt′ ĭk)
　-i·cal·ly
ec·to·plasm (ĕk′ tô·plăz′m)
　ec·to·plas·mic
　　　　　　　(ĕk′ tô·plăz′ mĭk)
Ec·ua·dor (ĕk′ wá·dôr)
ec·u·men·i·cal
　　　　　　　(ĕk′ û·mĕn′ ĭ·kâl)
ec·ze·ma (ĕk′ sĕ·mà)
E·dam cheese (ē′ dăm)
ed·dy (ĕd′ ĭ)
　ed·died ed·dy·ing
　ed·dies
e·del·weiss (ā′ dĕl·vīs)
E·den (ē′ d′n)
edge (ĕj)
　edg·ing edge·wise
　edg·y
ed·i·ble (ĕd′ ĭ·b′l)
　ed·i·bil·i·ty (ĕd′ ĭ·bĭl′ ĭ·tĭ)
e·dict (ē′ dĭkt)
ed·i·fice (ĕd′ ĭ·fĭs)
ed·i·fy (ĕd′ ĭ·fĭ)
　-fied -fy·ing
　ed·i·fi·ca·tion
　　　　　　　(ĕd′ ĭ·fĭ·kā′ shŭn)
ed·it (ĕd′ ĭt)
　-it·ed -it·ing
　e·di·tion (ê·dĭsh′ ŭn)
　ed·i·tor
　ed·i·to·ri·al (ĕd′ ĭ·tô′ rĭ·âl)
　-al·ly
ed·u·cate (ĕd′ û·kāt)
　-cat·ing
　ed·u·ca·ble (ĕd′ û·kà·b′l)
　ed·u·ca·tion (ĕd′ û·kā′ shŭn)
　-tion·al
　ed·u·ca·tive (ĕd′ û·kā′ tĭv)
　ed·u·ca·tor (ĕd′ û·kā′ tĕr)
e·duce (ê·dūs′)
　-duc·ing e·duc·i·ble

ee·rie (ē′ rĭ)
　ee·ri·ly -i·ness
ef·face (ê·fās′)
　ef·fac·ing ef·face·ment
ef·fect (ê·fĕkt′)
　(result; see affect)
　ef·fec·tive
ef·fec·tu·al (ê·fĕk′ tû·âl)
　ef·fec·tu·ate (-āt)
　-at·ing
ef·fem·i·nate (ê·fĕm′ ĭ·nĭt)
　ef·fem·i·na·cy (-nà·sĭ)
ef·fer·vesce (ĕf′ ĕr·vĕs′)
　-vesc·ing ef·fer·ves·cence
ef·fete (ê·fēt′)
ef·fi·ca·cy (ĕf′ ĭ·kà·sĭ)
　ef·fi·ca·cious (ĕf′ ĭ·kā′ shŭs)
ef·fi·cient (ê·fĭsh′ ĕnt)
　ef·fi·cien·cy
ef·fi·gy (ĕf′ ĭ·jĭ)
　-gies
ef·fort (ĕf′ ērt)
　ef·fort·less·ly
ef·fron·ter·y (ê·frŭn′ tĕr·ĭ)
　-ter·ies
ef·fu·sion (ê·fū′ zhŭn)
ef·fu·sive (ê·fū′ sĭv)
e·gal·i·tar·i·an
　　　　　　(ê·găl′ ĭ·târ′ ĭ·ấn)
egg·head (ĕg′ hĕd′)
egg·nog (ĕg′ nŏg′)
e·go (ē′ gō)
　e·go·cen·tric (ē′ gô·sĕn′ trĭk)
　e·go·ism (ē′ gô·ĭz′m)
　-ist
　e·go·tism (ē′ gô·tĭz′m)
　-tist
　e·go·tis·ti·cal (ē′ gô·tĭs′ tĭ·kâl)
e·gre·gious (ê·grē′ jŭs)
e·gress (ē′ grĕs)
e·gret (ē′ grĕt)
E·gypt (ē′ jĭpt)
　E·gyp·tian (ê·jĭp′ shấn)
ei·der down (ī′ dĕr)
eight·een (ā′ tēn′)
eight·y (ā′ tĭ)
　eight·ies eight·i·eth
Ein·stein the·o·ry
　　　　　　(īn′ stīn)
Ei·sen·how·er, Dwight D.
　　　　　　(ī′ z′n·hou′ ĕr)
ei·ther (ē′ thĕr)
e·jac·u·late (ê·jăk′ û·lāt)
　-lat·ing

e·jac·u·la·tion
    (ĕ·jăk′ ū·lā′ shŭn)
 e·jac·u·la·tor
e·ject   (ĕ·jĕkt′)
 e·jec·tion (-jĕk′ shŭn)
 e·jec·tor
eke   (ēk)
 ek·ing
e·lab·o·rate (ĕ·lăb′ ô·rĭt)
    adj.
    (-rāt) v.
 -rat·ing
 e·lab·o·rate·ly (-rĭt·lĭ)
 e·lab·o·ra·tion
    (ĕ·lăb′ ô·rā′ shŭn)
é·lan   (ā′ läɴ′)
e·lapse   (ĕ·lăps′)
 -laps·ing
e·las·tic   (ĕ·lăs′ tĭk)
 e·las·tic·i·ty (ĕ·lăs′ tĭs′ ĭ·tĭ)
e·late   (ĕ·lāt′)
 -lat·ing e·lat·ed·ly
 e·la·tion
el·bow   (ĕl′ bō)
 el·bow·room
el·der·ber·ry (ĕl′ dēr·bĕr′ ĭ)
 -ber·ries
eld·er·ly   (ĕl′ dēr·lĭ)
El Do·ra·do (ĕl dô·rä′ dō)
e·lect   (ĕ·lĕkt′)
 e·lec·tion (ĕ·lĕk′ shŭn)
 e·lec·tive e·lec·tor
 e·lec·tor·al col·lege
    (ĕ·lĕk′ tēr·ăl)
 e·lec·tor·ate (ĕ·lĕk′ tēr·ĭt)
e·lec·tric   (ĕ·lĕk′ trĭk)
 e·lec·tri·cal
 e·lec·tri·cian (ĕ·lĕk′ trĭsh′ ăn)
 e·lec·tric·i·ty (ĕ·lĕk′ trĭs′ ĭ·tĭ)
e·lec·tri·fy (ĕ·lĕk′ trĭ·fī)
 -fied   -fy·ing
 e·lec·tri·fi·ca·tion
    (ĕ·lĕk′ trĭ·fĭ·kā′ shŭn)
e·lec·tro·car·di·o·gram
    (ĕ·lĕk′ trô·kär′ dĭ·ô·grăm′)
e·lec·tro·cute (ĕ·lĕk′ trô·kūt)
 -cut·ing
 e·lec·tro·cu·tion
    (ĕ·lĕk′ trô·kū′ shŭn)
e·lec·trode (ĕ·lĕk′ trōd)
e·lec·tro·dy·nam·ics
    (ĕ·lĕk′ trô·dī·năm′ ĭks)
e·lec·trol·y·sis (ĕ·lĕk′ trŏl′ ĭ·sĭs)
e·lec·tro·lyt·ic (ĕ·lĕk′ trô·lĭt′ ĭk)

e·lec·tro·mag·net·ic
    (ĕ·lĕk′ trô·măg·nĕt′ ĭk)
e·lec·tron (ĕ·lĕk′ trŏn)
 e·lec·tron·ic (ĕ·lĕk′ trŏn′ ĭk)
e·lec·tro·plate (ĕ·lĕk′ trô·plāt′)
 -plat·ing
e·lec·tro·ther·a·py
    (ĕ·lĕk′ trô·thĕr′ ȧ·pĭ)
el·ee·mos·y·nar·y
    (ĕl′ ê·mŏs′ ĭ·nĕr′ ĭ)
el·e·gance (ĕl′ ê·gȧns)
 -gant
el·e·gy   (ĕl′ ê·jĭ)
 -gies
 el·e·gi·ac (ĕl′ ê·jī′ ăk)
 el·e·gize (ĕl′ ê·jīz)
 -giz·ing
el·e·ment (ĕl′ ê·mĕnt)
 el·e·men·tal (ĕl′ ê·mĕn′ tȧl)
 el·e·men·ta·ry (ĕl′ ê·mĕn′ tȧ·rĭ)
el·e·phant (ĕl′ ê·fȧnt)
 el·e·phan·tine (ĕl′ ê·făn′ tĭn)
el·e·vate (ĕl′ ê·vāt)
 -vat·ing
 el·e·va·tion (ĕl′ ê·vā′ shŭn)
 el·e·va·tor (ĕl′ ê·vā′ tēr)
e·lev·en   (ê·lĕv′ ĕn)
elf·in   (ĕl′ fĭn)
e·lic·it   (ê·lĭs′ ĭt)
 (to draw forth; see illicit)
 -it·ed   -it·ing
e·lide   (ê·līd′)
 -lid·ing
 e·li·sion (ê·lĭzh′ ŭn)
el·i·gi·ble (ĕl′ ĭ·jĭ·b′l)
 el·i·gi·bil·i·ty (ĕl′ ĭ·jĭ·bĭl′ ĭ·tĭ)
e·lim·i·nate (ê·lĭm′ ĭ·nāt)
 -nat·ing
 e·lim·i·na·tion
    (ê·lĭm′ ĭ·nā′ shŭn)
e·li·sion   (ê·lĭzh′ ŭn)
e·lite   (ā·lēt′)
e·lix·ir   (ê·lĭk′ sēr)
E·liz·a·be·than
    (ê·lĭz′ ȧ·bē′ thăn)
el·lipse   (ĕ·lĭps′)
 el·lip·sis el·lip·tic
 -ti·cal
el·o·cu·tion (ĕl′ ô·kū′ shŭn)
e·lon·gate (ê·lŏng′ gāt)
 -gat·ing
 e·lon·ga·tion
    (ê·lŏng′ gā′ shŭn)
e·lope   (ê·lōp′)
 -lop·ing e·lope·ment

el·o·quence (ĕl′ ŏ·kwĕns)
-quent
else·where (ĕls′ hwâr)
e·lu·ci·date (ė·lū′ sĭ·dāt)
-dat·ing
e·lu·ci·da·tion
(ė·lū′ sĭ·dā′ shŭn)
e·lude (ė·lūd′)
(evade; see *allude*)
-lud·ing
e·lu·sion (ė·lū′ zhŭn)
e·lu·sive (ė·lū′ sĭv)
(baffling; see *illusive*)
e·ma·ci·ate (ė·mā′ shĭ·āt)
(to make thin)
-at·ing
e·ma·ci·a·tion
(ė·mā′ sĭ·ā′ shŭn)
em·a·nate (ĕm′ á·nāt)
(to flow)
-nat·ing
em·a·na·tion (ĕm′ á·nā′ shŭn)
e·man·ci·pate (ė·măn′ sĭ·pāt)
(to free)
-pat·ing
e·man·ci·pa·tion
(ė·măn′ sĭ·pā′ shŭn)
e·mas·cu·late (ė·măs′ ků·lāt)
-lat·ing
e·mas·cu·la·tion
(ė·măs′ ků·lā′ shŭn)
em·balm (ĕm·bäm′)
em·bank·ment (ĕm·băngk′ mĕnt)
em·bar·go (ĕm·bär′ gō)
-goes
em·bark (ĕm·bärk′)
em·bar·ka·tion
(ĕm′ bär·kā′ shŭn)
em·bark·ment
em·bar·rass (ĕm·băr′ ás)
em·bar·rass·ment
em·bas·sy (ĕm′ bá·sĭ)
-bas·sies
em·bat·tle (ĕm·băt′ 'l)
-bat·tling
em·bed (ĕm·bĕd′)
-bed·ded -bed·ding
em·bel·lish (ĕm·bĕl′ ĭsh)
em·ber (ĕm′ bēr)
em·bez·zle (ĕm·bĕz′ 'l)
-bez·zling
em·bez·zle·ment
em·bez·zler
em·bit·ter (ĕm·bĭt′ ēr)
em·bla·zon (ĕm·blā′ z'n)

em·blem (ĕm′ blĕm)
em·blem·at·ic (ĕm′ blĕ·măt′ ĭk)
em·bod·y (ĕm·bŏd′ ĭ)
-bod·ied -bod·y·ing
em·bod·i·ment
(ĕm·bŏd′ ĭ·mĕnt)
em·bold·en (ĕm·bōl′ dĕn)
em·boss (ĕm·bŏs′)
em·brace (ĕm·brās′)
-brac·ing
em·broi·der (ĕm·broi′ dēr)
em·broi·der·y
em·broil (ĕm·broil′)
em·bry·o (ĕm′ brĭ·ō)
-os
em·bry·o·log·i·cal
(ĕm′ brĭ·ŏ·lŏj′ ĭ·kál)
em·bry·ol·o·gy
(ĕm′ brĭ·ŏl′ ŏ·jĭ)
em·bry·on·ic (ĕm′ brĭ·ŏn′ ĭk)
em·cee (ĕm′ sē′)
e·mend (ė·mĕnd′)
e·men·da·tion
(ē′ mĕn·dā′ shŭn)
em·er·ald (ĕm′ ēr·áld)
Em·er·ald Isle
e·merge (ė·mûrj′)
-merg·ing e·mer·gent,
-gence
e·mer·gen·cy (ė·mûr′ jĕn·sĭ)
-cies
e·mer·i·tus (ė·mĕr′ ĭ·tŭs)
e·merse (ė·mûrs′)
-mers·ing
e·mer·sion (ė·mûr′ shŭn)
em·er·y (ĕm′ ēr·ĭ)
e·met·ic (ė·mĕt′ ĭk)
em·i·grate (ĕm′ ĭ·grāt)
(to leave one's homeland; see
immigrate) -grat·ing
em·i·grant (-grănt)
em·i·gra·tion (ĕm′ ĭ·grā′ shŭn)
é·mi·gré (ā′ mē′ grā′)
em·i·nence (ĕm′ ĭ·nĕns)
em·i·nent do·main
em·is·sar·y (ĕm′ ĭ·sĕr′ ĭ)
em·is·sar·ies
e·mis·sion (ė·mĭsh′ ŭn)
e·mit (ė·mĭt′)
-mit·ted -mit·ting
e·mol·li·ent (ė·mŏl′ ĭ·ĕnt)
(lotion)
e·mol·u·ment (ė·mŏl′ û·mĕnt)
(wages)

e·mo·tion (ê·mō′ shŭn)
  e·mo·tion·al -al·ly
e·mo·tive (ê·mō′ tĭv)
em·pa·thy (ĕm′ pá·thĭ)
em·per·or (ĕm′ pĕr·ĕr)
em·pha·sis (ĕm′ fá·sĭs)
  pl. em·pha·ses (-sēz)
  em·pha·size -siz·ing
  em·phat·ic (ĕm·făt′ ĭk)
  -i·cal·ly
em·pire (ĕm′ pīr)
em·pir·ic (ĕm·pĭr′ ĭk)
  em·pir·i·cal
  em·pir·i·cism (-ĭ·sĭz′m)
em·place·ment (ĕm·plās′ mĕnt)
em·ploy (ĕm·ploi′)
  em·ploy·a·ble em·ploy·ee
  em·ploy·er em·ploy·ment
em·po·ri·um (ĕm·pō′ rĭ·ŭm)
em·pow·er (ĕm·pou′ ĕr)
emp·ty (ĕmp′ tĭ)
  -tied -ty·ing
  emp·ti·ly -ti·ness
em·py·re·an (ĕm′ pĭ·rē′ ăn)
em·u·late (ĕm′ ū·lât)
  -lat·ing
  em·u·la·tion (ĕm′ ū·lā′ shŭn)
  em·u·la·tive (ĕm′ ū·lā′ tĭv)
  em·u·la·tor (ĕm′ ū·lā′ tĕr)
e·mul·si·fy (ê·mŭl′ sĭ·fī)
  -fied -fy·ing
  e·mul·si·fi·ca·tion
    (ê·mŭl′ sĭ·fĭ·kā′ shŭn)
e·mul·sion (ê·mŭl′ shŭn)
en·a·ble (ĕn·ā′ b′l)
  -bling
en·act·ment (ĕn·ăkt′ mĕnt)
en·am·el (ĕn·ăm′ ĕl)
  -eled -el·ing
en·am·ored (ĕn·ăm′ ĕrd)
en·camp·ment (ĕn·kămp′ mĕnt)
en·ceph·a·lo·gram
    (ĕn·sĕf′ á·lô·grăm′)
en·chant (ĕn·chánt′)
  en·chant·ress
en·cir·cle (ĕn·sûr′ k′l)
  -cling en·cir·cle·ment
en·clasp (ĕn·klásp′)
en·clave (ĕn′ klāv)
en·close (ĕn·klōz′)
  -clos·ing
  en·clo·sure (ĕn·klō′ zhĕr)
en·co·mi·um (ĕn·kō′ mĭ·ŭm)
en·com·pass (ĕn·kŭm′ pás)
en·core (äng′ kōr)

en·coun·ter (ĕn·koun′ tĕr)
en·cour·age (ĕn·kûr′ ĭj)
  -ag·ing
  en·cour·age·ment
en·croach (ĕn·krōch′)
en·crust (ĕn·krŭst′)
en·cum·ber (ĕn·kŭm′ bĕr)
  en·cum·brance
en·cyc·li·cal (ĕn·sĭk′ lĭ·kǎl)
en·cy·clo·pe·di·a
    (ĕn·sī′ klô·pē′ dĭ·á)
  en·cy·clo·pe·dic
en·dan·ger (ĕn·dān′ jĕr)
en·dear·ing (ĕn·dēr′ ĭng)
en·deav·or (ĕn·dĕv′ ĕr)
en·dem·ic (ĕn·dĕm′ ĭk)
  en·dem·i·cal·ly
en·dive (ĕn′ dīv)
end·less·ly (ĕnd′ lĕs·lĭ)
en·do·crine (ĕn′ dô·krīn)
  en·do·cri·nol·o·gy
    (ĕn′ dô·krī·nŏl′ ô·jĭ)
en·dorse (ĕn·dôrs′)
  -dors·ing en·dors·a·ble
  en·dor·see (ĕn′ dôr·sē′)
  en·dorse·ment
en·dow·ment (ĕn·dou′ mĕnt)
en·due (ĕn·dū′)
  -du·ing
en·dure (ĕn·dūr′)
  -dur·ing en·dur·a·ble
  en·dur·ance
en·e·ma (ĕn′ ê·má)
en·e·my (ĕn′ ê·mĭ)
  -mies
en·er·gy (ĕn′ ĕr·jĭ)
  -gies
  en·er·get·ic (ĕn′ ĕr·jĕt′ ĭk)
  -i·cal·ly
  en·er·gize (ĕn′ ĕr·jīz)
  -giz·ing
en·er·vate (ĕn′ ĕr·vāt)
  (to deprive of nerve; see *innervate*)
  -vat·ing
  en·er·va·tion (ĕn′ ĕr·vā′ shŭn)
en·fee·ble (ĕn·fē′ b′l)
  -fee·bling
en·force (ĕn·fōrs′)
  -forc·ing en·force·a·ble
  en·force·ment
en·fran·chise (ĕn·frăn′ chīz)
  -chis·ing
  en·fran·chise·ment
en·gage (ĕn·gāj′)
  -gag·ing en·gage·ment

en·gen·der (ĕn·jĕn′ dĕr)
en·gine (ĕn′ jĭn)
en·gi·neer (ĕn′ jĭ·nēr′)
  en·gi·neer·ing
Eng·lish·man (ĭng′ glĭsh·mǎn)
en·grave (ĕn·grāv′)
  -grav·ing en·grav·er
en·gross (ĕn·grōs′)
en·gulf (ĕn·gŭlf′)
en·hance (ĕn·hȧns′)
  -hanc·ing en·hance·ment
e·nig·ma (ĕ·nĭg′ mȧ)
  e·nig·mat·ic (ē′ nĭg·mǎt′ ĭk)
  -i·cal·ly
en·join (ĕn·join′)
en·joy (ĕn·joi′)
  en·joy·a·ble en·joy·ment
en·large (ĕn·lärj′)
  -larg·ing en·large·ment
en·light·en·ment
  (ĕn·līt′ 'n·mĕnt)
en·list (ĕn·lĭst′)
  en·list·ment
en·liv·en (ĕn·lĭv′ ĕn)
en masse (ĕn·mȧs′)
en·mesh (ĕn·mĕsh′)
en·mi·ty (ĕn′ mĭ·tĭ)
  (ill will; see *amity*)
  -ties
en·no·ble (ĕ·nō′ b'l)
  -bling
en·nui (än′ wē)
e·nor·mous (ĕ·nôr′ mŭs)
  e·nor·mi·ty (ĕ·nôr′ mĭ·tĭ)
e·nough (ĕ·nŭf′)
en·plane (ĕn·plān′)
  -plan·ing
en·rage (ĕn·rāj′)
  -rag·ing
en·rap·ture (ĕn·rǎp′ tụr)
  -tur·ing
en·rich (ĕn·rĭch′)
en·roll (ĕn·rōl′)
  en·roll·ment
en route (än rōōt′)
en·sconce (ĕn·skŏns′)
  -sconc·ing
en·sem·ble (än·sŏm′ b'l)
en·shrine (ĕn·shrīn′)
  -shrin·ing
en·shroud (ĕn·shroud′)
en·sign (ĕn′ sīn)
en·slave·ment (ĕn·slāv′ mĕnt)
en·sue (ĕn·sū′)
  -su·ing

en·tail (ĕn·tāl′)
en·tan·gle (ĕn·tǎng′ g'l)
  -gling en·tan·gle·ment
en *tente cor·diale*
  (än′ tänt′ kôr′ dyál′)
en·ter (ĕn′ tēr)
  en·trant
en·ter·prise (ĕn′ tēr·prīz)
  -pris·ing
en·ter·tain (ĕn′ tēr·tān′)
  en·ter·tain·ing·ly
  en·ter·tain·ment
en·thrall (ĕn·thrôl′)
en·throne (ĕn·thrōn′)
  -thron·ing en·throne·ment
en·thu·si·asm (ĕn·thū′ zĭ·ǎz′m)
  en·thu·si·ast (ĕn·thū′ zĭ·ǎst)
  en·thu·si·as·tic
    (ĕn·thū′ zĭ·ǎs′ tĭk)
  -ti·cal·ly
en·tice (ĕn·tīs′)
  -tic·ing en·tice·ment
en·tire·ty (ĕn·tīr′ tĭ)
en·ti·tle (ĕn·tī′ t'l)
  -ti·tling
en·ti·ty (ĕn′ tĭ·tĭ)
  -ties
en·to·mol·o·gy (ĕn′ tô·mŏl′ ô·jĭ)
en·tou·rage (än·tōō·räzh′)
en·trails (ĕn′ trĕlz)
en·trance (ĕn′ trȧns) *n.*
en·trance (ĕn·trȧns′) *v.*
  -tranc·ing
en·trant (ĕn′ trȧnt)
en·treat (ĕn·trēt′)
  en·treat·ing·ly
  en·treat·y -treat·ies
en·tree (än′ trā)
en·trench·ment
  (ĕn·trĕnch·mĕnt)
en·tre·pre·neur
  (än′ trĕ·prĕ·nûr′)
en·trust (ĕn·trŭst′)
en·try (ĕn′ trĭ)
  -tries en·try·way
en·twine (ĕn·twīn′)
  -twin·ing
e·nu·mer·ate (ĕ·nū′ mēr·āt)
  -at·ing
  e·num·er·a·tion
    (ĕ·nū′ mēr·ā′ shŭn)
e·nun·ci·ate (ĕ·nŭn′ shĭ·āt)
  -at·ing
  e·nun·ci·a·tion
    (ĕ·nŭn′ sĭ·ā′ shŭn)

en·vel·op (ĕn·vĕl′ ŭp) v.
(to wrap up)
-oped -op·ing
en·vel·op·ment
en·ve·lope (ĕn′ vĕ·lōp) n.
(letter container)
en·ven·om (ĕn·vĕn′ ŭm)
en·vi·a·ble (ĕn′ vĭ·å·b′l)
en·vi·ous (ĕn′ vĭ·ŭs)
en·vi·ron·ment
(ĕn·vī′ rŭn·mĕnt)
en·vi·ron·men·tal
(ĕn·vī′ rŭn·mĕn′ tål)
en·vi·rons (ĕn·vī′ rŭnz)
en·vis·age (ĕn·vĭz′ ĭj)
-ag·ing
en·vi·sion (ĕn·vĭzh′ ŭn)
en·voy (ĕn′ voi)
en·vy (ĕn′ vĭ)
-vied -vy·ing
en·wrap (ĕn·răp′)
-wrapped -wrap·ping
en·zyme (ĕn′ zīm)
e·on (ē′ ŏn)
ep·au·let (ĕp′ ŏ·lĕt)
e·phem·er·al (ē·fĕm′ ĕr·ål)
ep·ic (ĕp′ ĭk)
ep·i·cure (ĕp′ ĭ·kūr)
ep·i·cu·re·an (ĕp′ ĭ·kû·rē′ ăn)
ep·i·dem·ic (ĕp′ ĭ·dĕm′ ĭk)
ep·i·der·mis (ĕp′ ĭ·dûr′ mĭs)
ep·i·gram (ĕp′ ĭ·grăm)
ep·i·gram·mat·ic
(ĕp′ ĭ·gră·măt′ ĭk)
ep·i·lep·sy (ĕp′ ĭ·lĕp′ sĭ)
ep·i·lep·tic (ĕp′ ĭ·lĕp′ tĭk)
ep·i·logue (ĕp′ ĭ·lŏg)
E·piph·a·ny (ē·pĭf′ å·nĭ)
E·pis·co·pa·li·an
(ē·pĭs′ kŏ·pā′ lĭ·ăn)
ep·i·sode (ĕp′ ĭ·sōd)
e·pis·tle (ē·pĭs′ ′l)
ep·i·taph (ĕp′ ĭ·tåf)
(tomb inscription)
ep·i·thet (ĕp′ ĭ·thĕt)
(nickname)
e·pit·o·me (ē·pĭt′ ŏ·mē)
e·pit·o·mize (ē·pĭt′ ŏ·mīz)
-miz·ing
ep·och (ĕp′ ŏk)
ep·och·al
eq·ua·ble (ĕk′ wå·b′l)
e·qual (ē′ kwål)
-qualed -qual·ing
e·qual·i·ty (ē·kwŏl′ ĭ·tĭ)

e·qual·ize -iz·ing
e·qual·ly
e·qua·nim·i·ty (ē′ kwå·nĭm′ ĭ·tĭ)
e·quate (ē·kwāt′)
-quat·ing
e·qua·tion (ē·kwā′ zhŭn)
e·qua·tor (ē·kwā′ tēr)
e·qua·to·ri·al (ē′ kwå·tō′ rĭ·ål)
e·ques·tri·an (ē·kwĕs′ trĭ·ăn)
e·qui·dis·tant (ē′ kwĭ·dĭs′ tånt)
e·qui·lat·er·al (ē′ kwĭ·lăt′ ĕr·ål)
-al·ly
e·qui·li·bra·tion
(ē′ kwĭ·lĭ·brā′ shŭn)
e·qui·lib·ri·um
(ē′ kwĭ·lĭb′ rĭ·ŭm)
e·quine (ē′ kwīn)
e·qui·nox (ē′ kwĭ·nŏks)
e·qui·noc·tial
(ē′ kwĭ·nŏk′ shål)
e·quip (ē·kwĭp′)
-quipped -quip·ping
eq·ui·page (ĕk′ wĭ·pĭj)
e·quip·ment
eq·ui·ta·ble (ĕk′ wĭ·tå·b′l)
eq·ui·ty (ĕk′ wĭ·tĭ)
-ties
e·quiv·a·lent (ē·kwĭv′ å·lĕnt)
-lence
e·quiv·o·cal (ē·kwĭv′ ŏ·kål)
-cal·ly
e·quiv·o·cate (ē·kwĭv′ ŏ·kāt)
-cat·ing
e·quiv·o·ca·tion
(ē·kwĭv′ ŏ·kā′ shŭn)
e·ra (ē′ rå)
e·rad·i·cate (ē·răd′ ĭ·kāt)
-cat·ing
e·rad·i·ca·ble (ē·răd′ ĭ·kå·b′l)
e·rad·i·ca·tion
(ē·răd′ ĭ·kā′ shŭn)
e·rad·i·ca·tor (ē·răd′ ĭ·kā′ tēr)
e·rase (ē·rās′)
-ras·ing e·ras·a·ble
e·ras·er
e·ra·sure (ē·rā′ zhēr)
e·rect (ē·rĕkt′)
e·rect·er
e·rec·tile (ē·rĕk′ tĭl)
e·rec·tion
er·go (ûr′ gō)
er·mine (ûr′ mĭn)
e·rode (ē·rōd′)
-rod·ing
e·ro·sion (ē·rō′ zhŭn)

e·rot·ic   (ê·rŏt′ ĭk)
err   (ûr)
er·rand   (ĕr′ ănd)
er·rant   (ĕr′ ănt)
  (wandering; see *arrant*)
er·rat·ic   (ĕ·răt′ ĭk)
  -i·cal·ly
er·ra·tum   (ĕ·rā′ tŭm)
  pl. er·ra·ta
er·ro·ne·ous   (ĕ·rō′ nê·ŭs)
er·ror   (ĕr′ ēr)
er·satz   (ĕr·zăts′)
erst·while   (ûrst′ hwīl′)
er·u·dite   (ĕr′ ŏŏ·dīt)
  er·u·di·tion   (ĕr′ ŏŏ·dĭsh′ ŭn)
e·rupt   (ê·rŭpt′)
  e·rup·tion   e·rup·tive
es·ca·la·tor   (ĕs′ kà·lā′ tēr)
es·ca·pade   (ĕs′ kà·pād′)
es·cape   (ĕs·kāp′)
  -cap·ing   es·cap·a·ble
  es·cape·ment   es·cap·ism, -ist
es·ca·role   (ĕs′ kà·rōl)
es·carp·ment   (ĕs·kärp′ mĕnt)
es·chew   (ĕs·chōō′)
es·cort   (ĕs′ kôrt) *n.*
            (ĕs·kôrt′) *v.*
es·crow   (ĕs′ krō′)
es·cutch·eon   (ĕs·kŭch′ ŭn)
Es·ki·mo   (ĕs′ kĭ·mō)
  -mos
es·o·ter·ic   (ĕs′ ô·tĕr′ ĭk)
es·pe·cial   (ĕs·pĕsh′ ăl)
  es·pe·cial·ly
Es·pe·ran·to   (ĕs′ pĕ·rän′ tō)
es·pi·o·nage   (ĕs′ pĭ·ô·nĭj)
es·pla·nade   (ĕs′ plà·nād′)
es·pouse   (ĕs·pouz′)
  -pous·ing   es·pous·al
es·prit de corps
            (ĕs′ prē′ dē kôr′)
es·py   (ĕs·pī′)
  -pied   -py·ing
es·quire   (ĕs·kwīr′)
es·say   (ĕ·sā′) *v.*
            (ĕs′ ā) *n.*
es·sence   (ĕs′ ĕns)
es·sen·tial   (ĕ·sĕn′ shăl)
  -tial·ly
es·tab·lish   (ĕs·tăb′ lĭsh)
es·tate   (ĕs·tāt′)
es·teem   (ĕs·tēm′)
es·ti·ma·ble   (ĕs′ tĭ·mà·b′l)
es·ti·mate   (ĕs′ tĭ·mât) *n.*
  -mat·ing   (-mât) *v.*

es·ti·ma·tion   (ĕs′ tĭ·mā′ shŭn)
es·top   (ĕs·tŏp′)
  -topped   -top·ping
  es·top·page
es·trange   (ĕs·trānj′)
  -trang·ing   es·trange·ment
es·tro·gen   (ĕs′ trŏ·jĕn)
  es·tro·gen·ic   (ĕs′ trŏ·jĕn′ ĭk)
es·tu·ar·y   (ĕs′ tû·ĕr′ ĭ)
  -ar·ies
et cet·er·a   (ĕt sĕt′ ēr·à)
etch·ing   (ĕch′ ĭng)
e·ter·nal   (ê·tûr′ năl)
  -nal·ly
e·ter·ni·ty   (ê·tûr′ nĭ·tĭ)
e·ther   (ē′ thēr)
e·the·re·al   (ê·thēr′ ê·ăl)
eth·ics   (ĕth′ ĭks)
  eth·i·cal
eth·nic   (ĕth′ nĭk)
e·thos   (ē′ thŏs)
eth·yl   (ĕth′ ĭl)
e·ti·ol·o·gy   (ē′ tĭ·ŏl′ ŏ·jĭ)
et·i·quette   (ĕt′ ĭ·kĕt)
E·ton jack·et   (ē′ t'n)
E·trus·can   (ê·trŭs′ kăn)
é·tude   (ā′ tūd)
et·y·mol·o·gy   (ĕt′ ĭ·mŏl′ ŏ·jĭ)
  et·y·mol·o·gist
eu·ca·lyp·tus   (û′ kà·lĭp′ tŭs)
Eu·cha·rist   (û′ kà·rĭst)
eu·chre   (û′ kēr)
Eu·clid   (û′ klĭd)
  Eu·clid·e·an   (û·klĭd′ ê·ăn)
eu·gen·ic   (û·jĕn′ ĭk)
eu·lo·gy   (û′ lô·jĭ)
  -gies
  eu·lo·gis·tic   (û′ lô·jĭs′ tĭk)
  eu·lo·gize   (û′ lô·jīz)
  -giz·ing
eu·nuch   (û′ nŭk)
eu·phe·mism   (û′ fê·mĭz′m)
  eu·phe·mis·tic   (û′ fê·mĭs′ tĭk)
  -ti·cal·ly
eu·phon·ic   (û·fŏn′ ĭk)
eu·pho·ri·a   (û·fō′ rĭ·à)
eu·re·ka   (û·rē′ kà)
Eu·ro·pe·an   (û′ rŏ·pē′ ăn)
Eu·sta·chi·an tube
            (û·stā′ kĭ·ăn)
eu·tha·na·si·a   (û′ thà·nā′ zhĭ·à)
e·vac·u·ate   (ê·văk′ û·āt)
  -at·ing
  e·vac·u·a·tion
            (ê·văk′ û·ā′ shŭn)

e·vac·u·ee (ĕ·văk′ ū·ē′)
e·vade (ĕ·vād′)
-vad·ing
e·val·u·ate (ĕ·văl′ ū·āt)
-at·ing
e·val·u·a·tion
    (ĕ·văl′ ū·ā′ shŭn)
ev·a·nes·cent (ĕv′ ȧ·nĕs′ ĕnt)
-cence
e·van·gel·i·cal
    (ē′ văn·jĕl′ ĭ·kɑl)
e·van·ge·list (ĕ·văn′ jĕ·lĭst)
e·vap·o·rate (ĕ·văp′ ŏ·rāt)
-rat·ing
e·vap·o·ra·tion
    (ĕ·văp′ ŏ·rā′ shŭn)
e·va·sion (ĕ·vā′ zhŭn)
e·va·sive -sive·ly
e·ven (ē′ vĕn)
e·ven·ly e·ven·ness
eve·ning (ēv′ nĭng)
e·vent (ĕ·vĕnt′)
e·vent·ful, -ful·ly, -ful·ness
e·ven·tide (ē′ vĕn·tīd′)
e·ven·tu·al (ĕ·vĕn′ tū·ɑl)
e·ven·tu·al·i·ty
    (ĕ·vĕn′ tū·ăl′ ĭ·tĭ)
e·ven·tu·al·ly
ev·er (ĕv′ ĕr)
the Ev·er·glades
ev·er·green ev·er·last·ing
ev·er·more
ev·er·y (ĕv′ ĕr·ĭ)
ev·er·y·bod·y
ev·er·y·day adj.
ev·er·y·one pron.
ev·er·y·thing ev·er·y·where
e·vict (ĕ·vĭkt′)
e·vic·tion (ĕ·vĭk′ shŭn)
ev·i·dence (ĕv′ ĭ·dĕns)
ev·i·dent·ly
e·vil (ē′ v′l)
e·vil·do·er -do·ing
e·vil·ly e·vil-mind·ed
e·vince (ĕ·vĭns′)
-vinc·ing e·vin·ci·ble
e·vis·cer·ate (ĕ·vĭs′ ĕr·āt)
-at·ing
e·vis·cer·a·tion
    (ĕ·vĭs′ ĕr·ā′ shŭn)
e·voke (ĕ·vōk′)
-vok·ing
ev·o·ca·tion (ĕv′ ŏ·kā′ shŭn)
e·voc·a·tive (ĕ·vŏk′ ȧ·tĭv)

ev·o·lu·tion (ĕv′ ŏ·lū′ shŭn)
ev·o·lu·tion·ar·y
e·volve (ĕ·vŏlv′)
-volv·ing
ex·ac·er·bate (ĕg·zăs′ ĕr·bāt)
-bat·ing
ex·ac·er·ba·tion
    (ĕg·zăs′ ĕr·bā′ shŭn)
ex·act (ĕg·zăkt′)
ex·act·ing ex·ac·tion
ex·ag·ger·ate (ĕg·zăj′ ĕr·āt)
-at·ing ex·ag·ger·a·tor
ex·ag·ger·a·tion
    (ĕg·zăj′ ĕr·ā′ shŭn)
ex·alt (ĕg·zôlt′)
ex·al·ta·tion (ĕg′ zôl·tā′ shŭn)
ex·am·ine (ĕg·zăm′ ĭn)
-in·ing
ex·am·i·na·tion
    (ĕg·zăm′ ĭ·nā′ shŭn)
ex·am·ple (ĕg·zăm′ p′l)
ex·as·per·ate (ĕg·zăs′ pĕr·āt)
-at·ing
ex·as·per·a·tion
    (ĕg·zăs′ pĕr·ā′ shŭn)
Ex·cal·i·bur (ĕks·kăl′ ĭ·bĕr)
ex·ca·vate (ĕks′ kȧ·vāt)
-vat·ing
ex·ca·va·tion
    (ĕks′ kȧ·vā′ shŭn)
ex·ca·va·tor
ex·ceed (ĕk·sēd′)
(to surpass; see accede)
ex·ceed·ing·ly
ex·cel (ĕk·sĕl′)
-celled -cel·ling
ex·cel·lent (ĕk′ sĕ·lĕnt)
-cel·lence
ex·cel·si·or (ĕk·sĕl′ sĭ·ôr)
ex·cept (ĕk·sĕpt′)
ex·cep·tion
ex·cep·tion·a·ble
ex·cep·tion·al, -al·ly
ex·cerpt (ĕk·sûrpt′) v.
    (ĕk′ sûrpt) n.
ex·cess (ĕk·sĕs′)
ex·ces·sive
ex·change (ĕks·chānj′)
ex·change·a·ble
ex·cheq·uer (ĕks·chĕk′ ĕr)
ex·cise (ĕk′ sīz) n.
-cis·ing (ĕk·sīz′) v.
ex·ci·sion (ĕk·sĭzh′ ŭn)
ex·cite (ĕk·sīt′)
-cit·ing

ex·cit·a·bil·i·ty
    (ĕk·sĭt′ a·bĭl′ ĭ·tĭ)
ex·cit·a·ble
ex·ci·ta·tion   (ĕk′ sĭ·tā′ shŭn)
ex·cit·ed·ly   ex·cite·ment
ex·claim   (ĕks·klām′)
ex·cla·ma·tion
    (ĕks′ klà·mā′ shŭn)
ex·clam·a·tor·y
    (ĕks·klăm′ à·tō′ rĭ)
ex·clude   (ĕks·klōōd′)
-clud·ing   ex·clu·sion
ex·clu·sive   -sive·ly
ex·com·mu·ni·cate
    (ĕks′ kŏ·mū′ nĭ·kāt)
-cat·ing
ex·co·ri·ate   (ĕks·kō′ rĭ·āt)
-at·ing
ex·cre·ment   (ĕks′ krĕ·mĕnt)
ex·cres·cence   (ĕks·krĕs′ ĕns)
ex·crete   (ĕks·krēt′)
-cret·ing   ex·cre·tion
ex·cre·to·ry   (ĕks′ krĕ·tō′ rĭ)
ex·cru·ci·at·ing
    (ĕks·krōō′ shĭ·āt′ ĭng)
ex·cru·ci·a·tion
    (ĕks·krōō′ shĭ·ā′ shŭn)
ex·cur·sion   (ĕks·kûr′ zhŭn)
ex·cuse   (ĕks·kūz′) v.
-cus·ing   (ĕks·kūs′) n.
ex·cus·a·ble   (ĕks·kūz′ à·b′l)
ex·e·cra·ble   (ĕk′ sĕ·krà·b′l)
ex·e·cute   (ĕk′ sĕ·kūt)
-cut·ing
ex·e·cu·tion   (ĕk′ sĕ·kū′ shŭn)
ex·ec·u·tive   (ĕg·zĕk′ û·tĭv)
ex·ec·u·tor   (ĕg·zĕk′ û·tĕr)
n. masc.
ex·ec·u·trix   (-trĭks) *n. fem.*
ex·e·ge·sis   (ĕk′ sĕ·jē′ sĭs)
pl. -ses   (sēz)
ex·em·pla·ry   (ĕg·zĕm′ plà·rĭ)
ex·em·pli·fy   (ĕg·zĕm′ plĭ·fī)
-fied   -fy·ing
ex·em·pli·fi·ca·tion
    (ĕg·zĕm′ plĭ·fĭ·kā′ shŭn)
ex·empt   (ĕg·zĕmpt′)
ex·empt·i·ble   ex·emp·tion
ex·er·cise   (ĕk′ sĕr·sīz)
-cis·ing
ex·ert   (ĕg·zûrt′)
ex·er·tion
ex·hale   (ĕks·hāl′)
-hal·ing   ex·hal·ant
ex·ha·la·tion   (ĕks′ hà·lā′ shŭn)

ex·haust   (ĕg·zôst′)
ex·haust·i·ble   ex·haus·tion
ex·haus·tive
ex·hib·it   (ĕg·zĭb′ ĭt)
-it·ed   -it·ing
ex·hib·i·tor
ex·hi·bi·tion   (ĕk′ sĭ·bĭsh′ ŭn)
-tion·ist
ex·hil·a·rate   (ĕg·zĭl′ à·rāt)
-rat·ing
ex·hil·a·ra·tion
    (ĕg·zĭl′ à·rā′ shŭn)
ex·hort   (ĕg·zôrt′)
ex·hor·ta·tion   (ĕg′ zôr·tā′ shŭn)
ex·hume   (ĕks·hūm′)
-hum·ing
ex·i·gen·cy   (ĕk′ sĭ·jĕn·sĭ)
ex·ig·u·ous   (ĕg·zĭg′ û·ŭs)
ex·ile   (ĕk′ sīl)
ex·ist   (ĕg·zĭst′)
ex·ist·ence   -ent
ex·is·ten·tial·ism
    (ĕg′ zĭs·tĕn′ shàl·iz′m)
ex·it   (ĕg′ sĭt)
ex·o·dus   (ĕk′ sŏ·dŭs)
ex·on·er·ate   (ĕg·zŏn′ ēr·āt)
-at·ing
ex·on·er·a·tion
    (ĕg·zŏn′ ēr·ā′ shŭn)
ex·o·ra·ble   (ĕk′ sŏ·rà·b′l)
ex·or·bi·tant   (ĕg·zôr′ bĭ·tănt)
-tance
ex·or·cise   (ĕk′ sôr·sīz)
(to expel)   -cis·ing
ex·ot·ic   (ĕks·ŏt′ ĭk)
ex·pand   (ĕks·pănd′)
ex·pand·a·ble
ex·panse   (ĕks·păns′)
ex·pan·sion   ex·pan·sive
ex·pa·tri·ate   (ĕks·pā′ trĭ·āt)
ex·pect·ant   (ĕks·pĕk′ tănt)
ex·pect·an·cy
ex·pec·ta·tion
    (ĕks′ pĕk·tā′ shŭn)
ex·pec·to·rate   (ĕks·pĕk′ tŏ·rāt)
-rat·ing   ex·pec·to·rant
ex·pec·to·ra·tion
    (ĕks·pĕk′ tŏ·rā′ shŭn)
ex·pe·di·ent   (ĕks·pē′ dĭ·ĕnt)
ex·pe·di·en·cy
ex·pe·dite   (ĕks′ pĕ·dīt)
-dit·ing   ex·pe·dit·er
ex·pe·di·tion   (ĕks′ pĕ·dĭsh′ ŭn)
ex·pe·di·tion·ar·y
ex·pe·di·tious   (ĕks′ pĕ·dĭsh′ ŭs)

ex·pel (ĕks·pĕl′)
-pelled -pel·ling
ex·pend·a·ble (ĕks·pĕn′ dá·b'l)
ex·pend·i·ture (ĕks·pĕn′ dĭ·tṳr)
ex·pense (ĕks·pĕns′)
ex·pen·sive -sive·ly
ex·pe·ri·ence (ĕks·pēr′ ĭ·ĕns)
ex·per·i·ment (ĕks·pĕr′ ĭ·mĕnt)
ex·per·i·men·tal
(ĕks·pĕr′ ĭ·mĕn′ tăl)
ex·per·i·men·ta·tion
(ĕks·pĕr′ ĭ·mĕn·tā′ shŭn)
ex·pert (ĕks·pûrt′) adj.
(ĕks′ pûrt) n.
ex·pi·ate (ĕks′ pĭ·āt)
-at·ing
ex·pi·a·tion (ĕks′ pĭ·ā′ shŭn)
ex·pi·ra·tion (ĕk′ spĭ·rā′ shŭn)
ex·plain (ĕks·plān′)
ex·plain·a·ble
ex·pla·na·tion
(ĕks′ plá·nā′ shŭn)
ex·plan·a·to·ry
(ĕks·plăn′ á·tō′ rĭ)
ex·ple·tive (ĕks·plĕ′ tĭv)
ex·pli·ca·to·ry (ĕks′ plĭ·ká·tō′ rĭ)
ex·plic·it (ĕks·plĭs′ ĭt)
ex·ploit (ĕks′ ploit) n.
(ĕks·ploit′) v.
ex·ploi·ta·tion
(ĕks′ ploi·tā′ shŭn)
ex·plore (ĕks·plōr′)
-plor·ing
ex·plo·ra·tion
(ĕks′ plŏ·rā′ shŭn)
ex·plor·a·to·ry
(ĕks·plōr′ á·tō′ rĭ)
ex·plor·er
ex·plo·sion (ĕks·plō′ zhŭn)
ex·plo·sive
ex·po·nent (ĕks·pō′ nĕnt)
ex·port (ĕks·pōrt′) v.
(ĕks′ pōrt) n.
ex·por·ta·tion
(ĕks′ pŏr·tā′ shŭn)
ex·pose (ĕks·pōz′) v.
-pos·ing
ex·po·sé (ĕks′ pŏ·zā′) n.
ex·po·si·tion (ĕks′ pŏ·zĭsh′ ŭn)
ex post fac·to (ĕks pōst făk′ tō)
ex·pos·tu·late (ĕks·pŏs′ tṳ·lāt)
-lat·ing
ex·pos·tu·la·tion
(ĕks·pŏs′ tṳ·lā′ shŭn)
ex·po·sure (ĕks·pō′ zhēr)

ex·pound (ĕks·pound′)
ex·press (ĕks·prĕs′)
ex·press·i·ble ex·pres·sion
ex·pres·sive ex·press·way
ex·pro·pri·ate (ĕks·prō′ prĭ·āt)
-at·ing
ex·pro·pri·a·tion
(ĕks·prō′ prĭ·ā′ shŭn)
ex·pul·sion (ĕks·pŭl′ shŭn)
ex·punge (ĕks·pŭnj′)
-pung·ing
ex·pur·gate (ĕks′ pĕr·gāt)
-gat·ing
ex·pur·ga·tion
(ĕks′ pĕr·gā′ shŭn)
ex·qui·site (ĕks′ kwĭ·zĭt)
ex·qui·site·ly
ex·tant (ĕks′ tănt)
(in existence; see extent)
ex·tem·po·ra·ne·ous
(ĕks·tĕm′ pŏ·rā′ nĕ·ŭs)
ex·tem·po·rize (ĕks·tĕm′ pŏ·rīz)
-riz·ing
ex·ten·sion (ĕks·tĕn′ shŭn)
ex·ten·sive (ĕks·tĕn′ sĭv)
-sive·ly
ex·tent (ĕks·tĕnt′)
(degree; see extant)
ex·ten·u·ate (ĕks·tĕn′ ṳ·āt)
-at·ing
ex·te·ri·or (ĕks·tēr′ ĭ·ēr)
ex·ter·mi·nate (ĕks·tûr′ mĭ·nāt)
-nat·ing -na·tor
ex·ter·mi·na·tion
(ĕks·tûr′ mĭ·nā′ shŭn)
ex·ter·nal (ĕks·tûr′ năl)
ex·ter·nal·ly
ex·tinct (ĕks·tĭngkt′)
ex·tinc·tion
ex·tin·guish (ĕks·tĭng′ gwĭsh)
ex·tin·guish·a·ble
ex·tin·guish·er
ex·tir·pate (ĕk′ stĕr·pāt)
-pat·ing
ex·tol (ĕks·tŏl′)
-tolled -tol·ling
ex·tort (ĕks·tôrt′)
ex·tor·tion -tion·ist
ex·tract (ĕks′ trăkt) n.
ex·tract (ĕks·trăkt′) v.
ex·trac·tion ex·trac·tive
ex·trac·tor
ex·tra·cur·ric·u·lar
(ĕks′ trá·kŭ·rĭk′ ů·lēr)

ex·tra·dite   (ĕks′ trȧ·dīt)
  -dit·ing
  ex·tra·di·tion
      (ĕks′ trȧ·dĭsh′ ŭn)
ex·tra·mar·i·tal
      (ĕks′ trȧ·măr′ ĭ·tăl)
ex·tra·ne·ous   (ĕks·trā′ nĕ·ŭs)
ex·traor·di·nar·y
      (ĕks·trôr′ dĭ·nĕr′ ĭ)
  ex·traor·di·nar·i·ly
      (ĕks·trôr′ dĭ·nĕr′ ĭ·lĭ)
ex·trap·o·late   (ĕks·trăp′ ŏ·lāt)
  -lat·ing
ex·tra·sen·so·ry perception
      (ĕks′ trȧ·sĕn′ sŏ·rĭ)
ex·tra·ter·ri·to·ri·al
      (ĕks′ trȧ·tĕr′ ĭ·tō′ rĭ·ăl)
ex·trav·a·gance
      (ĕks·trăv′ ȧ·găns)
ex·treme   (ĕks·trēm′)
  ex·treme·ly   ex·trem·ism
  ex·trem·ist
  ex·trem·i·ty   (ĕks·trĕm′ ĭ·tĭ)
ex·tri·cate   (ĕks′ trĭ·kāt)
  -cat·ing
  ex·tri·ca·ble   (ĕks′ trĭ·kȧ·b'l)
ex·trin·sic   (ĕks·trĭn′ sĭk)
ex·tro·vert   (ĕks′ trŏ·vûrt)
  ex·tro·ver·sion
      (ĕks′ trŏ·vûr′ shŭn)
ex·tru·sion   (ĕks·trōō′ zhŭn)
ex·u·ber·ant   (ĕg·zū′ bĕr·ȧnt)
  -ance
ex·ude   (ĕks·ūd′)
  -ud·ing
ex·ult   (ĕg·zŭlt′)
  ex·ult·an·cy   ex·ult·ant
  ex·ul·ta·tion   (ĕk′ sŭl·tā′ shŭn)
eye   (ī)
  eye·brow   eye·cup
  eye·let   eye·lid
  eye·shot   eye·strain
  eye·tooth   eye·wit·ness

F

fa·ble   (fā′ b'l)
fab·ric   (făb′ rĭk)
fab·ri·cate   (făb′ rĭ·kāt)
  -ca·ting
  fab·ri·ca·tion   (făb′ rĭ·kā′shŭn)
  fab·ri·ca·tor
fab·u·lous   (făb′ û·lŭs)
fa·çade   (fȧ·säd′)

face   (fās)
  fac·ing   face card
  face val·ue   fa·cial
fac·et   (făs′ ĕt)
  -et·ed
fa·ce·tious   (fȧ·sē′ shŭs)
  (joking; see *factious*)
fa·cial   (fā′ shăl)
fac·ile   (făs′ ĭl)
fa·cil·i·tate   (fȧ·sĭl′ ĭ·tāt)
  (help; see *felicitate*)
fa·cil·i·ty   (fȧ·sĭl′ ĭ·tĭ)
  -ties
fac·sim·i·le   (făk·sĭm′ ĭ·lē)
fac·tion   (făk′ shŭn)
  fac·tion·al
fac·tious   (făk′ shŭs)
  (dissenting; see *facetious*)
fac·tor   (făk′ tẽr)
fac·to·ry   (făk′ tô·rĭ)
  -ries
fac·to·tum   (făk·tō′ tŭm)
fac·tu·al   (făk′ tû·ăl)
  -al·ly
fac·ul·ty   (făk′ ŭl·tĭ)
  -ties
fad·dist   (făd·ĭst)
fag·ot   (făg′ ŭt)
  fag·ot·ing
Fahr·en·heit   (făr′ ĕn·hīt)
fail·ure   (fāl′ ûr)
faint   (fānt)
  (lose consciousness; see *feint*)
  faint·heart·ed
fair   (fâr)
  fair and square
  fair-mind·ed   fair-sized
  fair-trade a·gree·ment
  fair·way
fair·y   (fâr′ ĭ)
  fair·ies   fair·y·land
  fair·y tale
fait ac·com·pli (fĕ′ tȧ′ kôn′ plē′)
faith   (fāth)
  faith·ful, -ful·ly, -ful·ness
  faith·less
fak·er   (fāk′ ẽr)
  (fraud)
fa·kir   (fȧ·kẽr′)
  (yogi)
fal·con   (fôl′ kŭn)
fal·la·cy   (făl′ ȧ·sĭ)
  -cies
  fal·la·cious   (fȧ·lā′ shŭs)

fall·en (fôl′ ĕn)
fal·li·ble (făl′ ĭ·b'l)
 fal·li·bil·i·ty (făl′ ĭ·bĭl′ ĭ·tĭ)
Fal·lo·pi·an tube
 (fá·lō′ pĭ·ăn)
fall-out (fôl′ out′)
fal·low (făl′ ō)
false (fôls)
 false·heart·ed false·hood
 false·ly
fal·set·to (fôl·sĕt′ ō)
fal·si·fy (fôl′ sĭ·fī)
 -fied -fy·ing
fal·si·ty (fôl′ sĭ·tĭ)
 -ties
Fal·staff·i·an (fôl·stăf′ ĭ·ăn)
fal·ter·ing (fôl′ tẽr·ĭng)
fa·mil·iar (fá·mĭl′ yẽr)
 fa·mil·i·ar·i·ty
 (fá·mĭl′ ĭ·ăr′ ĭ·tĭ)
 fa·mil·iar·ize, -iz·ing
fam·i·ly (făm′ ĭ·lĭ)
 -lies
 fa·mil·ial (fá·mĭl′ yăl)
 fam·i·ly cir·cle
 fam·i·ly name
fam·ine (făm′ ĭn)
fam·ish (făm′ ĭsh)
fa·mous (fā′ mŭs)
fa·nat·ic (fá·năt′ ĭk)
 fa·nat·i·cal -cal·ly
 fa·nat·i·cism
fan·cy (făn′ sĭ)
 -cied -cy·ing
 fan·cier
 fan·ci·ful, -ful·ly, -ful·ness
 fan·cy dress fan·cy-free
 fan·cy·work
fan·dan·go (făn·dăng′ gō)
fan·fare (făn′ fâr)
fan·tas·tic (făn·tăs′ tĭk)
 -ti·cal·ly
fan·ta·sy (făn′ tá·sĭ)
 -sies
far (fär)
 far·a·way Far East
 far·fetched far-flung
 far-off adj. far-reach·ing
 far·see·ing far·sight·ed
farce (färs)
 far·ci·cal (fär′ sĭ·kăl)
fare·well (fâr′ wĕl′)
fa·ri·na (fá·rē′ ná)
farm (färm)
 farm hand farm·house

farm·yard
far·ther (fär′ thẽr)
 (refers only to spatial distance;
 see further) far·thest
fas·ci·nate (făs′ ĭ·nāt)
 -nat·ing
 fas·ci·na·tion (făs′ ĭ·nā′ shŭn)
fas·cism (făsh′ ĭz'm)
 fas·cist
fash·ion (făsh′ ŭn)
 fash·ion·a·ble fash·ion plate
fas·ten·ing (fás′ 'n·ĭng)
fas·tid·i·ous (făs·tĭd′ ĭ·ŭs)
fa·tal (fā′ tăl)
 fa·tal·i·ty (fá·tăl′ ĭ·tĭ)
 -ties fa·tal·is·tic
 fa·tal·ly
fate (fāt)
 fate·ful -ful·ly
fa·ther (fä′ thẽr)
 fa·ther-in-law fa·thers-in-law
 fa·ther·land fa·ther·less
 Fa·ther's Day
fath·om (făth′ ŭm)
 fath·om·a·ble fath·om·less
fa·tigue (fá·tēg′)
 -tigued -ti·guing
 fa·ti·ga·ble
fat·ten (făt′ 'n)
fat·u·ous (făt′ û·ŭs)
 fa·tu·i·ty (fá·tū′ ĭ·tĭ)
fau·cet (fô′ sĕt)
fault (fôlt)
 fault·find·ing fault·y
faun (fôn)
 (wood sprite; see fawn)
faux pas (fō′ pä′)
fa·vor (fā′ vẽr)
 fa·vor·a·ble
fa·vor·ite (fā′ vẽr·ĭt)
 fa·vor·it·ism
fawn (fôn)
 (young deer; see faun)
faze (fāz)
 (disconcert; see phase)
 faz·ing
fear (fẽr)
 fear·ful, -ful·ly, -ful·ness
 fear·some
fea·si·ble (fē′ zĭ·b'l)
 fea·si·bil·i·ty (fē′ zĭ·bĭl′ ĭ·tĭ)
feat (fēt)
 (deed; see fete)
feath·er (fĕth′ ẽr)
 feath·er·bed -bed·ding

feath·er·weight
fea·ture (fē′ tûr)
  -tur·ing   fea·ture·less
Feb·ru·ar·y (fĕb′ rŏŏ·ĕr′Ĭ)
feck·less (fĕk′ lĕs)
fe·cund (fē′ kŭnd)
  fe·cun·di·ty (fĕ·kŭn′ dĭ·tĭ)
fed·er·al (fĕd′ ĕr·ạl)
  fed·er·al·ist   fed·er·al·ly
fed·er·ate (fĕd′ ĕr·åt)
  -at·ing
  fed·er·a·tion (fĕd′ ĕr·ā′ shŭn)
fee·ble (fē′ b′l)
  fee·ble-mind·ed
  fee·ble·ness
  fee·bler, -blest, -bly
feed·back (fēd′ băk′)
feign (fān)
feint (fānt)
  (trick; see *faint*)
fe·lic·i·tate (fĕ·lĭs′ ĭ·tāt)
  (make happy; see *facilitate*)
  -tat·ing
  fe·lic·i·ta·tion
         (fĕ·lĭs′ ĭ·tā′ shŭn)
fe·lic·i·ty (fĕ·lĭs′ ĭ·tĭ)
  -ties   fe·lic·i·tous
fe·line (fē′ lĭn)
fel·low (fĕl′ ō)
  fel·low·ship
  fel·low trav·el·er
fel·on (fĕl′ ŭn)
  fe·lo·ni·ous (fĕ·lō′ nĭ·ŭs)
  fel·o·ny   -nies
fe·male (fē′ māl)
fem·i·nine (fĕm′ ĭ·nĭn)
  fem·i·nin·i·ty (fĕm′ ĭ·nĭn′ ĭ·tĭ)
fence (fĕns)
  fenc·ing   fence·less
fend·er (fĕn′ dēr)
fen·nel (fĕn′ ĕl)
fe·ral (fĕr′ ạl)
fer-de-lance (fâr′ dĕ·läNs)
fer·ment (fûr′ mĕnt) *n.*
fer·ment (fēr·mĕnt′) *v.*
  fer·men·ta·tion
         (fûr′ mĕn·tā′ shŭn)
fe·ro·cious (fĕ·rō′ shŭs)
  fe·roc·i·ty (fĕ·rŏs′ ĭ·tĭ)
fer·ret (fĕr′ ĕt)
Fer·ris wheel (fĕr′ Ĭs)
fer·rous (fĕr′ ŭs)
fer·ry (fĕr′ Ĭ)
  fer·ried   fer·ry·ing
  fer·ry·boat

fer·tile (fûr′ tĬl)
  fer·tile·ly
  fer·til·i·ty (fĕr·tĬl′ Ĭ·tĬ)
fer·ti·lize (fûr′ tĬ·līz)
  -liz·ing
  fer·ti·li·za·tion
         (fûr′ tĬ·lĬ·zā′ shŭn)
  fer·ti·liz·er
fer·vent (fûr′ vĕnt)
  -ven·cy
fer·vid (fûr′ vĬd)
fer·vor (fûr′ vēr)
fes·ti·val (fĕs′ tĬ·vạl)
fes·tive (fĕs′ tĬv)
  fes·tiv·i·ty (fĕs·tĬv′ Ĭ·tĬ)
  -ties
fes·toon (fĕs·tōōn′)
fetch (fĕch)
fete (fāt)
  (festival; see *feat*)
fet·id (fĕt′ Ĭd)
fe·tish (fē′ tĬsh)
fet·ter (fĕt′ ēr)
fe·tus (fē′ tŭs)
  -tus·es
feud (fūd)
feu·dal (fū′ dạl)
fe·ver (fē′ vēr)
  fe·ver·ish   fe·ver·rid·den
fi·an·cé (fē′ än·sā′)
  n. masc.
  fi·an·cée (fē′ än·sā′) *n. fem.*
fi·as·co (fĕ·ăs′ kō)
fi·at (fī′ ăt)
fi·ber (fī′ bĕr)
  fi·ber·board   Fi·ber·glas
  fi·brous
fick·le (fĬk′ ′l)
  fick·le·ness
fic·tion (fĬk′ shŭn)
  fic·tion·al   -al·ly
fic·ti·tious (fĬk·tĬsh′ ŭs)
fid·dle (fĬd′ ′l)
  fid·dling   fid·dle-fad·dle
  fid·dle·sticks
fi·del·i·ty (fĭ·dĕl′ Ĭ·tĬ)
fidg·et (fĬj′ ĕt)
  -et·ed   -et·ing
fi·du·ci·ar·y (fĭ·dū′ shĬ·ĕr′ Ĭ)
field (fēld)
fiend (fēnd)
  fiend·ish
fierce (fĕrs)
fi·er·y (fī′ rĬ)
  fi·er·i·er, -i·est, -i·ness

fi·es·ta (fĭ·ĕs′ tȧ)
fif·teen (fĭf′ tēn′)
  fif·teenth
fifth (fĭfth)
  fifth col·um·nist
fif·ty (fĭf′ tĭ)
  -ties   fif·ti·eth
  fif·ty·fold
fight·er (fīt′ ẽr)
fig·ment (fĭg′ mĕnt)
fig·ure (fĭg′ ûr)
  -ur·ing
  fig·u·ra·tion (fĭg′ û·rā′ shŭn)
  fig·ur·a·tive (fĭg′ ûr·ȧ·tĭv)
  fig·ure·head
  fig·u·rine (fĭg′ û·rēn′)
fil·a·ment (fĭl′ ȧ·mĕnt)
fil·bert (fĭl′ bêrt)
fil·i·al (fĭl′ ĭ·ȧl)
fil·i·bus·ter (fĭl′ ĭ·bŭs′ tẽr)
fil·i·gree (fĭl′ ĭ·grē)
Fil·i·pi·no (fĭl′ ĭ·pē′ nō)
  -nos
  But: Phil·ip·pine Is·lands
fil·let (fĭl′ ĕt)
fil·ly (fĭl′ ĭ)
  fil·lies
film (fĭlm)
  film·i·er, -i·est, -i·ness
  film·strip   film·y
fil·ter (fĭl′ tẽr)
  (porous article; see *philter*)
  fil·ter·a·bil·i·ty
      (fĭl′ tẽr·ȧ·bĭl′ ĭ·tĭ)
  fil·ter·a·ble
  fil·tra·tion (fĭl·trā′ shŭn)
filth·y (fĭl′ thĭ)
  filth·i·er, -i·est, -i·ly, -i·ness
fi·na·gler (fĭ·nā′ glẽr)
fi·nal (fī′ nȧl)
  fi·nal·i·ty (fī·nǎl′ ĭ·tĭ)
  fi·nal·ly
fi·na·le (fê·nä′ lȧ)
fi·nance (fĭ·nǎns′)
  -nanc·ing
  fi·nan·cial (fĭ·nǎn′ shȧl)
  fin·an·cier (fĭn′ ȧn·sẽr′)
fine (fīn)
  fine arts   fin·er·y
  fine·spun   fine-tooth comb
fi·nesse (fĭ·nĕs′)
fin·ger (fĭng′ gẽr)
  fin·ger bowl   fin·ger·nail
  fin·ger·print
fin·ick·y (fĭn′ ĭ·kĭ)

fi·nis (fī′ nĭs)
fin·ish (fĭn′ ĭsh)
fi·nite (fī′ nīt)
Fin·land (fĭn′ lȧnd)
  Finn   Finn·ish
fiord (fyôrd)
fire (fīr)
  fir·ing   fire·arm
  fire·bug   fire·brand
  fire·crack·er   fire-eat·er
  fire en·gine   fire es·cape
  fire ex·tin·guish·er
  fire·man   fire·place
  fire·plug   fire·pow·er
  fire·proof   fire·side
  fire·trap   fire·ward·en
  fire·wood   fire·works
fir·ma·ment (fûr′ mȧ·mĕnt)
first (fûrst)
  first aid   first base
  first-born   first class *n.*
  first-class *adj.*   first·hand
  first-rate
fis·cal (fĭs′ kȧl)
fish (fĭsh)
  fish·er·man   fish·er·y, -er·ies
  fish·hook   fish meal
  fish mon·ger
fis·sion (fĭsh′ ŭn)
  fis·sion·a·ble   fis·sion bomb
fis·sure (fĭsh′ ẽr)
fist·ic (fĭs′ tĭk)
  fist·i·cuffs
fit·ful (fĭt′ fŏŏl)
  -ful·ly   -ful·ness
five·fold (fīv′ fōld′)
fix·a·tion (fĭks·ā′ shŭn)
fix·ture (fĭks′ tûr)
fiz·zle (fĭz′ 'l)
  fiz·zling
flab·ber·gast (flăb′ ẽr·găst)
flab·by (flăb′ ĭ)
  flab·bi·ness
flac·cid (flăk′ sĭd)
flag (flăg)
  flagged   flag·ging
  flag·pole   flag·ship
  flag stop
flag·el·late (flăj′ ĕ·lāt)
  -el·lat·ing   flag·el·lant
flag·on (flăg′ ŭn)
fla·grant (flā′ grȧnt)
  -gran·cy
flair (flâr)
  (aptitude; see *flare*)

flake (flāk)
  flak·y   flak·i·er
  -i·est, -i·ly, -i·ness
flam·boy·ant (flăm·boi′ ănt)
  -an·cy
flame (flām)
  flam·ing   flame·proof
  flame throw·er
fla·min·go (flá·mĭng′ gō)
  -gos
flam·ma·ble (flăm′ á·b′l)
  flam·ma·bil·ity
          (flăm′ á·bĭl′ ĭ·tĭ)
flap·per (flăp′ ēr)
flare (flâr)
  (blaze; see *flair*)
  flare-up   flar·ing
flash (flăsh)
  flash·back   flash flood
  flash·light   flash·y,
  flash·i·er, -i·est, -i·ly, -i·ness
flat (flăt)
  flat·boat   flat·car
  flat-foot·ed
  Flat·head In·di·an
  flat·i·ron   flat·tened
  flat·top   flat·ware
flat·ter·y (flăt′ ēr·ĭ)
  flat·ter·ies   flat·ter·er
flaunt (flônt)
fla·vor (flā′ vēr)
  fla·vor·ful
flax·en (flăk′ s′n)
flea (flē)
  (insect)
  flea·bite
  flea-bit·ten
fledg·ling (flĕj′ lĭng)
flee (flē)
  (escape)
fleece (flēs)
fleet (flēt)
Flem·ish (flĕm′ ĭsh)
flesh·y (flĕsh′ ĭ)
  flesh·i·ness
fleur-de-lis (flûr′ dĕ·lē′)
flex·i·ble (flĕk′ sĭ·b′l)
  flex·i·bil·i·ty (flĕk′ sĭ·bĭl′ ĭ·tĭ)
flib·ber·ti·gib·bet
        (flĭb′ ēr·tĭ·jĭb′ ĕt)
flick·er (flĭk′ ēr)
fli·er (flī′ ēr)
flight (flīt)
  flight·y   flight·i·er
  -i·est, -i·ly, -i·ness

flim·sy (flĭm′ zĭ)
  flim·si·er, -si·est, -si·ly, -si·ness
flint·lock (flĭnt′ lŏk′)
flip·pant (flĭp′ ănt)
  flip·pan·cy
flir·ta·tion (flûr·tā′ shŭn)
  flir·ta·tious (flûr·tā′ shŭs)
float (flōt)
  flo·ta·tion (flō·tā′ shŭn)
floc·cu·late (flŏk′ û·lāt)
  -lat·ing
  floc·cu·la·tion (flŏk′ û·lā′ shŭn)
flog·ging (flŏg′ ĭng)
flood (flŭd)
  flood·gate   flood·light
  flood tide
floor (flōr)
  floor lead·er   floor show
  floor·walk·er
flop·house (flŏp′ hous′)
flop·py (flŏp′ ĭ)
flo·ral (flō′ răl)
flo·ri·cul·ture (flō′ rĭ·kŭl′ tûr)
flor·id (flŏr′ ĭd)
Flor·i·da (flŏr′ ĭ·dá)
  abbr. Fla.
  Flo·rid·i·an (flō·rĭd′ ĭ·ăn)
flo·rist (flō′ rĭst)
flo·ta·tion (flō·tā′ shŭn)
flo·til·la (flō·tĭl′ á)
flot·sam (flŏt′ săm)
flounce (flouns)
  flounc·ing
floun·der (floun′ dēr)
flour·ish (flûr′ ĭsh)
flow·age (flō′ ĭj)
flow·er (flou′ ēr)
  flow·er·i·ness   flow·er·pot
  flow·er·y
flown (flōn)
flu (flōō)
  (influenza)
fluc·tu·ate (flŭk′ tû·āt)
  -at·ing
  fluc·tu·a·tion (flŭk′tû·ā′ shŭn)
flue (flōō)
  (chimney)
flu·ent (flōō′ ĕnt)
  -en·cy
flu·id (flōō′ ĭd)
  flu·id·i·ty (flōō·ĭd′ ĭ·tĭ)
fluke (flōōk)
flum·mox (flŭm′ ŭks)
flunk·y (flŭngk′ ĭ)
  flunk·ies

flu·o·res·cent (flōō' ŏ·rĕs' ĕnt)
  -cence
flu·o·ri·date (flōō' ŏ·rĭ·dāt)
  -dat·ing
  flu·o·ri·da·tion
            (flōō' ŏ·rĭ·dā' shŭn)
flu·o·ri·nate (flōō' ŏ·rĭ·nāt)
  -nat·ing
  flu·o·ri·na·tion
            (flōō' ŏ·rĭ·nā' shŭn)
flu·o·ro·scope (flōō' ŏ·rŏ·skōp)
flur·ry (flûr' ĭ)
  flur·ries
flute (flōōt)
  flut·ist
flut·ter (flŭt' ĕr)
flux (flŭks)
fly (flī)
  flew   fly·ing
  flies   fly-by-night
  fly·ing fish fly·ing sau·cer
  fly·leaf   fly·pa·per
  fly·speck   fly·wheel
fo·cal (fō' kǎl)
fo·cus (fō' kŭs)
  -cused   -cus·ing
fod·der (fŏd' ĕr)
fog·gy (fŏg' ĭ)
  fog·gi·ness
fo·gy (fō' gĭ)
  ("old fogy")   -gies
foi·ble (foi' b'l)
foist (foist)
fo·li·age (fō' lĭ·ĭj)
fo·li·o (fō' lĭ·ō)
folk (fōk)
  folk dance   folk·lore
  folk mu·sic   folk tale
  folk·way
fol·li·cle (fŏl' ĭ·k'l)
fol·low (fŏl' ō)
  fol·low-through
  fol·low-up
fol·ly (fŏl' ĭ)
  fol·lies
fo·ment (fō·mĕnt')
  fo·men·ta·tion
            (fō' mĕn·tā' shŭn)
fon·dant (fŏn' dǎnt)
fon·dle (fŏn' d'l)
  -dling
fon·due (fŏn·dōō')
fool (fōōl)
  fool·er·y   -er·ies
  fool·har·dy   -di·ness

fool·proof   fool's gold
fool's par·a·dise
foot (fŏŏt)
  foot·age   (fŏŏt' ĭj)
  foot·ball   foot brake
  foot·bridge foot-can·dle
  foot·fall   foot·hill
  foot·hold   foot·lights
  foot·loose   foot·man
  foot·note   foot·print
  foot·rest   foot sol·dier
  foot·step   foot·stool
  foot·work
fop·per·y (fŏp' ĕr·ĭ)
for·age (fŏr' ĭj)
  -ag·ing
for·ay (fŏr' ā)
  -ay·ing
for·bear (fôr·bâr')
  for·bear·ance for·borne
for·bid (fŏr·bĭd')
  -bid·ding
  for·bade   (fŏr·bǎd')
  for·bid·den for·bid·ding·ly
force (fôrs)
  forc·ing   force·ful
  -ful·ly   -ful·ness
  for·ci·ble
for·ceps (fôr' sĕps)
Ford·ham (univ.) (fôr' dǎm)
fore- (fôr-)
  fore·arm
  fore·bode   -bod·ing
  fore·cast   fore·close
  fore·clo·sure fore·fa·thers
  fore·fin·ger fore·go
  fore·gone con·clu·sion
  fore·hand   fore·man
  fore·most   fore·noon
  fore·or·dain fore·quar·ter
  fore·run·ner fore·see·a·ble
  fore·shad·ow fore·stall
  fore·tell
for·eign (fŏr' ĭn)
fo·ren·sic (fŏ·rĕn' sĭk)
for·est (fŏr' ĕst)
  for·est·a·tion (fŏr' ĕs·tā' shŭn)
for·ev·er (fŏr·ĕv' ĕr)
for·feit (fôr' fĭt)
  -feit·ed   -feit·ing
  for·feit·a·ble for·fei·ture
forge (fôrj)
  forg·ing
for·ger·y (fôr' jĕr·ĭ)
  -ger·ies

for·get   (fŏr·gĕt′)
  -get·ting   for·get·ful
  -ful·ly   -ful·ness
  for·get-me-not   for·get·ta·ble
for·give   (fŏr·gĭv′)
  -giv·ing   for·giv·a·ble
  for·give·ness
for·go   (fŏr·gō′)
for·got   (fŏr·gŏt′)
  for·got·ten
for·lorn   (fŏr·lôrn′)
  for·lorn·ly   for·lorn·ness
for·mal   (fôr′ măl)
  for·mal·ism   for·mal·ly
  for·mal·i·ty   (fôr·măl′ ĭ·tĭ)
form·al·de·hyde
                    (fôr·măl′ dĕ·hīd)
for·mal·ize   fôr′ măl·īz)
  -iz·ing
  for·mal·i·za·tion
                    (fôr′ măl·ĭ·zā′ shŭn)
for·mat   (fôr′ măt)
for·ma·tion   (fôr·mā′ shŭn)
form·a·tive   (fôr′ mȧ·tĭv)
for·mi·da·ble   (fôr′ mĭ·dȧ·b′l)
For·mo·sa   (fôr·mō′ sȧ)
  (also: Taiwan)
for·mu·la   (fôr′ mŭ·lȧ)
  pl. -las or -lae (-lē)
for·mu·late   (fôr′ mŭ·lāt)
  -lat·ing
  for·mu·la·tion
                    (fôr′ mŭ·lā′ shŭn)
  for·mu·la·tor
for·sake   (fŏr·sāk′)
  -sak·ing   for·sak·en
for·syth·i·a   (fôr·sĭth′ ĭ·ȧ)
forth   (fōrth)
  forth·com·ing   forth·right
  forth·with
for·ti·eth   (fôr′ tĭ·ĕth)
for·ti·fy   (fôr′ tĭ·fī)
  -fied   -fy·ing
  for·ti·fi·ca·tion
                    (fôr′ tĭ·fĭ·kā′ shŭn)
for·tis·si·mo   (fôr·tĭs′ ĭ·mō)
for·ti·tude   (fôr′ tĭ·tūd)
Fort Lau·der·dale,
  Fla.   (fôrt lô′ dĕr·dāl)
fort·night   (fôrt′ nĭt)
for·tress   (fôr′ trĕs)
for·tu·i·tous   (fôr·tū′ ĭ·tŭs)
  for·tu·i·ty
for·tu·nate   (fôr′ tū̇·nĭt)
  -nate·ly

for·tune   (fôr′ tūn)
  for·tune hunt·er
  for·tune·tell·er
for·ty   (fôr′ tĭ)
  -ties   for·ti·eth
  for·ty·fold   for·ty·nin·er
fo·rum   (fō′ rŭm)
for·ward   (fôr′ wĕrd)
fos·sil   (fŏs′ ĭl)
  fos·sil·ized   (fŏs′ ĭ·līzd)
fought   (fôt)
foul   (foul)
  (dirty; see fowl)
  foul·mouthed   foul play
found   (found)
foun·da·tion   (foun·dā′ shŭn)
found·ry   (foun′ drĭ)
  -ries
foun·tain   (foun′ tĭn)
  foun·tain·head foun·tain pen
four   (fōr)
  four-di·men·sion·al
  four-flush·er   four-in-hand
  four-post·er   four·score
  four·some   four·square
  four-wheeled
four·teen   (fōr′ tēn′)
fowl   (foul)
  (poultry; see foul)
fox   (fŏks)
  fox·glove   fox·hole
  fox·hound   fox·tail
  fox ter·ri·er   fox·trot
  fox·y
foy·er   (foi′ ĕr)
fra·cas   (frā′ kȧs)
frac·tion   (frăk′ shŭn)
  frac·tion·al   -al·ly
frac·ture   (frăk′ tū̇r)
frag·ile   (frăj′ ĭl)
  -ile·ly
  fra·gil·i·ty   (frȧ·jĭl′ ĭ·tĭ)
frag·ment   (frăg′ mĕnt)
  frag·men·tar·y
  frag·men·ta·tion
                    (frăg′ mĕn·tā′ shŭn)
fra·grant   (frā′ grȧnt)
  -grance
frail   (frāl)
  frail·ty   -ties
frame-up   (frām′ ŭp′)
frame·work   (frām′ wŭrk′)
fran·chise   (frăn′ chīz)
  fran·chise·ment

Fran·co, Fran·cis·co
    (fräng′ kô,
    frän·thēs′ kô)
Fran·co·phile   (frăng′ kô·fĭl)
Frank·en·stein   (frăngk′ ĕn·stīn)
frank·furt·er   (frăngk′ fẽr·tẽr)
frank·in·cense   (frăngk′ ĭn·sĕns)
fran·tic   (frăn′ tĭk)
  fran·ti·cal·ly
frap·pé   (frȧ′ pā′)
fra·ter·nal   (frȧ·tûr′ nǎl)
  -nal·ly   fra·ter·nal·ism
fra·ter·ni·ty   (frȧ·tûr′ nĭ·tĭ)
  -ties
frat·er·nize   (frăt′ ẽr·nīz)
  -niz·ing
  frat·er·ni·za·tion
    (frăt′ ẽr·nĭ·zā′ shŭn)
fraud   (frôd)
  fraud·u·lent   -lence
fraught   (frôt)
Fräu·lein   (froi′ līn)
freak·ish   (frēk′ ĭsh)
freck·le   (frĕk′ 'l)
  -ling
Fred·er·icks·burg ,Va.
    (frĕd′ rĭks·bûrg)
free   (frē)
  fre·er
  free on board (f.o.b.)
  free·born   free-for-all
  free·hand *adj.*
  free-lance *adj. & v.*
  Free·ma·son   free·think·er
  free·way
  free-will of·fer·ing
free·dom   (frē′ dŭm)
freez·er   (frēz′ ẽr)
freight   (frāt)
  freight·age   freight·er
fren·zy   (frĕn′ zĭ)
  -zied   -zy·ing
fre·quent   (frē′ kwĕnt)
  -quen·cy
fres·co   (frĕs′ kō)
  -coes
fresh   (frĕsh)
  fresh·en   fresh-water *adj.*
  fresh·man
fret   (frĕt)
  fret·ted   fret·ting
  fret·ful, -ful·ly, -ful·ness
Freud·i·an   (froid′ ĭ·ǎn)
fri·ar   (frī′ ẽr)
  (churchman; see *fryer*)

fric·as·see   (frĭk′ ȧ·sē′)
fric·tion   (frĭk′ shŭn)
Fri·day   (frī′ dĭ)
fried   (frīd)
friend·ly   (frĕnd′ lĭ)
  friend·li·er, -li·est, -li·ness
frieze   (frēz)
  (ornamented band)
frig·ate   (frĭg′ ĭt)
fright   (frīt)
  -ful·ly   -ful·ness
  fright·en   fright·ful
frig·id   (frĭj′ ĭd)
  fri·gid·i·ty   (frĭ·jĭd′ ĭ·tĭ)
fri·jole   (frē′ hōl)
fringe   (frĭnj)
  fring·ing
frip·per·y   (frĭp′ ẽr·ĭ)
  frip·per·ies
frisk·y   (frĭs′ kĭ)
  frisk·i·er, -i·est, -i·ly, -i·ness
frit·ter   (frĭt′ ẽr)
friv·o·lous   (frĭv′ ô·lŭs)
  fri·vol·i·ty   (frĭ·vŏl′ ĭ·tĭ)
  -ties
frog·man   (frŏg′ măn)
frol·ic   (frŏl′ ĭk)
  frol·ick·er   frol·ick·y
  frol·ic·some
front·age   (frŭn′ tĭj)
fron·tal   (frŭn′ tǎl)
  -tal·ly
fron·tiers·man   (frŭn·tẽrz′ măn)
fron·tis·piece   (frŭn′ tĭs·pēs)
frost·bite   (frôst′ bīt′)
  frost·bit·ten   (-bĭt′ 'n)
froth·y   (frŏth′ ĭ)
  froth·i·ness
frown   (froun)
fro·zen   (frō′ z'n)
fru·gal   (froō′ gǎl)
  fru·gal·i·ty   (froō·găl′ ĭ·tĭ)
  fru·gal·ly
fruit   (froōt)
  -ful·ly   -ful·ness
  fruit·cake   fruit·ful
  fruit·less
fru·i·tion   (froō·ĭsh′ ŭn)
frus·trate   (frŭs′ trāt)
  -trat·ing
  frus·tra·tion   (frŭs·trā′ shŭn)
fry   (frī)
  fried   fry·ing
  fry·er (chicken; see *friar*)
fuch·sia   (fū′ shà)

fu·el (fū′ ĕl)
-eled -el·ing
fu·gi·tive (fū′ jĭ·tĭv)
fugue (fūg)
ful·crum (fŭl′ krŭm)
ful·fill (fŏŏl·fĭl′)
ful·fill·ment
full (fŏŏl)
full·back full-blood·eđ
full-blown full-fledged
full-sized ful·ly
ful·some (fŏŏl′ sŭm)
fum·ble (fŭm′ b′l)
-bling
fu·mi·gate (fū′ mĭ·gāt)
-gat·ing
fu·mi·ga·tion (fū′ mĭ·gā′ shŭn)
fu·mi·ga·tor
func·tion (fŭngk′ shŭn)
func·tion·al -al·ly
func·tion·ar·y
fun·da·men·tal
(fŭn′ đȧ·men′ tđl)
-tal·ly
fu·ner·al (fū′ nĕr·đl)
fu·ne·re·al (fū·nĕr′ ê·đl)
fun·gus (fŭng′ gŭs)
_pl._ fun·gi (fŭn′ jī)
fun·nel (fŭn′ ĕl)
fun·neled fun·nel·ing
fun·ny (fŭn′ ĭ)
fun·ni·est
fur (fûr)
fur·ry
fur·bish (fûr′ bĭsh)
fu·ri·ous (fū′ rĭ·ŭs)
furl (fûrl)
fur·long (fûr′ lŏng)
fur·lough (fûr′ lō)
fur·nace (fûr′ nĭs)
fur·nish·ings (fûr′ nĭsh·ĭngz)
fur·ni·ture (fûr′ nĭ·tůr)
fu·ror (fū′ rôr)
fur·ri·er (fûr′ ĭ·ẽr)
fur·row (fûr′ ō)
fur·ther (fûr′ thĕr)
(more distant in time, degree, or
quantity; see _farther_)
fur·ther·ance fur·ther·more
fur·ther·most fur·thest
fur·tive (fûr′ tĭv)
fu·ry (fū′ rĭ)
-ries
fuse (fūz)
fus·ing

fu·se·lage (fū′ zĕ·läzh′)
fu·sel oil (fū′ zĕl)
fu·si·ble (fū′ zĭ·b′l)
fu·sil·lade (fū′ zĭ·lād′)
fu·sion bomb (fū′ zhŭn)
fus·sy (fŭs′ ĭ)
fuss·i·ly -i·ness
fu·tile (fū′ tĭl)
fu·tile·ly
fu·til·i·ty (fū·tĭl′ ĭ·tĭ)
fu·ture (fū′ tůr)
fu·tu·ri·ty (fū·tū′ rĭ·tĭ)
fuz·zy (fŭz′ ĭ)

G

gab·ar·dine (găb′ ẽr·dēn′)
gad·a·bout (găd′ ȧ·bout′)
gad·fly (găd′ flī′)
-flies
gadg·et (găj′ ĕt)
Gael·ic (gāl′ ĭk)
(Irish; see _Gallic_)
gai·e·ty (gā′ ĕ·tĭ)
-ties
gai·ly (gā′ lĭ)
gain·ful (gān′ fŏŏl)
-ful·ly -ful·ness
gain·say (gān′ sā′)
gait (gāt)
(manner of walking; see _gate_)
gal·ax·y (găl′ đk·sĭ)
-ax·ies
ga·lac·tic (gȧ·lăk′ tĭk)
Gal·i·lee (găl′ ĭ·lē)
Gal·i·le·an (găl′ ĭ·lē′ đn)
gal·lant (găl′ đnt)
gal·lant·ry -ries
gal·le·on (găl′ ê·ŭn)
gal·ler·y (găl′ ẽr·ĭ)
gal·ler·ies
gal·ley (găl′ ĭ)
Gal·lic (găl′ ĭk)
(French; see _Gaelic_)
gal·lon (găl′ ŭn)
abbr. gal.
gal·lop (găl′ ŭp)
gal·loped gal·lop·ing
gall·stone (gôl′ stōn′)
Gal·lup poll (găl′ ŭp)
ga·lore (gȧ·lōr′)
ga·losh (gȧ·lŏsh′)
(overshoe; see _goulash_)

gal·va·nize   (găl′ vá·nīz)
-niz·ing
gal·van·ic   (găl·văn′ ĭk)
gal·va·ni·za·tion
    (găl′ vá·nĭ·zā′ shŭn)
Gal·ves·ton, Tex.
    (găl′ vĕs·tŭn)
gam·bit   (găm′ bĭt)
gam·ble   (găm′ b'l)
    (bet)   -bling
gam·bol   (găm′ bŭl)
    (frolic)   -boled, -bol·ing
game   (găm)
    game bird   game dog
    game fish   game·keep·er
    game laws   game·ster
    game ward·en   gam·y
gam·ma   (găm′ á)
    gam·ma glob·u·lin
    gam·ma rays
gam·ut   (găm′ ŭt)
Gan·dhi, Mo·han·das
    (gän′ dē,
    mō′ hán·däs)
    title: Ma·hat·ma   (má·hät′ má)
gan·gling   (găng′ glĭng)
gang·plank   (găng′ plăngk′)
gan·grene   (găng′ grēn)
    gan·gre·nous   (-grē′ nŭs)
gang·ster   (găng′ stēr)
ga·rage   (gá·räzh′)
gar·bage   (gär′ bĭj)
gar·den·er   (gär′ d'n·ēr)
gar·de·ni·a   (gär·dē′ nĭ·á)
gar·gle   (gär′ g'l)
    -gling
gar·goyle   (gär′ goil)
gar·ish   (gâr′ ĭsh)
gar·land   (gär′ lănd)
gar·lic   (gär′ lĭk)
    gar·lick·y
gar·nish·ee   (gär′ nĭsh·ē′)
gar·ri·son   (găr′ ĭ·sŭn)
gar·ru·lous   (găr′ û·lŭs)
    gar·ru·li·ty   (gá·rōō′ lĭ·tĭ)
gas   (găs)
    gas·e·ous   (găs′ ē·ŭs)
    gas·light   gas·o·line
    gas·sing   gas sta·tion
gas·ket   (găs′ kĕt)
gas·tric   (găs′ trĭk)
gas·tron·o·my   (găs·trŏn′ ŏ·mĭ)
    gas·tro·nom·ic
    (găs′ trŏ·nŏm′ ĭk)

gate   (gāt)
    (fence opening; see gait)
    gate·house   gate·keep·er
    gate·way
gath·er·ing   (găth′ ēr·ĭng)
gauche   (gōsh)
    gauche·ly
    gau·che·rie   (gō′ shē·rē′)
gaud·y   (gôd′ ĭ)
    gaud·i·er, -i·est, -i·ly, -i·ness
gauge   (gāj)
    gaug·ing
Gau·guin, Paul   (gō′ găN′)
gaunt   (gônt)
gaunt·let   (gônt′ lĕt)
gauze   (gôz)
    gauz·y
gav·el   (găv′ ĕl)
gawk·y   (gôk′ ĭ)
    gawk·i·ness
ga·zelle   (gá·zĕl′)
ga·zette   (gá·zĕt′)
    gaz·et·teer   (găz′ ĕ·tēr′)
gear·shift   (gēr′ shĭft′)
Gei·ger count·er
    (gī′ gēr)
gei·sha   (gā′ shá)
gel·a·tin   (jĕl′ á·tĭn)
    ge·lat·i·nous   (jē·lăt′ ĭ·nŭs)
gen·darme   (zhän·därm′)
gen·e·al·o·gy   (jĕn′ ē·ăl′ ŏ·jĭ)
    gen·e·al·o·gist
gen·er·al   (jĕn′ ēr·ăl)
    gen·er·al·is·si·mo
    (jĕn′ ēr·ăl·ĭs′ ĭ·mō)
    gen·er·al·i·za·tion
    (jĕn′ ēr·ăl·ĭ·zā′ shŭn)
    gen·er·al·ly
gen·er·ate   (jĕn′ ēr·āt)
    -at·ing
    gen·er·a·tion   (jĕn′ ēr·ā′ shŭn)
    gen·er·a·tive   (jĕn′ ēr·ā′ tĭv)
    gen·er·a·tor
ge·ner·ic   (jē·nĕr′ ĭk)
gen·er·ous   (jĕn′ ēr·ŭs)
    gen·er·os·i·ty   (jĕn′ ēr·ŏs′ ĭ·tĭ)
    -ties
gen·e·sis   (jĕn′ ē·sĭs)
ge·net·ics   (jē·nĕt′ ĭks)
    ge·net·i·cist   (jē·nĕt′ ĭ·sĭst)
Gen·ghis Khan   (jĕng′ gĭs kän′)
gen·ial   (jēn′ yăl)
    -ial·ly
    ge·ni·al·i·ty   (jē′ nĭ·ăl′ ĭ·tĭ)
gen·i·tal   (jĕn′ ĭ·tăl)

gen·i·tive   (jĕn′ ĭ·tĭv)
gen·ius   (jēn′ yŭs)
gen·o·cide   (jĕn′ ŏ·sīd)
gen·re   (zhän′ r′)
gen·teel   (jĕn·tēl′)
  -teel·ly
gen·tian   (jĕn′ shăn)
gen·tile   (jĕn′ tīl)
gen·til·i·ty   (jĕn·tĭl′ ĭ·tĭ)
gen·tle   (jĕn′ t′l)
  gen·tle·man   gen·tle·ness
  gen·tlest   gen·tly
gen·try   (jĕn′ trĭ)
gen·u·flect   (jĕn′ û·flĕkt)
  gen·u·flec·tion
     (jĕn′ û·flĕk′ shŭn)
gen·u·ine   (jĕn′ û·ĭn)
ge·nus   (jē′ nŭs)
  pl. gen·er·a   (jĕn′ ēr·ȧ)
ge·o·det·ic   (jē′ ŏ·dĕt′ ĭk)
ge·og·ra·phy   (jē·ŏg′ rȧ·fĭ)
  ge·og·ra·pher
  ge·o·graph·i·cal
     (jē′ ŏ·grăf′ ĭ·kȧl)
ge·ol·o·gy   (jē·ŏl′ ŏ·jĭ)
  ge·o·log·ic   (jē′ ŏ·lŏj′ ĭk)
  ge·ol·o·gist   (jē·ŏl′ ŏ·jĭst)
ge·om·e·try   (jē·ŏm′ ĕ·trĭ)
  ge·o·met·ric   (jē′ ŏ·mĕt′ rĭk)
  ge·o·met·ri·cal
     (jē′ ŏ·mĕt′ rĭ·kȧl)
ge·o·phys·ics   (jē′ ŏ·fĭz′ ĭks)
ge·o·po·lit·i·cal
     (jē′ ŏ·pŏ·lĭt′ ĭ·kȧl)
Geor·gia   (jôr′ jȧ)
  abbr. Ga.
  Geor·gi·an   (jôr′ jĭ·ȧn)
ge·ra·ni·um   (jē·rā′ nĭ·ŭm)
ger·i·at·rics   (jĕr′ ĭ·ăt′ rĭks)
ger·mane   (jûr·mān′)
ger·mi·cide   (jûr′ mĭ·sīd)
ger·mi·nal   (jûr′ mĭ·năl)
ger·mi·na·tion   (jûr′ mĭ·nā′ shŭn)
germ·proof   (jûrm′ prōōf′)
ger·ry·man·der   (gĕr′ ĭ·măn′ dēr)
ger·und   (jĕr′ ŭnd)
Ge·sta·po   (gĕ·stä′ pō)
ges·ta·tion   (jĕs·tā′ shŭn)
ges·tic·u·late   (jĕs·tĭk′ û·lāt)
  -lat·ing
  ges·tic·u·la·tion
     (jĕs·tĭk′ û·lā′ shŭn)
ges·ture   (jĕs′ tûr)
Ge·sund·heit   (gĕ·zōōnt′ hīt)
get·a·way   (gĕt′ ȧ·wä′)

get·ting   (gĕt′ ĭng)
gey·ser   (gī′ zēr)
Gha·na   (gä′ nȧ)
  Gha·na·ian   (gä′ nȧ·yȧn)
ghast·ly   (gȧst′ lĭ)
  ghast·li·er, -li·est, -li·ness
ghet·to   (gĕt′ ō)
  ghet·tos
ghost   (gōst)
  ghost·like   ghost·li·ness
  ghost·ly   ghost writ·er
  ghost·writ·ten
ghoul·ish   (gōōl′ ĭsh)
GI   (jē′ ī′)
  pl. GIs
gi·ant   (jī′ ȧnt)
gib·ber·ish   (jĭb′ ēr·ĭsh)
gibe   (jīb)
  (also *jibe*)   gib·ing
gib·let   (jĭb′ lĕt)
Gi·bral·tar   (jĭ·brôl′ tēr)
gid·dy   (gĭd′ ĭ)
  gid·di·ness
gi·gan·tic   (jĭ·găn′ tĭk)
gig·gle   (gĭg′ ′l)
  gig·gling   gig·gly
gig·o·lo   (jĭg′ ŏ·lō)
  -los
gild   (gĭld)
  (plate with gold; see *guild*)
  gilt-edged
gim·mick   (gĭm′ ĭk)
gin·ger   (jĭn′ jēr)
  gin·ger ale   gin·ger·bread
  gin·ger·snap
ging·ham   (gĭng′ ȧm)
gin·gi·vi·tis   (jĭn′ jĭ·vī′ tĭs)
gin rum·my   (jĭn′ rŭm′ ĭ)
gi·raffe   (jĭ·răf′)
gird·er   (gûr′ dēr)
gir·dle   (gûr′ d′l)
  -dling
girth   (gûrth)
gist   (jĭst)
give   (gĭv)
  giv·ing   give-and-take
  give·a·way
giz·zard   (gĭz′ ērd)
gla·cier   (glā′ shēr)
  gla·cial   (glā′ shȧl)
  gla·ci·a·tion   (glā′ sĭ·ā′ shŭn)
glad   (glăd)
  glad·den   glad·dest
  glad·ly
glad·i·a·tor   (glăd′ ĭ·ā′ tēr)

glad·i·o·la   (glăd′ ĭ·ō′ lá)
glam·our   (glăm′ ẽr)
   glam·or·ize   -iz·ing
   glam·or·ous
glance   (gláns)
   glanc·ing
glan·du·lar   (glăn′ dụ·lẽr)
glar·ing   (glâr′ ĭng)
Glas·gow, Scot·land
     (glăs′ kō)
glass   (glás)
   glass blow·er   glass·ful
   glass·ware
gleam·ing   (glēm′ ĭng)
glee club   (glē)
glee·ful   (glē′ fŏŏl)
glib·ness   (glĭb′ nĕs)
glide   (glīd)
   glid·ing
glim·mer   (glĭm′ ẽr)
glimpse   (glĭmps)
   glimps·ing
glis·ten   (glĭs′ 'n)
gloat·ing   (glōt′ ĭng)
glob·al   (glōb′ ăl)
   -al·ly
glob·u·lar   (glŏb′ ů·lẽr)
gloom·y   (glōōm′ ĭ)
   gloom·i·er, -i·est, -i·ly, -i·ness
glo·ri·fy   (glō′ rĭ·fī)
   -fied   -fy·ing
   glo·ri·fi·ca·tion
     (glō′ rĭ·fĭ·kā′ shŭn)
glo·ri·ous   (glō′ rĭ·ŭs)
glos·sa·ry   (glŏs′ á·rĭ)
   -ries
glos·sy   (glŏs′ ĭ)
   gloss·i·ness
Glouces·ter, Mass.
     (glŏs′ tẽr)
glow·worm   (glō′ wûrm′)
glu·cose   (glōō′ kōs)
glue   (glōō)
   glue·y   glu·ing
glum·ly   (glŭm′ lĭ)
glut·ton   (glŭt′ 'n)
   glut·ton·ous   (glŭt′ 'n·ŭs)
   glut·ton·y
glyc·er·in   (glĭs′ ẽr·ĭn)
gnarl   (närl)
gnash   (năsh)
gnat   (năt)
gnaw   (nô)
gnome   (nōm)
goad   (gōd)

goal   (gōl)
   goal·ee   (gōl′ ē)
gob·let   (gŏb′ lĕt)
gob·lin   (gŏb′ lĭn)
god   (gŏd)
   god·child   god·daugh·ter
   god·dess   god·fa·ther
   god·send
Goe·the, Jo·hann von
     (fôn gụ′ tĕ, yō′ hän)
go-get·ter   (gō′ gĕt′ ẽr)
gog·gles   (gŏg′ 'lz)
   gog·gle-eyed
Gogh, Vin·cent van
     (văn kŏk′, vĭn·sĕnt′)
gold   (gōld)
   gold·brick v.   gold dig·ger
   gold·fish
gold·en·rod   (gōl′ dĕn·rŏd′)
golf   (gŏlf)
   (game; see gulf)
   golf club
Go·li·ath   (gō·lī′ ăth)
Go·mor·rah   (gō·mŏr′ á)
gon·do·la   (gŏn′ dō·lá)
gon·or·rhe·a   (gŏn′ ŏ·rē′ á)
good   (gŏŏd)
   good-bye   good·heart·ed
   good-hu·mored good will
goose   (gōōs)
   goose·ber·ry   goose pim·ple
   goose step
go·pher   (gō′ fẽr)
gor·geous   (gôr′ jŭs)
go·ril·la   (gŏ·rĭl′ á)
   (ape; see guerrilla)
gos·pel   (gŏs′ pĕl)
gos·sa·mer   (gŏs′ á·mẽr)
gos·sip   (gŏs′ ĭp)
   gos·sip·ing   gos·sip·y
Go·tham   (gŏth′ ăm)
Goth·ic   (gŏth′ ĭk)
got·ten   (gŏt′ 'n)
gouge   (gouj)
   goug·ing
gou·lash   (gōō′ läsh)
   (Hungarian dish; see galosh)
gourd   (gōrd)
gour·met   (gŏŏr′ mā)
gout   (gout)
   gout·y
gov·ern·a·ble   (gŭv′ ẽr·ná·b'l)
gov·ern·ess   (gŭv′ ẽr·nĕs)

gov·ern·ment   (gŭv′ ĕrn·mĕnt)
  gov·ern·men·tal
          (gŭv′ ĕrn·mĕn′ t* al)
  -tal·ly
gov·er·nor   (gŭv′ ĕr·nĕr)
  gov·er·nor gen·er·al
  gov·er·nor·ship
gown   (goun)
grace   (grās)
  grace·ful, -ful·ly, -ful·ness
  grace·less
gra·cious   (grā′ shŭs)
gra·da·tion   (grȧ·dā′ shŭn)
  (series)
gra·di·ent   (grā′ dĭ·ĕnt)
grad·u·al   (grăd′ û·ȧl)
  -al·ly   -al·ness
grad·u·ate   (grăd′ û·āt)
  -at·ing
  grad·u·a·tion   (grăd′ û·ā′ shŭn)
  (commencement)
grain·y   (grān′ ĭ)
  grain·i·ness
gram   (grăm)
gram·mar   (grăm′ ĕr)
  gram·mar·i·an   (grȧ·mâr′ ĭ·ȧn)
  gram·mat·i·cal
        (grȧ·măt′ ĭ·kȧl)
  -cal·ly
gran·a·ry   (grăn′ ȧ·rĭ)
  -ries
grand   (grănd)
  grand·child   grand·dad
  grand·daugh·ter
  grand duke   grand·par·ent
  grand·son   grand·stand
gran·deur   (grăn′ dụr)
gran·dil·o·quence
    (grăn·dĭl′ ȯ·kwĕns)
gran·di·ose   (grăn′ dĭ·ōs)
  -ose·ly
gran·ite   (grăn′ ĭt)
grant-in-aid   (grănt′ ĭn·ād′)
  grants-in-aid
gran·u·late   (grăn′ û·lāt)
  -lat·ing
  gran·u·lar   (grăn′ û·lĕr)
grape   (grāp)
  grape·fruit   grape juice
  grape·shot   grape·vine
graph·ic   (grăf′ ĭk)
  graph·i·cal·ly
graph·ite   (grăf′ īt)
grap·ple   (grăp′ 'l)
  grap·pling hook

grass·hop·per   (grȧs′ hŏp′ ĕr)
grate   (grāt)
  grat·ing
grate·ful   (grāt′ fŏŏl)
  grate·ful·ly   -ful·ness
grat·i·fy   (grăt′ ĭ·fī)
  -fied   -fy·ing
  grat·i·fi·ca·tion
        (grăt′ ĭ·fĭ·kā′ shŭn)
grat·i·tude   (grăt′ ĭ·tūd)
gra·tu·i·ty   (grȧ·tū′ ĭ·tĭ)
  -ties
  gra·tu·i·tous   (grȧ·tū′ ĭ·tŭs)
grav·el   (grăv′ ĕl)
  -el·ly
grav·en im·age   (grāv′ ĕn)
grave·stone   (grāv′ stōn′)
grav·i·ty   (grăv′ ĭ·tĭ)
gra·vy   (grā′ vĭ)
  -vies
gray   (grā)
  gray·beard   gray·ness
grease   (grēs)
  greas·ing   greas·i·ness
  greas·y
great   (grāt)
  great-grand·fa·ther
  Great Lakes
  Great Smok·y Mts.
Gre·cian   (grē′ shȧn)
Gre·co, El   (ĕl grā′ kŏ)
greed·y   (grēd′ ĭ)
  greed·i·er, -i·est, -i·ly, -i·ness
green   (grēn)
  green·er·y   green-eyed
  green·gage   green·horn
  green·house
Green·wich Vil·lage
    (grĕn′ ĭch)
greet·ing   (grēt′ ĭng)
gre·gar·i·ous   (grē·gâr′ ĭ·ŭs)
Gre·go·ri·an cal·en·dar
    (grē·gō′ rĭ·ȧn)
grem·lin   (grĕm′ lĭn)
gre·nade   (grē·nād′)
gren·a·dier   (grĕn′ ȧ·dẹr′)
gren·a·dine   (grĕn′ ȧ·dēn′)
Gresh·am′s law   (grĕsh′ ȧmz)
grey·hound   (grā′ hound′)
grid·dle·cake   (grĭd′ 'l·kāk′)
grid·i·ron   (grĭd′ ī·ẽrn)
grief·-strick·en   (grēf′ strĭk′ ĕn)
grieve   (grēv)
  griev·ing
  griev·ance   (grēv′ ȧns)

griev·ous (grēv′ ŭs)
grill (grĭl)
  (to broil)
grille (grĭl)
  (a grating)
grim (grĭm)
  grim·mest grim·ly
gri·mace (grĭ·mās′)
  -mac·ing
grime (grīm)
  grim·i·ness grim·y
grin (grĭn)
  grinned grin·ning
grind·stone (grīnd′ stōn′)
grip (grĭp)
  gripped grip·ping
gripe (grīp)
  grip·ing
gris·ly (grĭz′ lĭ)
  gris·li·est gris·li·ness
gris·tle (grĭs′ ′l)
grist·mill (grĭst′ mĭl′)
griz·zly bear (grĭz′ ′lĭ)
gro·cer (grō′ sẽr)
  gro·cer·y -cer·ies
grog·gy (grŏg′ ĭ)
  grog·gi·ness
grom·met (grŏm′ ĕt)
gros·beak (grōs′ bēk′)
gros·grain rib·bon
    (grō′ grān′)
gro·tesque (grō·těsk′)
  -tesque·ly
grot·to (grŏt′ ō)
grouch·y (grouch′ ĭ)
  grouch·i·ness
ground (ground)
  ground floor ground hog
  ground·work
grouse (grous)
grov·el (grŏv′ ′l)
  -eled -el·ing
grown·up (grōn′ ŭp′) n.
growth (grōth)
grub (grŭb)
  grub·bi·ness grub·by
  grub·stake
grudge (grŭj)
  grudg·ing·ly
gru·el (grōō′ ĕl)
  gru·el·ing
grue·some (grōō′ sŭm)
grum·ble (grŭm′ b′l)
  -bling

Gua·da·lupe (gwŏd′ ′l·ōōp)
  Riv. & Mt., Tex.
Gua·de·loupe Is.,
  West In·dies (gwŏd′ ′l·ōōp)
Guan·tá·na·mo
    (gwän·tä′ nä·mŏ)
guar·an·tee (găr′ ăn·tē′)
  -tee·ing
  guar·an·tor (găr′ ăn·tôr)
guar·an·ty (găr′ ăn·tĭ)
  -ties
guard (gärd)
guard·i·an (gär′ dĭ·ăn)
Gua·te·ma·la (gwä′ tĕ·mä′ lá)
Gua·ya·quil, (gwä′ yä·kēl′)
  Ec·ua·dor
gu·ber·na·to·ri·al
    (gū′ bẽr·na·tō′ rĭ·ál)
Guern·sey (gûrn′ zĭ)
  -seys
guer·ril·la (gĕ·rĭl′ á)
  (irregular warrior; see gorilla)
guess·work (gĕs′ wûrk′)
guest (gĕst)
guf·faw (gŭ·fô′)
Gui·a·na (gĕ·ä′ ná)
  (S. Amer. region)
guide (gīd)
  guid·ing guid·a·ble
  guid·ance guide·book
  guide·post guid·ed mis·sile
guild (gĭld)
  (association; see gild)
guile (gīl)
  guile·less
guil·lo·tine (gĭl′ ō·tēn)
guilt·y (gĭl′ tĭ)
  guilt·i·ly
Guin·ea, Afr. (gĭn′ ĭ)
guin·ea pig (gĭn′ ĭ)
guise (gīz)
gui·tar (gĭ·tär′)
gulf (gŭlf)
  (separation; see golf)
gul·li·ble (gŭl′ ĭ·b′l)
gul·ly (gŭl′ ĭ)
  gul·lies
gum·bo (gŭm′ bō)
gun (gŭn)
  gun·man gun·ner
  gun·ner·y gun play
  gun pow·der gun·shot
gur·gle (gûr′ g′l)
  -gling
gus·to (gŭs′ tō)

gust·y   (gŭs′ tĭ)
  gust·i·ness
gut·ter·snipe   (gŭt′ ĕr·snĭp′)
gut·tur·al   (gŭt′ ĕr·ăl)
  -al·ly
guz·zle   (gŭz′ 'l)
  guz·zling
gym·na·si·um   (jĭm·nā′ zĭ·ŭm)
gym·nast   (jĭm′ năst)
  gym·nas·tic   (jĭm·năs′ tĭk)
gyn·e·col·o·gy   (jĭn′ ê·kŏl′ ô·jĭ)
  gyn·e·co·log·i·cal
       (jĭn′ ê·kô·lŏj′ ĭ·kăl)
gyp   (jĭp)
  gypped   gyp·ping
gyp·sum   (jĭp′ sŭm)
gyp·sy   (jĭp′ sĭ)
  -sies
gy·rate   (jī′ rāt)
  -rat·ing
  gy·ra·tion   (jī·rā′ shŭn)
  gy·ra·tor
gy·ro·scope   (jī′ rô·skōp)

H

ha·be·as cor·pus
    (hā′ bê·ăs kôr′ pŭs)
hab·er·dash·er·y
    (hăb′ ĕr·dăsh′ ĕr·ĭ)
hab·it   (hăb′ ĭt)
  hab·it·a·ble   hab·i·tat
  hab·i·ta·tion   (hăb′ ĭ·tā′ shŭn)
  ha·bit·u·al   (há·bĭt′ û·ăl)
  -al·ly
  ha·bit·u·a·tion
    (há·bĭt′ û·ā′ shŭn)
  ha·bit·u·é   (há·bĭt′ û·ā′)
ha·ci·en·da   (hăs′ ĭ·ĕn′ dá)
hack·neyed   (hăk′ nĭd)
had·dock   (hăd′ ŭk)
Ha·des   (hā′ dēz)
hag·gard   (hăg′ ērd)
hag·gle   (hăg′ 'l)
  hag·gling
Hague, The, Neth·er·lands
    (hāg)
hail   (hāl)
  hail·stone   hail·storm
hair   (hâr)
  hair·breadth   hair·dress·er
  hair·split·ter   hair·spring
  hair trig·ger   hair·y

Hai·ti   (hā′ tĭ)
  Hai·ti·an   (hā′ tĭ·ăn)
hal·cy·on   (hăl′ sĭ·ŭn)
hale   (hāl)
  (and hearty)
half   (hăf)
  pl. halves   half-and-half
  half·back   half-baked
  half-breed   half broth·er
  half-caste   half dol·lar
  half·heart·ed   half-hour
  half life   half-mast
  half-moon   half nel·son
  half sis·ter   half-tim·bered
  half·way   half-wit·ted
hal·i·but   (hăl′ ĭ·bŭt)
hal·i·to·sis   (hăl′ ĭ·tō′ sĭs)
hal·le·lu·jah   (hăl′ ê·lōō′ yá)
hall·mark   (hôl′ märk′)
hal·lowed ground
         (hăl′ ōd)
Hal·low·een   (hăl′ ô·ēn′)
hal·lu·ci·na·tion
    (há·lū′ sĭ·nā′ shŭn)
ha·lo   (hā′ lō)
  -los
hal·ter   (hôl′ tĕr)
halt·ing   (hôl′ tĭng)
halve   (hăv)
  halv·ing
hal·yard   (hăl′ yĕrd)
ham·burg·er   (hăm′ bûr·gĕr)
Ham·let   (hăm′ lĕt)
ham·mer and sick·le
    (hăm′ ĕr ănd sĭk′ 'l)
ham·mer·head shark
    (hăm′ ĕr·hĕd′)
ham·mock   (hăm′ ŭk)
ham·per   (hăm′ pĕr)
ham·ster   (hăm′ stĕr)
ham·string   (hăm′ strĭng′)
hand   (hănd)
  hand·bag   hand·bill
  hand·cuff   hand·ful
  hand gre·nade   hand·made
  hand-me-down   hand·out
  hand·spring   hand-to-mouth
  hand·writ·ing
hand·i·cap   (hăn′ dĭ·kăp)
  -capped   -cap·ping
hand·i·craft   (hăn′ dĭ·krăft)
hand·i·work   (hăn′ dĭ·wûrk′)
han·dle   (hăn′ d'l)
  -dling

hand·some (hăn′ sŭm)
-some·ly
hand·y (hăn′ dĭ)
hand·i·ly hand·y man
hang (hăng)
hang·nail hang·out
hang-o·ver
hang·ar (hăng′ ēr)
(for aircraft)
hang·er (hăng′ ēr)
(for clothes)
han·ker·ing (hăng′ kēr·ĭng)
han·som cab (hăn′ sŭm)
Ha·nuk·kah (hä′ nŏŏ·kä)
hap·haz·ard (hăp′ hăz′ ērd)
hap·pen·ing (hăp′ ĕn·ĭng)
hap·py (hăp′ ĭ)
hap·pi·er hap·pi·est
hap·pi·ly hap·pi·ness
hap·py-go-luck·y
har·a-kir·i (hăr′ ȧ·kĭr′ ĭ)
ha·rangue (hȧ·răng′)
-rangu·ing
har·ass (hăr′ ȧs)
har·ass·ment
har·bin·ger (här′ bĭn·jēr)
har·bor (här′ bēr)
hard (härd)
hard-bit·ten hard-boiled
hard·en hard·head·ed
hard·heart·ed hard·ship
hard·tack hard·ware
har·dy (här′ dĭ)
har·di·ness
hare·brained (hâr′ brānd′)
hare·lip (hâr′ lĭp′)
ha·rem (hä′ rĕm)
hark·en (här′ kĕn)
Har·le·quin (här′ lĕ·kwĭn)
har·lot (här′ lŏt)
harm·ful (härm′ fŏŏl)
-ful·ly -ful·ness
har·mon·i·ca (här·mŏn′ ĭ·kȧ)
har·mo·ny (här′ mŏ·nĭ)
-nies
har·mon·ic (här·mŏn′ ĭk)
har·mo·ni·ous (här·mŏ′ nĭ·ŭs)
har·mo·niz·ing
(här′ mŏ·nīz′ ĭng)
har·ness (här′ nĕs)
har·poon (här·pōōn′)
harp·si·chord (härp′ sĭ·kôrd)
har·row·ing (hăr′ ō·ĭng)
har·ry (hăr′ ĭ)
har·ried har·ry·ing

Har·vard (univ.) (här′ vērd)
har·vest·er (här′ vĕs·tēr)
has-been (hăz′ bĭn′)
ha·sen·pfef·fer (hä′ zĕn(p)fĕf′ ēr)
has·sock (hăs′ ŭk)
haste (hāst)
has·ten (hās′ ′n)
hast·y
hatch (hăch)
hatch·er·y (hăch′ ēr·ĭ)
hatch·et (hăch′ ĕt)
hatch·et-faced
hate·ful (hāt′ fŏŏl)
-ful·ly -ful·ness
ha·tred (hā′ trĕd)
Hat·ter·as, Cape, (hăt′ ēr·ȧs)
N.C.
haugh·ty (hô′ tĭ)
haugh·ti·er -ti·est
-ti·ly -ti·ness
haul (hôl)
haunch (hônch)
haunt (hônt)
Ha·van·a, Cu·ba
(hȧ·văn′ ȧ)
ha·ven (hā′ vĕn)
hav·er·sack (hăv′ ēr·săk)
hav·oc (hăv′ ŭk)
Ha·wai·i (hȧ·wī′ ê)
Ha·wai·ian (hȧ·wī′ ȧn)
hawk-eyed (hôk′ īd′)
haw·thorn (hô′ thôrn)
hay (hā)
hay fe·ver hay·fork
hay·loft hay·seed
hay·stack hay·wire
haz·ard·ous (hăz′ ēr·dŭs)
haze (hāz)
ha·zy
ha·zel·nut (hā′ z′l·nŭt′)
H-bomb (āch′ bŏm′)
head (hĕd)
head·ache head·dress
head·first head·gear
head-hunt·er head·light
head·line head·long
head·mas·ter
head-on col·li·sion
head·phone head·piece
head·quar·ters head·strong
head·wait·er head wind
heal (hēl)
(cure)
health·ful (hĕlth′ fŏŏl)
-ful·ly -ful·ness

health·y   (hĕl′ thĭ)
  health·i·ness
hear·say ev·i·dence
                             (hēr′ sā′)
hearse   (hûrs)
heart   (härt)
  heart·ache   heart·break·ing
  heart·burn   heart dis·ease
  heart·en·ing   heart·felt
  heart·less   heart-rend·ing
  heart-to-heart
hearth   (härth)
heat·er   (hēt′ ēr)
hea·then   (hē′ thĕn)
  hea·then·ish
heath·er   (hĕth′ ēr)
heave   (hēv)
  heav·ing
heav·en   (hĕv′ ĕn)
  heav·en·ward
heav·y   (hĕv′ ĭ)
  heav·i·er, -i·est, -i·ly, -i·ness
  heav·y-du·ty   heav·y·heart·ed
  heav·y·weight
He·bra·ic   (hē·brā′ ĭk)
heck·le   (hĕk′ 'l)
  -ling
hec·tic   (hĕk′ tĭk)
  hec·ti·cal·ly
hec·to·graph   (hĕk′ tȯ·gráf)
hedge   (hĕj)
  hedge·hog   hedge·row
he·don·ism   (hē′ dŏn·ĭz′m)
  he·don·ist
heed   (hēd)
  heed·ful, -ful·ly, -ful·ness
  heed·less
heel   (hēl)
  (foot part)
heft·y   (hĕf′ tĭ)
  heft·i·ness
He·ge·li·an   (hā·gā′ lĭ·ẟn)
he·gem·o·ny   (hē·jĕm′ ȯ·nĭ)
heif·er   (hĕf′ ēr)
heigh-ho   (hī′ hō′)
height   (hīt)
  height·en   (hīt′ 'n)
hei·nous   (hā′ nŭs)
heir   (âr)
  heir ap·par·ent
  heir·ess   heir·loom
hel·i·cal   (hĕl′ ĭ·kẟl)
hel·i·cop·ter   (hĕl′ ĭ·kŏp′ tēr)
he·li·o·trope   (hē′ lĭ·ȯ·trōp)
he·li·um   (hē′ lĭ·ŭm)

hell   (hĕl)
  hell·cat   hell-div·er
  hell-fire
Hel·len·ic   (hĕ·lĕn′ ĭk)
helm   (hĕlm)
hel·met   (hĕl′ mĕt)
  -met·ed
help   (hĕlp)
  help·ful, -ful·ly, -ful·ness
  help·less   help·mate
hel·ter-skel·ter   (hĕl′ tēr·skĕl′ tēr)
hem·i·sphere   (hĕm′ ĭ·sfēr)
  hem·i·spher·ic   (hĕm′ ĭ·sfĕr′ ĭk)
hem·lock   (hĕm′ lŏk)
he·mo·glo·bin   (hē′ mȯ·glō′ bĭn)
he·mo·phil·i·a   (hē′ mȯ·fĭl′ ĭ·ẟ)
  he·mo·phil·i·ac (-fĭl′ ĭ·ăk)
hem·or·rhage   (hĕm′ ȯ·rĭj)
hem·or·rhoid   (hĕm′ ȯ·roid)
hence·forth   (hĕns′ fôrth′)
  hence·for·ward
hench·man   (hĕnch′ mẟn)
hen·na   (hĕn′ ẟ)
  hen·naed   hen·na·ing
hen·pecked   (hĕn′ pĕkt′)
hep·a·ti·tis   (hĕp′ ẟ·tī′ tĭs)
Hep·ple·white   (hĕp′ 'l·hwīt)
her·ald   (hĕr′ ẟld)
  he·ral·dic   (hē·răl′ dĭk)
  her·ald·ry   (hĕr′ ẟld·rĭ)
herb   (ûrb)
  her·ba·ceous   (hûr·bā′ shŭs)
  herb·age   (ûr′ bĭj)
  her·biv·o·rous   (hûr·bĭv′ ȯ·rŭs)
her·cu·le·an   (hûr·kū′ lē·ẟn)
herds·man   (hûrdz′ mẟn)
here   (hēr)
  here·a·bout   here·aft·er
  here·at   here·by
  here·in   here·in·aft·er
  here·to·fore   here·unto
  here·up·on   here·with
he·red·i·tar·y   (hē·rĕd′ ĭ·tĕr′ ĭ)
he·red·i·ty   (hē·rĕd′ ĭ·tĭ)
Her·e·ford cat·tle
                             (hĕr′ ĕ·fērd)
her·e·sy   (hĕr′ ĕ·sĭ)
  -sies
  her·e·tic   (hĕr′ ĕ·tĭk)
  he·ret·i·cal   (hē·rĕt′ ĭ·kẟl)
her·it·age   (hĕr′ ĭ·tĭj)
her·met·ic   (hûr·mĕt′ ĭk)
  her·met·i·cal·ly sealed
her·mit   (hûr′ mĭt)
  her·mit·age   (hûr′ mĭ·tĭj)

her·ni·a (hûr′ nĭ·ȧ)
he·ro (hēr′ ō)
  -roes
  he·ro·ic (hē·rō′ ĭk)
  he·ro·i·cal·ly
  her·o·ine (hĕr′ ō·ĭn)
  her·o·ism (hĕr′ ō·ĭz′m)
  her·o·in (hĕr′ ō·ĭn)
    (drug)
her·on (hĕr′ ŭn)
    (bird)
her·ring·bone (hĕr′ ĭng·bōn′)
her·self (hûr·sĕlf′)
hes·i·tate (hĕz′ ĭ·tāt)
  -tat·ing
  hes·i·tan·cy (hĕz′ ĭ·tăn·sĭ)
  hes·i·tant (hĕz′ ĭ·tănt)
  hes·i·ta·tion (hĕz′ ĭ·tā′ shŭn)
Hes·sian (hĕsh′ ăn)
het·er·o·dox (hĕt′ ēr·ō·dŏks)
het·er·o·ge·ne·ous
    (hĕt′ ēr·ō·jē′ nē·ŭs)
  het·er·o·ge·ne·i·ty
    (-jē·nē′ ĭ·tĭ)
het·er·o·sex·u·al
    (hĕt′ ēr·ō·sĕk′ shōō·ȧl)
heu·ris·tic (hū·rĭs′ tĭk)
hew (hū)
    (cut; see hue)
  hewn (hūn)
hex·a·gon (hĕk′ sȧ·gŏn)
  hex·ag·o·nal (hĕks·ăg′ ō·nȧl)
hex·am·e·ter (hĕks·ăm′ ĕ·tēr)
hey·day (hā′ dā′)
hi·a·tus (hī·ā′ tŭs)
Hi·a·wa·tha (hī′ ȧ·wô′ thȧ)
hi·ber·nate (hī′ bēr·nāt)
  -nat·ing
  hi·ber·na·tion
    (hī′ bēr·nā′ shŭn)
hi·bis·cus (hī·bĭs′ kŭs)
hic·cup (hĭk′ ŭp)
hick·o·ry (hĭk′ ō·rĭ)
hid·den (hĭd′ 'n)
hide·bound (hīd′ bound′)
hid·e·ous (hĭd′ ē·ŭs)
hie (hī)
  hied hy·ing
hi·er·arch·y (hī′ ēr·är′ kĭ)
  -arch·ies
hi·er·o·glyph·ic
    (hī′ ēr·ō·glĭf′ ĭk)
hi-fi (hī′ fī′)
high (hī)
  high·ball high·born

high·brow
high-flown
high jump
high school
high-spir·it·ed
high-ten·sion
high fi·del·i·ty
high-fre·quen·cy
high·light
high-sound·ing
high-strung
high·way
hi·jack (hī′ jăk′)
hi·lar·i·ous (hĭ·lâr′ ĭ·ŭs)
  hi·lar·i·ty (hĭ·lăr′ ĭ·tĭ)
hill·bil·ly (hĭl′ bĭl′ ĭ)
Hi·ma·la·ya (mts.)
    (hĭ·mä′ lȧ·yȧ)
him·self (hĭm·sĕlf′)
hind·quar·ter (hīnd′ kwôr′ tēr)
hin·drance (hĭn′ drȧns)
hind·sight (hīnd′ sīt′)
Hin·du (hĭn′ dōō)
  Hin·du·ism (hĭn′ dōō·ĭz′m)
  Hin·du·sta·ni (hĭn′ dōō·stä′ nē)
hinge (hĭnj)
  hing·ing
hin·ter·land (hĭn′ tēr·lănd′)
Hip·po·crat·ic oath
    (hĭp′ ō·krăt′ ĭk)
hip·po·drome (hĭp′ ō·drōm)
hip·po·pot·a·mus
    (hĭp′ ō·pŏt′ ȧ·mŭs
  -mus·es
hir·a·ble (hīr′ ȧ·b'l)
hire·ling (hīr′ lĭng)
Hi·ro·hi·to (hē′ rō·hē′ tō)
hir·sute (hûr′ sūt)
his·ta·mine (hĭs′ tȧ·mēn)
his·tol·o·gy (hĭs·tŏl′ ō·jĭ)
his·to·ry (hĭs′ tō·rĭ)
  -ries
  his·to·ri·an (hĭs·tō′ rĭ·ăn)
  his·tor·ic (hĭs·tŏr′ ĭk)
  his·tor·i·cal (hĭs·tŏr′ ĭ·kȧl)
  -cal·ly
  his·to·ri·og·ra·pher
    (hĭs·tō′ rĭ·ŏg′ rȧ·fēr)
his·tri·on·ic (hĭs′ trĭ·ŏn′ ĭk)
hit-and-run (hĭt′ ănd run′)
hitch·hike (hĭch′ hīk′)
  -hik·ing
hith·er·to (hĭth′ ēr·tōō′)
hives (hīvz)
hoard (hōrd)
hoar·frost (hōr′ frŏst′)
hoarse (hōrs)
  hoarse·ly
hoar·y (hōr′ ĭ)
  hoar·i·ness
hoax (hōks)

hob·ble (hŏb′ ′l)
 hob·bling
hob·by (hŏb′ ĭ)
 hob·bies hob·by·horse
hob·gob·lin (hŏb′ gŏb′ lĭn)
hob·nail (hŏb′ nāl′)
hob·nob (hŏb′ nŏb′)
 -nobbed -nob·bing
ho·bo (hō′ bō)
 -boes
hock·ey (hŏk′ ĭ)
ho·cus-po·cus (hō′ kŭs·pō′ kŭs)
hod car·ri·er (hod)
hodge·podge (hŏj′ pŏj′)
hoe (hō)
 hoe·ing
hog·wash (hŏg′ wŏsh′)
hoi pol·loi (hoi′ pŏ·loi′)
hoist (hoist)
ho·kum (hō′ kŭm)
hold·up (hōld′ ŭp′)
hol·i·day (hŏl′ ĭ·dā)
ho·li·ness (hō′ lĭ·něs)
hol·lan·daise sauce
  (hŏl′ ăn·dāz′)
hol·low (hŏl′ ō)
hol·ly·hock (hŏl′ ĭ·hŏk)
hol·o·caust (hŏl′ ŏ·kôst)
hol·ster (hōl′ stĕr)
ho·ly (hō′ lĭ)
 ho·li·er ho·li·est
 ho·li·ness
hom·age (hŏm′ ĭj)
Hom·burg hat (hŏm′ bûrg)
home (hōm)
 home e·co·nom·ics
 home·made home·mak·er
 home run home·sick
 home·spun home·stead
 home·ward home·work
home·ly (hōm′ lĭ)
 home·li·ness
home·y (hōm′ ĭ)
hom·i·cide (hŏm′ ĭ·sīd)
 hom·i·cid·al (hŏm′ ĭ·sīd′ ăl)
hom·i·let·ic (hŏm′ ĭ·lĕt′ ĭk)
hom·i·ly (hŏm′ ĭ·lĭ)
 -lies
hom·i·ny grits (hŏm′ ĭ·nĭ)
ho·mo·ge·ne·ous
  (hō′ mŏ·jē′ nĕ·ŭs)
 ho·mo·ge·ne·i·ty
  (-jě·nē′ ĭ·tĭ)
ho·mog·e·nized milk
  (hō·mŏj′ ê·nīzd)

ho·mol·o·gous (hō·mŏl′ ŏ·gŭs)
hom·o·nym (hŏm′ ŏ·nĭm)
ho·mo·sex·u·al
  (hō′ mŏ·sĕk′ shŏŏ·ăl)
Hon·du·ras, (hŏn·dŏŏr′ ăs)
 Cen. Am.
hon·es·ty (ŏn′ ĕs·tĭ)
hon·ey (hŭn′ ĭ)
 hon·eyed hon·ey·bee
 hon·ey·comb
 hon·ey·dew mel·on
 hon·ey·moon hon·ey·suck·le
Hong Kong (hŏng′ kŏng′)
honk·y-tonk (hŏngk′ ĭ·tŏngk′)
hon·or (ŏn′ ēr)
 hon·or·a·ble
 hon·or·ar·y (ŏn′ ēr·ĕr′ ĭ)
hon·o·rar·i·um (ŏn′ ŏ·râr′ ĭ·ŭm)
hood·lum (hŏŏd′ lŭm)
hoo·doo (hōō′ dōō)
hood·wink (hŏŏd′ wĭngk)
hoo·ey (hōō′ ĭ)
hoof·er (hŏŏf′ ēr)
hook·up (hŏŏk′ ŭp′)
hook·y (hŏŏk′ ĭ)
hoo·li·gan (hōō′ lĭ·găn)
Hoo·sier (hōō′ zhēr)
hope·ful (hōp′ fŏŏl)
 -ful·ly -ful·ness
hop·per (hŏp′ ēr)
hop·scotch (hŏp′ skŏch′)
horde (hōrd)
ho·ri·zon (hō·rī′ z′n)
hor·i·zon·tal (hŏr′ ĭ·zŏn′ tăl)
 -tal·ly
hor·mone (hôr′ mōn)
hor·net (hôr′ nĕt)
hor·o·scope (hŏr′ ŏ·skōp)
hor·ren·dous (hŏ·rĕn′ dŭs)
hor·ri·ble (hŏr′ ĭ·b′l)
hor·rid (hŏr′ ĭd)
hor·ri·fy (hŏr′ ĭ·fī)
 -fied -fy·ing
 hor·ri·fi·ca·tion
  (hŏr′ ĭ·fĭ·kā′ shŭn)
hor·ror (hŏr′ ēr)
hors d'oeuvre (ôr′ dû′ vr′)
horse (hôrs)
 horse·back horse·fly
 horse·man·ship
 horse·pow·er horse-rad·ish
 horse sense horse·shoe
 hors·y
hor·ti·cul·ture (hôr′ tĭ·kŭl′ tûr)
ho·san·na (hō·zăn′ á)

ho·sier·y (hō′ zhēr· ĭ)
hos·pi·ta·ble (hŏs′ pĭ· tá· b'l)
 hos·pi·tal·i·ty (hŏs′ pĭ· tăl′ ĭ· tĭ)
hos·pi·tal (hŏs′ pĭt· ăl)
 hos·pi·tal·ize -iz·ing
hos·tage (hŏs′ tĭj)
hos·tel (hŏs′ tĕl)
 (inn; see *hostile*)
host·ess (hōs′ tĕs)
hos·tile (hŏs′ tĭl)
 (unfriendly; see *hostel*)
 hos·til·i·ty (hŏs·tĭl′ ĭ· tĭ)
 -ties
hot (hŏt)
 hot·bed hot-blood·ed
 hot dog hot·head·ed
 hot·house hot plate
 hot rod
ho·tel (hō·tĕl′)
hour·glass (our′ glás′)
house (hous)
 house·boat house·coat
 house·fly house·ful
 house·hold house·keep·er
 house or·gan house par·ty
 house·top house·warm·ing
 house·wife -wives
 house·work
hous·ing (houz′ ĭng)
hov·el (hŏv′ ĕl)
hov·er·ing (hŭv′ ēr· ĭng)
how·be·it (hou·bē′ ĭt)
how·ev·er (hou·ĕv′ ēr)
how·itz·er (hou′ ĭt·sēr)
howl (houl)
how·so·ev·er (hou′ sŏ·ĕv′ ēr)
hub·bub (hŭb′ ŭb)
huck·le·ber·ry (hŭk′ 'l·bĕr′ ĭ)
 -ber·ries
huck·ster (hŭk′ stēr)
hud·dle (hŭd′ 'l)
 hud·dling
hue (hū)
 (color; see *hew*)
 hue and cry
huge (hūj)
 huge·ness
Hu·gue·not (hū′ gĕ·nŏt)
hu·la (hōō′ lä)
hulk·ing (hŭl′ kĭng)
hul·la·ba·loo (hŭl′ á·bá·lōō′)
hu·man (hū′ măn)
 hu·mane (hū·mān′)
 hu·man·is·tic (hū′ măn·ĭs′ tĭk)

hu·man·i·tar·i·an
 (hū·măn′ ĭ·târ′ ĭ·ăn)
 hu·man·i·ty (hū·măn′ ĭ·tĭ)
 -ties
hum·ble (hŭm′ b'l)
 -bling
hum·bug (hŭm′ bŭg′)
hum·drum (hŭm′ drŭm′)
hu·mid (hū′ mĭd)
 hu·mid·i·fy (hū·mĭd′ ĭ·fĭ)
 -fied -fy·ing
 hu·mid·i·ty (hū·mĭd′ ĭ·tĭ)
hu·mi·dor (hū′ mĭ·dôr)
hu·mil·i·ate (hū·mĭl′ ĭ·āt)
 -at·ing
 hu·mil·i·a·tion
 (hū·mĭl′ ĭ·ā′ shŭn)
 hu·mil·i·ty (hū·mĭl′ ĭ·tĭ)
hum·ming·bird (hŭm′ ĭng·bûrd′)
hum·mock (hŭm′ ŭk)
hu·mor (hū′ mēr)
 hu·mor·ist hu·mor·ous
 hu·mor·esque (hū′ mēr·ĕsk′)
hu·mus (hū′ mŭs)
hunch·back (hŭnch′ băk′)
hun·dred (hŭn′ drĕd)
 hun·dred·fold
 hun·dred-per·cent·er
 hun·dredth hun·dred·weight
Hun·ga·ry (hŭng′ gá·rĭ)
 Hun·gar·i·an (hŭng·gâr′ ĭ·ăn)
hun·ger (hŭng′ gēr)
hun·gry (hŭng′ grĭ)
 hun·gri·ly
hunt·ress (hŭn′ trĕs)
hunts·man (hŭnts′ măn)
hur·dle (hûr′ d'l)
 (a barrier; or to leap a barrier; see
 hurtle) -dling
hur·dy-gur·dy (hûr′ dĭ·gûr′ dĭ)
hurl (hûrl)
hur·rah (hŏō·rô′)
 or: hur·ray (hŏō·rā′)
hur·ri·cane (hûr′ ĭ·kăn)
hur·ry (hûr′ ĭ)
 hur·ried hur·ry·ing
hurt·ful (hûrt′ fŏŏl)
 -ful·ly -ful·ness
hur·tle (hûr′ t'l)
 (to throw violently; see *hurdle*)
 -tling
hus·band (hŭz′ bǎnd)
husk·y (hŭs′ kĭ)
 hus·ki·ness
hus·sar (hŏŏ·zär′)

hus·sy   (hŭz′ ĭ)
  hus·sies
hus·tings   (hŭs′ tĭngz)
hus·tle   (hŭs′ 'l)
  -tling
hy·a·cinth   (hī′ á·sĭnth)
hy·brid   (hī′ brĭd)
  hy·brid·i·za·tion
                      (hī′ brĭd·ĭ·zā′ shŭn)
hy·drant   (hī′ drănt)
hy·drate   (hī′ drāt)
  -drat·ing
  hy·dra·tion   (hī·drā′ shŭn)
hy·drau·lic   (hī·drô′ lĭk)
  -li·cal·ly
hy·dro·car·bon
                      (hī′ drŏ·kär′ bŏn)
hy·dro·chlo·ric   (hī′ drŏ·klō′ rĭk)
hy·dro·dy·nam·ics
                      (hī′ drŏ·dī·năm′ ĭks)
hy·dro·e·lec·tric
                      (hī′ drŏ·ĕ·lĕk′ trĭk)
hy·dro·gen   (hī′ drŏ·jĕn)
  hy·dro·gen per·ox·ide
hy·dro·gen·ate   (hī′ drŏ·jĕn·āt)
  -at·ing
  hy·dro·gen·a·tion
                      (hī′ drŏ·jĕn·ā′ shŭn)
hy·drol·y·sis   (hī·drŏl′ ĭ·sĭs)
hy·drom·e·ter   (hī·drŏm′ ĕ·tēr)
hy·dro·pho·bi·a
                      (hī′ drŏ·fō′ bĭ·á)
hy·dro·ther·a·py
                      (hī′ drŏ·thĕr′ á·pĭ)
hy·drox·ide   (hī·drŏk′ sīd)
hy·giene   (hī′ jēn)
  hy·gi·en·ic   (hī′ jĭ·ĕn′ ĭk)
hy·men   (hī′ mĕn)
hymn   (hĭm)
  hym·nal   (hĭm′ năl)
  hym·nol·o·gy   (hĭm·nŏl′ ŏ·jĭ)
hy·per-   (hī′ pēr)
  hy·per·a·cid·i·ty
  hy·per·ac·tive hy·per·crit·i·cal
  hy·per·sen·si·tive
  hy·per·son·ic hy·per·ten·sion
hy·per·bo·le   (hī·pûr′ bŏ·lē)
hy·phen   (hī′ fĕn)
  hy·phen·a·tion
                      (hī′ fĕn·ā′ shŭn)
hyp·no·sis   (hĭp·nō′ sĭs)
  hyp·not·ic   (hĭp·nŏt′ ĭk)
  hyp·no·tist   (hĭp′ nŏ·tĭst)
  hyp·no·tize   (hĭp′ nŏ·tīz)
  -tiz·ing

hy·po·chon·dri·a
                      (hī′ pŏ·kŏn′ drĭ·á)
  hy·po·chon·dri·ac   (-ăk)
hy·poc·ri·sy   (hĭ·pŏk′ rĭ·sĭ)
  -sies
  hyp·o·crite   (hĭp′·ŏ·krĭt)
  hyp·o·crit·i·cal
                      (hĭp′ ŏ·krĭt′ ĭ·kál)
hy·po·der·mic   (hī′ pŏ·dûr′ mĭk)
hy·po·ten·sion   (hī′ pŏ·tĕn′ shŭn)
hy·pot·e·nuse   (hī·pŏt′ ĕ·nūs)
hy·po·thal·a·mus
                      (hī′ pŏ·thăl′ á·mŭs)
hy·poth·e·sis   (hī·pŏth′ ĕ·sĭs)
  pl. hy·poth·e·ses
  hy·poth·e·size   -siz·ing
  hy·po·thet·i·cal
                      (hī′ pŏ·thĕt′ ĭ·kál)
hys·sop   (hĭs′ ŭp)
hys·ter·ec·to·my
                      (hĭs′ tēr·ĕk′ tŏ·mĭ)
hys·te·ri·a   (hĭs·tēr′ ĭ·á)
  hys·ter·i·cal   (-tēr′ ĭ·kál)
  hys·ter·ics   (-tēr′ ĭks)

I

i·am·bic   (ĭ·ăm′ bĭk)
i·bi·dem   (ĭ·bī′ dĕm)
  abbr. ibid.
i·bis   (ī′ bĭs)
Ib·sen, Hen·rik
                      (ĭb′ s'n, hĕn′ rĭk)
ice   (īs)
  ice bag   ice·berg
  ice·boat   ice·break·er
  ice·cap   ice cream
  ice·house   ice·man
  ice pack
Ice·land   (īs′ lănd)
  Ice·lan·dic   (īs·lăn′ dĭk)
ich·thy·ol·o·gy   (ĭk′ thĭ·ŏl′ ŏ·jĭ)
i·ci·cle   (ī′ sĭk·'l)
ic·ing   (īs′ ĭng)
i·con   (ī′ kŏn)
  i·con·o·clast   (ī·kŏn′ ŏ·klăst)
  i·co·nog·ra·phy
                      (ī′ kŏ·nŏg′ rá·fĭ)
i·cy   (ī′ sĭ)
  i·ci·ly   (ī′ sĭ·lĭ)
I·da·ho   (ī′ dá·hō)
  abbr. Ida.
  I·da·ho·an   (-hō′ ăn)
i·de·a   (ī·dē′ á)

i·de·al (ĭ·dē′ ăl)
 i·de·al·ism
 i·de·al·is·tic (ĭ·dē′ ăl·ĭs′ tĭk)
 i·de·al·i·za·tion
  (ĭ·dē′ ăl·ĭ·zā′ shŭn)
 i·de·al·ly
i·de·a·tion (ĭ′ dē·ā′ shŭn)
i·den·ti·cal (ĭ·dĕn′ tĭ·kăl)
i·den·ti·fy (ĭ·dĕn′ tĭ·fī)
 -fied, -fy·ing
 i·den·ti·fi·ca·tion
  (ĭ·dĕn′ tĭ·fĭ·kā′ shŭn)
id·e·ol·o·gy (ĭd′ ê·ŏl′ ô·jĭ)
 -gies
 id·e·o·log·i·cal
  (ĭd′ ê·ô·ŏ·lŏj′ ĭ·kăl)
ides of March (ĭdz)
id·i·o·cy (ĭd′ ĭ·ô·sĭ)
id·i·om (ĭd′ ĭ·ŭm)
 id·i·o·mat·ic (ĭd′ ĭ·ô·măt′ ĭk)
 -i·cal·ly
 id·i·o·syn·cra·sy
  (ĭd′ ĭ·ô·sĭng′ krà·sĭ)
id·i·ot (ĭd′ ĭ·ŭt)
 id·i·o·cy (ĭd′ ĭ·ô·sĭ)
 id·i·ot·ic (ĭd′ ĭ·ŏt′ ĭk)
i·dle (ī′ d′l)
 (inactive; see idol, idyl)
 i·dle·ness
 i·dly
i·dol (ī′ dŭl)
 (deity; see idle, idyl)
 i·dol·a·ter (ĭ·dŏl′ à·tēr)
 i·dol·a·trous (ĭ·dŏl′ à·trŭs)
 i·dol·a·try (ĭ·dŏl′ à·trĭ)
 -tries
 i·dol·i·za·tion
  (ī′ dŭl·ĭ·zā′ shŭn)
 i·dol·ize (ī′ dŭl·īz)
 -iz·ing
i·dyl (ī′ dĭl)
 (literary work; see idle, idol)
 i·dyl·lic (ĭ·dĭl′ ĭk)
ig·loo (ĭg′ lōō)
ig·ne·ous (ĭg′ nê·ŭs)
ig·nite (ĭg·nīt′)
 -nit·ing ig·nit·i·ble
ig·ni·tion (ĭg·nĭsh′ ŭn)
ig·no·ble (ĭg·nō′ b′l)
ig·no·min·i·ous
  (ĭg′ nô·mĭn′ ĭ·ŭs)
 ig·no·min·y (ĭg′ nô·mĭn·ĭ)
 -min·ies
ig·no·ra·mus (ĭg′ nô·rā′ mŭs)

ig·no·rance (ĭg′ nô·răns)
 -rant
ig·nore (ĭg·nōr′)
 -nor·ing
i·gua·na (ĭ·gwä′ nà)
Il·i·ad (ĭl′ ĭ·ăd)
ill (ĭl)
 ill-ad·vised ill-bred
 ill-con·ceived ill-de·fined
 ill-fat·ed ill-got·ten
 ill-hu·mored ill-kept
 ill-man·nered ill-na·tured
 ill-starred ill tem·per
 ill-tem·pered ill-treat·ment
 ill-us·age
il·le·gal (ĭl·lē′ găl)
 -gal·ly
 il·le·gal·i·ty (ĭl′ lê·găl′ ĭ·tĭ)
il·leg·i·ble (ĭl·lĕj′ ĭ·b′l)
il·le·git·i·mate (ĭl′ lê·jĭt′ ĭ·mĭt)
 -ma·cy
il·lib·er·al (ĭl·lĭb′ ēr·ăl)
il·lic·it (ĭl·lĭs′ ĭt)
 (unlawful; see elicit)
il·lim·i·ta·ble (ĭl·lĭm′ ĭt·à·b′l)
Il·li·nois (ĭl′ ĭ·noi′)
 abbr. Ill.
 Il·li·nois·an (-noi′ ăn)
il·lit·er·a·cy (ĭl·lĭt′ ēr·à·sĭ)
 -er·ate
il·log·i·cal (ĭl·lŏj′ ĭ·kăl)
 -cal·ly
il·lume (ĭ·lūm′)
 il·lum·ing
il·lu·mi·nate (ĭ·lū′ mĭ·nāt)
 -nat·ing
 il·lu·mi·nant (ĭ·lū′ mĭ·nănt)
 il·lu·mi·na·tion
  (ĭ·lū′ mĭ·nā′ shŭn)
il·lu·sion (ĭ·lū′ zhŭn)
 (misconception; see allusion)
 il·lu·sion·al
il·lu·sive (ĭ·lū′ sĭv)
 (unreal; see elusive)
il·lu·so·ry (ĭ·lū′ sô·rĭ)
il·lus·trate (ĭl′ ŭs·trāt)
 -trat·ing
 il·lus·tra·tion (ĭl′ ŭs·trā′ shŭn)
 il·lus·tra·tive (ĭ·lŭs′ trà·tĭv)
 il·lus·tra·tor
il·lus·tri·ous (ĭ·lŭs′ trĭ·ŭs)
im·age (ĭm′ ĭj)
 im·age·ry (ĭm′ ĭj·rĭ)
im·ag·ine (ĭ·măj′ ĭn)
 -in·ing
 im·ag·i·na·ble

im·ag·i·nar·y
im·ag·i·na·tion
   (ĭ·măj′ ĭ·nā′ shŭn)
im·ag·i·na·tive
   (ĭ·măj′ ĭ·nā′ tĭv)
im·bal·ance (ĭm·băl′ ăns)
im·be·cile (ĭm′ bĕ·sĭl)
  im·be·cil·i·ty (ĭm′ bĕ·sĭl′ ĭ·tĭ)
im·bibe (ĭm·bīb′)
  -bib·ing
im·bro·glio (ĭm·brōl′ yō)
im·bue (ĭm·bū′)
  -bu·ing
im·i·tate (ĭm′ ĭ·tāt)
  -tat·ing
  im·i·ta·ble (ĭm′ ĭ·tȧ·b'l)
  im·i·ta·tive (ĭm′ ĭ·tā′ tĭv)
  im·i·ta·tor
im·mac·u·late (ĭ·măk′ û·lĭt)
  Im·mac·u·late Con·cep·tion
im·ma·nent (ĭm′ ȧ·nĕnt)
  (indwelling; see *imminent*)
  im·ma·nence
im·ma·te·ri·al (ĭm′ mȧ·tēr′ ĭ·ăl)
im·ma·ture (ĭm′ ȧ·tūr′)
  im·ma·tu·ri·ty
im·meas·ur·a·ble
   (ĭ·mĕzh′ ēr·ȧ·b'l)
im·me·di·ate (ĭ·mē′ dĭ·ĭt)
  im·me·di·a·cy (-dĭ·ȧ·sĭ)
  im·me·di·ate·ly
im·me·mo·ri·al
   (ĭm′ mĕ·mō′ rĭ·ăl)
im·mense (ĭ·mĕns′)
  im·men·si·ty
im·merse (ĭ·mûrs′)
  -mers·ing
  im·mer·sion (ĭ·mûr′ shŭn)
im·mi·grate (ĭm′ ĭ·grāt)
  (to enter a country; see *emigrate*)
  -grat·ing   im·mi·grant
  im·mi·gra·tion
   (ĭm′ ĭ·grā′ shŭn)
im·mi·nent (ĭm′ ĭ·nĕnt)
  (about to happen; see *immanent*)
  im·mi·nence
im·mo·bile (ĭm·mō′ bĭl)
  im·mo·bil·i·ty (ĭm′ ō·bĭl′ ĭ·tĭ)
  im·mo·bi·lized (ĭm·mō′ bĭ·līzd)
im·mod·er·ate (ĭm·mŏd′ ēr·ĭt)
im·mod·est (ĭm·mŏd′ ĕst)
im·mo·late (ĭm′ ō·lāt)
  -lat·ing
  im·mo·la·tion (ĭm′ ō·lā′ shŭn)

im·mor·al (ĭm·mŏr′ ăl)
  (not moral)
  im·mo·ral·i·ty
   (ĭm′ mŏ·răl′ ĭ·tĭ)
im·mor·tal (ĭ·môr′ tăl)
  (deathless)
  im·mor·tal·i·ty
   (ĭm′ ôr·tăl′ ĭ·tĭ)
  im·mor·tal·ize (ĭ·môr′ tăl·īz)
  -iz·ing
im·mov·a·ble (ĭm·mōōv′ ȧ·b'l)
im·mune (ĭ·mūn′)
  im·mu·ni·ty (ĭ·mū′ nĭ·tĭ)
  -ties
  im·mu·ni·za·tion
   (ĭm′ û·nĭ·zā′ shŭn)
im·mu·ta·ble (ĭ·mū′ tȧ·b'l)
im·pact·ed (ĭm·păk′ tĕd)
  im·pac·tion (ĭm·păk′ shŭn)
im·pair·ment (ĭm·pâr′ mĕnt)
im·pale (ĭm·pāl′)
  -pal·ing
im·pal·pa·ble (ĭm·păl′ pȧ·b'l)
im·part (ĭm·pärt′)
im·par·tial (ĭm·pär′ shăl)
  -tial·ly
  im·par·ti·al·i·ty
   (ĭm′ pär·shĭ·ăl′ ĭ·tĭ)
im·pass·a·ble (ĭm·pás′ ȧ·b'l)
im·passe (ĭm·pás′)
im·pas·sioned (ĭm·păsh′ ŭnd)
im·pas·sive (ĭm·păs′ ĭv)
im·pa·tient (ĭm·pā′ shĕnt)
  -tience
im·peach (ĭm·pēch′)
im·pec·ca·ble (ĭm·pĕk′ ȧ·b'l)
im·pe·cu·ni·ous
   (ĭm′ pĕ·kū′ nĭ·ŭs)
im·pede (ĭm·pēd′)
  -ped·ing
  im·ped·i·ment (ĭm·pĕd′ ĭ·mĕnt)
im·pel (ĭm·pĕl′)
  -pelled   -pel·ling
im·pend·ing (ĭm·pĕnd′ ĭng)
im·pen·e·tra·ble
   (ĭm·pĕn′ ĕ·trȧ·b'l)
  im·pen·e·tra·bil·i·ty
   (ĭm·pĕn′ ĕ·trȧ·bĭl′ ĭ·tĭ)
im·pen·i·tence (ĭm·pĕn′ ĭ·tĕns)
im·per·a·tive (ĭm·pĕr′ ȧ·tĭv)
im·per·cep·ti·ble
   (ĭm′ pĕr·sĕp′ tĭ·b'l)
im·per·cep·tive (-tĭv)
im·per·fect (ĭm·pûr′ fĕkt)

im·pe·ri·al (ĭm·pēr′ ĭ·ɑl)
im·pe·ri·al·is·tic
　　　　(ĭm·pēr′ ĭ·ɑl·ĭs′ tĭk)
im·pe·ri·ous (ĭm·pēr′ ĭ·ŭs)
im·per·ish·a·ble
　　　　(ĭm·pĕr′ ĭsh·ȧ·b′l)
im·per·ma·nent
　　　　(ĭm·pûr′ mȧ·nĕnt)
-nence
im·per·me·a·ble
　　　　(ĭm·pûr′ mē·ȧ·b′l)
im·per·son·al (ĭm·pûr′ sŭn·ɑl)
-al·ly
im·per·son·ate (ĭm·pûr′ sŭn·āt)
-at·ing
im·per·son·a·tion
　　　　(ĭm·pûr′ sŭn·ā′ shŭn)
im·per·son·a·tor
im·per·ti·nence
　　　　(ĭm·pûr′ tĭ·nĕns)
im·per·turb·a·ble
　　　　(ĭm′ pēr·tûr′ bȧ·b′l)
im·per·vi·ous (ĭm·pûr′ vĭ·ŭs)
im·pe·ti·go (ĭm′ pŏ·tī′ gō)
im·pet·u·ous (ĭm·pĕt′ û·ŭs)
(impulsive)
im·pet·u·os·i·ty
　　　　(ĭm·pĕt′ û·ŏs′ ĭ·tĭ)
im·pe·tus (ĭm′ pĕ·tŭs)
(momentum)
im·pi·e·ty (ĭm·pī′ ĕ·tĭ)
-ties
im·pi·ous (ĭm·pī′ ŭs)
im·pinge (ĭm·pĭnj)
-ping·ing
imp·ish (ĭmp′ ĭsh)
im·pla·ca·ble (ĭm·plā′ kȧ·b′l)
im·plant (ĭm·plȧnt′)
im·plau·si·ble (ĭm·plô′ zĭ·b′l)
im·ple·ment (ĭm′ plē·mĕnt)
im·ple·men·ta·tion
　　　　(ĭm′ plē·mĕn·tā′ shŭn)
im·pli·cate (ĭm′ plĭ·kāt)
-cat·ing
im·pli·ca·tion
　　　　(ĭm′ plĭ·kā′ shŭn)
im·plic·it (ĭm·plĭs′ ĭt)
im·plore (ĭm·plōr′)
-plor·ing
im·ply (ĭm·plī′)
-plied -ply·ing
im·po·lite (ĭm′ pŏ·līt′)
im·po·lite·ness
im·pol·i·tic (ĭm·pŏl′ ĭ·tĭk)

im·pon·der·a·ble
　　　　(ĭm·pŏn′ dĕr·ȧ·b′l)
im·port (ĭm·pōrt′) v.
　　　　(ĭm′ pōrt) n.
im·port·a·ble (ĭm·pōr′ tȧ·b′l)
im·por·ta·tion
　　　　(ĭm′ pŏr·tā′ shŭn)
im·por·tance (ĭm·pōr′ tȧns)
-tant
im·por·tu·nate (ĭm·pōr′ tû·nĭt)
im·por·tune (ĭm′ pŏr·tūn′)
im·pos·ing (ĭm·pōz′ ĭng)
im·po·si·tion (ĭm′ pŏ·zĭsh′ ŭn)
im·pos·si·ble (ĭm·pŏs′ ĭ·b′l)
-bly
im·pos·si·bil·i·ty
　　　　(ĭm·pŏs′ ĭ·bĭl′ ĭ·tĭ)
im·pos·tor (ĭm·pŏs′ tēr)
im·pos·ture (ĭm·pŏs′ tûr)
im·po·tent (ĭm′ pŏ·tĕnt)
-tence
im·pound (ĭm·pound′)
im·pov·er·ish (ĭm·pŏv′ ēr·ĭsh)
im·prac·ti·ca·ble
　　　　(ĭm·prăk′ tĭ·kȧ·b′l)
im·prac·ti·cal (ĭm·prăk′ tĭ·kɑl)
im·prac·ti·cal·i·ty
　　　　(ĭm·prăk′ tĭ·kăl′ ĭ·tĭ)
im·pre·cate (ĭm′ prē·kāt)
-cat·ing
im·pre·ca·tion
　　　　(ĭm′ prē·kā′ shŭn)
im·preg·na·ble
　　　　(ĭm·prĕg′ nȧ·b′l)
im·preg·nate (ĭm·prĕg′ nāt)
-nat·ing
im·pre·sa·ri·o (ĭm′ prȧ·sä′ rĭ·ō)
im·press (ĭm′ prĕs) n.
im·press (ĭm·prĕs′) v.
im·press·i·ble
im·pres·sion (ĭm·prĕsh′ ŭn)
im·pres·sion·a·ble
im·pres·sion·is·tic
　　　　(ĭm·prĕsh′ ŭn·ĭs′ tĭk)
im·pres·sive
im·pri·ma·tur (ĭm′ prĭ·mā′ tēr)
im·print (ĭm·prĭnt′) v.
　　　　(ĭm′ prĭnt) n.
im·pris·on (ĭm·prĭz′′n)
im·pris·on·ment
im·prob·a·ble (ĭm·prŏb′ ȧ·b′l)
im·prob·a·bil·i·ty
　　　　(ĭm′ prŏb·ȧ·bĭl′ ĭ·tĭ)
im·promp·tu (ĭm·prŏmp′ tū)
im·prop·er (ĭm·prŏp′ ēr)

im·pro·pri·e·ty
     (ĭm′ prŏ·prī′ ĕ·tĭ)
 -ties
im·prove   (ĭm·prōōv′)
 -prov·ing   im·prov·a·ble
 im·prove·ment
im·prov·i·dent (ĭm·prŏv′ ĭ·dĕnt)
 -dence
im·pro·vise   (ĭm′ prŏ·vīz)
 -vis·ing
 im·pro·vi·sa·tion
     (ĭm′ prŏ·vī·zā′ shŭn)
im·pru·dent   (ĭm·prōō′ dĕnt)
 -dence
im·pugn   (ĭm·pūn′)
im·pulse   (ĭm′ pŭls)
 im·pul·sion (ĭm·pŭl′ shŭn)
 im·pul·sive (ĭm·pŭl′ sĭv)
im·pu·ni·ty (ĭm·pū′ nĭ·tĭ)
im·pure   (ĭm·pūr′)
 im·pu·ri·ty -ties
im·pute   (ĭm·pūt′)
 -put·ing im·put·a·ble
 im·pu·ta·tion
     (ĭm′ pŭ·tā′ shŭn)
in·a·bil·i·ty (ĭn′ ȧ·bĭl′ ĭ·tĭ)
 -ties
in ab·sen·ti·a (ĭn ăb·sĕn′ shĭ·ȧ)
in·ac·ces·si·ble (ĭn′ ăk·sĕs′ ĭ·b'l)
in·ac·cu·ra·cy (ĭn·ăk′ ū·rȧ·sĭ)
 -cies
 in·ac·cu·rate -rate·ly
in·ac·tive (ĭn·ăk′ tĭv)
 in·ac·tiv·i·ty (ĭn′ ăk·tĭv′ ĭ·tĭ)
in·ad·e·quate (ĭn·ăd′ ē·kwĭt)
 -qua·cy
in·ad·mis·si·ble
     (ĭn′ ăd·mĭs′ ĭ·b'l)
in·ad·vert·ence
     (ĭn′ ăd·vûr′ tĕns)
 -ent
in·ad·vis·a·ble
     (ĭn′ ăd·vīz′ ȧ·b'l)
in·al·ien·a·ble (ĭn·āl′ yĕn·ȧ·b'l)
in·al·ter·a·ble (ĭn·ôl′ tẽr·ȧ·b'l)
in·am·o·ra·ta (ĭn·ăm′ ŏ·rä′ tȧ)
in·ane (ĭn·ān′)
 in·an·i·ty (ĭn·ăn′ ĭ·tĭ)
in·an·i·mate (ĭn·ăn′ ĭ·mȧt)
in·ap·peas·a·ble
     (ĭn′ ȧ·pēz′ ȧ·b'l)
in·ap·pli·ca·ble
     (ĭn·ăp′ lĭ·kȧ·b'l)
in·ap·pre·ci·a·ble
     (ĭn′ ȧ·prē′ shĭ·ȧ·b'l)

in·ap·pre·ci·a·tive
     (ĭn′ ȧ·prē′ shĭ·ā′ tĭv)
in·ap·proach·a·ble
     (ĭn′ ȧ·prōch′ ȧ·b'l)
in·ar·tic·u·late
     (ĭn′ är·tĭk′ ū·lȧt)
 -late·ly
in·ar·tis·tic (ĭn′ är·tĭs′ tĭk)
in·as·much as (ĭn′ ăz·mŭch′)
in·at·ten·tion (ĭn′ ȧ·tĕn′ shŭn)
in·at·ten·tive (ĭn′ ȧ·tĕn′ tĭv)
 -tive·ly
in·au·di·ble (ĭn·ô′ dĭ·b'l)
in·au·gu·ral (ĭn·ô′ gŭ·rȧl)
in·au·gu·rate (ĭn·ô′ gŭ·rāt)
 -rat·ing
 in·au·gu·ra·tion
     (ĭn·ô′ gŭ·rā′ shŭn)
in·aus·pi·cious
     (ĭn′ ôs·pĭsh′ ŭs)
in·born (ĭn′ bôrn′)
in·cal·cu·la·ble
     (ĭn·kăl′ kū·lȧ·b'l)
in·can·des·cent
     (ĭn′ kȧn·dĕs′ ĕnt)
 -cence
in·can·ta·tion (ĭn′ kăn·tā′ shŭn)
in·ca·pa·ble (ĭn·kā′ pȧ·b'l)
in·ca·pa·cious (ĭn′ kȧ·pā′ shŭs)
in·ca·pac·i·tate
     (ĭn′ kȧ·păs′ ĭ·tāt)
 -tat·ing
 in·ca·pac·i·ta·tion
     (ĭn′ kȧ·păs′ ĭ·tā′ shŭn)
in·car·cer·ate (ĭn·kär′ sẽr·āt)
 -at·ing
 in·car·cer·a·tion
     (ĭn·kär′ sẽr·ā′ shŭn)
in·car·nate (ĭn·kär′ nāt)
 in·car·na·tion
     (ĭn′ kär·nā′ shŭn)
in·cau·tious (ĭn·kô′ shŭs)
in·cen·di·ar·y (ĭn·sĕn′ dĭ·ĕr′ ĭ)
in·cense (ĭn·sĕns′) *v.*
 -cens·ing
     (ĭn′ sĕns) *n.*
in·cen·tive (ĭn·sĕn′ tĭv)
in·cep·tion (ĭn·sĕp′ shŭn)
in·ces·sant·ly (ĭn·sĕs′ ȧnt·lĭ)
in·cest (ĭn′ sĕst)
 in·ces·tu·ous (ĭn·sĕs′ tŭ·ŭs)
in·cho·ate (ĭn·kō′ ĭt)
in·ci·dent (ĭn′ sĭ·dĕnt)
 in·ci·dence
 in·ci·den·tal (ĭn′ sĭ·dĕn′ tȧl)
 -tal·ly

in·cin·er·ate (ĭn·sĭn′ĕr·āt)
  -at·ing   in·cin·er·a·tor
in·cip·i·ent (ĭn·sĭp′ĭ·ĕnt)
  -ence
in·cise (ĭn·sīz′)
  -cis·ing
  in·ci·sion (ĭn·sĭzh′ŭn)
  in·ci·sive (ĭn·sī′sĭv)
  in·ci·sor tooth (ĭn·sī′zĕr)
in·cite (ĭn·sīt′)
  -cit·ing   in·cite·ment
in·clem·ent (ĭn·klĕm′ĕnt)
in·cline (ĭn′ klīn) n.
in·cline (ĭn·klīn′) v.
  -clin·ing   in·clin·a·ble
  in·cli·na·tion (ĭn′ klĭ·nā′ shŭn)
in·clude (ĭn·klōōd′)
  -clud·ing
  in·clu·sion (ĭn·klōō′ zhŭn)
  in·clu·sive   -sive·ly
in·cog·ni·to (ĭn·kŏg′ nĭ·tō)
in·co·her·ent (ĭn′ kō·hĕr′ ĕnt)
  -ence
in·com·bus·ti·ble
      (ĭn′ kŏm·bŭs′ tĭ·b'l)
in·come (ĭn′ kŭm)
  in·com·ing (ĭn′ kŭm′ ĭng)
in·com·men·su·rate
      (ĭn′ kŏ·mĕn′ shŏŏ·rĭt)
  in·com·men·su·ra·ble
in·com·mo·di·ous
      (ĭn′ kŏ·mō′ dĭ·ŭs)
in·com·mu·ni·ca·ble
      (ĭn′ kŏ·mū′ nĭ·kȧ·b'l)
  in·com·mu·ni·ca·tive
in·com·mu·ni·ca·do
      (ĭn′ kŏ·mū′ nĭ·kä′ dō)
in·com·pa·ra·ble
      (ĭn·kŏm′ pȧ·rȧ·b'l)
in·com·pat·i·ble
      (ĭn′ kŏm·păt′ ĭ·b'l)
  in·com·pat·i·bil·i·ty
      (ĭn′ kŏm·păt′ ĭ·bĭl′ ĭ·tĭ)
in·com·pe·tence (ĭn·kŏm′ pĕ·tĕns)
  -tent
in·com·plete (ĭn′ kŏm·plēt′)
in·com·pli·ant (ĭn′ kŏm·plī′ ȧnt)
in·com·pre·hen·si·ble
      (ĭn′ kŏm·prē·hĕn′ sĭ·b'l)
in·con·ceiv·a·ble
      (ĭn′ kŏn·sēv′ ȧ·b'l)
in·con·clu·sive
      (ĭn′ kŏn·klōō′ sĭv)

in·con·gru·ous
      (ĭn·kŏng′ grōō·ŭs)
  in·con·gru·i·ty
      (ĭn′ kŏng·grōō′ ĭ·tĭ)
  -ties
in·con·se·quen·tial
      (ĭn·kŏn′ sĕ·kwĕn′ shȧl)
in·con·sid·er·ate
      (ĭn′ kŏn·sĭd′ ĕr·ĭt)
in·con·sist·ent
      (ĭn′ kŏn·sĭs′ tĕnt)
  -ten·cy
in·con·sol·a·ble
      (ĭn′ kŏn·sōl′ ȧ·b'l)
in·con·so·nant (ĭn·kŏn′ sŏ·nȧnt)
  -nance
in·con·spic·u·ous
      (ĭn′ kŏn·spĭk′ û·ŭs)
in·con·stant (ĭn·kŏn′ stȧnt)
  -stan·cy
in·con·test·a·ble
      (ĭn′ kŏn·tĕs′ tȧ·b'l)
in·con·ti·nent (ĭn·kŏn′ tĭ·nĕnt)
  -nence
in·con·tro·vert·i·ble
      (ĭn′ kŏn·trŏ·vûr′ tĭ·b'l)
in·con·ven·ient
      (ĭn′ kŏn·vēn′ yĕnt)
  -ience
in·cor·po·rat·ed
      (ĭn·kôr′ pŏ·rāt′ ĕd)
in·cor·rect·ly (ĭn′ kŏ·rĕkt′ lĭ)
in·cor·ri·gi·ble
      (ĭn·kŏr′ ĭ·jĭ·b'l)
  in·cor·ri·gi·bil·i·ty
      (ĭn·kŏr′ ĭ·jĭ·bĭl′ ĭ·tĭ)
in·cor·rupt·i·ble
      (ĭn′ kŏ·rŭp′ tĭ·b'l)
in·crease (ĭn′ krēs) n.
  -creas·ing (ĭn·krēs′) v.
in·cred·i·ble (ĭn·krĕd′ ĭ·b'l)
  in·cred·i·bil·i·ty
      (ĭn·krĕd′ ĭ·bĭl′ ĭ·tĭ)
in·cred·u·lous (ĭn·krĕd′ û·lŭs)
  in·cre·du·li·ty (ĭn′ krĕ·dū′ lĭ·tĭ)
in·cre·ment (ĭn′ krĕ·mĕnt)
in·crim·i·nat·ing
      (ĭn·krĭm′ ĭ·nāt′ ĭng)
in·crus·ta·tion (ĭn′ krŭs·tā′ shŭn)
in·cu·bate (ĭn′ kû·bāt)
  -bat·ing
  in·cu·ba·tion (ĭn′ kû·bā′ shŭn)
  in·cu·ba·tor (ĭn′ kû·bā′ tĕr)
in·cu·bus (ĭn′ kû·bŭs)

in·cul·cate   (ĭn·kŭl′ kāt)
-cat·ing
in·cul·ca·tion
          (ĭn′ kŭl·kā′ shŭn)
in·cul·pate   (ĭn·kŭl′ pāt)
-pat·ing
in·cum·bent   (ĭn·kŭm′ bĕnt)
-ben·cy
in·cur   (ĭn·kûr′)
-curred   -cur·ring
in·cur·a·ble   (ĭn·kûr′ à·b′l)
in·cur·sion   (ĭn·kûr′ zhŭn)
in·debt·ed·ness   (ĭn·dĕt′ ĕd·nĕs)
in·de·cen·cy   (ĭn·dē′ sĕn·sĭ)
in·de·ci·pher·a·ble
          (ĭn′ dē·sī′ fēr·à·b′l)
in·de·ci·sive   (ĭn′ dē·sī′ sĭv)
in·de·ci·sion   (ĭn′ dē·sĭzh′ ŭn)
in·dec·o·rous   (ĭn·dĕk′ ô·rŭs)
in·de·co·rum   (ĭn′ dē·kō′ rŭm)
in·deed   (ĭn·dēd′)
in·de·fat·i·ga·ble
          (ĭn′ dē·făt′ ĭ·gá·b′l)
in·de·fat·i·ga·bil·i·ty
          (ĭn′ dē·făt′ ĭ·gá·bĭl′ ĭ·tĭ)
in·de·fea·si·ble   (ĭn′ dē·fē′ zĭ·b′l)
in·de·fen·si·ble
          (ĭn′ dē·fĕn′ sĭ·b′l)
in·de·fin·a·ble
          (ĭn′ dē·fīn′ à·b′l)
in·def·i·nite   (ĭn·dĕf′ ĭ·nĭt)
-nite·ly
in·del·i·ble   (ĭn·dĕl′ ĭ·b′l)
in·del·i·cate   (ĭn·dĕl′ ĭ·kĭt)
-ca·cy
in·dem·ni·fy   (ĭn·dĕm′ nĭ·fī)
-fied   -fy·ing
in·dem·ni·ty   (ĭn·dĕm′ nĭ·tĭ)
-ties
in·den·ta·tion   (ĭn′ dĕn·tā′ shŭn)
in·den·ture   (ĭn·dĕn′ tûr)
in·de·pend·ence
          (ĭn′ dē·pĕn′ dĕns)
-dent
in·de·scrib·a·ble
          (ĭn′ dē·skrĭb′ à·b′l)
in·de·struct·i·ble
          (ĭn′ dē·strŭk′ tĭ·b′l)
in·de·ter·mi·na·ble
          (ĭn′ dē·tûr′ mĭ·nà·b′l)
in·de·ter·mi·nate
          (ĭn′ dē·tûr′ mĭ·nåt)
in·dex   (ĭn′ dĕks)
-dex·es
In·di·a ink   (ĭn′ dĭ·à)

In·di·an·a   (ĭn′ dĭ·ăn′ à)
abbr. Ind.
In·di·an·i·an   (ăn′ ĭ·ản)
in·di·cate   (ĭn′ dĭ·kāt)
-cat·ing
in·di·ca·tion   (ĭn′ dĭ·kā′ shŭn)
in·dic·a·tive   (ĭn·dĭk′ à·tĭv)
in·di·ca·tor
in·dict   (ĭn·dīt′)
in·dict·ment
in·dif·fer·ence   (ĭn·dĭf′ ēr·ĕns)
in·di·gence   (ĭn′ dĭ·jĕns)
in·dig·e·nous   (ĭn·dĭj′ ê·nŭs)
in·di·ges·tion   (ĭn·dĭ·jĕs′ chŭn)
in·di·gest·i·ble
in·dig·nant   (ĭn·dĭg′ nǎnt)
-nance
in·dig·na·tion
          (ĭn′ dĭg·nā′ shŭn)
in·dig·ni·ty   (ĭn·dĭg′ nĭ·tĭ)
-ties
in·di·go   (ĭn′ dĭ·gō)
in·di·rect   (ĭn′ dĭ·rĕkt′)
in·dis·cern·i·ble
          (ĭn′ dĭ·zûr′ nĭ·b′l)
in·dis·creet   (ĭn′ dĭs·krēt′)
in·dis·cre·tion
          (ĭn′ dĭs·krĕsh′ ŭn)
in·dis·crim·i·nate
          (ĭn′ dĭs·krĭm′ ĭ·nĭt)
in·dis·pen·sa·ble
          (ĭn′ dĭs·pĕn′ sà·b′l)
in·dis·posed   (ĭn′ dĭs·pōzd′)
in·dis·pu·ta·ble
          (ĭn·dĭs′ pû·tà·b′l)
in·dis·sol·u·ble
          (ĭn′ dĭ·sŏl′ û·b′l)
in·dis·tinct   (ĭn′ dĭs·tĭngkt′)
in·dis·tin·guish·a·ble
          (ĭn′ dĭs·tĭng′ gwĭsh·à·b′l)
in·di·vid·u·al   (ĭn′ dĭ·vĭd′ û·ål)
in·di·vid·u·al·ism, -al·ist
in·di·vid·u·al·i·ty
          (ĭn′ dĭ·vĭd′ û·ăl′ ĭ·tĭ)
in·di·vid·u·al·ize, -iz·ing
in·di·vid·u·al·ly
in·di·vis·i·ble   (ĭn′ dĭ·vĭz′ ĭ·b′l)
In·do·chi·na   (ĭn′ dô·chī′ nà)
in·doc·tri·nate   (ĭn·dŏk′ trĭ·nāt)
-nat·ing
in·doc·tri·na·tion
          (ĭn·dŏk′ trĭ·nā′ shŭn)
in·do·lent   (ĭn′ dô·lĕnt)
-lence

in·dom·i·ta·ble
    (ĭn·dŏm′ ĭ·tá·b'l)
In·do·ne·sia (ĭn′ dŏ·nē′ zhá)
in·doors (ĭn′ dōrz′)
in·du·bi·ta·ble (ĭn′·dū′ bĭ·tá·b'l)
in·duce (ĭn·dūs′)
  -duc·ing   in·duce·ment
in·duct (ĭn·dŭkt′)
  in·duc·tion (ĭn·dŭk′ shŭn)
  in·duc·tive   in·duc·tor
in·due (ĭn·dū′)
  -du·ing
in·dulge (ĭn·dŭlj′)
  -dulg·ing
  in·dul·gent   -gence
in·dus·try (ĭn′ dŭs·trĭ)
  -tries
  in·dus·tri·al (ĭn·dŭs′ trĭ·ăl)
  -al·ly   -al·ism
  in·dus·tri·al·ist
    (ĭn·dŭs′ trĭ·ăl·ĭst)
  in·dus·tri·al·i·za·tion
    (ĭn·dŭs′ trĭ·ăl·ĭ·zā′ shŭn)
  in·dus·tri·ous (ĭn·dŭs′ trĭ·ŭs)
in·dwell·ing (ĭn′ dwĕl′ ĭng)
in·e·bri·at·ed (ĭn·ē′ brĭ·āt′ ĕd)
  in·e·bri·a·tion
    (ĭn·ē′ brĭ·ā′ shŭn)
in·ed·i·ble (ĭn·ĕd′ ĭ·b'l)
in·ef·fa·ble (ĭn·ĕf′ á·b'l)
in·ef·face·a·ble
    (ĭn′ ĕ·fās′ á·b'l)
in·ef·fec·tive (ĭn′ ĕ·fĕk′ tĭv)
in·ef·fec·tu·al (ĭn′ ĕ·fĕk′ tû·ăl)
  in·ef·fec·tu·al·i·ty
    (ĭn′ ĕ·fĕk′ tû·ăl′ ĭ·tĭ)
in·ef·fi·ca·cious
    (ĭn′ ĕf·ĭ·kā′ shŭs)
  in·ef·fi·ca·cy (ĭn·ĕf′ ĭ·ká·sĭ)
in·ef·fi·cient (ĭn′ ĕ·fĭsh′ ĕnt)
  -cien·cy
in·e·las·tic (ĭn′ ĕ·lăs′ tĭk)
in·el·e·gance (ĭn·ĕl′ ĕ·gáns)
in·el·i·gi·ble (ĭn·ĕl′ ĭ·jĭ·b'l)
  in·el·i·gi·bil·i·ty
    (ĭn·ĕl′ ĭ·jĭ·bĭl′ ĭ·tĭ)
in·e·luc·ta·ble (ĭn′ ĕ·lŭk′ tá·b'l)
in·ept (ĭn·ĕpt′)
  in·ept·i·tude (ĭn·ĕpt′ ĭ·tūd)
in·e·qual·i·ty (ĭn′ ĕ·kwŏl′ ĭ·tĭ)
  -ties
in·eq·ui·ta·ble
    (ĭn·ĕk′ wĭ·tá·b'l)
in·eq·ui·ty (ĭn·ĕk′ wĭ·tĭ)
  -ties

in·e·rad·i·ca·ble
    (ĭn′ ĕ·răd′ ĭ·ká·b'l)
in·e·ras·a·ble (ĭn′ ĕ·rās′ á·b'l)
in·ert (ĭn·ûrt′)
in·er·tia (ĭn·ûr′ shá)
in·es·cap·a·ble
    (ĭn′ ĕs·kāp′ á·b'l)
in·es·sen·tial (ĭn′ ĕ·sĕn′ shál)
in·es·ti·ma·ble (ĭn·ĕs′ tĭ·má·b'l)
in·ev·i·ta·ble (ĭn·ĕv′ ĭ·tá·b'l)
  in·ev·i·ta·bil·i·ty
    (ĭn·ĕv′ ĭ·tá·bĭl′ ĭ·tĭ)
in·ex·cus·a·ble
    (ĭn′ ĕks·kūz′ á·b'l)
in·ex·haust·i·ble
    (ĭn′ ĕg·zôs′ tĭ·b'l)
in·ex·o·ra·ble (ĭn·ĕk′ sô·rá·b'l)
in·ex·pe·di·ent
    (ĭn′ ĕks·pē′ dĭ·ĕnt)
in·ex·pen·sive (ĭn′ ĕks·pĕn′ sĭv)
in·ex·pe·ri·enced
    (ĭn′ ĕks·pēr′ ĭ·ĕnst)
in·ex·pert (ĭn′ ĕks·pûrt′)
in·ex·pli·ca·ble
    (ĭn·ĕks′ plĭ·ká·b'l)
in·ex·press·i·ble
    (ĭn′ ĕks·prĕs′ ĭ·b'l)
  in·ex·pres·sive
in·ex·tri·ca·ble
    (ĭn·ĕks′ trĭ·ká·b'l)
in·fal·li·ble (ĭn·făl′ ĭ·b'l)
  in·fal·li·bil·i·ty
    (ĭn·făl′ ĭ·bĭl′ ĭ·tĭ)
in·fa·mous (ĭn′ fá·mŭs)
in·fa·my (ĭn′ fá·mĭ)
in·fant (ĭn′ fănt)
  in·fan·cy
  in·fan·ti·cide (ĭn·făn′ tĭ·sīd)
  in·fan·tile (ĭn′ făn·tīl)
in·fan·try (ĭn′ făn·trĭ)
  in·fan·try·man
in·fat·u·ate (ĭn·făt′ û·āt)
  -at·ing
  in·fat·u·a·tion
    (ĭn·făt′ û·ā′ shŭn)
in·fec·tion (ĭn·fĕk′ shŭn)
  in·fec·tious (ĭn·fĕk′ shŭs)
in·fer (ĭn·fûr′)
  -ferred   -fer·ring
  in·fer·ence (ĭn′ fēr·ĕns)
  in·fer·en·tial (ĭn′ fēr·ĕn′ shăl)
in·fe·ri·or (ĭn·fēr′ ĭ·ēr)
  in·fe·ri·or·i·ty com·plex
    (ĭn·fēr′ ĭ·ŏr′ ĭ·tĭ)
in·fer·nal (ĭn·fûr′ năl)

in·fer·no (ĭn·fûr′ nō)
in·fi·del (ĭn′ fĭ·dĕl)
in·fi·del·i·ty (ĭn′ fĭ·dĕl′ ĭ·tĭ)
in·field·er (ĭn′ fēl′ dēr)
in·fil·trate (ĭn·fĭl′ trāt)
-trat·ing
in·fil·tra·tion (ĭn′ fĭl·trā′ shŭn)
in·fi·nite (ĭn′ fĭ·nĭt)
in·fi·nite·ly
in·fin·i·tes·i·mal
         (ĭn′ fĭn·ĭ·tĕs′ ĭ·măl)
in·fin·i·tive (ĭn′ fĭn′ ĭ·tĭv)
in·fin·i·ty (ĭn′ fĭn′ ĭ·tĭ)
in·firm (ĭn·fûrm′)
in·fir·ma·ry (ĭn·fûr′ má·rĭ)
-ries
in·fir·mi·ty (ĭn·fûr′ mĭ·tĭ)
-ties
in·flame (ĭn·flām′)
-flam·ing
in·flam·ma·ble (ĭn·flăm′ á·b'l)
in·flam·ma·to·ry
         (ĭn·flăm′ á·tō′ rĭ)
in·flam·ma·tion (ĭn′ flă·mā′ shŭn)
in·flate (ĭn·flāt′)
-flat·ing   in·flat·a·ble
in·fla·tion (ĭn·flā′ shŭn)
in·fla·tion·ar·y
in·flec·tion (ĭn·flĕk′ shŭn)
-tion·al
in·flex·i·ble (ĭn·flĕk′ sĭ·b'l)
in·flex·i·bil·i·ty
         (ĭn·flĕk′ sĭ·bĭl′ ĭ·tĭ)
in·flict (ĭn·flĭkt′)
in·flic·tion (ĭn·flĭk′ shŭn)
in·flu·ence (ĭn′ flŏŏ·ĕns)
in·flu·en·tial (ĭn′ flŏŏ·ĕn′ shăl)
in·flu·en·za (ĭn′ flŏŏ·ĕn′ ză)
in·flux (ĭn′ flŭks)
in·form (ĭn·fôrm′)
in·form·ant (ĭn·fôr′ mănt)
in·for·ma·tion
         (ĭn′ fôr·mā′ shŭn)
in·form·a·tive (ĭn·fôr′ má·tĭv)
in·form·er
in·for·mal (ĭn·fôr′ măl)
-mal·ly
in·for·mal·i·ty
         (ĭn′ fôr·măl′ ĭ·tĭ)
in·frac·tion (ĭn·frăk′ shŭn)
in·fra·red (ĭn′ frá·rĕd′)
in·fre·quent (ĭn·frē′ kwĕnt)
-quen·cy
in·fringe (ĭn·frĭnj′)
-fring·ing   in·fringe·ment

in·fu·ri·ate (ĭn·fū′ rĭ·āt)
-at·ing
in·fuse (ĭn·fūz′)
-fus·ing
in·fu·sion (ĭn·fū′ zhŭn)
in·gen·ious (ĭn·jĕn′ yŭs)
(clever; see *ingenuous*)
in·gé·nue (ăn′ zhā′ nū′)
in·ge·nu·i·ty (ĭn′ jĕ·nū′ ĭ·tĭ)
in·gen·u·ous (ĭn·jĕn′ û·ŭs)
(frank; see *ingenious*)
in·gen·u·ous·ness
in·gest (ĭn·jĕst′)
in·ges·tion
in·glo·ri·ous (ĭn·glō′ rĭ·ŭs)
in·got i·ron (ĭng′ gŏt)
in·grained (ĭn′ grānd′)
in·grate (ĭn′ grāt)
in·grat·i·tude (ĭn·grăt′ ĭ·tūd)
in·gra·ti·ate (ĭn·grā′ shĭ·āt)
-at·ing
in·gra·ti·a·tion
         (ĭn·grā′ shĭ·ā′ shŭn)
in·gre·di·ent (ĭn·grē′ dĭ·ĕnt)
in·grown (ĭn′ grōn′)
in·hab·it (ĭn·hăb′ ĭt)
-ited   -it·ing
in·hab·it·able
in·hab·it·an·cy
         (ĭn·hăb′ ĭ·tăn·sĭ)
in·hab·it·ant
in·hale (ĭn·hāl′)
-hal·ing
in·hal·ant (ĭn·hāl′ ănt)
in·ha·la·tion (ĭn′ há·lā′ shŭn)
in·ha·la·tor (ĭn′ há·lā′ tēr)
in·her·ent (ĭn·hēr′ ĕnt)
-en·cy
in·her·it (ĭn·hĕr′ ĭt)
-it·ed   -it·ing
in·her·it·a·ble   in·her·it·ance
in·her·i·tor
in·hib·it (ĭn·hĭb′ ĭt)
-it·ed   -it·ing
in·hi·bi·tion (ĭn′ hĭ·bĭsh′ ŭn)
in·hib·i·tor
in·hib·i·to·ry (ĭn·hĭb′ ĭ·tō′ rĭ)
in·hos·pi·ta·ble
         (ĭn·hŏs′ pĭ·tá·b'l)
in·hu·man (ĭn·hū′ măn)
in·hu·man·i·ty
         (ĭn′ hū·măn′ ĭ·tĭ)
in·hu·man·ness
in·hu·mane (ĭn′ hû·mān′)
-mane·ly

in·hume (ĭn·hūm′)
  -hum·ing
in·im·i·cal (ĭn·ĭm′ ĭ·kə̆l)
in·im·i·ta·ble (ĭn·ĭm′ ĭ·tá·b'l)
in·iq·ui·tous (ĭ·nĭk′ wĭ·tŭs)
  in·iq·ui·ty -ties
in·i·tial (ĭ·nĭsh′ ă̆l)
  -tialed -tial·ing
  in·i·tial·ly
in·i·ti·ate (ĭ·nĭsh′ ĭ·āt)
  -at·ing
  in·i·ti·a·tion
    (ĭ·nĭsh′ ĭ·ā′ shŭn)
  in·i·ti·a·tive (ĭ·nĭsh′ ĭ·ā′ tĭv)
in·ject (ĭn·jĕkt′)
  in·jec·tion in·jec·tor
in·ju·di·cious (ĭn′ jōō·dĭsh′ ŭs)
in·junc·tion (ĭn·jŭngk′ shŭn)
in·jure (ĭn′ jĕr)
  -jur·ing
  in·ju·ri·ous (ĭn·jŏŏr′ ĭ·ŭs)
  in·ju·ry (ĭn′ jĕr·ĭ)
  -ries
in·jus·tice (ĭn·jŭs′ tĭs)
ink·ling (ĭngk′ lĭng)
in·laid (ĭn·lād′)
in·land (ĭn′ lănd)
in-law (ĭn′ lô′)
in·lay (ĭn′ lā′) n.
in·let (ĭn′ lĕt)
in·mate (ĭn′ māt)
in·most (ĭn′ mōst)
in·nards (ĭn′ ĕrdz)
in·nate (ĭn′ nāt)
in·ner·most (ĭn′ ĕr·mōst)
in·ner·vate (ĭ·nûr′ vāt)
  (to supply with nerves; see *ener-
  vate*)
  -vat·ing
  in·ner·va·tion (ĭn′ ĕr·vā′ shŭn)
in·ning (ĭn′ ĭng)
inn·keep·er (ĭn′ kēp′ ĕr)
in·no·cent (ĭn′ ŏ·sĕnt)
  -cence
in·noc·u·ous (ĭ·nŏk′ ŭ·ŭs)
in·no·vate (ĭn′ ŏ·vāt)
  -vat·ing
  in·no·va·tion (ĭn′ ŏ·vā′ shŭn)
  in·no·va·tor (ĭn′ ŏ·vā′ tĕr)
in·nu·en·do (ĭn′ ŭ·ĕn′ dō)
  -does
in·nu·mer·a·ble
    (ĭ·nū′ mĕr·á·b'l)
in·oc·u·late (ĭn·ŏk′ ŭ·lāt)
  -lat·ing

in·oc·u·la·tion
    (ĭn·ŏk′ ŭ·lā′ shŭn)
in·of·fen·sive (ĭn′ ŏ·fĕn′ sĭv)
in·op·er·a·ble (ĭn·ŏp′ ĕr·á·b'l)
in·op·er·a·tive (ĭn·ŏp′ ĕr·ā′ tĭv)
in·op·por·tune (ĭn·ŏp′ ŏr·tūn′)
  -tune·ly
in·or·di·nate (ĭn·ôr′ dĭ·nĭt)
in·or·gan·ic (ĭn′ ôr·găn′ ĭk)
in·put (ĭn′ pŏŏt′)
in·quest (ĭn′ kwĕst)
in·quire (ĭn·kwīr′)
  -quir·ing
  in·quir·y (ĭn·kwīr′ ĭ)
  -quir·ies
in·qui·si·tion (ĭn′ kwĭ·zĭsh′ ŭn)
in·quis·i·tive (ĭn·kwĭz′ ĭ·tĭv)
in·quis·i·tor (ĭn·kwĭz′ ĭ·tĕr)
  in·quis·i·to·ri·al
    (ĭn·kwĭz′ ĭ·tō′ rĭ·ăl)
in·rush·ing (ĭn′ rŭsh′ ĭng)
in·sane (ĭn·sān′)
  in·san·i·ty (ĭn·săn′ ĭ·tĭ)
in·sa·ti·a·ble (ĭn·sā′ shĭ·á·b'l)
in·scribe (ĭn·skrīb′)
  -scrib·ing
  in·scrip·tion (ĭn·skrĭp′ shŭn)
in·scru·ta·ble (ĭn·skrōō′ tá·b'l)
in·sect (ĭn′ sĕkt)
  in·sec·ti·cide (ĭn·sĕk′ tĭ·sīd)
in·se·cure (ĭn′ sĕ·kūr′)
  in·se·cu·ri·ty (ĭn′ sĕ·kū′ rĭ·tĭ)
in·sem·i·na·tion
    (ĭn·sĕm′ ĭ·nā′ shŭn)
in·sen·sate (ĭn·sĕn′ săt)
in·sen·si·ble (ĭn·sĕn′ sĭ·b'l)
in·sen·si·tive (ĭn·sĕn′ sĭ·tĭv)
in·sen·si·tiv·i·ty
    (ĭn·sĕn′ sĭ·tĭv′ ĭ·tĭ)
in·sep·a·ra·ble (ĭn·sĕp′ á·rá·b'l)
in·sert (ĭn·sûrt′) v.
  (ĭn′ sûrt) n.
  in·ser·tion (ĭn·sûr′ shŭn)
in·sid·i·ous (ĭn·sĭd′ ĭ·ŭs)
in·sight (ĭn′ sīt′)
in·sig·ni·a (ĭn·sĭg′ nĭ·á)
  n. pl.
  sing. in·sig·ne (-nē)
in·sig·nif·i·cant
    (ĭn′ sĭg·nĭf′ ĭ·kănt)
  -cance
in·sin·cere (ĭn′ sĭn·sēr′)
  -cere·ly
  in·sin·cer·i·ty (ĭn′ sĭn·sĕr′ ĭ·tĭ)

in·sin·u·ate (ĭn·sĭn′ ū·āt)
-at·ing
in·sin·u·a·tion
(ĭn·sĭn′ ū·ā′ shŭn)
in·sip·id (ĭn·sĭp′ ĭd)
in·sist (ĭn·sĭst′)
in·sist·ence (ĭn·sĭs′ těns)
-tent
in·so·far (ĭn′ sŏ·fär′)
in·sole (ĭn′ sōl′)
in·so·lent (ĭn′ sŏ·lĕnt)
-lence
in·sol·u·ble (ĭn·sŏl′ ū·b′l)
in·solv·a·ble (ĭn·sŏl′ vȧ·b′l)
in·sol·vency (ĭn·sŏl′ věn·sĭ)
in·som·nia (ĭn·sŏm′ nĭ·ȧ)
in·som·ni·ac (-ăk)
in·so·much as (ĭn′ sŏ·mŭch′)
in·sou·ci·ance (ĭn·sōō′ sĭ·ȧns)
in·spect (ĭn·spěkt′)
in·spec·tion (ĭn·spěk′ shŭn)
in·spec·tor
in·spire (ĭn·spīr′)
-spir·ing
in·spi·ra·tion·al
(ĭn′ spĭ·rā′ shŭn·ȧl)
in·spir·it (ĭn·spĭr′ ĭt)
in·sta·bil·i·ty (ĭn′ stȧ·bĭl′ ĭ·tĭ)
in·stall (ĭn·stôl′)
in·stal·la·tion (ĭn′ stȧ·lā′ shŭn)
in·stall·ment
in·stant (ĭn′ stȧnt)
-stance
in·stan·ta·ne·ous
(ĭn′ stȧn·tā′ ně·ŭs)
in·state (ĭn·stāt′)
-stat·ing
in·stead (ĭn·stěd′)
in·step (ĭn·stěp′)
in·sti·gate (ĭn·stĭ·gāt)
-gat·ing
in·sti·ga·tion (ĭn′ stĭ·gā′ shŭn)
in·sti·ga·tor
in·still (ĭn·stĭl′)
in·stinct (ĭn′ stĭngkt)
in·stinc·tive (ĭn·stĭngk′ tĭv)
in·sti·tute (ĭn′ stĭ·tūt)
-tut·ing
in·sti·tu·tion (ĭn′ stĭ·tū′ shŭn)
in·struct (ĭn·strŭkt′)
in·struc·tion (ĭn·strŭk′ shŭn)
-tion·al   in·struc·tive
in·struc·tor   in·struc·tress
in·stru·ment (ĭn′ strōō·měnt)

in·stru·men·tal
(ĭn′ strōō·měn′ tȧl)
in·stru·men·tal·i·ty
(ĭn′ strōō·měn·tăl′ ĭ·tĭ)
in·stru·men·ta·tion
(ĭn′ strōō·měn·tā′ shŭn)
in·sub·or·di·nate
(ĭn′ sŭ·bôr′ dĭ·nĭt)
in·sub·or·di·na·tion
(ĭn′ sŭ·bôr′ dĭ·nā′ shŭn)
in·sub·stan·tial
(ĭn′ sŭb·stăn′ shȧl)
-tial·ly
in·suf·fer·a·ble
(ĭn·sŭf′ ěr·ȧ·b′l)
in·suf·fi·cient (ĭn′ sŭ·fĭsh′ ěnt)
-cien·cy
in·su·lar (ĭn′ sŭ·lěr)
in·su·lar·i·ty (ĭn′ sŭ·lăr′ ĭ·tĭ)
in·su·late (ĭn′ sŭ·lāt)
-lat·ing
in·su·la·tion (ĭn′ sŭ·lā′ shŭn)
in·su·la·tor
in·su·lin (ĭn′ sŭ·lĭn)
in·sult (ĭn·sŭlt′) v.
(ĭn′ sŭlt) n.
in·su·per·a·ble
(ĭn·sū′ pěr·ȧ·b′l)
in·sup·port·a·ble
(ĭn′ sŭ·pōr′ tȧ·b′l)
in·sure (ĭn·shōōr′)
-sur·ing   in·sur·a·ble
in·sur·ance (ĭn·shōōr′ ȧns)
in·sur·gent (ĭn·sûr′ jěnt)
-gen·cy
in·sur·mount·a·ble
(ĭn′ sûr·moun′ tȧ·b′l)
in·sur·rec·tion (ĭn′ sŭ·rěk′ shŭn)
in·sus·cep·ti·ble
(ĭn′ sŭ·sěp′ tĭ·b′l)
in·tact (ĭn·tăkt′)
in·tagl·io (ĭn·tăl′ yō)
in·take (ĭn′ tāk′)
in·tan·gi·ble (ĭn·tăn′ jĭ·b′l)
in·te·ger (ĭn′ tě·jěr)
in·te·gral (ĭn′ tě·grȧl)
-gral·ly
in·te·grate (ĭn′ tě·grāt)
-grat·ing
in·te·gra·tion (ĭn′ tě·grā′ shŭn)
in·teg·ri·ty (ĭn·těg′ rĭ·tĭ)
in·tel·lect (ĭn′ tě·lěkt)
in·tel·lec·tu·al
(ĭn′ tě·lěk′ tū·ȧl)
-al·ly

in·tel·li·gent   (ĭn·tĕl′ ĭ·jĕnt)
-gence
in·tel·li·gent·si·a
    (ĭn·tĕl′ ĭ·jĕnt′ sĭ·á)
in·tel·li·gi·ble   (ĭn·tĕl′ ĭ·jĭ·b'l)
in·tel·li·gi·bil·i·ty
    (ĭn·tĕl′ ĭ·jĭ·bĭl′ ĭ·tĭ)
in·tem·per·ate   (ĭn·tĕm′ pēr·ĭt)
-ance
in·tend   (ĭn·tĕnd′)
in·tense   (ĭn·tĕns′)
in·ten·si·fy   -fied, -fy·ing
in·ten·si·ty
in·ten·sive   -sive·ly
in·tent   (ĭn·tĕnt′)
in·ten·tion   (ĭn·tĕn′ shŭn)
-tion·al
in·ter   (ĭn·tûr′)
-terred   -ter·ring
in·ter·ac·tion   (ĭn′ tēr·ăk′ shŭn)
in·ter·breed   (ĭn′ tēr·brēd′)
in·ter·cede   (ĭn′ tēr·sēd′)
-ced·ing
in·ter·cept   (ĭn′ tēr·sĕpt′)
in·ter·cep·tion in·ter·cep·tor
in·ter·ces·sion   (ĭn′ tēr·sĕsh′ ŭn)
in·ter·change   (ĭn′ tēr·chānj′)
-chang·ing
in·ter·change·a·ble
in·ter·com   (ĭn′ tēr·kŏm′)
in·ter·con·nec·tion
    (ĭn′ tēr·kŏ·nĕk′ shŭn)
in·ter·course   (ĭn′ tēr·kōrs)
in·ter·de·pend·ence
    (ĭn′ tēr·dĕ·pĕn′ dĕns)
in·ter·dict   (ĭn′ tēr·dĭkt′)
in·ter·est   (ĭn′ tēr·ĕst)
in·ter·est·ed·ly
in·ter·fere   (ĭn′ tēr·fĕr′)
-fer·ing
in·ter·fer·ence   (ĭn′ tēr·fĕr′ ĕns)
in·ter·im   (ĭn′ tēr·ĭm)
in·te·ri·or   (ĭn·tēr′ ĭ·ēr)
in·ter·ject   (ĭn′ tēr·jĕkt′)
in·ter·jec·tion
in·ter·lace   (ĭn′ tēr·lās′)
-lac·ing
in·ter·lard   (ĭn′ tēr·lärd′)
in·ter·lin·ing   (ĭn′ tēr·lĭn′ ĭng)
in·ter·lock   (ĭn′ tēr·lŏk′)
in·ter·loc·u·tor
    (ĭn′ tēr·lŏk′ ū·tēr)
in·ter·lop·er   (ĭn′ tēr·lōp′ ēr)
in·ter·lude   (ĭn′ tēr·lūd)

in·ter·mar·riage
    (ĭn′ tēr·măr′ ĭj)
in·ter·me·di·ar·y
    (ĭn′ tēr·mē′ dĭ·ĕr′ ĭ)
in·ter·me·di·ate
    (ĭn′ tēr·mē′ dĭ·ĭt)
in·ter·mez·zo   (ĭn′ tēr·mĕd′ zō)
in·ter·mi·na·ble
    (ĭn·tûr′ mĭ·ná·b'l)
in·ter·mis·sion   (ĭn′ tēr·mĭsh′ ŭn)
in·ter·mit·tent   (ĭn′ tēr·mĭt′ ĕnt)
-mit·ten·cy
in·ter·mix·ture   (ĭn′ tēr·mĭks′ tūr)
in·tern   (ĭn′ tûrn)
in·tern·ship
in·ter·nal   (ĭn·tûr′ năl)
-nal·ly
in·ter·na·tion·al
    (ĭn′ tēr·năsh′ ŭn·ăl)
in·ter·ne·cine   (ĭn′ tēr·nē′ sĭn)
in·tern·ment   (ĭn·tûrn′ mĕnt)
in·ter·phone   (ĭn′ tēr·fōn′)
in·ter·po·late   (ĭn·tûr′ pŏ·lāt)
-lat·ing
in·ter·po·la·tion
    (ĭn·tûr′ pŏ·lā′ shŭn)
in·ter·pose   (ĭn′ tēr·pōz′)
-pos·ing
in·ter·pret   (ĭn·tûr′ prĕt)
in·ter·pre·ta·tion
    (ĭn·tûr′ prĕ·tā′ shŭn)
in·ter·pret·er   in·ter·pre·tive
in·ter·reg·num
    (ĭn′ tēr·rĕg′ nŭm)
in·ter·ro·gate   (ĭn·tĕr′ ŏ·gāt)
-gat·ing   in·ter·ro·ga·tor
in·ter·rog·a·tive
    (ĭn′ tĕ·rŏg′ á·tĭv)
in·ter·rog·a·to·ry
    (ĭn′ tĕ·rŏg′ á·tō′ rĭ)
in·ter·rupt   (ĭn′ tĕ·rŭpt′)
in·ter·rup·tion
    (ĭn′ tĕ·rŭp′ shŭn)
in·ter·sect   (ĭn′ tēr·sĕkt′)
in·ter·sperse   (ĭn′ tēr·spûrs′)
-spers·ing
in·ter·sper·sion   (-spûr′ shŭn)
in·ter·state   (ĭn′ tēr·stāt′)
in·ter·stel·lar   (ĭn′ tēr·stĕl′ ēr)
in·ter·stice   (ĭn·tûr′ stĭs)
in·ter·sti·tial   (ĭn′ tēr·stĭsh′ ăl)
in·ter·val   (ĭn′ tēr·văl)
in·ter·vene   (ĭn′ tēr·vēn′)
-ven·ing
in·ter·ven·tion   (-vĕn′ shŭn)

in·ter·view (ĭn′ tẽr·vū)
  in·ter·view·er
in·ter·weave (ĭn′ tẽr·wēv′)
  -weav·ing
  in·ter·wo·ven (ĭn′ tẽr·wō′ vĕn)
in·tes·tate (ĭn·tĕs′ tāt)
in·tes·tine (ĭn·tĕs′ tĭn)
  in·tes·ti·nal (ĭn·tĕs′ tĭ·nắl)
in·ti·mate (ĭn′ tĭ·māt) v.
  -mat·ing
  in·ti·ma·tion (ĭn′ tĭ·mā′ shŭn)
in·ti·mate (ĭn′ tĭ·mĭt) adj.
  in·ti·ma·cy (ĭn′ tĭ·má·sĭ)
  in·ti·mate·ly (-mĭt·lĭ′)
in·tim·i·date (ĭn·tĭm′ ĭ·dāt)
  -dat·ing
in·tol·er·a·ble (ĭn·tŏl′ ẽr·á·b′l)
in·tol·er·ant (ĭn·tŏl′ ẽr·ắnt)
  -rance
in·to·na·tion (ĭn′ tŏ·nā′ shŭn)
in·tox·i·cate (ĭn·tŏk′ sĭ·kāt)
  -cat·ing
  in·tox·i·cant (ĭn·tŏk′ sĭ·kănt)
  in·tox·i·ca·tion
    (ĭn·tŏk′ sĭ·kā′ shŭn)
in·trac·ta·ble (ĭn·trăk′ tá·b′l)
in·tra·mu·ral (ĭn′ trá·mū′ rắl)
in·tran·si·gent (ĭn·trăn′ sĭ·jĕnt)
  -gen·cy
in·tran·si·tive (ĭn·trăn′ sĭ·tĭv)
in·tra·ve·nous (ĭn′ trá·vē′ nŭs)
in·trep·id (ĭn·trĕp′ ĭd)
in·tri·cate (ĭn′ trĭ·kĭt)
  -cate·ly
  in·tri·ca·cy (-ká·sĭ)
in·trigue (ĭn·trēg′)
  -tri·guing
in·trin·sic (ĭn·trĭn′ sĭk)
  in·trin·si·cal·ly
in·tro·duce (ĭn′ trŏ·dūs′)
  -duc·ing
in·tro·duc·tion
    (ĭn′ trŏ·dŭk′ shŭn)
  in·tro·duc·to·ry
    (ĭn′ trŏ·dŭk′ tŏ·rĭ)
in·tro·it (ĭn·trō′ ĭt)
in·tro·jec·tion (ĭn′ trŏ·jĕk′ shŭn)
in·tro·spec·tive (ĭn′ trŏ·spĕk′ tĭv)
in·tro·ver·sion (ĭn′ trŏ·vûr′ shŭn)
in·tro·vert (ĭn′ trŏ·vûrt′) n.
in·trude (ĭn·trōōd′)
  -trud·ing
  in·tru·sion (ĭn·trōō′ zhŭn)
  in·tru·sive (-sĭv)

in·tu·i·tion (ĭn′ tû·ĭsh′ ŭn)
  in·tu·i·tive (ĭn·tū′ ĭ·tĭv)
  in·tu·i·tive·ness
in·un·date (ĭn′ ŭn·dāt)
  -dat·ing
  in·un·da·tion (ĭn′ ŭn·dā′ shŭn)
in·ure (ĭn·ūr′)
  -ur·ing   in·ure·ment
in·vade (ĭn·vād′)
  -vad·ing
in·val·id (ĭn·văl′ ĭd) adj.
  (null)
  in·val·i·date (ĭn·văl′ ĭ·dāt)
  in·val·i·da·tion
    (ĭn·văl′ ĭ·dā′ shŭn)
in·va·lid (ĭn′ vá·lĭd)
  adj., n.; (sick)
  in·va·lid·ism
in·val·u·a·ble (ĭn·văl′ û·á·b′l)
in·var·i·a·ble (ĭn·vâr′ ĭ·á·b′l)
in·va·sion (ĭn·vā′ zhŭn)
in·vec·tive (ĭn·vĕk′ tĭv)
in·veigh (ĭn·vā′)
in·vei·gle (ĭn·vē′ g′l)
  -gling
in·vent (ĭn·vĕnt′)
  in·ven·tion (ĭn·vĕn′ shŭn)
  in·ven·tive
in·ven·to·ry (ĭn′ vĕn·tŏ′ rĭ)
  -ries
in·verse (ĭn·vûrs′)
  -verse·ly
in·ver·sion (ĭn·vûr′ shŭn)
in·vert (ĭn·vûrt′) v.
  (ĭn′ vûrt) n.
in·ver·te·brate (ĭn·vûr′ tĕ·brāt)
in·ves·ti·gate (ĭn·vĕs′ tĭ·gāt)
  -gat·ing
  in·ves·ti·ga·tion
    (ĭn·vĕs′ tĭ·gā′ shŭn)
  in·ves·ti·ga·tive
    (ĭn·vĕs′ tĭ·gā′ tĭv)
  in·ves·ti·ga·tor
    (ĭn·vĕs′ tĭ·gā′ tẽr)
in·ves·ti·ture (ĭn·vĕs′ tĭ·tûr)
in·vest·ment (ĭn·vĕst′ mĕnt)
in·ves·tor (ĭn·vĕs′ tẽr)
in·vet·er·ate (ĭn·vĕt′ ẽr·ĭt)
in·vid·i·ous (ĭn·vĭd′ ĭ·ŭs)
in·vig·or·at·ing
    (ĭn·vĭg′ ẽr·āt′ ĭng)
in·vin·ci·ble (ĭn·vĭn′ sĭ·b′l)
  in·vin·ci·bil·i·ty
    (ĭn·vĭn′ sĭ·bĭl′ ĭ·tĭ)
in·vi·o·la·ble (ĭn·vī′ ŏ·lá·b′l)
  in·vi·o·late (ĭn·vī′ ŏ·lāt)

in·vis·i·ble (ĭn·vĭz′ ĭ·b′l)
 in·vis·i·bil·i·ty
  (ĭn·vĭz′ ĭ·bĭl′ ĭ·tĭ)
in·vi·ta·tion (ĭn′ vĭ·tā′ shŭn)
in·vite (ĭn·vīt′)
 -vit·ing
in·vo·ca·tion (ĭn′ vô·kā′ shŭn)
in·voice (ĭn·vois)
in·voke (ĭn·vōk′)
 -vok·ing
 in·vo·ca·tion (ĭn′ vô·kā′ shŭn)
in·vol·un·tar·y (ĭn·vŏl′ ŭn·tĕr′ ĭ)
 in·vol·un·tar·i·ly
in·vo·lu·tion (ĭn′ vō·lū′ shŭn)
in·volve·ment (ĭn·vŏlv′ mĕnt)
in·vul·ner·a·ble
  (ĭn·vŭl′ nĕr·a·b′l)
 in·vul·ner·a·bil·i·ty
  (ĭn·vŭl′ nĕr·a·bĭl′ ĭ·tĭ)
in·ward (ĭn′ wĕrd)
i·o·dide (ī′ ô·dĭd)
 i·o·dine (ī′ ô·dīn)
i·on (ī′ ŏn)
 i·on·ic (ī·ŏn′ ĭk)
 i·on·ize (ī′ ŏn·īz)
 i·on·o·sphere (ī·ŏn′ ô·sfēr)
i·o·ta (ī·ō′ tá)
I·O·U (ī′ ō′ ū′)
I·o·wa (ī′ ô·wá)
 abbr. Ia.
 I·o·wan
I·Q (ī′ kū′)
 I·Qs
I·ra·ni·an (ī·rā′ nĭ·ăn)
I·ra·qi (ê·rä′ kê)
i·ras·ci·ble (ĭ·răs′ ĭ·b′l)
i·rate (ī′ rāt)
ire·ful (īr′ fôól)
ir·i·des·cent (ĭr′ ĭ·dĕs′ ĕnt)
 -cence
i·ris (ī′ rĭs)
I·rish·man (ī′ rĭsh·măn)
irk·some (ûrk′ sŭm)
i·ron (īr′ ẽrn)
 i·ron·clad i·ron cur·tain
 i·ron lung i·ron·work
i·ro·ny (ī′ rŏ·nĭ)
 i·ron·i·cal (ī·rŏn′ ĭ·kăl)
 -cal·ly
Ir·o·quois (ĭr′ ô·kwoi)
ir·ra·di·ate (ĭ·rā′ dĭ·āt)
 -at·ing
 ir·ra·di·a·tion (ĭ·rā′ dĭ·ā′ shŭn)
ir·ra·tion·al (ĭr′ răsh′ ŭn·ăl)

ir·ra·tion·al·i·ty
  (ĭr′ răsh′ ŭn·ăl′ ĭ·tĭ)
ir·re·claim·a·ble
  (ĭr′ rê·klām·′ a·b′l)
ir·rec·on·cil·a·ble
  (ĭr′ rĕk′ ŏn·sĭl′ a·b′l)
ir·re·cov·er·a·ble
  (ĭr′ rê·kŭv′ ẽr·a·b′l)
ir·re·deem·a·ble
  (ĭr′ rê·dēm′ a·b′l)
ir·re·duc·i·ble (ĭr′ rê·dūs′ ĭ·b′l)
ir·ref·u·ta·ble (ĭr·rĕf′ û·ta·b′l)
ir·reg·u·lar (ĭr·rĕg′ û·lẽr)
 ir·reg·u·lar·i·ty
  (ĭr·rĕg′ û·lăr′ ĭ·tĭ)
ir·rel·e·vant (ĭr·rĕl′ ê·vănt)
 -van·cy
ir·re·li·gious (ĭr′ rê·lĭj′ ŭs)
ir·re·me·di·a·ble
  (ĭr′ rê·mē′ dĭ·a·b′l)
ir·rep·a·ra·ble (ĭ·rĕp′ a·ra·b′l)
ir·re·place·a·ble
  (ĭr′ rê·plās′ a·b′l)
ir·re·press·i·ble
  (ĭr′ rê·prĕs′ ĭ·b′l)
ir·re·proach·a·ble
  (ĭr′ rê·prōch′ a·b′l)
ir·re·sist·i·ble (ĭr′ rê·zĭs′ tĭ·b′l)
ir·res·o·lute (ĭ·rĕz′ ô·lūt)
ir·re·spec·tive (ĭr·rê·spĕk′ tĭv)
ir·re·spon·si·ble
  (ĭr′ rê·spŏn′ sĭ·b′l)
 ir·re·spon·si·bil·i·ty
  (ĭr′ rê·spŏn′ sĭ·bĭl′ ĭ·tĭ)
ir·re·triev·a·ble
  (ĭr′ rê·trēv′ a·b′l)
ir·rev·er·ence (ĭr′ rĕv′ ẽr·ĕns)
ir·re·vers·i·ble (ĭr′ rê·vûr′ sĭ·b′l)
ir·rev·o·ca·ble (ĭ·rĕv′ ô·ka·b′l)
ir·ri·gate (ĭr′ ĭ·gāt)
 -gat·ing
 ir·ri·ga·ble (ĭr′ ĭ·ga·b′l)
 ir·ri·ga·tion (ĭr′ ĭ·gā′ shŭn)
ir·ri·ta·ble (ĭr′ ĭ·ta·b′l)
 ir·ri·ta·bil·i·ty
  (ĭr′ ĭ·ta·bĭl′ ĭ·tĭ)
ir·ri·tant (ĭr′ ĭ·tănt)
 -tan·cy
ir·ri·tate (ĭr′ ĭ·tāt)
 -tat·ing
 ir·ri·ta·tion (ĭr′ ĭ·tā′ shŭn)
ir·rup·tion (ĭ·rŭp′ shŭn)
 ir·rup·tive
i·sin·glass (ī′ zĭng·glás′)

Is·lam (ĭs′ lȧm)
  Is·lam·ic (ĭs·lăm′ ĭk)
is·land (ī′ lănd)
  is·land·er
isle (īl)
  (small island; see *aisle*)
  is·let (ī′ lĕt)
i·so·bar (ī′ sṓ·bär)
i·so·late (ī′ sṓ·lāt)
  -lat·ing
  i·so·la·tion (ī′ sṓ·lā′ shŭn)
i·sos·ce·les (ī·sŏs′ ĕ·lēz)
i·so·tope (ī′ sṓ·tōp)
Is·ra·el (ĭz′ rĭ·ĕl)
  Is·rae·li (ĭz·rā′ lĭ)
  Is·ra·el·ite (ĭz′ rĭ·ĕl·ĭt)
is·sue (ĭsh′ ū)
  is·su·ing
  is·su·ance (ĭsh′ ū·ȧns)
  is·su·ant
Is·tan·bul, Turk. (ĭs′ tăm·bōōl′)
isth·mus (ĭs′ mŭs)
I·tal·ian (ĭ·tăl′ yȧn)
i·tal·ic (ĭ·tăl′ ĭk)
  i·tal·i·cize (ĭ·tăl′ ĭ·sīz)
  -ciz·ing
i·tem·ize (ī′ tĕm·īz)
  -iz·ing
i·tin·er·ant (ĭ·tĭn′ ēr·ȧnt)
i·tin·er·ar·y (ĭ·tĭn′ ēr·ĕr′ ĭ)
  -ar·ies
its (ĭts)
  (belonging to it)
it's (ĭts)
  (it is, it has)
it·self (ĭt·sĕlf′)
i·vor·y (ī′ vṓ·rĭ)
i·vy (ī′ vĭ)
  i·vies

J

ja·bot (zhȧ′ bō′)
jack (jăk)
  jack-in-the-pul·pit
  jack·knife
  jack-of-all-trades
  jack-o′-lan·tern
  jack·pot   jack rab·bit
jack·al (jăk′ ôl)
jack·et (jăk′ ĕt)
jag·ged (jăg′ ĕd)
jag·uar (jăg′ wär)
jail·bird (jāl′ bûrd′)

Ja·mai·ca (jȧ·mā′ kȧ)
jam·bo·ree (jăm′ bŏ·rē′)
jan·i·tor (jăn′ ĭ·tēr)
  jan·i·to·ri·al (jăn′ ĭ·tō′ rĭ·ȧl)
Jan·u·ar·y (jăn′ ū·ĕr′ ĭ)
Jap·a·nese (jăp′ ȧ·nēz′)
jar·gon (jär′ gŏn)
jas·mine (jăz′ mĭn)
jaun·dice (jôn′ dĭs)
jaun·ty (jôn′ tĭ)
  jaun·ti·ly
jave·lin (jăv′ lĭn)
jaw·bone (jô′ bōn′)
jay·walk·er (jā′ wôk′ ēr)
jazz·y (jăz′ ĭ)
jeal·ous·y (jĕl′ ŭs·ĭ)
  -ous·ies
jeans (jēnz)
jeep (jēp)
Jef·fer·so·ni·an (jĕf′ ēr·sō′ nĭ·ȧn)
Je·ho·vah (jĕ·hō′ vȧ)
je·june (jĕ·jōōn′)
jel·ly (jĕl′ ĭ)
  jel·lied   jel·ly·ing
  jel·ly·fish
jeop·ard·y (jĕp′ ēr·dĭ)
  jeop·ard·ize   -iz·ing
jer·kin (jûr′ kĭn)
jerk·y (jûr′ kĭ)
  jerk·i·ness
jer·ry-built (jĕr′ ĭ·bĭlt′)
jer·sey (jûr′ zĭ)
  -seys
Je·ru·sa·lem (jĕ·rōō′ sȧ·lĕm)
jest·er (jĕs′ tēr)
Jes·u·it (jĕz′ ū·ĭt)
jet pro·pul·sion (jĕt)
jet·sam (jĕt′ săm)
jet·ti·son (jĕt′ ĭ·sŭn)
jet·ty (jĕt′ ĭ)
  jet·ties
jew·el (jōō′ ĕl)
  -eled   -el·ing
  jew·el·er   jew·el·ry
Jew·ry (jōō′ rĭ)
jew′s-harp (jōōz′ härp′)
Jez·e·bel (jĕz′ ĕ·bĕl)
jibe (jīb)
  jib·ing
jif·fy (jĭf′ ĭ)
jig·ger (jĭg′ ēr)
jig·saw puz·zle (jĭg′ sô′)
jin·gle (jĭng′ g′l)
  -gling

jin·go (jĭng′ gō)
  -goes   jin·go·ism
jin·rik·i·sha (jĭn·rĭk′ shä)
jit·ney (jĭt′ nĭ)
jock·ey (jŏk′ ĭ)
jo·cose (jō·kōs′)
  jo·cos·i·ty (jō·kŏs′ ĭ·tĭ)
joc·u·lar (jŏk′ ū·lẽr)
  joc·u·lar·i·ty (jŏk′ ū·lăr′ ĭ·tĭ)
joc·und (jŏk′ ŭnd)
  jo·cun·di·ty (jō·kŭn′ dĭ·tĭ)
jodh·purs (jŏd′ pẽrz)
jog·gle (jŏg′ 'l)
  jog·gling
Jo·han·nes·burg, S. Afr.
        (jō·hăn′ ĭs·bûrg)
John·son City, (jŏn′ s'n)
  N.Y., Tenn.
Johns·town, Pa. (jŏnz′ toun)
joie de vi·vre (zhwả′ dẽ·vẽ′ vr')
joint (joint)
  join·ture (join′ tůr)
jok·ing·ly (jōk′ ĭng·lĭ)
jol·li·ty (jŏl′ ĭ·tĭ)
  jol·li·ness
jon·quil (jŏng′ kwĭl)
jos·tle (jŏs′ 'l)
  -tling
jour·nal (jûr′ nɑ̆l)
  jour·nal·ese (jûr′ nɑ̆l·ēz′)
  jour·nal·ism
  jour·nal·is·tic (jûr′ nɑ̆l·ĭs′ tĭk)
jour·ney (jûr′ nĭ)
  -neys
joust (jŭst)
jo·vi·al (jō′ vĭ·ɑ̆l)
  -al·ly
jowl (joul)
joy·ful (joi′ fo͝ol)
  joy·ous (joi′ ŭs)
ju·bi·lant (jo͞o′ bĭ·lɑ̆nt)
  -lance
ju·bi·la·tion (jo͞o′ bĭ·lā′ shŭn)
ju·bi·lee (jo͞o′ bĭ·lē)
judge (jŭj)
  judg·ing
  judg·ment
ju·di·ca·ture (jo͞o′ dĭ·kɑ̆·tůr)
ju·di·cial (jo͞o·dĭsh′ ɑ̆l)
  -cial·ly
  ju·di·ci·ar·y (jo͞o·dĭsh′ ĭ·ẽr′ ĭ)
  ju·di·cious (jo͞o·dĭsh′ ŭs)
jug·ger·naut (jŭg′ ẽr·nôt)
jug·gler (jŭg′ lẽr)
jug·u·lar vein (jŭg′ ū·lẽr)

juice (jo͞os)
  juic·i·ness   juic·y
ju·jit·su (jo͞o·jĭt′ so͞o)
juke·box (jo͞ok′ bŏks′)
ju·lep (jo͞o′ lĕp)
ju·li·enne (jo͞o′ lĭ·ĕn′)
jum·bled (jŭm′ b'ld)
jum·bo (jŭm′ bō)
junc·tion (jŭngk′ shŭn)
junc·ture (jŭngk′ tůr)
jun·gle (jŭng′ g'l)
jun·ior (jo͞on′ yẽr)
ju·ni·per (jo͞o′ nĭ·pẽr)
jun·ket (jŭng′ kĕt)
jun·ta (jŭn′ tả)
ju·rid·i·cal (jo͞o·rĭd′ ĭ·kɑ̆l)
ju·ris·dic·tion (jo͝or′ ĭs·dĭk′ shŭn)
ju·ris·pru·dence
        (jo͝or′ ĭs·pro͞o′ dĕns)
ju·ry (jo͝or′ ĭ)
  ju·ries   ju·rist
  ju·ror
jus·tice (jŭs′ tĭs)
jus·ti·fy (jŭs′ tĭ·fĭ)
  -fied,   -fy·ing
  jus·ti·fi·a·ble (jŭs′ tĭ·fĭ′ ả·b'l)
  jus·ti·fi·ca·tion
        (jŭs′ tĭ·fĭ·kā′ shŭn)
ju·ve·nile (jo͞o′ vĕ·nĭl)
jux·ta·pose (jŭks′ tả·pōz′)
  jux·ta·po·si·tion
        (jŭks′ tả·pŏ·zĭsh′ ŭn)

K

kai·ser (kī′ zẽr)
kale (kāl)
ka·lei·do·scope (kả·lī′ dŏ·skŏp′)
kan·ga·roo (kăng′ gả·ro͞o′)
Kan·sas (kăn′ zɑ̆s)
  abbr. Kans. or Kan.
  Kan·san
ka·pok (kā′ pŏk)
ka·put (kä·po͝ot′)
kar·a·kul (kăr′ ả·kŭl)
ka·ty·did (kā′ tĭ dĭd′)
Kau·ai (is.) (kou′ ī)
kay·ak (kī′ ăk)
keel·boat (kēl′ bōt′)
keen·ness (kēn′ nĕs)
keep·sake (kēp′ sāk′)
kelp (kĕlp)
Ken·ne·dy, John F. and
  Jac·que·line (kĕn′ ĕ·dĭ)

ken·nel (kĕn′ ĕl)
Ken·tuck·y (kĕn·tŭk′ ĭ)
  abbr. Ky.
  Ken·tuck·i·an
Ken·ya (kĕn′ yȧ)
ker·chief (kûr′ chĭf)
ker·nel (kûr′ nĕl)
ker·o·sene (kĕr′ ô·sēn′)
ketch (kĕch)
ket·tle·drum (kĕt′ 'l·drŭm′)
key (kē)
  key·board key·hole
  key·note key sig·na·ture
  key·stone
khak·i (kăk′ ĭ)
khe·dive (kĕ·dēv′)
Khru·shchev, Ni·ki·ta
          (ⱪrŏŏsh·chôf′, nyĭ·kē′ tȧ)
kib·itz·er (kĭb′ ĭt·sẽr)
kick·back (kĭk′ băk′)
kid·nap (kĭd′ năp)
  -naped -nap·ing
  kid·nap·er
kid·ney (kĭd′ nĭ)
kill·deer (kĭl′ dḗr′)
kill-joy (kĭl′ joi′)
kiln (kĭl)
ki·lo- (kĭl′ ô-)
  kil·o·cy·cle kil·o·gram
  kil·o·me·ter kil·o·watt
  kil·o·watt-hour
ki·mo·no (kĭ·mō′ nȧ)
  -nos
kin·der·gar·ten
          (kĭn′ dẽr·gär′ t'n)
  kin·der·gart·ner
kind·heart·ed (kĭnd′ här′ tĕd)
kin·dle (kĭn′ d'l)
  -dling
kind·ly (kĭnd′ lĭ)
  kind·li·er -li·est, -li·ness
kin·dred (kĭn′ drĕd)
kin·e·scope (kĭn′ ê·skōp′)
kin·es·thet·ic (kĭn′ ĕs·thĕt′ ĭk)
ki·net·ic (kĭ·nĕt′ ĭk)
king·dom (kĭng′ dŭm)
king·fish·er (kĭng′ fĭsh′ ẽr)
kins·man (kĭnz′ mȧn)
ki·osk (kĕ·ŏsk′)
kirsch (kĭrsh)
kis·met (kĭz′ mĕt)
kitch·en (kĭch′ ĕn)
  kitch·en·ette (kĭch′ ĕ·nĕt′)
  kitch·en·ware
kit·ten (kĭt′ 'n)

klep·to·ma·ni·a
          (klĕp′ tô·mā′ nĭ·ȧ)
  klep·to·ma·ni·ac
          (-ăk)
klieg light (klēg)
klis·ter (klĭs′ tẽr)
knack (năk)
knap·sack (năp′ săk′)
knave (nāv)
  knav·er·y (nāv′ ẽr·ĭ)
  knav·ish
knead (nēd)
knee·cap (nē′ kăp′)
kneel (nēl)
  knelt (nĕlt)
knell (nĕl)
knick·ers (nĭk′ ẽrz)
knick·knack (nĭk′ năk′)
knife (nīf)
  pl. knives (nīvz)
knight (nīt)
  knight-er·rant knight·hood
knit (nĭt)
  knit·ting knit·wear
knob (nŏb)
  knob·by
knock (nŏk)
  knock·down knock·kneed
  knock·out
knoll (nōl)
knot (nŏt)
  knot·ted knot·ting
  knot·hole knot·ty
know (nō)
  know·a·ble know·how
  know·ing·ly known
knowl·edge (nŏl′ ĕj)
  knowl·edge·a·ble
          (nŏl′ ĕj·ȧ·b'l)
knuck·le (nŭk′ 'l)
ko·a·la (kô·ä′ lȧ)
Ko·dak (kō′ dăk)
  Ko·da·chrome
Ko·di·ak bear (kō′ dĭ·ăk)
kohl·ra·bi (kōl′ rä′ bĭ)
ko·sher (kō′ shẽr)
kow·tow (kō′ tou′)
kraft pa·per (kräft)
krem·lin (krĕm′ lĭn)
Ku·blai Khan (kū′ blī kän′)
ku·dos (kū′ dŏs)
Ku Klux Klan (kū klŭks klăn)
kum·quat (kŭm′ kwŏt)

L

la·bel (lā′ bĕl)
-beled -bel·ing
la·bor (lā′ bĕr)
la·bor·er
la·bo·ri·ous (lȧ·bō′ rĭ·ŭs)
la·bor·sav·ing la·bor un·ion
lab·o·ra·to·ry (lăb′ ȯ·rȧ·tō′ rĭ)
-ries
lab·y·rinth (lăb′ ĭ·rĭnth)
lac·er·ate (lăs′ ĕr·āt)
-at·ing
lac·er·a·tion (lăs′ ĕr·ā′ shŭn)
lach·ry·mal (lăk′ rĭ·mȧl)
lach·ry·mose (lăk′ rĭ·mōs)
lack·a·dai·si·cal
(lăk′ ȧ·dā′ zĭ·kȧl)
lack·ey (lăk′ ĭ)
-eys
lack·lus·ter (lăk′ lŭs′ tēr)
la·con·ic (lȧ·kŏn′ ĭk)
la·con·i·cal·ly
lac·quer (lăk′ ēr)
la·crosse (lȧ·krôs′)
lac·ta·tion (lăk·tā′ shŭn)
lac·tic ac·id (lăk′ tĭk)
lac·tose (lăk′ tōs)
lac·y (lās′ ĭ)
lac·i·ness
lad·der-back chair
(lăd′ ēr·băk′)
lad·en (lād′ ′n)
lad·ing (lād′ ĭng)
(bill of)
la·dle (lā′ d′l)
-dling
la·dy (lā′ dĭ)
-dies la·dy·fin·ger
la·dy-kill·er la·dy·like
la·dy's-slip·per
la·ger beer (lä′ gēr)
lag·gard (lăg′ ērd)
la·goon (lȧ·gōōn′)
lais·sez faire (lĕ′ sā′ fâr′)
la·i·ty (lā′ ĭ·tĭ)
lama (lä·mȧ)
(priest; see llama)
La·ma·ism (lä′ mȧ·ĭz′m)
lam·baste (lăm′ bāst′)
-bast·ing
lamb·skin (lăm′ skĭn′)
la·mé (lȧ′ mā′)

la·ment (lȧ′ mĕnt′)
lam·en·ta·ble (lăm′ ĕn·tȧ·b′l)
lam·en·ta·tion
(lăm′ ĕn·tā′ shŭn)
la·ment·ed (lȧ·mĕn′ tĕd)
lam·i·nate (lăm′ ĭ·nāt)
-nat·ing
lam·i·nar (lăm′ ĭ·nēr)
lam·i·na·tion (lăm′ ĭ·nā′ shŭn)
lamp·black (lămp′ blăk′)
lam·poon (lăm·pōōn′)
lam·poon·er·y
lam·prey eel (lăm′ prĭ)
lance (lăns)
lanc·ing
lan·cet (lăn′ sĕt)
land (lănd)
land-grant col·lege
land·hold·er land·lord
land·lub·ber land·own·er
land·scape land·slide
lan·guage (lăng′ gwĭj)
lan·guid (lăng′ gwĭd)
lan·guish·ing (lăng′ gwĭsh·ĭng)
lan·guor (lăng′ gēr)
lan·guor·ous (lăng′ gēr·ŭs)
lank·y (lăngk′ ĭ)
lank·i·ness
lan·o·lin (lăn′ ȯ·lĭn)
lan·tern (lăn′ tērn)
lan·yard (lăn′ yērd)
Laos (louz)
La·o·tian (lä·ō′ shȧn)
la·pel (lȧ·pĕl′)
lap·i·dar·y (lăp′ ĭ·dĕr′ ĭ)
lap·is laz·u·li (lăp′ ĭs lăz′ ū·lĭ)
Lap·land·er (lăp′ lăn·dēr)
Lapp
lapse (lăps)
laps·ing
lar·ce·ny (lär′ sĕ·nĭ)
-nies lar·ce·nist
lar·ce·nous
lard·er (lär′ dēr)
large·ly (lärj′ lĭ)
large-scale (lärj′ skāl′)
lar·gess (lär′ jĕs)
lar·ghet·to (lär·gĕt′ ō)
lar·go (lär′ gō)
lar·i·at (lär′ ĭ·ȧt)
lark·spur (lärk′ spŭr)
lar·va (lär′ vȧ)
pl. lar·vae (-vē)
lar·vi·cide (lär′ vĭ·sīd)
lar·yn·gi·tis (lăr′ ĭn·jī′ tĭs)

lar·ynx   (lăr′ ĭngks)
  pl. la·ryn·ges   (lȧ·rĭn′ jēz)
las·civ·i·ous   (lȧ·sĭv′ ĭ·ŭs)
las·si·tude   (lăs′ ĭ·tūd)
las·so   (lăs′ ō)
  las·soed   las·so·ing
  las·sos
last·ing·ly   (làst′ ĭng·lĭ)
latch·key   (lăch′ kē′)
la·teen sail   (lȧ·tēn′)
late·ly   (lāt′ lĭ)
la·tent   (lā′ tĕnt)
  la·ten·cy
lat·er·al   (lăt′ ēr·ȧl)
  -al·ly
la·tex   (lā′ tĕks)
lath·work   (láth′ wûrk′)
lat·i·tude   (lăt′ ĭ·tūd)
  lat·i·tu·di·nal   (lăt′ ĭ·tū′ dĭ·nȧl)
la·trine   (lȧ·trēn′)
lat·ter·most   (lăt′ ēr·mōst)
lat·tice   (lăt′ ĭs)
  lat·tice·work   lat·tic·ing
laud   (lôd)
  laud·a·ble
  laud·a·to·ry   (lôd′ ȧ·tō′ rĭ)
lau·da·num   (lô′ dȧ·nŭm)
laugh   (lăf)
  laugh·a·ble   laugh·ing·stock
  laugh·ter
launch   (lônch)
laun·der   (lôn′ dēr)
  laun·dress   (lôn′ drĕs)
  laun·dry   -dries
  laun·dry·man
lau·re·ate   (lô′ rė·ȧt)
lau·rel   (lô′ rĕl)
lav·a·liere   (lăv′ ȧ·lẽr′)
lav·a·to·ry   (lăv′ ȧ·tō′ rĭ)
  -ries
lav·en·der   (lăv′ ĕn·dēr)
lav·ish   (lăv′ ĭsh)
law   (lô)
  law-a·bid·ing   law break·er
  law·ful   -ful·ly
  -ful·ness   law·giv·er
  law·less·ness   law·mak·er
  law·suit
lawn mow·er   (lôn)
law·yer   (lô′ yēr)
lax·a·tive   (lăk′ sȧ·tĭv)
lax·i·ty   (lăk′ sĭ·tĭ)
lay·er   (lā′ ēr)
lay·man   (lā′ măn)
lay·off   (lā′ ôf′)

lay·o·ver   (lā′ ō′ vēr)
la·zy   (lā′ zĭ)
  la·zi·er   -zi·est
  -zi·ly   -zi·ness
  la·zy·bones   La·zy Su·san
leach   (lēch)
  (dissolve; see *leech*)
lead   (lēd) *v.*
lead   (lĕd) *n.*
  lead·en
  lead poi·son·ing
lead·er·ship   (lēd′ ēr·shĭp)
leaf   (lēf)
  leaves
  leaf·age   (lēf′ ĭj)
  leaf·hop·per   leaf·let
  leaf·y
league   (lēg)
leak   (lēk)
  (crack or hole; see *leek*)
  leak·age   (lēk′ ĭj)
  leak·y
lean-to   (lēn′ tōō′)
leap·frog   (lēp′ frŏg′)
leap year   (lēp yẽr)
learn·ed·ly   (lûr′ nĕd·lĭ)
lease·hold·er   (lēs′ hōl′ dēr)
leash   (lēsh)
least   (lēst)
leath·er   (lĕth′ ēr)
  Leath·er·ette   (lĕth′ ēr·ĕt′)
  leath·er·y
leav·en·ing   (lĕv′ ĕn·ĭng)
Leb·a·non   (lĕb′ ȧ·nŭn)
  Leb·a·nese   (lĕb′ ȧ·nēz′)
lech·er   (lĕch′ ēr)
  lech·er·ous   (lĕch′ ēr·ŭs)
  lech·er·y
lec·tern   (lĕk′ tērn)
lec·ture   (lĕk′ tu̇r)
  lec·tur·er
ledge   (lĕj)
ledg·er   (lĕj′ ēr)
leech   (lēch)
  (worm; see *leach*)
leek   (lēk)
  (plant; see *leak*)
leer·ing   (lẽr′ ĭng)
leer·y   (lẽr′ ĭ)
lee·ward   (lē′ wẽrd)
lee·way   (lē′ wā′)
left-hand·ed   (lĕft′ hăn′ dĕd)
left·ist   (lĕf′ tĭst)
leg·a·cy   (lĕg′ ȧ·sĭ)

le·gal (lē′ gắl)
  le·gal·i·ty (lĕ·gắl′ ĭ·tĭ)
  le·gal·ize -iz·ing
  le·gal·i·za·tion
        (lĕ′ gắl·ĭ·zā′ shŭn)
  le·gal·ly le·gal ten·der
leg·ate (lĕg′ ĭt)
  le·ga·tion (lĕ·gā′ shŭn)
leg·end (lĕj′ ĕnd)
  leg·end·ar·y (lĕj′ ĕn·dĕr′ ĭ)
leg·er·de·main (lĕj′ ēr·dĕ·mān′)
le·ger·i·ty (lĕ·jĕr′ ĭ·tĭ)
leg·gings (lĕg′ ĭngz)
leg·horn (lĕg′ hôrn)
leg·i·ble (lĕj′ ĭ·b'l)
  leg·i·bil·i·ty (lĕj′ ĭ·bĭl′ ĭ·tĭ)
le·gion (lē′ jŭn)
  le·gion·naire (lē′ jŭn·âr′)
leg·is·late (lĕj′ ĭs·lāt)
  -lat·ing
  leg·is·la·tion (lĕj′ ĭs·lā′ shŭn)
  leg·is·la·tive (lĕj′ ĭs·lā′ tĭv)
  leg·is·la·tor (lĕj′ ĭs·lā′ tēr)
  leg·is·la·ture (lĕj′ ĭs·lā′ ṭûr)
le·git·i·mate (lĕ·jĭt′ ĭ·mĭt)
  le·git·i·ma·cy
  le·git·i·ma·tion
      (lĕ·jĭt′ ĭ·mā′ shŭn)
  le·git·i·mize (lĕ·jĭt′ ĭ·mĭz)
  -miz·ing
leg·ume (lĕg′ ūm)
lei·sure (lē′ zhēr)
  lei·sure·li·ness lei·sure·ly
leit·mo·tiv (līt′ mȯ·tēf′)
lem·ming (lĕm′ ĭng)
lem·on (lĕm′ ŭn)
  lem·on·aḍe (lĕm′ ŭn·ād′)
le·mur (lē′ mēr)
lend-lease (lĕnd′ lēs′)
length (lĕngth)
  length·en lenghth·i·ness
  length·wise length·y
le·ni·ent (lē′ nĭ·ĕnt)
  -en·cy
len·i·ty (lĕn′ ĭ·tĭ)
lens (lĕnz)
  lens·es
Lent·en (lĕn′ tĕn)
len·til (lĕn′ tĭl)
leop·ard (lĕp′ ērd)
le·o·tard (lē′ ȯ·tärd)
lep·er (lĕp′ ēr)
  lep·ro·sy (lĕp′ rȯ·sĭ)
  lep·rous
Les·bi·an (lĕz′ bĭ·ḍn)

le·sion (lē′ zhŭn)
less (lĕs)
  less·en·ing less·er
les·see (lĕs·ē′)
  les·sor
les·son (lĕs′ 'n)
lest (lĕst)
let·down (lĕt′ ḍoun′)
le·thal (lē′ thắl)
  -thal·ly
le·thar·gic (lĕ·thär′ jĭk)
  le·thar·gi·cal·ly
leth·ar·gy (lĕth′ ēr·jĭ)
let·ter·head (lĕt′ ēr·hĕd′)
let·tuce (lĕt′ ĭs)
let·up (lĕt′ ŭp′)
leu·ke·mi·a (lū·kē′ mĭ·ḍ)
lev·ee (lĕv′ ė)
  (dike; see *levy*)
lev·el (lĕv′ ĕl)
  -eled -eling
  lev·el·er
  lev·el·ly lev·el·head·eḍ
le·ver (lē′ vēr)
  le·ver·age (lē′ vēr·ĭj)
le·vi·a·than (lĕ·vī′ ḍ·thắn)
Le·vi's (lē′ vīz)
lev·i·ty (lĕv′ ĭ·tĭ)
lev·y (lĕv′ ĭ)
  (to collect; see *levee*)
  lev·ied lev·y·ing
lewd·ness (lūd′ nĕs)
lex·i·cog·ra·phy
    (lĕk′ sĭ·kŏg′ rȧ·fĭ)
lex·i·con (lĕk′ sĭ·kŏn)
li·a·ble (lī′ ȧ·b'l)
  li·a·bil·i·ty (lī′ ȧ·bĭl′ ĭ·tĭ)
li·ai·son (lē′ ā·zŏn′)
li·ar (lī′ ēr)
li·ba·tion (lĭ·bā′ shŭn)
li·bel (lī′ bĕl)
  -beled -bel·ing
  li·bel·er li·bel·ous
lib·er·al (lĭb′ ēr·ắl)
  -al·ly lib·er·al·ism
  lib·er·al·i·ty (lĭb′ ēr·ắl′ ĭ·tĭ)
  lib·er·al·ize -iz·ing
lib·er·ate (lĭb′ ēr·āt)
  -at·ing lib·er·a·tor
lib·er·tar·i·an (lĭb′ ēr·târ′ ĭ·ḍn)
lib·er·tine (lĭb′ ēr·tēn)
lib·er·ty (lĭb′ ēr·tĭ)
  -ties
li·bi·do (lĭ·bī′ dō)
li·bid·i·nal (lĭ·bĭd′ ĭ·nắl)

li·bid·i·nous   (lĭ·bĭd′ ĭ·nŭs)
li·brar·y   (lī′ brĕr′ ĭ)
  -brar·ies
  li·brar·i·an   (lī·brâr′ ĭ·ăn)
li·bret·to   (lĭ·brĕt′ ō)
Lib·y·a   (lĭb′ ĭ·à)
lice   (līs)
li·cense   (lī′ sĕns)
  -cens·ing
  li·cen·see   (lī′ sĕn·sē′)
li·cen·tious   (lĭ·sĕn′ shŭs)
li·chen   (lī′ kĕn)
lic·it   (lĭs′ ĭt)
lic·o·rice   (lĭk′ ŏ·rĭs)
lie   (lī)
  lied   ly·ing
  li·ar
Lie·der·kranz   (lē′ dĕr·krănts′)
liege   (lēj)
lien   (lē·ĕn)
lieu   (lū)
lieu·ten·ant   (lū·tĕn′ ănt)
  -an·cy
life   (līf)
  pl. lives   life belt
  life·blood   life·boat
  life·guard   life·line
  life·long   life·sav·er
  life·sized   life·time
  life·work
lig·a·ment   (lĭg′ à·mĕnt)
lig·a·ture   (lĭg′ à·tûr)
light   (līt)
  light-fin·gered   light·head·ed
  light·heart·ed   light·house
  light-year
light·ning   (līt′ nĭng)
like   (līk)
  lik·ing   lik·a·ble
  like·ly   -li·hood
  like·ness   like·wise
li·lac   (lī′ lăk)
lil·y   (lĭl′ ĭ)
  lil·ies
  lil·y of the val·ley
limb   (lĭm)
lim·ber   (lĭm′ bĕr)
lim·bo   (lĭm′ bō)
  -boes
Lim·burg·er   (lĭm′ bûrg·ĕr)
lime·light   (līm′ līt′)
Lim·er·ick   (lĭm′ ĕr·ĭk)
lime·stone   (līm′ stōn′)
lime·wa·ter   (līm′ wô′ tĕr)

lim·it   (lĭm′ ĭt)
  -it·ed   -it·ing
  lim·i·ta·tion   (lĭm′ ĭ·tā′ shŭn)
  lim·it·less
limn   (lĭm)
lim·ou·sine   (lĭm′ ŏŏ·zēn′)
lim·pid   (lĭm′ pĭd)
lin·age   (līn′ ĭj)
  (alignment; see *lineage*)
linch·pin   (lĭnch′ pĭn′)
lin·den tree   (lĭn′ dĕn)
lin·e·age   (lĭn′ ê·ĭj)
  (ancestry; see *linage*)
lin·e·al   (lĭn′ ê·ăl)
lin·e·a·ment   (lĭn′ ê·à·mĕnt)
lin·e·ar meas·ure
           (lĭn′ ê·ēr)
line·man   (līn′ măn)
lin·en   (lĭn′ ĕn)
lin·ge·rie   (län′ zhē·rē)
lin·guist   (lĭng′ gwĭst)
  lin·guis·tics   (lĭng·gwĭs′ tĭks)
lin·i·ment   (lĭn′ ĭ·mĕnt)
lin·ing   (līn′ ĭng)
link·age   (lĭngk′ ĭj)
li·no·le·um   (lĭ·nō′ lê·ŭm)
Lin·o·type   (līn′ ō·tīp)
lin·seed oil   (lĭn′ sēd′)
li·on·ess   (lī′ ŭn·ĕs)
li·on·ize   (lī′ ŭn·īz)
  -iz·ing
liq·ue·fac·tion   (lĭk′ wê·făk′ shŭn)
liq·ue·fy   (lĭk′ wê·fī)
  -fied,   -fy·ing
  liq·ue·fi·a·ble   (lĭk′ wê·fī′ à·b'l)
li·queur   (lê·kûr′)
liq·uid   (lĭk′ wĭd)
liq·ui·date   (lĭk′ wĭ·dāt)
  -dat·ing
  liq·ui·da·tion
           (lĭk′ wĭ·dā′ shŭn)
liq·uor   (lĭk′ ēr)
lisle   (līl)
lis·some   (lĭs′ ŭm)
lis·ten   (lĭs′ 'n)
list·less   (lĭst′ lĕs)
lit·a·ny   (lĭt′ à·nĭ)
  -nies
li·ter   (lē′ tēr)
lit·er·a·cy   (lĭt′ ēr·à·sĭ)
lit·er·al   (lĭt′ ēr·ăl)
  -al·ly
lit·er·ar·y   (lĭt′ ēr·ĕr′ ĭ)
lit·er·ate   (lĭt′ ēr·ĭt)
  lit·er·a·ture   (lĭt′ ēr·à·tûr)

lithe (lĭth)
  lithe·ness
lith·o·graph (lĭth' ŏ·grȧf)
lit·i·gate (lĭt' ĭ·gāt)
  -gat·ing
  lit·i·gant (lĭt' ĭ·gȧnt)
  lit·i·ga·tion (lĭt' ĭ·gā' shŭn)
  li·ti·gious (lĭ·tĭj' ŭs)
lit·mus pa·per (lĭt' mŭs)
lit·ter (lĭt' ẽr)
lit·tle·ness (lĭt' 'l·nĕs)
lit·ur·gy (lĭt' ẽr·jĭ)
  -gies
  li·tur·gi·cal (lĭ·tûr' jĭ·kȧl)
live (lĭv) v.
  liv·ing (lĭv) adj.
  liv·a·ble (lĭv' ȧ·b'l)
live·li·hood (lĭv' lĭ·hŏŏd)
live·ly (lĭv' lĭ)
  live·li·er -li·est
  -li·ness
liv·en (lĭv' ĕn)
liv·er (lĭv' ẽr)
liv·er·wurst (lĭv' ẽr·wûrst')
liv·er·y sta·ble (lĭv' ẽr·ĭ)
live·stock (lĭv' stŏk')
liv·id (lĭv' ĭd)
liv·ing room (lĭv' ĭng)
liz·ard (lĭz' ẽrd)
lla·ma (lä' mȧ)
  (animal; see lama)
loaf (lōf)
  pl. loaves (lōvz)
loaf·er (lōf' ẽr)
loam (lōm)
loathe (lōth)
  loath·ing loath·some
lob·by (lŏb' ĭ)
  lob·bies lob·by·ist
lobe (lōb)
  lo·bar (lō' bẽr)
lob·lol·ly pine (lŏb' lŏl' ĭ)
lo·bot·o·my (lŏ·bŏt' ŏ·mĭ)
lob·ster (lŏb' stẽr)
lob·ule (lŏb' ūl)
lo·cal (lō' kȧl)
  lo·cal·ism
  lo·cal·i·ty (lŏ·kăl' ĭ·tĭ)
  -ties lo·cal·ize
  -iz·ing
lo·cate (lō' kāt)
  -cat·ing
  lo·ca·tion (lŏ·kā' shŭn)
lock·et (lŏk' ĕt)
lock·jaw (lŏk' jô')

lo·co·mo·tion (lō' kŏ·mō' shŭn)
lo·co·mo·tive (lō' kŏ·mō' tĭv)
lo·co·weed (lō' kŏ·wēd')
lo·cust (lō' kŭst)
lo·cu·tion (lŏ·kū' shŭn)
lode·star (lōd' stär')
lode·stone (lōd' stōn')
lodge (lŏj)
  lodg·ing
loft·y (lôf' tĭ)
  loft·i·ly -i·ness
lo·gan·ber·ry (lō' gȧn·bĕr' ĭ)
  -ber·ries
log·a·rithm (lŏg' ȧ·rĭth'm)
log·ger·head (lŏg' ẽr·hĕd')
log·ging (lŏg' ĭng)
log·ic (lŏj' ĭk)
  log·i·cal -cal·ly
  lo·gi·cian (lŏ·jĭsh' ȧn)
  lo·gis·tics (lŏ·jĭs' tĭks)
lo·gy (lō' gĭ)
  log·i·ness
Lo·hen·grin (lō' ĕn·grĭn)
loin·cloth (loin' klŏth')
loi·ter·er (loi' tẽr·ẽr)
lol·li·pop (lŏl' ĭ·pŏp)
lone·ly (lōn' lĭ)
  lone·li·ness
lone·some (lōn' sŭm)
  -some·ness
long (lŏng)
  long·bow long-dis·tance
  long·hand long-lived
  long-play·ing long·shore·man
  long-suf·fer·ing
  long-term bond
  long-wind·ed
lon·gev·i·ty (lŏn·jĕv' ĭ·tĭ)
lon·gi·tude (lŏn' jĭ·tūd)
  lon·gi·tu·di·nal
    (lŏn' jĭ·tū' dĭ·nȧl)
look·ing glass (lŏŏk' ĭng glȧs)
look·out (lŏŏk' out')
loom·ing (lōōm' ĭng)
loon·y (lōōn' ĭ)
  loon·i·ness
loop·hole (lōōp' hōl')
loose (lōōs)
  loose-joint·ed loose·ly
  loos·en loose·ness
loot·er (lōōt' ẽr)
lop-eared (lŏp' ẽrd')
lop·sid·ed (lŏp' sĭd' ĕd)
lo·qua·cious (lŏ·kwā' shŭs)
  lo·quac·i·ty (lŏ·kwăs' ĭ·tĭ)

lor·do·sis (lôr·dō′ sĭs)
lord·ship (lôrd′ shĭp)
lore (lōr)
Lor·e·lei (lôr′ ĕ·lī)
lor·gnette (lôr′ nyĕt′)
lose (lōōz) v.
los·ing
loss (lôs) n.
loss lead·er
lo·tion (lō′ shŭn)
lot·ter·y (lŏt′ ĕr·ĭ)
lot·ter·ies
lo·tus (lō′ tŭs)
loud (loud)
loud·mouthed loud-speak·er
Lou·i·si·an·a (lōō′ ĭ·zĭ·ăn′ à)
abbr. La.
Lou·i·si·an·i·an
or Lou·i·si·an·an
lounge (lounj)
loung·ing
louse (lous)
pl. lice (līs)
lous·y (louz′ ĭ)
lout·ish (lout′ ĭsh)
lou·ver (lōō′ vĕr)
lou·vered
love (lŭv)
lov·ing lov·a·ble
love·bird love·less
love·lorn love-mak·ing
love·sick
love·ly (lŭv′ lĭ)
love·li·er -li·est, -li·ness
low (lō)
low·born low·brow
low-pres·sure low tide
low·er·class·man
(lō′ ĕr·klâs′ măn)
low·ly (lō′ lĭ)
low·li·er -li·est, -li·ness
loy·al (loi′ ăl)
loy·al·ty
Loy·o·la, St. Ig·na·ti·us
(loi·ō′ là, Ĭg·nā′ shĭ·ŭs)
loz·enge (lŏz′ ĕnj)
lub·ber·ly (lŭb′ ĕr·lĭ)
lu·bri·cate (lū′ brĭ·kāt)
-cat·ing
lu·bri·cant (-brĭ·kănt)
lu·bri·ca·tion (lū′ brĭ·kā′ shŭn)
lu·bri·ca·tor
lu·cid (lū′ sĭd)
lu·cid·i·ty (lū·sĭd′ ĭ·tĭ)
luck·less (lŭk′ lĕs)

luck·y (lŭk′ ĭ)
luck·i·er -i·est
-i·ly -i·ness
lu·cra·tive (lū′ krá·tĭv)
lu·cre (lū′ kĕr)
lu·di·crous (lū′ dĭ·krŭs)
lug·gage (lŭg′ ĭj)
lu·gu·bri·ous (lù·gū′ brĭ·ŭs)
luke·warm (lūk′ wôrm′)
lull (lŭl)
lull·a·by (lŭl′ à·bī′)
-bied -by·ing
lum·ba·go (lŭm·bā′ gō)
lum·bar (lŭm′ bĕr)
(vertebra; see lumber)
lum·ber (lŭm′ bĕr)
(timber; see lumbar)
lum·ber·jack lum·ber·yard
lu·mi·nar·y (lū′ mĭ·nĕr′ ĭ)
-nar·ies
lu·mi·nes·cent (lū′ mĭ·nĕs′ ĕnt)
-cence
lu·mi·nous (lū′ mĭ·nŭs)
lu·mi·nos·i·ty (lū′ mĭ·nŏs′ ĭ·tĭ)
lum·mox (lŭm′ ŭks)
lump·y (lŭmp′ ĭ)
lump·i·ness
lu·na·cy (lū′ nà·sĭ)
lu·nar (lū′ nĕr)
lu·na·tic (lū′ nà·tĭk)
lunch·eon (lŭn′ chŭn)
lunch·eon·ette (lŭn′ chŭn·ĕt′)
lunge (lŭnj)
lung·ing
lung·fish (lŭng′ fĭsh′)
lu·pine (lū′ pĭn) n.
(flower)
lu·pine (lū′ pĭn) adj.
(wolfish)
lurch (lûrch)
lu·rid (lū′ rĭd)
lurk (lûrk)
lus·cious (lŭsh′ ŭs)
lus·ter·ware (lŭs′ tĕr·wâr′)
lust·ful (lŭst′ fōōl)
-ful·ly -ful·ness
lus·trous (lŭs′ trŭs)
lust·y (lŭs′ tĭ)
lust·i·er -i·est
-i·ly -i·ness
Lu·ther·an (lū′ thĕr·ăn)
Lux·em·bourg (lŭk′ sĕm·bûrg)
lux·u·ri·ant (lŭks·ū′ rĭ·ănt)
lux·u·ri·ance

lux·u·ri·ate (lŭks·ū′ rĭ·āt)
  -at·ing
lux·u·ry (lŭk′ shŏŏ·rĭ)
  -ries
lux·u·ri·ous (lŭks·ū′ rĭ·ŭs)
ly·ce·um (lī·sē′ ŭm)
lye (lī)
ly·ing-in (lī′ ĭng·ĭn′)
lymph (lĭmf)
  lym·phat·ic (lĭm·făt′ ĭk)
lynch law (lĭnch)
lynx (lĭngks)
ly·on·naise (lī′ ŭ·nāz′)
lyr·ic (lĭr′ ĭk)
  lyr·i·cal (lĭr′ ĭ·kăl)
  lyr·i·cism (lĭr′ ĭ·sĭz′m)

M

ma′am (măm)
ma·ca·bre (ma·kä′ b′r)
mac·ad·am (măk·ăd′ ăm)
  mac·ad·am·ize
          (măk·ăd′ ăm·īz)
mac·a·ro·ni (măk′ a·rō′ nĭ)
mac·a·roon (măk′ a·rōōn′)
ma·caw (ma·kô′)
Mc·Coy, the (ma·koi′)
ma·che·te (mä·chā′ tā)
Mach·i·a·vel·li·an
      (măk′ ĭ·a·vĕl′ ĭ·ăn)
mach·i·na·tion (măk′ ĭ·nā′ shŭn)
ma·chine (ma·shēn′)
  ma·chin·er·y ma·chine shop
  ma·chin·ist
mack·er·el (măk′ ĕr·ĕl)
Mack·i·naw coat
      (măk′ ĭ·nô)
Mac·mil·lan, Har·old
      (măk·mĭl′ ăn)
mac·ro·cosm (măk′ rŏ·kŏz′m)
mad·am (măd′ ăm)
mad·ame (ma′ dăm′)
  pl. mes·dames (mā′ dăm′)
mad·den·ing (măd′ ′n·ĭng)
Ma·dei·ra wine (ma·dēr′ a)
ma·de·moi·selle
      (măd′ mwa′ zĕl′)
ma·don·na (ma·dŏn′ a)
ma·dras (ma·drăs′)
mad·ri·gal (măd′ rĭ·găl)
mael·strom (māl′ strŏm)
ma·e·stro (mä·ĕ′ strŏ)
maf·fi·a (mäf′ fĕ·ä)

mag·a·zine (măg′ a·zēn′)
ma·gen·ta (ma·jĕn′ ta)
mag·got (măg′ ŭt)
mag·ic (măj′ ĭk)
  mag·i·cal -cal·ly
  ma·gi·cian (ma·jĭsh′ ăn)
mag·is·trate (măj′ ĭs·trāt)
  mag·is·te·ri·al
      (măj′ ĭs·tēr′ ĭ·ăl)
  mag·is·tra·cy (măj′ ĭs·tra·sĭ)
Mag·na Char·ta
      (măg′ na kär′ ta)
mag·na cum lau·de
      (măg′ na kŭm lô′ dē)
mag·nan·i·mous
      (măg·năn′ ĭ·mŭs)
  mag·na·nim·i·ty
      (măg′ na·nĭm′ ĭ·tĭ)
mag·nate (măg′ nāt)
mag·ne·sia (măg·nē′ sha)
  mag·ne·si·um
      (măg·nē′ shĭ·ŭm)
mag·net (măg′ nĕt)
  mag·net·ic (măg·nĕt′ ĭk)
  mag·net·ism mag·net·ize
Mag·nif·i·cat (măg·nĭf′ ĭ·kăt)
mag·ni·fi·ca·tion
      (măg′ nĭ·fĭ·kā′ shŭn)
mag·nif·i·cent (măg·nĭf′ ĭ·sĕnt)
  -cence
mag·nif·i·co (măg·nĭf′ ĭ·kō)
  -coes
mag·ni·fy (măg′ nĭ·fī)
  -fied -fy·ing
  mag·ni·fi·er
mag·ni·tude (măg′ nĭ·tūd)
mag·no·li·a (măg·nō′ lĭ·a)
mag·num o·pus
      (măg′ nŭm ō′ pŭs)
mag·pie (măg′ pī)
mag·uey (măg′ wā)
Mag·yar (măg′ yär)
ma·ha·ra·ja (ma·hä′ rä′ ja)
  n. masc.
  ma·ha·ra·ni (ma·hä′ rä′ nē)
  n. fem.
ma·hat·ma (ma·hät′ ma)
mah-jongg (mä′ jŏng′)
ma·hog·a·ny (ma·hŏg′ a·nĭ)
maid·en (mād′ ′n)
mail (māl)
  mail·a·ble mail·box
  mail·man
  mail-or·der house
mail·lot (ma′ yō′)

maim (mām)
Maine (mān)
  abbr. **Me.**
main·land (mān′ lănd′)
main·stay (mān′ stā′)
main·tain (mān·tān′)
  main·tain·a·ble
  main·te·nance (mān′ t'n·ăns)
maî·tre d'hô·tel (mâ′ trĕ dô′ tĕl′)
maize (māz)
  (corn; see *maze*)
maj·es·ty (măj′ ĕs·tĭ)
  -ties
ma·jes·tic (má·jĕs′ tĭk)
  -ti·cal·ly
ma·jor (mā′ jĕr)
ma·jor-do·mo (mā′ jĕr·dō′ mō)
ma·jor·ette (mā′ jĕr·ĕt′)
ma·jor league
ma·jor·i·ty (má·jŏr′ ĭ·tĭ)
  -ties
make (māk)
  mak·ing   make-be·lieve
  make·shift   make-up
mal·a·chite (măl′ á·kīt)
mal·ad·just·ed (măl′ ă·jŭs′ tĕd)
mal·a·dy (măl′ á·dĭ)
  -dies
ma·laise (mă·lāz′)
ma·lar·i·a (má·lâr′ ĭ·á)
Ma·lay·a (má·lā′ á)
mal·con·tent (măl′ kŏn·tĕnt′)
mal de mer (măl′ dĕ mâr′)
mal·e·fac·tor (măl′ ĕ·făk′ tĕr)
ma·lev·o·lent (má·lĕv′ ô·lĕnt)
mal·fea·sance (măl·fē′ zăns)
mal·for·ma·tion
    (măl′ fôr·mā′ shŭn)
mal·ice (măl′ ĭs)
ma·li·cious (má·lĭsh′ ŭs)
ma·lign (má·līn′)
  ma·lig·nan·cy (má·lĭg′ năn·sĭ)
  ma·lig·nant
ma·lin·ger (má·lĭng′ gĕr)
  ma·lin·ger·er
mal·lard (măl′ ĕrd)
mal·le·a·ble (măl′ ĕ·á·b'l)
  mal·le·a·bil·i·ty
    (măl′ ĕ·á·bĭl′ ĭ·tĭ)
mal·let (măl′ ĕt)
malm·sey wine (măm′ zĭ)
mal·nu·tri·tion
    (măl′ nû·trĭsh′ ŭn)
mal·prac·tice (măl′ prăk′ tĭs)
malt (môlt)

Mal·thu·sian (măl·thū′ zhăn)
malt·ose (môl′ tōs)
mam·ba snake (măm′ bä)
mam·mal (măm′ ăl)
  mam·ma·li·an (mă·mā′ lĭ·ăn)
  mam·ma·ry (măm′ á·rĭ)
mam·mon (măm′ ŭn)
mam·moth (măm′ ŭth)
man (măn)
  manned   man·ning
  man-at-arms   man-eat·er
  man·ful   -ful·ly
  -ful·ness   man·hole
  man·hood   man·kind
  man·ly   -li·ness
  man·nish   man-of-war
  man·pow·er
man·a·cle (măn′ á·k'l)
  -cling
man·age (măn′ ĭj)
  -ag·ing
  man·age·a·bil·i·ty
    (măn′ ĭj·á·bĭl′ ĭ·tĭ)
  man·age·a·ble man·age·ment
  man·ag·er   man·ag·er·ess
man·a·ge·ri·al
    (măn′ á·jĕr′ ĭ·ăl)
  -al·ly
ma·ña·na (mä·nyä′ nä)
man·a·tee (măn′ á·tē′)
man·da·mus, writ of
    (măn·dā′ mŭs)
man·da·rin (măn′ dá·rĭn)
man·date (măn′ dāt)
man·da·to·ry (măn′ dá·tō′ rĭ)
man·di·ble (măn′ dĭ·b'l)
man·do·lin (măn′ dô·lĭn)
ma·neu·ver (má·nōō′ vĕr)
  ma·neu·ver·a·bil·i·ty
    (má·nōō′ vĕr·á·bĭl′ ĭ·tĭ)
  ma·neu·ver·a·ble
man·ga·nate (măng′ gá·nāt)
man·ga·nese (măng′ gá·nēs)
man·gle (măng′ g'l)
  -gling
man·go (măng′ gō)
  -goes
man·gy (mān′ jĭ)
  man·gi·ness
ma·ni·a (mā′ nĭ·á)
ma·ni·ac (mā′ nĭ·ăk)
ma·ni·a·cal (má·nī′ á·kăl)
ma·nic (mā′ nĭk)
  ma·nic-de·pres·sive

man·i·cure   (măn′ ĭ·kūr)
man·i·cur·ist
man·i·fest   (măn′ ĭ·fĕst)
man·i·fes·ta·tion
    (măn′ ĭ·fĕs·tā′ shŭn)
man·i·fest·ly
man·i·fes·to   (măn′ ĭ·fĕs′ tō)
man·i·fold   (măn′ ĭ·fōld)
Ma·nil·a paper   (má·nĭl′ á)
ma·nip·u·late   (má·nĭp′ û·lāt)
-lat·ing
ma·nip·u·la·tion
    (má·nĭp′ û·lā′ shŭn)
ma·nip·u·la·tive
    (má·nĭp′ û·lā′ tĭv)
ma·nip·u·la·tor
    (-lā′ tēr)
man·na   (măn′ á)
man·ne·quin   (măn′ ĕ·kĭn)
man·ner   (măn′ ēr)
    (way of acting; see *manor*)
man·ner·ism
man·ner·ly   -li·ness
man·or   (măn′ ēr)
    (house of an estate; see *manner*)
ma·no·ri·al   (má·nō′ rĭ·ăl)
man·sard roof   (măn′ särd)
manse   (măns)
man·sion   (măn′ shŭn)
man·tel   (măn′ t'l)
    (fireplace framework; see *mantle*)
man·tel·piece
man·til·la   (măn·tĭl′ á)
man·tle   (măn′ t'l)
    (cloak; see *mantel*)
man·u·al   (măn′ û·ăl)
man·u·al·ly
man·u·fac·ture   (măn′ û·făk′ tûr)
-tur·ing
man·u·fac·tur·er
ma·nure   (má·nūr′)
man·u·script   (măn′ û·skrĭpt)
Manx cat   (măngks)
man·y-sid·ed   (mĕn′ ĭ·sīd′ ĕd)
Ma·o·ri   (mä′ ō·rĭ)
Mao Tse-tung   (mä′ ō·dzŭ′ dŏŏng′)
map   (măp)
    mapped   map·ping
ma·ple sir·up   (mā′ p'l)
ma·ra·ca   (mä·rä′ kä)
mar·a·schi·no cher·ry
    (măr′ á·skē′ nō)
mar·a·thon   (măr′ á·thŏn)
ma·raud·er   (má·rôd′ ēr)

mar·ble   (mär′ b'l)
    -bling   mar·ble·ize
mar·chion·ess   (mär′ shŭn·ĕs)
Mar·di gras   (mär′ dĕ grä′)
mar·ga·rine   (mär′ já·rĭn)
mar·gin   (mär′ jĭn)
    mar·gin·al
mar·i·gold   (măr′ ĭ·gōld)
mar·i·jua·na   (măr′ ĭ·wä′ ná)
ma·rim·ba   (má·rĭm′ bá)
mar·i·nade   (măr′ ĭ·nād′)
mar·i·nate   (măr′ ĭ·nāt)
    -nat·ing
ma·rine   (má·rēn′)
mar·i·ner   (măr′ ĭ·nēr)
mar·i·o·nette   (măr′ ĭ·ō·nĕt′)
mar·i·tal   (măr′ ĭ·tăl)
    (matrimonial; see *martial*)
mar·i·tal·ly
mar·i·time   (măr′ ĭ·tīm)
mar·jo·ram   (mär′ jō·răm)
mark·ed·ly   (mär′ kĕd·lĭ)
mar·ket   (mär′ kĕt)
    -ket·ed   -ket·ing
mar·ket·a·ble   mar·ket place
    mar·ket val·ue
marks·man·ship
    (märks′ măn·shĭp)
mark·up   (märk′ ŭp′)
marl   (märl)
mar·lin   (mär′ lĭn)
mar·ma·lade   (mär′ má·lād)
mar·mo·set   (mär′ mō·zĕt)
mar·mot   (mär′ mŭt)
ma·roon   (má·rōōn′)
mar·quee   (mär·kē′)
mar·quis   (mär′ kwĭs)
mar·qui·sette   (mär′ kĭ·zĕt′)
mar·riage   (măr′ ĭj)
    mar·riage·a·bil·i·ty
    (măr′ ĭj·á·bĭl′ ĭ·tĭ)
    mar·riage·a·ble
    (măr′ ĭj·á·b'l)
mar·row   (măr′ ō)
mar·ry   (măr′ ĭ)
    mar·rieđ   mar·ry·ing
mar·shal   (mär′ shăl)
    -shaled   -shal·ing
marsh·mal·low   (märsh′ măl′ ō)
mar·su·pi·al   (mär·sū′ pĭ·ăl)
mar·ten   (mär′ tĕn)
    (mammal; see *martin*)
mar·tial   (mär′ shăl)
    (warlike; see *marital*)

Mar·ti·an   (mär′ shĭ·ăn)
  (of Mars)
mar·tin   (mär′ tĭn)
  (bird; see *marten*)
mar·ti·net   (mär′ tĭ·nĕt′)
mar·tyr   (mär′ tēr)
  mar·tyr·dom
mar·vel   (mär′ vĕl)
  -veled   -vel·ing
  mar·vel·ous   (mär′ vĕl·ŭs)
Marx·ist   (märk′ sĭst)
Mar·y·land   (mĕr′ ĭ·lănd)
  abbr. Md.   Mar·y·land·er
mas·car·a   (măs·kăr′ ȧ)
mas·cot   (măs′ kŏt)
mas·cu·line   (măs′ kŭ·lĭn)
  mas·cu·lin·i·ty
     (măs′ kŭ·lĭn′ ĭ·tĭ)
mas·och·ism   (măz′ ŏk·ĭz′m)
  mas·och·ist   (-ĭst)
ma·son   (mā′ s′n)
  ma·son·ic   (mȧ·sŏn′ ĭk)
  ma·son·ry
Ma·son-Dix·on line
     (mā′ s′n·dĭk′ s′n)
mas·quer·ade   (măs′ kĕr·ād′)
Mas·sa·chu·setts
     (măs′ ȧ·choo̅′ sĕts)
  abbr. Mass.
mas·sa·cre   (măs′ ȧ·kĕr)
  mas·sa·cred   (-kĕrd)
  mas·sa·cring   (-krĭng)
mas·sage   (mȧ·săzh′)
  mas·sag·ing
mas·seur   (mă·sûr′)
  mas·seuse   (mă·sûz′) *fem.*
mas·sive   (măs′ ĭv)
  mas·sive·ly
mas·ter   (más′ tĕr)
  mas·ter·dom   mas·ter-at-arms
  mas·ter·ful, -ful·ly, -ful·ness
  mas·ter·ly   mas·ter·piece
  mas·ter stroke mas·ter·work
  mas·ter·y
mast·head   (mást′ hĕd′)
mas·ti·cate   (măs′ tĭ·kāt)
  -cat·ing
  mas·ti·ca·tion
     (măs′ tĭ·kā′ shŭn)
mas·tiff   (más′ tĭf)
mas·to·don   (măs′ tŏ·dŏn)
mas·toid   (măs′ toid)
mat·a·dor   (măt′ ȧ·dôr)
match·less   (măch′ lĕss)
match·mak·er   (măch′ māk′ ĕr)

ma·te·ri·al   (mȧ·tēr′ ĭ·ăl)
  (substance; see *matériel*)
  ma·te·ri·al·ism
  ma·te·ri·al·ist   ma·te·ri·al·ize
  ma·te·ri·al·ly
ma·té·ri·el   (mȧ·tēr′ ĭ·ĕl′)
  (equipment; see *material*)
ma·ter·nal   (mȧ·tûr′ năl)
  ma·ter·nal·ly
  ma·ter·ni·ty   (mȧ·tûr′ nĭ·tĭ)
math·e·mat·ics
     (măth′ ĕ·măt′ ĭks)
  math·e·mat·i·cal, -cal·ly
  math·e·ma·ti·cian
     (măth′ ĕ·mȧ·tĭsh′ ăn)
mat·in   (măt′ ĭn)
  mat·in·al   (măt′ ĭ·năl)
mat·i·nee   (măt′ ĭ·nā′)
ma·tri·arch   (mā′ trĭ·ärk)
  ma·tri·arch·y   (mā′ trĭ·är′ kĭ)
ma·tric·u·late   (mȧ·trĭk′ û·lāt)
  -lat·ing
  ma·tric·u·la·tion
     (mȧ·trĭk′ û·lā′ shŭn)
mat·ri·mo·ny   (măt′ rĭ·mō′ nĭ)
  mat·ri·mo·ni·al
     (măt′ rĭ·mō′ nĭ·ăl)
  -al·ly
ma·trix   (mā′ trĭks)
  pl. ma·tri·ces   (mā′ trĭ·sēz)
ma·tron   (mā′ trŭn)
  ma·tron·ly   -li·ness
mat·ter   (măt′ ĕr)
  mat·ter-of-fact *adj.*
mat·ting   (măt′ ĭng)
mat·tress   (măt′ rĕs)
ma·ture   (mȧ·tūr′)
  -tur·ing
  mat·u·ra·tion   (măt′ û·rā′ shŭn)
  ma·ture·ly
  ma·tu·ri·ty   (mȧ·tū′ rĭ·tĭ)
maud·lin   (môd′ lĭn)
Mau·i is., Ha·wai·i
     (mou′ ē)
maul·er   (môl′ ĕr)
Maun·dy Thurs·day
     (môn′ dĭ)
Mau·re·ta·ni·a, Afr.
     (mô′ rĕ·tā′ nĭ·ȧ)
mau·so·le·um   (mô′ sȯ·lē′ ŭm)
mauve   (mōv)
mav·er·ick   (măv′ ĕr·ĭk)
mawk·ish   (môk′ ĭsh)
max·im   (măk′ sĭm)
max·i·mal   (măk′ sĭ·măl)

max·i·mum (măk′ sĭ·mŭm)
  pl. max·i·ma
  max·i·mize -miz·ing
may·hem (mā′ hĕm)
may·on·naise (mā′ ŏ·nāz′)
may·or (mā′ ẽr)
  may·or·al·ty (mā′ ẽr·ăl·tĭ)
maze (māz)
  (labyrinth; see *maize*)
ma·zur·ka (mȧ·zûr′ kȧ)
mead (mēd)
  (fermented drink; see *meed*)
mead·ow (mĕd′ ō)
mea·ger (mē′ gẽr)
meal·time (mēl′ tīm′)
meal·y (mēl′ ĭ)
  meal·i·ness meal·y·mouthed
mean (mēn)
  (intend; see *mien*)
  mean·ing·less mean·ness
  mean·time mean·while
me·an·der·ing (mē·ăn′ dẽr·ĭng)
mea·sles (mē′ z’lz)
meas·ure (mĕzh′ ẽr)
  -ur·ing
  meas·ur·a·bil·i·ty
                (mĕzh′ ẽr·ȧ·bĭl′ ĭ·tĭ)
  meas·ur·a·ble meas·ure·less
  meas·ure·ment
meat (mēt)
  (food; see *meet, mete*)
meat·y (mēt′ ĭ)
  meat·i·er, -i·est, -i·ness
me·chan·ic (mē·kăn′ ĭk)
  me·chan·i·cal
  mech·a·nism (mĕk′ ȧ·nĭz′m)
  mech·a·nis·tic (mĕk′ ȧ·nĭs′ tĭk)
  mech·a·nize (mĕk′ ȧ·nīz)
med·al (mĕd′ ’l)
  med·al·ist
  me·dal·lion (mē·dăl′ yŭn)
med·dle (mĕd′ ’l)
  med·dling med·dler
  med·dle·some
me·di·a (mē′ dĭ·ȧ)
  pl. of me·di·um
me·di·an (mē′ dĭ·ȧn)
me·di·ate (mē′ dĭ·āt)
  -at·ing
  me·di·a·tion (mē′ dĭ·ā′ shŭn)
  me·di·a·tor
med·i·cal (mĕd′ ĭ·kȧl)
med·i·cate (mĕd′ ĭ·kāt)
  -cat·ing

med·i·ca·tion
                (mĕd′ ĭ·kā′ shŭn)
med·i·ca·tive (mĕd′ ĭ·kā′ tĭv)
med·i·cine (mĕd′ ĭ·sĭn)
  me·dic·i·nal (mē·dĭs′ ĭ·nȧl)
  -nal·ly
me·di·e·val (mē′ dĭ·ē′ vȧl)
me·di·o·cre (mē′ dĭ·ō′ kẽr)
  me·di·oc·ri·ty (mē′ dĭ·ŏk′ rĭ·tĭ)
med·i·tate (mĕd′ ĭ·tāt)
  -tat·ing
  med·i·ta·tion (mĕd′ ĭ·tā′ shŭn)
  med·i·ta·tive (mĕd′ ĭ·tā′ tĭv)
  med·i·ta·tor
Med·i·ter·ra·ne·an (sea)
                (mĕd′ ĭ·tĕ·rā′ nē·ȧn)
me·di·um (mē′ dĭ·ŭm)
  pl. me·di·ums (in general sense)
  pl. me·di·a (as in "communica-
    tions media" and in scientific
    sense)
med·ley (mĕd′ lĭ)
  -leys
Me·du·sa (mē·dū′ sȧ)
meed (mēd)
  (reward; see *mead*)
meek (mēk)
meer·schaum (mẽr′ shŭm)
meet (mēt)
  (come upon; see *meat, mete*)
meet·ing·house (mēt′ ĭng·hous′)
meg·a·cy·cle (mĕg′ ȧ·sī′ k’l)
meg·a·lo·ma·ni·a
                (mĕg′ ȧ·lō·mā′ nĭ·ȧ)
meg·a·phone (mĕg′ ȧ·fōn)
meg·a·ton (mĕg′ ȧ·tŭn′)
Meis·ter·sing·er
                (mīs′ tẽr·sĭng′ ẽr)
mel·an·cho·li·a
                (mĕl′ ȧn·kō′ lĭ·ȧ)
  mel·an·chol·ic (-kŏl′ ĭk)
  mel·an·chol·y (-kŏl′ ĭ)
Mel·a·ne·sia (mĕl′ ȧ·nē′ zhȧ)
mé·lange (mā′ länzh′)
me·lee (mā′ lā′)
mel·lif·lu·ent (mē·lĭf′ lōō·ĕnt)
  -ence mel·lif·lu·ous
mel·low (mĕl′ ō)
mel·o·dra·ma (mĕl′ ŏ·drä′ mȧ)
  mel·o·dra·mat·ic
                (mĕl′ ŏ·drȧ·măt′ ĭk)
mel·o·dy (mĕl′ ŏ·dĭ)
  -dies
  me·lo·dic (mē·lŏd′ ĭk)
  me·lo·di·ous (mē·lō′ dĭ·ŭs)

mel·on (mĕl′ ŭn)
melt (mĕlt)
  melt·a·ble   melt·ing pot
mem·brane (mĕm′ brān)
  mem·bra·nous (mĕm′ brȧ·nŭs)
me·men·to (mĕ·mĕn′ tō)
  -tos
mem·o (mĕm′ ō)
  -os
mem·oir (mĕm′ wăr)
mem·o·ra·ble (mĕm′ ō·rȧ·b'l)
  mem·o·ra·bil·i·a
    (mĕm′ ō·rȧ·bĭl′ ĭ·ȧ)
  mem·o·ra·bil·i·ty
    (mĕm′ ō·rȧ·bĭl′ ĭ·tĭ)
mem·o·ran·dum
    (mĕm′ ō·răn′ dŭm)
  pl. -dums *or* -da
me·mo·ri·al (mĕ·mō′ rĭ·ăl)
  me·mo·ri·al·ize
mem·o·ry (mĕm′ ō·rĭ)
  -ries
  mem·o·ri·za·tion
    (mĕm′ ō·rĭ·zā′ shŭn)
  mem·o·rize   -iz·ing
men·ace (mĕn′ ĭs)
  men·ac·ing·ly
mé·nage (mā·näzh′)
me·nag·er·ie (mĕ·năj′ ĕr·ĭ)
men·da·cious (mĕn·dā′ shŭs)
  men·dac·i·ty (mĕn·dăs′ ĭ·tĭ)
Men·del's law (mĕn′ dĕlz)
  Men·de·li·an (mĕn·dē′ lĭ·ăn)
men·di·cant (mĕn′ dĭ·kȧnt)
  -can·cy
me·ni·al (mē′ nĭ·ăl)
  -al·ly
men·in·gi·tis (mĕn′ ĭn·jī′ tĭs)
men·o·pause (mĕn′ ō·pôz)
men·stru·ate (mĕn′ strōō·āt)
  -at·ing   men·stru·al
  men·stru·a·tion
    (mĕn′ strōō·ā′ shŭn)
men·su·ra·tion
    (mĕn′ shōō·rā′ shŭn)
men·tal (mĕn′ tăl)
  men·tal·i·ty (mĕn·tăl′ ĭ·tĭ)
  men·tal·ly
men·thol (mĕn′ thōl)
  men·tho·lat·ed
    (mĕn′ thō·lāt′ ĕd)
men·tion (mĕn′ shŭn)
  men·tion·a·ble
men·tor (mĕn′ tẽr)

men·u (mĕn′ ū)
  -us
Meph·i·stoph·e·les
    (mĕf′ ĭ·stŏf′ ĕ·lēz)
mer·can·tile (mûr′ kȧn·tĭl)
  mer·can·til·ism
    (mûr′ kȧn·tĭl·ĭz′m)
mer·ce·nar·y (mûr′ sĕ·nĕr′ ĭ)
  nari·es
mer·cer·ized thread
    (mûr′ sẽr′ ĭzd)
mer·chan·dise (mûr′ chȧn·dīz)
mer·chant (mûr′ chȧnt)
Mer·cu·ro·chrome
    (mûr·kū′ rō·krōm′)
mer·cu·ry (mûr′ kū·rĭ)
  mer·cu·ri·al (mûr·kū′ rĭ·ăl)
  mer·cu·ric (mûr·kū′ rĭk)
  mer·cu·ry-va·por lamp
mer·cy (mûr′ sĭ)
  -cies
  mer·ci·ful, -ful·ly, -ful·ness
  mer·ci·less   -less·ness
mere (mẽr)
  mere·ly
mer·e·tri·cious (mĕr′ ĕ·trĭsh′ ŭs)
mer·gan·ser duck
    (mẽr·găn′ sẽr)
merge (mûrj)
  merg·ing   mer·gence
  merg·er
me·rid·i·an (mĕ·rĭd′ ĭ·ăn)
me·ringue (mĕ·răng′)
mer·it (mĕr′ ĭt)
  -it·ed   -it·ing
  mer·i·to·ri·ous
    (mĕr′ ĭ·tō′ rĭ·ŭs)
mer·maid (mûr′ mād′)
mer·ry (mĕr′ ĭ)
  mer·ri·ment   mer·ri·ly
  mer·ry-go-round
  mer·ry·mak·er
me·sa (mā′ sȧ)
Me·sa·bi (iron range)
    (mĕ·sä′ bĭ)
mes·cal (mĕs·kăl′)
mes·mer·ize (mĕz′ mẽr·ĭz)
  -iz·ing
  mes·mer·ism (mĕz′ mẽr·ĭz′m)
mes·quite (mĕs·kēt′)
mes·sage (mĕs′ ĭj)
  mes·sen·ger (mĕs′ ĕn·jẽr)
Mes·si·ah (mĕ·sī′ ȧ)
  Mes·si·an·ic (mĕs′ ĭ·ăn′ ĭk)
mess kit (mĕs)

mess·mate (mĕs′ māt′)
mess·y (mĕs′ ĭ)
 mess·i·ness
mes·ti·zo (mĕs·tē′ zō)
 -zos
me·tab·o·lism (mĕ·tăb′ ŏ·lĭz′m)
 met·a·bol·ic (mĕt′ à·bŏl′ ĭk)
met·al (mĕt′ 'l)
 (substance; see *mettle*)
 me·tal·lic (mĕ·tăl′ ĭk)
 met·al·lur·gist (mĕt′ 'l·ûr′ jĭst)
 met·al·lur·gy (mĕt′ 'l·ûr′ jĭ)
 met·al·ware met·al·work·er
met·a·mor·pho·sis
 (mĕt′ à·môr′ fŏ·sĭs)
 pl. met·a·mor·pho·ses
 met·a·mor·phic
 (mĕt′ à·môr′ fĭk)
met·a·phor (mĕt′ à·fēr)
 met·a·phor·i·cal
 (mĕt′ à·fŏr′ ĭ·kàl)
met·a·phys·ics (mĕt′ à·fĭz′ ĭks)
 met·a·phys·i·cal (-fĭz′ ĭ·kàl)
 met·a·phy·si·cian (-fĭ·zĭsh′ ắn)
met·a·tar·sal (mĕt′ à·tär′ sàl)
mete (mēt)
 (allot; see *meat*, *meet*)
 met·ing
me·te·or (mē′ tĕ·ēr)
 me·te·or·ic (mē′ tĕ·ŏr′ ĭk)
 me·te·or·ite (mē′ tĕ·ēr·īt)
me·te·or·ol·o·gy
 (mē′ tĕ·ēr·ŏl′ ŏ·jĭ)
 me·te·or·o·log·i·cal
 (mē′ tĕ·ŏr·ŏ·lŏj′ ĭ·kàl)
 me·te·or·ol·o·gist
 (mē′ tĕ·ēr·ŏl′ ŏ·jĭst)
me·ter (mē′ tēr)
meth·ane (mĕth′ ān)
meth·od (mĕth′ ŭd)
 me·thod·i·cal (mĕ·thŏd′ ĭ·kàl)
 meth·od·o·log·i·cal
 (mĕth′ ŭd·ŏ·lŏj′ ĭ·kàl)
 meth·od·ol·o·gy
 (mĕth′ ŭd·ŏl′ ŏ·jĭ)
Meth·od·ist (mĕth′ ŭd·ĭst)
Me·thu·se·lah (mĕ·thū′ zĕ·là)
meth·yl (mĕth′ ĭl)
 meth·yl·ene
me·tic·u·lous (mĕ·tĭk′ ŭ·lŭs)
met·ric (mĕt′ rĭk)
 met·ri·cal
met·ro·nome (mĕt′ rŏ·nōm)
me·trop·o·lis (mĕ·trŏp′ ŏ·lĭs)

met·ro·pol·i·tan
 (mĕt′ rŏ·pŏl′ ĭ·tăn)
met·tle (mĕt′ 'l)
 (spirit; see *metal*)
mez·za·nine (mĕz′ à·nēn)
mez·zo-so·pra·no
 (mĕd′ zŏ·sŏ·prä′ nō)
mi·as·ma (mĭ·ăz′ mà)
mi·ca (mī′ kà)
Mich·i·gan (mĭsh′ ĭ·gắn)
 abbr. Mich.
 Mich·i·gan·ite *or*
 Mich·i·gan·der
 (mĭsh′ ĭ·găn′ dēr)
micro- (mī′ krŏ-)
 mi·cro·a·nal·y·sis
 mi·cro·cosm (mī′ krŏ·kŏz′m)
 mi·cro·cos·mic
 mī′ krŏ·kŏz′ mĭk
 mi·cro·film mi·cro·groove
 mi·crom·e·ter (mī·krŏm′ ĕ·tēr)
 mi·cro·or·gan·ism
 (mī′ krŏ·ôr′ găn·ĭz′m)
 mi·cro·phone mi·cro·print
 mi·cro·scope (mī′ krŏ·skōp)
 mi·cro·scop·ic (-skŏp′ ĭk)
 mi·cro·wave
mi·crobe (mī′ krōb)
mi·cron (mī′ krŏn)
mid- (mĭd-)
 mid-chan·nel mid-con·ti·nent
 mid·day mid·land
 mid-o·cean mid·night
 mid-point mid·riff
 mid·ship·man mid·sum·mer
 mid·way mid·week
 Mid·west Mid·west·ern·er
 mid·wife mid·win·ter
 mid·year
Mi·das (mī′ dàs)
mid·dle (mĭd′ 'l)
 mid·dle age mid·dle-aged
 mid·dle class *n.*
 mid·dle-class *adj.*
 mid·dle ear Mid·dle East
 mid·dle·man mid·dle·weight
 Mid·dle West
 Mid·dle West·ern·er
mid·dling (mĭd′ lĭng)
mid·dy blouse (mĭd′ ĭ)
midg·et (mĭj′ ĕt)
mid·riff (mĭd′ rĭf)
midst (mĭdst)
mien (mēn)
 (demeanor; see *mean*)

might (mĭt)
  (strength; see *mite*)
might·y (mĭt′ ĭ)
  might·i·er, -i·est, -i·ly, -i·ness
mi·gnon·ette (mĭn′ yŭn·ĕt′)
mi·graine head·ache
          (mī′ grān)
mi·grate (mī′ grāt)
  -grat·ing
mi·grant (mī′ grănt)
mi·gra·tion (mī·grā′ shŭn)
mi·gra·to·ry (mī′ grá·tō′ rĭ)
mi·ka·do (mĭ·kä′ dō)
mi·la·dy (mĭ·lā′ dĭ)
mil·dew (mĭl′ dū)
mile·age (mīl′ ĭj)
mile·stone (mīl′ stōn′)
mi·lieu (mē′ lyû′)
mil·i·tar·y (mĭl′ ĭ·tĕr′ ĭ)
  mil·i·tan·cy (-tăn·sĭ)
  mil·i·tant (-tănt)
  mil·i·ta·rist (mĭl′ ĭ·tá·rĭst)
  mil·i·ta·ris·tic
        (mĭl′ ĭ·tá·rĭs′ tĭk)
  mil·i·ta·rize -riz·ing
  mil·i·tate -tat·ing
mi·li·tia (mĭ·lĭsh′ á)
milk (mĭlk)
  milk·man
  milk of mag·ne·sia
  milk shake milk·sop
  milk weed milk·y
mil·len·ni·um (mĭ·lĕn′ ĭ·ŭm)
  pl. mil·len·nia mil·len·ni·al
mil·le·pede (mĭl′ ė·pēd)
mil·let (mĭl′ ĕt)
mil·li·me·ter (mĭl′ ĭ·mē′ tĕr)
mil·li·ner (mĭl′ ĭ·nĕr)
  mil·li·ner·y (-nĕr′ ĭ)
mil·lion (mĭl′ yŭn)
  mil·lion·aire (mĭl′ yŭn·âr′)
  mil·lionth
mill·stone (mĭl′ stōn′)
mill·wright (mĭl′ rīt′)
mi·lord (mĭ·lôrd′)
Mil·wau·kee, Wis.
        (mĭl·wô′ kė)
mime (mīm)
  mi·met·ic (mĭ·mĕt′ ĭk)
mim·e·o·graph (mĭm′ ė·ô·gráf′)
mim·ic (mĭm′ ĭk)
  mim·ick·er mim·ic·ry
mi·mo·sa (mĭ·mō′ sá)
min·a·ret (mĭn′ á·rĕt′)
mince·meat (mĭns′ mēt′)

minc·ing·ly (mĭn′ sĭng·lĭ)
mind (mīnd)
  mind·ful, -ful·ly, -ful·ness
  mind·less mind read·er
  mind's eye
min·er (mīn′ ĕr)
  (one who mines; see *minor*)
min·er·al (mĭn′ ĕr·ál)
  min·er·al·ize -iz·ing
  min·er·al·og·i·cal
        (mĭn′ ĕr·ál·ŏj′ ĭ·kál)
  min·er·al·o·gy
        (mĭn′ ĕr·ăl′ ŏ·jĭ)
mi·ne·stro·ne soup
        (mė·ná·strō′ nå)
min·gle (mĭng′ g'l)
  -gling
min·i·a·ture (mĭn′ ĭ·á·tůr)
min·i·mum (mĭn′ ĭ·mŭm)
  min·i·mal (-mál)
  min·i·mize -miz·ing
min·ing (mīn′ ĭng)
min·ion (mĭn′ yŭn)
min·is·ter (mĭn′ ĭs·tĕr)
  min·is·te·ri·al (mĭn′ ĭs·tĕr′ ĭ·ál)
  min·is·tra·tion (mĭn′ ĭs·trā′ shŭn)
  min·is·try (mĭn′ ĭs·trĭ)
  -tries
Min·ne·ap·o·lis, (mĭn′ ė·ăp′ ŏ·lĭs)
  Minn.
Min·ne·so·ta (mĭn′ ė·sō′ tá)
  abbr. Minn. Min·ne·so·tan
min·now (mĭn′ ō)
mi·nor (mī′ nĕr)
  (under age; see *miner*)
mi·nor·i·ty (mĭ·nŏr′ ĭ·tĭ)
  -ties
min·strel (mĭn′ strĕl)
mint·age (mĭn′ tĭj)
mint ju·lep (mĭnt)
min·u·et (mĭn′ û·ĕt′)
mi·nus (mī′ nŭs)
mi·nus·cule (mĭ·nŭs′ kŭl)
min·ute (mĭn′ ĭt)
  (time unit) min·ute·man
mi·nute (mĭ·nūt′)
  (little) mi·nute·ly
mi·nu·ti·a (mĭ·nū′ shĭ·á)
  pl. mi·nu·tiae (-ē)
minx (mĭngks)
  minx·es
mir·a·cle (mĭr′ á·k'l)
  mi·rac·u·lous (mĭ·răk′ û·lŭs)
mi·rage (mĭ·räzh′)
mire (mīr)

mir·ror (mĭr′ ēr)
  mir·rored   mir·ror·ing
mirth (mûrth)
  mirth·ful, -ful·ly, -ful·ness
mis·al·li·ance (mĭs′ ă·lī′ ăns)
mis·an·thrope (mĭs′ ăn·thrōp)
  mis·an·throp·ic
    (mĭs′ ăn·thrŏp′ ĭk)
mis·be·got·ten (mĭs′ bĕ·gŏt′ 'n)
mis·cal·cu·la·tion
    (mĭs′ kăl·kū·lā′ shŭn)
mis·car·riage (mĭs·kăr′ ĭj)
mis·ce·ge·na·tion
    (mĭs′ ĕ·jĕ·nā′ shŭn)
mis·cel·la·ne·ous
    (mĭs′ ĕ·lā′ nĕ·ŭs)
  mis·cel·la·ny (mĭs′ ĕ·lā′ nĭ)
mis·chief (mĭs′ chĭf)
  mis·chie·vous (mĭs′ chĭ·vŭs)
mis·con·cep·tion
    (mĭs′ kŏn·sĕp′ shŭn)
mis·con·strue (mĭs′ kŏn·strōō′)
  -stru·ing
mis·de·mean·or
    (mĭs′ dĕ·mēn′ ēr)
mi·ser (mī′ zēr)
mis·er·a·ble (mĭz′ ēr·a·b'l)
mis·fea·sance (mĭs·fē′ zăns)
mis·hap (mĭs·hăp′)
mis·in·ter·pre·ta·tion
    (mĭs′ ĭn·tûr′ prĕ·tā′ shŭn)
mis·judg·ment (mĭs·jŭj′ mĕnt)
mis·man·age·ment
    (mĭs·măn′ ĭj·mĕnt)
mis·no·mer (mĭs·nō′ mēr)
mi·sog·y·ny (mĭ·sŏj′ ĭ·nĭ)
mis·rep·re·sen·ta·tion
    (mĭs′ rĕp·rĕ·zĕn·tā′ shŭn)
mis·sal (mĭs′ ăl)
  (devotional book; see *missile*)
mis·shap·en (mĭs·shāp′ ĕn)
mis·sile (mĭs′ ĭl)
  (self-propelling weapon; see *missal*)
mis·sion (mĭsh′ ŭn)
mis·sion·ar·y (mĭsh′ ŭn·ĕr′ ĭ)
  -aries
Mis·sis·sip·pi (mĭs′ ĭ·sĭp′ ĭ)
  abbr. Miss.
  Mis·sis·sip·pi·an
mis·sive (mĭs′ ĭv)
Mis·sou·ri (mĭ·zŏŏr′ ĭ)
  abbr. Mo. Mis·sou·ri·an
mis·spell (mĭs·spĕl′)

mis·state (mĭs·stāt′)
  mis·stat·ing
mis·step (mĭs·stĕp′)
  mis·stepped mis·step·ping
mis·take (mĭs·tāk′)
  -tak·ing   mis·tak·a·ble
  mis·tak·en
mis·tle·toe (mĭs′ 'l·tō)
mis·tress (mĭs′ trĕs)
mis·un·der·stand·ing
    (mĭs′ ŭn·dēr·stănd′ ĭng)
mite (mīt)
  (a bit; see *might*)
mi·ter (mī′ tēr)
mit·i·gate (mĭt′ ĭ·gāt)
  -gat·ing   mit·i·gant
  mit·i·ga·tion (mĭt′ ĭ·gā′ shŭn)
  mit·i·ga·tor
mitt (mĭt)
mit·ten (mĭt′ 'n)
mix (mĭks)
  mix·ture (mĭks′ tŭr)
  mix-up
mne·mon·ics (nē·mŏn′ ĭks)
moat (mōt)
  (ditch; see *mote*)
mo·bile (mō′ bĭl) *adj.*
  mo·bil·i·ty (mō·bĭl′ ĭ·tĭ)
mo·bile (mō′ bēl) *n.*
mo·bi·lize (mō′ bĭ·līz)
  -liz·ing
  mo·bi·li·za·tion
    (mō′ bĭ·lĭ·zā′ zhŭn)
mob·oc·ra·cy (mŏb·ŏk′ ra·sĭ)
moc·ca·sin (mŏk′ a·sĭn)
mock (mŏk)
  mock·er·y mock-he·ro·ic
  mock·ing·bird
mod·al (mōd′ ăl)
  (pertaining to mode; see *model*)
mod·el (mŏd′ 'l)
  (design; see *modal*)
  -eled   -el·ing
mod·er·ate (mŏd′ ēr·ĭt)
  mod·er·ate·ly
  mod·er·a·tion (mŏd′ēr·ā′shŭn)
  mod·er·a·tor (mŏd′ ēr·ā′ tēr)
mod·ern (mŏd′ ērn)
  mod·ern·is·tic (mŏd′ ēr·nĭs′ tĭk)
  mo·der·ni·ty (mŏ·dûr′ nĭ·tĭ)
  mod·ern·i·za·tion
    (mŏd′ ēr·nĭ·zā′ shŭn)
mod·ern·ize (mŏd′ ēr·nīz)
  -iz·ing   mod·ern·ness

mod·est   (mŏd′ ĕst)
  mod·est·ly   mod·es·ty
mod·i·cum   (mŏd′ ĭ·kŭm)
mod·i·fy   (mŏd′ ĭ·fī)
  -fied,   -fy·ing
  mod·i·fi·a·ble (mŏd′ ĭ·fī′ à·b′l)
  mod·i·fi·ca·tion
         (mŏd′ ĭ·fī·kā′ shŭn)
  mod·i·fi·er
mod·ish   (mŏd′ ĭsh)
mo·diste   (mō·dēst′)
mod·u·late   (mŏd′ û·lāt)
  -lat·ing
  mod·u·la·tion   (mŏd′ û·lā′shŭn)
  mod·u·la·tor
mo·dus o·pe·ran·di
    (mō′ dŭs ŏp′ ĕ·răn′ dī)
mo·gul   (mō′ gŭl)
mo·hair   (mō′ hâr′)
Mo·ham·med·an
    (mō·hăm′ ĕ·dăn)
Mo·hawk   (mō′ hôk)
moi·ré   (mwá′ rā′)
moist   (moist)
  mois·ten   (mois′ ′n)
  mois·ture   (mois′ tŭr)
  mois·ture·proof
  mois·tur·ize -iz·ing
mo·lar   (mō′ lẽr)
mo·las·ses   mō·lăs′ ĕz
mold   (mōld)
  mold·a·ble   mold·ing
  mold·y
mol·e·cule   (mŏl′ ĕ·kūl)
  mo·lec·u·lar (mō·lĕk′ û·lẽr)
mole·hill   (mōl′ hĭl′)
mo·lest   (mō·lĕst′)
  mo·les·ta·tion
    (mō′ lĕs·tā′ shŭn)
  mo·lest·er
mol·li·fy   (mŏl′ ĭ·fī)
  -fied,   -fy·ing
  mol·li·fi·ca·tion
    (mŏl′ ĭ·fī·kā′ shŭn)
mol·lusk   (mŏl′ ŭsk)
mol·ly·cod·dle   (mŏl′ ĭ·kŏd′ ′l)
  -cod·dling
mol·ten   (mōl′ tĕn)
mo·lyb·de·num
    (mō·lĭb′ dĕ·nŭm)
mo·ment   (mō′ mĕnt)
mo·men·tar·y   (mō′ mĕn·tĕr′ ĭ)
  mo·men·tar·i·ly
mo·men·tous   (mō·mĕn′ tŭs)

mo·men·tum   (mō·mĕn′ tŭm)
  pl. mo·men·ta
Mo·na Li·sa   (mō′ nà lē′ zà)
mon·arch   (mŏn′ ẽrk)
  mo·nar·chic   (mō·när′ kĭk)
  mon·arch·y   (mŏn′ ẽr·kĭ)
  -arch·ies
mon·as·ter·y   (mŏn′ ăs·tĕr′ ĭ)
  -ter·ies
mo·nas·tic   (mō·năs′ tĭk)
  mo·nas·ti·cism
    (mō·năs′ tĭ·sĭz′m)
mon·e·tar·y   (mŏn′ ĕ·tĕr′ ĭ)
  mon·e·tar·i·ly
mon·e·tize   (mŏn′ ĕ·tīz)
  -tiz·ing
mon·ey   (mŭn′ ĭ)
  mon·eyed
  mon·ey-chang·er
  mon·ey·lend·er
  mon·ey-mak·ing
  mon·ey or·der
mon·ger   (mŭng′ gẽr)
Mon·gol   (mŏng′ gŏl)
  Mon·go·lian (mŏng·gōl′ yăn)
  Mon·gol·oid   (mŏng′ gŏl·oid)
mon·goose   (mŏng′ gōōs)
mon·grel   (mŭng′ grĕl)
mon·i·ker   (mŏn′ ĭ·kẽr)
mon·i·tor   (mŏn′ ĭ·tẽr)
monk   (mŭngk)
  monk·er·y   monk·ish
mon·key   (mŭng′ kĭ)
  -keys   mon·key·shine
  mon·key wrench
mon·o·chro·ma·tic
    (mŏn′ ŏ·krō·măt′ ĭk)
mon·o·cle   (mŏn′ ŏ·k′l)
mo·nog·a·my   (mō·nŏg′ à·mĭ)
  mo·nog·a·mist (-mĭst)
  mo·nog·a·mous (-mŭs)
mon·o·gram   (mŏn′ ŏ·grăm)
  mon·o·gram·mat·ic
    (mŏn′ ŏ·grà·măt′ ĭk)
mon·o·graph   (mŏn′ ŏ·gráf)
mo·nog·y·ny   (mō·nŏj′ ĭ·nĭ)
mon·o·lith·ic   (mŏn′ ŏ·lĭth′ ĭk)
mon·o·logue   (mŏn′ ŏ·lŏg)
mon·o·man·ia   (mŏn′ ŏ·mā′ nĭ·à)
mo·nop·o·ly   (mō·nŏp′ ŏ·lĭ)
  -lies
  mo·nop·o·lis·tic
    (mō·nŏp′ ŏ·lĭs′ tĭk)
  mo·nop·o·lize, -liz·ing

mon·o·syl·la·ble (mŏn′ ô· sĭl′ á· b'l)

mon·o·syl·lab·ic (mŏn′ ô· sĭ· lăb′ ĭk)

mon·o·the·ism (mŏn′ ô· thē· ĭz′m)

mon·o·the·is·tic (mŏn′ ô· thē· ĭs′ tĭk)

mon·o·tone (mŏn′ ô· tōn)

mo·not·o·nous (mô· nŏt′ ô· năs)

mo·not·o·ny (mô· nŏt′ ô· nĭ)

mon·ox·ide (mŏn· ŏk′ sīd)

mon·sieur (mē· syû′)

mon·si·gnor (mŏn· sē′ nyôr)

mon·soon (mŏn· sōōn′)

mon·ster (mŏn′ stēr)

mon·stros·i·ty (mŏn· strŏs′ ĭ· tĭ)
-ties

mon·strous (mŏn′ strŭs)

mon·tage (mŏn· täzh′)

Mon·tan·a (mŏn· tăn′ á)
abbr. Mont. Mon·tan·an

Mon·te Car·lo (mŏn′ tê kär′ lō)

Mon·te·rey, Calif. (mŏn′ tĕ· rā′)

Mon·ter·rey, Mex. (mŏn′ tĕ· rā′)

month·ly (mŭnth′ lĭ)
-lies

mon·u·ment (mŏn′ û· mĕnt)

mon·u·men·tal (mŏn′ û· mĕn′ tál)

mood·y (mōōd′ ĭ)
mood·i·er, -i·est, -i·ly, -i·ness

moon (mōōn)
moon·beam moon·light
moon·shine moon·stone
moon·struck

moor·age (mōōr′ ĭj)

Moor·ish (mōōr′ ĭsh)

moose (mōōs)
n. sing. & pl.

moot court (mōōt)

mope (mōp)
mop·ing mop·ish

mop·pet (mŏp′ ĕt)

mo·raine (mô· rān′)

mor·al (mŏr′ ál)
(ethical)
mor·al·ist
mor·al·is·tic (mŏr′ ál· ĭs′ tĭk)
mor·al·i·ty (mô· răl′ ĭ· tĭ)
mor·al·i·za·tion (mŏr′ ál· ĭ· zā′ shăn)
mor·al·i·zer mor·al·ly

mo·rale (mô· rál′)
(zeal)

mo·rass (mô· răs′)

mor·a·to·ri·um (môr′ á· tō′ rĭ· ŭm)
pl. mor·a·to·ri·a

mo·ray eel (mô· rā′)

mor·bid (môr′ bĭd)
mor·bid·i·ty (môr· bĭd′ ĭ· tĭ)

mor·dant (môr′ dănt)
-dan·cy

more·o·ver (mōr· ō′ vēr)

mo·res (mō′ rēz)
(customs)

mor·ga·nat·ic (môr′ gá· năt′ ĭk)

morgue (môrg)

mor·i·bund (môr′ ĭ· bŭnd)

Mor·mon (môr′ mŭn)

morn·ing (môr′ nĭng)
(early day; see mourning)
morn·ing-glo·ry
morn·ing star

Mo·roc·can (mô· rŏk′ ăn)

mo·roc·co leath·er (mô· rŏk′ ō)

mo·ron (mō′ rŏn)
mo·ron·ic (mô· rŏn′ ĭk)

mo·rose (mô· rōs′)
mo·rose·ly

mor·phine (môr′ fēn)

mor·phol·o·gy (môr· fŏl′ ô· jĭ)
mor·pho·log·i·cal (môr′ fô· lŏj′ ĭ· kál)

Mor·ris chair (mŏr′ ĭs)

mor·row (mŏr′ ō)

Morse code (môrs)

mor·sel (môr′ sĕl)

mor·tal (môr′ tál)
mor·tal·i·ty (môr· tăl′ ĭ· tĭ)
mor·tal·ly

mor·tar (môr′ tēr)
mor·tar·board

mort·gage (môr′ gĭj)
-gag·ing

mort·ga·gee (môr′ gĭ· jē′)
mort·ga·gor

mor·ti·cian (môr· tĭsh′ ăn)

mor·ti·fy (môr′ tĭ· fī)
-fied -fy·ing

mor·ti·fi·ca·tion (môr′ tĭ· fĭ· kā′ shŭn)

mor·tise (môr′ tĭs)

mor·tu·ar·y (môr′ tû· ĕr′ ĭ)
-ar·ies

mo·sa·ic (mô· zā′ ĭk)

Mo·selle wine   (mō·zĕl′)
Mo·ses   (mō′ zĭz)
   Mo·sa·ic law   (mō·zā′ ĭk)
mo·sey   (mō′ zĭ)
  -sey·ing
Mos·lem   (mŏz′ lĕm)
mosque   (mŏsk)
mos·qui·to   (mŭs·kē′ tō)
  -toes
moss   (mŏs)
most·ly   (mōst′ lĭ)
mote   (mōt)
  (particle; see *moat*)
mo·tel   (mō·tĕl′)
mo·tet   (mō·tĕt′)
moth ball   (mŏth bôl)
moth-eat·en   (mŏth′ ēt′ 'n)
moth·er   (mŭth′ ēr)
  Mother Goose   moth·er·hood
  moth·er-in-law   moth·ers-in-law
  moth·er·land
  moth·er·ly   -li·ness
  moth·er-of-pearl
  Moth·er's Day
  moth·er tongue
mo·tif   (mō·tēf′)
mo·tile   (mō′ tĭl)
  mo·til·i·ty   (mō·tĭl′ ĭ·tĭ)
mo·tion   (mō′ shŭn)
  mo·tion·less   mo·tion pic·ture
  mo·tion-pic·ture pro·jec·tor
mo·ti·vate   (mō′ tĭ·vāt)
  -vat·ing
  mo·ti·va·tion   (mō′ tĭ·vā′ shŭn)
mo·tive   (mō′ tĭv)
mot·ley   (mŏt′ lĭ)
mo·tor   (mō′ tēr)
  mo·tor·boat   mo·tor·cade
  mo·tor·cy·cle   -cy·clist
  mo·tor-driv·en   mo·tor·drome
  mo·tor·ist   mo·tor·ized
  mo·tor·man
mot·tled   (mŏt′ 'ld)
mot·to   (mŏt′ ō)
  mot·toes
mound   (mound)
mount   (mount)
  mount·a·ble
moun·tain   (moun′ tĭn)
  moun·tain·eer   (moun′ tĭ·nēr′)
  moun·tain lau·rel
  moun·tain·ous   (moun′ tĭ·nŭs)
  moun·tain·side
moun·te·bank   (moun′ tē·băngk)

mourn·ful   (mōrn′ fŏŏl)
  -ful·ly   -ful·ness
mourn·ing   (mōrn′ ĭng)
  (lamentation; see *morning*)
  mourn·ing dove
mouse   (mous)
  pl. mice   (mīs)
mousse   (mōōs)
mousse·line de soie
       (mōōs′ lēn′ dĕ swä′)
mous·y   (mous′ ĭ)
  mous·i·ness
mouth   (mouth)
  mouth·ful   -fuls
  mouth or·gan   mouth·piece
mou·ton coat   (mōō′ tŏn)
move   (mōōv)
  mov·ing
  mov·a·bil·i·ty
       (mōōv·à·bĭl′ ĭ·tĭ)
  mov·a·ble   (mōōv′ à·b'l)
  move·ment
mov·ie   (mōōv′ ĭ)
  mov·ing pic·ture
mow·er   (mō′ ēr)
Mo·zam·bique,   (mō′ zăm·bēk′)
  Afr.
mu·ci·lage   (mū′ sĭ·lĭj)
  mu·ci·lag·i·nous
       (mū′ sĭ·lăj′ ĭ·nŭs)
muck·rak·er   (mŭk′ rāk′ ēr)
mu·cous mem·brane
       (mū′ kŭs)
mud·dle   (mŭd′ 'l)
  mud·dling
  mud·dle·head·ed
mud·dy   (mŭd′ ĭ)
  mud·di·ness
mud·guard   (mŭd′ gärd′)
mud·sling·er   (mŭd′ slĭng′ ēr)
muff   (mŭf)
muf·fin   (mŭf′ ĭn)
muf·fle   (mŭf′ 'l)
  muf·fling   muf·fler
muf·ti   (mŭf′ tĭ)
mug·gy   (mŭg′ ĭ)
  mug·gi·ness
mug·wump   (mŭg′ wŭmp′)
muk·luk   (mŭk′ lŭk)
mu·lat·to   (mù·lăt′ ō)
  -lat·toes
mul·ber·ry   (mŭl′ bĕr′ ĭ)
  -ber·ries
mulch   (mŭlch)
mulct   (mŭlkt)

mule (mūl)
  mule skin·ner
  mu·le·teer (mū' lĕ·tẽr')
  mul·ish
mulled ci·der (mŭld)
mul·let (mŭl' ĕt)
mul·ti·far·i·ous (mŭl' tĭ·fâr' ĭ·ŭs)
mul·ti·fold (mŭl' tĭ·fōld)
Mul·ti·graph (mŭl' tĭ·gráf)
mul·ti·lat·er·al
      (mŭl' tĭ·lăt' ẽr·ál)
  -al·ly
mul·ti·lin·e·ar (mŭl' tĭ·lĭn' ê·ẽr)
mul·ti·mil·lion·aire
      (mŭl' tĭ·mĭl' yŭn·âr')
mul·ti·par·tite (mŭl' tĭ·pär' tīt)
mul·ti·ple (mŭl' tĭ·p'l)
  mul·ti·ple scle·ro·sis
  mul·ti·pli·ci·ty
      (mŭl' tĭ·plĭs' ĭ·tĭ)
mul·ti·ply (mŭl' tĭ·plī)
  -plied   -ply·ing
  mul·ti·pli·cand
      (mŭl' tĭ·plĭ·kănd')
  mul·ti·pli·ca·tion
      (mŭl' tĭ·plĭ·kā' shŭn)
  mul·ti·pli·er
mul·ti·tude (mŭl' tĭ·tūd)
  mul·ti·tu·di·nous
      (mŭl' tĭ·tū' dĭ·nŭs)
mum·ble (mŭm' b'l)
  -bling
mum·bo jum·bo
      (mŭm' bō jŭm' bō)
mum·mer (mŭm' ẽr)
mum·mi·fy (mŭm' ĭ·fī)
  -fied   -fy·ing
  mum·mi·fi·ca·tion
      (mŭm' ĭ·fĭ·kā' shŭn)
mum·my (mŭm' ĭ)
  mum·mies
mumps (mŭmps)
mun·dane (mŭn' dān)
  mun·dane·ly
mu·nic·i·pal (mū·nĭs' ĭ·pál)
  mu·nic·i·pal·i·ty
      (mū·nĭs' ĭ·păl' ĭ·tĭ)
mu·nif·i·cent (mū·nĭf' ĭ·sĕnt)
  -cence
mu·ni·tions (mū·nĭsh' ŭnz)
mu·ral (mū' rál)
mur·der (mûr' dẽr)
  mur·der·er   mur·der·ess
  mur·der·ous (-ŭs)

murk·y (mûr' kĭ)
  murk·i·ness
mur·mur (mûr' mẽr)
  -mured   -mur·ing
mus·ca·tel (mŭs' ká·tĕl')
mus·cle (mŭs' 'l)
  (body tissue; see *mussel*)
  -cling   mus·cle-bound
mus·cu·lar (mŭs' kŭ·lẽr)
  mus·cu·lar dys·tro·phy
  mus·cu·lar·i·ty
      (mŭs' kŭ·lăr' ĭ·tĭ)
  mus·cu·la·ture
      (mŭs' kŭ·lá·tûr)
muse (mūz)
  mus·ing
mu·sette bag (mū·zĕt')
mu·se·um (mū·zē' ŭm)
mush·room (mŭsh' rōōm)
mu·sic (mū' zĭk)
  mu·si·cal (mū' zĭ·kál)
  -cal·ly
  mu·si·cale (mū' zĭ·kál')
  mu·si·cian (mū·zĭsh' án)
musk deer (mŭsk)
mus·keg (mŭs' kĕg)
mus·kel·lunge (mŭs' kĕ·lŭnj)
mus·ket (mŭs' kĕt)
  mus·ket·eer (mŭs' kĕ·tẽr')
  mus·ket·ry
musk·mel·on (mŭsk' mĕl' ŭn)
musk ox (mŭsk)
musk·rat (mŭsk' răt')
mus·lin (mŭz' lĭn)
mus·sel (mŭs' 'l)
  (shellfish; see *muscle*)
mus·tache (mŭs·tásh')
  mus·ta·chio (mŭs·tä' shō)
  -chioed
mus·tard (mŭs' tẽrd)
mus·ter (mŭs' tẽr)
mus·ty (mŭs' tĭ)
  mus·ti·ness
mu·ta·ble (mū' tá·b'l)
  mu·ta·bil·i·ty (mū' tá·bĭl' ĭ·tĭ)
mu·ti·late (mū' tĭ·lāt)
  -lat·ing
  mu·ti·la·tion (mū' tĭ·lā' shŭn)
  mu·ti·la·tor
mu·ti·ny (mū' tĭ·nĭ)
  -nies, -nied, -ny·ing
  mu·ti·neer (mū' tĭ·nẽr')
  mu·ti·nous
mutt (mŭt)
mut·ter (mŭt' ẽr)

mut·ton (mŭt′ 'n)
mu·tu·al (mū′ tụ·ḓl)
 -al·ly
 mu·tu·al·i·ty (mū′ tụ·ăl′ ĭ·tĭ)
muz·zle (mŭz′ 'l)
 muz·zling muz·zle-load·er
my·o·pi·a (mī·ō′ pĭ·ḁ)
 my·op·ic (mī·ŏp′ ĭk)
myr·i·ad (mĭr′ ĭ·ḓd)
myrrh (mûr)
myr·tle (mûr′ t'l)
my·self (mī·sĕlf′)
mys·te·ri·ous (mĭs·tẽr′ ĭ·ŭs)
 mys·ter·y (mĭs′ tẽr·ĭ)
 -ter·ies
mys·tic (mĭs′ tĭk)
 mys·ti·cal mys·ti·cism
mys·ti·fy (mĭs′ tĭ·fī)
 -fied -fy·ing
 mys·ti·fi·ca·tion
  (mĭs′ tĭ·fĭ·kā′ shŭn)
myth (mĭth)
 myth·i·cal myth·i·cal·ly
 myth·o·log·i·cal
  (mĭth′ ō·lŏj′ ĭ·kḓl)
 my·thol·o·gy (mī·thŏl′ ō·jĭ)
 -gies

N

na·dir (nā′ dẽr)
nag·ging (năg′ ĭng)
na·ïve (nä·ēv′)
 na·ïve·ly
 na·ïve·té (nä·ēv′ tā′)
na·ked (nā′ kĕd)
 na·ked·ness
nam·by-pam·by
  (năm′ bĭ·păm′ bĭ)
name (nām)
 nam·ing nam·a·ble
 name·less name·ly
 name·sake
na·palm bomb (nā′ päm)
naph·tha (năf′ thḁ)
 naph·tha·lene (năf′ thḁ·lēn)
 naph·thol (năf′ thōl)
nap·kin (năp′ kĭn)
Na·po·le·on Bo·na·parte
  (nḁ·pō′ lē·ŭn bō′ nḁ·pärt)
 Na·po·le·on·ic wars
  (nḁ·pō′ lē·ŏn′ ĭk)
nar·cis·sus (när·sĭs′ ŭs)
 nar·cis·sis·tic (när′ sĭ·sĭs′ tĭk)

nar·co·sis (när·kō′ sĭs)
nar·co·syn·the·sis
  (när′ kō·sĭn′ thē·sĭs)
nar·cot·ic (när·kŏt′ ĭk)
 nar·co·tize (när′ kō·tīz)
 tiz·ing
Nar·ra·gan·sett (bay)
  (năr′ ḁ·găn′ sĕt)
nar·rate (nă·rāt′)
 nar·rat·ing
 nar·ra·tion (nă·rā′ shŭn)
 nar·ra·tive (năr′ ḁ·tĭv)
 -tive·ly
 nar·ra·tor (nă·rā′ tẽr)
nar·row (năr′ ō)
 nar·row-gauge
 nar·row-mind·ed
 nar·row·ness
na·sal (nā′ zḓl)
 na·sal·i·ty (nā·zăl′ ĭ·tĭ)
 na·sal·ize -iz·ing
 na·sal·ly
nas·cent (năs′ ĕnt)
Nas·sau (năs′ ô)
nas·tur·tium (năs·tûr′ shŭm)
nas·ty (năs′ tĭ)
 nas·ti·er, -ti·est, -ti·ly, -ti·ness
na·tal (nā′ tḓl)
na·ta·to·ri·um (nā′ tḁ·tō′ rĭ·ŭm)
na·tion (nā′ shŭn)
na·tion·al (năsh′ ŭn·ḓl)
 na·tion·al·ism
 na·tion·al·is·tic
  (năsh′ ŭn·ḓl·ĭs′ tĭk)
 na·tion·al·i·ty
  (năsh′ ŭn·ăl′ ĭ·tĭ)
 -ties
 na·tion·al·i·za·tion
  (năsh′ ŭn·ḓl·ĭ·zā′ shŭn)
 na·tion·al·ize (năsh′ ŭn·ḓl·ĭz)
 -iz·ing na·tion·al·ly
na·tive (nā′ tĭv)
 na·tive·ly
 na·tiv·is·tic (nā′ tĭv·ĭs′ tĭk)
 na·tiv·i·ty (nā·tĭv′ ĭ·tĭ)
nat·ty (năt′ ĭ)
 nat·ti·ly
nat·u·ral (năt′ û·rḓl)
 nat·u·ral·ism nat·u·ral·ist
 nat·u·ral·is·tic
  (năt′ û·rḓl·ĭs′ tĭk)
 nat·u·ral·i·za·tion
  (năt′ û·rḓl·ĭ·zā′ shŭn)
 nat·u·ral·ize -iz·ing
 nat·u·ral·ly nat·u·ral·ness

na·ture (nā′ tŭr)
na·tur·o·path (nā′ tŭr·ŏ·păth′)
naugh·ty (nô′ tĭ)
 naugh·ti·er -ti·est
 -ti·ly -ti·ness
nau·se·a (nô′ shē·à)
 nau·se·ate (nô′ shē·āt)
 -at·ing
 nau·se·a·tion (nô′ shē·ā′ shŭn)
 nau·seous (nô′ shŭs)
nau·ti·cal (nô′ tĭ·kǎl)
nau·ti·lus (nô′ tĭ·lŭs)
na·val (nā′ vǎl)
 (of ships; see *navel*)
nave (nāv)
na·vel (nā′ vĕl)
 (umbilicus; see *naval*)
 na·vel or·ange
nav·i·gate (nǎv′ ĭ·gāt)
 -gat·ing
 nav·i·ga·bil·i·ty
  (nǎv′ ĭ·gà·bĭl′ ĭ·tĭ)
 nav·i·ga·ble (nǎv′ ĭ·gà·b′l)
 nav·i·ga·tion (nǎv′ ĭ·gā′ shŭn)
 -tion·al nav·i·ga·tor
na·vy (nā′ vĭ)
 -vies
Naz·a·rene (nǎz′ à·rēn′)
Na·zi (nä′ tsē)
 Na·zism (nä′ tsĭz′m)
Ne·an·der·thal man
  (nē·ǎn′ dēr·tǎl′)
Ne·a·pol·i·tan (nē′ à·pŏl′ ĭ·tǎn)
neap tide (nēp)
near (nĕr)
 near·by Near East
 near·est near·ly
 near·ness
 near·sight·ed·ness
neat·ness (nēt′ nĕs)
neat′s-foot oil (nēts′ fŏŏt′)
Ne·bras·ka (nē·brǎs′ kà)
 abbr. Nebr., Neb.
 Ne·bras·kan
neb·u·la (nĕb′ û·là)
 pl. neb·u·lae (-lē)
 neb·u·lar (-lēr)
neb·u·lous (nĕb′ û·lŭs)
nec·es·sar·y (nĕs′ ĕ·sĕr′ ĭ)
 nec·es·sar·i·ly (nĕs′ ĕ·sĕr′ ĭ·lĭ)
 ne·ces·si·tate (nē·sĕs′ ĭ·tāt)
 -tat·ing
 ne·ces·si·tous (nē·sĕs′ ĭ·tŭs)
 ne·ces·si·ty (nē·sĕs′ ĭ·tĭ)
 -ties

neck·er·chief (nĕk′ ēr·chĭf)
neck·lace (nĕk′ lĭs)
neck·tie (nĕk′ tī′)
ne·crol·o·gy (nĕ·krŏl′ ŏ·jĭ)
nec·ro·man·cy (nĕk′ rŏ·mǎn′ sĭ)
nec·tar (nĕk′ tēr)
nec·tar·ine (nĕk′ tēr·ēn′)
need (nēd)
 need·ful need·i·est
 need·less -less·ly
 need·y
nee·dle (nē′ d′l)
 nee·dle-point lace
 nee·dle·work
ne′er-do-well (nâr′ dŏŏ·wĕl′)
ne·far·i·ous (nē·fâr′ ĭ·ŭs)
ne·gate (nē·gāt′)
 -gat·ing
 ne·ga·tion (nē·gā′ shŭn)
neg·a·tive (nĕg′ à·tĭv)
 neg·a·tive·ly neg·a·tiv·ism
neg·lect (nĕg·lĕkt′)
 neg·lect·ful, -ful·ly, -ful·ness
neg·li·gee (nĕg′ lĭ·zhā′)
neg·li·gent (nĕg′ lĭ·jĕnt)
 -gence
neg·li·gi·ble (nĕg′ lĭ·jĭ·b′l)
 neg·li·gi·bil·i·ty
  (nĕg′ lĭ·jĭ·bĭl′ ĭ·tĭ)
ne·go·ti·ate (nē·gō′ shĭ·āt)
 -at·ing
 ne·go·ti·a·bil·i·ty
  (nē·gō′ shĭ·à·bĭl′ ĭ·tĭ)
 ne·go·ti·a·ble
  (nē·gō′ shĭ·à·b′l)
 ne·go·ti·a·tion
  (nē·gō′ shĭ·ā′ shŭn)
 ne·go·ti·a·tor
Ne·gro (nē′ grō)
 -groes Ne·groid
Neh·ru, Ja·wa·har·lal
  (nā′ rŏŏ, jà·wä′ hàr·lǎl)
neigh (nā)
neigh·bor (nā′ bēr)
 neigh·bor·hood
 neigh·bor·ly -li·ness
nei·ther (nē′ thēr)
nem·a·tode (nĕm′ à·tōd)
nem·e·sis (nĕm′ ē·sĭs)
 pl. nem·e·ses
ne·o- (nē′ ŏ)
 ne·o-Cath·o·lic
 ne·o·clas·sic ne·o-Goth·ic
 ne·o-Hel·len·ic
 ne·o·im·pres·sion·ism

ne·o·lith·ic   ne·o·phyte
ne·o·plasm   Ne·o·pla·ton·ic
ne·o·prene
Ne·o-Scho·las·tic
Ne·o·zo·ic
neph·ew   (nĕf′ ū)
ne·phri·tis   (nĕ·frī′ tĭs)
  ne·phrit·ic   (nĕ·frĭt′ ĭk)
nep·o·tism   (nĕp′ ô·tĭz′m)
Nep·tune   (nĕp′ tūn)
nerve   (nûrv)
  nerve·less   nerve-rack·ing
  nerv·ous   nerv·ous·ness
  nerv·y
nes·tle   (nĕs′ ′l)
  -tling
neth·er·most   (nĕth′ ĕr·mōst)
net·ting   (nĕt′ ĭng)
net·tle   (nĕt′ ′l)
net·work   (nĕt′ wûrk′)
neu·ral·gia   (nû·răl′ jà)
neu·ras·the·ni·a
                    (nū′ răs·thē′ nĭ·à)
neu·ri·tic   (nû·rĭt′ ĭk)
  neu·ri·tis   (nû·rī′ tĭs)
neu·rol·o·gy   (nû·rŏl′ ô·jĭ)
  neu·ro·log·i·cal (nū′ rô·lŏj′ ĭ·kăl)
neu·ro·psy·cho·sis
                    (nū′ rô·sī·kō′ sĭs)
neu·ro·sis   (nû·rō′ sĭs)
  pl. neu·ro·ses   (-sēz)
neu·rot·ic   (nû·rŏt′ ĭk)
neu·ter   (nū′ tĕr)
neu·tral   (nū′ trăl)
  neu·tral·i·ty   (nû·trăl′ ĭ·tĭ)
  neu·tral·i·za·tion
                    (nū′ trăl·ĭ·zā′ shŭn)
  neu·tral·ize   -iz·ing
  neu·tral·iz·er
neu·tron   (nū′ trŏn)
Ne·va·da   (nĕ·văd′ à)
  abbr. Nev.   Ne·va·dan
nev·er·the·less   (nĕv′ ĕr·thē·lĕs′)
new   (nū)
  new·born   new·com·er
  new·fan·gled   new-fash·ioned
  new·ly-wed   new·ness
new·el   (nū′ ĕl)
New·found·land
                    (nū′ fŭnd·lănd′)
New Guin·ea   (nū gĭn′ ĭ)
New Hamp·shire
                    (nū hăm(p)′ shĕr)
  abbr. N.H.

New Heb·ri·des   (nū hĕb′ rĭ·dēz)
New Jer·sey   (nū jûr′ zĭ)
  abbr. N.J.   New Jer·sey·ite
New Mex·i·co   (nū mĕk′ sĭ·kō)
  abbr. N. Mex.   New Mex·i·can
news   (nūz)
  news·cast·er   news·let·ter
  news·man
  news·pa·per·man
  news·print   news·reel
  news·stand   news·y
New York   (nū yôrk′)
  abbr. N.Y.
New Zea·land   (nū zē′ lănd)
  abbr. N.Z.
nex·us   (nĕk′ sŭs)
ni·a·cin   (nī′ à·sĭn)
Ni·ag·a·ra   (nī·ăg′ à·rà)
nib·ble   (nĭb′ ′l)
  nib·bling
Nic·a·ra·gua   (nĭk′ à·rä′ gwà)
Ni·cene (creed)   (nī·sēn′)
ni·ce·ty   (nī′ sĕ·tĭ)
  -ties
niche   (nĭch)
nick·el   (nĭk′ ĕl)
nick·el·o·de·on   (nĭk′ ĕl·ō′ dē·ŭn)
nick·name   (nĭk′ nām′)
nic·o·tine   (nĭk′ ô·tēn)
nic·o·tin·ic ac·id
                    (nĭk′ ô·tĭn′ ĭk)
niece   (nēs)
Ni·ge·ri·a, Afr.   (nī·jĕr′ ĭ·à)
nig·gard·ly   (nĭg′ ĕrd·lĭ)
nig·gling   (nĭg′ ′lĭng)
nigh   (nī)
night   (nīt)
  night blind·ness
  night·cap   night club
  night crawl·er   night·fall
  night·gown   night·hawk
  night·in·gale   night·latch
  night·long   night·mare
  night owl   night·shade
  night·shirt   night·time
  night·wear
night·in·gale   (nīt′ ĭn·gāl)
ni·hil·ism   (nī′ ĭ·lĭz′m)
  ni·hil·ist   (nī′ ĭ·lĭst)
Ni·ke mis·sile   (nī′ kē)
nil   (nĭl)
nim·ble   (nĭm′ b′l)
  nim·ble·ness   nim·bly
nim·bus   (nĭm′ bŭs)

nine (nīn)
  nine·fold   nine·pins
  ninth
nine·teen (nīn′ tēn′)
nine·ty (nīn′ tĭ)
  -ties   nine·ti·eth
  nine·ty·fold
nip·ple (nĭp′ 'l)
Nip·pon·ese (nĭp′ ǒ·nēz′)
nip·py (nĭp′ ĭ)
  nip·pi·ness
nir·va·na (nĭr·vä′ nȧ)
ni·sei (nē′ sā′)
  n. sing. & pl.
ni·trate (nī′ trāt)
ni·tric ac·id (nī′ trĭk)
ni·tride (nī′ trīd)
ni·tri·fy (nī′ trĭ·fī)
  -fied   -fy·ing
ni·trite (nī′ trīt)
ni·tro·gen (nī′ trǒ·jěn)
  ni·tro·gen·ize (nī′ trǒ·jěn·īz)
  ni·trog·e·nous (nī·trǒj′ ě·nŭs)
ni·tro·glyc·er·in
         (nī′ trǒ·glĭs′ ěr·ĭn)
ni·trous ox·ide (nī′ trŭs)
nit·wit (nĭt′ wĭt′)
No·bel prize (nō·běl′)
no·ble (nō′ b'l)
  no·bil·i·ty (nō·bĭl′ ĭ·tĭ)
  no·ble·man   no·ble·ness
  no·bly
no·blesse o·blige
        (nō′ blěs′ ǒ′ blēzh′)
no·bod·y (nō′ bǒd·ĭ)
noc·tur·nal (nŏk·tûr′ nǎl)
  -nal·ly
noc·turne (nŏk′ tûrn)
noc·u·ous (nŏk′ û·ŭs)
node (nōd)
nod·ule (nŏd′ ūl)
no·el (nō·ěl′)
nog·gin (nŏg′ ĭn)
noise (noiz)
  noise·less   noise·mak·er
  nois·y   nois·i·er
  -i·est, -i·ly, -i·ness
noi·some (noi′ sŭm)
no·mad (nō′ mǎd)
  no·mad·ic (nō·mǎd′ ĭk)
nom de plume (nŏm′ dē plōōm′)
no·men·cla·ture
        (nō′ měn·klā′ tửr)
nom·i·nal (nŏm′ ĭ·nǎl)
  -nal·ly

nom·i·nate (nŏm′ ĭ·nāt)
  -nat·ing
  nom·i·na·tion
        (nŏm′ ĭ·nā′ shŭn)
  nom·i·na·tor
  nom·i·nee (nŏm′ ĭ·nē′)
nom·i·na·tive (nŏm′ ĭ·nȧ·tĭv)
non- (nŏn)
  non·ab·sorb·ent
  non·ac·cept·ance
  non·ag·gres·sive
  non·al·co·ho·lic
  non-Ar·y·an
  non·be·liev·er
  non·bel·lig·er·ent
  non·bloom·ing
  non·cha·lance
  non-Chris·tian
  non·co·er·cive
  non·com·bat·ant
  non·com·bus·ti·ble
  non·com·mis·sioned
  non·com·mit·tal
  non·com·mu·nist
  non·com·pet·i·tive
  non·com·pli·ance
  non·con·duc·tor
  non·con·form·ist
  non·con·tro·ver·sial
  non·cor·ro·sive
  non·de·script
  non·e·lec·tive
  non·en·ti·ty
  non·es·sen·tial
  non·ex·ist·ence
  non·fea·sance
  non·fic·tion
  non·in·ter·ven·tion
  non·ir·ri·tant
  non·mem·ber
  non·me·tal·lic
  non·ob·jec·tive
  non·par·ti·san
  non·pay·ment
  non·pro·duc·tive
  non·prof·it
  non·rec·og·ni·tion
  non·re·cur·ring
  non·re·new·a·ble
  non·res·i·dent, -den·tial
  non·re·stric·tive
  non·sec·tar·i·an
  non·stra·te·gic
  non·tech·ni·cal
  non·tox·ic

non·trans·fer·a·ble

non·typ·i·cal

non·vi·o·lence

non·cha·lant   (nŏn′ shá·lănt)

-lance

non·pa·reil   (nŏn′ pá·rĕl′)

non·plus   (nŏn′ plŭs)

-plused   -plus·ing

non·sense   (nŏn′ sĕns)

-sen·si·cal

non se·qui·tur   (nŏn sĕk′ wĭ·tēr)

noo·dle   (nōō′ d'l)

no one   (nō′ wŭn′)

noose   (nōōs)

norm   (nôrm)

nor·mal   (nôr′ măl)

nor·mal·cy

nor·mal·i·ty   (nôr·măl′ ĭ·tĭ)

nor·mal·ly

nor·ma·tive   (nôr′ má·tĭv)

Norse·man   (nôrs′ măn)

north   (nôrth)

north·east   north·east·er·ly

north·er·ly   north·ern·er

north·ern lights

north·ern·most

north·land   North Pole

north·ward

north·west·er·ly

North Car·o·li·na

          (nôrth kăr′ ŏ·lī′ ná)

abbr. N.C.,   N. Car.

North Car·o·lin·i·an

          (-kăr′ ŏ·lĭn′ ĭ·ăn)

North Da·ko·ta   (nôrth dá·kō′ tá)

abbr. N. Dak.

North Da·ko·tan

Nor·we·gian   (nôr·wē′ jăn)

nose   (nōz)

nose·bleed   nose dive

nose-dive *v.*   nose·gay

nose·piece   nos·y

nos·tal·gi·a   (nŏs·tăl′ jĭ·á)

nos·tal·gic

nos·tril   (nŏs′ trĭl)

nos·trum   (nŏs′ trŭm)

no·ta·ble   (nō′ tá·b'l)

no·ta·bil·i·ty   (nō′ tá·bĭl′ ĭ·tĭ)

no·ta·ry   (nō′ tá·rĭ)

-ries   no·ta·ry pub·lic

no·ta·rize   (nō′ tá·rīz)

-riz·ing

no·ta·tion   (nŏ·tā′ shŭn)

no·ta·tion·al

notch   (nŏch)

note·book   (nōt′ bŏŏk′)

note·wor·thy   (nōt′ wûr′ thĭ)

no·tice   (nō′ tĭs)

-tic·ing   no·tice·a·ble

no·ti·fy   (nō′ tĭ·fī)

-fied   -fy·ing

no·ti·fi·ca·tion

          (nō′ tĭ·fĭ·kā′ shŭn)

no·ti·fi·er

no·tion   (nō′ shŭn)

no·to·ri·e·ty   (nō′ tô·rī′ ĕ·tĭ)

no·to·ri·ous   (nō·tō′ rĭ·ŭs)

No·tre Dame, U. of

          (nō′ tēr dām′)

no-trump   (nō′ trŭmp′)

not·with·stand·ing

          (nŏt′ wĭth·stăn′ dĭng)

nou·gat   (nōō′ gát)

nought   (nôt)

noun   (noun)

nour·ish   (nûr′ ĭsh)

nour·ish·ment

No·va Sco·tia   (nō′ vá skō′ shá)

nov·el   (nŏv′ ĕl)

nov·el·ette   (nŏv′ ĕl·ĕt′)

nov·el·ist

no·vel·la   (nŏ·vĕl′ lä)

nov·el·ty   -ties

No·vem·ber   (nŏ·vĕm′ bēr)

no·ve·na   (nō·vē′ ná)

pl. no·ve·nae   (-nē)

nov·ice   (nŏv′ ĭs)

no·vi·ti·ate   (nŏ·vĭsh′ ĭ·ăt)

No·vo·cain   (nō′ vō·kān)

now·a·days   (nou′ á·dāz′)

no·where   (nō′ hwâr)

nox·ious   (nŏk′ shŭs)

noz·zle   (nŏz′ 'l)

nth de·gree   (ĕnth)

nu·ance   (nū·äns′)

nub·bin   (nŭb′ ĭn)

nu·bile   (nū′ bĭl)

nu·bil·i·ty   (nū·bĭl′ ĭ·tĭ)

nu·cle·ar   (nū′ klĕ·ēr)

nu·cle·ar en·er·gy

nu·cle·ar fis·sion

nu·cle·ar phys·ics

nu·cle·on   (nū′ klĕ·ŏn)

nu·cle·us   (nū′ klĕ·ŭs)

pl. nu·cle·i   (-ī)

nude   (nūd)

nud·ism   nud·ist

nu·di·ty

nug·get   (nŭg′ ĕt)

nui·sance   (nū′ săns)

null (nŭl)
  (and void)

nul·li·fi·ca·tion
          (nŭl′ ĭ·fĭ·kā′ shŭn)
nul·li·fy (nŭl′ ĭ·fĭ)
  -fied   -fy·ing
nul·li·ty (nŭl′ ĭ·tĭ)
numb (nŭm)
  numb·ly   numb·ness
num·ber (nŭm′ bēr)
  num·ber·less
nu·mer·a·ble (nū′ mēr·à·b'l)
nu·mer·al (nū′ mēr·ǎl)
nu·mer·ate (nū′ mēr·āt)
  -at·ing
  nu·mer·a·tion
          (nū·mēr·ā′ shŭn)
nu·mer·i·cal (nŭ·mēr′ ĭ·kǎl)
  -cal·ly
nu·mer·ol·o·gy (nū·mēr·ŏl′ ô·jĭ)
nu·mer·ous (nū′ mēr·ŭs)
nu·mis·mat·ics (nū′ mĭz·măt′ ĭks)
num·skull (nŭm′ skŭl′)
nun (nŭn)
  nun·nery
nun·ci·o (nŭn′ shĭ·ō)
nup·tial (nŭp′ shǎl)
nurse (nûrs)
  nurs·ing   nurse·maid
  nurs·er·y (nûr′ sēr·ĭ)
  -er·ies
  nurs·er·y rhyme
nur·ture (nûr′ tụr)
  -tur·ing
nut·crack·er (nŭt′ krăk′ ēr)
nut·hatch (nŭt′ hăch′)
nut·meg (nŭt′ mĕg)
nu·tri·a (nū′ trĭ·à)
nu·tri·ent (nū′ trĭ·ĕnt)
  nu·tri·ment (nū′ trĭ·mĕnt)
  nu·tri·tion (nŭ·trĭsh′ ŭn)
  nu·tri·tion·al (nū·trĭsh′ ŭn·ǎl)
  -al·ly
  nu·tri·tious (nŭ·trĭsh′ ŭs)
  nu·tri·tive (nū′ trĭ·tĭv)
nut·shell (nŭt′ shĕl′)
nuz·zle (nŭz′ 'l)
  nuz·zling
Ny·as·a·land, Afr.
          (nĭ·ăs′ à·lănd′)
ny·lon (nī′ lŏn)
nymph (nĭmf)
nym·pho·ma·ni·ac
          (nĭm′ fô·mā′ nĭ·ăk)

O

oaf·ish (ōf′ ĭsh)
O·a·hu is., Ha·wai·i
          (ô·ä′ hōō)
oak·en (ōk′ ĕn)
oars·man (ōrz′ mǎn)
o·a·sis (ô·ā′ sĭs)
  pl. o·a·ses (-sēz)
oath (ōth)
oat·meal (ōt′ mēl′)
ob·bli·ga·to (ŏb′ lĭ·gä′ tō)
ob·du·rate (ŏb′ dû·rǎt)
  ob·du·ra·cy
o·be·di·ent (ô·bē′ dĭ·ĕnt)
  -ence
o·bei·sance (ô·bā′ sǎns)
ob·e·lisk (ŏb′ ĕ·lĭsk)
o·bese (ô·bēs′)
  o·bes·i·ty (ô·bēs′ ĭ·tĭ)
o·bey (ô·bā′)
  -beyed   -bey·ing
ob·fus·cate (ŏb·fŭs′ kāt)
  -cat·ing
  ob·fus·ca·tion
          (ŏb′ fŭs·kā′ shŭn)
o·bit·u·ar·y (ô·bĭt′ û·ĕr′ ĭ)
  -ar·ies
ob·ject (ŏb′ jĕkt) n.
ob·ject (ŏb·jĕkt′) v.
  ob·jec·ti·fy (ŏb·jĕk′ tĭ·fĭ)
  -fied
  ob·jec·tion (ŏb·jĕk′ shŭn)
  ob·jec·tion·a·ble
  ob·jec·tive -tive·ly
  ob·jec·tiv·ism
  ob·jec·tiv·i·ty (ŏb′ jĕk·tĭv′ ĭ·tĭ)
  ob·jec·tor
ob·jet d'art (ôb′ zhĕ′ där′)
  ob·jets d'art (ôb′ zhĕ′ där′)
ob·late (ŏb′ lāt)
  ob·la·tion (ŏb·lā′ shŭn)
ob·li·gate (ŏb′ lĭ·gāt)
  -gat·ing
  ob·li·ga·tion (ŏb′ lĭ·gā′ shŭn)
  ob·lig·a·to·ry (ŏb·lĭg′ à·tō′ rĭ)
o·blige (ô·blīj′)
  -blig·ing
o·blique (ŏb·lēk′)
  -blique·ly
ob·lit·er·ate (ŏb·lĭt′ ēr·āt)
  -at·ing
  ob·lit·er·a·tion
          (ŏb·lĭt′ ēr·ā′ shŭn)

ob·liv·i·on (ŏb·lĭv′ ĭ·ŭn)
  ob·liv·i·ous (ŏb·lĭv′ ĭ·ŭs)
ob·long (ŏb′ lŏng)
ob·lo·quy (ŏb′ lŏ·kwĭ)
  -quies
ob·nox·ious (ŏb·nŏk′ shŭs)
o·boe (ō′ bō)
  o·bo·ist
ob·scene (ŏb·sēn′)
  -scene·ly
  ob·scen·i·ty (ŏb·sĕn′ ĭ·tĭ)
  -ties
ob·scur·ant·ism
      (ŏb·skūr′ ăn·tĭz'm)
ob·scure (ŏb·skūr′)
  ob·scu·ri·ty (ŏb·skū′ rĭ·tĭ)
ob·se·qui·ous (ŏb·sē′ kwĭ·ŭs)
ob·se·quies (ŏb′ sĕ·kwĭz)
ob·serve (ŏb·zûrv′)
  -serv·ing   ob·serv·a·ble
  ob·serv·ant   -ance
  ob·ser·va·tion
      (ŏb′ zēr·vā′ shŭn)
  -tion·al
  ob·serv·a·to·ry
      (ŏb·zûr′ va·tō′ rĭ)
  -ries   ob·serv·er
ob·sess (ŏb·sĕs′)
  ob·ses·sion   ob·ses·sive
ob·sid·i·an (ŏb·sĭd′ ĭ·ăn)
ob·so·lete (ŏb′ sŏ·lēt)
  ob·so·les·cent (ŏb′ sŏ·lĕs′ ĕnt)
  -cence
ob·sta·cle (ŏb′ stá·k'l)
ob·stet·rics (ŏb·stĕt′ rĭks)
  ob·stet·ri·cal (ŏb·stĕt′ rĭ·kăl)
  ob·ste·tri·cian
      (ŏb′ stĕ·trĭsh′ ăn)
ob·sti·nate (ŏb′ stĭ·nĭt)
  ob·sti·na·cy (-ná·sĭ)
  ob·sti·nate·ly
ob·strep·er·ous
      (ŏb·strĕp′ ĕr·ŭs)
ob·struct (ŏb·strŭkt′)
  ob·struct·er   ob·struc·tion
  ob·struc·tion·ist
ob·tain (ŏb·tān′)
  ob·tain·a·ble
ob·trude (ŏb·trōōd′)
  -trud·ing
  ob·tru·sion (ŏb·trōō′ zhŭn)
  ob·tru·sive (ŏb·trōō′ sĭv)
  -sive·ness
ob·tuse (ŏb·tūs′)
  -tuse·ness

ob·verse (ŏb·vûrs′)
  ob·verse·ly   ob·ver·sion
ob·vi·ate (ŏb′ vĭ·āt)
  -at·ing
ob·vi·ous (ŏb′ vĭ·ŭs)
oc·a·ri·na (ŏk′ á·rē′ ná)
oc·ca·sion (ŏ·kā′ zhŭn)
  oc·ca·sion·al   -al·ly
oc·ci·dent (ŏk′ sĭ·dĕnt)
  oc·ci·den·tal (ŏk′ sĭ·dĕn′ tăl)
oc·cip·i·tal (ŏk·sĭp′ ĭ·tăl)
oc·clude (ŏ·klōōd′)
  oc·clud·ing
  oc·clu·sion (ŏ·klōō′ zhŭn)
oc·cult (ŏ·kŭlt′)
  oc·cult·ism
oc·cu·pant (ŏk′ û·pănt)
  -pan·cy
oc·cu·pa·tion (ŏk′ û·pā′ shŭn)
  oc·cu·pa·tion·al, -al·ly
oc·cu·py (ŏk′ û·pĭ)
  -pied   -py·ing
oc·cur (ŏ·kûr′)
  oc·curred   oc·cur·ring
  oc·cur·rence
o·cean (ō′ shăn)
  o·ce·an·ic (ō′ shĕ·ăn′ ĭk)
  o·ce·a·nog·ra·phy
      (ō′ shĕ·á·nŏg′ rá·fĭ)
o·ce·lot (ō′ sĕ·lŏt)
o·cher (ō′ kĕr)
o'clock (ŏ·klŏk′)
oc·ta·gon (ŏk′ tá·gŏn)
  oc·tag·o·nal (ŏk·tăg′ ŏ·năl)
  -nal·ly
oc·ta·he·dron (ŏk′ tá·hē′ drŭn)
oc·tane (ŏk′ tān)
oc·tave (ŏk′ tāv)
oc·tet (ŏk·tĕt′)
Oc·to·ber (ŏk·tō′ bĕr)
oc·to·ge·nar·i·an
      (ŏk′ tŏ·jĕ·nâr′ ĭ·ăn)
oc·to·pus (ŏk′ tŏ·pŭs)
  -pus·es
oc·to·roon (ŏk′ tŏ·rōōn′)
oc·u·lar (ŏk′ û·lĕr)
oc·u·list (ŏk′ û·lĭst)
odd (ŏd)
  odd·i·ty (ŏd′ ĭ·tĭ)
  odd·ly   odd·ment
  odds and ends
ode (ōd)
o·di·ous (ō′ dĭ·ŭs)
  o·di·um (ō′ dĭ·ŭm)
o·dom·e·ter (ŏ·dŏm′ ĕ·tĕr)

o·dor (ō′ dẽr)
  o·dor·if·er·ous
            (ō′ dẽr·ĭf′ ẽr·ŭs)
  o·dor·less
  o·dor·ous (ō′ dẽr·ŭs)
od·ys·sey (ŏd′ ĭ·sĭ)
Oed·i·pus com·plex
            (ĕd′ ĭ·pŭs)
oes·trus (ĕs′ trŭs)
off (ðf)
  off and on   off·cast
  off-chance   off-col·or
  off·hand   off·ing
  off·set   off·set·ting
  off·shoot   off·shore
  off side   off·spring
of·fal (ŏf′ ăl)
of·fend (ð·fĕnd′)
  of·fend·er
of·fense (ð·fĕns′)
  of·fen·sive   -sive·ly
of·fer (ðf′ ẽr)
  of·fer·ing
of·fer·to·ry (ðf′ ẽr·tō′ rĭ)
of·fice (ðf′ ĭs)
  of·fice boy
  of·fice·hold·er (ðf′ ĭs·hōl′ dẽr)
  of·fi·cer (ðf′ ĭ·sẽr)
of·fi·cial (ð·fĭsh′ ăl)
  of·fi·cial·dom   of·fi·cial·ly
of·fi·ci·ate (ð·fĭsh′ ĭ·āt)
  -at·ing
of·fi·ci·a·tion
      (ð·fĭsh′ ĭ·ā′ shŭn)
  of·fi·ci·a·tor
of·fi·cious (ð·fĭsh′ ŭs)
of·ten (ðf′ ĕn)
  of·ten·er   of·ten·est
  of·ten·times
o·gre (ō′ gẽr)
  o·gre·ish (ō′ gẽr·ĭsh)
O·hi·o (ō·hī′ ō)
  abbr. O.   O·hi·o·an
ohm (ōm)
oil·skin (oil′ skĭn′)
oil·y (oil′ ĭ)
  oil·i·ness
oint·ment (oint′ mĕnt)
O.K. (ō′ kā′)
  (also okay)   O.K.′ d
  O·K.′ ing
O·ki·na·wa Is. (ō′ kĭ·nä′ wá)
O·kla·ho·ma (ō′ klá·hō′ má)
  abbr. Okla.   O·kla·ho·man
o·kra (ō′ krá)

old (ōld)
  old coun·try   old-fash·ioned
  old-fo·gy·ish   Old Glo·ry
  old maid·ish
  Old Tes·ta·ment
  old-tim·er   old wives′ tale
  old-world adj.
old·ster (ōld′ stẽr)
o·le·ag·i·nous (ō′ lê·ăj′ ĭ·nŭs)
o·le·an·der (ō′ lê·ăn′ dẽr)
o·le·o·mar·ga·rine
      (ō′ lê·ð·mär′ ja·rĭn)
ol·fac·to·ry (ŏl·făk′ tô·rĭ)
ol·i·garch (ŏl′ ĭ·gärk)
  ol·i·gar·chic (ŏl′ ĭ·gär′ kĭk)
  -chi·cal
  ol·i·garch·y (ŏl′ ĭ·gär′ kĭ)
  -chies
O·lym·pic (ð·lĭm′ pĭk)
  O·lym·pi·an
o·me·ga (ð·mē′ gá)
om·e·let (ŏm′ ĕ·lĕt)
  o·men (ō′ mĕn)
om·i·nous (ŏm′ ĭ·nŭs)
o·mis·sion (ð·mĭsh′ ŭn)
o·mit (ð·mĭt′)
  -mit·ted   -mit·ting
om·ni·bus (ŏm′ nĭ·bŭs)
om·nip·o·tent (ŏm·nĭp′·ð·tĕnt)
  -tence
om·ni·pres·ent (ŏm′ nĭ·prĕz′ ĕnt)
om·nis·cient (ŏm·nĭsh′ ĕnt)
  -cience
om·niv·o·rous (ŏm·nĭv′ ô·rŭs)
once (wŭns)
on·com·ing (ŏn′ kŭm′ ĭng)
one (wŭn)
  one-horse town one·self
  one-sid·ed   one·time
  one-track mind one-way street
on·er·ous (ŏn′ ẽr·ŭs)
on·ion·skin (ŭn′ yŭn·skĭn′)
on·look·er (ŏn′ lŏŏk′ ẽr)
on·ly (ŏn′ lĭ)
on·o·mat·o·poe·ia
      (ŏn′ ð·măt′ ð·pē′ yá)
on·set (ŏn′ sĕt′)
on·slaught (ŏn′ slôt′)
on·to (ŏn′ tōō)
on·tol·o·gy (ŏn·tŏl′ ð·jĭ)
  on·to·log·i·cal (ŏn′ tô·lŏj′ ĭ·kăl)
o·nus (ō′ nŭs)
on·ward (ŏn′ wẽrd)
on·yx (ŏn′ ĭks)

ooze (ōōz)
  ooz·ing
o·pac·i·ty (ŏ·păs′ ĭ·tĭ)
o·pal (ō′ păl)
o·pal·es·cent (ō′ păl·ĕs′ ĕnt)
  -cence
o·paque (ŏ·pāk′)
  o·paque·ness
o·pen (ō′ pĕn)
  o·pen-air *adj.*
  o·pen-and-shut case
  o·pen·er   o·pen-eyed
  o·pen·hand·ed
  o·pen house   o·pen let·ter
  o·pen-mind·ed o·pen·work
op·er·a (ŏp′ ĕr·à)
  op·er·a·tic (ŏp′ ĕr·ăt′ ĭk)
op·er·a·ble (ŏp′ ĕr·à·b′l)
op·er·ate (ŏp′ ĕr·āt)
  -at·ing
  op·er·a·tion (ŏp′ ĕr·ā′ shŭn)
  -tion·al
  op·er·a·tive (ŏp′ ĕr·ā′ tĭv)
  op·er·a·tor
op·er·et·ta (ŏp′ ĕr·ĕt′ à)
oph·thal·mol·o·gist
    (ŏf′ thăl·mŏl′ ŏ·jĭst)
o·pi·ate (ō′ pĭ·āt)
o·pine (ŏ·pīn′)
  -pin·ing
o·pin·ion (ŏ·pĭn′ yŭn)
  o·pin·ion·at·ed
    (ŏ·pĭn′ yŭn·āt′ ĕd)
  o·pin·ion·a·tive
    (ŏ·pĭn′ yŭn·ā′ tĭv)
o·pi·um (ō′ pĭ·ŭm)
o·pos·sum (ŏ·pŏs′ ŭm)
op·po·nent (ŏ·pō′ nĕnt)
op·por·tune (ŏp′ ŏr·tūn′)
  op·por·tune·ly
op·por·tun·ism (ŏp′ ŏr·tūn′ ĭz′m)
  op·por·tun·ist
  op·por·tun·is·tic
    (ŏp′ ŏr·tūn·ĭs′ tĭk)
op·por·tu·ni·ty (ŏp′ ŏr·tū′ nĭ·tĭ)
  -ties
op·pose (ŏ·pōz′)
  op·pos·ing   op·pos·a·ble
op·po·site (ŏp′ ŏ·zĭt)
  op·po·site·ly
  op·po·si·tion (ŏp′ ŏ·zĭsh′ ŭn)

op·pro·bri·ous (ŏ·prō′ brĭ·ŭs)
  op·pro·bri·um
op·tic (ŏp′ tĭk)
  op·ti·cal
  op·ti·cian (ŏp·tĭsh′ ăn)
op·ti·mism (ŏp′ tĭ·mĭz′m)
  op·ti·mist
  op·ti·mis·tic (ŏp′ tĭ·mĭs′ tĭk)
  -ti·cal·ly
op·ti·mum (ŏp′ tĭ·mŭm)
op·tion (ŏp′ shŭn)
  op·tion·al   -al·ly
op·tom·e·try (ŏp·tŏm′ ĕ·trĭ)
  op·tom·e·trist (ŏp·tŏm′ ĕ·trĭst)
op·u·lence (ŏp′ û·lĕns)
  -lent
o·pus (ō′ pŭs)
  pl. op·e·ra (ŏp′ ĕ·rà)
or·a·cle (ŏr′ à·k′l)
  o·rac·u·lar (ŏ·răk′ û·lēr)
o·ral (ō′ răl)
  (spoken; see *aural*)
  o·ral·ly
or·ange (ŏr′ ĕnj)
  or·ange·ade (ŏr′ ĕnj·ād′)
  or·ange pe·koe
o·rang·u·tan (ŏ·răng′ ōō·tăn′)
o·rate (ŏ·rāt′)
  -rat·ing
  o·ra·tion (ŏ·rā′ shŭn)
  or·a·tor (ŏr′ à·tēr)
  or·a·tor·i·cal (ŏr′ à·tŏr′ ĭ·kăl)
  or·a·to·ry (ŏr′ à·tō′ rĭ)
or·a·to·ri·o (ŏr′ à·tō′ rĭ·ō)
or·bit (ŏr′ bĭt)
  -bit·ed   -bit·ing
  or·bit·al
or·chard (ŏr′ chĕrd)
or·ches·tra (ŏr·kĕs·trà)
  or·ches·tral (ŏr·kĕs′ trăl)
  or·ches·trate (ŏr′ kĕs·trāt)
  or·ches·tra·tion
    (ŏr′ kĕs·trā′ shŭn)
or·chid (ŏr′ kĭd)
or·dain (ŏr·dān′)
or·deal (ŏr·dēl′)
or·der (ŏr′ dĕr)
  or·der·ly   -li·ness
or·di·nal (ŏr′ dĭ·năl)
or·di·nance (ŏr′ dĭ·năns)
  (law; see *ordnance*)
or·di·nary (ŏr′ dĭ·nĕr′ ĭ)
  or·di·nar·i·ly -i·ness
or·di·nate (ŏr′ dĭ·năt)
  -nat·ing

or·di·na·tion   (ôr′ dĭ·nā′ shŭn)
ord·nance   (ôrd′ nŭns)
   (military supplies: see *ordnance*)
or·dure   (ôr′ dụr)
Or·e·gon   (ŏr′ ê·gŏn)
   abbr. Oreg. *or* Ore.
Or·e·go·ni·an   (ŏr′ ê·gō′ nĭ·ɑn)
or·gan   (ôr′ gɑn)
   or·gan·ic   (ôr·găn′ ĭk)
   or·gan·ism   (ôr′ gɑn·ĭz′m)
   or·gan·ist
or·gan·dy   (ôr′ găn·dĭ)
   -dies
or·gan·ize   (ôr′ găn·īz)
   -iz·ing   or·gan·iz·able
   or·gan·i·za·tion
      (ôr′ gɑn·ĭ·zā′ shŭn)
   or·gan·iz·er
or·gan·za   (ôr·găn′ zȧ)
or·gasm   (ôr′ găz′m)
or·gy   (ôr′ jĭ)
   -gies
   or·gi·as·tic   (ôr′ jĭ·ăs′ tĭk)
o·ri·ent   (ō′ rĭ·ĕnt)
   o·ri·en·tal   (ō′ rĭ·ĕn′ tɑl)
o·ri·en·ta·tion   (ō′ rĭ·ĕn·tā′ shŭn)
or·i·fice   (ŏr′ ĭ·fĭs)
or·i·gin   (ŏr′ ĭ·jĭn)
o·rig·i·nal   (ô·rĭj′ ĭ·nɑl)
   o·rig·i·nal·i·ty
      (ô·rĭj′ ĭ·năl′ ĭ·tĭ)
   o·rig·i·nal·ly
o·rig·i·nate   (ô·rĭj′ ĭ·nāt)
   -nat·ing
   o·rig·i·na·tion
      (ô·rĭj′ ĭ·nā′ shŭn)
   o·rig·i·na·tor
o·ri·ole   (ō′ rĭ·ōl)
or·i·son   (ŏr′ ĭ·zŭn)
or·lon   (ôr′ lŏn)
or·na·ment   (ôr′ nȧ·mĕnt)
   or·na·men·tal   (ôr′ nȧ·mĕn′ tɑl)
   -tal·ly
   or·na·men·ta·tion
      (ôr′ nȧ·mĕn·tā′ shŭn)
or·nate   (ôr·nāt′)
   or·nate·ly   -nate·ness
or·ner·y   (ôr′ nêr·ĭ)
   or·ner·i·ness
or·ni·thol·o·gy   (ôr′ nĭ·thŏl′ ô·jĭ)
or·phan   (ôr′ fɑn)
   or·phan·age
or·tho·don·tist   (ôr′ thô·dŏn′ tĭst)
or·tho·dox·y   (ôr′ thô·dŏk′ sĭ)
   -dox·ies

or·tho·gen·ic   (ôr′ thô·jĕn′ ĭk)
or·thog·ra·phy   (ôr·thŏg′ rȧ·fĭ)
or·tho·pe·dics   (ôr′ thô·pē′ dĭks)
os·cil·late   (ŏs′ ĭ·lāt)
   (vibrate; see *osculate*)
   -cil·lat·ing
   os·cil·la·tion   (ŏs′ ĭ·lā′ shŭn)
   os·cil·la·tor   (ŏs′ ĭ·lā′ tēr)
os·cu·late   (ŏs′ kû·lāt)
   (to kiss; see *oscillate*)
   -lat·ing
   os·cu·la·tion   (ŏs′ kû·lā′ shŭn)
os·mo·sis   (ŏs·mō′ sĭs)
   os·mot·ic   (ŏs·mŏt′ ĭk)
os·prey   (ŏs′ prĭ)
   -preys
os·si·cle   (ŏs′ ĭ·k′l)
os·si·fy   (ŏs′ ĭ·fī)
   -fied   -fy·ing
   os·si·fi·ca·tion
      (ŏs′ ĭ·fĭ·kā′ shŭn)
os·ten·si·ble   (ŏs·tĕn′ sĭ·b′l)
os·ten·ta·tion   (ŏs′ tĕn·tā′ shŭn)
   os·ten·ta·tious   (-shŭs)
os·te·o·path   (ŏs′ tê·ô·păth)
os·tra·cize   (ŏs′ trȧ·sīz)
   -ciz·ing
   os·tra·cism   (ŏs′ trȧ·sĭz′m)
os·trich   (ŏs′ trĭch)
oth·er·wise   (ŭth′ ēr·wīz′)
oth·er·world·ly
      (ŭth′ ēr·wûrld′ lĭ)
o·ti·ose   (ō′ shĭ·ōs)
Ot·ta·wa, Can.   (ŏt′ ȧ·wȧ)
ot·ter   (ŏt′ ēr)
Ot·to·man   (ŏt′ ô·mɑn)
ought   (ôt)
   (bound by duty; see *aught*)
Oui·ja board   (wē′ jȧ)
ounce   (ouns)
our·selves   (our·sĕlvz′)
oust   (oust)
   oust·er
out   (out)
   out-and-out   out·bal·ance
   out·board   out·break
   out·burst   out·cast
   out·class   out·come
   out·crop   out·cry
   out·dis·tance   out·do
   out·doors   out·er·most
   out·field   out·fit·ter
   out·go·ing   out·growth
   out·land·ish   out·last
   out·law   out·let

out·line   out·look
out·ly·ing   out·ma·neu·ver
out·mod·ed   out-of-date
out-of-door   out-of-the-way
out·pa·tient   out·post
out·pour·ing   out·put
out·rage   out·ra·geous
out·reach   out·rig·ger
out·right   out·sell
out·set   out·sid·er
out·size   out·skirts
out·smart   out·spo·ken
out·spo·ken·ness
out·spread   out·stand·ing
out·strip   out·ward
out·weigh   out·wit
o·va·ry   (ō′ vȧ·rǐ)
   -ries
o·va·tion   (ȯ·vā′ shŭn)
ov·en   (ŭv′ ĕn)
o·ver   (ō′ vẽr)
   o·ver·act   o·ver-all
   o·ver·alls   o·ver·awed
   o·ver·bear·ing   o·ver·board
   o·ver·cast
   o·ver·de·vel·op·ment
   o·ver·dose   o·ver·draft
   o·ver·ex·po·sure
   o·ver·haul   o·ver·head
   o·ver·lap·ping   o·ver·lay
   o·ver·look   o·ver·night
   o·ver·pass
   o·ver·pow·er·ing
   o·ver·pro·duc·tion
   o·ver·rate   o·ver·reach
   o·ver·ride   o·ver·rul·ing
   o·ver·run   o·ver·seas
   o·ver·seer   o·ver·shoe
   o·ver·sight   o·ver·sup·ply
   o·ver-the-count·er
   o·ver·throw   o·ver·time
   o·ver·tone   o·ver·ween·ing
   o·ver·weight   o·ver·whelm·ing
   o·ver·work   o·ver·wrought
o·vert   (ō′ vûrt)
o·ver·ture   (ō′ vẽr·tụ̄r)
o·vip·a·rous   (ȯ·vǐp′ ȧ·rŭs)
o·vum   (ō′ vŭm)
   pl. o·va
owe   (ō)
   ow·ing
owl·ish   (oul′ ǐsh)
own·er·ship   (ōn′ ẽr·shǐp)
ox   (ŏks)
   pl. ox·en

ox·al·ic   (ŏks·ăl′ ǐk)
ox·eye dai·sy   (ŏks′ ī′)
ox·i·da·tion   (ŏk′ sǐ·dā′ shŭn)
ox·ide   (ŏk′ sīd)
ox·i·dize   (ŏk′ sǐ·dīz)
   -diz·ing
ox·tail   (ŏks′ tāl′)
ox·y·gen   (ŏk′ sǐ·jĕn)
oys·ter   (ois′ tẽr)
o·zone   (ō′ zōn)

P

pab·u·lum   (păb′ û·lŭm)
pace·mak·er   (pās′ māk′ ẽr)
pach·y·derm   (păk′ ǐ·dûrm)
pac·i·fy   (păs′ ǐ·fī)
   -fied   -fy·ing
   pa·cif·ic   (pȧ·sǐf′ ǐk)
   pac·i·fi·ca·tion
        (păs′ ǐ·fǐ·kā′ shŭn)
   pac·i·fi·er   pac·i·fist
pack·age   (păk′ ǐj)
   -ag·ing
pack·et   (păk′ ĕt)
pack·ing house   (păk′ ǐng)
pack·sack   (păk′ săk′)
pack·sad·dle   (păk′ săd′ ′l)
pact   (păkt)
pad·ding   (păd′ ǐng)
pad·dle wheel   (păd′ ′l)
pad·dock   (păd′ ŭk)
pad·lock   (păd′ lŏk′)
pa·dre   (pä′ drǐ)
pae·an   (pē′ ȧn)
pa·gan   (pā′ găn)
   pa·gan·ism
pag·eant   (păj′ ĕnt)
   pag·eant·ry
pag·i·na·tion   (păj′ ǐ·nā′ shŭn)
pa·go·da   (pȧ·gō′ dȧ)
paid   (pād)
pail·ful   (pāl′ fòòl)
pain   (pān)
   (punishment; see pane)
   pain·ful   -ful·ly
   -ful·ness   pain·less
   pains·tak·ing
paint·brush   (pănt′ brŭsh′)
paint·ing   (pănt′ ǐng)
pair   (pâr)
   (two; see pear)
Pais·ley print   (pāz′ lǐ)
pa·ja·ma   (pȧ·jă′ mȧ)

Pak·i·stan (păk′ ĭ·stăn′)
  Pak·i·stan·i (-ĭ)
pal·ace (păl′ ĭs)
  pa·la·tial (pá·lā′ shál)
pal·a·din (păl′ á·dĭn)
pal·at·a·ble (păl′ ĭt·á·b′l)
  pal·at·a·bil·i·ty
    (păl′ ĭt·á·bĭl′ ĭ·tĭ)
pal·ate (păl′ ĭt)
  (roof of mouth; see *palette, pallet*)
  pal·a·tal (păl′ á·tál)
pa·la·tial (pá·lā′ shál)
  -tial·ly
pal·a·tine (păl′ á·tīn)
pa·lav·er (pá·lăv′ ẽr)
pale (pāl)
  pale·face pale·ness
pa·le·o- (pā′ lē·ŏ-)
  pa·le·o·bot·a·ny
    (-bŏt′ á·nĭ)
  pa·le·o·lith·ic (-lĭth′ ĭk)
  pa·le·on·tol·o·gy
    (pā′ lĕ·ŏn·tŏl′ ŏ·jĭ)
  Pa·le·o·zo·ic era
    (-zō′ ĭk)
  pa·le·o·zo·ol·o·gy
    (-zŏ·ŏl′ ŏ·jĭ)
pal·ette (păl′ ĕt)
  (painter's board; see *palate,
  pallet*)
  pal·ette knife
pal·frey (pôl′ frĭ)
pal·i·sade (păl′ ĭ·sād′)
pal·la·di·um (pá·lā′ dĭ·ŭm)
Pal·las Ath·e·na
  (păl′ ás á·thē′ ná)
pall·bear·er (pôl′ bâr′ ẽr)
pal·let (păl′ ĕt)
  (bed; see *palate, palette*)
pal·li·ate (păl′ ĭ·āt)
  -at·ing
  pal·li·a·tion (păl′ ĭ·ā′ shŭn)
  pal·li·a·tive (păl′ ĭ·ā′ tĭv)
pal·lid (păl′ ĭd)
pal·lor (păl′ ẽr)
pal·met·to (păl·mĕt′ ō)
palm·is·try (päm′ ĭs·trĭ)
pal·my·ra (păl·mī′ rá)
pal·o·mi·no (păl′ ŏ·mē′ nō)
pal·pa·ble (păl′ pá·b′l)
pal·pi·tate (păl′ pĭ·tāt)
  -tat·ing
  pal·pi·ta·tion (păl′ pĭ·tā′ shŭn)
pal·sy (pôl′ zĭ)
  -sied

pal·try (pôl′ trĭ)
  pal·tri·ness
pam·pas (păm′ páz)
pam·per (păm′ pẽr)
pam·phlet (păm′ flĕt)
  pam·phlet·eer (păm′ flĕt·ēr′)
pan·a·ce·a (păn′ á·sē′ á)
Pan·a·ma (păn′ á·mô)
  Pan·a·ma hat
  Pan·a·ma·ni·an
    (păn′ á·mā′ nĭ·ăn)
Pan-A·mer·i·can
    (păn′ á·mĕr′ ĭ·kăn)
pan·a·tel·la (păn′ á·tĕl′ á)
pan·cake (păn′ kāk′)
pan·chro·mat·ic
    (păn′ krŏ·măt′ ĭk)
pan·cra·ti·um (păn·krā′ shĭ·ŭm)
pan·cre·as (păn′ krĕ·ás)
  pan·cre·at·ic juice
    (păng′ krĕ·ăt′ ĭk)
pan·da (păn′ dá)
pan·dem·ic (păn·dĕm′ ĭk)
pan·de·mo·ni·um
    (păn′ dĕ·mō′ nĭ·ŭm)
pan·der (păn′ dẽr)
  pan·der·er
Pan·do·ra′s box (păn·dō′ ráz)
pan·dow·dy (păn·dou′ dĭ)
pane (pān)
  (a panel; glass; see *pain*)
pan·e·gyr·ic (păn′ ĕ·jĭr′ ĭk)
pan·el (păn′ ĕl)
  -eled -el·ing
  pan·el·ist
pan·han·dle (păn′ hăn′ d′l)
  -dling
Pan·hel·len·ic (păn′ hĕ·lĕn′ ĭk)
pan·ic (păn′ ĭk)
  -icked -ick·ing
  pan·ick·y pan·ic-strick·en
pan·nier (păn′ yẽr)
pan·o·ply (păn′ ŏ·plĭ)
  -plies pan·o·plied
pan·o·ra·ma (păn′ ŏ·rä′ má)
  pan·o·ram·ic (-răm′ ĭk)
pan·sy (păn′ zĭ)
  -sies
pan·ta·loon (păn′ tá·lōōn′)
pan·the·ism (păn′ thē·ĭz′m)
  pan·the·is·tic (păn′ thē·ĭs′ tĭk)
pan·the·on (păn′ thē·ŏn)
pan·ther (păn′ thẽr)
  pan·ther·ess
pant·ing (pănt′ ĭng)

pan·to·mime   (pănʹ tŏ·mīm)
  pan·to·mim·ic
          (pănʹ tŏ·mīmʹ ĭk)
  pan·to·mim·ist
pan·to·then·ic ac·id
          (pănʹ tŏ·thĕnʹ ĭk)
pan·try   (pănʹ trĭ)
  -tries
pant·y   (pănʹ tĭ)
  pant·ies   pant·y gir·dle
  pant·y·waist
Pan·zer di·vi·sion
          (pănʹ tsēr)
pa·pa·cy   (pāʹ pȧ·sĭ)
  pa·pal   (pāʹ pȧl)
pa·paw   (pȧ·pôʹ)
pa·pay·a   (pȧ·pīʹ ȧ)
pa·per   (pāʹ pēr)
  pa·per·back   pa·per·board
  pa·per cut·ter   pa·per knife
  pa·per-thin   pa·per·weight
  pa·per work
pa·pier-mâ·ché
        (pāʹ pĕr·mȧ·shāʹ)
pa·pil·la   (pȧ·pĭlʹ ȧ)
  pl. pa·pil·lae   (-ē)
  pap·il·lar·y   (păpʹ ĭ·lĕrʹ Ĭ)
pa·poose   (pă·po͞osʹ)
pa·pri·ka   (pȧ·prēʹ kȧ)
pa·py·rus   (pȧ·pīʹ rŭs)
  pl. pa·py·ri   (-rī)
par·a·ble   (părʹ ȧ·bʹl)
  pa·rab·o·la   (pȧ·răbʹ ŏ·lȧ)
  par·a·bol·ic   (părʹ ȧ·bŏlʹ ĭk)
  -i·cal·ly
  pa·rab·o·loid   (pȧ·răbʹ ŏ·loid)
par·a·chute   (părʹ ȧ·shōͦt)
  -chut·ist
pa·rade   (pȧ·rādʹ)
  -rad·ing
par·a·digm   (părʹ ȧ·dĭm)
par·a·dise   (părʹ ȧ·dīs)
par·a·dox   (părʹ ȧ·dŏks)
  par·a·dox·i·cal
        (părʹ ȧ·dŏkʹ sĭ·kȧl)
  -cal·ly
par·af·fin   (părʹ ȧ·fĭn)
par·a·gon   (părʹ ȧ·gŏn)
par·a·graph   (părʹ ȧ·grăf)
Par·a·guay   (părʹ ȧ·gwī)
par·a·keet   (părʹ ȧ·kēt)
par·a·lax   (părʹ ȧ·lăks)
  par·al·lac·tic   (părʹ ȧ·lăkʹ tĭk)
par·al·lel   (părʹ ȧ·lĕl)
  -al·leled   -al·lel·ing

par·al·lel·o·gram
        (părʹ ȧ·lĕlʹ ŏ·grăm)
pa·ral·y·sis   (pȧ·rălʹ ĭ·sĭs)
par·a·lyt·ic   (părʹ ȧ·lĭtʹ ĭk)
par·a·lyze   (părʹ ȧ·līz)
  -lyz·ing
par·a·me·ci·um
        (părʹ ȧ·mēʹ shĭ·ŭm)
  pl. par·a·me·ci·a
pa·ram·e·ter   (pȧ·rămʹ ĕ·tēr)
par·a·mount   (părʹ ȧ·mount)
par·a·mour   (părʹ ȧ·mŏͦr)
par·a·noi·a   (părʹ ȧ·noiʹ ȧ)
  par·a·noi·ac   (-ăk)
par·a·pet   (părʹ ȧ·pĕt)
  -pet·ed
par·a·pher·na·li·a
        (părʹ ȧ·fēr·nāʹ lĭ·ȧ)
par·a·phrase   (părʹ ȧ·frāz)
  phras·ing
  par·a·phras·tic
        (părʹ ȧ·frăsʹ tĭk)
par·a·ple·gi·a   (părʹ ȧ·plēʹ jĭ·ȧ)
  par·a·pleg·ic   (-plĕjʹ ĭk)
par·a·psy·chol·o·gy
        (părʹ ȧ·sī·kŏlʹ ŏ·jĭ)
par·a·site   (părʹ ȧ·sīt)
  par·a·sit·ic   (părʹ ȧ·sĭtʹ ĭk)
  -i·cal
  par·a·sit·ism   (părʹ ȧ·sītʹ ĭz'm)
  par·a·si·tol·o·gy
        (părʹ ȧ·sī·tŏlʹ ŏ·jĭ)
par·a·sym·pa·thet·ic
        (părʹ ȧ·sĭmʹ pȧ·thĕtʹ Ĭk)
par·a·troop·er   (părʹ ȧ·trōͦpʹ ēr)
par·boil   (pärʹ boilʹ)
par·cel   (pärʹ sĕl)
  -celed   -cel·ing
  par·cel post
par·chee·si   (pär·chēʹ zĭ)
parch·ment   (pärchʹ mĕnt)
par·don   (pärʹ d'n)
  par·don·a·ble   par·don·er
pare   (pâr)
  par·ing
par·ent   (pârʹ ĕnt)
  par·ent·age   (pârʹ ĕn·tĭj)
  pa·ren·tal   (pȧ·rĕnʹ tȧl)
  par·ent·hood
pa·ren·the·sis   (pȧ·rĕnʹ thĕ·sĭs)
  pl. pa·ren·the·ses   (-sēz)
  par·en·thet·ic   (părʹ ĕn·thĕtʹ Ĭk)
  -i·cal·ly
pa·re·sis   (pȧ·rēʹ sĭs)
pa·ret·ic   (pȧ·rĕtʹ ĭk)

par ex·cel·lence
    (pär ĕk′ sĕ·läns)
par·fait (pär fā′)
pa·ri·ah (pȧ·rī′ ȧ)
pa·ri·e·tal (pȧ·rī′ ĕ·tȧl)
par·i·mu·tu·el (pär′ ĭ-mū′ tụ·ĕl)
par·ish (pär′ ĭsh)
   par·ish·ion·er (pȧ·rĭsh′ ŭn·ẽr)
par·i·ty (păr′ ĭ·tĭ)
par·ka (pär′ kȧ)
park·way (pärk′ wā′)
par·lance (pär′ lȧns)
par·lay (pär′ lā)
  (bet; see *parley*)
par·ley (pär′ lĭ)
  (conversation; see *parlay*)
par·lia·ment (pär′ lĭ·mĕnt)
  par·lia·men·tar·i·an
    (pär′ lĭ·mĕn·târ′ ĭ·ăn)
  par·lia·men·ta·ry
    (pär′ lĭ·mĕn′ tá·rĭ)
par·lor (pär′ lẽr)
  par·lor car   par·lor·maid
Par·me·san cheese
    (pär′ mĕ·zăn′)
Par·nas·sus (pär·năs′ ŭs)
pa·ro·chi·al (pȧ·rō′ kĭ·ȧl)
par·o·dy (păr′ ŏ·dĭ)
  -dies
  par·o·died   -dy·ing
  par·o·dist
pa·role (pȧ·rōl′)
  pa·rol·ee (pȧ·rōl′ ē′)
par·ox·ysm (păr′ ŏk·sĭz′m)
par·quet (pär·kā′)
par·ri·cide (păr′ ĭ·sīd)
  -cid·al
Par·ris Is., S.C. (păr′ ĭs)
par·rot (păr′ ŭt)
  par·rot·ed   par·rot·ing
par·ry (păr′ ĭ)
  par·ried   par·ry·ing
parse (pärs)
  pars·ing
par·si·mo·ni·ous
    (pär′ sĭ·mō′ nĭ·ŭs)
  par·si·mo·ny (pär′ sĭ·mō′ nĭ)
pars·ley (pärs′ lĭ)
pars·nip (pärs′ nĭp)
par·son (pär′ s'n)
  par·son·age (-ĭj)
par·take (pär·tāk′)
  tak·ing
par·the·no·gen·e·sis
    (pär′ thĕ·nŏ·jĕn′ ĕ·sĭs)

Par·the·non (pär′ thĕ·nŏn)
par·tial (pär′ shȧl)
  par·ti·al·i·ty (pär′ shĭ·ăl′ ĭ·tĭ)
  par·tial·ly
par·tic·i·pate (pär·tĭs′ ĭ·pāt)
  -pat·ing
  par·tic·i·pant (-pȧnt)
  par·tic·i·pa·tion
    (pär·tĭs′ ĭ·pā′ shŭn)
  par·tic·i·pa·tor
par·ti·ci·ple (pär′ tĭ·sĭ·p'l)
  par·ti·cip·i·al (pär′ tĭ·sĭp′ ĭ·ȧl)
par·ti·cle (pär′ tĭ·k'l)
par·tic·u·lar (pẽr·tĭk′ û·lẽr)
  par·tic·u·lar·i·ty
    (pẽr·tĭk′ û·lăr′ ĭ·tĭ)
  par·tic·u·lar·ize
   -iz·ing   par·tic·u·lar·ly
par·ti·san (pär′ tĭ·zȧn)
  par·ti·san·ship
par·ti·tion (pär·tĭsh′ ŭn)
  par·ti·tion·ment
par·ti·tive (pär′ tĭ·tĭv)
part·ner (pärt′ nẽr)
  part·ner·ship
par·tridge (pär′ trĭj)
par·tu·ri·tion (pär′ tụ·rĭsh′ ŭn)
par·ty (pär′ tĭ)
  -ties
par·ve·nu (pär′ vĕ·nū)
pas·chal lamb (păs′ kȧl)
pa·sha (pȧ·shä′)
pasque·flow·er (păsk′ flou′ ẽr)
pass·a·ble (pás′ ȧ·b'l)
pas·sage (păs′ ĭj)
  pas·sage·way
Pas·sa·ic, N.J. (pȧ·sā′ ĭk)
pass·book (pás′ bŏŏk′)
pas·sé (pă·sā′)
pas·sen·ger pi·geon
    (păs′ ĕn·jẽr)
pass·er-by (pás′ ẽr·bī′)
pas·sion (păsh′ ŭn)
  pas·sion·ate (-ĭt)
  -ate·ly   pas·sion·flow·er
  pas·sion·less   Pas·sion play
pas·sive (păs′ ĭv)
  pas·sive·ly
  pas·siv·i·ty (pă·sĭv′ ĭ·tĭ)
pass·key (pás′ kē′)
pass·port (pás′ pōrt)
paste (păst)
  past·ing   paste·board
  past·y
pas·tel (păs′ tĕl′)

pas·teur·ize   (păs′ tẽr· īz)
  -iz·ing
  pas·teur·i·za·tion
         (păs′ tẽr·ĭ·zā′ shŭn)
pas·tiche   (păs· tēsh′)
pas·time   (păs′ tīm′)
pas·tor   (păs′ tẽr)
  pas·tor·ate   (-ĭt)
pas·to·ral   (păs′ tŏ·răl)
  (rural; see *pastorale*)
pas·to·ra·le   (păs′ tŏ·rä′ lå)
  (music; see *pastoral*)
  pl. -ra·li   (-rä′ lē)
pas·tra·mi   (păs· trä′ mĭ)
pas·try   (păs′ trĭ)
  -tries
pas·ture   (păs′ tûr)
  -tur·ing
  pas·tur·age   (-ĭj)
patch·work   (păch′ wûrk′)
pâ·té de foie gras
    (pä′ tā′ dĕ fwä′ grä′)
pa·tel·la   (pà·tĕl′ å)
  pl. pa·tel·lae   (-ē)
pat·en   (păt′ ĕn)
pat·ent   (păt′ ĕnt)
  pat·ent·a·ble
  pat·ent·ee   (păt′ ĕn·tē′)
  pa·tent·ly   pat·en·tor
pa·ter·fa·mil·i·as
    (pä′ tẽr·fà·mĭl′ ĭ·ăs)
pa·ter·nal   (pà·tûr′ năl)
  pa·ter·nal·is·tic
    (pà·tûr′ năl·ĭs′ tĭk)
  pa·ter·ni·ty   (pà·tûr′ nĭ·tĭ)
pa·ter·nos·ter   (pä′ tẽr·nŏs′ tẽr)
Pat·er·son, N. J.   (păt′ ẽr·s′n)
pa·thet·ic   (pà·thĕt′ ĭk)
  -i·cal·ly
  pa·thet·ic fal·la·cy
path·find·er   (păth′ fīn′ dẽr)
pa·thol·o·gy   (pà·thŏl′ ŏ·jĭ)
  -gies
  path·o·log·i·cal
    (păth′ ŏ·lŏj′ ĭ·kăl)
  pa·thol·o·gist   (pà·thŏl′ ŏ·jĭst)
pa·thos   (pā′ thŏs)
pa·tient   (pā′ shĕnt)
  pa·tience
pat·i·na   (păt′ ĭ·nà)
pat·i·o   (păt′ ĭ·ō)
pat·ois   (păt′ wä)
pa·tri·arch   (pā′ trĭ·ärk)
  pa·tri·ar·chal   (pä′ trĭ·är′ kăl)
  pa·tri·arch·y   -arch·ies

pa·tri·cian   (pà· trĭsh′ ăn)
pat·ri·mo·ny   (păt′ rĭ·mō′ nĭ)
pa·tri·ot   (pä′ trĭ·ŭt)
  pa·tri·ot·ic   (pā′ trĭ·ŏt′ ĭk)
  -i·cal·ly
  pa·tri·ot·ism   (pā′ trĭ·ŭt·ĭz′m)
pa·trol   (pà·trōl′)
  -trolled,   -trol·ling
  pa·trol·man   pa·trol wag·on
pa·tron   (pā′ trŭn)
  pa·tron·age   (pā′ trŭn·ĭj)
  pa·tron·ess   (pā′ trŭn·ĕs)
  pa·tron·ize
  pa·tron·iz·ing·ly
pat·ro·nym·ic   (păt′ rŏ·nĭm′ ĭk)
pa·troon   (pà·troon′)
pat·ter   (păt′ ẽr)
pat·tern   (păt′ ẽrn)
pat·ty shell   (păt′ ĭ)
pau·ci·ty   (pô′ sĭ·tĭ)
Paul·ist   (pôl′ ĭst)
paunch·y   (pôn′ chĭ)
pau·per   (pô′ pẽr)
  pau·per·ize   -iz·ing
pause   (pôz)
  paus·ing
pav·an   (păv′ ăn)
pave·ment   (pāv′ mĕnt)
pa·vil·ion   (pà·vĭl′ yŭn)
pav·ing   (pāv′ ĭng)
pawn·bro·ker   (pôn′ brō′ kẽr)
Paw·nee· In·di·ans
    (pô′ nē′)
pay   (pā)
  pay·a·ble
  pay·ee   (pā′ ē′)
  pay·er   pay·mas·ter
  pay·ment   pay·off
  pay·roll
peace   (pēs)
  peace·a·ble
  peace·ful, -ful·ly, -ful·ness
  peace·mak·er peace of·fer·ing
  peace of·fi·cer
peach   (pēch)
pea·cock   (pē′ kŏk′)
pea·hen   (pē′ hĕn′)
pea jack·et   (pē)
peaked   (pēk′ ĕd)
  (thin; see *peeked*)
peal·ing   (pēl′ ĭng)
  (of a bell; see *peeling*)
pea·nut   (pē′ nŭt′)
pearl   (pûrl)
  (gem; see *purl*)

pearl·y (pûr′ lĭ)
peas·ant (pĕz′ ănt)
peas·ant·ry
peb·ble (pĕb′ 'l)
peb·bly
pe·can (pĕ·kăn′)
pec·ca·dil·lo (pĕk′ à·dĭl′ ō)
-dil·loes
pec·ca·ry (pĕk′ à·rĭ)
pec·tin (pĕk′ tĭn)
pec·tic ac·id
pec·to·ral (pĕk′ tô·răl)
pe·cul·iar (pĕ·kūl′ yẽr)
pe·cu·li·ar·i·ty
(pĕ·kū′ lĭ·ăr′ ĭ·tĭ)
-ties
pe·cu·ni·ar·y (pĕ·kū′ nĭ·ĕr′ ĭ)
ped·a·gogue (pĕd′ à·gŏg)
ped·a·gog·ic (pĕd′ à·gŏj′ ĭk)
-i·cal
ped·a·go·gy (pĕd′ à·gō′ jĭ)
ped·al (pĕd′ ăl)
(on a bike; see *peddle*)
-aled -al·ing
ped·ant (pĕd′ ănt)
pe·dan·tic (pĕ·dăn′ tĭk)
-ti·cal·ly
ped·ant·ry (pĕd′ ănt·rĭ)
ped·dle (pĕd′ 'l)
(sell; see *pedal*)
ped·dling ped·dler
ped·es·tal (pĕd′ ĕs·tăl)
pe·des·tri·an (pĕ·dĕs′ trĭ·ăn)
pe·di·at·rics (pē′ dĭ·ăt′ rĭks)
pe·di·a·tri·cian
(pē′ dĭ·à·trĭsh′ ăn)
ped·i·cure (pĕd′ ĭ·kūr)
ped·i·gree (pĕd′ ĭ·grē)
peeked (pēkt)
(looked; see *peaked*)
peel·ing (pēl′ ĭng)
(of an apple; see *pealing*)
Peep·ing Tom (pēp′ ĭng)
peer (pẽr)
(an equal; see *pier*)
peer·age (pẽr′ ĭj)
peer·less
peeve (pēv)
peev·ing pee·vish
pee·wee (pē′ wē)
Peg·a·sus (pĕg′ à·sŭs)
peign·oir (pān·wär′)
pe·jo·ra·tive (pē′ jô·rā′ tĭv)
-tive·ly
Pe·king·ese (pē′ kĭng·ēz′)

pe·koe (pē′ kō)
pelf (pĕlf)
pel·i·can (pĕl′ ĭ·kăn)
pel·la·gra (pĕ·lā′ grà)
pel·let (pĕl′ ĕt)
pell-mell (pĕl′ mĕl′)
pel·lu·cid (pĕ·lū′ sĭd)
pel·vic (pĕl′ vĭk)
pel·vis
pem·mi·can (pĕm′ ĭ·kăn)
pe·nal (pē′ năl)
pe·nal code
pe·nal·ize -iz·ing
pen·al·ty (pĕn′ ăl·tĭ)
-ties
pen·ance (pĕn′ ăns)
pence (pĕns)
pen·chant (pĕn′ chănt)
pen·cil (pĕn′ sĭl)
-ciled -cil·ing
pend·ant (pĕn′ dănt)
(ornament; see *pendent*)
pend·ent (pĕn′ dĕnt)
(suspended; see *pendant*)
pend·en·cy
pend·ing (pĕnd′ ĭng)
pen·du·lous (pĕn′ dụ·lŭs)
pen·du·lum (pĕn′ dụ·lŭm)
pen·e·trate (pĕn′ ĕ·trāt)
-trat·ing
pen·e·tra·ble (pĕn′ ĕ·trá·b'l)
pen·e·trant (pĕn′ ĕ·trănt)
pen·e·tra·tion
(pĕn′ ĕ·trā′ shŭn)
pen·e·tra·tive (pĕn′ ĕ·trā′ tĭv)
pen·guin (pĕn′ gwĭn)
pen·hold·er (pĕn′ hōl′ dẽr)
pen·i·cil·lin (pĕn′ ĭ·sĭl′ ĭn)
pen·in·su·la (pĕn·ĭn′ sụ·là)
pen·in·su·lar (-lẽr)
pen·i·tent (pĕn′ ĭ·tĕnt)
-tence
pen·i·ten·tial (pĕn′ ĭ·tĕn′ shăl)
pen·i·ten·tia·ry
(pĕn′ ĭ·tĕn′ shá·rĭ)
-ries
pen·knife (pĕn′ nīf′)
pen·man·ship (pĕn′ măn·shĭp)
pen·nant (pĕn′ ănt)
pen·ni·less (pĕn′ ĭ·lĕs)
Penn·syl·va·nia
abbr. Pa. or Penna.
Penn·syl·va·nian

pen·ny   (pĕn′ ĭ)
  pen·nies
  pen·ni·less   (pĕn′ ĭ·lĕs)
  pen·ny an·te   pen·ny·weight
  pen·ny-wise
pe·nol·o·gy   (pĕ·nŏl′ ō·jĭ)
pen·sion   (pĕn′ shŭn)
  pen·sion·er
pen·ta-   (pĕn′ tȧ-)
  pen·ta·gon   (pĕn′ tȧ·gŏn)
  pen·tag·o·nal   (pĕn·tăg′ ō·nȧl)
  pen·ta·he·dron
                       (pĕn′ tȧ·hē′ drŭn)
  pen·tam·e·ter   (pĕn·tăm′ ĕ·tẽr)
  Pen·ta·teuch   (pĕn′ tȧ·tūk)
  pen·tath·lon   (pĕn·tăth′ lŏn)
  Pen·te·cos·tal   (pĕn′ tĕ·kŏs′ tȧl)
pent·house   (pĕnt′ hous′)
pe·nu·che   (pĕ·nōō′ chĕ)
pe·nul·ti·mate   (pĕ·nŭl′ tĭ·mĭt)
pe·nu·ri·ous   (pĕ·nū′ rĭ·ŭs)
  pen·u·ry   (pĕn′ û·rĭ)
pe·on   (pē′ ŏn)
  pe·on·age   (pē′ ŏn·ĭj)
pe·o·ny   (pē′ ō·nĭ)
  -nies
peo·ple   (pē′ p'l)
  -pling
pep·lum   (pĕp′ lŭm)
pep·per   (pĕp′ ẽr)
  pep·per·corn   pep·per·mint
  pep·per·y
pep·sin   (pĕp′ sĭn)
  pep·tic   (pĕp′ tĭk)
pep·tone   (pĕp′ tōn)
per·ad·ven·ture
                       (pûr′ ăd·vĕn′ tûr)
per·am·bu·late
                       (pẽr·ăm′ bû·lāt)
  -lat·ing
  per·am·bu·la·tion
                       (pẽr·ăm′ bû·lā′ shŭn)
  per·am·bu·la·tor
                       (pẽr·ăm′ bû·lā′ tẽr)
per an·num   (pẽr ăn′ ŭm)
per·bo·rate   (pûr·bō′ rāt)
per·cale   (pẽr·kāl′)
per cap·i·ta   (pẽr·kăp′ ĭ·tȧ)
per·ceive   (pẽr·sēv′)
  -ceiv·ing   per·ceiv·a·ble
per cent   (pẽr sĕnt′)
  per·cent·age   (pẽr·sĕn′ tĭj)
  per·cen·tile   (pẽr·sĕn′ tĭl)
per·cept   (pûr′ sĕpt)
per·cep·ti·ble   (pẽr·sĕp′ tĭ·b'l)

per·cep·tion   (pẽr·sĕp′ shŭn)
per·cep·tive   (pẽr·sĕp′ tĭv)
perch   (pûrch)
per·chance   (pẽr·chȧns′)
per·cip·i·ent   (pẽr·sĭp′ ĭ·ĕnt)
  -ence
per·co·late   (pûr′ kō·lāt)
  -lat·ing   per·co·la·tor
per·cus·sion   (pẽr·kŭsh′ ŭn)
per·di·tion   (pẽr·dĭsh′ ŭn)
per·dur·a·ble   (pûr·dūr′ ȧ·b'l)
per·e·gri·nate   (pẽr′ ĕ·grĭ·nāt)
  -nat·ing
  per·e·gri·na·tion
                       (pẽr′ ĕ·grĭ·nā′ shŭn)
per·emp·to·ry   (pẽr·ĕmp′ tō·rĭ)
  per·emp·to·ri·ly
per·en·ni·al   (pẽr·ĕn′ ĭ·ȧl)
  per·en·ni·al·ly
per·fect   (pûr′ fĕkt) adj.
  per·fect par·ti·ci·ple
per·fect   (pẽr·fĕkt′) v.
  per·fect·i·bil·i·ty
                       (pẽr·fĕk′ tĭ·bĭl′ ĭ·tĭ)
  per·fect·i·ble
  per·fec·tion   (pẽr·fĕk′ shŭn)
  per·fec·tion·ist
per·fec·to   (pẽr·fĕk′ tō)
per·fi·dy   (pûr′ fĭ·dĭ)
  -dies
  per·fid·i·ous   (pẽr·fĭd′ ĭ·ŭs)
per·fo·rate   (pûr′ fō·rāt)
  -rat·ing
  per·fo·ra·tion
                       (pûr′ fō·rā′ shŭn)
per·force   (pẽr·fōrs′)
per·form   (pẽr·fôrm′)
  per·form·a·ble   per·form·ance
per·fume   (pẽr·fūm′)
  -fum·ing
per·func·to·ry   (pẽr·fŭngk′ tō·rĭ)
  per·func·to·ri·ly
  per·func·to·ri·ness
per·haps   (pẽr·hăps′)
Per·i·cles   (pĕr′ ĭ·klēz)
  Per·i·cle·an   (pĕr′ ĭ·klē′ ȧn)
per·i·gee   (pĕr′ ĭ·jē)
per·i·he·li·on   (pĕr′ ĭ·hē′ lĭ·ŏn)
per·il   (pĕr′ ĭl)
  -iled   -il·ing
  per·il·ous   (pĕr′ ĭ·lŭs)
per·im·e·ter   (pĕ·rĭm′ ĕ·tẽr)
per·i·ne·um   (pĕr′ ĭ·nē′ ŭm)
pe·ri·od   (pẽr′ ĭ·ŭd)
  pe·ri·od·ic   (pẽr′ ĭ·ŏd′ ĭk)

pe·ri·od·i·cal (pĕr′ ĭ·ŏd′ ĭ·kăl)
-cal·ly
pe·ri·o·dic·i·ty
         (pĕr′ ĭ·ŏ·dĭs′ ĭ·tĭ)
per·i·os·te·um (pĕr′ ĭ·ŏs′ tĕ·ŭm)
per·i·pa·tet·ic (pĕr′ ĭ·pȧ·tĕt′ ĭk)
pe·riph·er·y (pĕ·rĭf′ ēr·ĭ)
-er·ies
pe·riph·er·al (pĕ·rĭf′ ēr·ăl)
per·i·scope (pĕr′ ĭ·skōp)
per·i·scop·ic (pĕr′ ĭ·skŏp′ ĭk)
per·ish (pĕr′ ĭsh)
per·ish·a·ble
per·i·stal·sis (pĕr′ ĭ·stăl′ sĭs)
per·i·stal·tic (-tĭk)
per·i·to·ni·tis (pĕr′ ĭ·tȯ·nī′ tĭs)
per·i·wig (pĕr′ ĭ·wĭg)
per·i·win·kle (pĕr′ ĭ·wĭng′ k'l)
per·jure (pûr′ jẽr)
-jur·ing   per·jur·er
per·ju·ry
perk·y (pûrk′ ĭ)
per·ma·nent (pûr′ mȧ·nĕnt)
-nence
per·man·ga·nate
        (pĕr·măng′ gȧ·nāt)
per·me·ate (pûr′ mĕ·āt)
-at·ing
per·me·a·bil·i·ty
        (pûr′ mĕ·ȧ·bĭl′ ĭ·tĭ)
per·me·a·ble (pûr′ mĕ·ȧ·b'l)
per·mis·si·ble (pĕr·mĭs′ ĭ·b'l)
per·mis·si·bil·i·ty
        (pĕr·mĭs′ ĭ·bĭl′ ĭ·tĭ)
per·mis·sion (pĕr·mĭsh′ ŭn)
per·mis·sive (pĕr·mĭs′ ĭv)
-mis·sive·ly
per·mit (pĕr·mĭt′) v.
-mit·ted   -mit·ting
per·mit (pûr′ mĭt) n.
per·mute (pĕr·mūt′)
-muting
per·mu·ta·tion
        (pûr′ mŭ·tā′ shŭn)
per·ni·cious a·ne·mi·a
        (pĕr·nĭsh′ ŭs)
per·nick·et·y (pĕr·nĭk′ ĕ·tĭ)
per·o·rate (pĕr′ ŏ·rāt)
-rat·ing
per·o·ra·tion (pĕr′ ŏ·rā′ shŭn)
per·ox·ide (pŏk′ sīd)
per·pen·dic·u·lar
        (pûr′ pĕn·dĭk′ û·lēr)
per·pe·trate (pûr′ pĕ·trāt)
-trat·ing

per·pe·tra·tion
        (pûr′ pĕ·trā′ shŭn)
per·pe·tra·tor
per·pet·u·al (pĕr·pĕt′ û·ȧl)
-al·ly
per·pet·u·ate (pĕr·pĕt′ û·āt)
-at·ing
per·pet·u·a·tion
        (pĕr·pĕt′ û·ā′ shŭn)
per·pe·tu·i·ty (pûr′ pĕ·tū′ ĭ·tĭ)
per·plex (pĕr·plĕks′)
per·se·cute (pûr′ sĕ·kūt)
-cut·ing
per·se·cu·tion
        (pûr′ sĕ·kū′ shŭn)
per·se·cu·tor
per·se·vere (pûr′ sĕ·vẽr′)
-ver·ing   per·se·ver·ance
Per·sian lamb (pûr′ zhȧn)
per·si·flage (pûr′ sĭ·fläzh)
per·sim·mon (pĕr·sĭm′ ŭn)
per·sist (pĕr·sĭst′)
per·sis·tence   -tent
per·son (pûr′ s'n)
per·son·a·ble (pûr′ sŭn·ȧ·b'l)
per·son·age (-ĭj)
per·son·al·i·ty
        (pûr′ sŭ·năl′ ĭ·tĭ)
-ties
per·son·al·ize, -iz·ing
per·son·al·ly
per·so·na non gra·ta
        (pĕr·sō′ nȧ nŏn grā′ tȧ)
per·son·al (pûr′ sŭn·ăl)
(private; see *personnel*)
per·son·i·fy (pĕr·sŏn′ ĭ·fī)
-fied   -fy·ing
per·son·i·fi·ca·tion
        (pĕr·sŏn′ ĭ·fī·kā′ shŭn)
per·son·nel (pûr′ sŏ·nĕl′)
(employees; see *personal*)
per·spec·tive (pĕr·spĕk′ tĭv)
(n.; appearance; see *prospective*)
per·spi·ca·cious
        (pûr′ spĭ·kā′ shŭs)
per·spi·cac·i·ty
        (pûr′ spĭ·kăs′ ĭ·tĭ)
per·spi·cu·i·ty (pûr′ spĭ·kū′ ĭ·tĭ)
per·spire (pĕr·spīr′)
-spir·ing
per·spi·ra·tion
        (pûr′ spĭ·rā′ shŭn)
per·suade (pĕr·swād′)
-suad·ing   per·suad·a·ble
per·suad·er

per·sua·sion (-swā′ zhŭn)
per·sua·sive
per·sua·sive·ness
per·tain (pĕr·tān′)
per·ti·na·cious (pûr′ tĭ·nā′ shŭs)
per·ti·nac·i·ty (-năs′ ĭ·tĭ)
per·ti·nent (pûr′ tĭ·nĕnt)
 -nence
per·turb (pĕr·tûrb′)
 per·turb·a·ble
 per·tur·ba·tion
  (pûr′ tĕr·bā′ shŭn)
pe·ruke (pĕ·rōōk′)
pe·ruse (pĕ·rōōz′)
 -rus·ing
 pe·rus·al (pĕ·rōōz′ ăl)
per·vade (pĕr·vād′)
 -vad·ing per·va·sion
 per·va·sive
per·verse (pĕr·vûrs′)
 per·verse·ly
per·ver·sion (pĕr·vûr′ zhŭn)
per·vert (pĕr·vûrt′) v
per·vert (pûr′ vûrt) n
pe·so (pā′ sō)
 -sos
pes·si·mism (pĕs′ ĭ·mĭz′m)
 pes·si·mist
 pes·si·mis·ti·cal·ly
  (pĕs′ ĭ·mĭs′ tĭ·kăl·ĭ)
pes·ti·cide (pĕs′ tĭ·sīd)
pes·tif·er·ous (pĕs·tĭf′ ēr·ŭs)
pes·ti·lent (pĕs′ tĭ·lĕnt)
 -lence
 pes·ti·len·tial (pĕs′ tĭ·lĕn′ shăl)
pes·tle (pĕs′ ′l)
pet·al (pĕt′ ′l)
pe·tard (pĕ·tärd′)
pet·cock (pĕt′ kŏk′)
pe·tite (pĕ·tēt′)
pe·ti·tion (pĕ·tĭsh′ ŭn)
 pe·ti·tion·ar·y
 pe·ti·tion·er
pet·it ju·ry (pĕt′ ĭ)
pe·tits fours (pĕ·tē′ fōōr′)
pet·ri·fy (pĕt′ rĭ·fī)
 -fied -fy·ing
pe·tro·le·um (pĕ·trō′ lĕ·ŭm)
pe·trol·o·gy (pĕ·trŏl′ ŏ·jĭ)
pet·ti·coat (pĕt′ ĭ·kōt)
pet·ti·fog (pĕt′ ĭ·fŏg)
 -fogged -fog·ging
 pet·ti·fog·ger
pet·ty (pĕt′ ĭ)
 pet·ti·ness pet·ty cash

pet·ty lar·ce·ny
pet·u·lant (pĕt′ ū·lănt)
 -lance -lan·cy
pe·tu·ni·a (pĕ·tū′ nĭ·á)
pew (pū)
pew·ter (pū′ tēr)
pha·lanx (fā′ lăngks)
 -lanx·es
phal·lus (făl′ ŭs)
 phal·lic (făl′ ĭk)
phan·tom (făn′ tŭm)
Phar·aoh (fâr′ ō)
Phar·i·see (fâr′ ĭ·sē)
 phar·i·sa·i·cal (fâr′ ĭ·sā′ ĭ·kăl)
phar·ma·cy (fär′ má·sĭ)
 -cies
 phar·ma·ceu·ti·cal
  (fär′ má·sū′ tĭ·kăl)
 phar·ma·cist (fär′ má·sĭst)
 phar·ma·col·o·gy
  (fär′ má·kŏl′ ŏ·jĭ)
phar·ynx (fär′ ĭngks)
 pl. pha·ryn·ges
  (fá·rĭn′ jēz)
phase (fāz)
 (aspect; see faze)
pheas·ant (fĕz′ ănt)
phe·no·bar·bi·tal
  (fē′ nŏ·bär′ bĭ·tôl)
phe·nom·e·non (fē·nŏm′ ē·nŏn)
 pl. phe·nom·e·na
 phe·nom·e·nal
Phil·a·del·phi·a,
 Pa. (fĭl′ á·dĕl′ fĭ·á)
phi·lan·der·er (fĭ·lăn′ dēr·ēr)
phi·lan·thro·py
  (fĭ·lăn′ thrŏ·pĭ)
 phil·an·throp·ic
  (fĭl′ ăn·thrŏp′ ĭk)
 phil·an·throp·ist
phi·lat·e·ly (fĭ·lăt′ ē·lĭ)
 phi·lat·e·list (fĭ·lăt′ ē·lĭst)
phil·har·mon·ic
  (fĭl′ ēr·mŏn′ ĭk)
Phil·ip, Prince, Duke of
 Ed·in·burgh
  (fĭl′ ĭp;
  ĕd′ ′n·bûr′ ō)
phi·lip·pic (fĭ·lĭp′ ĭk)
Phil·ip·pine (is.) (fĭl′ ĭ·pēn)
 But: Fil·i·pi·no
Phi·lis·tine (fĭ·lĭs′ tĭn)
phil·o·den·dron
  (fĭl′ ŏ·dĕn′ drŏn)

phi·lol·o·gy   (fĭ·lŏl′ ô·jĭ)
   phi·lol·o·gist
phi·los·o·phy   (fĭ·lŏs′ ô·fĭ)
   -phies   phi·los·o·pher
   phil·o·soph·i·cal
        (fĭl′ ô·sŏf′ ĭ·kăl)
   phi·los·o·phize
phil·ter   (fĭl′ tẽr)
   (as in *love philter;* see *filter*)
phlegm   (flĕm)
   phleg·mat·ic   (flĕg·măt′ ĭk)
phlo·gis·tic   (flô·jĭs′ tĭk)
phlo·gis·ton   (flô·jĭs′ tŏn)
phlox   (flŏks)
pho·bi·a   (fō′ bĭ·å)
   pho·bic   (fō′ bĭk)
phoe·be   (fē′ bè)
Phoe·ni·cian   (fē·nĭsh′ ăn)
Phoe·nix, Ariz.   (fē′ nĭks)
pho·net·ic   (fô·nĕt′ ĭk)
   pho·net·i·cal·ly
phon·ics   (fŏn′ ĭks)
pho·no·graph   (fō′ nô·gráf)
phos·gene   (fŏz′ jēn)
phos·phate   (fŏs′ fāt)
phos·pho·res·cence
        (fŏs′ fô·rĕs′ ĕns)
   -cent
phos·pho·rus   (fŏs′ fô·rŭs)
   phos·phor·ic   (fŏs·fŏr′ ĭk)
pho·to   (fō′ tō)
   -toed, -to·ing, -tos
pho·to·e·lec·tric
        (fō′ tô·ė·lĕk′ trĭk)
pho·to·en·grav·ing
        (fō′ tô·ĕn·grāv′ ĭng)
pho·to·flood lamp
        (fō′ tô·flŭd′)
pho·to·gen·ic   (fō′ tô·jĕn′ ĭk)
pho·to·graph   (fō′ tô·gráf)
   pho·tog·ra·pher
        (fô·tŏg′ rá·fẽr)
   pho·to·graph·ic
        (fō′ tô·grăf′ ĭk)
   pho·tog·ra·phy
        (fô·tŏg′ rá·fĭ)
pho·to·gra·vure (fō′ tô·grá·vūr′)
pho·to·mu·ral   (fō′ tô·mū′ rǎl)
pho·to-off·set   (fō′ tô·ôf′ sĕt′)
pho·to·sen·si·tive
        (fō′ tô·sĕn′ sĭ·tĭv)
pho·to·sphere   (fō′ tô·sfẽr)
Pho·to·stat   (fō′ tô·stăt)
pho·to·syn·the·sis
        (fō′ tô·sĭn′ thĕ·sĭs)

phrase   (frāz)
   phras·ing   phras·al
   phra·se·o·log·i·cal
        (frā′ zė·ô·lŏj′ ĭ·kǎl)
   phra·se·ol·o·gy
        (frā′ zė·ŏl′ ô·jĭ)
phre·net·ic   (frė·nĕt′ ĭk)
phre·nol·o·gy   (frė·nŏl′ ô·jĭ)
phy·log·e·ny   (fĭ·lŏj′ ė·nĭ)
phy·lum   (fī′ lŭm)
   pl. phy·la
phys·ic   (fĭz′ ĭk)
phys·i·cal   (fĭz′ ĭ·kǎl)
   phys·i·cal ther·a·py
phy·si·cian   (fĭ·zĭsh′ ǎn)
phys·ics   (fĭz′ ĭks)
   phys·i·cist   (fĭz′ ĭ·sĭst)
phys·i·og·no·my
        (fĭz′ ĭ·ŏg′ nô·mĭ)
   -mies
phys·i·ol·o·gy   (fĭz′ ĭ·ŏl′ ô·jĭ)
   phys·i·o·log·i·cal
        (fĭz′ ĭ·ô·lŏj′ ĭ·kǎl)
phys·i·o·ther·a·py
        (fĭz′ ĭ·ô·thĕr′ á·pĭ)
phy·sique   (fĭ·zēk′)
pi·a·nis·si·mo   (pė′ á·nĭs′ ĭ·mō)
pi·an·o   (pĭ·ăn′ ō)
   -os
   pi·an·ist   (pĭ·ăn′ ĭst)
pi·az·za   (pĭ·ăz′ á)
pi·ca   (pī′ ká)
pic·a·resque   (pĭk′ á·rĕsk′)
pic·a·yune   (pĭk′ á·yōōn′)
   pic·a·yun·ish
Pic·ca·dil·ly   (pĭk′ á·dĭl′ ĭ)
pic·ca·lil·li   (pĭk′ á·lĭl′ ĭ)
pic·co·lo   (pĭk′ ô·lō)
   -los
pick·a·back   (pĭk′ á·băk′)
pick·a·nin·ny   (pĭk′ á·nĭn′ ĭ)
   -nin·nies
pick·ax   (pĭk′ ăks′)
   -ax·es
pick·er·el   (pĭk′ ẽr·ĕl)
   pick·er·el·weed
pick·et   (pĭk′ ĕt)
   -et·ed   -et·ing
   pick·et·er
pick·le   (pĭk′ ′l)
   -ling
pick·pock·et   (pĭk′ pŏk′ ĕt)
pick·up   (pĭk′ ŭp′)
pic·nic   (pĭk′ nĭk)
   -nicked   -nick·ing

pic·nick·er
pic·to·graph   (pĭk′ tô·gráf)
pic·to·ri·al   (pĭk·tō′ rĭ·ȧl)
 -al·ly
pic·ture   (pĭk′ tụ̆r)
 -tur·ing
pic·tur·esque   (pĭk′ tụ̆r·ĕsk′)
pid·dling   (pĭd′ lĭng)
pidg·in Eng·lish
                      (pĭj′ ĭn)
pie·bald   (pī′ bôld′)
piece   (pēs)
 piec·ing   piece·meal
 piece·work
pièce de ré·sis·tance
                (pyĕs′ dē rā′ zēs′ täns′)
pied   (pīd)
pied·mont   (pēd′ mŏnt)
pier   (pēr)
 (breakwater; see *peer*)
pierce   (pērs)
 pierc·ing
pi·e·ty   (pī′ ĕ·tĭ)
 -ties
pig   (pĭg)
 pig·head·ed   pig i·ron
 pig·pen   pig·skin
 pig·sty   -sties
 pig·tail
pi·geon   (pĭj′ ŭn)
 pi·geon-breast·ed
 pi·geon·hole   pi·geon-toed
pig·gy bank   (pĭg′ ĭ)
pig·ment   (pĭg′ mĕnt)
 pig·men·tar·y   (pĭg′ mĕn·tĕr′ ĭ)
 pig·men·ta·tion
                 (pĭg′ mĕn·tā′ shŭn)
pi·las·ter   (pĭ·lăs′ tēr)
pi·lau   (pĭ·lō′)
pil·chard   (pĭl′ chērd)
pile driv·er   (pīl)
pil·fer   (pĭl′ fēr)
 pil·fer·age   pil·fer·er
pil·grim   (pĭl′ grĭm)
 pil·grim·age   (pĭl′ grĭ·mĭj)
 Pil·grim Fa·thers
pil·ing   (pīl′ ĭng)
pil·lage   (pĭl′ ĭj)
pil·lar   (pĭl′ ēr)
pill·box   (pĭl′ bŏks′)
pil·lo·ry   (pĭl′ ô·rĭ)
 -ries
pil·low   (pĭl′ ō)
 pil·low·case   pil·low slip

pi·lot   (pī′ lŭt)
 -lot·ed   -lot·ing
Pilt·down man   (pĭlt′ doun′)
pi·men·to   (pĭ·mĕn′ tō)
 -tos
pim·per·nel   (pĭm′ pēr·nĕl)
pim·ple   (pĭm′ p'l)
 -ply
pin·a·fore   (pĭn′ ȧ·fōr′)
pin·ball ma·chine
                      (pĭn′ bôl′)
pince-nez   (păns′ nā′)
pin·cers   (pĭn′ sērz)
pinch hit·ter   (pĭnch)
pin·cush·ion   (pĭn′ kŏŏsh′ ŭn)
pine·al gland   (pĭn′ ē·ȧl)
pine·ap·ple   (pĭn′ ăp′ 'l)
pin·feath·er   (pĭn′ fĕth′ ēr)
Ping-pong   (pĭng′ pŏng′)
pin·hole   (pĭn′ hōl′)
pin·ion   (pĭn′ yŭn)
pink·eye   (pĭngk′ ī′)
pin·nace   (pĭn′ ĭs)
pin·na·cle   (pĭn′ ȧ·k'l)
pin·nate   (pĭn′ āt)
pi·noch·le   (pē′ nŭk′ 'l)
pin·point   (pĭn′ point′)
pin·tail duck   (pĭn′ tāl′)
pin·to   (pĭn′ tō)
pin-up   (pĭn′ ŭp′)
pi·o·neer   (pī′ ô·nēr′)
pi·ous   (pī′ ŭs)
 pi·e·ty   (pī′ ĕ·tĭ)
pipe   (pīp)
 pip·ing   pipe dream
 pipe·line   pipe or·gan
pi·pette   (pĭ·pĕt′)
pi·quant   (pē′ kȧnt)
 pi·quan·cy   (pē′ kȧn·sĭ)
pique   (pēk)
pi·qué   (pĕ·kā′)
pi·ra·nha fish   (pĭ·rän′ yȧ)
pi·rate   (pī′ rĭt)
 pi·ra·cy   (pī′ rȧ·sĭ)
pir·ou·ette   (pĭr′ ŏŏ·ĕt′)
 -ett·ing
pis·ca·to·ri·al   (pĭs′ kȧ·tō′ rĭ·ȧl)
pis·tach·i·o   (pĭs·tăsh′ ĭ·ō)
pis·til   (pĭs′ tĭl)
 (plant part; see *pistol*)
pis·tol   (pĭs′ t'l)
 (firearm; see *pistil*)
pis·ton ring   (pĭs′ tŭn)
pitch   (pĭch)
 pitch-black

pitch·blende (pĭch′ blĕnd′)
pitch·er pitch·fork
pitch pipe
pit·e·ous (pĭt′ ē·ŭs)
pit·fall (pĭt′ fôl′)
pith·y (pĭth′ ĭ)
pit·i·a·ble (pĭt′ ĭ·à·b'l)
pit·i·ful (pĭt′ ĭ·fōŏl)
    -ful·ly -ful·ness
pit·i·less (pĭt′ ĭ·lĕs)
pi′ ton (pē′ tôN′)
pit·tance (pĭt′ ăns)
Pitts·burg, Kans. (pĭts′ bûrg)
Pitts·burgh, Pa. (pĭts′ bûrg)
pi·tu·i·tar·y gland
                    (pĭ·tū′ ĭ·tĕr′ ĭ)
pit·y (pĭt′ ĭ)
    pit·ied pit·y·ing
    pit·e·ous (pĭt′ ē·ŭs)
    pit·i·a·ble
    pit·i·ful, -ful·ly, -ful·ness
    pit·i·less
piv·ot (pĭv′ ŭt)
    -ot·ed -ot·ing
    piv·ot·al
pix·y (pĭk′ sĭ)
    pix·ies
piz·za (pēt′ sá)
    piz·ze·ri·a (pēt′ sĕ·rē′ à)
plac·ard (plăk′ ärd)
pla·cate (plā′ kāt)
    -cat·ing
pla·ce·bo (plà·sē′ bō)
place·ment (plās′ mĕnt)
pla·cen·ta (plà·sĕn′ tá)
    pla·cen·tal
plac·er min·ing (plăs′ ēr)
plac·id (plăs′ ĭd)
    pla·cid·i·ty (plà·sĭd′ ĭ·tĭ)
plack·et (plăk′ ĕt)
pla·gi·a·rism (plā′ jĭ·à·rĭz'm)
    pla·gi·a·rist pla·gi·a·rize
    pla·gi·ar·y
plague (plāg)
plaid (plăd)
plain (plān)
    plain-clothes man
    plains·man
plaint (plānt)
plain·tiff (plān′ tĭf)
plain·tive (plān′ tĭv)
    plain·tive·ly
plait·ing (plāt′ ĭng)
plane (plān)
    plane an·gle

plane ge·om·e·try
plan·et (plăn′ ĕt)
    plan·e·tar·y (plăn′ ĕ·tĕr′ ĭ)
plan·e·tar·i·um
                    (plăn′ ĕ·târ′ ĭ·ŭm)
    pl. plan·e·tar·i·a
plank (plăngk)
plank·ton (plăngk′ tŏn)
    plank·ton·ic (plăngk·tŏn′ ĭk)
pla·no·graph (plā′ nŏ·gráf)
plan·tain (plăn′ tĭn)
plan·ta·tion (plăn·tā′ shŭn)
plaque (plăk)
plas·ma (plăz′ má)
plas·ter (plăs′ tēr)
    plas·ter·board plas·ter cast
    plas·ter of Par·is
plas·tic (plăs′ tĭk)
    plas·tic·i·ty (plăs·tĭs′ ĭ·tĭ)
    plas·tic sur·ger·y
plate (plāt)
    plat·ing plate·ful
    plate glass plate·let
pla·teau (plà·tō′)
plat·en (plăt′ 'n)
plat·form (plăt′ fôrm′)
plat·i·num (plăt′ ĭ·nŭm)
plat·i·tude (plăt′ ĭ·tūd)
    plat·i·tu·di·nous
                    (plăt′ ĭ·tū′ dĭ·nŭs)
Pla·ton·ic (plà·tŏn′ ĭk)
pla·toon (plà·tōōn′)
plat·ter (plăt′ ēr)
plat·y·pus (plăt′ ĭ·pŭs)
    -pus·es
plau·dit (plô′ dĭt)
plau·si·ble (plô′ zĭ·b'l)
    plau·si·bil·i·ty
                    (plô′ zĭ·bĭl′ ĭ·tĭ)
play (plā)
    play·bill play·boy
    play·ful, -ful·ly, -ful·ness
    play·go·er play·ground
    play-off play·wright
    play·writ·ing
pla·za (plä′ zà)
plea (plē)
plead (plēd)
    plead·a·ble
pleas·ant (plĕz′ ánt)
    pleas·ance pleas·ant·ry
    -ries
please (plēz)
    pleas·ing

pleas·ure (plězh′ ēr)
  pleas·ur·a·ble
pleat (plēt)
ple·be·ian (plě·bē′ yăn)
pleb·i·scite (plěb′ ĭ·sīt)
pledge (plěj)
  pledg·ing
  pledg·ee (plěj′ ē′)
Pleis·to·cene (plīs′ tô·sēn)
ple·na·ry (plē′ nȧ·rĭ)
plen·i·po·ten·ti·ar·y
    (plěn′ ĭ·pô·těn′ shĭ·ěr′ ĭ)
plen·te·ous (plěn′ tě·ŭs)
plen·ti·ful (plěn′ tĭ·fŏŏl)
  -ful·ly   -ful·ness
pleth·o·ra (plěth′ ô·rȧ)
pleu·ri·sy (plŏŏr′ ĭ·sĭ)
plex·us (plěk′ sŭs)
pli·a·ble (plī′ ȧ·b′l)
  pli·a·bil·i·ty (plī′ ȧ·bĭl′ ĭ·tĭ)
  pli·a·ble·ness
pli·ant (plī′ ănt)
  pli·an·cy
pli·ers (plī′ ērz)
plight (plīt)
plinth (plĭnth)
Pli·o·cene (plī′ ô·sēn)
plod (plŏd)
  plod·ded   plod·ding
plot·ter (plŏt′ ēr)
plov·er (plŭv′ ēr)
plow·share (plou′ shâr′)
pluck·y (plŭk′ ĭ)
  pluck·i·ness
plum·age (plŏŏm′ ĭj)
plumb (plŭm)
  plumb·er   plumb·ing
  plumb line
plume (plŏŏm)
  plum·age
plum·met (plŭm′ ět)
  plum·met·ed   plum·met·ing
plun·der (plŭn′ dēr)
plunge (plŭnj)
  plung·ing
plu·per·fect (plŏŏ′ pûr′ fěkt)
plu·ral (plŏŏr′ ăl)
  plu·ral·is·tic (plŏŏr′ ăl·ĭs′ tĭk)
  plu·ral·i·ty (plŏŏ·răl′ ĭ·tĭ)
plus (plŭs)
plu·toc·ra·cy (plŏŏ·tŏk′ rȧ·sĭ)
  plu·to·crat (plŏŏ′ tô·krăt)
plu·to·ni·um (plŏŏ·tō′ nĭ·ŭm)
ply (plī)
  plied   ply·ing

ply·wood
Ply·mouth rock (plĭm′ ŭth)
pneu·mat·ic (nŭ·măt′ ĭk)
pneu·mo·ni·a (nŭ·mō′ nĭ·ȧ)
poach·er (pōch′ ēr)
pock·et (pŏk′ ět)
  -et·ed   -et·ing
  pock·et·book   pock·et·knife
  pock·et mon·ey
  pock·et ve·to
pock·mark (pŏk′ märk′)
  pock-marked
po·di·um (pō′ dĭ·ŭm)
  pl. po·di·a
po·et (pō′ ět)
  po·em
  po·et·ic (pô·ět′ ĭk)
  po·et·i·cal (pô·ět′ ĭ·kȧl)
  -cal·ly   po·et·ic li·cense
  po·et lau·re·ate
  po·et·ry
po·grom (pô·grŏm′)
poign·ant (poin′ yȧnt)
  poign·an·cy
poin·set·ti·a (poin·sět′ ĭ·ȧ)
point·less (point′ lěs)
poi·son (poi′ z′n)
  poi·son i·vy   poi·son·ous
  poi·son su·mac
poke bon·net (pōk)
po·ker face (pō′ kēr)
po·lar (pō′ lēr)
  po·lar bear
  po·lar·i·ty (pô·lăr′ ĭ·tĭ)
Po·la·ris (pô·lā′ rĭs)
po·lar·ize (pō′ lēr·īz)
  -iz·ing
  po·lar·i·za·tion
    (pō′ lēr·ĭ·zā′ shŭn)
Po·lar·oid (pō′ lēr·oid)
pole (pōl)
  (long piece of wood; see *poll*)
po·lem·ic (pô·lěm′ ĭk)
  po·lem·i·cist (pô·lěm′ ĭ·sĭst)
pole·star (pōl′ stär′)
pole vault·er (pōl)
  pole-vault *v.*
po·lice·man (pô·lēs′ mȧn)
pol·i·cy (pŏl′ ĭ·sĭ)
  -cies   pol·i·cy·hold·er
po·li·o (pō′ lĭ·ō)
  po·li·o·my·e·li·tis
    (pō′ lĭ·ô·mī′ ě·lī′ tĭs)
pol·ish (pŏl′ ĭsh)

po·lite   (pô·līt′)
  po·lite·ly
pol·i·tics   (pŏl′ ĭ·tĭks)
  po·lit·i·cal   (pô·lĭt′ ĭ·kǎl)
  pol·i·ti·cian   (pŏl′ ĭ·tĭsh′ ǎn)
  po·lit·i·co   (pô·lĭt′ ĭ·kō)
  -cos
pol·i·ty   (pŏl′ ĭ·tĭ)
pol·ka   (pō(l)′ kà)
  pol·ka dot
poll   (pōl)
  (survey; see *pole*)
  poll·ee   poll·ster
  poll tax
pol·len   (pŏl′ ĕn)
pol·li·nate   (pŏl′ ĭ·nāt)
  -nat·ing
  pol·li·na·tion   (pŏl′ ĭ·nā′ shŭn)
pol·li·wog   (pŏl′ ĭ·wŏg)
pol·lute   (pô·lūt′)
  pol·lut·ing
  pol·lu·tion   (pô·lū′ shŭn)
Pol·ly·an·na   (pŏl′ ĭ·ǎn′ à)
po·lo   (pō′ lō)
  po·lo coat   po·lo shirt
pol·o·naise   (pŏl′ ô·nāz′)
pol·ter·geist   (pŏl′ tĕr·gīst′)
pol·troon   (pŏl·trōōn′)
pol·y·an·dry   (pŏl′ ĭ·ǎn′ drĭ)
pol·y·chro·mat·ic
    (pŏl′ ĭ·krō·mǎt′ ĭk)
pol·y·eth·yl·ene
    (pŏl′ ĭ·ĕth′ ĭ·lēn)
po·lyg·a·my   (pô·lĭg′ à·mĭ)
  po·lyg·a·mist   po·lyg·a·mous
pol·y·glot   (pŏl′ ĭ·glŏt)
pol·y·gon   (pŏl′ ĭ·gŏn)
  po·lyg·o·nal   (pô·lĭg′ ô·nǎl)
pol·y·gy·ny   (pô·lĭj′ ĭ·nĭ)
Pol·y·ne·sian   (pŏl′ ĭ·nē′ shǎn)
pol·yp   (pŏl′ ĭp)
pol·y·phon·ic   (pŏl′ ĭ·fŏn′ ĭk)
pol·y·tech·nic   (pŏl′ ĭ·tĕk′ nĭk)
po·made   (pô·mād′)
pome·gran·ate   (pŏm′ grăn′ ĭt)
pom·pa·dour   (pŏm′ pà·dōr)
pom·pa·no   (pŏm′ pà·nō)
pom·pon   (pŏm′ pŏn)
pomp·ous   (pŏmp′ ŭs)
  pom·pos·i·ty   (pŏm·pŏs′ ĭ·tĭ)
pon·cho   (pŏn′ chō)
  -chos
pon·der   (pŏn′ dĕr)
  pon·der·a·ble   pon·der·ous
pon·gee   (pŏn·jē′)

pon·tiff   (pŏn′ tĭf)
  pon·tif·i·cal   (pŏn·tĭf′ ĭ·kǎl)
  pon·tif·i·cate   (pŏn·tĭf′ ĭ·kāt)
  -cat·ing
pon·toon   (pŏn·tōōn′)
po·ny   (pō′ nĭ)
  -nies
poo·dle   (pōō′ d′l)
pooh-pooh   (pōō′ pōō′)
pope   (pōp)
  pop·er·y   pop·ish
pop·lar   (pŏp′ lĕr)
pop·lin   (pŏp′ lĭn)
pop·py   (pŏp′ ĭ)
  pop·pies
pop·u·lace   (pŏp′ û·lĭs)
pop·u·lar   (pŏp′ û·lĕr)
  pop·u·lar·i·ty   (pŏp′ û·lăr′ ĭ·tĭ)
  pop·u·lar·i·za·tion
    (pŏp′ û·lĕr·ĭ·zā′ shŭn)
  pop·u·lar·ize   -izing
pop·u·late   (pŏp′ û·lāt)
  -lat·ing
  pop·u·la·tion   (pŏp′ û·lā′ shŭn)
Pop·u·list   (pŏp′ û·lĭst)
pop·u·lous   (pŏp′ û·lŭs)
por·ce·lain   (pōr′ sĕ·lĭn)
por·cu·pine   (pôr′ kû·pīn)
pore   (pōr)
  por·ing (*n.*: a tiny opening;
    v.: to study; see *pour*)
  po·ros·i·ty   (pô·rŏs′ ĭ·tĭ)
  po·rous   (pō′ rŭs)
por·no·graph·ic
    (pôr′ nô·grăf′ ĭk)
por·poise   (pôr′ pŭs)
por·ridge   (pôr′ ĭj)
port·a·ble   (pōr′ tà·b′l)
  port·a·bil·i·ty   (pōr′ tà·bĭl′ ĭ·tĭ)
por·tage   (pōr′ tĭj)
por·tal   (pōr′ tǎl)
por·tend   (pōr·tĕnd′)
  por·tent   (pōr′ tĕnt)
  por·ten·tous   (pōr·tĕn′ tŭs)
por·ter·house steak
    (pōr′ tĕr·hous′)
port·fo·li·o   (pōrt·fō′ lĭ·ō)
  -os
por·ti·co   (pōr′ tĭ·kō)
  -coes
por·tion   (pōr′ shŭn)
port·land ce·ment
    (pōrt′ lǎnd)
port·ly   (pōrt′ lĭ)
  port·li·ness

port·man·teau   (pōrt·măn′ tō)
por·trait   (pōr′ trāt)
  por·trai·ture   (pōr′ trȧ·tụ̄r)
por·tray   (pōr·trā′)
  por·tray·a·ble por·tray·al
Por·tu·guese   (pōr′ tụ·gēz)
pos·it   (pŏz′ ĭt)
  -it·ed   -it·ing
po·si·tion   (pŏ·zĭsh′ ŭn)
pos·i·tive   (pŏz′ ĭ·tĭv)
  pos·i·tive·ly   -tive·ness
  pos·i·tiv·ism
pos·se   (pŏs′ ė)
pos·sess   (pŏ·zĕs′)
  pos·ses·sion pos·ses·sive
  pos·ses·sive·ness
  pos·ses·sor
pos·si·ble   (pŏs′ ĭ·b'l)
  pos·si·bil·i·ty   (pŏs′ ĭ·bĭl′ ĭ·tĭ)
pos·sum   (pŏs′ ŭm)
post-   (pōst-)
  post card post·date
  post ex·change
  post·grad·u·ate
  post·haste
  post·hu·mous   (pŏs′ tụ·mŭs)
  post·im·pres·sion·ism
  post·lude post·man
  post·mark post·mas·ter
  post me·rid·i·em
        (-mė·rĭd′ ĭ·ĕm)
  post·mis·tress post-mor·tem
  post·na·tal post of·fice
  post·or·bit·al post·paid
  post·pon·a·ble (pōst·pōn′ ȧ·b'l)
  post·pone·ment
  post-Rev·o·lu·tion·ar·y
  post·script post·war
post·age   (pōs′ tĭj)
post·al   (pōs′ tȧl)
post·er   (pōs′ tēr)
pos·te·ri·or   (pŏs·tēr′ ĭ·ēr)
pos·ter·i·ty   (pŏs·tĕr′ ĭ·tĭ)
pos·tu·late   (pŏs′ tụ·lȧt)
  -lat·ing
pos·ture   (pŏs′ tụ̄r)
  pos·tur·al
po·sy   (pō′ zĭ)
  -sies
pot-   (pŏt-)
  pot·bel·ly -bel·lied
  pot·boil·er pot·hole
  pot·latch pot liq·uor
  pot·luck pot·pie
  pot shot

po·ta·ble   (pō′ tȧ·b'l)
pot·ash   (pŏt′ ăsh′)
po·tas·si·um   (pŏ·tăs′ ĭ·ŭm)
  car·bon·ate chlo·rate
  chlo·ride hy·drox·ide
  per·man·ga·nate
po·ta·tion   (pō·tā′ shŭn)
po·ta·to   (pŏ·tā′ tō)
  -toes po·ta·to bee·tle
  po·ta·to chips
po·tent   (pō′ tĕnt)
  po·ten·cy
po·ten·tate   (pō′ tĕn·tāt)
po·ten·tial   (pŏ·tĕn′ shȧl)
  -tial·ly
  po·ten·ti·al·i·ty
      (pŏ·tĕn′ shĭ·ăl′ ĭ·tĭ)
pot·pour·ri   (pō′ pōō′ rē′)
pot·sherd   (pŏt′ shûrd′)
pot·tage   (pŏt′ ĭj)
pot·ter·y   (pŏt′ ēr·ĭ)
pouch   (pouch)
Pough·keep·sie, (pŏ·kĭp′ sĭ)
  N. Y.
poul·tice   (pōl′ tĭs)
poul·try   (pōl′ trĭ)
pounce   (pouns)
  pounc·ing
pound   (pound)
  pound·age pound·cake
  pound-fool·ish
pour   (pōr)
  (to flow; see *pore*)
pousse-ca·fé   (pōōs′ kȧ′ fā′)
pout   (pout)
pout·er pi·geon (pout′ ēr)
pov·er·ty   (pŏv′ ēr·tĭ)
  pov·er·ty-strick·en
pow·der   (pou′ dēr)
  pow·der horn pow·der room
pow·er   (pou′ ēr)
  pow·er am·pli·fi·er
  pow·er·boat pow·er-driv·en
  pow·er·ful, -ful·ly, -ful·ness
  pow·er·less
pow·wow   (pou′ wou′)
pox   (pŏks)
prac·ti·ca·ble (prăk′ tĭ·kȧ·b'l)
  prac·ti·ca·bil·i·ty
      (prăk′ tĭ·kȧ·bĭl′ ĭ·tĭ)
prac·ti·cal   (prăk′ tĭ·kȧl)
  prac·ti·cal·i·ty
      (prăk′ tĭ·kăl′ ĭ·tĭ)
  prac·ti·cal·ly

prac·tice (prăk′ tĭs)
-tic·ing
prac·ti·tion·er (prăk·tĭsh′ ŭn·ẽr)
Prae·to·ri·an guard
(prē·tō′ rĭ·ἀn)
prag·mat·ic (prăg·măt′ ĭk)
prag·mat·i·cal·ly
prag·ma·tism (prăg′ mἀ·tĭz'm)
prai·rie (prâr′ ĭ)
prai·rie schoon·er
praise (prāz)
prais·ing
praise·wor·thy, -wor·thi·ness
pra·line (prä′ lēn)
prance (práns)
pranc·ing
prank·ish (prăngk′ ĭsh)
prate (prāt)
prat·ing
prat·tle (prăt′ 'l)
prat·tling
prawn (prôn)
pray (prā)
(entreat; see prey)
prayer (prâr)
pray·ing man·tis
(prā′ ĭng măn′ tĭs)
preach (prēch)
preach·er preach·ment
pre·am·ble (prē′ ăm′ b'l)
Pre-Cam·bri·an
(prē′ kăm′ brĭ·ἀn)
pre·can·cel (prē·kăn′ sĕl)
-celed -cel·ing
pre·car·i·ous (prē·kâr′ ĭ·ŭs)
pre·cau·tion (prē·kô′ shŭn)
-tion·ar·y
pre·cede (prē·sēd′)
-ced·ing
pre·ced·ence (prē·sēd′ ĕns)
pre·ced·ent (prē·sēd′ ĕnt)
(going before)
prec·e·dent (prĕs′ ê·dĕnt)
(setting an example)
pre·cept (prē′ sĕpt)
pre·cinct (prē′ sĭngkt)
pre·cious (prĕsh′ ŭs)
prec·i·pice (prĕs′ ĭ·pĭs)
pre·cip·i·tant (prē·sĭp′ ĭ·tἀnt)
pre·cip·i·tate (prē·sĭp′ ĭ·tāt)
-tat·ing
pre·cip·i·ta·tion
(prē·sĭp′ ĭ·tā′ shŭn)
pre·cip·i·tous (prē·sĭp′ ĭ·tŭs)

pré·cis (prā·sē′)
(summary; see precise)
pre·cise (prē·sĭs′)
(sharply defined; se précis)
pre·cise·ly
pre·ci·sion (prē·sĭzh′ ŭn)
pre·clude (prē·klōōd′)
-clud·ing
pre·clu·sion (-klōō′ zhŭn)
pre·co·cious (prē·kō′ shŭs)
pre·con·cep·tion
(prē′ kŏn·sĕp′ shŭn)
pre·con·di·tion
(prē′ kŏn·dĭsh′ ŭn)
-tion·ing
pre·cur·sor (prē·kûr′ sẽr)
pred·a·tor (prĕd′ ἀ·tẽr)
pred·a·to·ry (prĕd′ ἀ·tō′ rĭ)
pred·e·ces·sor (prĕd′ ê·sĕs′ ẽr)
pre·des·ti·na·tion
(prē·dĕs′ tĭ·nā′ shŭn)
pre·des·tine (prē·dĕs′ tĭn)
-tin·ing
pre·de·ter·mine
(prē′ dĕ·tûr′ mĭn)
-min·ing
pre·dic·a·ment
(prē·dĭk′ ἀ·mĕnt)
pred·i·cate (prĕd′ ĭ·kāt) v.
-cat·ing (-kĭt) adj., n.
pred·i·ca·tion
(prĕd′ ĭ·kā′ shŭn)
pre·dict (prē·dĭkt′)
pre·dict·a·ble
pre·dic·tion (prē·dĭk′ shŭn)
pre·dic·tive pre·dic·tor
pre·di·lec·tion (prē′ dĭ·lĕk′ shŭn)
pre·dom·i·nant
(prē·dŏm′ ĭ·nἀnt)
nance
pre·dom·i·nate (-nāt)
-nat·ing
pre·dom·i·na·tion
(prē·dŏm′ ĭ·nā′ shŭn)
pre·em·i·nent (prē·ĕm′ ĭ·nĕnt)
pre·em·i·nence
pre-empt (prē·ĕmpt′)
pre-emp·tion pre-emp·tive
pre-emp·to·ry
preen (prēn)
pre-ex·ist·ence (prē′ ĕg·zĭs′ tĕns)
pre·fab·ri·cate (prē·făb′ rĭ·kāt)
-cat·ing
pre·fab·ri·ca·tion
(prē′ făb·rĭ·kā′ shŭn)

pref·ace   (prĕf′ ĭs)
-ac·ing
pre·fect   (prē′ fĕkt)
pre·fec·ture
pre·fer   (prĕ·fûr′)
-ferred   -fer·ring
pref·er·a·ble   (prĕf′ ēr·a·b′l)
pref·er·ence   (prĕf′ ēr·ĕns)
pref·er·en·tial
      (prĕf′ ēr·ĕn′ shăl)
pre·fer·ment   (prĕ·fûr′ mĕnt)
pre·ferred stock   (prĕ·fûrd′)
preg·nant   (prĕg′ nănt)
preg·nan·cy
pre·hen·sile   (prĕ·hĕn′ sĭl)
pre·his·tor·ic   (prē′ hĭs·tŏr′ ĭk)
prej·u·dice   (prĕj′ ŏŏ·dĭs)
prej·u·di·cial
      (prĕj′ ŏŏ·dĭsh′ ăl)
prel·ate   (prĕl′ ĭt)
prel·a·cy   (-a·sĭ)
prel·a·ture   (-a·tûr)
pre·lim·i·nar·y
      (prĕ·lĭm′ ĭ·nĕr′ ĭ)
-nar·ies
pre·lim·i·nar·i·ly
      (prĕ·lĭm′ ĭ·nĕr′ ĭ·lĭ)
prel·ude   (prĕl′ ūd)
pre·ma·ture   (prē′ ma·tūr′)
pre·ma·ture·ly
pre·med·i·cal   (prē·mĕd′ ĭ·kăl)
pre·med·i·tate   (prĕ·mĕd′ ĭ·tāt)
-tat·ing
pre·med·i·ta·tion
      (prē′ mĕd·ĭ·tā′ shŭn)
pre·mi·er   (prē′ mĭ·ēr)
(chief officer; see première)
pre·*mière*   (prĕ·mĕr′)
(first showing; see *premier*)
prem·ise   (prĕm′ ĭs)
pre·mi·um   (prē′ mĭ·ŭm)
pre·mo·lar   (prē·mō′ lēr)
pre·mo·ni·tion   (prē′ mŏ·nĭsh′ ŭn)
pre·mon·i·to·ry
      (prē·mŏn′ ĭ·tō′ rĭ)
pre·na·tal   (prē·nā′ tăl)
pre·oc·cu·pa·tion
      (prē·ŏk′ û·pā′ shŭn)
pre·oc·cu·py   (prē·ŏk′ û·pī)
-pied,   -py·ing
pre·or·dain   (prē′ ôr·dān′)
pre·or·di·na·tion
      (prē′ ôr·dĭ·nā′ shŭn)
prep school   (prĕp)

pre·pare   (prĕ·pâr′)
-par·ing
prep·a·ra·tion
      (prĕp′ a·rā′ shŭn)
pre·par·a·tive   (prĕ·păr′ a·tĭv)
pre·par·a·to·ry
      (prĕ·păr′ a·tō′ rĭ)
pre·par·ed·ness
      (prĕ·păr′ ĕd·nĕs)
pre·pay   (prē·pā′)
-paid   -pay·ing
pre·pay·ment
pre·pon·der·ance
      (prĕ·pŏn′ dēr·dns)
-ant
prep·o·si·tion
      (prĕp′ ŏ·zĭsh′ ŭn)
-tion·al
pre·pos·ses·sing
      (prē′ pŏ·zĕs′ ĭng)
pre·pos·ter·ous
      (prĕ·pŏs′ tēr·ŭs)
pre·req·ui·site   (prĕ·rĕk′ wĭ·zĭt)
pre·rog·a·tive   (prĕ·rŏg′ a·tĭv)
pres·age   (prĕs′ ĭj) *n.*
pre·sage   (prĕ·sāj′) *v.*
-sag·ing
Pres·by·te·ri·an
      (prĕz′ bĭ·tēr′ ĭ·ăn)
pres·by·ter·y   (prĕz′ bĭ·tēr′ ĭ)
-ter·ies
pre·school   (prĕ·skōōl′)
pre·sci·ence   (prē′ shĭ·ĕns)
pre·scind   (prĕ·sĭnd′)
pre·scribe   (prĕ·skrīb′)
(dictate; see *proscribe*)
-scrib·ing
pre·scrip·tion   (prĕ·skrĭp′ shŭn)
pres·ence   (prĕz′ ĕns)
pre·sent   (prĕ·zĕnt′) *v.*
pre·sent·a·ble
pres·ent·a·tion
      (prĕz′ ĕn·tā′ shŭn)
pres·ent   (prĕz′ ĕnt) *n., adj.*
pre·sen·ti·ment
      (prĕ·zĕn′ tĭ·mĕnt)
pre·sent·ment   (prĕ·zĕnt′ mĕnt)
pre·serv·a·tive   (prĕ·zûr′ va·tĭv)
pre·serve   (prĕ·zûrv′)
-serv·ing   pre·serv·a·ble
pres·er·va·tion
      (prĕz′ ēr·vā′ shŭn)
pre·side   (prĕ·zīd′)
-sid·ing

pres·i·dent　　(prĕz′ ĭ·dĕnt)
　pres·i·den·cy
　pres·i·den·tial
　　　　　　(prĕz′ ĭ·dĕn′ shăl)
pre·si·di·o　　(prĕ·sē′ dĭ·ō)
pre·sid·i·um　　(prĕ·sĭd′ ĭ·ŭm)
press a·gent　　(prĕs)
pres·sure　　(prĕsh′ ēr)
　pres·sur·ize　　-iz·ing
pres·ti·dig·i·ta·tion
　　　　　　(prĕs′ tĭ·dĭj′ ĭ·tā′ shŭn)
　-ta·tor
pres·tige　　(prĕs·tēzh′)
pres·to　　(prĕs′tō)
pre·sume　　(prĕ·zūm′)
　-sum·ing　　pre·sum·a·ble
　pre·sum·ed·ly
　pre·sump·tion
　　　　　　(prĕ·zŭmp′ shŭn)
　pre·sump·tive　　(-zŭmp′ tĭv)
　pre·sump·tu·ous
　　　　　　(-zŭmp′ tū·ŭs)
pre·sup·pose　　(prē′ sŭ·pōz′)
　-sup·pos·ing
　pre·sup·po·si·tion
　　　　　　(prē′ sŭp·ō·zĭsh′ ŭn)
pre·tend　　(prē·tĕnd′)
　pre·tend·er
　pre·tense　　(prē·tĕns′)
　pre·ten·sion　　(prē·tĕn′ shŭn)
　pre·ten·tious　　(prē·tĕn′ shŭs)
pre·ter·nat·u·ral
　　　　　　(prē′ tēr·năt′ û·răl)
pre·text　　(prē′ tĕkst)
pret·ti·fy　　(prĭt′ ĭ·fī)
　-fied　　-fy·ing
pret·ty　　(prĭt′ ĭ)
　pret·ti·er　　pret·ti·est
　pret·ti·ly　　pret·ti·ness
pre·vail　　(prē·vāl′)
　-vailed　　vail·ing
　prev·a·lent　　(prĕv′ ȧ·lĕnt)
pre·var·i·cate　　(prē·văr′ ĭ·kāt)
　-cat·ing　　pre·var·i·ca·tor
pre·vent　　(prē·vĕnt′)
　pre·vent·a·tive
　　　　　　(prē·vĕn′ tȧ·tĭv)
　pre·ven·tive　　(prē·vĕn′ tĭv)
pre·view　　(prē′ vū′)
pre·vi·ous　　(prē′ vĭ·ŭs)
prey　　(prā)
　(victim; see pray)
price·less　　(prīs′ lĕs)
prick·le　　(prĭk′ ′l)
　-ling　　prick·ly heat

pride·ful　　(prīd′ fŏŏl)
　-ful·ly　　-ful·ness
priest　　(prēst)
　priest·ess　　priest·hood
　priest·ly　　-li·ness
prig　　(prĭg)
　prig·gish
pri·ma·cy　　(prī′ mȧ·sĭ)
pri·ma don·na　　(prē′ mȧ dŏn′ ȧ)
pri·ma-fa·ci·e ev·i·dence
　　　　　　(prī′ mȧ fā′ shĭ·ē)
pri·mal　　(prī′ măl)
pri·ma·ry　　(prī′ mĕr·ĭ)
　-ries
　pri·ma·ri·ly　　(prī′ mĕr·ĭ·lĭ)
pri·mate　　(prī′ mĭt)
prim·er　　(prĭm′ ēr)
　(book)
pri·me·val　　(prī·mē′ văl)
prim·i·tive　　(prĭm′ ĭ·tĭv)
pri·mo·gen·i·ture
　　　　　　(prī′ mō·jĕn′ ĭ·tûr)
pri·mor·di·al　　(prī·môr′ dĭ·ăl)
prim·rose　　(prĭm′ rōz′)
prince·ly　　(prĭns′ lĭ)
prin·cess　　(prĭn′ sĕs)
prin·ci·pal　　(prĭn′ sĭ·păl)
　(adj., highest-ranking;
　n., school official; see principle)
　prin·ci·pal·i·ty
　　　　　　(prĭn′ sĭ·păl′ ĭ·tĭ)
　prin·ci·pal·ly
prin·ci·ple　　(prĭn′ sĭ·p′l) n.
　(rule; see principal)
　prin·ci·pled
print·a·ble　　(prĭnt′ ȧ·b′l)
pri·or　　(prī′ ēr)
　pri·or·ess
　pri·or·i·ty　　(prī·ŏr′ ĭ·tĭ)
　-ties
prism　　(prĭz′m)
pris·mat·ic　　(prĭz·măt′ ĭk)
pris·on　　(prĭz′ ′n)
　pris·on·er
pris·sy　　(prĭs′ ĭ)
pris·tine　　(prĭs′ tēn)
prith·ee　　(prĭth′ ē)
pri·vate　　(prī′ vĭt)
　pri·va·cy　　(-vȧ·sĭ)
pri·va·tion　　(prī·vā′ shŭn)
priv·i·lege　　(prĭv′ ĭ·lĭj)
priv·y coun·cil　　(prĭv′ ĭ)
prize　　(prīz)
　priz·ing　　prize fight·er

prob·a·ble   (prŏb′ a·b'l)
   prob·a·bil·i·ty
          (prŏb′ a·bĭl′ ĭ·tĭ)
   prob·a·bly
pro·bate   (prō′ bāt)
   pro·ba·tion   (prō·bā′ shŭn)
   pro·ba·tion·er
          (prō·bā′ shŭn·ẽr)
probe   (prōb)
  prob·ing
prob·i·ty   (prŏb′ ĭ·tĭ)
prob·lem   (prŏb′ lĕm)
   prob·lem·at·i·cal
          (prŏb′ lĕm·ăt′ ĭ·kăl)
pro·bos·cis   (prō·bŏs′ ĭs)
pro·caine   (prō·kān′)
pro·ce·dure   (prō·sē′ dụr)
   pro·ce·dur·al
pro·ceed   (prō·sēd′) v.
pro·ceeds   (prō′ sēdz) n.
proc·ess   (prŏs′ ĕs)
pro·ces·sion   (prō·sĕsh′ ŭn)
  -ces·sion·al
pro·claim   (prō·klām′)
   proc·la·ma·tion
          (prŏk′ la·mā′ shŭn)
pro·cliv·i·ty   (prō·klĭv′ ĭ·tĭ)
  -ties
pro·con·sul   (prō·kŏn′ sŭl)
pro·cras·ti·nate
          (prō·krăs′ tĭ·nāt)
  -nat·ing
   pro·cras·ti·na·tion
          (prō·krăs′ tĭ·nā′ shŭn)
   pro·cras·ti·na·tor
pro·cre·ate   (prō′ krē·āt)
  -at·ing
   pro·cre·a·tion
          (prō′ krē·ā′ shŭn)
   pro·cre·a·tor
proc·tor   (prŏk′ tẽr)
proc·u·ra·tor   (prŏk′ û·rā′ tẽr)
   proc·u·ra·cy   (prŏk′ û·ra·sĭ)
pro·cure   (prō·kūr′)
  -cur·ing   pro·cure·ment
   pro·cur·er
prod·i·gal   (prŏd′ ĭ·găl)
   prod·i·gal·i·ty
          (prŏd′ ĭ·găl′ ĭ·tĭ)
pro·di·gious   (prō·dĭj′ ŭs)
prod·i·gy   (prŏd′ ĭ·jĭ)
  -gies
pro·duce   (prō·dūs′) v.
  -duc·ing   pro·duc·er
   pro·duc·i·ble

prod·uce   (prŏd′ ūs) n.
prod·uct   (prŏd′ ŭkt)
   pro·duc·tion   (prō·dŭk′ shŭn)
   pro·duc·tive   (prō·dŭk′ tĭv)
   pro·duc·tiv·i·ty
          (prō′ dŭk·tĭv′ ĭ·tĭ)
pro·fane   (prō·fān′)
  -fan·ing
   prof·a·na·tion
          (prŏf′ a·nā′ shŭn)
   pro·fan·i·ty   (prō·făn′ ĭ·tĭ)
pro·fess   (prō·fĕs′)
   pro·fess·ed·ly
pro·fes·sion   (prō·fĕsh′ ŭn)
   pro·fes·sion·al
pro·fes·sor   (prō·fĕs′ ẽr)
   pro·fes·sor·ate   (prō·fĕs′ ẽr·ĭt)
   pro·fes·so·ri·al
          (prō′ fĕ·sō′ rĭ·ăl)
prof·fer   (prŏf′ ẽr)
   prof·fered   prof·fer·ing
pro·fi·cient   (prō·fĭsh′ ĕnt)
   pro·fi·cien·cy
pro·file   (prō′ fīl)
prof·it   (prŏf′ ĭt)
  (gain; see *prophet*)
  -it·ed   -it·ing
   prof·it·a·ble
   prof·it-and-loss state·ment
   prof·it·eer   (prŏf′ ĭ·tẽr′)
   prof·it·less
prof·li·gate   (prŏf′ lĭ·gåt)
   prof·li·ga·cy   (-gå·sĭ)
pro·found   (prō·found′)
   pro·fun·di·ty   (prō·fŭn′ dĭ·tĭ)
  -ties
pro·fuse   (prō·fūs′)
   pro·fuse·ly
   pro·fu·sion   (-fū′ zhŭn)
pro·gen·i·tor   (prō·jĕn′ ĭ·tẽr)
prog·e·ny   (prŏj′ ĕ·nĭ)
prog·no·sis   (prŏg·nō′ sĭs)
  pl. prog·no·ses   (-sēz)
   prog·nos·tic   (prŏg·nŏs′ tĭk)
   prog·nos·ti·cate
          (prŏg·nŏs′ tĭ·kāt)
  -cat·ing
pro·gram   (prō′ grăm)
   pro·gram·mat·ic
          (prō′ grå·măt′ ĭk)
prog·ress   (prŏg′ rĕs) n.
pro·gress   (prō·grĕs′) v.
   pro·gres·sion   (prō·grĕsh′ ŭn)
   pro·gres·sive   -sive·ly

pro·hib·it (prô·hĭb′ ĭt)
-it·ed -it·ing
pro·hi·bi·tion (prō′ ĭ·bĭsh′ ŭn)
pro·hib·i·tive (prô·hĭb′ ĭ·tĭv)
pro·hib·i·to·ry
      (prô·hĭb′ ĭ·tō′ rĭ)
pro·ject (prô·jĕkt′) v.
pro·jec·tile (prô·jĕk′ tĭl)
pro·jec·tion (prô·jĕk′ shŭn)
pro·jec·tive (prô·jĕk′ tĭv)
pro·jec·tor (prô·jĕk′ tĕr)
proj·ect (prŏj′ ĕkt) n.
pro·lac·tin (prô·lăk′ tĭn)
pro·le·tar·i·an (prō′ lĕ·târ′ ĭ·ăn)
pro·le·tar·i·at
pro·lif·er·ate (prô·lĭf′ ĕr·āt)
-at·ing
pro·lif·er·a·tion
      (prô·lĭf′ ĕr·ā′ shŭn)
pro·lif·ic (prô·lĭf′ ĭk)
pro·lif·i·cal·ly
pro·lix (prô·lĭks′)
pro·lix·i·ty (prô·lĭk′ sĭ·tĭ)
pro·logue (prō′ lŏg)
pro·long (prô·lŏng′)
prom·e·nade (prŏm′ ĕ·nād′)
prom·i·nence (prŏm′ ĭ·nĕns)
-nent
pro·mis·cu·ous (prô·mĭs′ kû·ŭs)
prom·is·cu·i·ty
      (prŏm′ ĭs·kū′ ĭ·tĭ)
prom·ise (prŏm′ ĭs)
-is·ing
prom·is·so·ry (prŏm′ ĭ·sō′ rĭ)
prom·on·to·ry (prŏm′ ŭn·tō′ rĭ)
-ries
pro·mote (prô·mōt′)
-mot·ing pro·mot·er
pro·mo·tion
prompt (prŏmpt)
prompt·ness
pro·mul·gate (prô·mŭl′ gāt)
-gat·ing
pro·mul·ga·tion
      (prō′ mŭl·gā′ shŭn)
pro·mul·ga·tor
prone (prōn)
prone·ness
prong·horn (prŏng′ hôrn′)
pro·noun (prō′ noun)
pro·nounce (prô·nouns′)
-nounc·ing
pro·nounce·a·ble
pro·nounc·ed·ly
pro·nounce·ment

pro·nun·ci·a·tion
      (prô·nŭn′ sĭ·ā′ shŭn)
proof (proof)
proof·read·er
prop·a·gan·da (prŏp′ à·găn′ dà)
prop·a·gan·dist
prop·a·gan·dize
-diz·ing
prop·a·gate (prŏp′ à·gāt)
-gat·ing
prop·a·ga·tion
      (prŏp′ à·gā′ shŭn)
prop·a·ga·tor
pro·pane (prō′ pān)
pro·pel (prô·pĕl′)
-pelled -pel·ling
pro·pel·lant (prô·pĕl′ ănt)
pro·pel·ler
pro·pen·si·ty (prô·pĕn′ sĭ·tĭ)
-ties
prop·er (prŏp′ ĕr)
prop·er·ty (prŏp′ ĕr·tĭ)
-ties prop·er·tied
proph·e·cy (prŏf′ ĕ·sĭ) n.
-cies
proph·e·sy (prŏf′ ĕ·sī) v.
-sied -sy·ing
proph·e·si·er
proph·et (prŏf′ ĕt)
(seer; see profit)
proph·et·ess
pro·phet·ic (prô·fĕt′ ĭk)
pro·phy·lac·tic
      (prō′ fĭ·lăk′ tĭk)
pro·phy·lax·is (-lăk′ sĭs)
pro·pin·qui·ty (prô·pĭng′ kwĭ·tĭ)
pro·pi·ti·ate (prô·pĭsh′ ĭ·āt)
-at·ing
pro·pi·ti·a·tion
      (prô·pĭsh′ ĭ·ā′ shŭn)
pro·pi·tious (prô·pĭsh′ ŭs)
pro·pi·tious·ness
pro·po·nent (prô·pō′ nĕnt)
pro·por·tion (prô·pōr′ shŭn)
pro·por·tion·al
pro·por·tion·ate
      (-ĭt)
pro·pose (prô·pōz′)
-pos·ing pro·pos·al
prop·o·si·tion (prŏp′ ô·zĭsh′ ŭn)
-tion·al
pro·pound (prô·pound′)
pro·pri·e·tor (prô·prī′ ĕ·tĕr)
pro·pri·e·tar·y
      (prô·prī′ ĕ·tĕr′ ĭ)

pro·pri·e·ty   (prô·prī′ ĕ·tĭ)
-ties
pro·pul·sion   (prô·pŭl′ shŭn)
pro·pul·sive
pro·rate   (prō′ rāt′)
-rat·ing
pro·ra·tion   (prô·rā′ shŭn)
pro·sa·ic   (prô·zā′ ĭk)
pro·sa·i·cal·ly
pro·sce·ni·um   (prô·sē′ nĭ·ŭm)
pro·scribe   (prô·skrīb′)
   (condemn; see *prescribe*)
pro·scrip·tion   (-skrĭp′ shŭn)
pros·e·cute   (prŏs′ ĕ·kūt)
-cut·ing
pros·e·cu·tion
         (prŏs′ ĕ·kū′ shŭn)
pros·e·cu·tor
pros·e·lyte   (prŏs′ ĕ·līt)
pro·slav·er·y   (prô·slāv′ ēr·ĭ)
pros·o·dy   (prŏs′ ô·dĭ)
pros·pect   (prŏs′ pĕkt)
pro·spec·tive   (prô·spĕk′ tĭv)
   adj. (confidently expected; see *perspective*)
pro·spec·tus   (prô·spĕk′ tŭs)
pros·per   (prŏs′ pēr)
pros·per·i·ty   (prŏs·pēr′ ĭ·tĭ)
pros·per·ous
pros·tate gland   (prŏs′ tāt)
pros·ti·tute   (prŏs′ tĭ·tūt)
pros·ti·tu·tion
         (prŏs′ tĭ·tū′ shŭn)
pros·trate   (prŏs′ trāt)
pros·tra·tion   (prŏs·trā′ shŭn)
pros·y   (prōz′ ĭ)
pro·tag·o·nist   (prô·tăg′ ô·nĭst)
pro·tect   (prô·tĕkt′)
pro·tec·tion   (prô·tĕk′ shŭn)
pro·tec·tion·ism
pro·tec·tive tar·iff
pro·tec·tor   pro·tec·tress
pro·tec·tor·ate
         (prô·tĕk′ tēr·ĭt)
pro·té·gé   (prō′ tĕ·zhā)
pro·te·in   (prō′ tĕ·ĭn)
pro tem·po·re   (prō tĕm′ pô·rĕ)
pro·test   (prô·tĕst′) *v.*
         (prō′ tĕst) *n.*
prot·es·ta·tion
         (prŏt′ ĕs·tā′ shŭn)
Prot·es·tant   (prŏt′ ĕs·tănt)
pro·to·col   (prō′ tô·kŏl)
pro·ton   (prō′ tŏn)
pro·to·plasm   (prō′ tô·plăz′m)

pro·to·type   (prō′ tô·tīp)
pro·to·zo·an   (prō′ tô·zō′ ăn)
pro·to·zo·ic   (-ĭk)
pro·trude   (prô·trood′)
-trud·ing
pro·tru·sion   (prô·troo′ zhŭn)
pro·tu·ber·ance
         (prô·tū′ bēr·ăns)
-ant
proud   (proud)
prove   (proov)
prov·ing   prov·a·ble
prov·en
prov·en·der   (prŏv′ ĕn·dēr)
prov·erb   (prŏv′ ûrb)
pro·ver·bi·al   (prô·vûr′ bĭ·ăl)
pro·vide   (prô·vīd′)
-vid·ing   pro·vid·er
prov·i·dence   (prŏv′ ĭ·dĕns)
-dent
prov·i·den·tial
         (prŏv′ ĭ·dĕn′ shăl)
prov·ince   (prŏv′ ĭns)
pro·vin·cial   (prô·vĭn′ shăl)
-cial·ism
pro·vi·sion   (prô·vĭzh′ ŭn)
pro·vi·sion·al, -al·ly
pro·vi·sion·er
pro·vi·so   (prô·vī′ zō)
-sos
pro·voke   (prô·vōk′)
-vok·ing
prov·o·ca·tion
         (prŏv′ ô·kā′ shŭn)
pro·voc·a·tive   (prô·vŏk′ à·tĭv)
-tive·ly   pro·vok·er
pro·vost mar·shal
         (prō′ vō)
prow·ess   (prou′ ĕs)
prowl·er   (proul′ ēr)
prox·im·i·ty   (prŏks·ĭm′ ĭ·tĭ)
prox·y   (prŏk′ sĭ)
prox·ies
prude   (prood)
prud·er·y   prud·ish
pru·dent   (proo′ dĕnt)
-dence
prun·ing hook   (proon′ ĭng)
pru·ri·ent   (proor′ ĭ·ĕnt)
-ence
Prus·sian blue   (prŭsh′ ăn)
prus·sic ac·id   (prŭs′ ĭk)
pry   (prī)
pried   pry·ing
pry·er

psalm (säm)
  psalm·ist
  psal·mo·dy (săl′ mõ·dĭ)
Psal·ter (sôl′ tẽr)
pseu·do·nym (sū′ dõ·nĭm)
pso·ri·a·sis (sõ·rī′ ȧ·sĭs)
psy·chi·a·try (sī·kī′ ȧ·trĭ)
  psy·chi·at·ric (sī′ kĭ·ăt′ rĭk)
  psy·chi·a·trist (sī·kī′ ȧ·trĭst)
psy·chic (sī′ kĭk)
psy·cho- (sī′ kõ-)
  psy·cho·a·nal·y·sis
  psy·cho·an·a·lyt·i·cal
  psy·cho·an·a·lyze, -lyz·ing
  psy·cho·dra·ma
  psy·cho·mo·tor
  psy·cho·neu·ro·sis
  psy·cho·neu·rot·ic
  psy·cho·path·ic
  psy·cho·so·mat·ic
  psy·cho·sur·ger·y
  psy·cho·ther·a·peu·tics
  psy·cho·ther·a·py
psy·chol·o·gy (sī·kŏl′ õ·jĭ)
  psy·cho·log·i·cal
       (sī′ kõ·lŏj′ ĭ·kăl)
psy·chom·e·try (sī·kŏm′ ê·trĭ)
psy·cho·sis (sī·kõ′ sĭs)
  pl. -ses
ptar·mi·gan (tär′ mĭ·gȧn)
pter·o·dac·tyl (tẽr′ õ·dăk′ tĭl)
Ptol·e·my (tŏl′ ĕ·mĭ)
  Ptol·e·ma·ic (tŏl′ ê·mā′ ĭk)
pto·maine (tõ′ mān)
pu·ber·ty (pū′ bẽr·tĭ)
pu·bic (pū′ bĭk)
pub·lic (pŭb′ lĭk)
  pub·lic-ad·dress sys·tem
  pub·lic·ly
pub·li·ca·tion (pŭb′ lĭ·kā′ shŭn)
pub·li·cize (pŭb′ lĭ·sīz)
  -ciz·ing
  pub·li·cist (pŭb′ lĭ·sĭst)
  pub·lic·i·ty (pŭb·lĭs′ ĭ·tĭ)
pub·lish (pŭb′ lĭsh)
  pub·lish·a·ble pub·lish·er
puck·er (pŭk′ ẽr)
puck·ish (pŭk′ ĭsh)
pud·ding (pŏŏd′ ĭng)
pud·dle (pŭd′ ′l)
pudg·y (pŭj′ ĭ)
pueb·lo (pwĕb′ lõ)
  -los
pu·er·ile (pū′ ẽr·ĭl)
  pu·er·il·i·ty (pū′ ẽr·ĭl′ ĭ·tĭ)

Puer·to Ri·co (pwĕr′ tŭ rē′ kõ)
  Puer·to Ri·can
puf·fin (pŭf′ ĭn)
puff·y (pŭf′ ĭ)
  puff·i·ness
Pu·get (sound) (pū′ jĕt)
pu·gil·ist (pū′ jĭ·lĭst)
pug·na·cious (pŭg·nā′ shŭs)
  pug·nac·i·ty (pŭg·năs′ ĭ·tĭ)
pu·is·sance (pū′ ĭ·sȧns)
  pu·is·sant
pul·chri·tude (pŭl′ krĭ·tūd)
  pul·chri·tu·di·nous
      (pŭl′ krĭ·tū′ dĭ·nŭs)
pul·let (pŏŏl′ ĕt)
pul·ley (pŏŏl′ ĭ)
Pull·man car (pŏŏl′ mȧn)
pull-o·ver (pŏŏl′ õ′ vẽr)
pul·mo·nar·y (pŭl′ mõ·nĕr′ ĭ)
Pul·mo·tor (pŭl′ mõ′ tẽr)
pul·pit (pŏŏl′ pĭt)
pulp·wood (pŭlp′ wŏŏd′)
pul·que (pŏŏl′ kȧ)
pul·sate (pŭl′ sāt)
  -sat·ing
  pul·sa·tion (pŭl·sā′ shŭn)
pul·ver·ize (pŭl′ vĕr·īz)
  -iz·ing
pu·ma (pū′ mȧ)
pum·ice (pŭm′ ĭs)
pum·per·nick·el
      (pŭm′ pĕr·nĭk′ ′l)
pump·kin (pŭmp′ kĭn)
punch·ing bag (pŭnch′ ĭng)
punc·til·i·ous (pŭngk·tĭl′ ĭ·ŭs)
punc·tu·al (pŭngk′ tū·ȧl)
  -al·ly
  punc·tu·al·i·ty
      (pŭngk′ tū·ăl′ ĭ·tĭ)
punc·tu·ate (pŭngk′ tū·āt)
  -at·ing
  punc·tu·a·tion
      (pŭngk′ tū·ā′ shŭn)
punc·ture (pŭngk′ tūr)
  -tur·ing punc·tur·a·ble
pun·dit (pŭn′ dĭt)
pun·gent (pŭn′ jĕnt)
  pun·gen·cy
pun·ish (pŭn′ ĭsh)
  pun·ish·a·ble pun·ish·ment
pu·ni·tive (pū′ nĭ·tĭv)
pun·ster (pŭn′ stẽr)
pu·pa (pū′ pȧ)
  pl. pu·pae (-pē)
pu·pil (pū′ p′l)

pup·pet   (pŭp′ ĕt)
  pup·pet·ry
pup·py   (pŭp′ ĭ)
  pup·pies
pur·blind   (pûr′ blīnd′)
pur·chase   (pûr′ chĭs)
  -chas·ing pur·chas·a·ble
Pur·due (univ.)   (pĕr·dū′)
pure   (pūr)
  pure·bred pure·ly
  pu·ri·fi·ca·tion
       (pū′ rĭ·fĭ·kā′ shŭn)
  pu·ri·fi·er   pu·ri·fy
  -fied, -fy·ing pu·ri·ty
pu·rée   (pŭ·rā′)
pur·ga·tive   (pûr′ gȧ·tĭv)
pur·ga·to·ry   (pûr′ gȧ·tō′ rĭ)
  pur·ga·to·ri·al
       (pûr′ gȧ·tō′ rĭ·ȧl)
purge   (pûrj)
  purg·ing
Pu·ri·tan   (pū′ rĭ·tăn)
  pu·ri·tan·i·cal
      (pū′ rĭ·tăn′ ĭ·kăl)
purl   (pûrl)
  (knitting stitch; see *pearl*)
pur·lieu   (pûr′ lū)
pur·loin   (pûr·loin′)
pur·ple   (pûr′ p′l)
pur·port   (pûr·pōrt′) *v.*
       (pûr′ pōrt) *n.*
pur·pose   (pûr′ pŭs)
  pur·pose·ful, -ful·ly, -ful·ness
  pur·pose·less pur·pose·ly
  pur·pos·ive
purr   (pûr)
purse   (pûrs)
purs·lane   (pûrs′ lān)
pur·sue   (pĕr·sū′)
  -su·ing
  pur·su·ance   (pĕr·sū′ ȧns)
  pur·su·ant   pur·su·er
  pur·suit   (pĕr·sūt′)
pur·vey   (pûr·vā′)
  pur·vey·ance pur·vey·or
pur·view   (pûr′ vū)
pus   (pŭs)
  pus·sy
push   (pŏŏsh)
  push-but·ton *adj.*
  push·cart   push·o·ver
pu·sil·lan·i·mous
      (pū′ sĭ·lăn′ ĭ·mŭs)
  pu·sil·la·nim·i·ty
      (pū′ sĭ·lȧ·nĭm′ ĭ·tĭ)

puss·y·foot   (pŏŏs′ ĭ·fŏŏt′)
pus·tule   (pŭs′ tūl)
pu·tre·fy   (pū′ trĕ·fī)
  -fied   -fy·ing
  pu·tre·fac·tion
      (pū′ trĕ·făk′ shŭn)
pu·tres·cent   (pū·trĕs′ ĕnt)
pu·trid   (pū′ trĭd)
putt   (pŭt)
put·tee   (pŭt′ ĭ)
  (legging; see *putty*)
put·ty   (pŭt′ ĭ)
  (cement; see *puttee*)
puz·zle   (pŭz′ ′l)
  puz·zling   puz·zle·ment
Pyg·my   (pĭg′ mĭ)
py·lon   (pī′ lŏn)
py·lo·rus   (pī·lō′ rŭs)
  py·lor·ic   (pī·lŏr′ ĭk)
py·or·rhe·a   (pī′ ŏ·rĕ′ ȧ)
pyr·a·mid   (pĭr′ ȧ·mĭd)
pyre   (pīr)
Py·rex   (pī′ rĕks)
py·ri·tes   (pī·rī′ tēz)
py·ro·ma·ni·ac
      (pī′ rŏ·mā′ nĭ·ăk)
py·ro·tech·nics
      (pī′ rŏ·tĕk′ nĭks)
Pyr·rhic vic·to·ry
      (pĭr′ ĭk)
py·thon   (pī′ thŏn)

Q

quack   (kwăk)
  quack·er·y   quack grass
quad·ran·gle   (kwŏd′ răng′ g′l)
quad·rant   (kwŏd′ rȧnt)
quad·ri·lat·er·al
      (kwŏd′ rĭ·lăt′ ĕr·ȧl)
quad·roon   (kwŏd·rōōn′)
quad·ru·ped   (kwŏd′ rŏŏ·pĕd)
quad·ru·ple   (kwŏd′ rŏŏ·p′l)
quad·ru·plet   (kwŏd′ rŏŏ·plĕt)
quad·ru·pli·cate
      (kwŏd·rōō′ plĭ·kāt)
quaff   (kwáf)
quag·mire   (kwăg′ mīr)
quail   (kwāl)
quaint   (kwānt)
Quak·er   (kwāk′ ēr)
qual·i·fy   (kwŏl′ ĭ·fī)
  -fied   -fy·ing

qual·i·fi·ca·tion
    (kwŏl' ĭ·fĭ·kā' shŭn)
qual·i·fi·er
qual·i·ty (kwŏl' ĭ·tĭ)
  -ties
  qual·i·ta·tive (kwŏl' ĭ·tā' tĭv)
qualm (kwäm)
quan·da·ry (kwŏn' dȧ·rĭ)
  -ries
quan·ti·fy (kwŏn' tĭ·fī)
  -fied -fy·ing
quan·ti·ty (kwŏn' tĭ·tĭ)
  -ties
  quan·ti·ta·tive
    (kwŏn' tĭ·tā' tĭv)
quan·tum theory
    (kwŏn' tŭm)
quar·an·tine (kwŏr' ȧn·tēn)
quar·rel (kwŏr' ĕl)
  quar·reled quar·rel·ing
  quar·rel·some
quar·ry (kwŏr' ĭ)
  quar·ried quar·ry·ing
quar·ter (kwŏr' tēr)
  quar·ter·back quar·ter-deck
  quar·ter·mas·ter
quar·ter·ly (kwôr' tēr·lĭ)
  -lies
quar·tet (kwôr·tĕt')
quar·to (kwôr' tō)
  -tos
quartz (kwôrts)
quartz·ite (kwôrts' īt)
qua·si-ju·di·cial
    (kwā' sī·jōō·dĭsh' ȧl)
quat·rain (kwŏt' rān)
quat·re·foil (kăt' ēr·foil')
qua·ver (kwā' vēr)
quay (kwā)
quea·sy (kwē' zĭ)
  quea·si·ness
queen (kwēn)
  queen·ly -li·ness
queer (kwēr)
quell (kwĕl)
quench (kwĕnch)
quer·u·lous (kwĕr' ū·lŭs)
que·ry (kwēr' ĭ)
  -ries
quest (kwĕst)
ques·tion (kwĕs' chŭn)
  ques·tion·a·ble
  ques·tion·er ques·tion·ing·ly
  ques·tion·naire (kwĕs' chŭn·âr')
quet·zal (kĕt·säl')

queue (kū)
  (waiting line; see *cue*)
  queu·ing
quib·ble (kwĭb' 'l)
  quib·bling
quick (kwĭk)
  quick·en quick-fir·ing
  quick-freeze quick·sand
  quick·sil·ver quick-wit·ted
quid·di·ty (kwĭd' ĭ·tĭ)
quid pro quo (kwĭd prō kwō)
quies·cent (kwī·ĕs' ĕnt)
  quies·cence
qui·et (kwī' ĕt)
  qui·et·er qui·et·ly
  qui·e·tude (kwī' ĕ·tūd)
  qui·e·tus (kwī·ē' tŭs)
quill (kwĭl)
quilt (kwĭlt)
quince (kwĭns)
qui·nine (kwī' nīn)
quin·sy (kwĭn' zĭ)
quint·es·sence (kwĭnt·ĕs' ĕns)
quin·tet (kwĭn·tĕt')
quin·til·lion (kwĭn·tĭl' yŭn)
quin·tu·ple (kwĭn' tū·p'l)
quin·tu·plet (kwĭn' tū·plĕt)
quin·tu·pli·cate
    (kwĭn·tū' plĭ·kāt)
quip (kwĭp)
  quipped quip·ping
  quip·ster
quire (kwīr)
quirk (kwûrk)
quirt (kwûrt)
quis·ling (kwĭz' lĭng)
quit (kwĭt)
  quit·ting quit·tance
  quit·ter
quite (kwīt)
quiv·er (kwĭv' ēr)
Quix·ote, Don (kē·hō' tȧ, dŏn)
  quix·ot·ic (kwĭks·ŏt' ĭk)
quiz (kwĭz)
  quizzed quiz·zing
  quiz·zes
quiz·zi·cal (kwĭz' ĭ·kȧl)
  quiz·zi·cal·ly
quoits (kwoits)
quon·dam (kwŏn' dăm)
quo·rum (kwō' rŭm)
quo·ta (kwō' tȧ)
quote (kwōt)
  quot·ing quot·a·ble
  quo·ta·tion (kwō·tā' shŭn)

quoth (kwōth)
quo·tid·i·an (kwŏ·tĭd′ ĭ·ɑn)
quo·tient (kwō′ shĕnt)

R

rab·bet joint (răb′ ĕt)
rab·bi (răb′ ī)
 rab·bin·i·cal (rɑ·bĭn′ ĭ·kɑl)
rab·bit (răb′ ĭt)
 rab·bit fe·ver rab·bit punch
rab·ble (răb′ 'l)
Rab·e·lai·si·an
  (răb′ ĕ·lā′ zĭ·ɑn)
rab·id (răb′ ĭd)
ra·bies (rā′ bēz)
rac·coon (ră·kōōn′)
ra·cial (rā′ shɑl)
rac·ism (răs′ ĭz'm)
 rac·ist
rack·et (răk′ ĕt)
 rack·et·eer (răk′ ĕ·tēr′)
rac·on·teur (răk′ ŏn·tûr′)
rac·y (rās′ ĭ)
 rac·i·ness
ra·dar (rā′ där)
 ra·dar·scope (rā′ där)
Rad·cliffe (coll.) (răd′ klĭf)
ra·di·ant (rā′ dĭ·ɑnt)
 ra·di·ance
ra·di·ate (rā′ dĭ·āt)
 -at·ing
 ra·di·a·tion (rā′ dĭ·ā′ shŭn)
 ra·di·a·tor (rā′ dĭ·ā′ tĕr)
rad·i·cal (răd′ ĭ·kɑl)
 rad·i·cal·ism rad·i·cal·ly
ra·di·o·ac·tive (rā′ dĭ·ō·ăk′ tĭv)
 ra·di·o·ac·tiv·i·ty
  (-ăk·tĭv′ ĭ·tĭ)
ra·di·ol·o·gy (rā′ dĭ·ŏl′ ō·jĭ)
 ra·di·o·log·i·cal
  (rā′ dĭ·ō·lŏj′ ĭ·kɑl)
ra·di·o·sen·si·tive
  (rā′ dĭ·ō·sĕn′ sĭ·tĭv)
ra·di·o·sonde (rā′ dĭ·ō·sŏnd′)
ra·di·o·tel·e·gram
  (rā′ dĭ·ō·tĕl′ ĕ·grăm)
ra·di·o·ther·a·py
  (rā′ dĭ·ō·thĕr′ ɑ·pĭ)
rad·ish (răd′ ĭsh)
ra·di·um (rā′ dĭ·ŭm)
ra·di·us (rā′ dĭ·ŭs)
 pl. ra·di·i (-ī)
raf·fi·a (răf′ ĭ·ɑ)

raff·ish (răf′ ĭsh)
raf·fle (răf′ 'l)
 raf·fling
raft·er (răf′ tĕr)
rag·a·muf·fin (răg′ ɑ·mŭf′ ĭn)
rag·ged (răg′ ĕd)
rag·lan (răg′ lɑn)
ra·gout (ră·gōō′)
rag·weed (răg′ wēd′)
raid·er (rād′ ēr)
rail·ing (rāl′ ĭng)
rail·ler·y (rāl′ ēr·ĭ)
rail·road (rāl′ rōd′)
rail·way (rāl′ wā′)
rai·ment (rā′ mĕnt)
rain (rān)
 (falling drops of water; see *reign*,
 rein)
 rain·bow rain·coat
 rain·drop rain·fall
 rain gauge rain·proof
 rain·storm rain wa·ter
 rain·y
Rai·nier, Mt. (rɑ·nēr′)
raise (rāz)
 (awaken; see *raze*)
 rais·ing
rai·sin (rā′ z'n)
ra·ja (rā′ jɑ)
rak·ish (răk′ ĭsh)
ral·ly (răl′ ĭ)
 ral·lied ral·ly·ing
ram·bler (răm′ blēr)
ram·e·kin (răm′ ĕ·kĭn)
ram·i·fi·ca·tion
  (răm′ ĭ·fĭ·kā′ shŭn)
ram-jet en·gine (răm′ jĕt′)
ram·page (răm·pāj′)
 -pag·ing
ramp·ant (răm′ pɑnt)
ram·part (răm′ pärt)
ram·rod (răm′ rŏd′)
ram·shack·le (răm′ shăk′ 'l)
ranch house (rănch)
ran·cid (răn′ sĭd)
ran·cor (răng′ kĕr)
 ran·cor·ous (răng′ kĕr·ŭs)
ran·dom (răn′ dŭm)
range (rānj)
 rang·ing rang·er
 rang·y, rang·i·er, -i·est, -i·ness
ran·kle (răng′ k'l)
 -kling
ran·sack (răn′ săk)
ran·som (răn′ sŭm)

rant (rănt)
ra·pa·cious (rá·pā′ shŭs)
  ra·pac·i·ty (rá·păs′ ĭ·tĭ)
rap·id (răp′ ĭd)
  rap·id-fire
  ra·pid·i·ty (rá·pĭd′ ĭ·tĭ)
ra·pi·er (rā′ pĭ·ẽr)
rap·ine (răp′ ĭn)
Rap·pa·han·nock (riv.)
       (răp′ á·hăn′ ŭk)
rap·port (ră′ pôr′)
rapt (răpt)
rap·ture (răp′ tûr)
  rap·tur·ous (răp′ tûr·ŭs)
rar·e·fy (râr′ ĕ·fĭ)
  -fied -fy·ing
rare·ly (râr′ lĭ)
rar·i·ty (răr′ ĭ·tĭ)
  -ties
ras·cal (răs′ kǎl)
  ras·cal·i·ty (răs·kăl′ ĭ·tĭ)
  ras·cal·ly
rash·er (răsh′ ẽr)
rasp·ber·ry (răz′ bĕr′ ĭ)
  -ber·ries
rasp·ing (răs′ pĭng)
ratch·et (răch′ ĕt)
rate (rāt)
  rat·ing rat·a·ble
rath·skel·ler (räts′ kĕl′ ẽr)
rat·i·fy (răt′ ĭ·fĭ)
  -fied -fy·ing
  rat·i·fi·ca·tion
       (răt′ ĭ·fĭ·kā′ shŭn)
  rat·i·fi·er
ra·tio (rā′ shō)
ra·ti·oc·i·na·tion
       (răsh′ ĭ·ŏs′ ĭ·nā′ shŭn)
ra·tion·al (răsh′ ŭn·ǎl)
  ra·tion·al·is·tic
       (răsh′ ŭn·ǎl·ĭs′ tĭk)
  ra·tion·al·i·ty
       (răsh′ ŭn·ăl′ ĭ·tĭ)
ra·tion·ale (răsh′ ŭn·ăl′)
ra·tion·al·ize (răsh′ ŭn·ǎl·īz)
  -iz·ing
  ra·tion·al·i·za·tion
       (răsh′ ŭn·ǎl·ĭ·zā′ shŭn)
rat·tan (ră·tăn′)
rat·tle (răt′ ′l)
  rat·tling rat·tle·brained
  rat·tle·snake
rat·trap (răt′ trăp′)
rau·cous (rô′ kŭs)

rav·age (răv′ ĭj)
  -ag·ing
rav·el (răv′ ĕl)
  -eled -el·ing
rav·en·ing (răv′ ĕn·ĭng)
rav·en·ous (răv′ ĕn·ŭs)
ra·vi·o·li (rä·vyô·lĕ)
rav·ish·ing (răv′ ĭsh·ĭng)
raw (rô)
  raw·boned raw·hide
  raw ma·te·ri·al
ray·on (rā′ ŏn)
raze (răz)
  (demolish; see *raise*)
  raz·ing
ra·zor (rā′ zẽr)
re·ab·sorb (rē′ ǎb·sôrb′)
reach (rēch)
re·act (rē·ăkt′)
  re·ac·tion (rē·ăk′ shŭn)
  re·ac·tion·ar·y
      (rē·ăk′ shŭn·ĕr′ ĭ)
  re·ac·tor (rē·ăk′ tẽr)
read (rēd)
  (peruse; see *reed*)
read·a·ble (rēd′ á·b′l)
  read·a·bil·i·ty (rēd′ á·bĭl′ ĭ·tĭ)
read·er·ship (rēd′ ẽr·shĭp)
read·i·ly (rĕd′ ĭ·lĭ)
read·i·ness (rĕd′ ĭ·nĕs)
re·ad·just·ment (rē′ ǎ·jŭst′ mĕnt)
re·ad·mis·sion (rē′ ǎd·mĭsh′ ŭn)
re·ad·mit (rē′ ǎd·mĭt′)
  -mit·ted -mit·ting
  re·ad·mit·tance
      (rē′ ǎd·mĭt′ ǎns)
read·y (rĕd′ ĭ)
  read·ied read·y·ing
  read·i·er, -i·est, -i·ly, -i·ness
  read·y-made read·y-to-wear
re·af·firm (rē′ ǎ·fûrm′)
  re·af·fir·ma·tion
      (rē′ ăf·ẽr·mā′ shŭn)
re·a·gent (rē·ā′ jĕnt)
re·al (rē′ ǎl)
  (actual; see *reel*)
  re·al es·tate
  re·al·is·tic (rē′ ǎl·ĭs′ tĭk)
  re·al·i·ty (rē·ăl′ ĭ·tĭ)
re·al·ize (rē′ ǎl·īz)
  -iz·ing re·al·iz·a·ble
  re·al·i·za·tion
      (rē′ ǎl·ĭ·zā′ shŭn)
re·al·lo·ca·tion
      (rē′ ăl·ô·kā′ shŭn)

re·al·ly (rē′ ăl·ĭ)
realm (rĕlm)
re·al·ty (rē′ ăl·tĭ)
  re·al·tor (rē′ ăl·tēr)
ream (rēm)
reap·er (rēp′ ēr)
re·ap·pear·ance
        (rē′ ă·pēr′ ăns)
re·ap·point (rē′ ă·point′)
re·ar·ma·ment (rē·är′ mà·mĕnt)
re·ar·range·ment
        (rē′ ă·rānj′ mĕnt)
rea·son (rē′ z'n)
  -soned   -son·ing
  rea·son·a·ble
re·as·sem·ble (rē′ ă·sĕm′ b'l)
  -bling
re·as·sign (rē′ ă·sīn′)
re·as·sure (rē′ ă·shŏor′)
  -as·sur·ing
re·a·wak·en (rē′ à·wāk′ ĕn)
re·bate (rē′ bāt)
  -bat·ing
re·bel (rē·bĕl′) v.
  -belled   -bel·ling
reb·el (rĕb′ ĕl) n., adj.
re·bel·lion (rē·bĕl′ yŭn)
re·bel·lious (rē·bĕl′ yŭs)
re·birth (rē·bûrth′)
re·bound (rē·bound′)
re·buff (rē·bŭf′)
re·buke (rē·būk′)
re·bus (rē′ bŭs)
re·but (rē·bŭt′)
  -but·ted   -but·ting
  re·but·tal (rē·bŭt′ ăl)
re·cal·ci·trant (rē·kăl′ sĭ·trănt)
  -trance
re·call·a·ble (rē·kôl′ à·b'l)
re·cant (rē·kănt′)
re·cap (rē·kăp′)
  -capped   -cap·ping
  re·cap·pa·ble
re·ca·pit·u·late
        (rē′ kà·pĭt′ û·lāt)
  -lat·ing
re·ca·pit·u·la·tion
        (rē′ kà·pĭt′ û·lā′ shŭn)
re·cede (rē·sēd′)
  -ced·ing
re·ceipt (rē·sēt′)
re·ceive (rē·sēv′)
  -ceiv·ing   re·ceiv·a·ble
  re·ceiv·er·ship

re·cent (rē′ sĕnt)
  re·cen·cy   re·cent·ly
re·cep·ta·cle (rē·sĕp′ tà·k'l)
re·cep·tion (rē·sĕp′ shŭn)
  re·cep·tion·ist
re·cep·tive (rē·sĕp′ tĭv)
  re·cep·tive·ness
  re·cep·tiv·i·ty (rē· sĕp·tĭv′ ĭ·tĭ)
re·cep·tor (rē·sĕp′ tēr)
re·ces·sion (rē·sĕsh′ ŭn)
  re·ces·sion·al   re·ces·sive
rec·i·pe (rĕs′ ĭ·pē)
re·cip·i·ent (rē·sĭp′ ĭ·ĕnt)
  -ence
re·cip·ro·cal (rē·sĭp′ rŏ·kăl)
  re·cip·ro·cate, -cat·ing
  re·cip·ro·ca·tion
        (rē·sĭp′ rŏ·kā′ shŭn)
  rec·i·proc·i·ty (rĕs′ ĭ·prŏs′ ĭ·tĭ)
re·cite (rē·sīt′)
  -cit·ing   re·cit·al
  rec·i·ta·tion (rĕs′ ĭ·tā′ shŭn)
reck·less (rĕk′ lĕs)
reck·on (rĕk′ ŭn)
  reck·on·ing
re·claim (rē·klām′)
  re·claim·a·ble
  rec·la·ma·tion
        (rĕk′ là·mā′ shŭn)
re·clin·er (rē·klīn′ ēr)
re·cluse (rē·klōōs′)
rec·og·ni·tion (rĕk′ ŏg·nĭsh′ ŭn)
rec·og·nize (rĕk′ ŏg·nīz)
  -niz·ing   rec·og·niz·a·ble
re·coil (rē·koil′)
  -coiled   -coil·ing
re·col·lect (rĕk′ ŏ·lĕkt′)
rec·om·mend (rĕk′ ŏ·mĕnd′)
  rec·om·men·da·tion
        (rĕk′ ŏ·mĕn·dā′ shŭn)
re·com·mit (rē′ kŏ·mĭt′)
  -com·mit·ted   -com·mit·ting
  re·com·mit·ment
rec·om·pense (rĕk′ ŏm·pĕns)
rec·on·cile (rĕk′ ŏn·sīl)
  -cil·ing   rec·on·cil·a·ble
  rec·on·cil·i·a·tion
        (rĕk′ ŏn·sĭl′ ĭ·ā′ shŭn)
rec·on·dite (rĕk′ ŭn·dīt)
re·con·di·tioned
        (rē′ kŏn·dĭsh′ ŭnd)
re·con·nais·sance
        (rē·kŏn′ ĭ·sàns)
rec·on·noi·ter (rĕk′ ŏ·noi′ tēr)
re·con·sid·er (rē′ kŏn·sĭd′ ēr)

re·con·sti·tute   (rē·kŏn′ stǐ·tūt)
  -tut·ing
re·con·struc·tion
                (rē′ kŏn·strŭk′ shŭn)
re·con·vene   (rē′ kŏn·vēn′)
  -ven·ing
re·con·vert   (rē′ kŏn·vûrt′)
  re·con·ver·sion
                (rē′ kŏn·vûr′ shŭn)
re·cord   (rĕ·kôrd′) v.
rec·ord   (rĕk′ ĕrd) n.
re·coup   (rĕ·kōōp′)
re·course   (rĕ·kōrs′)
re·cov·er   (rĕ·kŭv′ ĕr)
  re·cov·er·a·ble
  re·cov·er·y
rec·re·ant   (rĕk′ rĕ·ănt)
rec·re·a·tion   (rĕk′ rĕ·ā′ shŭn)
re·crim·i·na·tion
                (rĕ·krĭm′ ĭ·nā′ shŭn)
re·cru·des·cence
                (rē′ krōō·dĕs′ ĕns)
re·cruit   (rĕ·krōōt′)
  re·cruit·er   re·cruit·ment
rec·tal   (rĕk′ tăl)
rec·tan·gle   (rĕk′ tăng′ g′l)
  rec·tan·gu·lar
                (rĕk·tăng′ gŭ·lēr)
rec·ti·fy   (rĕk′ tǐ·fī)
  -fied   -fy·ing
  rec·ti·fi·a·ble
rec·ti·lin·e·ar   (rĕk′ tǐ·lǐn′ ĕ·ēr)
rec·ti·tude   (rĕk′ tǐ·tūd)
rec·tor   (rĕk′ tēr)
  rec·tor·y   -tor·ies
rec·tum   (rĕk′ tŭm)
re·cum·bent   (rĕ·kŭm′ bĕnt)
  -ben·cy
re·cu·per·ate   (rĕ·kū′ pēr·āt)
  -at·ing
  re·cu·per·a·tion
                (rĕ·kū′ pēr·ā′ shŭn)
  re·cu·per·a·tive
                (rĕ·kū′ pēr·ā′ tǐv)
re·cur   (rĕ·kûr′)
  -curred   -cur·ring
  re·cur·rence   re·cur·rent
red   (rĕd)
  red-blood·ed   red·coat
  red·den   red·dish
  red-hand·ed   red·head
  red-hot   red-let·ter day
  red o·cher   red·skin
  red tape

re·deem   (rĕ·dēm′)
  re·deem·a·ble   re·deem·er
re·demp·tion   (rĕ·dĕmp′ shŭn)
re·demp·tive   (rĕ·dĕmp′ tǐv)
re·de·vel·op·ment
                (rē′ dĕ·vĕl′ ŭp·mĕnt)
red·in·gote   (rĕd′ ĭng·gōt)
re·dis·cov·er·y
                (rē′ dǐs·kŭv′ ĕr·ǐ)
red·o·lent   (rĕd′ ô·lĕnt)
  -lence
re·dou·ble   (rē·dŭb′ ′l)
  -bling
re·doubt·a·ble   (rĕ·dout′ à·b′l)
re·dound   (rĕ·dound′)
re·dress   (rĕ·drĕs′)
re·duce   (rĕ·dūs′)
  -duc·ing   re·duc·i·ble
  re·duc·tion   (rĕ·dŭk′ shŭn)
re·dun·dant   (rĕ·dŭn′ dănt)
  -dan·cy
re·du·pli·ca·tion
                (rĕ·dū′ plǐ·kā′ shŭn)
re·ech·o   (rē·ĕk′ ō)
reed   (rēd)
  (grass; see read)
re·ed·u·ca·tion
                (rē·ĕd′ û·kā′ shŭn)
reef   (rēf)
reek   (rēk)
reel   (rēl)
  (dance; see real)
re·e·lect   (rē′ ĕ·lĕkt′)
re·e·mer·gence   (rē′ ĕ·mûr′ jĕns)
re·em·ploy   (rē′ ĕm·ploi′)
re·en·act   (rē′ ĕn·ăkt′)
re·en·gage   (rē′ ĕn·gāj′)
  -gag·ing
re·en·list·ment   (rē′ ĕn·lǐst′ mĕnt)
re·en·ter   (rē·ĕn′ tēr)
  re·en·try   -tries
re·es·tab·lish   (rē′ ĕs·tăb′ lǐsh)
re·ex·am·ine   (rē′ ĕg·zăm′ ǐn)
  -in·ing
re·fer   (rĕ·fûr′)
  -ferred   -fer·ring
  ref·er·a·ble   (rĕf′ ĕr·à·b′l)
  re·fer·ral
ref·er·ee   (rĕf′ ĕr·ē′)
ref·er·ence   (rĕf′ ĕr·ĕns)
ref·er·en·dum   (rĕf′ ĕr·ĕn′ dŭm)
re·fill·a·ble   (rē·fĭl′ à·b′l)
re·fine   (rĕ·fīn′)
  -fin·ing   re·fine·ment
  re·fin·er·y   -er·ies

re·flect   (rĕ·flĕkt′)
  re·flec·tion   re·flec·tive
  re·flec·tive·ness
  re·flec·tor
re·flex   (rē′ flĕks)
re·for·est·a·tion
                    (rē′ fôr·ĕs·tā′ shŭn)
re·form   (rĕ·fôrm′)
  re·form·a·ble
  ref·or·ma·tion
                    (rĕf′ ôr·mā′ shŭn)
re·form·a·to·ry
                    (rĕ·fôr′ mȧ·tō′ rĭ)
  -ries
re·fract   (rĕ·frăkt′)
  re·frac·tion   re·frac·tive
re·frac·to·ry   (rĕ·frăk′ tô·rĭ)
re·frain   (rĕ·frān′)
re·fresh·ment   (rĕ·frĕsh′ mĕnt)
re·frig·er·ate   (rĕ·frĭj′ ĕr·āt)
  -at·ing   re·frig·er·a·tor
re·frig·er·a·tion
                    (rĕ·frĭj′ ĕr·ā′ shŭn)
ref·uge   (rĕf′ ūj)
ref·u·gee   (rĕf′ ū·jē′)
re·fund   (rē·fŭnd′)
re·fur·bish   (rē·fûr′ bĭsh)
re·fuse   (rĕ·fūz′) v.
  -fus·ing
  re·fus·al   (rĕ·fūz′ ăl)
ref·use   (rĕf′ ūs) adj., n.
re·fute   (rĕ·fūt′)
  -fut·ing
  ref·u·ta·ble   (rĕf′ ū·tȧ·b'l)
  ref·u·ta·tion   (rĕf′ ū·tā′ shŭn)
re·gal   (rē′ găl)
  -gal·ly
re·gale   (rĕ·gāl′)
  -gal·ing   re·gale·ment
re·ga·li·a   (rĕ·gā′ lĭ·ȧ)
re·gard·ing   (rĕ·gärd′ ĭng)
re·gat·ta   (rĕ·găt′ ȧ)
re·gen·er·a·tion
                    (rĕ·jĕn′ ĕr·ā′ shŭn)
re·gent   (rē′ jĕnt)
  -gen·cy
re·gime   (rȧ·zhēm′)
reg·i·men   (rĕj′ ĭ·mĕn)
reg·i·ment   (rĕj′ ĭ·mĕnt)
  reg·i·men·tal   (rĕj′ ĭ·mĕn′ tăl)
  reg·i·men·ta·tion
                    (rĕj′ ĭ·mĕn·tā′ shŭn)
re·gion   (rē′ jŭn)
  re·gion·al

reg·is·ter   (rĕj′ ĭs·tēr)
  reg·is·trant   (-trănt)
  reg·is·trar   (-trär)
  reg·is·tra·tion   (rĕj′ ĭs·trā′ shŭn)
  reg·is·try
re·gress   (rĕ·grĕs′)
  re·gres·sive   re·gres·sion
re·gret   (rĕ·grĕt′)
  -gret·ted   -gret·ting
  re·gret·ful, -ful·ly, -ful·ness
  re·gret·ta·ble
reg·u·lar   (rĕg′ û·lēr)
  reg·u·lar·i·ty   (rĕg′ û·lăr′ ĭ·tĭ)
  reg·u·lar·ize   -iz·ing
reg·u·late   (rĕg′ û·lāt)
  -lat·ing
  reg·u·la·tion   (rĕg′ û·lā′ shŭn)
  reg·u·la·tive   (rĕg′ û·lā′ tĭv)
  reg·u·la·tor   (rĕg′ û·lā′ tēr)
  reg·u·la·to·ry   (rĕg′ û·lȧ·tō′ rĭ)
re·gur·gi·tate   (rĕ·gûr′ jĭ·tāt)
  -tat·ing
re·ha·bil·i·tate
                    (rē′ hȧ·bĭl′ ĭ·tāt)
  -tat·ing
  re·ha·bil·i·ta·tion
                    (rē′ hȧ·bĭl′ ĭ·tā′ shŭn)
re·hearse   (rĕ·hûrs′)
  -hears·ing   re·hears·al
Reich   (rīk)
reign   (rān)
  (royal authority; see rain, rein)
re·im·burse·ment
                    (rē′ ĭm·bûrs′ mĕnt)
rein   (rān)
  (bridle strap; see rain, reign)
re·in·car·na·tion
                    (rē′ ĭn·kär·nā′ shŭn)
rein·deer   (rān′ dēr′)
re·in·force·ment
                    (rē′ ĭn·fôrs′ mĕnt)
re·in·sert   (rē′ ĭn·sûrt′)
re·in·state·ment
                    (rē′ ĭn·stāt′ mĕnt)
re·in·te·grate   (rĕ·ĭn′ tĕ·grāt)
  -grat·ing
re·in·tro·duce   (rē′ ĭn·trô·dūs′)
  -duc·ing
re·in·vest   (rē′ ĭn·vĕst′)
re·is·sue   (rē·ĭsh′ ū)
  -is·su·ing
re·it·er·ate   (rĕ·ĭt′ ĕr·āt)
  -at·ing
  re·it·er·a·tion
                    (rĕ·ĭt′ ĕr·ā′ shŭn)

re·ject (rĕ·jĕkt′)
  re·jec·tion (rĕ·jĕk′ shŭn)
re·joice (rĕ·jois′)
  -joic·ing
re·join·der (rĕ·join′ dĕr)
re·ju·ve·nate (rĕ·jōō′ vĕ·nāt)
  -nat·ing
  re·ju·ve·na·tion
         (rĕ·jōō′ vĕ·nā′ shŭn)
re·kin·dle (rĕ·kĭn′ d′l)
  -dling
re·lapse (rĕ·lăps′)
  -laps·ing
re·late (rĕ·lāt′)
  -lat·ing
re·la·tion (rĕ·lā′ shŭn)
  re·la·tion·ship
rel·a·tive (rĕl′ a·tĭv)
  rel·a·tiv·i·ty (rĕl′ a·tĭv′ ĭ·tĭ)
re·lax (rĕ·lăks′)
  re·lax·a·tion (rē′ lăk·sā′ shŭn)
  re·lax·er
re·lay (rĕ·lā′)
  -layed   -lay·ing
re·lease (rĕ·lēs′)
  -leas·ing
rel·e·gate (rĕl′ ĕ·gāt)
  -gat·ing
  rel·e·ga·tion (rĕl′ ĕ·gā′ shŭn)
re·lent (rĕ·lĕnt′)
  re·lent·less
rel·e·vant (rĕl′ ĕ·vănt)
  -vance,   -van·cy
re·li·a·ble (rĕ·lī′ a·b′l)
  re·li·a·bil·i·ty (rĕ·lī′ a·bĭl′ ĭ·tĭ)
re·li·ant (rĕ·lī′ ănt)
  re·li·ance
rel·ic (rĕl′ ĭk)
re·lief (rĕ·lēf′)
re·lieve (rĕ·lēv′)
  -liev·ing   re·liev·a·ble
re·li·gion (rĕ·lĭj′ ŭn)
  re·li·gious
re·lin·quish (rĕ·lĭng′ kwĭsh)
rel·ish (rĕl′ ĭsh)
re·lo·ca·tion (rē′ lō·kā′ shŭn)
re·luc·tant (rĕ·lŭk′ tănt)
  -tance
re·ly (rĕ·lī′)
  -lied   -ly·ing
Rem·brandt van Rijn
        (rĕm′ brănt văn rīn′)
re·main (rĕ·mān′)
  re·main·der
re·mand (rĕ·mánd′)

re·mark·a·ble (rĕ·märk′ ka·b′l)
re·mar·riage (rĕ·măr′ ĭj)
rem·e·dy (rĕm′ ĕ·dĭ)
  -died, -dies, -dy·ing
  re·me·di·a·ble (rĕ·mē′ dĭ·a·b′l)
  re·me·di·al (rĕ·mē′ dĭ·ăl)
  rem·e·di·less
re·mem·ber (rĕ·mĕm′ bĕr)
  re·mem·brance (-brăns)
re·mind·er (rĕ·mīn′ dĕr)
rem·i·nisce (rĕm′ ĭ·nĭs′)
  -nis·cing   rem·i·nis·cence
  rem·i·nis·cent
re·miss (rĕ·mĭs′)
re·mis·sion (rĕ·mĭsh′ ŭn)
re·mit (rĕ·mĭt′)
  -mit·ted   -mit·ting
  re·mit·ta·ble   re·mit·tal
  re·mit·tance   re·mit·tent
  re·mit·tor
rem·nant (rĕm′ nănt)
re·mod·el (rē·mŏd′ ′l)
  -eled   -el·ing
re·mon·strate (rĕ·mŏn′ strāt)
  -strat·ing
  re·mon·strance
        (rĕ·mŏn′ străns)
re·morse (rĕ·môrs′)
  re·morse·ful, -ful·ly, -ful·ness
  re·morse·less
re·mote (rĕ·mōt′)
  -mote·ly   -mote·ness
re·move (rĕ·mōōv′)
  -mov·ing   re·mov·a·ble
  re·mov·al
re·mu·ner·a·tion
      (rĕ·mū′ nĕr·ā′ shŭn)
  re·mu·ner·a·tive
        (rĕ·mū′ nĕr·ā′ tĭv)
ren·ais·sance (rĕn′ ĕ·zäns′)
  Ren·ais·sance art
ren·der (rĕn′ dĕr)
ren·dez·vous (rän′ dĕ·vōō)
ren·di·tion (rĕn·dĭsh′ ŭn)
ren·e·gade (rĕn′ ĕ·gād)
re·nege (rĕ·nĕg′)
  -neg·ing
re·ne·go·ti·ate
      (rē′ nĕ·gō′ shĭ·āt)
  -at·ing
  re·ne·go·ti·a·ble
      (rē′ nĕ·gō′ shĭ·a·b′l)
re·new·al (rĕ·nū′ ăl)
ren·net (rĕn′ ĕt)

re·nom·i·nate   (rē·nŏm′ ĭ·nāt)
  -nat·ing
re·nounce   (rē·nouns′)
  -nounc·ing   re·nounce·ment
ren·o·vate   (rĕn′ ō·vāt)
  -vat·ing
  ren·o·va·tion   (rĕn′ ō·vā′ shŭn)
re·nown   (rē·noun′)
  re·nowned   (-nound)
rent·al   (rĕn′ tăl)
re·nun·ci·a·tion
            (rē·nŭn′ sĭ·ā′ shŭn)
re·oc·cu·py   (rē·ŏk′ ū·pī)
  -pied   -py·ing
  re·oc·cu·pa·tion
            (rē′ ŏk·ū·pā′ shŭn)
re·o·pen   (rē·ō′ pĕn)
re·or·der   (rē·ôr′ dēr)
re·or·gan·i·za·tion
            (rē′ ôr·găn·ĭ·zā′ shŭn)
re·pair   (rē·pâr′)
rep·a·ra·tion   (rĕp′ a·rā′ shŭn)
rep·ar·tee   (rĕp′ ēr·tē′)
re·past   (rē·păst′)
re·pay   (rē·pā′)
  -paid   -pay·ing
  re·pay·a·ble   re·pay·ment
re·peal   (rē·pēl′)
  -pealed   -peal·ing
  re·peal·a·ble
re·peat   (rē·pēt′)
  re·peat·ed·ly   re·peat·er
re·pel   (rē·pĕl′)
  -pelled   -pel·ling
  re·pel·lent
re·pent   (rē·pĕnt′)
  re·pent·ance
re·per·cus·sion
            (rē′ pēr·kŭsh′ ŭn)
rep·er·toire   (rĕp′ ēr·twär′)
rep·er·to·ry   (rĕp′ ēr·tō′ rĭ)
rep·e·ti·tion   (rĕp′ ĕ·tĭsh′ ŭn)
  rep·e·ti·tious
re·pet·i·tive   (rē·pĕt′ ĭ·tĭv)
re·place   (rē·plās′)
  -plac·ing   re·place·a·ble
  re·place·ment
re·plen·ish   (rē·plĕn′ ĭsh)
re·plete   (rē·plēt′)
  re·ple·tion   (rē·plē′ shŭn)
rep·li·ca   (rĕp′ lĭ·ka)
rep·li·ca·tion   (rĕp′ lĭ·kā′ shŭn)
re·ply   (rē·plī′)
  -plied   -ply·ing

re·port   (rē·pōrt′)
  re·port·a·ble   re·port·er
  rep·or·to·ri·al   (rĕp′ ôr·tō′ rĭ·ǎl)
re·pose   (rē·pōz′)
  -pos·ing   re·pose·ful
re·pos·i·to·ry   (rē·pŏz′ ĭ·tō′ rĭ)
  -ries
re·pos·sess   (rē′ pō·zĕs′)
  re·pos·ses·sion
rep·re·hend   (rĕp′ rē·hĕnd′)
rep·re·hen·si·ble
            (rĕp′ rē·hĕn′ sĭ·b′l)
rep·re·sent   (rĕp′ rē·zĕnt′)
  rep·re·sent·a·ble
  rep·re·sen·ta·tion
            (rĕp′ rē·zĕn·tā′ shŭn)
  rep·re·sent·a·tive
            (rĕp′ rē·zĕn′ tá·tĭv)
re·press   (rē·prĕs′)
  re·pres·sion   (rē·prĕsh′ ŭn)
  re·pres·sive
re·prieve   (rē·prēv′)
  -priev·ing
re·pri·mand   (rĕp′ rĭ·mànd)
re·pris·al   (rē·prīz′ ǎl)
re·proach·ful   (rē·prōch′ fŏŏl)
  -ful·ly   -ful·ness
rep·ro·bate   (rĕp′ rō·bāt)
  rep·ro·ba·tion
            (rĕp′ rō·bā′ shŭn)
re·pro·duce   (rē′ prō·dūs′)
  -duc·ing   re·pro·duc·i·ble
  re·pro·duc·tion
            (rē′ prō·dŭk′ shŭn)
  re·pro·duc·tive
            (rē′ prō·dŭk′ tĭv)
re·proof   (rē·prōōf′) n.
re·prove   (rē·prōōv′) v.
  -prov·ing
rep·tile   (rĕp′ tĭl)
  rep·til·i·an   (rĕp·tĭl′ ĭ·ǎn)
re·pub·lic   (rē·pŭb′ lĭk)
  re·pub·li·can
re·pu·di·ate   (rē·pū′ dĭ·āt)
  -at·ing
  re·pu·di·a·tion
            (rē·pū′ dĭ·ā′ shŭn)
re·pug·nant   (rē·pŭg′ nǎnt)
  -nance
re·pulse   (rē·pŭls′)
  -puls·ing
  re·pul·sion   (rē·pŭl′ shŭn)
  re·pul·sive   -sive·ness
rep·u·ta·ble   (rĕp′ ū·tá·b′l)

rep·u·ta·bil·i·ty
(rĕp′ ū·tȧ·bĭl′ ĭ·tĭ)
rep·u·ta·tion (rĕp′ ū·tā′ shŭn)
re·put·ed·ly (rē·pūt′ ĕd·lĭ)
re·quest (rē·kwĕst′)
re·qui·em (rē′ kwĭ·ĕm)
re·quire·ment (rē·kwīr′ mĕnt)
req·ui·site (rĕk′ wĭ·zĭt)
req·ui·si·tion (rĕk′ wĭ·zĭsh′ ŭn)
re·quite (rē·kwīt′)
re·quit·al
re·sale (rē·sāl′)
re·sal·a·ble
re·scind (rē·sĭnd′)
re·scis·sion (rē·sĭzh′ ŭn)
res·cue (rĕs′ kū)
-cu·ing
re·search (rē·sûrch′)
re·sem·ble (rē·zĕm′ b'l)
-bling
re·sem·blance (rē·zĕm′ blȧns)
re·sent (rē·zĕnt′)
re·sent·ful, -ful·ly, -ful·ness
re·sent·ment
res·er·va·tion (rĕz′ ēr·vā′ shŭn)
re·serve (rē·zûrv′)
-serv·ing re·serv·ed·ly
re·serv·ist
res·er·voir (rĕz′ ēr·vwôr)
re·set·tle·ment (rē·sĕt′ 'l·mĕnt)
re·side (rē·zīd′)
-sid·ing
res·i·dent (rĕz′ ĭ·dĕnt)
res·i·dence
res·i·den·tial (rĕz′ ĭ·dĕn′ shȧl)
res·i·due (rĕz′ ĭ·dū)
re·sid·u·al (rē·zĭd′ ū·ȧl)
re·sign (rē·zīn′)
res·ig·na·tion (rĕz′ ĭg·nā′ shŭn)
re·sign·ed·ly (rē·zīn′ ĕd·lĭ)
re·sil·i·ent (rē·zĭl′ ĭ·ĕnt)
re·sil·i·ence
res·in (rĕz′ ĭn)
res·in·ous (rĕz′ ĭ·nŭs)
re·sist (rē·zĭst′)
re·sis·tance (rē·zĭs′ tȧns)
re·sis·tant re·sist·i·ble
re·sis·tive re·sis·tor
res·o·jet en·gine
(rĕz′ ô·jĕt′)
res·o·lute (rĕz′ ô·lūt)
-lute·ly
res·o·lu·tion (rĕz′ ô·lū′ shŭn)
re·solve (rē·zŏlv′)
-solv·ing re·solv·a·ble

res·o·nant (rĕz′ ô·nȧnt)
-nance res·o·na·tor
re·sort (rē·zôrt′)
re·sound (rē·zound′)
re·source (rē·sōrs′)
re·source·ful, -ful·ly, -ful·ness
re·spect (rē·spĕkt′)
re·spect·a·bil·i·ty
(rē·spĕk′ tȧ·bĭl′ ĭ·tĭ)
re·spect·a·ble (rē·spĕk′ tȧ·b'l)
re·spect·er
re·spect·ful, -ful·ly, -ful·ness
re·spect·ing
re·spec·tive -tive·ly
res·pi·ra·tion (rĕs′ pĭ·rā′ shŭn)
res·pi·ra·tor (rĕs′ pĭ·rā′ tēr)
re·spir·a·to·ry (rē·spīr′ ȧ·tō′ rĭ)
res·pite (rĕs′ pĭt)
re·splend·ent (rē·splĕn′ dĕnt)
-ence
re·spond·ent (rē·spŏn′ dĕnt)
re·sponse (rē·spŏns′)
re·spon·si·ble (rē·spŏn′ sĭ·b'l)
re·spon·si·bil·i·ty
(rē·spŏn′ sĭ·bĭl′ ĭ·tĭ)
re·spon·sive (rē·spŏn′ sĭv)
-sive·ness
res·tau·rant (rĕs′ tô·rȧnt)
res·tau·ra·teur (rĕs′ tô·rä·tûr′)
(NOTE: no n)
rest·ful (rĕst′ fool)
-ful·ly -ful·ness
res·ti·tu·tion (rĕs′ tĭ·tū′ shŭn)
res·tive (rĕs′ tĭv)
rest·less (rĕst′ lĕs)
res·to·ra·tion (rĕs′ tô·rā′ shŭn)
re·stor·a·tive (rē·stōr′ ȧ·tĭv)
re·strain (rē·strān′)
re·strain·a·ble re·straint
re·strict (rē·strĭkt′)
re·stric·tion (rē·strĭk′ shŭn)
re·stric·tive (rē·strĭk′ tĭv)
re·sult (rē·zŭlt′)
re·sult·ant
re·sume (rē·zūm′) v.
-sum·ing
ré·su·mé (rā′ zŭ·mā′) n.
re·sump·tion (rē·zŭmp′ shŭn)
re·sur·gent (rē·sûr′ jĕnt)
-gence
res·ur·rect (rĕz′ ŭ·rĕkt′)
res·ur·rec·tion
(rĕz′ ŭ·rĕk′ shŭn)
re·sus·ci·tate (rē·sŭs′ ĭ·tāt)
-tat·ing

re·sus·ci·ta·tion
      (rê·sŭs′ ĭ·tā′ shŭn)
re·sus·ci·ta·tor
      (rê·sŭs′ ĭ·tā′ tẽr)
re·tail (rē′ tāl)
  re·tail·er
re·tain (rê·tān′)
  re·tain·a·ble   re·tain·er
re·tal·i·ate (rê·tăl′ ĭ·āt)
  -at·ing
re·tal·i·a·tion
      (rê·tăl′ ĭ·ā′ shŭn)
re·tal·i·a·tive (rê·tăl′ ĭ·ā′ tĭv)
re·tal·i·a·to·ry
      (rê·tăl′ ĭ·à·tō′ rĭ)
re·tard (rê·tärd′)
  re·tar·da·tion (rê′ tär·dā′ shŭn)
retch (rĕch)
  (vomit; see *wretch*)
re·ten·tion (rê·tĕn′ shŭn)
  re·ten·tive
ret·i·cent (rĕt′ ĭ·sĕnt)
  -cence
ret·i·na (rĕt′ ĭ·nà)
ret·i·nue (rĕt′ ĭ·nū)
re·tire (rê·tīr′)
  -tir·ing   re·tire·ment
re·tort (rê·tôrt′)
re·touch (rē·tŭch′)
re·tract (rê·trăkt′)
  re·tract·a·ble   re·trac·tion
re·tread (rē·trĕd′)
re·treat (rê·trēt′)
re·trench·ment (rê·trĕnch′ mĕnt)
re·tri·al   – (rê·trī′ ăl)
ret·ri·bu·tion (rĕt′ rĭ·bū′ shŭn)
re·trieve (rê·trēv′)
  -triev·ing   re·triev·a·ble
  re·triev·er
ret·ro·ac·tive (rĕt′ rō·ăk′ tĭv)
ret·ro·ces·sion (rĕt′ rō·sĕsh′ ŭn)
ret·ro·gres·sion
      (rĕt′ rō·grĕsh′ ŭn)
ret·ro·spect (rĕt′ rō·spĕkt)
ret·ro·ver·sion (rĕt′ rō·vûr′ shŭn)
re·turn (rê·tûrn′)
  re·turn·a·ble
re·un·ion (rê·ūn′ yŭn)
re·u·nite (rē′ û·nīt′)
  -nit·ing
rev (rĕv)
  revved   rev·ving
re·vamp (rē·vămp′)
re·veal (rê·vēl′)
  -vealed   -veal·ing

re·veal·a·ble   re·veal·ment
rev·eil·le (rĕv′ ĕ·lĭ)
rev·el (rĕv′ ĕl)
  -eled   -el·ing
  rev·el·ry
rev·e·la·tion (rĕv′ ĕ·lā′ shŭn)
re·venge (rê·vĕnj′)
  -veng·ing   re·venge·ful
re·e·nue (rĕv′ ĕ·nū)
re·ver·ber·ate (rê·vûr′ bẽr·āt)
  -at·ing
  re·ver·ber·a·tion
      (rê·vûr′ bẽr·ā′ shŭn)
re·vere (rê·vẽr′)
  -ver·ing
rev·er·end (rĕv′ ẽr·ĕnd)
rev·er·ent (rĕv′ ẽr·ĕnt)
  rev·er·ence
rev·er·ie (rĕv′ ẽr·ĭ)
re·verse (rê·vûrs′)
  -vers·ing   re·ver·sal
  re·vers·i·ble
re·ver·sion (rê·vûr′ shŭn)
re·vert (rê·vûrt′)
  re·vert·i·ble
re·view (rê·vū′)
  (survey; see *revue*)
re·vile (rê·vīl′)
  -vil·ing   re·vile·ment
re·vise (rê·vīz′)
  -vis·ing
  re·vi·sion (rê·vĭzh′ ŭn)
re·vi·tal·ize (rê·vī′ tǎl·īz)
  -iz·ing
  re·vi·tal·i·za·tion
      (rē′ vī·tǎl·ĭ·zā′ shŭn)
re·viv·al (rê·vīv′ ăl)
  re·viv·al·ist
re·vive (rê·vīv′)
  -viv·ing
re·viv·i·fy (rê·vīv′ ĭ·fī)
  -fied,   -fy·ing
re·voke (rê·vōk′)
  -vok·ing
  rev·o·ca·ble (rĕv′ ô·kà·b'l)
re·volt·ing (rê·vōl′ tĭng)
rev·o·lu·tion (rĕv′ ô·lū′ shŭn)
  rev·o·lu·tion·ar·y
  rev·o·lu·tion·ize, -iz·ing
re·volv·er (rê·vŏl′ vẽr)
re·vue (rê·vū′)
  (burlesque; see *review*)
re·vul·sion (rê·vŭl′ shŭn)
re·ward (rê·wôrd′)

rhap·so·dy (răp′ sŏ·dĭ)
-dies
rhap·so·dize -diz·ing
Rhen·ish (rĕn′ ĭsh)
rhe·o·stat (rē′ ŏ·stăt)
rhet·o·ric (rĕt′ ŏ·rĭk)
rhe·tor·i·cal (rĕ·tŏr′ ĭ·kăl)
rhet·o·ri·cian (rĕt′ ŏ·rĭsh′ ăn)
rheu·ma·tism (rōō′ mä·tĭz′m)
rheu·mat·ic (rōō·măt′ ĭk)
rheu·ma·toid ar·thri·tis
(rōō′ mä·toid)
Rh fac·tor (är′ ăch′)
Rh-neg·a·tive Rh-pos·i·tive
rhine·stone (rīn′ stōn′)
Rhine wine (rīn)
rhi·ni·tis (rī·nī′ tĭs)
rhi·noc·er·os (rī·nŏs′ ĕr·ŏs)
Rhode Is·land (rōd ī′ lănd)
abbr. R. I.
Rhode Is·land·er
Rho·de·sia (rŏ·dē′ zhä)
Rhodes schol·ar·ship
(rōdz)
rhom·bus (rŏm′ bŭs)
rhu·barb (rōō′ bärb)
rhyme (rīm)
rhym·ing
rhythm (rĭth′m)
rhyth·mic (rĭth′ mĭk)
-mi·cal
Ri·al·to (rĭ·ăl′ tō)
rib·ald (rĭb′ ăld)
rib·ald·ry (-rĭ)
rib·bing (rĭb′ĭng)
rib·bon (rĭb′ŭn)
ri·bo·fla·vin (rī′ bō·flā′ vĭn)
rich·es (rĭch′ ĕz)
rick·ets (rĭk′ ĕts)
rick·et·y (rĭk′ ĕ·tĭ)
rick·ey (rĭk′ ĭ)
rick·rack (rĭk′ răk′)
rick·sha (rĭk′ shä)
ric·o·chet (rĭk′ ŏ·shā′)
-cheted -chet·ing
rid·dance (rĭd′ ăns)
rid·dle (rĭd′ ′l)
rid·dling
ride (rīd)
rid·ing
rid·den (rĭd′ ′n)
ridge (rĭj)
rid·i·cule (rĭd′ ĭ·kūl)
-cul·ing
ri·dic·u·lous (rĭ·dĭk′ û·lŭs)

rife (rīf)
rif·fle (rĭf′ ′l)
(shuffle; see rifle)
rif·fling
riff·raff (rĭf′ răf′)
ri·fle (rī′ f′l)
(gun; see riffle)
-fling ri·fle·man
rift (rĭft)
rig·ging (rĭg′ ĭng)
right (rīt)
(correct; see rite, wright, write)
right an·gle right-an·gled
right·eous (rī′ chŭs)
right·ful, -ful·ly, -ful·ness
right-hand·ed
right of way (pl. rights of way)
rig·id (rĭj′ ĭd)
ri·gid·i·ty (rĭ·jĭd′ ĭ·tĭ)
rig·ma·role (rĭg′ mä·rōl)
rig·or (rĭg′ ĕr)
ri·gor mor·tis (rĭg′ ĕr môr′ tĭs)
rig·or·ous (rĭg′ ĕr·ŭs)
ring (rĭng)
ring·lead·er ring·mas·ter
ring·side ring·worm
rinse (rĭns)
rins·ing
Rio de Ja·nei·ro,
Bra·zil (rē′ ō dĕ jä·nā′ rō)
Ri·o Grande (riv.)
(rē′ ŏ gränd′)
ri·ot (rī′ ŭt)
-ot·ed -ot·ing
ri·o·ter ri·ot·ous
rip·cord (rĭp′ kôrd′)
rip·en (rĭp′ ĕn)
rip·ple (rĭp′ ′l)
rip·pling
rip-roar·ing (rĭp′ rôr′ ĭng)
Rip van Win·kle
(rĭp′ văn wĭng′ k′l)
rise (rīz)
ris·ing
ris·en (rĭz′ ′n)
risk·y (rĭs′ kĭ)
risk·i·ness
ri·sot·to (rĕ·sôt′ tō)
ris·qué (rĭs·kā′)
rite (rīt)
(liturgy; see right, wright, write)
rit·u·al (rĭt′ û·ăl)
rit·u·al·is·tic (rĭt′ û·ăl·ĭs′ tĭk)
rit·u·al·ly

ri·val (rī′ vål)
-valed -val·ing
ri·val·ry
Ri·vie·ra (rĕ·vyä′ rä)
riv·u·let (rĭv′ ū·lĕt)
roach (rōch)
road (rōd)
road·bed road·block
road·house road·run·ner
road·way
roam (rōm)
roan (rōn)
Ro·a·noke, Va. (rō′ å·nōk)
roar·ing (rōr′ ĭng)
roast (rōst)
rob·ber·y (rŏb′ ĕr·ĭ)
rob·ber·ies
rob·in (rŏb′ ĭn)
Rob·in·son Cru·soe
(rŏb′ ĭn·s'n krōō′ sō)
ro·bot (rō′ bŏt)
ro·bust (rō·bŭst′)
rock (rŏk)
rock bot·tom n.
rock-bot·tom adj.
rock gar·den rock-ribbed
rock salt
Rock·e·fel·ler, John
(rŏk′ ĕ·fĕl′ ĕr)
rock·er (rŏk′ ĕr)
rock·et (rŏk′ ĕt)
rock·et launch·er
rock·et·ry
rock·y (rŏk′ ĭ)
rock·i·er, -i·est, -i·ly, -i·ness
Rock·ies (mts.)
ro·co·co (rō·kō′ kō)
ro·dent (rō′ dĕnt)
ro·de·o (rō′ dĕ·ō)
roe (rō)
(doe; eggs; see row)
roent·gen (rûnt′ gĕn)
rogue (rōg)
ro·guer·y (rō′ gĕr·ĭ)
rogues' gal·ler·y
ro·guish
roil (roil)
roil·ing
roist·er (rois′ tĕr)
role (rōl)
(actor's part; see roll)
roll (rōl)
(revolve; see role)
roll·back roll call

roll·er (rōl′ ĕr)
roll·er bear·ing
roll·er coast·er
roll·er skate
rol·lick·ing (rŏl′ ĭk·ĭng)
rol·y-pol·y (rō′ lĭ·pō′ lĭ)
ro·maine let·tuce
(rō·mān′)
Ro·man Cath·o·lic (church)
(rō′ mǎn kǎth′ ō·lĭk)
ro·mance (rō·mǎns′)
Ro·man·esque (rō′ mǎn·ĕsk′)
Ro·ma·nia (rō·mǎn′ yå)
ro·man·tic (rō·mǎn′ tĭk)
ro·man·ti·cal·ly
ro·man·ti·cize (-tĭ·sīz)
Ro·me·o (rō′ mĕ·ō)
romp·er (rŏmp′ ĕr)
ron·do (rŏn′ dō)
-dos
roof·ing (rōōf′ ĭng)
rook·er·y (rōōk′ ĕr·ĭ)
-er·ies
rook·ie (rōōk′ ĭ)
room (rōōm)
room·ette (rōōm·ĕt′)
room·ful room·i·ness
room·mate room·y
Roo·se·velt, Frank·lin D.
(rō′ zĕ·vĕlt)
roost·er (rōōs′ tĕr)
root (rōōt)
(stem; see rout, route)
root beer root·er
root·less
rop·y (rōp′ ĭ)
rop·i·ness
Roque·fort cheese
(rōk′ fĕrt)
Ror·schach test (rōr′ shäk)
ro·sa·ry (rō′ zå·rĭ)
-ries
rose (rōz)
rose·bud rose-col·ored
rose·mar·y rose wa·ter
rose·wood
ro·se·ate (rō′ zĕ·åt)
Ro·set·ta stone (rō·zĕt′ å)
ro·sette (rō·zĕt′)
Rosh Ha·sha·na
(rōsh hä·shä′ nä)
ros·in (rŏz′ ĭn)
ros·ter (rŏs′ tĕr)
ros·trum (rŏs′ trŭm)
pl. ros·tra

ros·y (rōz′ ĭ)
  ros·i·er, -i·est, -i·ly, -i·ness
ro·ta·ry (rō′ tȧ·rĭ)
ro·tate (rō′ tāt)
  -tat·ing
  ro·ta·tion (rȯ·tā′ shŭn)
  ro·ta·tor
ro·te·none (rō′ t′n·ōn)
ro·tis·se·rie (rȯ′ tĕs·rē′)
ro·to·gra·vure (rō′ tȯ·grȧ·vūr′)
ro·to sec·tion (rō′ tȯ)
rot·ten (rŏt′ ′n)
  rot·ten·ness
ro·tund (rȯ·tŭnd′)
  ro·tun·di·ty (rȯ·tŭn′ dĭ·tĭ)
ro·tun·da (rȯ·tŭn′ dȧ)
rou·é (rōō·ā′)
rouge (rōōzh)
rough (rŭf)
  rough·age
  rough-and-read·y
  rough·hew   rough·house
  rough·neck   rough·rid·er
  rough·shod
rou·lette (rōō·lĕt′)
round (round)
  round·a·bout   round rob·in
  round-shoul·dered
  round steak   Round Ta·ble
  round trip   round·up
roun·de·lay (roun′ dĕ·lā)
rouse (rouz)
  rous·ing
Rous·seau, Jean Jacques
        (rōō′ sō′)
roust·a·bout (roust′ ȧ·bout′)
rout (rout)
  (conquer; see route)
route (rōōt)
  (path; see root, rout)
  rout·ing
rou·tine (rōō·tēn′)
rov·er (rōv′ ẽr)
row (rō)
  (propel with oars; see roe)
row·boat (rō′ bŏt′)
row·dy (rou′ dĭ)
  row·dy·ish
roy·al (roi′ ȧl)
  roy·al·ist   roy·al·ty
rub·ber (rŭb′ ẽr)
  rub·ber·neck   rub·ber-stamp
rub·bish (rŭb′ ĭsh)
rub·ble (rŭb′ ′l)
rub·down (rŭb′ doun′)

ru·bel·la (rōō·bĕl′ ȧ)
Ru·bi·con (rōō′ bĭ·kŏn)
ru·bric (rōō′ brĭk)
ruche (rōōsh)
  ruch·ing
ruck·sack (rŭk′ săk′)
ruc·tion (rŭk′ shŭn)
rud·der (rŭd′ ẽr)
rud·dy (rŭd′ ĭ)
  rud·di·ness
rude (rōōd)
  rude·ly   rude·ness
ru·di·ment (rōō′ dĭ·mĕnt)
  ru·di·men·ta·ry
       (rōō′ dĭ·mĕn′ tȧ·rĭ)
rue (rōō)
  ru·ing
  rue·ful, -ful·ly, -ful·ness
ruffed grouse (rŭft)
ruf·fi·an (rŭf′ ĭ·ᵭn)
ruf·fle (rŭf′ ′l)
  ruf·fling   ruf·fly
Rug·by foot·ball
       (rŭg′ bĭ)
rug·ged (rŭg′ ĕd)
ru·in (rōō′ ĭn)
  ru·in·a·tion (rōō′ ĭ·nā′ shŭn)
  ru·in·ous (rōō′ ĭ·nŭs)
rul·er (rōōl′ ẽr)
rul·ing (rōōl′ ĭng)
rum·ba (rōōm′ bä)
rum·ble (rŭm′ b′l)
  -bling
ru·mi·nant (rōō′ mĭ·nᵭnt)
ru·mi·nate (rōō′ mĭ·nāt)
  -nat·ing
  ru·mi·na·tion
       (rōō′ mĭ·nā′ shŭn)
rum·mage (rŭm′ ĭj)
rum·my (rŭm′ ĭ)
ru·mor (rōō′ mẽr)
rum·ple (rŭm′ p′l)
  -pling
rum·pus room (rŭm′ pŭs)
rum·run·ner (rŭm′ rŭn′ ẽr)
run (rŭn)
  ran   run·ning
  run·a·way   run-down
  run-on   run·way
run·ci·ble spoon
       (rŭn′ sĭ·b′l)
rune (rōōn)
  ru·nic
run·ner-up (rŭn′ ẽr·ŭp′)
rup·ture (rŭp′ tŭr)

ru·ral (rŏor′ dl)
ruse (rōoz)
rus·set (rŭs′ ĕt)
Rus·sian (rŭsh′ ån)
rus·tic (rŭs′ tĭk)
rus·tle (rŭs′ ′l)
   -tling   rus·tler
rust·y (rŭs′ tĭ)
   rust·i·ness
ru·ta·ba·ga (rŏo′ tå·bă′ gå)
ruth·less (rōoth′ lĕs)
rye (rī)
Ryu·kyu (is.) (rĭ·ōo′ kū)

S

Sab·bath (săb′ dth)
sab·bat·i·cal (så·băt′ ĭ·kdl)
sa·ber (sā′ bĕr)
sa·ble (sā′ b′l)
sab·o·tage (săb′ ŏ·täzh′)
   sab·o·teur (săb′ ŏ·tûr′)
sac·cha·rine (săk′ å·rĭn)
sac·er·do·tal (săs′ ĕr·dō′ tdl)
sa·chem (sā′ chĕm)
sa·chet (să·shā′)
sack·cloth (săk′ klŏth′)
sa·cral (sā′ krdl)
sac·ra·ment (săk′ rå·mĕnt)
   sac·ra·men·tal
   (săk′ rå·mĕn′ tdl)
sa·cred (sā′ krĕd)
sac·ri·fice (săk′ rĭ·fīs)
   -fic·ing
   sac·ri·fi·cial (săk′ rĭ·fĭsh′ dl)
   sac·ri·fi·cial·ly
sac·ri·lege (săk′ rĭ·lĕj)
   sac·ri·le·gious (săk′ rĭ·lē′ jŭs)
sa·cro·il·i·ac (sā′ krŏ·ĭl′ ĭ·ăk)
sac·ro·sanct (săk′ rŏ·săngkt)
sad·den (săd′ ′n)
sad·dle (săd′ ′l)
   sad·dling   sad·dle·bag
   sad·dle·soap
sad·ism (săd′ ĭz′m)
   sad·ist
   sa·dis·tic (så·dĭs′ tĭk)
   -ti·cal·ly
sa·fa·ri (så·fä′ rĭ)
safe (sāf)
   safe·break·er   safe-con·duct
   safe-de·pos·it box
   safe·guard   safe·keep·ing

safe·ty (sāf′ tĭ)
   safe·ty belt   safe·ty ra·zor
   safe·ty valve   safe·ty zone
saf·fron (săf′ rŭn)
sa·ga (sä′ gå)
sa·ga·cious (så·gā′ shŭs)
   sa·gac·i·ty (så·găs′ ĭ·tĭ)
sage·brush (sāj′ brŭsh′)
sa·hib (sä′ ĭb)
sail (sāl)
   sailed   sail·ing
   sail·boat   sail·or
saint·ed (sān′ tĕd)
St. John (riv., Me.)
   (sånt jŏn′)
St. Johns (riv., Fla.)
   (sånt jŏnz′)
St. Law·rence (sånt lô′ rĕns)
Saint Pat·rick's (sånt păt′ rĭks)
St. Vi·tus's dance
   (sånt vī′ tŭs·ĭz)
sa·laam (så·läm′)
sa·la·cious (så·lā′ shŭs)
sal·ad (săl′ dd)
sal·a·man·der (săl′ å·măn′ dĕr)
sa·la·mi (sä·lä′ mĕ)
sal·a·ry (săl′ å·rĭ)
   -ried   -ries
sale (sāl)
   sal·a·ble   sales·man
   sales tax
sa·li·ent (sā′ lĭ·ĕnt)
   sa·li·ence
sa·line (sā′ līn)
   sa·lin·i·ty (så·lĭn′ ĭ·tĭ)
sa·li·va (så·lī′ vå)
   sal·i·var·y (săl′ ĭ·vĕr′ ĭ)
   sal·i·vate (săl′ ĭ·vāt)
   -vat·ing
   sal·i·va·tion (săl′ ĭ·vā′ shŭn)
sal·low (săl′ ō)
sal·ma·gun·di (săl′ må·gŭn′ dĭ)
salm·on (săm′ ŭn)
sa·lon (så′ lôn′)
   (drawing room; see saloon)
sa·loon (så·lōon′)
   (alehouse; see salon)
sal·so·da (săl′ sō′ då)
salt·cel·lar (sôlt′ sĕl′ ĕr)
salt·pe·ter (sôlt′ pē′ tĕr)
salt·y (sôl′ tĭ)
   salt·i·ness
sa·lu·bri·ous (så·lū′ brĭ·ŭs)
sal·u·tar·y (săl′ û·tĕr′ ĭ)

sa·lu·ta·to·ri·an

    (sȧ·lū' tȧ·tō' rĭ·ǎn)

sa·lute   (sȧ·lūt')

  -lut·ing

  sal·u·ta·tion   (săl' û·tā' shŭn)

sal·vage   (săl' vĭj)

  (save; see *selvage*)

  -vag·ing

sal·va·tion   (săl·vā' shŭn)

salve   (săv)

sal·vo   (săl' vō)

  -vos

Sa·mar·i·tan   (sȧ·măr' ĭ·tǎn)

same·ness   (sām' nĕs)

Sa·mo·a   (sȧ·mō' ȧ)

sam·o·var   (săm' ŏ·vär)

sam·pan   (săm' păn)

sam·ple   (săm' p'l)

  -pling   sam·pler

sam·u·rai   (săm' ŏŏ·rī)

san·a·to·ri·um   (săn' ȧ·tō' rĭ·ŭm)

  pl. san·a·to·ri·a

sanc·ti·fy   (săngk' tĭ·fī)

  -fied,   -fy·ing

sanc·ti·mo·ni·ous

    (săngk' tĭ·mō' nĭ·ŭs)

sanc·tion   (săngk' shŭn)

sanc·ti·ty   (săngk' tĭ·tĭ)

  -ties

sanc·tu·ar·y   (săngk' tū·ĕr' ĭ)

  -ar·ies

sanc·tum sanc·to·rum

    (săngk' tŭm săngk·tō' rŭm)

sand   (sănd)

  sand·bag   sand bar

  sand·blast   sand·bur

  sand-lot base·ball

  sand·pa·per   sand·stone

  sand·storm

san·dal   (săn' dǎl)

  san·dal·wood

sand·wich   (sănd' wĭch)

sane   (sān)

  sane·ly

San·for·ized   (săn' fẽr·ĭzd)

San Fran·cis·co,

  Calif.   (săn' frăn·sĭs' kō)

sang-froid   (sän' frwä')

san·guine   (săng' gwĭn)

  san·gui·nar·y   (săng' gwĭ·nĕr' ĭ)

  san·guin·e·ous

    (săng·gwĭn' ê·ŭs)

san·i·tar·i·um   (săn' ĭ·târ' ĭ·ŭm)

san·i·tar·y   (săn' ĭ·tĕr' ĭ)

san·i·ta·tion   (săn' ĭ·tā' shŭn)

san·i·ty   (săn' ĭ·tĭ)

San·skrit   (săn' skrĭt)

sans-ser·if   (sănz' sĕr' ĭf)

San·ta Claus   (săn' tȧ klôz)

San·ti·a·go, Chile

    (săn' tĭ·ä' gō)

São Pau·lo, Bra·zil

    (souɴm pou' lŏŏ)

sa·pi·ent   (sā' pĭ·ĕnt)

  -ence

sap·o·dil·la   (săp' ŏ·dĭl' ȧ)

sap·phire   (săf' īr)

sap·sa·go   (săp' sȧ·gō)

Sar·a·cen   (săr' ȧ·sĕn)

sar·casm   (sär' kăz'm)

  sar·cas·tic   (sär·kăs' tĭk)

sar·coph·a·gus

    (sär·kŏf' ȧ·gŭs)

  pl. sar·coph·a·gi (-jī)

sar·dine   (sär·dēn')

sar·don·ic   (sär·dŏn' ĭk)

  sar·don·i·cal·ly

sar·gas·so   (sär·găs' ō)

sa·ri   (sä' rē)

sa·rong   (sȧ·rông')

sar·sa·pa·ril·la

    (săs' pȧ·rĭl' ȧ)

sar·to·ri·al   (sär·tō' rĭ·ǎl)

Sas·katch·e·wan,

  Can.   (săs·kăch' ě·wŏn)

sas·sa·fras   (săs' ȧ·frăs)

Sa·tan   (sā' tǎn)

  sa·tan·ic   (sȧ·tăn' ĭk)

satch·el   (săch' ĕl)

sate   (sāt)

  sat·ing

sa·teen   (sȧ·tēn')

sat·el·lite   (săt' ě·līt)

sa·ti·ate   (sā' shĭ·āt)

  -at·ing

  sa·ti·a·ble   (sā' shĭ·ȧ·b'l)

  sa·ti·e·ty   (sȧ·tī' ě·tĭ)

sat·in   (săt' ĭn)

sat·ire   (săt' īr)

  sa·tir·ic   (sȧ·tĭr' ĭk)

  sat·i·rist   (săt' ĭ·rĭst)

  sat·i·rize   (săt' ĭ·rīz)

  -riz·ing

sat·is·fac·tion   (săt' ĭs·făk' shŭn)

sat·is·fac·to·ry

    (săt' ĭs·făk' tŏ·rĭ)

  sat·is·fac·to·ri·ly, -i·ness

sat·is·fy   (săt' ĭs·fī)

  -fied   -fy·ing

sat·u·rate   (săt′ û·rāt)
  -rat·ing
  sat·u·ra·tion   (săt′ û·rā′ shŭn)
sat·ur·nine   (săt′ ẽr·nīn)
sat·yr   (săt′ ẽr)
sauce   (sôs)
  sauce·pan   sau·cer
  sau·cy
Sa·u·di A·ra·bi·a
                  (sà·ōō′ dĭ à·rā′ bĭ·à)
sauer·kraut   (sour′ krout′)
Sault Sainte Ma·rie,
  Mich.   (sōō′ sânt má·rē′)
saun·ter   (sôn′ tẽr)
sau·sage   (sô·sĭj)
sau·té   (sō·tā′)
  sau·téed   sau·té·ing
sau·terne   (sō·tûrn′)
sav·age   (săv′ ĭj)
  sav·age·ly
  sav·age·ry   (săv′ ĭj·rĭ)
sa·van·na   (sà·văn′ à)
Sa·van·nah, Ga.
                  (sà·văn′ à)
sa·vant   (sá·vänt′)
sav·ior   (sāv′ yẽr)
sa·voir-faire   (sá′ vwár′ fâr′)
sa·vor   (sā′ vẽr)
  -vored   -vor·ing
  sa·vor·less   sa·vor·y
sa·voy cab·bage
                  (sà·voi′)
saw·mill   (sô′ mĭl′)
saw-toothed   (sô′ tōōtht′)
saw·yer   (sô′ yẽr)
sax·o·phone   (săk′ sô·fōn)
scab·bard   (skăb′ ẽrd)
sca·brous   (skā′ brŭs)
scaf·fold·ing   (skăf′ ŭld·ĭng)
scal·a·wag   (skăl′ à·wăg)
scald   (skôld)
scale   (skāl)
  scal·ing   scal·a·ble
  scal·lion   (skăl′ yŭn)
  scal·lop   (skŏl′ ŭp)
  scal·loped
scalp   (skălp)
scal·pel   (skăl′ pĕl)
scal·y   (skāl′ ĭ)
  scal·i·ness
scam·per   (skăm′ pẽr)
scan   (skăn)
  scanned   scan·ning
scan·dal   (skăn′ dál)
  scan·dal·ize   -iz·ing

scan·dal·mon·ger (-mŭng′ gẽr)
scan·dal·ous   (-ŭs)
Scan·di·na·vi·an
                  (skăn′ dĭ·nā′ vĭ·ăn)
scant·y   (skăn′ tĭ)
  scant·i·ly   -i·ness
scape·goat   (skāp′ gōt′)
scar   (skär)
  scarred   scar·ring
scarce   (skârs)
  scarce·ly
  scar·ci·ty   (skâr′ sĭ·tĭ)
scare   (skâr)
  scar·ing   scare·crow
  scar·y
scarf   (skärf)
  pl. scarves
scar·let   (skär′ lĕt)
scathe   (skāth)
  scath·ing·ly
scat·ter·brain   (skăt′ ẽr·brān′)
scav·enge   (skăv′ ĕnj)
  -eng·ing   scav·en·ger
sce·nar·i·o   (sē·nâr′ ĭ·ō)
  sce·nar·ist   (sē·nâr′ ĭst)
scene   (sēn)
  scen·er·y   (sēn′ ẽr·ĭ)
  sce·nic   (sē′ nĭk)
scent   (sĕnt)
scep·ter   (sĕp′ tẽr)
sched·ule   (skĕd′ ŭl)
  -ul·ing
scheme   (skēm)
  schem·ing
  sche·mat·ic   (skĕ·măt′ ĭk)
  schem·er
Sche·nec·ta·dy,   (skĕ·nĕk′ tá·dĭ)
  N. Y.
scher·zo   (skĕr′ tsō)
schism   (sĭz′m)
  schis·mat·ic   (sĭz·măt′ ĭk)
schist   (shĭst)
schiz·oid   (skĭz′ oid)
schiz·o·phre·ni·a
                  (skĭz′ ô·frē′ nĭ·à)
  schiz·o·phren·ic (-frĕn′ ĭk)
schmaltz   (shmôlts)
schnapps   (shnăps)
schnau·zer   (shnou′ zẽr)
schol·ar   (skŏl′ ẽr)
  schol·ar·ship
scho·las·tic   (skô·lăs′ tĭk)
  scho·las·ti·cism
                  (skô·lăs′ tĭ·sĭz′m)

school (skōōl)
  school·boy   school·house
  school·mas·ter school·room
  school·teach·er
  school·work
schoon·er (skōōn′ ẽr)
schoi·tische (shŏt′ ĭsh)
schuss (shŏŏs)
Schwei·tzer, Al·bert
         (shvī′ tsẽr)
sci·at·i·ca (sī·ăt′ ĭ·ká)
  sci·at·ic nerve
sci·ence (sī′ ĕns)
  sci·en·tif·ic (sī′ ĕn·tĭf′ ĭk)
  -i·cal·ly   sci·en·tist
scim·i·tar (sĭm′ ĭ·tẽr)
scin·til·late (sĭn′ tĭ·lāt)
  -til·lat·ing
  scin·til·la·tion (sĭn′ tĭ·lā′ shŭn)
sci·on (sī′ ŭn)
scis·sors (sĭz′ ẽrz)
scle·ro·sis (sklĕ·rō′ sĭs)
scoff (skŏf)
scone (skōn)
scoot·er (skōōt′ ẽr)
scope (skōp)
scorch (skôrch)
scorn·ful (skôrn′ fŏŏl)
  -ful·ly   -ful·ness
Scor·pi·o (skôr′ pĭ·ō)
scor·pi·on (skôr′ pĭ·ŭn)
Scotch (skŏch)
scot-free (skŏt′ frē′)
Scots·man (skŏts′ mán)
Scot·tish (skŏt′ ĭsh)
scoun·drel (skoun′ drĕl)
  scoun·drel·ly
scour (skour)
scourge (skûrj)
scout·mas·ter (skout′ más′ tẽr)
scowl (skoul)
  scowled   scowl·ing
scrab·ble (skrăb′ ′l)
scrag·gy (skrăg′ ĭ)
scram·ble (skrăm′ b′l)
  -bling
scrap·book (skrăp′ bŏŏk′)
scrap·py (skrăp′ ĭ)
scratch (skrăch)
scrawl (skrôl)
  scrawl·y
scraw·ny (skrô′ ni)
scream (skrēm)
screech (skrēch)
screen·play (skrēn′ plā′)

screw (skrōō)
scrib·ble (skrĭb′ ′l)
  scrib·bling
scribe (skrīb)
scrim·mage (skrĭm′ ĭj)
  scrim·mag·ing
scrimp (skrĭmp)
scrip (skrĭp)
  (money; see *script*)
script (skrĭpt)
  (manuscript; see *scrip*)
  script-writ·er
scrip·ture (skrĭp′ tûr)
  scrip·tur·al
scroll (skrōl)
scrounge (skrounj)
  scroung·ing
scrub·by (skrŭb′ ĭ)
scruff (skrŭf)
scru·ple (skrōō′ p′l)
  scru·pu·lous (skrōō′ pŭ·lŭs)
scru·ti·ny (skrōō′ tĭ·nĭ)
  -nies
  scru·ti·nize   -niz·ing
scuff (skŭf)
scuf·fle (skŭf′ ′l)
  scuf·fling
scul·ler·y (skŭl′ ẽr·ĭ)
scul·lion (skŭl′ yŭn)
sculp·tor (skŭlp′ tẽr)
  sculp·tress   sculp·ture
  sculp·tur·al
scum (skŭm)
  scum·my
scup·per·nong (skŭp′ ẽr·nŏng)
scur·ril·ous (skûr′ ĭ·lŭs)
scur·ry (skûr′ ĭ)
  scur·ried   scur·ry·ing
scur·vy (skûr′ vĭ)
scut·tle (skŭt′ ′l)
  scut·tling
  scut·tle·butt (skŭt′ ′l·bŭt′)
scythe (sīth)
sea (sē)
  sea·board   sea·coast
  sea·far·ing   sea·go·ing
  sea gull   sea·man
  sea·plane   sea·scape
  sea·shore   sea·sick·ness
  sea·side   sea ur·chin
  sea wall   sea·ward
  sea·wor·thy
seal·skin (sēl′ skĭn′)
seam (sēm)
  seam·less   seam·y

seam·stress (sĕm′ strĕs)
sé·ance (sā′ äns′)
sear (sēr)
search (sûrch)
  search·light   search war·rant
sea·son (sē′ z′n)
  sea·son·a·ble
  sea·son·al   -al·ly
  sea·son·ing   sea·son tick·et
Se·at·tle, Wash. (sē·ăt′ ′l)
se·cede (sē·sēd′)
  -ced·ing
se·ces·sion (sē·sĕsh′ ŭn)
  se·ces·sion·ist
se·clude (sē·klōōd′)
  -clud·ing
  se·clu·sion (-klōō′ zhŭn)
sec·ond (sĕk′ ŭnd)
  sec·ond·ar·y   sec·ond-class
  sec·ond fid·dle   sec·ond·hand
  sec·ond na·ture
  sec·ond-rate   sec·ond sight
se·cret (sē′ krĕt)
  se·cre·cy (sē′ krĕ·sĭ)
  se·cre·tive (sē·krē′ tĭv)
sec·re·tar·i·at (sĕk′ rē·târ′ ĭ·ăt)
sec·re·tar·y (sĕk′ rē·tĕr′ ĭ)
  -tar·ies
  sec·re·tar·i·al (sĕk′ rē·târ′ ĭ·ăl)
  sec·re·tar·y·ship
se·crete (sē·krēt′)
  -cret·ing
  se·cre·tion (sē·krē′ shŭn)
se·cre·tive (sē·krē′ tĭv)
sect (sĕkt)
sec·tar·i·an (sĕk·târ′ ĭ·ăn)
sec·tion (sĕk′ shŭn)
  sec·tion·al
sec·tor (sĕk′ tĕr)
sec·u·lar (sĕk′ ū·lĕr)
  sec·u·lar·ize   -iz·ing
se·cure (sē·kūr′)
  -cur·ing
  se·cure·ly   -cure·ness
  se·cu·ri·ty   -ties
se·dan (sē·dăn′)
se·date (sē·dāt′)
  se·date·ly
se·da·tion (sē·dā′ shŭn)
sed·a·tive (sĕd′ à·tĭv)
sed·en·tar·y (sĕd′ ĕn·tĕr′ ĭ)
sedge (sĕj)
sed·i·ment (sĕd′ ĭ·mĕnt)
  sed·i·men·ta·ry
      (sĕd′ ĭ·mĕn′ tà·rĭ)

sed·i·men·ta·tion
      (sĕd′ ĭ·mĕn·tā′ shŭn)
se·di·tion (sē·dĭsh′ ŭn)
  se·di·tious (-ŭs)
se·duce (sē·dūs′)
  -duc·ing   se·duce·ment
  se·duc·i·ble
se·duc·tion (sē·dŭk′ shŭn)
  se·duc·tive   -tive·ly
  se·duc·tress
sed·u·lous (sĕd′ ū·lŭs)
seed·ling (sēd′ lĭng)
seed·y (sēd′ ĭ)
  seed·i·ness
see·ing (sē′ ĭng)
seem·ing·ly (sēm′ ĭng·lĭ)
seem·ly (sēm′ lĭ)
  seem·li·ness
seep·age (sēp′ ĭj)
se·er (sē′ ĕr)
seer·suck·er (sēr′ sŭk′ ĕr)
see·saw (sē′ sô′)
seethe (sēth)
  seeth·ing
seg·ment (sĕg′ mĕnt)
  seg·men·tar·y
  seg·men·ta·tion
      (sĕg′ mĕn·tā′ shŭn)
seg·re·gate (sĕg′ rē·gāt)
  -gat·ing
  seg·re·ga·tion (sĕg′ rē·gā′ shŭn)
seine (sān)
  sein·ing
seis·mo·graph (sīz′ mŏ·gráf)
seize (sēz)
  seiz·ing   seiz·a·ble
  sei·zure (sē′ zhĕr)
sel·dom (sĕl′ dŭm)
se·lect (sē·lĕkt′)
  se·lec·tee (sē·lĕk′ tē′)
  se·lec·tion   se·lec·tive
  se·lec·tiv·i·ty (sē·lĕk′ tĭv′ ĭ·tĭ)
se·le·ni·um (sē·lē′ nĭ·ŭm)
self (sĕlf)
  self-a·base·ment
  self-ad·dressed
  self-cen·tered
  self-con·fi·dence
  self-con·scious
  self-con·trol
  self-de·ni·al
  self-dis·ci·pline
  self-ev·i·dent
  self-ex·plan·a·to·ry
  self-ex·pres·sion

self·ful·fill·ment
self·in·dul·gence
self-made
self-pit·y
self-pres·er·va·tion
self-pro·tec·tion
self-re·li·ance
self-re·spect·ing
self-right·eous
self-sac·ri·fice
self·same
self-sat·is·fied
self-styled
self-sup·port·ing
sell·out (sĕl′ out′)
Selt·zer wa·ter (sĕlt′ sēr)
sel·vage (sĕl′ vĭj)
  (fabric edge; see *salvage*)
se·man·tics (sĕ·măn′ tĭks)
sem·a·phore (sĕm′ à·fōr)
sem·blance (sĕm′ blăns)
se·men (sē′ mĕn)
se·mes·ter (sĕ·mĕs′ tēr)
sem·i- (sĕm′ ĭ-)
sem·i·au·to·mat·ic
sem·i·cir·cle   sem·i·co·lon
sem·i·fi·nal·ist
sem·i·month·ly
sem·i·pre·cious
sem·i·week·ly
sem·i·nal (sĕm′ ĭ·năl)
sem·i·nar (sĕm′ ĭ·när′)
sem·i·nar·y (sĕm′ ĭ·nĕr′ ĭ)
  -nar·ies
Sem·i·nole (sĕm′ ĭ·nōl)
Se·mit·ic (sĕ·mĭt′ ĭk)
sem·o·li·na (sĕm′ ō·lē′ nȧ)
sen·ate (sĕn′ ĭt)
sen·a·tor (sĕn′ à·tēr)
sen·a·to·ri·al (sĕn′ à·tō′ rĭ·ăl)
send-off (sĕnd′ ŏf′)
Sen·e·gal, (sĕn′ ĕ·gôl′)
  Repub. of
se·nile (sē′ nīl)
  se·nil·i·ty (sĕ·nĭl′ ĭ·tĭ)
sen·ior (sĕn′ yēr)
  sen·ior·i·ty (sēn·yŏr′ ĭ·tĭ)
sen·na (sĕn′ à)
se·ñor (sā·nyôr′)
sen·sa·tion (sĕn·sā′ shŭn)
  sen·sa·tion·al
sense (sĕns)
  sens·ing   sense·less
sen·si·ble (sĕn′ sĭ·b'l)
  sen·si·bil·i·ty (sĕn′ sĭ·bĭl′ ĭ·tĭ)

sen·si·tive (sĕn′ sĭ·tĭv)
  sen·si·tive·ness
  sen·si·tiv·i·ty (sĕn′ sĭ·tĭv′ ĭ·tĭ)
sen·si·tize (sĕn′ sĭ·tīz)
  -tiz·ing
sen·so·ry (sĕn′ sō·rĭ)
sen·su·al (sĕn′ shŏŏ·ăl)
  -al·ly
  sen·su·al·i·ty (sĕn′ shŏŏ·ăl′ ĭ·tĭ)
  sen·su·ous
sen·tence (sĕn′ tĕns)
sen·ten·tious (sĕn·tĕn′ shŭs)
sen·tient (sĕn′ shĕnt)
  sen·ti·ence (sĕn′ shĭ·ĕns)
sen·ti·ment (sĕn′ tĭ·mĕnt)
  sen·ti·men·tal (sĕn′ tĭ·mĕn′ tăl)
  sen·ti·men·tal·i·ty (sĕn′ tĭ·mĕn·tăl′ ĭ·tĭ)
sen·ti·nel (sĕn′ tĭ·nĕl)
sen·try (sĕn′ trĭ)
  -tries
sep·a·ra·ble (sĕp′ à·rà·b'l)
  sep·a·ra·bil·i·ty (sĕp′ à·rà·bĭl′ ĭ·tĭ)
sep·a·rate (sĕp′ à·rāt)
  -rat·ing   sep·a·rate·ly
  sep·a·ra·tion (sĕp′ à·rā′ shŭn)
  sep·a·ra·tist (sĕp′ à·rā′ tĭst)
  sep·a·ra·tor (sĕp′ à·rā′ tēr)
se·pi·a (sē′ pĭ·à)
Sep·tem·ber (sĕp·tĕm′ bēr)
sep·tet (sĕp·tĕt′)
sep·tic (sĕp′ tĭk)
sep·tu·a·ge·nar·i·an (sĕp′ tũ·à·jĕ·nâr′ ĭ·ăn)
sep·tum (sĕp′ tŭm)
  pl. sep·ta
sep·ul·cher (sĕp′ ŭl·kēr)
  se·pul·chral (sĕ·pŭl′ krăl)
se·quel (sē′ kwĕl)
se·quence (sē′ kwĕns)
  se·quen·tial (sĕ·kwĕn′ shăl)
se·ques·ter (sĕ·kwĕs′ tēr)
  se·ques·tra·tion (sē′ kwĕs·trā′ shŭn)
se·quin (sē′ kwĭn)
se·quoi·a (sĕ·kwoi′ à)
se·ragl·io (sĕ·răl′ yō)
se·ra·pe (sĕ·rä′ pā)
ser·a·phim (sĕr′ à·fĭm)
ser·e·nade (sĕr′ ĕ·nād′)
  -nad·ing
ser·en·dip·i·ty (sĕr′ ĕn·dĭp′ ĭ·tĭ)

se·rene   (sĕ·rēn′)
  se·rene·ly
  se·ren·i·ty   (sĕ·rĕn′ ĭ·tĭ)
serf·dom   (sûrf′ dŭm)
serge   (sûrj)
  (fabric; see *surge*)
ser·geant   (sär′ jĕnt)
  ser·geant at arms
se·ri·al   (sēr′ ĭ·ăl)
  (in a series; see *cereal*)
  se·ri·al·i·za·tion
       (sēr′ ĭ·ăl·ĭ·zā′ shŭn)
  se·ri·al·ize   -iz·ing
se·ries   (sēr′ ēz)
  n. sing. & pl.
ser·if   (sĕr′ ĭf)
se·ri·ous   (sēr′ ĭ·ŭs)
ser·mon   (sûr′ mŭn)
  ser·mon·ize -iz·ing
ser·pent   (sûr′ pĕnt)
  ser·pen·tine (sûr′ pĕn·tēn)
ser·rat·ed   (sĕr′ āt·ĕd)
se·rum   (sēr′ ŭm)
serv·ant   (sûr′ vănt)
serv·ice   (sûr′ vĭs)
  -ic·ing
  serv·ice·a·bil·i·ty
       (sûr′ vĭs·à·bĭl′ ĭ·tĭ)
  serv·ice·a·ble (sûr′ vĭs·à·b′l)
  serv·ice·man   serv·ice sta·tion
ser·vile   (sûr′ vĭl)
  ser·vil·i·ty (sĕr· vĭl′ ĭ·tĭ)
ser·vi·tude   (sûr′ vĭ·tūd)
ses·a·me seed   (sĕs′ à·mĕ)
ses·qui·cen·ten·nial
       (sĕs′ kwĭ·sĕn·tĕn′ ĭ·ăl)
ses·sion   (sĕsh′ ŭn)
  (meeting; see *cession*)
set   (sĕt)
  set·back   set·ter
  set·ting   set-to
  set·up
set·tee   (sĕ·tē′)
set·tle   (sĕt′ ′l)
  set·tling   set·tle·ment
  set·tler
sev·en·fold   (sĕv′ ĕn·fōld′)
sev·en·teen   (sĕv′ ĕn·tēn′)
sev·en·ty   (sĕv′ ĕn·tĭ)
  -ties   sev·en·ti·eth
sev·er   (sĕv′ ēr)
  -ered   -er·ing
sev·er·al   (sĕv′ ēr·ăl)
  sev·er·al·ly
sev·er·ance   (sĕv′ ēr·ăns)

se·vere   (sĕ·vēr′)
  se·vere·ly
  se·ver·i·ty   (sĕ·vĕr′ ĭ·tĭ)
sew·age   (sū′ ĭj)
sew·er   (sū′ ēr)
sewn   (sōn)
sex·tet   (sĕks·tĕt′)
sex·ton   (sĕks′ tŭn)
sex·u·al   (sĕk′ shŏŏ·ăl)
  -al·ly
  sex·u·al·i·ty
       (sĕk′ shŏŏ·ăl′ ĭ·tĭ)
shab·by   (shăb′ ĭ)
  shab·bi·ly   shab·bi·ness
shack·le   (shăk′ ′l)
  shack·ling
shad·dock   (shăd′ ŭk)
shad·ow   (shăd′ ō)
  shad·ow·box   shad·ow·y
shad·y   (shād′ ĭ)
  shad·i·ness
shaft   (sháft)
shag   (shăg)
  shag·gy   shag rug
shah   (shä)
shake   (shāk)
  shak·ing   shak·a·ble
  shake·down   shake-up
Shake·speare, Wil·liam
       (shāk′ spēr)
  Shake·spear·e·an
       (shāk·spēr′ ē·ăn)
shak·y   (shāk′ ĭ)
  shak·i·ness
shale   (shāl)
shal·lot   (shà·lŏt′)
shal·low   (shăl′ ō)
sha·man   (shä′ măn)
sham·bles   (shăm′ b′lz)
shame   (shām)
  sham·ing   shame·faced
  shame·fac·ed·ly
  shame·ful, -ful·ly, -ful·ness
  shame·less
sham·poo   (shăm·pōō′)
  -pooed   -poo·ing
sham·rock   (shăm′ rŏk)
shang·hai   (shăng·hī′)
  -haied   -hai·ing
Shan·gri-La   (shăng′ grē·lä′)
Shan·tung   (shăn·tŭng′)
shan·ty   (shăn′ tĭ)
  -ties
shape·less   (shāp′ lĕs)

shape·ly (shāp'lĭ)
  shape·li·ness
share·crop·per (shâr' krŏp' ẽr)
share·hold·er (shâr' hōl' dẽr)
shark·skin (shärk' skĭn')
sharp (shärp)
  sharp·en·er sharp-eyed
  sharp·shoot·er sharp-sight·ed
  sharp-wit·ted
Shas·ta dai·sy (shăs' tȧ)
shat·ter (shăt' ẽr)
Sha·vi·an (shā' vĭ·ăn)
shawl (shôl)
Shaw·nee (shô·nē')
sheaf (shēf)
  pl. sheaves (shēvz)
shear (shẽr)
  (to cut; see *sheer*)
  shorn
sheath (shēth) *n.*
sheathe (shēth) *v.*
  sheath·ing
shed (shĕd)
  shed·ding
sheen (shēn)
sheep (shēp)
  sheep·herd·er sheep·ish
  sheep·shank sheeps·head
  sheep·shear·ing
  sheep·skin
sheer (shẽr)
  (transparent; see *shear*)
sheet (shēt)
sheik (shēk)
  sheik·dom
shelf (shĕlf)
  pl. shelves
shell (shĕl)
  shell·fire shell·fish
  shell shock
shel·lac (shĕ·lăk')
  shel·lacked shel·lack·ing
shel·ter (shĕl' tẽr)
shelve (shĕlv)
  shelv·ing
Shen·an·do·ah riv.
         (shĕn' ȧn·dō' ȧ)
she·nan·i·gans
         (shĕ·năn' ĭ·gănz)
shep·herd (shĕp' ẽrd)
sher·bet (shûr' bĕt)
sher·iff (shĕr' ĭf)
sher·ry (shĕr' ĭ)
  sher·ries

Shet·land po·ny
         (shĕt' lănd)
shib·bo·leth (shĭb' ō·lĕth)
shield (shēld)
shift·less (shĭft' lĕs)
shift·y (shĭf' tĭ)
  shift·i·ness
shil·le·lagh (shĭ·lā' lĕ)
shil·ling (shĭl' ĭng)
shil·ly-shal·ly (shĭl' ĭ·shăl' ĭ)
shim·mer (shĭm' ẽr)
shim·my (shĭm' ĭ)
shine (shīn)
  shin·ing shin·y
  shone
shin·gle (shĭng' g'l)
  -gling
Shin·to (shĭn' tō')
  Shin·to·ist
ship (shĭp)
  shipped ship·ping
  ship·board ship·load
  ship·mate ship·pa·ble
  ship·shape ship·wreck
shirk (shûrk)
  shirk·er
shirr (shûr)
shirt·waist (shûrt' wāst')
shiv·er (shĭv' ẽr)
  -ered, -er·ing shiv·er·y
shoal (shōl)
shock (shŏk)
  shock ab·sorb·er
  shock ther·a·py
shod·dy (shŏd' ĭ)
  shod·di·ness
shoe (shōō)
  shoe·ing shoe·horn
  shoe·lace shoe·mak·er
  shoe·shop shoe·string
  shoe tree
shop (shŏp)
  shopped shop·ping
  shop·keep·er shop·lift·er
  shop·walk·er shop·win·dow
  shop·worn
shorn (shōrn)
short (shôrt)
  short·cake short·change
  short cir·cuit short·com·ing
  short cut short·hand
  short·hand·ed Short·horn
  short-lived (shôrt' līvd')
  short shrift short·sight·ed
  short·stop short sto·ry

short-tem·pered

short-term   short-wave *adj.*

short-wind·ed

short·age   (shôrt' ĭj)

short·en·ing   (shôr' t'n·ĭng)

shot·gun   (shŏt' gŭn')

shot-put   (shŏt' pŏŏt')

should   (shŏŏd)

should·n't

shoul·der   (shōl' dĕr)

shout   (shout)

shove   (shŭv)

shov·ing

shov·el   (shŭv' 'l)

-eled   -el·ing

show   (shō)

show bill   show·boat

show·case   show·down

show·man·ship

show-off   show·room

show·er   (shou' ĕr)

show·er·y

show·y   (shō' ĭ)

show·i·ly   -i·ness

shrank   (shrăngk)

shrap·nel   (shrăp' nĕl)

shred   (shrĕd)

shred·ded   shred·ding

shred·der

shrew   (shrōō)

shrew·ish

shrewd   (shrōōd)

shriek   (shrēk)

shrift   (shrĭft)

shrike   (shrīk)

shrill   (shrĭl)

shrimp   (shrĭmp)

shrine   (shrīn)

Shrin·er

shrink   (shrĭngk)

shrink·age   (shrĭngk' ĭj)

shrunk·en

shriv·el   (shrĭv' 'l)

-eled   -el·ing

shroud   (shroud)

shrub   (shrŭb)

shrub·ber·y

shrunk·en   (shrŭngk' ĕn)

shuck   (shŭk)

shud·der   (shŭd' ĕr)

shuf·fle   (shŭf' 'l)

shuf·fling   shuf·fle·board

shun   (shŭn)

shunned   shun·ning

shunt   (shŭnt)

shut·down   (shŭt' doun')

shut-in   (shŭt' ĭn')

shut·out   (shŭt' out')

shut·ter   (shŭt' ĕr)

shut·tle·cock   (shŭt' 'l·kŏk')

shy   (shī)

shied   shy·ing

shi·er   shy·ly

shy·ness

shy·ster   (shī' stĕr)

Si·a·mese cat   (sī' a·mēz')

sib·i·lant   (sĭb' ĭ·lănt)

-lance

sib·ling   (sĭb' lĭng)

sick   (sĭk)

sick·bed   sick·en·ing

sick·ly   -li·ness

sick·ness

side   (sīd)

sid·ing   side·board

side·burns   side·car

side is·sue   side·light

side·long   side·split·ting

side-step   side stroke

side·swipe   side·track

side·walk   side·ways

side·wind·er

si·de·re·al   (sī·dĕr' ē·ăl)

si·dle   (sī' d'l)

-dling

siege   (sēj)

si·er·ra   (sī·ĕr' a)

si·es·ta   (sī·ĕs' ta)

sieve   (sĭv)

sift   (sĭft)

sigh   (sī)

sight   (sīt)

(view; see *cite*, *site*)

sight bill   sight·less

sight·ly   -li·ness

sign   (sīn)

sign·board   sign·post

sig·nal   (sĭg' năl)

sig·nal·ize   -iz·ing

sig·nal·man

sig·na·to·ry   (sĭg' na·tō' rĭ)

sig·na·ture   (sĭg' na·tụr)

sig·net ring   (sĭg' nĕt)

sig·nif·i·cant   (sĭg·nĭf' ĭ·kănt)

-cance

sig·ni·fi·ca·tion

                    (sĭg' nĭ·fĭ·kā' shŭn)

sig·ni·fy   (sĭg' nĭ·fī)

-fied   -fy·ing

si·lage   (sī' lĭj)

si·lence (sī′ lĕns)
  si·lenc·er   si·lent
sil·hou·ette (sĭl′ ŏŏ·ĕt′)
sil·i·ca gel (sĭl′ ĭ·kạ)
sil·i·cate (sĭl′ ĭ·kāt)
sil·i·con (sĭl′ ĭ·kŏn)
silk·en (sĭl′ kĕn)
silk·y (sĭl′ kĭ)
  silk·i·ly   -i·ness
sil·ly (sĭl′ ĭ)
  sil·li·ness
si·lo (sī′ lō)
  -los
sil·ver·ware (sĭl′ vĕr·wâr′)
sim·i·an (sĭm′ ĭ·ạn)
sim·i·lar (sĭm′ ĭ·lĕr)
  sim·i·lar·i·ty (sĭm′ ĭ·lăr′ ĭ·tĭ)
sim·i·le (sĭm′ ĭ·lē)
si·mil·i·tude (sĭ·mĭl′ ĭ·tūd)
sim·mer (sĭm′ ĕr)
sim·o·ny (sĭm′ ŏ·nĭ)
sim·ple (sĭm′ p'l)
  sim·plic·i·ty (sĭm·plĭs′ ĭ·tĭ)
  sim·pli·fi·ca·tion
      (sĭm′ plĭ·fĭ·kā′ shŭn)
  sim·pli·fy, -fied, -fy·ing
  sim·ply
sim·u·late (sĭm′ ū·lāt)
  -lat·ing
  sim·u·la·tion (sĭm′ ū·lā′ shŭn)
si·mul·ta·ne·ous
      (sī′ mŭl·tā′ nĕ·ŭs)
since (sĭns)
sin·cere (sĭn·sĕr′)
  sin·cere·ly
  sin·cer·i·ty (sĭn·sĕr′ ĭ·tĭ)
si·ne·cure (sī′ nĕ·kūr)
sin·ew (sĭn′ ū)
  sin·ew·y
sin·ful (sĭn′ fŏŏl)
  -ful·ly   -ful·ness
sing (sĭng)
  sing·a·ble
singe (sĭnj)
  singe·ing
sin·gle (sĭng′ g'l)
  sin·gle-breast·ed
  sin·gle file   sin·gle-hand·ed
  sin·gle-mind·ed
  sin·gle·ness   sin·gly
sin·gle·ton (sĭng′ g'l·tŭn)
sing·song (sĭng′ sŏng′)
sin·gu·lar (sĭng′ gŭ·lĕr)
  sin·gu·lar·i·ty
      (sĭng′ gŭ·lăr′ ĭ·tĭ)

sin·is·ter (sĭn′ ĭs·tĕr)
sink·age (sĭngk′ ĭj)
sin·ner (sĭn′ ĕr)
sin·u·ous (sĭn′ ū·ŭs)
si·nus (sī′ nŭs)
  si·nus·i·tis (sī′ nŭs·ī′ tĭs)
Sioux Cit·y, Ia. (sōō)
si·phon (sī′ fŏn)
si·ren (sī′ rĕn)
sir·loin (sûr′ loin′)
si·roc·co (sĭ·rŏk′ ō)
sir·up (sĭr′ ŭp)
  sir·up·y
si·sal (sī′ sạl)
sis·ter-in-law (sĭs′ tĕr·ĭn·lô′)
  pl. sis·ters-in-law
site (sīt)
  (location; see sight, cite)
sit·ter (sĭt′ ĕr)
sit·u·ate (sĭt′ ū·āt)
  -at·ing
  sit·u·a·tion (sĭt′ ū·ā′ shŭn)
sitz bath (sĭts)
six·pence (sĭks′ pĕns)
six·teenth (sĭks′ tēnth′)
sixth (sĭksth)
six·ty (sĭks′ tĭ)
  -ties   six·ti·eth
size (sīz)
  siz·ing   siz·a·ble
siz·zle (sĭz′ 'l)
  siz·zling
skate (skāt)
  skat·ing
skeet (skēt)
skein (skān)
skel·e·ton (skĕl′ ĕ·tŭn)
  skel·e·tal
sketch (skĕch)
  sketch·book   sketch·y
skew·er (skū′ ĕr)
ski (skē)
  skied   ski·ing
  ski·er
skill (skĭl)
  skill·ful, -ful·ly, -ful·ness
skim milk (skĭm)
skimp·y (skĭmp′ ĭ)
  skimp·i·ness
skin (skĭn)
  skinned,   skin·ning
  skin-deep   skin div·ing
  skin·flint   skin·tight
skin·ny (skĭn′ ĭ)
  skin·ni·ness

skip·per (skĭp′ ẽr)
skir·mish (skûr′ mĭsh)
skirt (skûrt)
skit·tish (skĭt′ ĭsh)
skit·tles (skĭt′ 'lz)
skul·dug·ger·y (skŭl·dŭg′ ẽr·ĭ)
skulk (skŭlk)
skull (skŭl)
  skull·cap
skunk (skŭngk)
sky (skī)
  skies   sky·lark
  sky·light   sky line
  sky·scrap·er   sky·ward
  sky·writ·ing
slack (slăk)
  slack·en
slake (slāk)
  slak·ing
sla·lom (slä′ lŭm)
slan·der (slăn′ dẽr)
  slan·der·er   slan·der·ous
slant·wise (slănt′ wīz′)
slap·dash (slăp′ dăsh′)
slap·stick (slăp′ stĭk′)
slat·tern·ly (slăt′ ẽrn·lĭ)
slaugh·ter (slô′ tẽr)
  slaugh·ter·house
Slav (släv)
slave (slāv)
  slav·ing   slave·hold·er
  slav·er·y   slav·ey
  slav·ish
slay·er (slā′ ẽr)
slea·zy (slā′ zĭ)
sled·ding (slĕd′ ĭng)
sledge ham·mer
                   (slĕj)
sleek (slēk)
sleep (slēp)
  sleep·walk·er   sleep·i·ly
  sleep·i·ness   sleep·y
sleet (slēt)
sleeve (slēv)
  sleeve·less
sleigh (slā)
sleight of hand (slīt)
slen·der·ize (slĕn′ dẽr·īz)
  -iz·ing
sleuth (slōōth)
slew (slōō)
  (killed; see slough)
slice (slīs)
  slic·ing
slick·er (slĭk′ ẽr)

slight (slīt)
slime (slīm)
  slim·y
sling·shot (slĭng′ shŏt′)
slink·y (slĭngk′ ĭ)
slip·knot (slĭp′ nŏt′)
slip·page (slĭp′ ĭj)
slip·per·y (slĭp′ ẽr·ĭ)
  slip·per·i·ness
slip·shod (slĭp′ shŏd′)
sliv·er (slĭv′ ẽr)
sloe-eyed (slō′ īd′)
sloe gin (slō)
slo·gan (slō′ găn)
sloop (slōōp)
slope (slōp)
  slop·ing
slop·py (slŏp′ ĭ)
  slop·pi·ly   slop·pi·ness
sloth·ful (slôth′ fŏŏl)
slouch (slouch)
slough
  (when pron. slŭf, means to cast
  off; when pron. slōō, means
  swamp or inlet; see slew)
Slo·vak (slō′ văk)
slov·en·ly (slŭv′ ĕn·lĭ)
  slov·en·li·ness
slow·down (slō′ doun′)
sludge (slŭj)
slug·gard (slŭg′ ẽrd)
slug·gish (slŭg′ ĭsh)
sluice (slōōs)
  sluic·ing
slum·ber (slŭm′ bẽr)
  slum·ber·ous
slur (slûr)
  slurred   slur·ring
sly (slī)
  sli·est   sly·ness
smack (smăk)
small (smôl)
  small change   small-mind·ed
  small·pox   small talk
smart (smärt)
smash·up (smăsh′ ŭp′)
smat·ter·ing (smăt′ ẽr·ĭng)
smear (smẽr)
smel·ling salts (smĕl′ ĭng)
smelt (smĕlt)
smelt·er (smĕl′ tẽr)
smile (smīl)
  smil·ing
smirch (smûrch)
smirk (smûrk)

smite	(smīt)	snow	(snō)
smit·ing		snow·ball	snow·bound
smit·ten	(smĭt′ 'n)	snow-blind	snow-capped
smith·er·eens	(smĭth′ ĕr·ēnz′)	snow·drift	snow·flake
smock	(smŏk)	snow·plow	snow·shoe
smog	(smŏg)	snow·storm	snow·y
smoke	(smōk)	snug·gle	(snŭg′ 'l)
smok·ing	smoke·house	snug·gling	
smoke screen	smoke·stack	so-and-so	(sō′ ănd·sō′)
smok·y		soap	(sōp)
smol·der	(smōl′ dĕr)	soap·box	soap op·e·ra
smooth	(smōōth)	soap·suds	
smor·gas·bord	(smôr′ gȧs·bôrd′)	soar·ing	(sōr′ ĭng)
smoth·er	(smŭth′ ēr)	so·be·it	(sō·bē′ ĭt)
smudge	(smŭj)	so·ber	(sō′ bĕr)
smudg·ing	smudg·y	so·bri·e·ty	(sȯ·brī′ ĕ·tĭ)
smug	(smŭg)	so·bri·quet	(sō′ brĭ·kā)
smug·gest	smug·ly	so-called	(sō′ kôld′)
smug·gle	(smŭg′ 'l)	soc·cer	(sŏk′ ēr)
smug·gling	smug·gler	so·cia·ble	(sō′ shȧ·b'l)
smut	(smŭt)	so·cia·bil·i·ty	(sō′ shȧ·bĭl′ ĭ·tĭ)
smut·ty		so·cial	(sō′ shȧl)
snack	(snăk)	so·cial·ism	
sna·fu	(snă·fōō′)	so·cial·is·tic	(sō′ shȧl·ĭs′ tĭk)
-fued	-fu·ing	so·cial·ite	(sō′ shȧl·īt)
snail	(snāl)	so·cial·ized	
snail-paced		so·ci·e·ty	(sȯ·sī′ ĕ·tĭ)
snap·drag·on	(snăp′ drăg′ ŭn)	-ties	
snap·per	(snăp′ ēr)	so·ci·e·tal	(sȯ·sī′ ĕ·tȧl)
snap·shot	(snăp′ shŏt′)	so·ci·ol·o·gy	(sō′ sĭ·ŏl′ ȯ·jĭ)
snare drum	(snâr)	so·ci·o·log·i·cal	
snarl·ing	(snärl′ ĭng)		(sō′ sĭ·ȯ·lŏj′ ĭ·kȧl)
sneak·ers	(snēk′ ērz)	so·ci·ol·o·gist	(sō′ sĭ·ŏl′ ȯ·jĭst)
sneak·y	(snēk′ ĭ)	sock·et	(sŏk′ ĕt)
sneak·i·ly		Soc·ra·tes	(sŏk′ rȧ·tēz)
sneer·ing	(snēr′ ĭng)	So·crat·ic	(sȯ·krăt′ ĭk)
sneeze	(snēz)	so·dal·i·ty	(sȯ·dăl′ ĭ·tĭ)
sneez·ing		-ties	
snick·er	(snĭk′ ēr)	sod·den	(sŏd′ 'n)
snif·fle	(snĭf′ 'l)	sod·den·ness	
snif·fling		so·di·um	(sō′ dĭ·ŭm)
snip·pet	(snĭp′ ĕt)	so·di·um bi·car·bon·ate	
snitch	(snĭch)	so·di·um car·bon·ate	
sniv·el	(snĭv′ 'l)	so·di·um chlo·ride	
-eled	-el·ing	so·di·um hy·drox·ide	
snob	(snŏb)	so·di·um ni·trate	
snob·ber·y	snob·bish	Sod·om	(sŏd′ ŭm)
snoop·y	(snōōp′ ĭ)	(and Gomorrah)	
snooze	(snōōz)	sod·om·y	(sŏd′ ŭm·ĭ)
snooz·ing		soft	(sôft)
snore	(snōr)	soft·ball	soft·heart·ed
snor·ing		soft-ped·al	soft-shell
snor·kel	(snôr′ kĕl)	soft-soap	soft-spo·ken
snout	(snout)	sog·gy	(sŏg′ ĭ)
		sog·gi·ness	

soil·age   (soil′ ĭj)
soi·ree   (swä·rā′)
so·journ   (sō·jûrn′)
sol·ace   (sŏl′ ĭs)
so·lar   (sō′ lēr)
   so·lar·i·um   (sō·lâr′ ĭ·ŭm)
   so·lar plex·us
sol·der·ing i·ron
         (sŏd′ ēr·ĭng)
sol·dier   (sōl′ jēr)
sole   (sōl)
   sole·ly
sol·e·cism   (sŏl′ ĕ·sĭz′m)
sol·emn   (sŏl′ ĕm)
   so·lem·ni·ty   (sō·lĕm′ nĭ·tĭ)
   -ties
   sol·em·nize   (sŏl′ ĕm·nīz)
   -niz·ing
so·lic·it   (sō·lĭs′ ĭt)
   -it·ed   -it·ing
   so·lic·i·ta·tion
       (sō·lĭs′ ĭ·tā′ shŭn)
   so·lic·i·tor
so·lic·it·ous   (sō·lĭs′ ĭ·tŭs)
   so·lic·i·tude   (sō·lĭs′ ĭ·tūd)
sol·id   (sŏl′ ĭd)
   sol·i·dar·i·ty   (sŏl′ ĭ·dăr′ ĭ·tĭ)
   so·lid·i·fy   (sō·lĭd′ ĭ·fī)
   -fied   -fy·ing
   sol·id·i·ty   (sō·lĭd′ ĭ·tĭ)
so·lil·o·quy   (sō·lĭl′ ō·kwĭ)
   pl. -quies
   so·lil·o·quize   (sō·lĭl′ ō·kwīz)
   -quiz·ing
sol·i·taire   (sŏl′ ĭ·târ)
sol·i·tar·y   (sŏl′ ĭ·tĕr′ ĭ)
   sol·i·tar·i·ness
sol·i·tude   (sŏl′ ĭ·tūd)
so·lo   (sō′ lō)
   -los   so·lo·ist
Sol·o·mon   (sŏl′ ō·mŭn)
sol·stice   (sŏl′ stĭs)
sol·u·ble   (sŏl′ ū·b′l)
   sol·u·bil·i·ty   (sŏl′ ū·bĭl′ ĭ·tĭ)
so·lu·tion   (sō·lū′ shŭn)
solve   (sŏlv)
   solv·ing
   solv·a·bil·i·ty   (sŏl′ vå·bĭl′ ĭ·tĭ)
   solv·a·ble
sol·vent   (sŏl′ vĕnt)
   sol·ven·cy
So·ma·li·land, Afr.
       (sō·mä′ lĕ·lănd′)
so·mat·ic   (sō·măt′ ĭk)
som·ber   (sŏm′ bēr)

som·bre·ro   (sŏm·brâr′ ō)
some   (sŭm)
   some·bod·y   some·one
   some·thing   some·times
   some·where
som·er·sault   (sŭm′ ēr·sôlt)
som·nam·bu·list
       (sŏm·năm′ bû·lĭst)
so·nar   (sō′ när)
so·na·ta   (sō·nä′ tå)
song·ster   (sŏng′ stēr)
   song·stress
son·ic   (sŏn′ ĭk)
son-in-law   (sŭn′ ĭn·lô′)
   pl. sons-in-law
son·net   (sŏn′ ĕt)
   son·net·eer   (sŏn′ ĕ·tēr′)
so·no·rous   (sō·nō′ rŭs)
   so·nor·i·ty   (sō·nŏr′ ĭ·tĭ)
soothe   (sōōth̸)
   sooth·ing
sooth·say·er   (sōōth′ sā′ ēr)
soot·y   (sŏŏt′ ĭ)
   soot·i·ness
soph·ism   (sŏf′ ĭz′m)
so·phis·ti·cat·ed
       (sō·fĭs′ tĭ·kāt′ ĕd)
   so·phis·ti·ca·tion
       (sō·fĭs′ tĭ·kā′ shŭn)
soph·ist·ry   (sŏf′ ĭs·trĭ)
   -ries
soph·o·more   (sŏf′ ō·mōr)
   soph·o·mor·ic   (sŏf′ ō·mŏr′ ĭk)
so·po·rif·ic   (sō′ pō·rĭf′ ĭk)
so·pran·o   (sō·prăn′ ō)
   -os
Sor·bonne   (sôr·bŏn′)
sor·cer·y   (sôr′ sēr·ĭ)
   sor·cer·er   sor·cer·ess
sor·did   (sôr′ dĭd)
sore·ly   (sōr′ lĭ)
sor·ghum   (sôr′ gŭm)
so·ror·i·ty   (sō·rŏr′ ĭ·tĭ)
   -ties
sor·rel   (sŏr′ ĕl)
sor·row   (sŏr′ ō)
   sor·row·ful, -ful·ly, -ful·ness
sor·ry   (sŏr′ ĭ)
   sor·ri·er   sor·ri·est
sor·tie   (sôr′ tē)
sot·tish   (sŏt′ ĭsh)
sou·brette   (sōō·brĕt′)
souf·flé   (sōō′ flā′)
sought   (sôt)

soul   (sōl)
   soul·ful, -ful·ly, -ful·ness
   soul·less
sound   (sound)
   sound·proof
soup   (sōōp)
soup·çon   (sōōp′ soɴ′)
sour   (sour)
   sour·dough
source   (sôrs)
souse   (sous)
south   (south)
   south·east
   south·er·ly   (sŭth′ ẽr·lĭ)
   south·ern·er   (sŭth′ ẽr·nẽr)
   south·ern·most
          (sŭth′ ẽrn·mōst)
   south·paw   South Pole
   south·ward   south·west·ern
South Car·o·li·na
       (south kăr′ ō·lī′ nȧ)
   abbr. S. C.
   South Car·o·lin·i·an
       (-kăr′ ō·lĭn′ĭ·ȧn)
South Da·ko·ta   (south dȧ·kō′ tȧ)
   abbr. S. Dak.
   South Da·ko·tan
sou·ve·nir   (sōō′ vě·nẽr′)
sou′west·er   (sou′ wěs′ tẽr)
sov·er·eign   (sŏv′ ẽr·ĭn)
   sov·er·eign·ty
so·vi·et   (sō′ vĭ·ět)
soy·bean   (soi′ bēn′)
space·ship   (spās′ shĭp′)
spa·cious   (spā′ shŭs)
spa·ghet·ti   (spȧ·gĕt′ ĭ)
span·gle   (spăng′ g′l)
Span·iard   (spăn′ yẽrd)
span·iel   (spăn′ yěl)
Span·ish   (spăn′ ĭsh)
span·ner   (spăn′ ẽr)
spare   (spâr)
   spar·ing   spare·ness
   spare·ribs
spar·kle   (spär′ k′l)
   -kling
spar·row   (spăr′ ō)
sparse   (spärs)
   sparse·ly
Spar·tan   (spär′ t′n)
spasm   (spăz′m)
   spas·mod·ic   (spăz·mŏd′ ĭk)
spas·tic   (spăs′ tĭk)
spa·tial   (spā′ shȧl)
   spa·tial·ly

spat·ter   (spăt′ ẽr)
spat·u·la   (spăt′ ū·lȧ)
spawn   (spôn)
speak·eas·y   (spēk′ ēz′ ĭ)
spear·mint   (spẽr′ mĭnt′)
spe·cial   (spĕsh′ ȧl)
   spe·cial·ist
   spe·cial·i·za·tion
       (spĕsh′ ȧl·ĭ·zā′ shŭn)
   spe·cial·ize   -iz·ing
   spe·cial·ty
spe·cie   (spē′ shĭ)
   (coin; see *species*)
spe·cies   (spē′ shĭz)
   (kind, variety; see *specie*)
spe·cif·ic   (spē·sĭf′ ĭk)
   spe·cif·i·cal·ly
spec·i·fy   (spĕs′ ĭ·fī)
   -fied   -fy·ing
   spec·i·fi·a·ble   (spĕs′ ĭ·fī′ ȧ·b′l)
   spec·i·fi·ca·tion
       (spĕs′ ĭ·fĭ·kā′ shŭn)
spec·i·men   (spĕs′ ĭ·měn)
spe·cious   (spē′ shŭs)
speck·led   (spĕk′ ′ld)
spec·ta·cle   (spĕk′ tȧ·k′l)
spec·tac·u·lar   (spĕk·tăk′ ū·lẽr)
spec·ta·tor   (spĕk·tā′ tẽr)
spec·ter   (spĕk′ tẽr)
   spec·tral   (spĕk′ trȧl)
spec·tro·scope   (spĕk′ trō·skōp)
spec·trum   (spĕk′ trŭm)
   pl. spec·tra
spec·u·late   (spĕk′ ū·lāt)
   -lat·ing
   spec·u·la·tion
       (spĕk′ ū·lā′ shŭn)
   spec·u·la·tive   (spĕk′ ū·lā′ tĭv)
   spec·u·la·tor
speech   (spēch)
speed   (spēd)
   speed·boat   speed·i·ly
   speed in·di·ca·tor
   speed lim·it
   speed·om·e·ter
       (spēd·ŏm′ ě·tẽr)
   speed·way   speed·y
spell·bound   (spĕl′ bound′)
spell·ing   (spĕl′ ĭng)
spend·thrift   (spĕnd′ thrĭft′)
sperm   (spûrm)
sper·ma·ce·ti   (spûr′ mȧ·sē′ tĭ)
spew   (spū)
sphag·num   (sfăg′ nŭm)

sphere	(sfēr)
spher·al	spher·i·cal
sphinc·ter	(sfĭngk′ tēr)
sphinx	(sfĭngks)
spick-and-span	(spĭk′ ănd·spăn′)
spic·y	(spĭs′ ĭ)
spic·i·er, -i·est, -i·ly, -i·ness	
spi·der	(spī′ dēr)
spiel	(spēl)
spig·ot	(spĭg′ ŭt)
spike·let	(spīk′ lĕt)
spill·age	(spĭl′ ĭj)
spin·ach	(spĭn′ ĭch)
spi·nal	(spī′ năl)
spin·dle	(spĭn′ d′l)
spin·dly	
spine·less	(spīn′ lĕs)
spin·et	(spĭn′ ĕt)
spin·ner·et	(spĭn′ ēr·ĕt)
spin·ning wheel	
	(spĭn′ ĭng)
spin·ster	(spĭn′ stēr)
spin·y	(spĭn′ ĭ)
spi·ral	(spī′ răl)
-raled	-ral·ing
spi·ral·ly	
spir·it	(spĭr′ ĭt)
spir·it·ed	spir·it·less
spir·it·u·al	(spĭr′ ĭt·û·ăl)
spir·it·u·al·i·ty	
	(spĭr′ ĭt·û·ăl′ ĭ·tĭ)
spite·ful	(spīt′ fŏŏl)
-ful·ly	-ful·ness
spit·fire	(spĭt′ fīr′)
spit·tle	(spĭt′ ′l)
spit·toon	(spĭ·tŏŏn′)
spleen	(splēn)
splen·did	(splĕn′ dĭd)
splen·dor	(splĕn′ dēr)
splice	(splīs)
splic·ing	
splin·ter	(splĭn′ tēr)
split-lev·el	(splĭt′ lĕv′ ĕl)
spoil	(spoil)
spoiled	spoil·ing
spoil·age	(spoil′ ĭj)
spo·ken	(spō′ kĕn)
spokes·man	(spōks′ măn)
sponge	(spunj)
spong·ing	sponge·cake
spon·gy	
spon·sor	(spŏn′ sēr)
spon·ta·ne·ous	(spŏn·tā′ nĕ·ŭs)
spon·ta·ne·i·ty	
	(spŏn′ tá·nē′ ĭ·tĭ)

spoof	(spŏŏf)
spoon·ful	(spŏŏn′ fŏŏl)
spoon·fuls	
spoor	(spŏŏr)
(animal track; see *spore*)	
spo·rad·ic	(spô·răd′ ĭk)
spore	(spōr)
(germ; see *spoor*)	
sport	(spōrt)
spor·tive	sports·man·like
sports·wear	sport·y
spot·light	(spŏt′ līt′)
spot·ty	(spŏt′ ĭ)
spouse	(spous)
spout	(spout)
sprain	(sprān)
sprawl·ing	(sprôl′ ĭng)
spread	(sprĕd)
spright·ly	(sprīt′ lĭ)
spright·li·ness	
spring	(sprĭng)
spring·board	spring·time
sprin·kle	(sprĭng′ k′l)
-kling	
sprint	(sprĭnt)
sprite	(sprīt)
sprock·et wheel	(sprŏk′ ĕt)
sprout	(sprout)
spruce	(sprŏŏs)
spry	(sprī)
spri·est	spry·ness
spu·ri·ous	(spū′ rĭ·ŭs)
spurn	(spûrn)
spurt	(spûrt)
sput·nik	(spŏŏt′ nĭk)
sput·ter	(spŭt′ ēr)
spu·tum	(spū′ tŭm)
spy·glass	(spī′ glăs′)
squab	(skwŏb)
squab·ble	(skwŏb′ ′l)
squab·bling	
squad	(skwŏd)
squad·ron	(skwŏd′ rŭn)
squal·id	(skwŏl′ ĭd)
squall	(skwôl)
squal·or	(skwŏl′ ēr)
squan·der	(skwŏn′ dēr)
square	(skwâr)
squar·ing	square dance
square·ly	square-rig·ger
squash	(skwŏsh)
squat	(skwŏt)
squatted	squat·ting
squat·ter	
squaw	(skwô)

squawk	(skwôk)
squeak	(skwēk)
squeal	(skwēl)
squeal·er	
squeam·ish	(skwēm′ ĭsh)
squee·gee	(skwē′ jē)
squeeze	(skwēz)
squeez·ing	
squelch	(skwĕlch)
squib	(skwĭb)
squid	(skwĭd)
squint	(skwĭnt)
squire	(skwīr)
squir·ing	
squirm	(skwûrm)
squir·rel	(skwûr′ ĕl)
squirt	(skwûrt)
sta·ble	(stā′ b'l)
sta·bil·i·ty	(sta·bĭl′ ɩ·tĭ)
sta·bil·ize	-iz·ing
sta·bly	
stac·ca·to	(sta·kä′ tō)
sta·di·um	(stā′ dĭ·ŭm)
staff	(stàf)
stage	(stāj)
stag·ing	stage·coach
stage fright	stage·hand
stage man·ag·er	
stage-struck	stag·y
stag·ger	(stăg′ ēr)
stag·nant	(stăg′ nånt)
stag·nate	(stăg′ nāt)
-nat·ing	
stag·na·tion	(stăg·nā′ shŭn)
staid	(stād)
stain·less	(stān′ lĕs)
stair·way	(stâr′ wā′)
stake	(stāk)
(post; see *steak*)	
sta·lac·tite	(sta·lăk′ tīt)
sta·lag·mite	(sta·lăg′ mīt)
stale·mate	(stāl′ māt′)
Sta·lin·ist	(stā′ lĭn·ĭst)
stalk	(stôk)
stall	(stôl)
stal·lion	(stăl′ yŭn)
stal·wart	(stôl′ wērt)
sta·men	(stā′ mĕn)
stam·i·na	(stăm′ ĭ·nà)
stam·mer	(stăm′ ēr)
stam·pede	(stăm·pēd′)
-ped·ing	
stance	(stăns)
stan·chion	(stăn′ shŭn)

stand	(stănd)
stand·ee	(stăn·dē′)
stand-in	stand·out
stand·still	
stand·ard	(stăn′ dĕrd)
stand·ard-bear·er	
stand·ard·i·za·tion	
(stăn′ dĕr·dĭ·zā′ shŭn)	
stand·ard·ize	-iz·ing
stan·za	(stăn′ zà)
sta·ple	(stā′ p'l)
star	(stär)
star·board	star·fish
star·let	star·light
star·lit	star·ry
star sap·phire	
starch	(stärch)
star·ling	(stär′ lĭng)
star·tle	(stär′ t'l)
-tling	
starve	(stärv)
starv·ing	
star·va·tion	(stär·vā′ shŭn)
state	(stāt)
stat·ing	state·hood
state·house	state·less
state·ly	-li·ness
state·ment	states′ rights
state·room	
state′s at·torn·ey	
state′s ev·i·dence	
states·man·like	
stat·ic	(stăt′ ĭk)
sta·tion	(stā′ shŭn)
sta·tion·mas·ter	
sta·tion wag·on	
sta·tion·ar·y	(stā′ shŭn·ĕr′ ĭ)
(unmoving; see *stationery*)	
sta·tion·er·y	(stā′ shŭn·ĕr′ ĭ)
(paper; see *stationary*)	
sta·tis·tics	(sta·tĭs′ tĭks)
stat·u·ar·y	(stăt′ û·ĕr′ ĭ)
stat·ue	(stăt′ ū)
stat·u·esque	(stăt′ û·ĕsk′)
stat·u·ette	(stăt′ û·ĕt′)
stat·ure	(stăt′ ûr)
sta·tus	(stā′ tŭs)
stat·ute	(stăt′ ūt)
stat·u·to·ry	(stăt′ û·tō′ rĭ)
stead·fast	(stĕd′ fàst)
stead·y	(stĕd′ ĭ)
stead·i·ness	
steak	(stāk)
(meat; see *stake*)	

steal   (stēl)
  (take feloniously; see *steel*)
  stole   steal·ing
stealth·y   (stĕl′ thĭ)
  stealth·i·ness
steam   (stēm)
  steam·boat   steam en·gine
  steam-roll·er   steam·ship
steel   (stēl)
  (metal; see *steal*)
  steel·head   steel wool
  steel·y
steep   (stēp)
stee·ple   (stē′ p′l)
  stee·ple·chase   stee·ple jack
steer   (stēr)
steer·age   (stēr′ ĭj)
stein   (stīn)
stel·lar   (stĕl′ ēr)
stench   (stĕnch)
sten·cil   (stĕn′ sĭl)
  -ciled   -cil·ing
ste·nog·ra·pher
               (stē·nŏg′ rȧ·fēr)
  sten·o·graph·ic
          (stĕn′ ō·grăf′ ĭk)
  sten·o·type   (stĕn′ ō·tīp)
sten·to·ri·an   (stĕn·tō′ rĭ·ȧn)
step   (stĕp)
  (pace; see *steppe*)
  stepped,   step·ping
  step·child   step·fa·ther
  step·par·ent   step·ping·stone
steppe   (stĕp)
  (Russian plains; see *step*)
ster·e·o·phon·ic
        (stĕr′ ĕ·ō·fŏn′ ĭk)
ster·e·op·ti·con
        (stĕr′ ĕ·ŏp′ tĭ·kŏn)
ster·e·o·scope   (stĕr′ ĕ·ō·skōp′)
ster·e·o·type   (stĕr′ ĕ·ō·tīp′)
ster·ile   (stĕr′ ĭl)
  ste·ril·i·ty   (stĕ·rĭl′ ĭ·tĭ)
  ster·i·li·za·tion
        (stĕr′ ĭ·lĭ·zā′ shŭn)
  ster·i·lize   -iz·ing
ster·ling   (stûr′ lĭng)
stern   (stûrn)
  stern·ness
ster·num   (stûr′ nŭm)
steth·o·scope   (stĕth′ ō·skōp)
  steth·o·scop·ic
        (stĕth′ ō·skŏp′ ĭk)
ste·ve·dore   (stē′ vĕ·dōr′)

Ste·ven·son, Ad·lai E.
      (stē′ vĕn·s′n, ăd′ lā)
stew·ard   (stū′ ērd)
  stew·ard·ess
stick·ler   (stĭk′ lēr)
stick·pin   (stĭk′ pĭn′)
stick-to-it·ive·ness
      (stĭk′ tōō′ ĭt·ĭv·nĕs)
stiff·en   (stĭf′ ĕn)
sti·fle   (stī′ f′l)
  -fling
stig·ma   (stĭg′ mȧ)
  stig·ma·tize   -tiz·ing
stig·ma·tism   (stĭg′ mȧ·tĭz′m)
stilt·ed   (stĭl′ tĕd)
stim·u·late   (stĭm′ û·lāt)
  -lat·ing
  stim·u·lant   (-lȧnt)
  stim·u·la·tion
        (stĭm′ û·lā′ shŭn)
  stim·u·la·tive   (stĭm′ û·lā′ tĭv)
  stim·u·la·tor
stim·u·lus   (stĭm′ û·lŭs)
  pl. stim·u·li   (-lī)
sting·y   (stĭn′ jĭ)
  sting·i·ness
sti·pend   (stī′ pĕnd)
stip·ple   (stĭp′ ′l)
  stip·pling
stip·u·late   (stĭp′ û·lāt)
  -lat·ing
  stip·u·la·tion   (stĭp′ û·lā′ shŭn)
stir·rup   (stîr′ ŭp)
stitch   (stĭch)
stock   (stŏk)
  stock·bro·ker   stock ex·change
  stock·hold·er   stock mar·ket
  stock·pile
stock·ade   (stŏk·ād′)
stock·i·net   (stŏk′ ĭ·nĕt′)
stock·ing   (stŏk′ ĭng)
stodg·y   (stŏj′ ĭ)
  stodg·i·ness
sto·gie   (stō′ gĭ)
sto·ic   (stō′ ĭk)
  sto·i·cal·ly
stok·er   (stōk′ ēr)
sto·len   (stō′ lĕn)
stol·id   (stŏl′ ĭd)
  sto·lid·i·ty   (stō·lĭd′ ĭ·tĭ)
stom·ach   (stŭm′ ák)
stone   (stōn)
  stone·cut·ter   stone-deaf
  stone·mas·on·ry
  stone·ware   ston·y

stooge (stooj)
stool pi·geon (stool)
stop (stŏp)
  stopped stop·ping
  stop·cock stop·gap
  stop light stop·o·ver
  stop·page stop·per
stor·age (stôr′ ĭj)
store·keep·er (stôr′ kēp′ ẽr)
sto·ry (stō′ rĭ)
  -ries
  (story of a building sometimes
  spelled *storey*)
  sto·ried sto·ry·tell·er
stout·heart·ed (stout′ här′ tĕd)
stove·pipe (stōv′ pīp′)
stow·a·way (stō′ á·wā′)
strad·dle (străd′ ′l)
  strad·dling
strag·gly (străg′ lĭ)
straight (strāt)
  (without curves; see *strait*)
  straight·a·way straight·en
  straight·for·ward
strain·er (strān′ ẽr)
strait (strāt)
  (tight, narrow; see *straight*)
  strait·jack·et strait-laced
strange (strānj)
  strange·ly strange·ness
stran·gle (străng′ g′l)
  -gling stran·gle hold
  stran·gu·la·tion
    (străng′ gū·lā′ shŭn)
strap·ping (străp′ ĭng)
strat·e·gy (străt′ ĕ·jĭ)
  -gies
  strat·a·gem (străt′ á·jĕm)
  stra·te·gic (strá·tē′ jĭk)
  strat·e·gist (străt′ ĕ·jĭst)
strat·i·fy (străt′ ĭ·fī)
  -fied -fy·ing
  strat·i·fi·ca·tion
    (străt′ ĭ·fĭ·kā′ shŭn)
strat·o·sphere (străt′ ŏ·sfẽr)
stra·tum (strā′ tŭm)
  pl. -ta
stra·tus (strā′ tŭs)
  pl. -ti (-tī)
straw·ber·ry (strô′ bĕr′ ĭ)
  -ber·ries
streak·y (strēk′ ĭ)
  streak·i·ness
stream·lined (strēm′ līnd′)
street·car (strēt′ kär′)

strength (strĕngth)
  strength·ened
stren·u·ous (strĕn′ ū·ŭs)
strep·to·coc·cus
    (strĕp′ tŏ·kŏk′ ŭs)
  pl. strep·to·coc·ci (-kŏk′ sī)
strep·to·my·cin
    (strĕp′ tŏ·mī′ sĭn)
stress (strĕs)
stretch (strĕch)
  stretch·a·ble
strewn (strōōn)
stri·at·ed (strī′ āt·ĕd)
  stri·a·tion (strī·ā′ shŭn)
strick·en (strĭk′ ĕn)
strict (strĭkt)
stric·ture (strĭk′ tŭr)
stri·dent (strī′ dĕnt)
  -dence -den·cy
strife (strīf)
strike (strīk)
  strik·ing strike·break·er
strin·gent (strĭn′ jĕnt)
  -gen·cy
string·y (strĭng′ ĭ)
striped (strīpt)
strip·ling (strĭp′ lĭng)
stroke (strōk)
  strok·ing
stroll·er (strōl′ ẽr)
strong (strŏng)
  strong-arm strong·box
  strong-willed
stron·ti·um (strŏn′ shĭ·ŭm)
struc·ture (strŭk′ tŭr)
  struc·tur·al
stru·del (shtrōō′ dĕl)
strug·gle (strŭg′ ′l)
  strug·gling
strum (strŭm)
  strummed strum·ming
strum·pet (strŭm′ pĕt)
strych·nine (strĭk′ nĭn)
stub·ble (stŭb′ ′l)
  stub·bly
stub·born (stŭb′ ẽrn)
  stub·born·ly stub·born·ness
stuc·co (stŭk′ ō)
stu·dent (stū′ dĕnt)
stu·di·o (stū′ dĭ·ō)
  -os
stu·di·ous (stū′ dĭ·ŭs)
stud·y (stŭd′ ĭ)
  stud·ied stud·ies
  stud·y·ing

stuff·ing (stŭf′ ĭng)
stuff·y (stŭf′ ĭ)
  stuff·i·ly -i·ness
stul·ti·fy (stŭl′ tĭ·fī)
  -fied -fy·ing
  stul·ti·fi·ca·tion
    (stŭl′ tĭ·fĭ·kā′ shŭn)
stum·ble (stŭm′ b′l)
  -bling
stun·ning (stŭn′ ĭng)
stu·pe·fy (stū′ pĕ·fī)
  -fied -fy·ing
  stu·pe·fac·tion
    (stū′ pĕ·făk′ shŭn)
stu·pen·dous (stū·pĕn′ dŭs)
stu·pid (stū′ pĭd)
  stu·pid·i·ty (stū·pĭd′ ĭ·tĭ)
stu·por (stū′ pĕr)
  stu·por·ous
stur·dy (stûr′ dĭ)
  stur·di·ly -di·ness
stur·geon (stûr′ jŭn)
stut·ter (stŭt′ ĕr)
sty (stī)
  sties
style (stīl)
  styl·ing styl·ish
  styl·ist
  sty·lis·tic (stī·lĭs′ tĭk)
  styl·ize -iz·ing
sty·lus (stī′ lŭs)
sty·mie (stī′ mĭ)
  -mied -my·ing
styp·tic (stĭp′ tĭk)
suave (swäv)
  suave·ly suave·ness
  suav·i·ty (swäv′ ĭ·tĭ)
sub·al·tern (sŭ·bôl′ tĕrn)
sub·com·mit·tee
    (sŭb′ kŏ·mĭt′ ê)
sub·con·scious (sŭb·kŏn′ shŭs)
sub·con·trac·tor
    (sŭb·kŏn′ trăk·tĕr)
sub·due (sŭb·dū′)
  -du·ing
sub·ject (sŭb·jĕkt) v.
    (sŭb′ jĕkt) adj.,n.
  sub·jec·tive (sŭb·jĕk′ tĭv)
  -tive·ly
  sub·jec·tiv·i·ty
    (sŭb′ jĕk·tĭv′ ĭ·tĭ)
sub·ju·gate (sŭb′ jōō·gāt)
  -gat·ing
sub·junc·tive (sŭb·jŭngk′ tĭv)

sub·lease (sŭb′ lēs′)
  -leas·ing
sub·li·mate (sŭb′ lĭ·māt)
  -mat·ing
  sub·li·ma·tion
    (sŭb′ lĭ·mā′ shŭn)
sub·lime (sŭb·līm′)
  sub·lime·ly
  sub·lim·i·ty (sŭb·lĭm′ ĭ·tĭ)
sub·lim·i·nal (sŭb·lĭm′ ĭ·nǎl)
  -nal·ly
sub·mar·gin·al (sŭb·mär′ jĭ·nǎl)
  -al·ly
sub·ma·rine (sŭb′ má·rēn′)
sub·merge (sŭb·mûrj′)
  -merg·ing
  sub·mer·gence (sŭb·mûr′ jĕns)
sub·merse (sŭb·mûrs′)
  -mers·ing sub·mers·i·ble
sub·mis·sion (sŭb·mĭsh′ ŭn)
sub·mis·sive (sŭb·mĭs′ ĭv)
  sub·mis·sive·ness
sub·mit (sŭb·mĭt′)
  -mitted -mit·ting
sub·nor·mal (sŭb·nôr′ mǎl)
  sub·nor·mal·i·ty
    (sŭb′ nôr·măl′ ĭ·tĭ)
sub·or·di·nate (sǔ·bôr′ dĭ·nĭt)
    adj., n
    (-nāt) v.
  -nat·ing
  sub·or·di·na·tion
    (sǔ·bôr′ dĭ·nā′ shŭn)
sub·orn (sŭb·ôrn′)
sub·poe·na (sŭb·pē′ nà)
sub·scribe (sŭb·skrīb′)
  -scrib·ing
  sub·scrip·tion
    (sŭb·skrĭp′ shŭn)
sub·se·quent (sŭb′ sê·kwĕnt)
  -quence
sub·ser·vi·ent (sŭb·sûr′ vĭ·ĕnt)
  -ence
sub·side (sŭb·sīd′)
  -sid·ing
sub·sid·i·ar·y (sŭb·sĭd′ ĭ·ĕr′ ĭ)
  -ar·ies
sub·si·dy (sŭb′ sĭ·dĭ)
  -dies
  sub·si·dize (sŭb′ sĭ·dĭ·zā′ shŭn)
    -diz·ing
sub·si·dize
sub·sist·ence (sŭb·sĭs′ tĕns)
sub·soil (sŭb′ soil′)
sub·spe·cies (sŭb·spē′ shĭz)

sub·stance	(sŭb′ stăns)
sub·stand·ard	(sŭb·stăn′ dĕrd)
sub·stan·tial	(sŭb·stăn′ shăl)
-tial·ly	
sub·stan·ti·ate	(sŭb·stăn′ shĭ·āt)
-at·ing	
sub·stan·ti·a·tion	
	(sŭb·stăn′ shĭ·ā′ shŭn)
sub·stan·tive	(sŭb′ stăn·tĭv)
sub·sti·tute	(sŭb′ stĭ·tūt)
-tut·ing	
sub·stra·tum	(sŭb·strā′ tŭm)
sub·struc·ture	(sŭb·strŭk′ tŭr)
sub·ter·fuge	(sŭb′ tēr·fūj)
sub·ter·ra·ne·an	
	(sŭb′ tĕ·rā′ nĕ·ăn)
sub·tle	(sŭt′ 'l)
sub·tle·ness	
sub·tle·ty, -ties	(sŭt′ 'l·tĭ)
sub·tly	(sŭt′ lĭ)
sub·tract	(sŭb·trăkt′)
sub·trac·tion	
sub·trop·i·cal	(sŭb·trŏp′ ĭ·kăl)
sub·urb	(sŭb′ ûrb)
sub·ur·ban	(sŭb·ûr′ băn)
sub·ur·ban·ite	(sŭb·ûr′ băn·ĭt)
sub·ur·bi·a	(sŭb·ûr′ bĭ·à)
sub·ver·sive	(sŭb·vûr′ sĭv)
sub·ver·sion	
sub·vert	(sŭb·vûrt′)
sub·vert·er	
suc·ceed	(sŭk·sēd′)
suc·cess	(sŭk·sĕs′)
suc·cess·ful, -ful·ly, -ful·ness	
suc·ces·sion	(sŭk·sĕsh′ ŭn)
suc·ces·sive	(sŭk·sĕs′ ĭv)
suc·ces·sive·ly suc·ces·sor	
suc·cinct	(sŭk·sĭngkt′)
suc·cor	(sŭk′ ēr)
suc·co·tash	(sŭk′ ŏ·tăsh)
suc·cu·lent	(sŭk′ û·lĕnt)
-lence	
suc·cumb	(sŭ·kŭm′)
suck·ling	(sŭk′ lĭng)
suc·tion	(sŭk′ shŭn)
sud·den	(sŭd′ 'n)
sud·den·ly sud·den·ness	
suds·y	(sŭd′ zĭ)
sue	(sū)
su·ing	
suède	(swād)
su·et	(sū′ ĕt)
suf·fer	(sŭf′ ēr)
suf·fer·ance	(sŭf′ ēr·ăns)

suf·fice	(sŭ·fīs′)
suf·fic·ing	
suf·fi·cient	(sŭ·fĭsh′ ĕnt)
-cien·cy	
suf·fix	(sŭf′ ĭks)
suf·fo·cate	(sŭf′ ŏ·kāt)
-cat·ing	
suf·fo·ca·tion	(sŭf′ ŏ·kā′ shŭn)
suf·frage	(sŭf′ rĭj)
suf·fra·gette	(sŭf′ rà·jĕt′)
suf·fuse	(sŭ·fūz′)
suf·fus·ing	
suf·fu·sion	(sŭ·fū′ zhŭn)
sug·ar	(shŏŏg′ ēr)
sug·ar-coat	sug·ar·plum
sug·ar·y	
sug·gest	(sŭg·jĕst′)
sug·gest·i·ble	
sug·ges·tion	(sŭg·jĕs′ chŭn)
sug·ges·tive	-tive·ness
su·i·cide	(sū′ ĭ·sīd)
su·i·cid·al	(sū′ ĭ·sīd′ ăl)
suit·a·ble	(sūt′ à·b'l)
suit·a·bil·i·ty	(sūt′ à·bĭl′ ĭ·tĭ)
suit·case	(sūt′ kās′)
suite	(swēt)
(retinue; see *sweet*)	
suit·or	(sūt′ ēr)
sul·fa	(sŭl′ fà)
sul·fa·nil·a·mide	
	(sŭl′ fà·nĭl′ à·mīd)
sul·fate	(sŭl′ fāt)
sul·fide	(sŭl′ fīd)
sul·fite	(sŭl′ fīt)
sul·fur	(sŭl′ fēr)
sul·fur di·ox·ide	
sul·fu·ric ac·id	(sŭl·fū′ rĭk)
sul·fu·rous	
sulk·y	(sŭl′ kĭ)
sulk·i·ness	
sul·len	(sŭl′ ĕn)
sul·len·ly	sul·len·ness
sul·tan	(sŭl′ tăn)
sul·tan·a	(sŭl·tăn′ à)
sul·try	(sŭl′ trĭ)
sul·tri·ness	
su·mac	(shŏŏ′ măk)
sum·ma·ry	(sŭm′ à·rĭ)
-ries	
sum·ma·ri·ly	(sŭm′ à·rĭ·lĭ)
sum·ma·ri·za·tion	
	(sŭm′ à·rĭ·zā′ shŭn)
sum·ma·rize	-riz·ing
sum·mer	(sŭm′ ēr)
sum·mer·house	

sum·mer·time sum·mer·y
sum·mit (sŭm′ ĭt)
sum·mon (sŭm′ ŭn)
sum·mon·er
sump·tu·ous (sŭmp′ tū̇·ŭs)
sun (sŭn)
sunned sun·ning
sun bath sun·burn
sun·di·al sun-dried
sun·fast sun·flow·er
sun·glass·es sun lamp
sun·light sun·ny
sun·rise sun·set
sun·shade sun·shine
sun·stroke sun·up
sun·dae (sŭn′ dĭ)
sun·der (sŭn′ dēr)
sunk·en (sŭngk′ ĕn)
su·per (sū′ pēr)
su·per·a·bun·dance
(sū′ pēr·a·bŭn′ dăns)
su·per·an·nu·ate
(sū′ pēr·ăn′ ū·āt)
su·perb (sù·pûrb′)
su·per·car·go (sū′ pēr·kär′ gō)
su·per·cil·i·ous
(sū′ pēr·sĭl′ ĭ·ŭs)
su·per·e·go (sū′ pēr·ē′ gō)
su·per·fi·cial (sū′ pēr·fĭsh′ ăl)
-cial·ly
su·per·fi·ci·al·i·ty
(sū′ pēr·fĭsh′ ĭ·ăl′ ĭ·tĭ)
-ties
su·per·flu·ous (sù·pûr′ flŏŏ·ŭs)
su·per·flu·i·ty
(sū′ pēr·flŏŏ′ ĭ·tĭ)
-ties
su·per·high·way
(sū′ pēr·hĭ′ wā′)
su·per·hu·man
(sū′ pēr·hū′ măn)
su·per·im·pose (sū′ pēr·ĭm·pōz′)
-pos·ing
su·per·in·tend (sū′ pēr·ĭn·tĕnd′)
su·per·in·tend·ent
su·pe·ri·or (sù·pē̇r′ ĭ·ēr)
su·pe·ri·or·i·ty
(sù·pē̇r′ ĭ·ŏr′ ĭ·tĭ)
su·per·la·tive (sù·pûr′ lá·tĭv)
-tive·ly
su·per·mar·ket
(sū′ pēr·mär′ kĕt)
su·per·nu·mer·ar·y
(sū′ pēr·nū′ mēr·ĕr′ ĭ)
-ar·ies

su·per·sat·u·rate
(sū′ pēr·săt′ ū̇·rāt)
-rat·ing
su·per·sede (sū′ pēr·sēd′)
-sed·ing
su·per·ses·sion (-sĕsh′ ŭn)
su·per·son·ic (sū′ pēr·sŏn′ ĭk)
su·per·sti·tion (sū′ pēr·stĭsh′ ŭn)
su·per·sti·tious
su·per·struc·ture
(sū′ pēr·strŭk′ tūr)
su·per·vise (sū′ pēr·vīz′)
-vis·ing su·per·vi·sor
su·per·vi·so·ry
(sū′ pēr·vĭ′ zō·rĭ)
su·pine (sù·pīn′)
sup·per (sŭp′ ēr)
sup·plant (sŭ·plánt′)
sup·ple (sŭp′ ′l)
sup·ple·ness
sup·ple·ment (sŭp′ lê·mĕnt)
sup·ple·men·tal
(sŭp′ lê·mĕn′ tăl)
sup·ple·men·ta·ry
(sŭp′ lê·mĕn′ tá·rĭ)
sup·pli·ant (sŭp′ lĭ·ănt)
-ance
sup·pli·cant (sŭp′ lĭ·kănt)
sup·pli·cate (sŭp′ lĭ·kāt)
-cat·ing
sup·ply (sŭ·plī′)
sup·plied sup·ply·ing
sup·pli·er sup·plies
sup·port (sŭ·pōrt′)
sup·port·a·ble sup·port·er
sup·pose (sŭ·pōz′)
sup·pos·ing sup·pos·a·ble
sup·pos·ed·ly
sup·po·si·tion (sŭp′ ō·zĭsh′ ŭn)
sup·po·si·tion·al
sup·pos·i·to·ry (sŭ·pŏz′ ĭ·tō′ rĭ)
-ries
sup·press (sŭ·prĕs′)
sup·press·i·ble
sup·pres·sion (-prĕsh′ ŭn)
sup·pres·sive
su·preme (sù·prēm′)
su·prem·a·cy (sù·prĕm′ á·sĭ)
su·preme·ly
sur·cease (sûr·sēs′)
sur·charge (sûr′ chärj′) **n.**
sure·ly (shŏŏr′ lĭ)
sure·ty (shŏŏr′ tĭ)
-ties

sur·face (sûr' fĭs)
  -fac·ing
surf·board (sûrf' bôrd')
sur·feit (sûr' fĭt)
  -feit·ed
surge (sûrj)
  (to swell; see *serge*)
  surg·ing
sur·geon (sûr' jŭn)
sur·ger·y (sûr' jĕr·ĭ)
  sur·gi·cal (sûr' jĭ·kăl)
  -cal·ly
sur·ly (sûr' lĭ)
  sur·li·ness
sur·mise (sûr·mīz')
  -mis·ing
sur·mount (sûr·mount')
  sur·mount·a·ble
sur·name (sûr' nām')
sur·pass (sĕr·pås')
  sur·pass·a·ble
sur·plice (sûr' plĭs)
  (vestment; see *surplus*)
sur·plus (sûr' plŭs)
  (excess; see *surplice*)
sur·prise (sĕr·prīz')
  -pris·ing
sur·re·al·ism (sŭ·rē' ăl·ĭz'm)
sur·ren·der (sŭ·rĕn' dĕr)
sur·rep·ti·tious (sûr' ĕp·tĭsh' ŭs)
sur·rey (sûr' ĭ)
sur·ro·gate (sûr' ŏ·gāt)
sur·round (sŭ·round')
sur·tax (sûr' tăks')
sur·veil·lance (sûr·vāl' ăns)
sur·vey (sĕr·vā') v.
    (sûr' vā) n.
  sur·vey·or (sĕr·vā' ĕr)
sur·vive (sĕr·vīv')
  -viv·ing   sur·viv·al
  sur·vi·vor
sus·cep·ti·ble (sŭ·sĕp' tĭ·b'l)
  sus·cep·ti·bil·i·ty
    (sŭ·sĕp' tĭ·bĭl' ĭ·tĭ)
sus·pect (sŭs' pĕkt) n.
    (sŭs·pĕkt')
    adj., v.
sus·pend (sŭs·pĕnd')
sus·pend·er (sŭs·pĕn' dĕr)
sus·pen·sion (sŭs·pĕn' shŭn)
sus·pi·cious (sŭs·pĭsh' ŭs)
  sus·pi·cion (sŭs·pĭsh' ŭn)
sus·tain·ing (sŭs·tān' ĭng)
sus·te·nance (sŭs' tĕ·năns)
su·ture (sū' tûr)

su·ze·rain·ty (sū' zĕ·răn·tĭ)
svelte (svĕlt)
swab·ber (swŏb' ĕr)
swad·dling clothes
    (swŏd' lĭng)
swag·ger (swăg' ĕr)
Swa·hi·li (swä·hē' lĕ)
swain (swān)
swal·low (swŏl' ŏ)
swa·mi (swä' mĭ)
swank·y (swăngk' ĭ)
swan's-down (swŏnz' doun')
swarth·y (swôr' thĭ)
  swarth·i·ness
swash·buck·ler (swŏsh' bŭk' lĕr)
swas·ti·ka (swŏs' tĭ·kä)
swatch (swŏch)
swat·ter (swŏt' ĕr)
sway-backed (swā' băkt')
Swa·zi·land (swä' zĕ·lănd')
swear (swâr)
sweat (swĕt)
  sweat·i·ness   sweat shirt
  sweat·shop
sweat·er (swĕt' ĕr)
Swede (swēd)
  Swed·ish
sweep·stake (swēp' stāk')
sweet (swēt)
  (agreeable; see *suite*)
  sweet·bread   sweet·bri·er
  sweet·en·ing   sweet·meats
  sweet po·ta·to sweet Wil·liam
swel·ter·ing (swĕl' tĕr·ĭng)
swept (swĕpt)
swerve (swûrv)
  swerv·ing
swill (swĭl)
swim (swĭm)
  swam   swim·ming
  swim·mer
swin·dler (swĭn' dlĕr)
swine (swīn)
  swin·ish
swirl (swûrl)
switch (swĭch)
  switch·back   switch·board
  switch·man
swiv·el (swĭv' 'l)
  -eled,   -el·ing
swol·len (swōl' ĕn)
sword (sôrd)
  sword·fish   swords·man
syc·a·more (sĭk' à·mōr)

syc·o·phant   (sĭk′ ŏ·fănt)
  -phan·cy
syl·la·ble   (sĭl′ à·b'l)
  syl·lab·ic   (sĭ·lăb′ ĭk)
  syl·lab·i·ca·tion
             (sĭ·lăb′ ĭ·kā′ shŭn)
  syl·lab·i·fy   (sĭ·lăb′ ĭ·fĭ)
  -fied   -fy·ing
syl·la·bus   (sĭl′ à·bŭs)
  -bus·es
syl·lo·gism   (sĭl′ ŏ·jĭz′m)
  syl·lo·gis·tic   (sĭl′ ŏ·jĭs′ tĭk)
sylph   (sĭlf)
  sylph·like
syl·van   (sĭl′ văn)
sym·bi·o·sis   (sĭm′ bĭ·ō′ sĭs)
  sym·bi·ot·ic   (-ŏt′ ĭk)
sym·bol   (sĭm′ bŭl)
  (emblem; see *cymbal*)
  sym·**bol**·ic   (sĭm·bŏl′ ĭk)
  sym·bol·i·cal   (sĭm·bŏl′ ĭ·kǎl)
  -cal·ly   sym·bol·ism
  sym·bol·ize   -iz·ing
sym·met·ri·cal   (sĭ·mĕt′ rĭ·kǎl)
  -cal·ly
sym·me·try   (sĭm′ ĕ·trĭ)
sym·pa·thy   (sĭm′ pà·thĭ)
  -thies
  sym·pa·thet·ic
            (sĭm′ pà·thĕt′ ĭk)
  sym·pa·thize   -thiz·ing
sym·pho·ny   (sĭm′ fŏ·nĭ)
  -nies
  sym·phon·ic   (sĭm·fŏn′ ĭk)
sym·po·si·um   (sĭm·pō′ zĭ·ŭm)
  pl. sym·po·si·a
symp·tom   (sĭmp′ tŭm)
  symp·to·mat·ic
            (sĭmp′ tŏ·mǎt′ ĭk)
syn·a·gogue   (sĭn′ à·gŏg)
syn·chro·mesh   (sĭng′krŏ·mĕsh′)
syn·chro·nize   (sĭng′ krŏ·nīz)
  -niz·ing
  syn·chro·ni·za·tion
         (sĭng′ krŏ·nĭ·zā′ shŭn)
syn·co·pa·tion
         (sĭng′ kŏ·pā′ shŭn)
syn·di·cate   (sĭn′ dĭ·kåt) *n.*
  -cat·ing   (-kāt) *v.*
syn·drome   (sĭn′ drōm)
syn·od   (sĭn′ ŭd)
syn·o·nym   (sĭn′ ŏ·nĭm)
  syn·on·y·mous
         (sĭ·nŏn′ ĭ·mŭs)

syn·op·sis   (sĭ·nŏp′ sĭs)
  pl. -ses
  syn·op·tic   (sĭ·nŏp′ tĭk)
syn·tax   (sĭn′ tăks)
syn·the·sis   (sĭn′ thĕ·sĭs)
  pl. -ses
  syn·the·size   (sĭn′ thĕ·sīz)
  -siz·ing
  syn·thet·ic   (sĭn·thĕt′ ĭk)
  syn·thet·i·cal·ly
syph·i·lis   (sĭf′ ĭ·lŭs)
sy·rin·ga   (sĭ·rĭng′ gà)
syr·inge   (sĭr′ ĭnj)
  sy·rin·ge·al   (sĭ·rĭn′ jĕ·ǎl)
syr·inx   (sĭr′ ĭngks)
  pl. syr·in·ges   (sĭ·rĭn′ jēz)
sys·tem   (sĭs′ tĕm)
  sys·tem·at·ic   (sĭs′ tĕm·ăt′ ĭk)
  -i·cal·ly
  sys·tem·a·**tize**   (sĭs′ tĕm·à·**tīz**)
  -tiz·ing

T

Ta·bas·co   (tà·băs′ kō)
tab·er·nac·le   (tăb′ ẽr·năk′l)
tab·leau   (tăb′ lō)
  pl. tab·leaux   (-lōz)
ta·ble·cloth   (tā′ b'l·klŏth′)
ta·ble d'hôte   (tà′ blĕ dōt′)
ta·ble·spoon   (tā′ b'l·spōōn′)
  ta·ble·spoon·ful, -fuls
tab·let   (tăb′ lĕt)
tab·loid   (tăb′ loid)
ta·boo   (tà·bōō′)
  -booed   -boo·ing
ta·bor   (tā′ bẽr)
tab·u·late   (tăb′ ù·lăt)
  -lat·ing
  tab·u·lar   (tăb′ ù·lẽr)
  tab·u·la·tion   (tăb′ ù·lā′ shŭn)
  tab·u·la·tor
tac·it   (tăs′ ĭt)
tac·i·turn   (tăs′ ĭ·tûrn)
  tac·i·tur·ni·ty   (tăs′ ĭ·tûr′ nĭ·tĭ)
tack·le   (tăk′l)
  -ling
tact   (tăkt)
  tact·ful, -ful·ly, -ful·ness
  tact·less   -less·ness
tac·tics   (tăk′ tĭks)
  tac·ti·cal   (tăk′ tĭ·kǎl)
  -cal·ly
  tac·ti·cian   (tăk·tĭsh′ ǎn)

tac·tile (tăk′ tĭl)
tad·pole (tăd′ pōl′)
taf·fe·ta (tăf′ ĕ·tả)
Ta·hi·ti·an (tả·hē′ tĭ·ản)
tail (tāl)
  tailed, tail·ing
  tail·first tail·less
  tail·piece tail spin
  tail wind
tai·lor (tā′ lĕr)
  tai·lor·ing tai·lor-made
taint (tānt)
Tai·wan (tī·wän′)
  (*also* Formosa)
Taj Mahal (täj mả·häl′)
talc (tălk)
tal·cum pow·der
  (tăl′ kŭm)
tal·ent (tăl′ ĕnt)
tale·tell·er (tāl′ tĕl′ ẽr)
tal·is·man (tăl′ ĭs·mản)
talk·a·tive (tôk′ ả·tĭv)
  -tive·ness
Tal·la·has·see, Fla.
  (tăl′ ả·hăs′ ĕ)
tal·low (tăl′ ō)
tal·ly·ho (tăl′ ĭ·hō′)
Tal·mud (tăl′ mŭd)
tal·on (tăl′ ŭn)
tam·a·rack (tăm′ ả·răk)
tam·bou·rine (tăm′ bŏŏ·rēn′)
tame (tām)
  tam·ing tam·a·ble
  tame·ly
Tam·ma·ny Hall (tăm′ ả·nĭ)
tamp·er (tăm′ pẽr)
tam·pon (tăm′ pŏn)
tan·a·ger (tăn′ ả·jẽr)
tan·dem (tăn′ dĕm)
Tan·gan·yi·ka (tăn′ găn·yē′ kả)
tan·gent (tăn′ jĕnt)
  tan·gen·tial (tăn·jĕn′ shăl)
tan·ge·rine (tăn′ jĕ·rēn′)
tan·gi·ble (tăn′ jĭ·b′l)
tan·gle (tăng′ g′l)
  -gling
tang·y (tăng′ ĭ)
  tang·i·ness
tank·ard (tăngk′ ẽrd)
tan·ner·y (tăn′ ẽr·ĭ)
  tan·ner·ies
tan·nic ac·id (tăn′ ĭk)
tan·ta·lize (tăn′ tả·līz)
  -liz·ing
tan·ta·mount (tăn′ tả·mount′)

tan·trum (tăn′ trŭm)
Tao·ism (tou′ ĭz′m)
ta·pa cloth (tä′ pä)
ta·per (tā′ pẽr)
  (candle; see *tapir*)
tap·es·try (tăp′ ĕs·trĭ)
  -tries
tape·worm (tāp′ wûrm′)
tap·i·o·ca (tăp′ ĭ·ō′ kả)
ta·pir (tā′ pẽr)
  (animal; see *taper*)
tap·ster (tăp′ stẽr)
tar·an·tel·la (tăr′ ản·tĕl′ ả)
  (dance)
ta·ran·tu·la (tả·răn′ tŭ·lả)
  (spider)
tar·dy (tär′ dĭ)
  tar·di·ly -i·ness
tar·get (tär′ gĕt)
tar·iff (tăr′ ĭf)
tar·nish (tär′ nĭsh)
  tar·nish·a·ble
ta·ro root (tä′ rō)
tar·pau·lin (tär·pô′ lĭn)
tar·pon (tär′ pŏn)
tar·ra·gon (tăr′ ả·gŏn)
tar·ry (tăr′ ĭ)
  tar·ried tar·ry·ing
tar·tan (tär′ tản)
tar·tar (tär′ tẽr)
  (cream of tartar)
tar·tare sauce (tär′ tẽr)
task·mas·ter (tásk′ más′ tẽr)
tas·sel (tăs′ ′l)
  tas·seled tas·sel·ing
taste (tāst)
  tast·ing
  taste·ful, -ful·ly, -ful·ness
  taste·less
  tast·i·ly -i·ness
  tast·y
tat·tered (tăt′ ẽrd)
tat·tle (tăt′ ′l)
  tat·tling tat·tle·tale
tat·too (tă·tōō′)
  tat·tooed tat·too·ing
taught (tôt)
  (instructed; see *taut*)
taunt (tônt)
taupe (tōp)
taut (tôt)
  (tight; see *taught*)
tau·tol·o·gy (tô·tŏl′ ô·jĭ)
  -gies

tau·to·log·i·cal
    (tô′ tŏ·lŏj′ ĭ·kăl)
tav·ern   (tăv′ ẽrn)
taw·dry   (tô′ drĭ)
  taw·dri·ness
taw·ny   (tô′ nĭ)
  taw·ni·ness
tax   (tăks)
  tax·a·ble
  tax·a·tion   (tăks·ā′ shŭn)
  tax-ex·empt   tax·gath·er·er
  tax·pay·er
tax·i   (tăk′ sĭ)
  tax·is   tax·i·cab
tax·i·der·mist   (tăk′ sĭ·dûr′ mĭst)
Tchai·kov·sky, Pe·ter Il·ich
    (chī·kôf′ skĭ)
teach   (tēch)
  teach·a·bil·i·ty
    (tēch′ à·bĭl′ ĭ·tĭ)
  teach·a·ble   teach·er
tea·cup·ful   (tē′ kŭp·fŏŏl′)
  -fuls
teak·wood   (tēk′ wŏŏd′)
team   (tēm)
  team·mate   team·ster
  team·work
tea·pot   (tē′ pŏt′)
tear·ful   (tẽr′ fŏŏl)
  -ful·ly   -ful·ness
tease   (tēz)
  teas·ing
tea·spoon·ful   (tē′ spŏŏn·fŏŏl′)
  -fuls
teat   (tēt)
tech·ni·cal   (tĕk′ nĭ·kăl)
  -cal·ly
  tech·ni·cal·i·ty
    (tĕk′ nĭ·kăl′ ĭ·tĭ)
  tech·ni·cian   (tĕk·nĭsh′ ăn)
Tech·ni·col·or   (tĕk′ nĭ·kŭl′ ẽr)
tech·nique   (tĕk·nēk′)
tech·nol·o·gy   (tĕk·nŏl′ ŏ·jĭ)
  -gies
  tech·no·log·i·cal
    (tĕk′ nŏ·lŏj′ ĭ·kăl)
  -cal·ly
  tech·nol·o·gist   (tĕk·nŏl′ ŏ·jĭst)
te·di·ous   (tē′ dĭ·ŭs)
  te·di·um   (tē′ dĭ·ŭm)
teem·ing   (tēm′ ĭng)
  (crowded)
teen-ag·er   (tēn′ āj′ ẽr)
tee shirt   (tē)
teeth   (tēth) n. pl.

teethe   (tēth) v.
  teeth·ing
tee·to·tal·er   (tē·tō′ t′lẽr)
Te·hran, I·ran   (tĕ·hrän′)
Tel A·viv, Is·ra·el
    (tĕl′ à·vēv′)
tel·e·cast   (tĕl′ ĕ·kăst′)
  tel·e·cast·er
tel·e·graph   (tĕl′ ĕ·gráf)
tel·e·ol·o·gy   (tĕl′ ĕ·ŏl′ ŏ·jĭ)
te·lep·a·thy   (tĕ·lĕp′ à·thĭ)
tel·e·phone   (tĕl′ ĕ·fōn)
tel·e·scope   (tĕl′ ĕ·skōp)
  tel·e·scop·ic   (tĕl′ ĕ·skŏp′ ĭk)
tel·e·type   (tĕl′ ĕ·tīp)
tel·e·vi·sion   (tĕl′ ĕ·vĭzh′ ŭn)
  tel·e·view·er
  tel·e·vise   -vis·ing
tell·tale   (tĕl′ tāl′)
te·mer·i·ty   (tĕ·mĕr′ ĭ·tĭ)
tem·per   (tĕm′ pẽr)
tem·per·a   (tĕm′ pẽr·à)
tem·per·a·ment
    (tĕm′ pẽr·à·mĕnt)
  tem·per·a·men·tal
    (tĕm′ pẽr·à·mĕn′ tăl)
  -tal·ly
tem·per·ance   (tĕm′ pẽr·ăns)
tem·per·ate   (tĕm′ pẽr·ĭt)
  -ate·ly
tem·per·a·ture   (tĕm′ pẽr·à·tûr)
tem·pest   (tĕm′ pĕst)
  tem·pes·tu·ous
    (tĕm·pĕs′ tṳ·ŭs)
tem·plate   (tĕm′ plĭt)
tem·ple   (tĕm′ p′l)
tem·po·ral   (tĕm′ pŏ·răl)
  tem·po·ral·ly
tem·po·rar·y   (tĕm′ pŏ·rĕr′ ĭ)
  tem·po·rar·i·ly
    (tĕm′ pŏ·rĕr′ ĭ·lĭ)
tem·po·rize   (tĕm′ pŏ·rīz)
  -riz·ing
tempt   (tĕmpt)
  tempt·a·ble
  temp·ta·tion   (tĕmp·tā′ shŭn)
  tempt·er   tempt·ress
ten·a·ble   (tĕn′ à·b′l)
te·na·cious   (tĕ·nā′ shŭs)
te·nac·i·ty   (tĕ·năs′ ĭ·tĭ)
ten·ant   (tĕn′ ănt)
  -an·cy
tend·en·cy   (tĕn′ dĕn·sĭ)
  -cies
ten·den·tious   (tĕn·dĕn′ shŭs)

tend·er   (těn′ dẽr)
  ten·der·foot   ten·der·heart·ed
  ten·der·loin
ten·don   (těn′ dŭn)
ten·dril   (těn′ drĭl)
Ten·e·brae   (těn′ ĕ·brē)
ten·e·ment   (těn′ ĕ·měnt)
ten·et   (těn′ ĕt)
ten·fold   (těn′ fōld′)
Ten·nes·see   (těn′ ĕ·sē′)
  abbr. Tenn.
  Ten·nes·see·an   (-sē′ ǎn)
ten·nis   (těn′ ĭs)
ten·or   (těn′ ẽr)
ten·pins   (těn′ pĭnz′)
tense   (těns)
  tense·ly   tense·ness
  ten·si·ty   (těn′ sĭ·tĭ)
ten·sile strength   (těn′ sĭl)
ten·sion   (těn′ shŭn)
ten·sor   (těn′ sẽr)
ten·ta·cle   (těn′ tȧ·k'l)
ten·ta·tive   (těn′ tȧ·tĭv)
  ten·ta·tive·ly, -tive·ness
ten·ter·hooks   (těn′ tẽr·hŏŏks′)
ten·u·ous   (těn′ û·ŭs)
ten·ure   (těn′ ûr)
te·pee   (tē′ pē)
tep·id   (těp′ ĭd)
te·qui·la   (tȧ·kē′ lä)
ter·ma·gant   (tûr′ mȧ·gǎnt)
ter·mi·na·ble   (tûr′ mĭ·nȧ·b'l)
ter·mi·nal   (tûr′ mĭ·nǎl)
ter·mi·nate   (tûr′ mĭ·nāt)
  -nat·ing
  ter·mi·na·tion
                    (tûr′ mĭ·nā′ shŭn)
ter·mi·nol·o·gy
                    (tûr′ mĭ·nŏl′ ō·jĭ)
  ter·mi·no·log·i·cal
                    (tûr′ mĭ·nō·lŏj′ ĭ·kǎl)
ter·mi·nus   (tûr′ mĭ·nŭs)
  pl. ter·mi·ni   (-nī)
ter·mite   (tûr′ mĭt)
tern   (tûrn)
  (bird; see turn)
ter·race   (těr′ ĭs)
ter·ra cot·ta   (těr′ ȧ·kŏt′ ȧ) n.
  ter·ra-cot·ta adj.
ter·rain   (tě·rān′)
ter·ra·pin   (těr′ ȧ·pĭn)
ter·raz·zo   (těr·rät′ tsō)
ter·res·tri·al   (tě·rěs′ trĭ·ǎl)
ter·ri·ble   (těr′ ĭ·b'l)
  ter·ri·ble·ness ter·ri·bly

ter·ri·er   (těr′ ĭ·ẽr)
ter·rif·ic   (tě·rĭf′ ĭk)
  ter·rif·i·cal·ly
ter·ri·fy   (těr′ ĭ·fī)
  -fied,   -fy·ing
ter·ri·to·ri·al   (těr′ ĭ·tō′ rĭ·ǎl)
  ter·ri·to·ry   (těr′ ĭ·tō′ rĭ)
ter·ror   (těr′ ẽr)
  ter·ror·ize   -iz·ing
ter·ry cloth   (těr′ ĭ)
terse   (tûrs)
  terse·ness
ter·ti·ar·y   (tûr′ shĭ·ěr′ ĭ)
tes·ta·ment   (těs′ tȧ·měnt)
tes·ti·cle   (těs′ tĭ·k'l)
tes·ti·fy   (těs′ tĭ·fī)
  -fied,   -fy·ing
  tes·ti·fi·er
tes·ti·mo·ny   (těs′ tĭ·mō′ nĭ)
  -nies
  tes·ti·mo·ni·al
                    (těs′ tĭ·mō′ nĭ·ǎl)
tet·a·nus   (tět′ ȧ·nŭs)
tête-à-tête   (tāt′ ȧ·tāt′)
teth·er   (těth′ ẽr)
tet·ra·chlo·ride   (tět′ rȧ·klō′ rīd)
tet·ra·he·dron   (tět′ rȧ·hē′ drŭn)
tet·ral·o·gy   (tě·trǎl′ ō·jĭ)
  -gies
te·tram·e·ter   (tě·trǎm′ ĕ·tẽr)
te·trarch   (tē′ trärk)
Teu·ton·ic   (tū·tŏn′ ĭk)
Tex·as   (těk′ sǎs)
  abbr. Tex.
  Tex·an   (těk′ sǎn)
text·book   (těkst′ bŏŏk′)
tex·tile   (těks′ tĭl)
tex·tu·al   (těks′ tṷ·ǎl)
tex·ture   (těks′ tûr)
  tex·tur·al
Thai·land   (tī′ lǎnd)
than   (thǎn)
  (other, else; "none other than
  yourself"; see then)
thank   (thǎngk)
  thank·ful, -ful·ly, -ful·ness
  thank·less
Thanks·giv·ing   (thǎnks·gĭv′ ĭng)
thatched   (thǎcht)
the·a·ter   (thē′ ȧ·tẽr)
  the·a·ter-in-the-round
the·at·ri·cal   (thě·ǎt′ rĭ·kǎl)
  -cal·ly
theft   (thěft)

their (thâr)
  (of them; see *there*)
  theirs
the·ism (thē′ ĭz′m)
  the·is·tic (thē·ĭs′ tĭk)
theme (thēm)
  the·mat·ic (thē·măt′ ĭk)
them·selves (thĕm·sĕlvz′)
then (thĕn)
  (at that time; see *than*)
thence (thĕns)
  thence·forth thence·for·ward
the·oc·ra·cy (thē·ŏk′ rȧ·sĭ)
the·ol·o·gy (thē·ŏl′ ō·jĭ)
  the·o·lo·gi·an (thē′ ō·lō′ jĭ·ȧn)
  the·o·log·i·cal (thē′ ō·lŏj′ ĭ·kȧl)
  -cal·ly
the·o·rem (thē′ ō·rĕm)
the·o·ry (thē′ ō·rĭ)
  -ries
  the·o·ret·i·cal (thē′ ō·rĕt′ ĭ·kȧl)
  -cal·ly
  the·o·re·ti·cian
      (thē′ ō·rē·tĭsh′ ȧn)
  the·o·rist (thē′ ō·rĭst)
  the·o·rize -riz·ing
the·os·o·phy (thē·ŏs′ ō·fĭ)
ther·a·peu·tic (thĕr′ ȧ·pū′ tĭk)
  ther·a·peu·ti·cal·ly
ther·a·py (thĕr′ ȧ·pĭ)
there (thâr)
  (in that place; see *their*)
there·a·bouts there·aft·er
there·by there·fore
there·in there·in·aft·er
there·in·to there·of
there·on there·un·der
there·un·to there·up·on
there·with
ther·mal (thûr′ mȧl)
ther·mo·dy·nam·ics
      (thûr′ mō·dĭ·năm′ ĭks)
ther·mom·e·ter
      (thĕr·mŏm′ ĕ·tēr)
ther·mo·nu·cle·ar
      (thûr′ mō·nū′ klē·ēr)
Ther·mos bot·tle
      (thûr′ mŏs)
ther·mo·stat (thûr′ mō·stăt)
  ther·mo·stat·i·cal·ly
      (thûr′ mō·stăt′ ĭ·kȧl·ĭ)
the·sau·rus (thē·sô′ rŭs)
these (thēz)
the·sis (thē′ sĭs)
  pl. the·ses (-sēz)

Thes·pi·an (thĕs′ pĭ·ȧn)
thi·a·mine (thī′ ȧ·mēn)
thick·ened (thĭk′ ĕnd)
thick·et (thĭk′ ĕt)
thick-skinned (thĭk′ skĭnd′)
thief (thēf) *n.*
  pl. thieves (thēvz)
thieve (thēv) *v.*
  thiev·ing thiev·er·y
  thiev·ish
thigh·bone (thī′ bōn′)
thim·ble·ful (thĭm′ b′l·fŏŏl)
thin (thĭn)
  thin·ly thin·ness
  thin·ner thin·ning
  thin-skinned
think·a·ble (thĭngk′ ȧ·b′l)
third (thûrd)
  third class
  third-class *adj. & adv.*
  third de·gree third-rate
thirst·y (thûrs′ tĭ)
  thirst·i·er, -i·est, -i·ly, -i·ness
thir·teen (thûr′ tēn′)
thir·ty (thûr′ tĭ)
  -ties thir·ti·eth
this·tle (thĭs′ ′l)
thith·er (thĭth′ ēr)
thong (thŏng)
tho·rax (thō′ răks)
  tho·rac·ic (thō·răs′ ĭk)
tho·ri·um (thō′ rĭ·ŭm)
thor·ough (thûr′ ō)
  thor·ough·bred
  thor·ough·go·ing
  thor·ough·ness
though (thō)
thought (thôt)
  thought·ful, -ful·ly, -ful·ness
  thought·less, -less·ly, -less·ness
thou·sand (thou′ zȧnd)
  thou·sand·fold thou·sandth
thrall·dom (thrôl′ dŭm)
thread·bare (thrĕd′ bâr′)
threat·en (thrĕt′ ′n)
three (thrē)
  three-di·men·sion·al
  three-pen·ny
  three-point land·ing
  three·some
thresh·er (thrĕsh′ ēr)
thresh·old (thrĕsh′ ōld)
thrice (thrīs)
thrift·y (thrĭf′ tĭ)
  thrift·i·er, -i·est, -i·ly, -i·ness

thrill·ing (thrĭl′ ĭng)
thriv·ing (thrĭv′ ĭng)
throat (thrōt)
throes (thrōz)
throm·bo·sis (thrŏm·bō′ sĭs)
throt·tle (thrŏt′ 'l)
through (thrōō)
  through·out
throw (thrō)
  throw·a·way throw·back
thug (thŭg)
  thug·gish
thumb (thŭm)
  thumb·nail thumb·tack
thun·der (thŭn′ dĕr)
  thun·der·bird thun·der·bolt
  thun·der·clap thun·der·cloud
  thun·der·head thun·der·ous
  thun·der·show·er
  thun·der·struck
thwart (thwôrt)
thyme (tīm)
  (seasoning; see time)
thy·mus gland (thī′ mŭs)
thy·roid gland (thī′ roid)
thy·self (thĭ·sĕlf′)
ti·ar·a (tĭ·âr′ ȧ)
Ti·bet·an (tĭ·bĕt′ ȧn)
tic (tĭk)
  (twitching; see tick)
tick (tĭk)
  (parasite; see tic)
tick·et (tĭk′ ĕt)
tick·le (tĭk′ 'l)
  -ling
  tick·lish (tĭk′ lĭsh)
tick·tack·toe (tĭk′ tăk·tō′)
tid·bit (tĭd′ bĭt′)
tid·dly·winks (tĭd′ 'l·ĭ·wĭngks′)
tide (tīd)
  tid·al (tīd′ ȧl)
  tide·wa·ter
ti·dy (tī′ dĭ)
  -died -dy·ing
  ti·di·er, -i·est, -i·ly, -i·ness
tie (tī)
  tied ty·ing
  tie-up
tier (tēr)
  (row)
tiff (tĭf)
tight (tīt)
  tight·en tight·fist·ed
  tight-lipped tight·rope
ti·gress (tī′ grĕs)

Ti·jua·na, Mex. (tê·hwä′ nä)
tile (tīl)
  til·ing
till (tĭl)
  till·a·ble
  till·age (tĭl′ ĭj)
tim·bale (tĭm′ bȧl)
tim·ber (tĭm′ bĕr)
  (wood; see timbre)
tim·bre (tĭm′ bĕr)
  (tone; see timber)
Tim·buk·tu (tĭm·bŭk′ tōō)
time (tīm)
  (period, occasion; see thyme)
  tim·ing time-hon·ored
  time·keep·er time·less
  time·li·ness time·ly
  time·piece time·sav·ing
  time·ta·ble time·worn
  time zone
tim·id (tĭm′ ĭd)
  ti·mid·i·ty (tĭ·mĭd′ ĭ·tĭ)
tim·or·ous (tĭm′ ēr·ŭs)
tim·pa·ni (tĭm′ pȧ·nē)
tinc·ture (tĭngk′ tụr)
tin·der·box (tĭn′ dĕr·bŏks′)
tine (tīn)
tin (tĭn)
  tin foil tin·ny
  tin-pan al·ley tin·type
tinge (tĭnj)
  tinge·ing
tin·gle (tĭng′ g'l)
  -gling
tin·sel (tĭn′ sĕl)
  -seled
ti·ny (tī′ nĭ)
  ti·ni·er, -i·est, -i·ness
tip-off (tĭp′ ôf′)
Tip·pe·rar·y (tĭp′ ĕ·râr′ ĭ)
tip·pler (tĭp′ lēr)
tip·ster (tĭp′ stēr)
tip·toe (tĭp′ tō′)
  -toe·ing
ti·rade (tī′ rād)
tire (tīr)
  tir·ing tired·ness
  tire·less
  tire·some -some·ly
tis·sue (tĭsh′ ū)
Ti·tan·ic (tī·tăn′ ĭk)
tithe (tĭth)
  tith·ing
ti·tian (tĭsh′ ȧn)

tit·il·late (tĭt′ ĭ·lāt)
  -il·lat·ing
  tit·il·la·tion (tĭt′ ĭ·lā′ shŭn)
ti·tle (tī′ t'l)
  -tling
  ti·tle·hold·er
  ti·tlist (tī′ tlĭst)
tit·mouse (tĭt′ mous′)
ti·trate (tī′ trāt)
  -trat·ing
  ti·tra·tion (tī·trā′ shŭn)
tit·u·lar (tĭt′ û·lēr)
to (tōō)
  (toward; see *too, two*)
toad·stool (tōd′ stōōl′)
toad·y (tōd′ ĭ)
  toad·ied   toad·y·ing
to-and-fro (tōō′ ₫nd·frō′)
toast·mas·ter (tōst′ más′ tēr)
to·bac·co (tô·bắk′ ō)
  -bac·cos
to·bog·gan (tô·bŏg′ ₫n)
to·day (tōō·dā′)
tod·dy (tŏ′ dĭ)
  (hot toddy)   tod·dies
to-do (tōō·dōō′)
toe (tō)
  toe·ing   toe dance *n.*
  toe hold   toe·nail
to·ga (tō′ gá)
to·geth·er (tōō·gĕth′ ēr)
togged (tŏgd)
tog·gle switch (tŏg′ 'l)
toil (toil)
  toil·er   toil·worn
toi·let (toi′ lĕt)
toi·lette (toi·lĕt′)
To·kay wine (tô·kā′)
to·ken (tō′ kĕn)
tol·er·a·ble (tŏl′ ēr·á·b'l)
tol·er·ant (tŏl′ ēr·₫nt)
  -ance
tol·er·ate (tŏl′ ēr·āt)
  -at·ing
  tol·er·a·tion (tŏl′ ēr·ā′ shŭn)
toll (tōl)
  toll booth   toll·gate
  toll·keep·er   toll road
Tol·stoy, Le·o (tŏl·stoi′)
tom·a·hawk (tŏm′ á·hôk)
to·ma·to (tô·mā′ tō)
  -toes
tomb·stone (tōōm′ stōn′)
tom·boy·ish (tŏm′ boi′ ĭsh)
tome (tōm)
tom·fool·er·y (tŏm′ fōōl′ ēr·ĭ)

to·mor·row (tōō·mŏr′ ō)
tom-tom (tŏm′ tŏm′)
ton·al (tōn′ ₫l)
  to·nal·i·ty (tô·nál′ ĭ·tĭ)
tone·less (tōn′ lĕs)
tongue (tŭng)
  tongue-tied
ton·ic (tŏn′ ĭk)
  to·nic·i·ty (tô·nĭs′ ĭ·tĭ)
to·night (tōō·nīt′)
ton·nage (tŭn′ ĭj)
ton·sil (tŏn′ sĭl)
  ton·sil·lec·to·my
         (tŏn′ sĭ·lĕk′ tô·mĭ)
  ton·sil·li·tis (tŏn′ sĭ·līr′ tĭs)
ton·sure (tŏn′ shēr)
  ton·so·ri·al (tŏn·sō′ rĭ·₫l)
too (tōō)
  (also; see *to, two*)
tool·mak·er (tōōl′ māk′ ēr)
tooth (tōōth)
  tooth·ache   tooth·brush
  tooth·less   tooth·pick
top (tŏp)
  top·coat   top·flight
  top hat   top-heav·y
  top·most   top·notch
  top·per   top·sail
  top se·cret   top ser·geant
  top·soil
to·paz (tō′ păz)
top·ic (tŏp′ ĭk)
  top·i·cal (tŏp′ ĭ·k₫l)
to·pog·ra·phy (tô·pŏg′ rá·fĭ)
to·pol·o·gy (tô·pŏl′ ô·jĭ)
top·ple (tŏp′ 'l)
  top·pling
top·sy-tur·vy (tŏp′ sĭ·tûr′ vĭ)
toque (tōk)
to·rah (tō′ rä)
torch·bear·er (tôrch′ bâr′ ēr)
tor·e·a·dor (tŏr′ ê·á·dôr′)
tor·ment (tôr·mĕnt′) *v.*
  (tôr′ mĕnt) *n.*
tor·men·tor (tôr·mĕn′ tēr)
tor·na·do (tôr·nā′ dō)
  -does
tor·pe·do (tôr·pē′ dō)
  -does
tor·por (tôr′ pēr)
tor·pid (tôr′ pĭd)
torque (tôrk)
tor·rent (tŏr′ ĕnt)
  tor·ren·tial (tô·rĕn′ sh₫l)
tor·rid (tŏr′ ĭd)

tor·sion (tôr′shŭn)
tor·so (tôr′sō)
-sos
tor·til·la (tôr·tē′yä)
tor·toise (tôr′tŭs)
tor·tu·ous (tôr′tṵ·ŭs)
tor·ture (tôr′tûr)
-tur·ing tor·tur·er
To·ry (tō′rĭ)
-ries
toss·up (tŏs′ŭp′)
to·tal (tō′tăl)
to·tal·i·ty (tō·tăl′ĭ·tĭ)
-ties
to·tal·ize -iz·ing
to·tal·ly
to·tal·i·tar·i·an
(tō·tăl′ĭ·târ′ĭ·ăn)
to·tem (tō′tĕm)
to·tem·ic (tō·tĕm′ĭk)
tou·can (tōō·kän′)
touch (tŭch)
touch·a·ble touch·down
touch·y
tou·ché (tōō′shā′)
tough (tŭf)
tough·ened
tou·pee (tōō·pā′)
tour de force (tōōr′ dĕ fôrs′)
tour·ist (tōōr′ĭst)
tour·ism
tour·na·ment (tōōr′nȧ·mĕnt)
tour·ney (tōōr′nĭ′)
-neys
tour·ni·quet (tōōr′nĭ·kĕt)
tou·sled (tou′z′ld)
to·ward (tō′ĕrd)
tow·el (tou′ĕl)
-eled -el·ing
tow·er (tou′ĕr)
-ered -er·ing
tow·head (tō′hĕd′)
tow·line (tō′līn′)
town (toun)
town cri·er town hall
town·ship towns·peo·ple
tox·ic (tŏk′sĭk)
tox·ic·i·ty (tŏks·ĭs′ĭ·tĭ)
tox·in (tŏk′sĭn)
trace (trās)
trac·ing trace·a·ble
trac·er·y
tra·che·a (trā′kĕ·ȧ)
trac·ta·ble (trăk′tȧ·b′l)

trac·ta·bil·i·ty
(trăk′tȧ·bĭl′ĭ·tĭ)
trac·tion (trăk′shŭn)
trac·tor (trăk′tēr)
trade (trād)
trad·ing trade-in
trade·mark trade name
trade school trades·man
trade wind
tra·di·tion (trȧ·dĭsh′ŭn)
tra·di·tion·al, -al·ly
tra·di·tion·al·ist
traf·fic (trăf′ĭk)
traf·ficked traf·fick·ing
trag·e·dy (trăj′ĕ·dĭ)
-dies
tra·ge·di·an (trȧ·jē′dĭ·ăn)
trag·ic (trăj′ĭk)
trag·i·cal·ly
trag·i·com·ic (trăj′ĭ·kŏm′ĭk)
trail·er (trāl′ēr)
train (trān)
train·a·ble
train·ee (trān·ē′)
trait (trāt)
trai·tor (trā′tēr)
trai·tor·ous
tra·jec·to·ry (trȧ·jĕk′tō·rĭ)
tram·meled (trăm′ĕld)
tram·ple (trăm′p′l)
-pling
tram·po·line (trăm′pō·lĭn)
tram·way (trăm′wā′)
trance (trăns)
tran·quil (trăng′kwĭl)
tran·quil·iz·er
tran·quil·li·ty (trăn·kwĭl′ĭ·tĭ)
tran·quil·ly
trans·act (trăns·ăkt′)
trans·ac·tion
trans·at·lan·tic
(trăns′ăt·lăn′tĭk)
tran·scend (trăn·sĕnd′)
tran·scend·ent (trăn·sĕn′dĕnt)
-ence
tran·scen·den·tal
(trăn′sĕn·dĕn′tăl)
tran·scribe (trăn·skrīb′)
-scrib·ing
tran·scrip·tion
(trăn·skrĭp′shŭn)
tran·sept (trăn′sĕpt)
trans·fer (trăns·fûr′)
-ferred -fer·ring
trans·fer·a·ble

trans·fer·ence (trăns·fûr′ ĕns)
trans·fig·u·ra·tion
    (trăns·fĭg′. û·rā′ shŭn)
trans·fixed (trăns·fĭkst′)
trans·for·ma·tion
    (trăns′ fôr·mā′ shŭn)
trans·form·er (trăns·fôr′ mĕr)
trans·fu·sion (trăns·fū′ zhŭn)
trans·gress (trăns·grĕs′)
 trans·gres·sion (-grĕsh′ ŭn)
 trans·gres·sor (-grĕs′ ĕr)
tran·sience (trăn′ shĕns)
 -sient
tran·sis·tor (trăn·zĭs′ tĕr)
trans·it (trăn′ sĭt)
tran·si·tion (trăn·zĭsh′ ŭn)
 tran·si·tion·al
tran·si·tive (trăn′ sĭ·tĭv)
tran·si·to·ry (trăn′ sĭ·tō′ rĭ)
trans·late (trăns·lāt′)
 -lat·ing trans·lat·a·ble
 trans·la·tion trans·la·tor
trans·lit·er·a·tion
    (trăns·lĭt′ ĕr·ā′ shŭn)
trans·lu·cent (trăns·lū′ sĕnt)
 -cence
trans·mi·gra·tion
    (trăns′ mĭ·grā′ shŭn)
trans·mit (trăns·mĭt′)
 -mit·ted -mit·ting
 trans·mit·tal (trăns·mĭt′ ăl)
 trans·mit·ter
trans·mute (trăns·mūt′)
 -mut·ing
tran·som (trăn′ sŭm)
trans·par·ent (trăns·pâr′ ĕnt)
 -en·cy
tran·spire (trăn·spīr′)
 -spir·ing
trans·plant (trăns·plănt′)
trans·port (trăns·pōrt′)
 trans·port·a·ble
 trans·por·ta·tion
    (trăns′ pŏr·tā′ shŭn)
trans·pose (trăns·pōz′)
 -pos·ing
 trans·po·si·tion
    (trăns′ pŏ·zĭsh′ ŭn)
Trans·vaal, S. Afr.
    (trăns·väl′)
trans·verse (trăns·vûrs′)
tra·peze (trá·pēz′)
trap·per (trăp′ ĕr)
Trap·pist (trăp′ ĭst)

trau·ma (trô′ má)
 trau·mat·ic (trô·măt′ ĭk)
trav·ail (trăv′ āl)
trav·el (trăv′ ĕl)
 -eled -el·ing
 trav·el·er
 trav·e·logue (trăv′ ĕ·lŏg)
trav·erse (trăv′ ĕrs)
 -vers·ing trav·ers·a·ble
trav·es·ty (trăv′ ĕs·tĭ)
 -ties
trawl·er (trôl′ ĕr)
treach·er·y (trĕch′ ĕr·ĭ)
 -er·ies treach·er·ous
trea·cle (trē′ k′l)
 trea·cly
trea·dle (trĕd′ ′l)
tread·mill (trĕd′ mĭl′)
trea·son (trē′ z′n)
 trea·son·a·ble trea·son·ous
treas·ure (trĕzh′ ĕr)
 treas·ur·er treas·ur·y
treat (trēt)
 treat·a·ble treat·ment
trea·tise (trē′ tĭs)
trea·ty (trē′ tĭ)
 -ties
tre·ble (trĕb′ ′l)
 tre·ble clef
tree·top (trē′ tŏp′)
tre·foil (trē′ foil)
trek (trĕk)
 trekked trek·king
trel·lis (trĕl′ ĭs)
trem·ble (trĕm′ b′l)
 -bling
tre·men·dous (trē·mĕn′ dŭs)
trem·o·lo (trĕm′ ō·lō)
trem·or (trĕm′ ĕr)
trem·u·lous (trĕm′ ū·lŭs)
trench·ant (trĕn′ chănt)
trep·i·da·tion (trĕp′ ĭ·dā′ shŭn)
tres·pass·er (trĕs′ pás·ĕr)
tres·tle (trĕs′ ′l)
tri·ad (trī′ ăd)
tri·al (trī′ ăl)
tri·an·gle (trī′ ăng′ g′l)
 tri·an·gu·lar (trī·ăng′ gû·lĕr)
Tri·as·sic (trī·ăs′ ĭk)
tribe (trīb)
 trib·al tribes·man
trib·u·la·tion (trĭb′ û·lā′ shŭn)
trib·une (trĭb′ ŭn)
 tri·bu·nal (trī·bū′ năl)

trib·u·tar·y (trĭb′ û·tĕr′ Ĭ)
  -tar·ies
trib·ute (trĭb′ ût)
trice (trīs)
tri·ceps (trī′ sĕps)
tri·chi·na (trĭ·kī′ nȧ)
  trich·i·no·sis (trĭk′ Ĭ·nō′ sĬs)
trick·er·y (trĭk′ ẽr·Ĭ)
trick·le (trĭk′ ′l)
  -ling
tri·col·or (trī′ kŭl′ ẽr)
tri·cot (trē′ kō)
tri·cy·cle (trī′ sĬk·′l)
tri·dent (trī′ dĕnt)
tri·en·ni·al (trī·ĕn′ Ĭ·ȧl)
tri·fling (trī′ flĭng)
trig·ger (trĭg′ ẽr)
tri·lin·gual (trī·lĭng′ gwȧl)
tril·lion (trĭl′ yŭn)
  (number)
tril·li·um (trĭl′ Ĭ·ŭm)
  (flower)
tril·o·gy (trĭl′ ȯ·jĬ)
  -gies
trim·ming (trĭm′ Ĭng)
trin·i·ty (trĭn′ ĭ·tĬ)
trin·ket (trĭng′ kĕt)
tri·o (trē′ ō)
  -os
tri·par·tite (trī·pär′ tĪt)
tri·ple (trĭp′ ′l)
  -pling
tri·plet (trĭp′ lĕt)
tri·ply
trip·li·cate (trĭp′ lĬ·kȧt)
tri·pod (trī′ pŏd)
trip·tych (trĭp′ tĬk)
trite (trīt)
  trite·ness
tri·umph (trī′ ŭmf)
  tri·um·phal (trī·ŭm′ fȧl)
  tri·um·phant (trī·ŭm′ fȧnt)
tri·um·vi·rate (trī·ŭm′ vĬ·rȧt)
triv·et (trĭv′ ĕt)
triv·i·a (trĭv′ Ĭ·ȧ)
triv·i·al (trĭv′ Ĭ·ȧl)
  triv·i·al·i·ty (trĭv′ Ĭ·ăl′ Ĭ·tĬ)
  triv·i·al·ly
trod·den (trŏd′ ′n)
troi·ka (troi′ kȧ)
trol·ley (trŏl′ Ĭ)
  trol·leys
trol·lop (trŏl′ ŭp)
trom·bone (trŏm′ bōn)

troop (troͦp)
  (boy scouts, soldiers; see *troupe*)
tro·phy (trō′ fĬ)
  -phies
trop·ic (trŏp′ Ĭk)
  trop·i·cal
tro·pism (trō′ pĬz′m)
trop·o·sphere (trŏp′ ȯ·sfẽr)
trot·ter (trŏt′ ẽr)
trou·ba·dour (troͦ′ bȧ·dŏͦr)
trou·ble (trŭb′ ′l)
  -bling trou·ble·some
  trou·blous
trough (trŏf)
troupe (troͦp)
  (actors; see *troop*)
trou·sers (trou′ zẽrz)
trous·seau (troͦ′ sō′)
  pl. trous·seaux (-sō′)
trout (trout)
trow·el (trou′ ĕl)
  -eled -el·ing
tru·ant (troͦ′ ȧnt)
  -an·cy
truce (troͦs)
truck·age (trŭk′ Ĭj)
truck·le (trŭk′ ′l)
  -ling
truc·u·lence (trŭk′ û·lĕns)
trudge (trŭj)
  trudg·ing
trudg·en stroke (trŭj′ ĕn)
true (troͦ)
  true·love true·ness
  tru·ism tru·ly
truf·fle (trŭf′ ′l)
trum·pet·er (trŭm′ pĕt·ẽr)
trun·cate (trŭng′ kāt)
  -cat·ing
trun·dle bed (trŭn′ d′l)
trun·nion (trŭn′ yŭn)
truss (trŭs)
trus·tee (trŭs·tē′)
  (one holding property in trust;
  see *trusty*)
  trus·tee·ship
trust·ful (trŭst′ fŏͦl)
  -ful·ly -ful·ness
trust·wor·thy (trŭst′ wûr′ thĬ)
  -wor·thi·ness
trust·y (trŭs′ tĬ)
  (convict allowed special privi-
  leges; see *trustee*)
  trust·ies

truth·ful	(trooth′ fool)	
-ful·ly	-ful·ness	
try	(trī)	
tried	try·ing	
try·out		
tryst·ing place	(trĭs′ tĭng)	
tsar	(zär)	
(or czar)		
tset·se fly	(tsĕt′ sĕ)	
tu·ba	(tū′ bȧ)	
pl. tu·bae	(-bē)	
tub·ba·ble	(tŭb′ ȧ·b′l)	
tu·ber·cu·lar	(tû·bûr′ kû·lẽr)	
tu·ber·cu·lo·sis		
	(tû·bûr′ kû·lō′ sĭs)	
tu·ber·ous	(tū′ bẽr·ŭs)	
tub·ing	(tūb′ ĭng)	
tu·bu·lar	(tū′ bû·lẽr)	
Tuc·son, Äriz.	(too·sŏn′)	
Tu·dor	(tū′ dẽr)	
Tues·day	(tūz′ dĭ)	
tuft·ed	(tŭf′ tĕd)	
tu·i·tion	(tû·ĭsh′ ŭn)	
tu·la·re·mi·a	(too′ lȧ·rē′ mĭ·ȧ)	
tu·lip	(tū′ lĭp)	
tum·ble-down	(tŭm′ b′l·doun′)	
tum·ble·weed	(tŭm′ b′l·wēd′)	
tu·mor	(tū′ mẽr)	
tu·mult	(tū′ mŭlt)	
tu·mul·tu·ous	(tû·mŭl′ tû·ŭs)	
tu·na fish	(too′ nȧ)	
tun·dra	(toon′ drȧ)	
tune·ful	(tūn′ fool)	
-ful·ly	-ful·ness	
tune·less		
tung·sten	(tŭng′ stĕn)	
tu·nic	(tū′ nĭk)	
tun·ing fork	(tūn′ ĭng)	
Tu·ni·si·a	(tû·nĭzh′ ĭ·ȧ)	
tun·nel	(tŭn′ ĕl)	
tun·neled	tun·nel·ing	
tur·ban	(tûr′ bȧn)	
(headdress)		
tur·bine	(tûr′ bĭn)	
(rotary engine)		
tur·bo·jet en·gine		
	(tûr′ bȯ·jĕt′)	
tur·bu·lent	(tûr′ bû·lĕnt)	
-lence		
tu·reen	(tû·rēn′)	
turf	(tûrf)	
tur·gid	(tûr′ jĭd)	
tur·gid·i·ty	(tûr·jĭd′ ĭ·tĭ)	
tur·key	(tûr′ kĭ)	
-keys		

Turk·ish	(tûr′ kĭsh)	
tur·mer·ic	(tûr′ mẽr·ĭk)	
tur·moil	(tûr′ moil)	
turn	(tûrn)	
(revolve; see tern)		
turn·a·bout	turn·coat	
turn·key	turn·out	
turn·o·ver	turn·pike	
turn·plate	turn·stile	
turn·ta·ble		
tur·nip	(tûr′ nĭp)	
tur·pen·tine	(tûr′ pĕn·tīn)	
tur·pi·tude	(tûr′ pĭ·tūd)	
tur·quoise	(tûr′ koiz)	
tur·ret	(tûr′ ĕt)	
tur·ret·ed		
tur·tle	(tûr′ t′l)	
tur·tle·back	tur·tle-neck adj.	
tus·sle	(tŭs′ ′l)	
tus·sling		
tu·te·lage	(tū′ tĕ·lĭj)	
tu·te·lar·y	(tū′ tĕ·lẽr′ ĭ)	
tu·tor	(tū′ tẽr)	
tu·tor·age	(tū′ tẽr·ĭj)	
tu·to·ri·al	(tû·tō′ rĭ·ȧl)	
tux·e·do	(tŭk·sē′ dō)	
-dos		
twad·dle	(twŏd′ ′l)	
twain	(twān)	
twang	(twăng)	
tweak	(twēk)	
tweed	(twēd)	
tweet·er	(twēt′ ẽr)	
tweez·ers	(twē₄′ ẽrz)	
twelfth	(twĕlfth)	
twen·ty	(twĕn′ tĭ)	
-ties	twen·ti·eth	
twen·ty-twen·ty		
twice	(twīs)	
twi·light	(twī′ līt′)	
twinge	(twĭnj)	
twing·ing		
twin·kle	(twĭng′ k′l)	
-kling		
twirl	(twûrl)	
twist·er	(twĭs′ tẽr)	
twitch	(twĭch)	
two	(too)	
(pair; see to, too)		
two-by-four	two-faced	
two-fist·ed	two·fold	
two·some	two-way	
ty·coon	(tī·koon′)	
ty·ing	(tī′ ĭng)	
tyke	(tīk)	

tym·pan·ic (tǐm·păn′ ǐk)
type (tīp)
  typ·ing type·script
  type·set·ter type·writ·er
ty·phoid (tī′ foid)
ty·phoon (tī· fōōn′)
ty·phus (tī′ fŭs)
typ·i·cal (tǐp′ ǐ· kăl)
  typ·i·cal·ly -cal·ness
typ·i·fy (tǐp′ ǐ· fī)
  -fied -fy·ing
typ·ist (tīp′ ǐst)
ty·pog·ra·phy (tī· pŏg′ rá· fǐ)
  ty·po·graph·i·cal
    (tī′ pŏ· grăf′ ǐ· kăl)
tyr·an·ny (tǐr′ á· nǐ)
  -an·nies
  ty·ran·ni·cal (tǐ· răn′ ǐ· kăl)
  tyr·an·nize -an·niz·ing
  tyr·an·nous
ty·rant (tī′ rănt)
ty·ro (tī′ rō)
  -ros

U

u·biq·ui·tous (ū· bǐk′ wǐ· tŭs)
  u·biq·ui·ty (-tǐ)
U-boat (ū′ bōt′)
ud·der (ŭd′ ĕr)
ugh (ŭ)
ug·ly (ŭg′ lǐ)
  ug·li·er, -li·est, -li·ness
u·ku·le·le (ū′ kū· lā′ lĕ)
ul·cer (ŭl′ sĕr)
  ul·ce·ra·tion (ŭl′ sĕr· ā′ shŭn)
  ul·cer·ous
ul·te·ri·or (ŭl· tēr′ ǐ· ĕr)
ul·ti·mate (ŭl′ tǐ· mǐt)
  -mate·ly
ul·ti·ma·tum (ŭl′ tǐ· mā′ tŭm)
ul·tra- (ŭl′ trá-)
  ul·tra·con·serv·a·tive
  ul·tra·lib·er·al ul·tra·ma·rine
  ul·tra·mod·ern
  ul·tra·vi·o·let
U·lys·ses (ū· lǐs′ ēz)
um·ber (ŭm′ bĕr)
um·bil·i·cal cord
  (ŭm· bǐl′ ǐ· kăl)
um·brage (ŭm′ brǐj)
um·brel·la (ŭm· brĕl′ á)
um·laut (ōōm′ lout)
um·pire (ŭm′ pīr)

un·a·ble (ŭn· ā′ b'l)
un·a·bridged (ŭn′ á· brǐjd′)
un·ac·count·a·ble
  (ŭn′ á· koun′ tá· b'l)
un·ac·cus·tomed
  (ŭn′ á· kŭs′ tŭmd)
un·af·fect·ed (ŭn′ á· fĕk′ tĕd)
un-A·mer·i·can
  (ŭn′ á· mĕr′ ǐ· kăn)
u·na·nim·i·ty (ū′ ná· nǐm′ ǐ· tǐ)
  u·nan·i·mous (ū· năn′ ǐ· mŭs)
un·as·sum·ing (ŭn′ á· sūm′ ǐng)
un·a·void·a·ble
  (ŭn′ á· void′ á· b'l)
un·be·com·ing
  (ŭn′ bē· kŭm′ ǐng)
un·be·knownst (ŭn′ bē· nōnst′)
un·bi·ased (ŭn· bī′ ást)
un·bid·den (ŭn· bǐd′ 'n)
un·bri·dled (ŭn· brī′ d'ld)
un·can·ny (ŭn· kăn′ ǐ)
un·cer·e·mo·ni·ous
  (ŭn′ sĕr· ē· mō′ nǐ· ŭs)
un·cer·tain·ty (ŭn· sûr′ tǐn· tǐ)
  -ties
un·chris·tian (ŭn· krǐs′ chăn)
un·civ·i·lized (ŭn· sǐv′ ǐ· līzd)
un·clas·si·fi·a·ble
  (ŭn· klăs′ ǐ· fī′ á· b'l)
un·cle (ŭng′ k'l)
un·com·fort·a·ble
  (ŭn· kŭm′ fērt· á· b'l)
un·com·mit·ted (ŭn′ kŏ· mǐt′ ĕd)
un·com·mon (ŭn· kŏm′ ŭn)
  un·com·mon·ly
  un·com·mon·ness
un·com·mu·ni·ca·tive
  (ŭn′ kŏ· mū′ nǐ· kā′ tǐv)
un·com·pro·mis·ing
  (ŭn· kŏm′ prŏ· mīz′ ǐng)
un·con·cern·ed·ly
  (ŭn′ kŏn· sûr′ nĕd·lǐ)
un·con·di·tion·al
  (ŭn′ kŏn· dǐsh′ ŭn· ál)
un·con·scion·a·ble
  (ŭn· kŏn′ shŭn· á· b'l)
un·con·scious (ŭn· kŏn′ shŭs)
un·con·sti·tu·tion·al
  (ŭn′ kŏn· stǐ· tū′ shŭn· ál)
un·couth (ŭn· kōōth′)
unc·tion (ŭngk′ shŭn)
unc·tu·ous (ŭngk′ tū· ŭs)
un·daunt·ed (ŭn· dôn′ tĕd)
un·de·mon·stra·tive
  (ŭn′ dē· mŏn′ strá· tǐv)

un·de·ni·a·ble   (ŭn′ dĕ·nī′ à·b'l)
un·der   (ŭn′ dĕr)
  un·der·brush   un·der·clothes
  un·der·cur·rent
  un·der·es·ti·mate
  un·der·ex·po·sure
  un·der·grad·u·ate
  un·der·hand·ed
  un·der·lie   -ly·ing
  un·der·neath
  un·der·nour·ished
  un·der·pin·ning
  un·der·priv·i·leged
  un·der·rate   un·der·signed
  un·der·stand·a·ble
  un·der·stood   un·der·tow
  un·der·weight   un·der·writ·er
un·de·sir·a·ble
    (ŭn′ dĕ·zīr′ à·b'l)
un·do·ing   (ŭn·dōō′ ĭng)
un·doubt·ed·ly
    (ŭn·dout′ ĕd·lĭ)
un·du·la·tion   (ŭn′ dŭ·lā′ shŭn)
un·du·ly   (ŭn·dū′ lĭ)
un·dy·ing   (ŭn·dī′ ĭng)
un·eas·i·ness   (ŭn·ēz′ ĭ·nĕs)
un·em·ploy·a·ble
    (ŭn′ ĕm·ploi′ à·b'l)
un·e·qual   (ŭn·ē′ kwăl)
  -qualed   un·e·qual·ly
un·e·quiv·o·cal
    (ŭn′ ē·kwĭv′ ō·kăl)
  -cal·ly
un·err·ing   (ŭn·ûr′ ĭng)
un·e·ven·ness   (ŭn·ē′ vĕn·nĕs)
un·ex·pur·gat·ed
    (ŭn·ĕks′ pēr·gāt′ ĕd)
un·faith·ful   (ŭn·fāth′ fōōl)
  -ful·ly,   -ful·ness
un·fa·mil·i·ar·i·ty
    (ŭn′ fà·mĭl′ ĭ·ăr′ ĭ·tĭ)
un·fas·ten   (ŭn·fás′ 'n)
un·fa·vor·a·ble
    (ŭn·fā′ vĕr·à·b'l)
un·feigned   (ŭn·fānd′)
un·fet·tered   (ŭn·fĕt′ ērd)
un·flinch·ing   (ŭn·flĭn′ chĭng)
un·for·get·ta·ble
    (ŭn′ fôr·gĕt′ à·b'l)
un·for·tu·nate·ly
    (ŭn·fôr′ tŭ·nĭt·lĭ)
un·friend·li·ness
    (ŭn·frĕnd′ lĭ·nĕs)
un·furled   (ŭn·fûrld′)

un·gain·li·ness
    (ŭn·gān′ lĭ·nĕs)
un·grace·ful   (ŭn·grās′ fōōl)
un·grate·ful   (ŭn·grāt′ fōōl)
un·hap·pi·ness   (ŭn·hăp′ ĭ·nĕs)
un·har·nessed   (ŭn·här′ nĕst)
un·hinged   (ŭn·hĭnjd′)
un·hur·ried   (ŭn·hûr′ ĭd)
u·ni·cam·er·al
    (ū′ nĭ·kăm′ ēr·ăl)
u·ni·corn   (ū′ nĭ·kôrn)
u·ni·fi·ca·tion   (ū′ nĭ·fĭ·kā′ shŭn)
u·ni·form·i·ty   (ū′ nĭ·fôr′ mĭ·tĭ)
u·ni·fy   (ū′ nĭ·fī)
  -fied,   -fy·ing
u·ni·lat·er·al   (ū′ nĭ·lăt′ ēr·ăl)
un·im·peach·a·ble
    (ŭn′ ĭm·pēch′ à·b'l)
un·ion·ize   (ŭn′ yŭn·īz)
  -iz·ing
u·nique   (û·nēk′)
  -nique·ly
u·ni·son   (ū′ nĭ·sŭn)
u·nit   (ū′ nĭt)
u·ni·tar·y   (ū′ nĭ·tĕr′ ĭ)
u·nite   (û·nīt′)
  -nit·ing
u·ni·ty   (ū′ nĭ·tĭ)
  -ties
u·ni·ver·sal   (ū′ nĭ·vûr′ săl)
  -sal·ly
u·ni·ver·sal·i·ty
    (ū′ nĭ·vûr·săl′ ĭ·tĭ)
u·ni·verse   (ū′ nĭ·vûrs)
u·ni·ver·si·ty   (ū′ nĭ·vûr′ sĭ·tĭ)
  -ties
un·kempt   (ŭn·kĕmpt′)
un·know·a·ble   (ŭn·nō′ à·b'l)
un·leash   (ŭn·lēsh′)
un·less   (ŭn·lĕs′)
un·like·ly   (ŭn·līk′ lĭ)
  un·like·li·hood
un·lim·it·ed   (ŭn·lĭm′ ĭ·tĕd)
un·men·tion·a·ble
    (ŭn·mĕn′ shŭn·à·b'l)
un·mer·ci·ful   (ŭn·mûr′ sĭ·fōōl)
un·mis·tak·a·ble
    (ŭn′ mĭs·tāk′ à·b'l)
un·mit·i·gat·ed
    (ŭn·mĭt′ ĭ·gāt′ ĕd)
un·named   (ŭn·nāmd′)
un·nat·u·ral   (ŭn·năt′ û·răl)
un·nec·es·sar·y
    (ŭn·nĕs′ ĕ·sĕr′ ĭ)
un·nerv·ing   (ŭn·nûrv′ ĭng)

un·num·bered (ŭn·nŭm′ bērd)
un·oc·cu·pied (ŭn·ŏk′ û·pīd)
un·par·al·leled (ŭn·păr′ ă·lĕld)
un·plumbed (ŭn·plŭmd′)
un·prec·e·dent·ed
     (ŭn·prĕs′ ĕ·dĕn′ tĕd)
un·prej·u·diced
     (ŭn·prĕj′ ŏŏ·dĭst)
un·prin·ci·pled
     (ŭn·prĭn′ sĭ·p′ld)
un·pro·nounce·a·ble
     (ŭn′ prŏ·nouns′ ă·b′l)
un·qual·i·fied (ŭn·kwŏl′ ĭ·fīd)
un·ques·tion·a·ble
     (ŭn·kwĕs′ chŭn·ă·b′l)
un·rav·eled (ŭn·răv′ ĕld)
un·re·al·i·ty (ŭn′ rē·ăl′ ĭ·tĭ)
un·rea·son·a·ble
     (ŭn·rē′ z′n·ă·b′l)
un·re·con·struct·ed
     (ŭn′ rē·kŏn·strŭk′ tĕd)
un·re·lent·ing (ŭn·rē·lĕn′ tĭng)
un·re·mit·ting (ŭn′ rē·mĭt′ ĭng)
un·right·eous (ŭn·rī′ chŭs)
un·ri·valed (ŭn·rī′ văld)
un·ruf·fled (ŭn·rŭf′ ′ld)
un·rul·y (ŭn·rōōl′ ĭ)
 un·rul·i·ness
un·sat·u·rat·ed
     (ŭn·săt′ û·rāt′ ĕd)
un·sa·vor·y (ŭn·sā′ vēr·ĭ)
 un·sa·vor·i·ness
un·sea·son·a·ble
     (ŭn·sē′ z′n·ă·b′l)
un·seem·ly (ŭn·sēm′ lĭ)
un·shack·led (ŭn·shăk′ ′ld)
un·sheathe (ŭn·shēth′)
 -sheath·ing
un·skill·ful (ŭn·skĭl′ fŏŏl)
un·so·cia·ble (ŭn·sō′ shă·b′l)
un·so·phis·ti·cat·ed
     (ŭn′ sŏ·fĭs′ tĭ·kāt′ ĕd)
un·spar·ing (ŭn·spâr′ ĭng)
un·speak·a·ble (ŭn·spēk′ ă·b′l)
un·spot·ted (ŭn·spŏt′ ĕd)
un·sub·stan·tial
     (ŭn′ sŭb·stăn′ shăl)
un·suit·a·ble (ŭn·sūt′ ă·b′l)
un·tan·gled (ŭn·tăng′ g′ld)
un·tie (ŭn·tī′)
 -tied   -ty·ing
un·til (ŭn·tĭl′)
un·time·ly (ŭn·tīm′ lĭ)
un·ti·tled (ŭn·tī′ t′ld)
un·touch·a·ble (ŭn′ tŭch′ ă·b′l)

un·to·ward (ŭn·tō′ ērd)
un·tram·meled (ŭn·trăm′ ĕld)
un·truth·ful (ŭn·trōōth′ fŏŏl)
un·tu·tored (ŭn·tū′ tērd)
un·u·su·al (ŭn·ū′ zhŏŏ·ăl)
 un·u·su·al·ly
un·ut·ter·a·ble (ŭn·ŭt′ ēr·ă·b′l)
un·want·ed (ŭn·wŏnt·ĕd)
 (not desired; see *unwonted*)
un·war·rant·a·ble
     (ŭn·wŏr′ ăn·tă·b′l)
un·war·y (ŭn·wâr′ ĭ)
 -war·i·ness
un·whole·some
     (ŭn·hōl′ sŭm)
un·wield·y (ŭn·wēl′ dĭ)
un·wit·ting (ŭn·wĭt′ ĭng)
un·wont·ed (ŭn·wŭn′ tĕd)
 (unaccustomed; see *unwanted*)
un·world·li·ness
     (ŭn·wûrld′ lĭ·nĕs)

up (ŭp)

up·braid·ing   up·date
up·grade   up·heav·al
up·hol·ster·y   up·lift·ing
up·right   up·roar·i·ous
up·stairs   up-to-date *adj.*
up·town   up·ward
up·per (ŭp′ ēr)
up·per-class   up·per·most
u·ra·ni·um (û·rā′ nĭ·ŭm)
ur·ban (ûr′ băn)
ur·ban·i·za·tion
     (ûr′ băn·ĭ·zā′ shŭn)
ur·ban·ize   -iz·ing
ur·bane (ûr·bān′)
ur·bane·ly
ur·chin (ûr′ chĭn)
urge (ûrj)
urg·ing
ur·gent (ûr′ jĕnt)
 -gen·cy
u·ri·nal (ū′ rĭ·năl)
u·ri·nar·y (ū′ rĭ·nĕr′ ĭ)
urn (ûrn)
Ur·sa Ma·jor (ûr′ să mā′ jēr)
U·ru·guay (ū′ rŭ·gwī)
 U·ru·guay·an
use (ūs) *n.*
    (ūz) *v.*

us·ing
us·a·ble (ūz′ ă·b′l)
us·age (ūs′ ĭj)
use·ful (ūs′ fŏŏl)
 -ful·ly   -ful·ness

use·less (ūs′ lĕs)
ush·er (ŭsh′ ēr)
u·surp (ū·zûrp′)
  u·surp·a·tion (ū′ zēr·pā′ shŭn)
u·su·ry (ū′ zhŏō·rǐ)
  u·su·rer (ū′ zhŏō·rēr)
  u·su·ri·ous (ū·zhŏōr′ ǐ·ŭs)
U·tah (ū′ tô)
  U·tah·an
u·ten·sil (ū·tĕn′ sǐl)
u·ter·ine (ū′ tēr·ǐn)
u·til·i·tar·i·an (ū·tǐl′ ǐ·târ′ ǐ·ǎn)
u·til·i·ty (ū·tǐl′ ǐ·tǐ)
  -ties
u·ti·lize (ū′ tǐ·līz)
  -liz·ing   u·ti·liz·a·ble
  u·ti·li·za·tion
    (ū′ tǐ·lǐ·zā′ shŭn)
ut·most (ŭt′ mōst)
U·to·pi·an (ū·tō′ pǐ·ǎn)
ut·ter (ŭt′ ēr)
  ut·ter·a·ble   ut·ter·ance
  ut·ter·ly   ut·ter·most
u·vu·la (ū′ vū·lá)

V

va·cant (vā′ kǎnt)
  va·can·cy
  va·cate (vā′ kāt)
  -cat·ing
va·ca·tion (vá·kā′ shŭn)
vac·ci·nate (vǎk′ sǐ·nāt)
  -nat·ing
  vac·ci·na·tion
    (vǎk′ sǐ·nā′ shŭn)
vac·cine (vǎk′ sēn)
vac·il·late (vǎs′ ǐ·lāt)
  -il·lat·ing
  vac·il·la·tion (vǎs′ ǐ·lā′ shŭn)
vac·u·ous (vǎk′ ū·ŭs)
  va·cu·i·ty (vá·kū′ ǐ·tǐ)
vac·u·um clean·er
    (vǎk′ ū·ŭm)
vag·a·bond (vǎg′ á·bŏnd)
va·gar·y (vá·gâr′ ǐ)
  gar·ies
va·gi·na (vá·jī′ ná)
va·gran·cy (vā′ grǎn·sǐ)
vague (vāg)
  vague·ly
vain (vān)
  (empty; conceited; see *vane, vein*)
vain·glo·ri·ous (vān′ glō′ rǐ·ŭs)

val·ance (vǎl′ ǎns)
  (drapery; see *valence*)
val·e·dic·to·ry (vǎl′ ė·dǐk′ tô·rǐ)
  val·e·dic·to·ri·an
    (vǎl′ ė·dǐk·tō′ rǐ·ǎn)
va·lence (vā′ lĕns)
  (of chemical elements; see *valance*)
val·en·tine (vǎl′ ĕn·tīn)
val·et (vǎl′ ĕt)
val·iant (vǎl′ yǎnt)
  -iance
val·id (vǎl′ ǐd)
  val·i·date   -dat·ing
  va·lid·i·ty (vá·lǐd′ ǐ·tǐ)
va·lise (vá·lēs′)
Val·kyr·ie (vǎl·kǐr′ ǐ)
val·ley (vǎl′ ǐ)
val·or (vǎl′ ēr)
  val·or·ous
Val·pa·rai·so, (vǎl′ pá·rā′ zō)
  Chile
val·ue (vǎl′ ū)
  -u·ing
  val·u·a·ble (vǎl′ ū·á·b′l)
  val·u·a·tion (vǎl′ ū·ā′ shŭn)
  val·ue·less
vam·pire (vǎm′ pīr)
van·dal (vǎn′ dǎl)
Van·der·bilt (univ.)
    (vǎn′ dēr·bǐlt)
Van·dyke (beard)
    (vǎn·dīk′)
vane (vān)
  (weathercock; see *vain, vein*)
van·guard (vǎn′ gärd′)
va·nil·la (vá·nǐl′ á)
van·ish (vǎn′ ǐsh)
van·i·ty (vǎn′ ǐ·tǐ)
  -ties
van·quish (vǎng′ kwǐsh)
van·tage (vǎn′ tǐj)
vap·id (vǎp′ ǐd)
va·por (vā′ pēr)
  va·por·ize   -iz·ing
  va·por·ous
var·i·a·ble (vâr′ ǐ·á·b′l)
  var·i·a·bil·i·ty
    (vâr′ ǐ·á·bǐl′ ǐ·tǐ)
var·i·ant (vâr′ ǐ·ǎnt)
  -ance
var·i·a·tion (vâr′ ǐ·ā′ shŭn)
var·i·cose vein (vǎr′ ǐ·kōs)
var·ied (vâr′ ǐd)
var·i·e·gat·ed (vâr′ ǐ·ė·gāt′ ĕd)

va·ri·e·ty   (va·rī′ ĕ·tĭ)
-ties
var·i·ous   (vâr′ ĭ·ŭs)
var·let   (vär′ lĕt)
var·si·ty   (vär′ sĭ·tĭ)
var·y   (vâr′ ĭ)
    var·ied, var·ies, var·y·ing
vas·cu·lar   (văs′ kū·lẽr)
vas·o·mo·tor   (văs′ ō·mō′ tẽr)
vas·sal   (văs′ ăl)
    vas·sal·age
Vas·sar (coll.)   (văs′ ẽr)
Vat·i·can   (văt′ ĭ·kăn)
vau·de·ville   (vō′ dĕ·vĭl)
vault·ed   (vôl′ tĕd)
veal   (vēl)
vec·tor   (vĕk′ tẽr)
veer·ing   (vẽr′ ĭng)
veg·e·ta·ble   (vĕj′ ĕ·tá·b'l)
    veg·e·tar·i·an (vĕj′ ĕ·târ′ ĭ·ăn)
veg·e·tate   (vĕj′ ĕ·tāt)
    -tat·ing
    veg·e·ta·tion   (vĕj′ ĕ·tā′ shŭn)
    veg·e·ta·tive   (vĕj′ ĕ·tā′ tĭv)
ve·he·ment   (vē′ ĕ·mĕnt)
    -mence
ve·hi·cle   (vē′ ĭ·k'l)
    ve·hic·u·lar   (vĕ·hĭk′ û·lẽr)
veil·ing   (vāl′ ĭng)
vein   (vān)
    (fissure; see vain, vane)
vel·lum   (vĕl′ ŭm)
ve·loc·i·pede   (vĕ·lŏs′ ĭ·pēd)
ve·loc·i·ty   (vĕ·lŏs′ ĭ·tĭ)
    -ties
ve·lours   (vĕ·lŏōr′)
vel·vet   (vĕl′ vĕt)
vel·vet·een   (vĕl′ vĕ·tēn′)
ve·nal   (vē′ năl)
    (mercenary; see venial)
    ve·nal·i·ty   (vē·năl′ ĭ·tĭ)
ven·det·ta   (vĕn·dĕt′ á)
ven·dor   (vĕn′ dẽr)
ven·due   (vĕn′ dū)
ve·neer   (vĕ·nẽr′)
ven·er·ate   (vĕn′ ẽr·āt)
    -at·ing
    ven·er·a·ble   (vĕn′ ẽr·á·b'l)
    ven·er·a·tion   (vĕn′ ẽr·ā′ shŭn)
ve·ne·re·al   (vĕ·nẽr′ ĕ·ăl)
    ven·er·y   (vĕn′ ẽr·ĭ)
Ve·ne·tian   (vĕ·nē′ shăn)
venge·ance   (vĕn′ jăns)
venge·ful   (vĕnj′ fŏōl)
    -ful·ly   -ful·ness

ve·ni·al   (vē′ nĭ·ăl)
    (excusable; see venal)
ven·i·son   (vĕn′ ĭ·z'n)
ven·om   (vĕn′ ŭm)
    ven·om·ous   (vĕn′ ŭm·ŭs)
ve·nous   (vē′ nŭs)
    (of veins; see Venus)
ven·ti·late   (vĕn′ tĭ·lāt)
    -lat·ing
    ven·ti·la·tion (vĕn′ tĭ·lā′ shŭn)
    ven·ti·la·tor
ven·tral   (vĕn′ trăl)
ven·tril·o·quist
                    (vĕn·trĭl′ ô·kwĭst)
ven·ture   (vĕn′ tụr)
    -tur·ing   ven·ture·some
    ven·tur·ous
ven·ue   (vĕn′ ū)
Ve·nus   (vē′ nŭs)
    (goddess of beauty; planet; see
    venous)
ve·ra·cious   (vĕ·rā′ shŭs)
ve·rac·i·ty   (vĕ·răs′ ĭ·tĭ)
ve·ran·da   (vĕ·răn′ dá)
ver·bal   (vûr′ băl)
    -bal·ly
    ver·bal·i·za·tion
                    (vûr′ băl·ĭ·zā′ shŭn)
    ver·bal·ize   -iz·ing
ver·ba·tim   (vûr·bā′ tĭm)
ver·be·na   (vẽr·bē′ ná)
ver·bi·age   (vûr′ bĭ·ĭj)
ver·bose   (vûr·bōs′)
    ver·bos·i·ty   (vûr·bŏs′ ĭ·tĭ)
ver·bo·ten   (fĕr·bō′ tĕn)
ver·dant   (vûr′ dănt)
    -dan·cy
ver·dict   (vûr′ dĭkt)
ver·dure   (vûr′ dụr)
verge   (vûrj)
    verg·ing
ver·i·fy   (vĕr′ ĭ·fī)
    -fied   -fy·ing
    ver·i·fi·a·ble (vĕr′ ĭ·fī′ á·b'l)
ver·i·ly   (vĕr′ ĭ·lĭ)
ver·i·si·mil·i·tude
                    (vĕr′ ĭ·sĭ·mĭl′ ĭ·tūd)
ver·i·ta·ble   (vĕr′ ĭ·tá·b'l)
ver·i·ty   (vĕr′ ĭ·tĭ)
    -ties
ver·mi·cel·li   (vûr′ mĭ·sĕl′ ĭ)
ver·mil·ion   (vẽr·mĭl′ yŭn)
ver·min   (vûr′ mĭn)
Ver·mont   (vẽr·mŏnt′)
    abbr. Vt.   Ver·mont·er

ver·mouth   (vĕr·mōōth′)
ver·nac·u·lar   (vĕr·năk′ û·lēr)
ver·nal e·qui·nox
        (vûr′ nǎl)
Ver·sailles   (vĕr·sālz)
ver·sa·tile   (vûr′ sȧ·tĭl)
   ver·sa·til·i·ty   (vûr′ sȧ·tĭl′ ĭ·tĭ)
verse   (vûrs)
   vers·ing
   ver·si·fi·ca·tion
        (vûr′ sĭ·fĭ·kā′ shŭn)
   ver·si·fy   (vûr′ sĭ·fī)
   -fied   -fy·ing
ver·sion   (vûr′ shŭn)
ver·sus   (vûr′ sŭs)
ver·te·bra   (vûr′ tĕ·brȧ)
   pl. ver·te·brae   (-brē)
   ver·te·bral   (vûr′ tĕ·brǎl)
ver·te·brate   (vûr′ tĕ·brȧt)
ver·tex   (vûr′ tĕks)
ver·ti·cal   (vûr′ tĭ·kǎl)
ver·ti·go   (vûr′ tĭ·gō)
ves·pers   (vĕs′ pērz)
ves·sel   (vĕs′ ′l)
ves·tal   (vĕs′ tǎl)
vest·ee   (vĕs′ tē′)
ves·ti·bule   (vĕs′ tĭ·būl)
ves·tige   (vĕs′ tĭj)
   ves·tig·i·al   (vĕs·tĭj′ ĭ·ǎl)
vest·ment   (vĕst′ mĕnt)
ves·try   (vĕs′ trĭ)
   -tries
ves·ture   (vĕs′ tụr)
vetch   (vĕch)
vet·er·an   (vĕt′ ēr·ǎn)
vet·er·i·nar·i·an
        (vĕt′ ēr·ĭ·nâr′ ĭ·ǎn)
   vet·er·i·nar·y   (vĕt′ ēr·ĭ·nĕr′ ĭ)
ve·to   (vē′ tō)
   -toes
vex·a·tion   (vĕks·ā′ shŭn)
   vex·a·tious   (vĕks·ā′ shŭs)
vi·a   (vī′ ȧ)
vi·a·ble   (vī′ ȧ·b′l)
vi·a·duct   (vī′ ȧ·dŭkt)
vi·al   (vī′ ǎl)
vi·and   (vī′ ǎnd)
vi·brant   (vī′ brǎnt)
   -bran·cy
vi·brate   (vī′ brāt)
   -brat·ing
vi·bra·tion   (vī·brā′ shŭn)
vi·bra·tor   (vī′ brā·tēr)
vi·bra·to   (vē·brä′ tô)

vic·ar   (vĭk′ ēr)
   vic·ar·age   (-ĭj)
   vic·ar·ate   (vĭk′ ēr·ȧt)
vi·car·i·ous   (vī·kâr′ ĭ·ŭs)
vice   (vīs)
   (in the place of; evil; see *vise*)
vice-   (vīs)
   vice-ad·mi·ral   vice-chan·cel·lor
   vice·ge·rent   (vīs′ jẽr′ ĕnt)
   vice-pres·i·dent
   vice·roy
vice ver·sa   (vī′ sĕ vûr′ sȧ)
vi·cin·i·ty   (vĭ·sĭn′ ĭ·tĭ)
   -ties
vi·cious   (vĭsh′ ŭs)
vi·cis·si·tude   (vĭ·sĭs′ ĭ·tūd)
vic·tim   (vĭk′ tĭm)
   vic·tim·i·za·tion
        (vĭk′ tĭm·ĭ·zā′ shŭn)
   vic·tim·ize   -iz·ing
vic·tor   (vĭk′ tēr)
   vic·to·ri·ous   (vĭk·tō′ rĭ·ŭs)
   vic·to·ry   -ries
Vic·tro·la   (vĭk·trō′ lȧ)
vict·ual   (vĭt′ ′l)
vi·cu·ña   (vĭ·kōōn′ yȧ)
vid·e·o   (vĭd′ ê·ō)
vie   (vī)
   vied   vy·ing
Vi·et·nam·ese   (vê·ĕt′ nä·mēz′)
view·point   (vū′ point′)
vig·il   (vĭj′ ĭl)
   vig·i·lance   (vĭj′ ĭ·lǎns)
   -lant
   vig·i·lan·te   (vĭj′ ĭ·lăn′ tê)
vi·gnette   (vĭn·yĕt′)
vig·or   (vĭg′ ēr)
   vig·or·ous   (vĭg′ ēr·ŭs)
vi·king   (vī′ kĭng)
vile   (vīl)
   vile·ness
vil·i·fy   (vĭl′ ĭ·fī)
   -fied   -fy·ing
   vil·i·fier
vil·la   (vĭl′ ȧ)
vil·lage   (vĭl′ ĭj)
vil·lain   (vĭl′ ĭn)
   (scoundrel; see *villein*)
   vil·lain·ous
vil·lein   (vĭl′ ĭn)
   (serf; see *villain*)
   vil·len·age
vin·ai·grette sauce
        (vĭn′ ȧ·grĕt′)

Vin·ci, da, Le·o·nar·do
    (dä věn′ chě, lä·ô·när′ dô)
vin·ci·ble   (vĭn′ sĭ·b'l)
vin·di·cate   (vĭn′ dĭ·kāt)
  -cat·ing
  vin·di·ca·tion
        (vĭn′ dĭ·kā′ shŭn)
vin·dic·tive   (vĭn·dĭk′ tĭv)
vin·e·gar   (vĭn′ ě·gēr)
vine·yard   (vĭn′ yērd)
vin·tage   (vĭn′ tĭj)
vi·nyl   (vī′ nĭl)
vi·o·la   (vě·ō′ lȧ)
vi·o·la·ble   (vī′ ô·lȧ·b'l)
vi·o·late   (vī′ ô·lāt)
  -lat·ing
  vi·o·la·tion   (vī′ ô·lā′ shŭn)
vi·o·lence   (vī′ ô·lěns)
  -lent
vi·o·let   (vī′ ô·lět)
vi·o·lin   (vī′ ô·lĭn′)
  vi·o·lin·ist
vi·o·lon·cel·lo
    (vē′ ô·lŏn·chěl′ ō)
vi·per   (vī′ pēr)
vi·ra·go   (vĭ·rā′ gō)
  -goes
vir·e·o   (vĭr′ ě·ō)
  -os
vir·gin   (vûr′ jĭn)
  vir·gin·al   (vûr′ jĭ·nȧl)
  vir·gin·i·ty   (vēr·jĭn′ ĭ·tĭ)
Vir·gin·ia   (vēr·jĭn′ yȧ)
  abbr. Va.
  Vir·gin·ian   (vēr·jĭn′ yȧn)
  Vir·gin·ia reel
vir·ile   (vĭr′ ĭl)
  vi·ril·i·ty   (vĭ·rĭl′ ĭ·tĭ)
vir·tu·al   (vûr′ tû·ȧl)
  -al·ly
vir·tue   (vûr′ tū)
  vir·tu·ous   (vûr′ tû·ŭs)
vir·tu·os·i·ty   (vûr′ tû·ŏs′ ĭ·tĭ)
  vir·tu·o·so   (vûr′ tû·ô′ sō)
vir·u·lence   (vĭr′ û·lěns)
  -lent
vi·rus   (vī′ rŭs)
vi·sa   (vē′ zȧ)
vis·age   (vĭz′ ĭj)
vis-à-vis   (vē′ zȧ·vē′)
vis·cer·al   (vĭs′ ēr·ȧl)
vis·cose   (vĭs′ kōs)
  vis·cos·i·ty   (vĭs·kŏs′ ĭ·tĭ)
  vis·cous   (vĭs′ kŭs)
vis·count   (vī′ kount′)

vise   (vīs)
  (device for holding work; see *vice*)
vis·i·ble   (vĭz′ ĭ·b'l)
  vis·i·bil·i·ty   (vĭz′ ĭ·bĭl′ ĭ·tĭ)
vi·sion   (vĭzh′ ŭn)
  vi·sion·al   vi·sion·ar·y
vis·it   (vĭz′ ĭt)
  -it·ed   vis·it·a·ble
  vis·it·ant   (vĭz′ ĭ·tȧnt)
  vis·it·a·tion   (vĭz′ ĭ·tā′ shŭn)
  vis·i·tor
vi·sor   (vī′ zēr)
  (front of a cap; see *vizier*)
vis·ta   (vĭs′ tȧ)
vis·u·al   (vĭzh′ û·ȧl)
  vis·u·al·ize   -iz·ing
vi·tal   (vī′ tȧl)
  vi·tal·i·ty   (vī·tăl′ ĭ·tĭ)
  vi·tal·ize   -iz·ing
  vi·tal·ly
vi·ta·**min**   (vī′ tȧ·mĭn)
vi·ti·ate   (vĭsh′ ĭ·āt)
  -at·ing
vit·re·ous   (vĭt′ rě·ŭs)
vit·ri·fy   (vĭt′ rĭ·fī)
  -fied   -fy·ing
vit·ri·ol   (vĭt′ rĭ·ŭl)
vi·tu·per·ate   (vĭ·tū′ pēr·āt)
  -at·ing
  vi·tu·per·a·tion
        (vĭ·tū′ pēr·ā′ shŭn)
  vi·tu·per·a·tive
        (vĭ·tū′ pēr·ā′ tĭv)
vi·va·cious   (vī·vā′ shŭs)
  vi·vac·i·ty   (vī·văs′ ĭ·tĭ)
viv·id   (vĭv′ ĭd)
viv·i·sec·tion   (vĭv′ ĭ·sěk′ shŭn)
vix·en·ish   (vĭk′ s'n·ĭsh)
vi·zier   (vĭ·zēr′)
  (high official; see *visor*)
vo·cab·u·lar·y   (vô·kăb′ û·lēr′ ĭ)
  -lar·ies
vo·cal   (vō′ kȧl)
  vo·cal·ist
  vo·cal·ize   -iz·ing
  vo·cal·ly
vo·ca·tion   (vô·kā′ shŭn)
  vo·ca·tion·al
vo·cif·er·ous   (vô·sĭf′ ēr·ŭs)
vod·ka   (vŏd′ kȧ)
vogue   (vōg)
voice   (vois)
  voic·ing   voice·less
void   (void)
  void·a·ble

voile	(voil)
vol·a·tile	(vŏl′ à·tĭl)
vol·a·til·i·ty	(vŏl′ à·tĭl′ ĭ·tĭ)
vol·a·til·ize	-iz·ing
vol·ca·no	(vŏl·kā′ nō)
-noes	
vol·can·ic	(vŏl·kăn′ ĭk)
vo·li·tion	(vô·lĭsh′ ŭn)
Volks·wa·gen	(fôlks′ vä′ gĕn)
vol·ley	(vŏl′ ĭ)
vol·leys	vol·ley·ball
volt·age	(vōl′ tĭj)
vol·u·ble	(vŏl′ û·b′l)
vol·u·bil·i·ty	(vŏl′ û·bĭl′ ĭ·tĭ)
vol·ume	(vŏl′ yŭm)
vo·lu·mi·nous	(vô·lū′ mĭ·nŭs)
vol·un·tar·y	(vŏl′ ŭn·tĕr′ ĭ)
vol·un·tar·i·ly	
vol·un·teer	(vŏl′ ŭn·tĕr′)
vo·lup·tu·ous	(vô·lŭp′ tû·ŭs)
vo·lup·tu·ar·y	(vô·lŭp′ tû·ĕr′ ĭ)
vom·it	(vŏm′ ĭt)
-it·ed	-it·ing
voo·doo	(vōō′ dōō)
vo·ra·cious	(vô·rā′ shŭs)
vo·rac·i·ty	(vô·răs′ ĭ·tĭ)
vor·tex	(vôr′ tĕks)
-tex·es	
vor·ti·cal	(vôr′ tĭ·kăl)
vo·ta·ry	(vō′ tà·rĭ)
-ries	
vot·ing ma·chine	
	(vōt′ ĭng)
vo·tive	(vō′ tĭv)
vouch·er	(vouch′ ĕr)
vouch·safe	(vouch·sāf′)
vow·el	(vou′ ĕl)
voy·age	(voi′ ĭj)
voy·a·ger	
vul·can·ize	(vŭl′ kăn·īz)
-iz·ing	
vul·gar	(vŭl′ gĕr)
vul·gar·i·an	(vŭl·gâr′ ĭ·ăn)
vul·gar·i·ty	(vŭl·găr′ ĭ·tĭ)
-ties	
vul·gar·ize	-iz·ing
Vul·gate	(vŭl′ gāt)
vul·ner·a·ble	(vŭl′ nĕr·à·b′l)
vul·ner·a·bil·i·ty	
	(vŭl′ nĕr·à·bĭl′ ĭ·tĭ)
vul·ture	(vŭl′ tûr)
vy·ing	(vī′ ĭng)

W

wad·dle	(wŏd′ ′l)
wad·dling	
wa·fer	(wā′ fĕr)
waf·fle	(wŏf′ ′l)
waft	(wáft)
wa·ger	(wā′ jĕr)
-gered	-ger·ing
wag·gish	(wăg′ ĭsh)
Wag·ne·ri·an	(väg·nēr′ ĭ·ăn)
wag·on	(wăg′ ŭn)
waif	(wāf)
Wai·ki·ki beach	
	(wī′ kĭ·kē′)
wail	(wāl)
(to lament; see wale, whale)	
wail·ing	
wain·scot	(wān′ skŭt)
-scot·ing	
waist·line	(wāst′ līn′)
wait·ress	(wāt′ rĕs)
waive	(wāv)
(to forgo)	waiv·ing
waiv·er	
wake·ful	(wāk′ fōōl)
-ful·ly	-ful·ness
wak·en	(wāk′ ĕn)
wale	(wāl)
(rib in fabric; see wail, whale)	
walk·ie-talk·ie	(wôk′ ĭ·tôk′ ĭ)
walk·out	(wôk′ out′)
wal·la·by	(wŏl′ à·bĭ)
-bies	
wal·let	(wŏl′ ĕt)
wall·eyed pike	(wôl′ īd′)
wall·flow·er	(wôl′ flou′ ĕr)
wal·lop·ing	(wŏl′ ŭp·ĭng)
wal·low	(wŏl′ ō)
wall·pa·per	(wôl′ pā′ pĕr)
wal·nut	(wôl′ nŭt)
wal·rus	(wôl′ rŭs)
waltz	(wôlts)
wam·pum	(wŏm′ pŭm)
wan·der·er	(wŏn′ dĕr·ĕr)
wan·der·lust	(wŏn′ dĕr·lŭst′)
wane	(wān)
wan·ing	
wan·gle	(wăng′ g′l)
-gling	
wan·ton	(wŏn′ tŭn)
wan·ton·ly	wan·ton·ness
war	(wôr)
war·fare	war·head

war·mon·ger   war·time
war·bler   (wôr' blĕr)
war·den   (wôr' d'n)
ward·robe   (wôrd' rōb')
ware·house   (wâr' hous')
war·i·ness   (wâr' ĭ·nĕs)
warm   (wôrm)
   warm-blood·ed   warm·heart·ed
   warmth
warn·ing   (wôrn' ĭng)
war·rant   (wŏr ɑnt)
   war·rant·a·ble   war·rant·eɖ
   war·rant·y   (wŏr' ɑn·tĭ)
   war·rant·ies
war·ri·or   (wŏr' ĭ·ĕr)
war·y   (wâr' ĭ)
   war·i·er, -i·est, -i·ly, -i·ness
wash   (wŏsh)
   wash·board   wash·cloth
   washed-up
   wash·er·wom·an
   wash·out   wash·room
wasp·ish   (wŏsp' ĭsh)
was·sail   (wŏs' 'l)
Was·ser·mann test
     (wŏs' ĕr·mɑn)
waste   (wāst)
   wast·ing   wast·age
   waste·bas·ket
   waste·ful, -ful·ly, -ful·ness
   waste·pa·per
wast·rel   (wās' trĕl)
watch   (wŏch)
   watch·dog
   watch·ful, -ful·ly, -ful·ness
   watch·mak·er   watch·man
   watch·word
wa·ter   (wô' tĕr)
   wa·ter-cooled   wa·ter·course
   wa·ter·fall   wa·ter·fowl
   wa·ter·front   wa·ter lil·y
   wa·ter·line
   wa·ter·log   -logged
   wa·ter main   wa·ter·mel·on
   wa·ter me·ter   wa·ter·proof
   wa·ter·side   wa·ter-sol·u·ble
   wa·ter·spout   wa·ter sup·ply
   wa·ter·tight   wa·ter tow·er
   wa·ter va·por   wa·ter·way
   wa·ter·y
watt   (wŏt)
   watt·age   (wŏt' ĭj)
   watt-hour
wat·tle   (wŏt' 'l)
wa·ver·ing   (wā' vĕr·ĭng)

wav·y   (wāv' ĭ)
   wav·i·ness
wax·en   (wăk' sĕn)
wax·wing   (wăks' wĭng')
wax·work   (wăks' wûrk')
wax·y   (wăk' sĭ)
   wax·i·ness
way   (wā)
   way·far·er   (wā' fâr' ĕr)
   way·far·ing   way·laid
   way·lay   way·side
   way·ward·ness
weak   (wēk)
   weak·ened   weak-kneeɖ
   weak·ling
wealth   (wĕlth)
   wealth·i·ly   -i·ness
wean   (wēn)
weap·on   (wĕp' ŭn)
wea·ri·some   (wẽr' ĭ·sŭm)
   -some·ly
wea·ry   (wẽr' ĭ)
   -ried,   -ry·ing
   wea·ri·ly   wea·ri·ness
wea·sel   (wē' z'l)
weath·er   (wĕth' ĕr)
   weath·er-beat·en
   weath·er·cock   weath·er gauge
   weath·er·man   weath·er·proof
   weath·er vane   weath·er-wise
weave   (wēv)
   weav·ing
web·bing   (wĕb' ĭng)
wed·ding   (wĕd' ĭng)
wedge   (wĕj)
   wedg·ing
Wedg·ie   (wĕj' ĭ)
Wedg·wood ware
     (wĕj' wŏŏd)
wed·lock   (wĕd' lŏk)
Wednes·day   (wĕnz' dĭ)
week   (wēk)
   week·day   week end
   week-end *adj.*   week·ly, -lies
wee·vil   (wē' v'l)
weigh   (wā)
   weight·y
weird   (wẽrd)
wel·come   (wĕl' kŭm)
weld   (wĕld)
wel·fare   (wĕl' fâr')
well   (wĕl)
(NOTE: When "well" combinations come before a noun, they
are usually hyphenated, as in

"well-acted play.") When "well" combinations come after a verb, the hyphen is usually dropped, as in "The play was *well acted.*"

well-be·ing	well·born
well-bred	well-fa·vored
well-found·ed	well-groomed
well-known	well-mean·ing
well-nigh	well off
well-read	well·spring
well-thought-of	well-to-do
well-wish·er	

Welsh rab·bit (wĕlsh răb′ ĭt)
 (*often incorrectly written* Welsh rarebit)
wel·ter·weight (wĕl′ tẽr·wāt′)
wench (wĕnch)
wept (wĕpt)
weren't (wûr′ 'nt)
were·wolf (wẽr′ wo͝olf′)
Wes·ley·an (wĕs′ lĭ·ăn)
west·er·ly (wĕs′ tẽr·lĭ)
 -lies
west·ern·er (wĕs′ tẽr·nẽr)
west·ern·most (wĕs′ tẽrn·mōst)
West·min·ste Ab·bey
   (wĕst′ mĭn′ stẽr)
West Vir·gin·ia
   (wĕst vẽr·jĭn′ yȧ)
 abbr. W. Va.
 West Vir·gin·ian
west·ward (wĕst′ wẽrd)
whale (hwāl)
 (cetacean; see *wail, wale*)
whale·bone (hwāl′ bōn′)
wharf (hwôrf)
 pl. wharves
what (hwŏt)
 what·ev·er what·not
 what·so·ev·er
wheat (hwēt)
whee·dle (hwē′ d'l)
 -dling
wheel (hwēl)
 wheel·bar·row wheel base
 wheel chair wheel·wright
wheeze (hwēz)
 wheez·ing wheez·i·ness
 wheez·y
whelp (hwĕlp)
when (hwĕn)
 when·ev·er when·so·ev·er
whence (hwĕns)
where (hwâr)
 where·a·bouts where·as

where·at	where·by
where·fore	where·from
where·in	where·in·to
where·of	where·on
where·so·ev·er	where·to
where·un·to	where·up·on
wher·ev·er	where·with
where·with·al	

wher·ry (hwĕr′ ĭ)
 wher·ries
wheth·er (hwĕth′ ẽr)
 (either, if; see *whither*)
whet·stone (hwĕt′ stōn′)
which (hwĭch)
 which·ev·er
whiff (hwĭf)
Whig (hwĭg)
 Whig·gish
while (hwīl)
 whilst (hwīlst)
whim·per (hwĭm′ pẽr)
whim·sey (hwĭm′ zĭ)
 whim·si·cal (hwĭm′ zĭ·kăl)
whine (hwīn)
 whin·ing whin·y
whin·ny (hwĭn′ ĭ)
 whin·nied whin·ny·ing
whip (hwĭp)
 whipped whip·ping
 whip·cord whip·stitch
whip·per·snap·per
   (hwĭp′ ẽr·snăp′ ẽr)
whip·pet (hwĭp′ ĕt)
whip·poor·will (hwĭp′ po͝or·wĭl′)
whirl (hwûrl)
 whirl·a·bout
 whirl·i·gig (hwûr′ lĭ·gĭg′)
 whirl·pool whirl·wind
whisk broom (hwĭsk)
whis·ky (hwĭs′ kĭ)
 -kies
whis·per·ing (hwĭs′ pẽr·ĭng)
whist (hwĭst)
whis·tle (hwĭs′ 'l)
 -tling
white (hwīt)
 white·cap white-col·lar *adj.*
 whit·ed sep·ul·cher
 white·fish white-head·ed
 white lie whit·en·er
 white·ness white oak
 white sauce white·wash
whith·er (hwĭth′ ẽr)
 (to what place; see *whether*)

whit·tle (hwĭt' 'l)
  whit·tling

whiz (hwĭz)
  whizzed   whiz·zing

whoa (hwō)

who·dun·it (hōō' dŭn' ĭt)

who·ev·er (hōō·ĕv' ēr)

whole (hōl)
  whole·heart·ed whole·ness
  whole·sale   whole·some
  whole-wheat *adj.*
  whol·ly

whom (hōōm)

whoop·ee (hwōōp' ē)

whoop·ing cough
          (hōōp' ĭng)

whop·per (hwŏp' ēr)

whore (hōr)
  whore·mon·ger whor·ish

whorl (hwûrl)

who's (hōōz)
  (contraction of *who is:* "Look
  who's here!")

whose (hōōz)
  (possessive of *who:* "*Whose* coat
  is this?")

who·so (hōō' sō)

who·so·ev·er (hōō' sō·ĕv' ēr)

Wich·i·ta, Kan. (wĭch' ĭ·tô)

wick·ed (wĭk' ĕd)
  wick·ed·ness

wick·er (wĭk' ēr)

wick·et (wĭk' ĕt)

wide (wīd)
  wide-an·gle lens
  wide-a·wake wide·ly
  wid·en·ing wide-o·pen
  wide·spread

wid·ow (wĭd' ō)
  wid·ow·er

width (wĭdth)

wield·y (wēl' dĭ)

wife (wīf)
  pl. wives wife·ly

wig·gle (wĭg' 'l)
  wig·gling wig·gly

wig·wam (wĭg' wŏm)

wild·cat (wīld' kăt')
  wild·cat·ter

wil·der·ness (wĭl' dēr·nĕs)

wild·fire (wīld' fīr')

wile (wīl)
  wil·i·ness wil·y

Wilkes-Bar·re, Pa.
        (wĭlks' băr' ĕ)

Wil·lam·ette (wĭ·lăm' ĕt)
  (riv., Ore.)

will·ful (wĭl' fōōl)
  -ful·ly   -ful·ness

will-o'-the-wisp (wĭl' ŏ·thĕ·wĭsp')

wil·low·y (wĭl' ŏ·ĭ)

wil·ly-nil·ly (wĭl' ĭ·nĭl' ĭ)

Wil·mette, Ill. (wĭl·mĕt')

wim·ple (wĭm' p'l)

wince (wĭns)
  winc·ing

winch (wĭnch)

Win·ches·ter (wĭn' chĕs' tēr)

wind (wĭnd)
  wind-blown wind·fall
  wind·jam·mer wind·lass
  wind·pipe wind·shield
  wind-swept wind tun·nel

win·dow (wĭn' dō)
  win·dow·pane win·dow sill

Wind·sor tie (wĭn' zēr)

wine (wīn)
  wine·bib·ber (wīn' bĭb' ēr)
  wine cel·lar wine·glass
  win·er·y -er·ies
  wine·skin win·y

wing·spread (wĭng' sprĕd')

Win·ni·peg, Can.
        (wĭn' ĭ·pĕg)

win·now (wĭn' ō)

win·some (wĭn' sŭm)

win·ter (wĭn' tēr)
  win·ter·green
  win·ter·ize -iz·ing
  win·ter·time win·ter wheat
  win·try

wip·er (wīp' ēr)

wire (wīr)
  wir·ing wire-haired
  wire·less Wire·pho·to
  wire tap·per wir·y

Wis·con·sin (wĭs·kŏn' s'n)
  abbr. Wis. Wis·con·sin·ite

wis·dom (wĭz' dŭm)

wise·a·cre (wīz' ā' kēr)

wise·crack (wīz' krăk')

wish·ful (wĭsh' fōōl)
  -ful·ly   -ful·ness

wis·ta·ri·a (wĭs·tā' rĭ·ä)

wist·ful (wĭst' fōōl)
  -ful·ly   -ful·ness

witch (wĭch)
  witch·craft witch doc·tor
  witch·er·y witch ha·zel

with (wĭth)
  with·al (wĭth·ôl′)
  with·draw   with·hold·ing
  with·in   with·out
  with·stand
with·er (wĭth′ ĕr)
wit·ness (wĭt′ nĕs)
wit·ti·cism (wĭt′ ĭ·sĭz′m)
wiz·ard (wĭz′ ĕrd)
wiz·ened (wĭz′ ′nd)
wob·ble (wŏb′ ′l)
  wob·bling   wob·bly
woe·be·gone (wō′ bĕ·gŏn′)
woe·ful (wō′ fōōl)
  -ful·ly   -ful·ness
wol·ver·ine (wōōl′ vĕr·ēn′)
wom·an (wōōm′ ăn)
  pl. wom·en
  wom·an·hood   wom·an·ish
  wom·an·kind   wom·an·li·ness
  wom·an·ly   wom·en·folk
womb (wōōm)
wom·bat (wŏm′ băt)
won·der (wŭn′ dĕr)
  won·der·ful, -ful·ly, -ful·ness
  won·der·land   won·der·ment
  won·der-strick·en
won·drous (wŭn′ drŭs)
wont (wŭnt)
won't (wōnt)
woo (wōō)
  wooed   woo·ing
wood·bine (wōōd′ bīn′)
wood·craft (wōōd′ krăft′)
wood·en (wōōd′ ′n)
  wood·en·ness
wood·peck·er (wōōd′ pĕk′ ĕr)
woods·man (wōōdz′ măn)
woof·er (wōōf′ ĕr)
wool·en (wōōl′ ĕn)
wool·ly (wōōl′ ĭ)
  wool·li·ness
wooz·y (wōōz′ ĭ)
Worces·ter, Mass.
        (wōōs′ tĕr)
Worces·ter·shire sauce
        (wōōs′ tĕr·shĭr)
word·y (wûr′ dĭ)
  word·i·ness
work (wûrk)
  work·a·ble   work·a·day
  work·bench   work·day
  work·house   work·man·ship
  work·out   work·shop
  work·week

world (wûrld)
  world·ling   world-wea·ry
  world-wide
world·ly (wûrld′ lĭ)
  world·li·ness   world·ly-wise
worm·wood (wûrm′ wōōd′)
worn-out (wōrn′ out′)
wor·ry (wûr′ ĭ)
  wor·ried   wor·ry·ing
  wor·ri·er   wor·ri·ment
  wor·ri·some
worse (wûrs)
  wors·en
wor·ship (wûr′ shĭp)
  -shiped   -ship·ing
  wor·ship·er   wor·ship·ful
worst (wûrst)
wor·sted (wōōs′ tĕd)
worth·while (wûrth′ hwĭl′)
wor·thy (wûr′ thĭ)
  wor·thi·er, -i·est, -i·ly, -i·ness
would (wōōd)
  would-be   would·n't
wound (wōōnd)
  (injury; pron. *wound* when past of
  wind)
wo·ven (wō′ vĕn)
wraith (rāth)
wran·gler (răng′ glĕr)
wrap·per (răp′ ĕr)
wrath·ful (răth′ fōōl)
  -ful·ly   -ful·ness
wreak (rēk)
  (give free play to)
wreath (rēth) *n.*
wreathe (rēth) *v.*
  wreath·ing
wreck (rĕk)
  (ruin)   wreck·age
wren (rĕn)
wrench (rĕnch)
wrest (rĕst)
wres·tler (rĕs′ lĕr)
wretch (rĕch)
  (miserable person; see *retch*)
wretch·ed (rĕch′ ĕd)
  wretch·ed·ness
wrig·gle (rĭg′ ′l)
  wrig·gling   wrig·gly
wright (rīt)
  (workman; see *right, rite, write*)
wrin·kle (rĭng′ k'l)
  -kling
wrist (rĭst)
  wrist·band   wrist watch

writ   (rĭt)

write   (rīt)
   (inscribe; see *right, rite, wright*)
   writ·ing
   writ·er's cramp
   write-up
   writ·ten   (rĭt′ 'n)

writhe   (rīth)
   writh·ing

wrong   (rông)
   wrong·do·er   wrong·ful

wrought   (rôt)

wry   (rī)
   wry·ly   wry·ness

Wy·o·ming   (wī·ō′ mĭng)
   abbr. Wyo.   Wy·o·ming·ite

yolk   (yōk)
   (yellow of an egg; see *yoke*)

yon·der   (yŏn′ dẽr)

York·shire pud·ding
               (yôrk′ shĭr)

young   (yŭng)

yours   (yŏŏrz)

your·self   (yŏŏr·sĕlf′)
   your·selves

youth·ful   (yōōth′ fŏŏl)
   -ful·ly   -ful·ness

yowl   (youl)

yuc·ca plant   (yŭk′ ȧ)

Yu·go·sla·vi·a   (yōō′ gŏ·slä′ vĭ·ȧ)
   Yu·go·slav

yule·tide   (yōōl′ tīd′)

X

xen·o·pho·bi·a   (zĕn′ ŏ·fō′ bĭ·ȧ)

X ray   (ĕks′ rā′)
   X-ray ther·a·py

xy·lo·phone   (zī′ lŏ·fōn)

Y

yachts·man   (yŏts′ mȧn)

Yan·kee   (yăng′ kê)

yard·age   (yär′ dĭj)

yard·stick   (yärd′ stĭk′)

yarn-dyed   (yärn′ dīd′)

yawn   (yôn)

year   (yẽr)
   year·book   year·ling
   year·long   year·ly

yearn·ing   (yûr′ nĭng)

yeast   (yēst)

yel·low   (yĕl′ ō)

yelp   (yĕlp)

yen   (yĕn)

yeo·man   (yō′ mȧn)

yes·ter·day   (yĕs′ tẽr·dĭ)

yew tree   (yōō)

Yid·dish   (yĭd′ ĭsh)

yield   (yēld)

yo·del   (yō′ d'l)
   -deled   -del·ing

yo·ga   (yō′ gȧ)

yo·ghurt   (yō′ gŏŏrt)

yo·gi   (yō′ gē)

yoke   (yōk)
   (frame; see *yolk*)

yo·kel   (yō′ kĕl)

Z

za·ny   (zā′ nĭ)
   za·ni·ness

Zan·zi·bar   (zăn′ zĭ·bär)

zeal   (zēl)
   zeal·ot   (zĕl′ ŭt)
   zeal·ous   (zĕl′ ŭs)

ze·bra   (zē′ brȧ)

ze·nith   (zē′ nĭth)

zep·pe·lin   (zĕp′ ĕ·lĭn)

ze·ro   (zēr′ ō)
   -ros

zest·ful   (zĕst′ fŏŏl)
   -ful·ly   -ful·ness

Zeus   (zūs)

zig·gu·rat   (zĭg′ ŏŏ·răt)

zig·zag   (zĭg′ zăg′)
   -zagged   -zag·ging

zinc ox·ide   (zĭngk)

zin·ni·a   (zĭn′ ĭ·ȧ)

Zi·on·ism   (zī′ ŭn·ĭz'm)

zip·per   (zĭp′ ẽr)

zir·con   (zûr′ kŏn)

zith·er   (zĭth′ ẽr)

zo·di·ac   (zō′ dĭ·ăk)

zom·bi   (zŏm′ bĭ)
   -bis

zone   (zōn)
   zon·ing   zon·al

zo·ol·o·gy   (zŏ·ŏl′ ŏ·jĭ)
   zo·o·log·i·cal   (zō′ ŏ·lŏj′ ĭ·kȧl)

Zo·ro·as·tri·an   (zō′ rŏ·ăs′ trĭ·ȧn)

zuc·chi·ni   (zōō·kē′ nê)

Zu·lu   (zōō′ lōō)

zwie·back   (tsvē′ bäk′)